Lecture Notes in Computer Science

Vol. 88: Mathematical Foundations of Computer Science 1980. Proceedings, 1980. Edited by P. Dembiński. VIII, 723 pages. 1980.

Vol. 89: Computer Aided Design - Modelling, Systems Engineering, CAD-Systems. Proceedings, 1980. Edited by J. Encarnacao. XIV, 461 pages. 1980.

Vol. 90: D. M. Sandford, Using Sophisticated Models in Resolution Theorem Proving.
XI, 239 pages. 1980

Vol. 91: D. Wood, Grammar and L Forms: An Introduction. IX, 314 pages. 1980.

Vol. 92: R. Milner, A Calculus of Communication Systems. VI, 171 pages. 1980.

Vol. 93: A. Nijholt, Context-Free Grammars: Covers, Normal Forms, and Parsing. VII, 253 pages. 1980.

Vol. 94: Semantics-Directed Compiler Generation. Proceedings, 1980. Edited by N. D. Jones. V, 489 pages. 1980.

Vol. 95: Ch. D. Marlin, Coroutines. XII, 246 pages. 1980.

Vol. 96: J. L. Peterson, Computer Programs for Spelling Correction: VI, 213 pages. 1980.

Vol. 97: S. Osaki and T. Nishio, Reliability Evaluation of Some Fault-Tolerant Computer Architectures. VI, 129 pages. 1980.

Vol. 98: Towards a Formal Description of Ada. Edited by D. Bjørner and O. N. Oest. XIV, 630 pages. 1980.

Vol. 99: I. Guessarian, Algebraic Semantics. XI, 158 pages. 1981.

Vol. 100: Graphtheoretic Concepts in Computer Science. Edited by H. Noltemeier. X, 403 pages. 1981.

Vol. 101: A. Thayse, Boolean Calculus of Differences. VII, 144 pages. 1981.

Vol. 102: J. H. Davenport, On the Integration of Algebraic Functions. 1–197 pages. 1981.

Vol. 103: H. Ledgard, A. Singer, J. Whiteside, Directions in Human Factors of Interactive Systems. VI, 190 pages. 1981.

Vol. 104: Theoretical Computer Science. Ed. by P. Deussen. VII, 261 pages. 1981.

Vol. 105: B. W. Lampson, M. Paul, H. J. Siegert, Distributed Systems – Architecture and Implementation. XIII, 510 pages. 1981.

Vol. 106: The Programming Language Ada. Reference Manual. X, 243 pages. 1981.

Vol. 107: International Colloquium on Formalization of Programming Concepts. Proceedings. Edited by J. Diaz and I. Ramos. VII, 478 pages. 1981.

Vol. 108: Graph Theory and Algorithms. Edited by N. Saito and T. Nishizeki. VI, 216 pages. 1981.

Vol. 109: Digital Image Processing Systems. Edited by L. Bolc and Zenon Kulpa. V, 353 pages. 1981.

Vol. 110: W. Dehning, H. Essig, S. Maass, The Adaptation of Virtual Man-Computer Interfaces to User Requirements in Dialogs. X, 142 pages. 1981.

Vol. 111: CONPAR 81. Edited by W. Händler. XI, 508 pages. 1981.

Vol. 112: CAAP '81. Proceedings. Edited by G. Astesiano and C. Böhm. VI, 364 pages. 1981.

Vol. 113: E.-E. Doberkat, Stochastic Automata: Stability, Nondeterminism, and Prediction. IX, 135 pages. 1981.

Vol. 114: B. Liskov, CLU, Reference Manual. VIII, 190 pages. 1981.

Vol. 115: Automata, Languages and Programming. Edited by S. Even and O. Kariv. VIII, 552 pages. 1981.

Vol. 116: M. A. Casanova, The Concurrency Control Problem for Database Systems. VII, 175 pages. 1981.

Vol. 117: Fundamentals of Computation Theory. Proceedings, 198 Edited by F. Gécseg. XI, 471 pages. 1981.

Vol. 118: Mathematical Foundations of Computer Science 198 Proceedings, 1981. Edited by J. Gruska and M. Chytil. XI, 589 page 1981.

Vol. 119: G. Hirst, Anaphora in Natural Language Understandin A Survey. XIII, 128 pages. 1981.

Vol. 120: L. B. Rall, Automatic Differentiation: Techniques and Appl cations. VIII, 165 pages. 1981.

Vol. 121: Z. Zlatev, J. Wasniewski, and K. Schaumburg, Y12M Sc lution of Large and Sparse Systems of Linear Algebraic Equations IX, 128 pages. 1981.

Vol. 122: Algorithms in Modern Mathematics and Computer Science Proceedings, 1979. Edited by A. P. Ershov and D. E. Knuth. XI, 48 pages. 1981.

Vol. 123: Trends in Information Processing Systems. Proceedings 1981. Edited by A. J. W. Duijvestijn and P. C. Lockemann. XI, 349 pages. 1981.

Vol. 124: W. Polak, Compiler Specification and Verification. XIII 269 pages. 1981.

Vol. 125: Logic of Programs. Proceedings, 1979. Edited by E Engeler. V, 245 pages. 1981.

Vol. 126: Microcomputer System Design. Proceedings, 1981. Edited by M. J. Flynn, N. R. Harris, and D. P. McCarthy. VII, 397 pages. 1982

Voll. 127: Y.Wallach, Alternating Sequential/Parallel Processing X, 329 pages. 1982.

Vol. 128: P. Branquart, G. Louis, P. Wodon, An Analytical Description of CHILL, the CCITT High Level Language. VI, 277 pages. 1982.

Vol. 129: B. T. Hailpern, Verifying Concurrent Processes Using Temporal Logic. VIII, 208 pages. 1982.

Vol. 130: R. Goldblatt, Axiomatising the Logic of Computer Programming. XI, 304 pages. 1982.

Vol. 131: Logics of Programs. Proceedings, 1981. Edited by D. Kozen. VI, 429 pages. 1982.

Vol. 132: Data Base Design Techniques I: Requirements and Logical Structures. Proceedings, 1978. Edited by S.B. Yao, S.B. Navathe, J.L. Weldon, and T.L. Kunii. V, 227 pages. 1982.

Vol. 133: Data Base Design Techniques II: Proceedings, 1979. Edited by S.B. Yao and T.L. Kunii. V, 229–399 pages. 1982.

Vol. 134: Program Specification. Proceedings, 1981. Edited by J. Staunstrup. IV, 426 pages. 1982.

Vol. 135: R.L. Constable, S.D. Johnson, and C.D. Eichenlaub, An Introduction to the PL/CV2 Programming Logic. X, 292 pages. 1982.

Vol. 136: Ch. M. Hoffmann, Group-Theoretic Algorithms and Graph Isomorphism. VIII, 311 pages. 1982.

Vol. 137: International Symposium on Programming. Proceedings, 1982. Edited by M. Dezani-Ciancaglini and M. Montanari. VI, 406 pages. 1982.

Vol. 138: 6th Conference on Automated Deduction. Proceedings, 1982. Edited by D.W. Loveland. VII, 389 pages. 1982.

Vol. 139: J. Uhl, S. Drossopoulou, G. Persch, G. Goos, M. Dausmann, G. Winterstein, W. Kirchgässner, An Attribute Grammar for the Semantic Analysis of Ada. IX, 511 pages. 1982.

Vol. 140: Automata, Languages and programming. Edited by M. Nielsen and E.M. Schmidt. VII, 614 pages. 1982.

Vol. 141: U. Kastens, B. Hutt, E. Zimmermann, GAG: A Practical Compiler Generator. IV, 156 pages. 1982.

Lecture Notes in Computer Science

Edited by G. Goos and J. Hartmanis

174

EUROSAM 84

International Symposium on
Symbolic and Algebraic Computation
Cambridge, England, July 9 – 11, 1984

Edited by John Fitch

Springer-Verlag
Berlin Heidelberg New York Tokyo 1984

Editor

John Fitch
School of Mathematics, University of Bath
Claverton Down, Bath, BA2 7AY, England

CR Subject Classifications (1982): I1, J2

ISBN 3-540-13350-X Springer-Verlag Berlin Heidelberg New York Tokyo
ISBN 0-387-13350-X Springer-Verlag New York Heidelberg Berlin Tokyo

Printing and binding: Beltz Offsetdruck, Hemsbach/Bergstr.
2145/3140-543210

PREFACE

Eurosam '84 is the third of a series of international Computer Algebra conferences held in Europe every five years. Co-sponsored by ACM SIGSAM, it is also the third of a series of international conferences receiving SAME sponsorship or co-sponsorship. The program consists of an invited banquet address, the presentation of thirty-seven submitted papers in twelve sessions and demonstrations of various Computer Algebra systems. Also, ample time has been provided for the informal exchange of ideas among the attendees.

The meeting was originally organized by Anthony C. Hearn, representing SIGSAM and J. A. van Hulzen, representing SAME. J. A. van Hulzen and R. D. Jenks were instrumental in the planning phases of the meeting and for the appointments of key people in the various committees. The members of the program committee did an excellent job in reading and evaluating a large amount of papers in a very short time span. John Fitch did an excellent job in putting together the very attractive and valuable Proceedings you have in your hands. James Davenport has worked very hard in making the our stay at Queens' College a pleasant one. J. Marti handled our accounts conscientiously. Everyone is familiar with the excellent job done by our Publicity Chairman, Patrizia Gianni. We also acknowledge the support that came from the staff at Queens' College, and the staff at ACM headquarters. To all: thank you very much!

Michael Rothstein

July, 1984

ORGANIZING COMMITTEE

SIGSAM Chairman	**A.C.Hearn, Rand Corporation, U.S.A**
SAME Chairman	**J.A.Van Hulzen, Technische Hogeschool, Twente, The Netherlands**
Conference Chairmen	**J.A.Van Hulzen, Technische Hogeschool, Twente, The Netherlands**
	R.D.Jenks, IBM Research, Yorktown Heights, U.S.A
Program Chairmen	**M.Mignotte, Université de Strasbourg, France**
	M.Rothstein, Kent State University, U.S.A
Program Committee	**D.Barton, University of California, Berkeley, U.S.A**
	K.Geddes, University of Waterloo, Canada
	L.Hornfeldt, University of Stockholm, Sweden
	D.Lazard, Université de Poitiers, France
	C.Sims, Rutgers University, U.S.A
	J.Smit, Technische Hogeschool, Twente, The Netherlands
	B.Trager, IBM Research, Yorktown Heights, U.S.A
Local Arrangements	**J.H.Davenport, University of Bath, England**
Proceedings Editor	**J.P.Fitch, University of Bath, England**

EUROSAM 84 was organized by ACM SIGSAM and SAME

CONTENTS

Introduction 1

DIFFERENTIAL EQUATIONS

Homogeneous Linear Difference Equation (Frobenius – Boole Method) 2
J. Della Dora, IMAG, Grenoble, France
E. Tournier, IMAG, Grenoble, France

An Experiment Toward a General Quadrature for Second Order Linear Ordinary Differential Equations by Symbolic Computation.................... 13
S. Watanabe, Tsuda College, Kodaira, Japan

Operational Calculus Techniques for Solving Differential Equations......... 23
N. Glinos, Rensselaer Polytechnic Institute, N.Y., U.S.A.
B.D. Saunders, Rensselaer Polytechnic Institute, N.Y., U.S.A.

APPLICATIONS 1

On the Application of Symbolic Computation to Nonlinear Control Theory.. 35
G. Cesareo, University of Rome II, Italy
R. Marino, University of Rome II, Italy

Quartic Equations and Algorithms for Riemann Tensor Classification......... 47
J.E. Åman, Queen Mary College, London, England
R.A. d'Inverno, University of Southampton, England
G.C. Joly, Queen Mary College, London, England
M.A.H. MacCallum, Queen Mary College, London, England

Symbolic Computation and the Dirichlet Problem............................. 59
R.W. Wilkerson, University of Florida, U.S.A.

SIMPLIFICATION AND ALGORITHM IMPLEMENTATION

Simplification of Polynomials in *n* Variables.............................. 64
G. Viry, Centre de Recherche en Informatique de Nancy, France

On The Equivalence of Hierarchical and Non-Hierarchical Rewriting on Conditional Term Rewriting Systems.. 74
M. Navarro, Euskal Herriko Unibersitatea, Donostia, Spain
F. Orejas, Universitat Politecnica, Barcelona, Spain

Implementation of a *p-adic* Package for Polynomial Factorization and Other Related Operations.. 86
P.S. Wang, Kent State University, Ohio, U.S.A.

ALGEBRAIC NUMBER COMPUTATION

Computations on Curves.. 100
C. Dicrescenzo, IMAG, Grenoble, France
D. Duval, IMAG, Grenoble, France

Detecting Torsion Divisors on Curves of Genus 2............................ 108
T.G. Berry, Universidad Simón Bolívar, Caracas, Venezuela

Computation in Radical Extensions.. 115
H. Najid-Zejli, IMAG, Grenoble, France

LANGUAGES FOR SYMBOLIC COMPUTING

A Primer: 11 Keys to New Scratchpad... 123
R.D. Jenks, IBM Research, Yorktown Heights, N.Y., U.S.A.

A Pure and Really Simple Initial Functional Algebraic Language............ 148
J.P. Fitch, University of Bath, England
J.A. Padget, University of Bath, England

APPLICATIONS 2

Code Generation and Optimization for Finite Element Analysis.............. 237
P.S. Wang, Kent State University, Ohio, U.S.A.
T.Y.P. Chang, University of Akron, Ohio, U.S.A.
J.A. van Hulzen, Twente University of Technology, The Netherlands

A Comparison of Algorithms for the Symbolic Computation of
Padé Approximants.. 248
S.R. Czapor, University of Waterloo, Ontario, Canada
K.O. Geddes, University of Waterloo, Ontario, Canada

Automatic Error Cumulation Control.................................. 260
B.J.A. Hulshof, Twente University of Technology, The Netherlands
J.A. van Hulzen, Twente University of Technology, The Netherlands

FACTORIZATION AND GCD COMPUTATIONS

Polynomial Factorization by Root Approximation...................... 272
A.K. Lenstra, Centrum voor Wiskunde en Informatica, Amsterdam, The Netherlands

Effective Hilbert Irreducibility..................................... 277
E. Kaltofen, University of Toronto, Ontario, Canada

GCDHEU: Heuristic Polynomial GCD Algorithm Based on Integer GCD
Computation... 285
B.W. Char, University of Waterloo, Ontario, Canada
K.O. Geddes, University of Waterloo, Ontario, Canada
G.H. Gonnet, University of Waterloo, Ontario, Canada

A New Lifting Process for the Multivariate Polynomial Factorization....... 297
D. Lugiez, IMAG, Grenoble, France

GROEBNER BASIS ALGORITHMS

Some Effectivity Problems in Polynomial Ideal Theory....................... 159
M. Giusti, Ecole Polytechnique, Palaiseau, France

Upper and Lower Bounds for the Degree of Groebner Bases.................... 172
H.M. Möller, FernUniversität Hagen, West Germany
F. Mora, Università di Genova, Italy

On the Complexity of the Groebner-Bases Algorithm over K[x,y,z]........... 184
F. Winkler, Johannes Kepler Universität, Linz, Austria

Algorithms for Computing Groebner Bases of Polynomial Ideals over
Various Euclidean Rings.. 195
A. Kandri-Rody, Rensselaer Polytechnic Institute, N.Y., U.S.A.
& University Mohammed-V, Rabat, Morocco
D. Kapur, General Electric Company, Schenectady, N.Y., U.S.A

COMPUTATIONAL GROUP THEORY

Computations with Rational Subsets of Confluent Groups..................... 207
R.H. Gilman, Stevens Institute of Technology, Hoboken, N.J., U.S.A.

CAMAC2: A Portable System for Combinatorial and Algebraic Computation..... 213
J.S. Leon, University of Illinois at Chicago, U.S.A.

Polynomial Time Algorithms for Galois Groups.............................. 225
S. Landau, Wesleyan University, Middletown, CT., U.S.A

NUMBER THEORY ALGORITHMS

Explicit Construction of the Hilbert Class Fields of Imaginary Quadratic Fields with Class Numbers 7 and 11 310
E. Kaltofen, University of Toronto, Ontario, Canada
N. Yui, University of Toronto, Ontario, Canada

On a Simple Primality Testing Algorithm 321
M.-D.A. Huang, Princeton University, N.J., U.S.A.

A Criterion for the Equivalence of Two Ideals 333
J. Buchmann, Universität zu Köln, West Germany

INTEGRATION

$y' + fy = g$ 341
J.H. Davenport, University of Bath, England

Integration in Finite Terms with Special Functions: A Progress Report 351
G.W. Cherry, University of Delaware, U.S.A.
B.F. Caviness, University of Delaware, U.S.A.

A Note on the Risch Differential Equation 359
E. Kaltofen, University of Toronto, Ontario, Canada

SOLUTION OF EQUATIONS

Approximation by Continued Fraction of a Polynomial Real Root 367
K. Thull, Heidelberg, West Germany

On the Automatic Resolution of Certain Diophantine Equations 378
M. Mignotte, Université Louis Pasteur, Strasbourg, France

On Pseudo-Resultants 386
M. Rothstein, Kent State University, Ohio, U.S.A.

AUTHOR INDEX

Aman 47
Berry 108
Buchmann 333
Caviness 351
Cesareo 35
Chang 237
Char 285
Cherry 351
Czapor 248
Davenport 341
Della Dora 2
Dicrescenzo 100
Duval 100
Fitch 148
Geddes 248, 285
Gilman 207
Giusti 159
Glinos 23
Gonnet 285
Huang 321
Hulshof 260
van Hulzen 237, 260
d'Inverno 47
Jenks 123
Joly 47
Kaltofen 277, 310, 359
Kandri-Rody 195
Kapur 195
Landau 225
Lenstra 272
Leon 213
Lugiez 297
MacCallum 47

Marino 35
Mignotte 378
Möller 172
Mora 172
Najid-Zejli 115
Navarro 74
Orejas 74
Padget 148
Rothstein 386
Saunders 23
Thull 367
Tournier 2
Viry 64
Wang 86, 237
Watanabe 13
Wilkerson 59
Winkler 184
Yui 310

INTRODUCTION

For the fourth time Springer-Verlag have published the proceedings of a Computer Algebra conference in their Lecture Notes in Computer Science series. This volume follows directly the 1979 "Symbolic & Algebraic Computation" EUROSAM 79 conference (LNCS 72) in being an international conference organized in Europe with American support and participation. As can be seen from the index the international range includes South America, Asia and Africa as well as North America and Europe.

As in all the previous volumes the richness and diversity of symbolic computation can be seen. As well as descriptions of new algebraic systems there are new application areas and advances in established ones. But the largest part of the conference is dedicated to the mathematical background to our subject. In part this is the use of the powerful tool that automated manipulation provides, to understand further how to solve for example differential equations. The use of new mathematical techniques is greatly in evidence in the developement of new algorithms for performing the calculations required in algebraic computation. This is a trend that can be seen in all the previous conferences.

These lecture notes should be of interest to anyone who may need to perform tedious algebra, as well as the pure mathematician who wishes to see the uses to which that subject can be put. From the various subjects and individual papers it should be possible to realise the scope of opportunity that computer algebra provides. While the material here is primarily research results at the frontiers of our knowledge, when taken with the previous Lecture Notes (LNCS 79, 144 and 162) it gives an educational program for a variety of workers in other fields

John Fitch

HOMOGENEOUS LINEAR DIFFERENCE EQUATION

(FROBENIUS - BOOLE METHOD)

J. Della Dora and E. Tournier
Institut IMAG - Laboratoire TIM3
BP 68 - 38402 Saint Martin d'Hères Cedex (France)

INTRODUCTION

Why study linear difference equation ?

Let $$L := \sum_{i=0}^{n} a_i \, \delta^i$$

be a linear difference operator with polynomial coefficients ($a \in k[x]$) and δ the operator of translation :

$$\delta u(x) = u(x-1)$$

In many domains, linear difference equations are of great importance. And this is fundamental in, at least, two ways :

1st - the study of asymptotic solution of linear differential equations in the neighbourhood of irregular singularities ([1], [2]).

2nd - the use of these relations to compute the previous solutions (for example to generate the Bessel functions J_n of 1st order...).

Even if the study of such equations started long time ago, with Leonard Euler and his work on the Γ function solution of the equation $u(x+1) = x\,u(x)$; we have not yet any satisfactory theory at our disposal, not even concerning the notion of solutions (cf. Ramis [4]). The algorithmic studies are also very poor.
The study of asymptotic solutions of L may be undertaken in two ways :

-a generalization of the method of Galbrun [5], Poincaré [6], and especially Birkhoff [7]. This study has been undertaken by Duval [12] and Loday [13].

-a suitable use of an operational method of Boole [10] which leads, more easily than that of Birkhoff, to an algorithmic treatment. At the present time, however this study is not yet sufficient to take into account all the degenerate solutions.

In this paper, we present a study of the second approach which will contain :

1) The π and ρ operators of Boole.
2) The Boole-Frobenius method.
3) The Newton polygon of linear difference equation and a classification.
4) Algorithms.
5) Conclusion.

) THE π AND ρ OPERATORS OF BOOLE

..1 - Definition of these operators

The two fundamental operators of this theory are the following :

$$\pi u(x) = x(u(x)-u(x-1))$$

$$\rho u(x) = \frac{\Gamma(x+1)}{\Gamma(x)} u(x-1)$$

They have the following properties :

(P1) : If m is a positive integer

$$(\rho+\pi)^m u(x) = x^m u(x)$$

$$\rho^m u(x) = \Gamma(x+1)\Gamma^{-1}(x-m+1)u(x-m)$$

If ρ^m is applied to the function identically equals to 1 we get :

$$\rho^m 1 = \Gamma(x+1)\Gamma^{-1}(x-m+1)$$

The following theorem is of great importance in applications.

Theorem 1 :

If P is an element of $k[x]$

$$P(\pi)\rho^m = \rho^m P(\pi+m)$$

In particular, if $\rho^m.1 = \frac{\Gamma(x+1)}{\Gamma(x-m+1)}$ we see that $P(\pi)\rho^m = P(m)\rho^m$.

The fundamental idea of the Boole method is to replace the 2 operators (multiplication by x and the operator δ of translation) which define L, by the two operators π and ρ.

First we notice that

(P2) : $$x\ u(x) = (\pi+\rho)\ u(x)$$

that leads to give a general expression of a polynomial P(x) with respect to π and ρ.

We have :

Theorem 2 :

If ∇ is the operator $\nabla u(x) = u(x)-u(x-1)$ and if $P \in k[x]$ and degree of $P=n$, then

$$P(\pi+\rho) = P(\pi) + \frac{\nabla P(\pi)}{1!} \rho + \ldots + \frac{\nabla^n P(\pi)}{n!} \rho^n$$

In practice, a recurrence is used to compute x^m.

1) $x = \pi+\rho$

2) If $x^n = \pi^n + g_1^n(\pi)\rho + \ldots + g_{n-1}^n(\pi)\rho^{n-1} + \rho^n \quad (g_i^n \in k[x])$

then $x^{n+1} = x^n(\pi+\rho) = \pi^{n+1} + g_1^{n+1}(\pi)\rho + \ldots + \rho^{n+1}$

so $$g_i^{n+1} = g_{i-1}^n + (\pi-i)\, g_i^n$$

Remark :

In this method, the simplification of difference expression leads to use rewriting rules in non commutative variables. The most important rule is

$$\rho^m \pi^n = (\pi-m)^n \rho^m$$

1.2 - Formal series of faculte

We define the $\mathbb{C}$-vector space of meromorphic formal series of faculte MF(x). For that, we have to define the following symbol :

(P3) : $$(x)_\lambda = \frac{\Gamma(x+1)}{\Gamma(x-\lambda+1)}$$

in which λ is any complex constant and Γ the usual Euler function.
In particular, if n is a positive integer we have :

$(x)_n = x(x-1) \ldots (x-n+1)$

$(x)_o = 1$

$(x)_{-n} = \dfrac{1}{(x+1)\ldots(x+n)}$

Definition

We call meromorphic formal serie of faculté, any formal serie of the form :

$$\sum_{n \geq n_o} a_n(x)_n, \; n_o \text{ belonging to } \mathbb{Z}$$

The set of these series forms a $\mathbb{C}$-vertor space which contains a special vector sub-space :

$F_2(x)$: $\mathbb{C}$-vector space of series having the form $\sum_{n\geq 0} a_n (x)_n$. These series are known by the name of factorial series of 2nd kind or Newton series.

In the same way, we can introduce the $\mathbb{C}$-vector space of factorial series of 1st kind. These series have the form : $\sum_{n\geq 0} a_n (x)_{-n}$.

With $F_1(x)$ and $F_2(x)$ we form the generalized spaces $GF_1(x)$ and $GF_2(x)$ of series having the form $\sum_{n\geq 0} a_n (x)_{-n+\lambda}$ and $\sum_{n\geq 0} a_n (x)_{n+\lambda}$.

2) THE BOOLE-FROBENIUS METHOD

The aim of this method is to follow the technique of Frobenius for linear differential equations solutions (cf. [1], [2]).

2.1 - The different steps of the method

Let $L = \sum_{i=0}^{n} a_i \delta^i$ be the initial difference operator.

1st step :

we form $x^{(n)}\, L = L_1$ then $\qquad L_1 = \sum_{i=0}^{n} a_i(x)\; x(x-1)\ldots(x-n+1)\delta^i$

from (P1) we have $\qquad L_1 = \sum_{i=0}^{n} a_i(x)\; (x-i+1)\ldots(x-n+1)\rho^i$

that we will note $\qquad L_1 = \sum_{i=0}^{n} b_i(x)\rho^i$

2nd step :

We look for solutions of the form

$$u(x)=\mu^x\, v(x)$$

this leads to the operator

$$L_\mu = \sum_{i=0}^{n} b_i(x)\; \mu^{n-i}\rho^i$$

3rd step :

We change into the variable π :

$$L_\mu = \sum_{i=0}^{n} \mu^{n-i} b_i(\pi+\rho)\rho^i$$

By applying theorem 2, and, if n_i = degree(b_i), we write :

$$b_i(\pi+\rho) = b_i(\pi) + \ldots + \frac{\nabla^{n_i} b_i(\pi)}{n_i!}\,\rho^{n_i}$$

then

$$L_\mu = \sum_{i=0}^{n} \mu^{n-i}\; \Big(\sum_{j=0}^{n_i} \frac{\nabla^j b_i(\pi)}{j!}\,\rho^j\Big)\rho^i$$

Noting $m = \max_{i=0,\dots,n} (i+n_i)$ we obtain

$$L_\mu = \sum_{i=0}^{m} f_i(\pi,\mu)\rho^i$$

with $f_i(\pi,\mu)$ belonging to $k(\mu)[x]$

4th step :

In this step, we use the following lemma :

Lemma : Whatever ν belonging to $\mathbb{C}$, we have :

1) $$\rho((x)_\nu) = (x)_{\nu+1}$$

2) $$\pi((x\ )_\nu) = \nu(x)_\nu$$

The action of L_μ on a symbolic power $(x)_\nu$ is then :

$$L_\mu((x)_\nu) = (\sum_{i=0}^{m} f_i(\pi,\mu)\rho^i)(x)_\nu$$

(P4) :
$$= \sum_{i=0}^{m} f_i(\pi,\mu)(x)_{\nu+i}$$

$$= \sum_{i=0}^{m} f_i(\nu+i,\mu)(x)_{\nu+i}$$

2.2 - Search for formal series solutions

2.2.1 - Solutions belonging to $GF_2(x)$:

We try solutions of the form

$$v = \sum_{j=0}^{+\infty} a_j(x)_{j+\nu}\ .$$

Using the linearity of the operator L_μ , we have :

$$L_\mu v = \sum_{j=0}^{+\infty} a_j\ L_\mu((x)_{-j+\nu})$$

$$= \sum_{j=0}^{+\infty} a_j(\sum_{j=0}^{m} f_i(\nu-j+i,\mu)(x)_{\nu-j+i})$$

By identification, we obtain two linear systems, which, under certain hypotheses, determine the a_i.

1st system

(S1) :
$$\begin{cases} a_o\ f_m(\nu+m,\mu) = 0 \\ \vdots \\ a_o\ f_1(\nu+1,\mu) +\dots+ a_{m-1}\ f_m(\nu+1,\mu) = 0 \end{cases}$$

2nd sub-system

The second infinite sub-system is nothing other than the linear difference equation :

$$(S2) : \quad a_{m+s} f_m(\nu-s,\mu) + \ldots + a_s f_o(\nu-s,\mu) = 0 \qquad (s = 0,1,\ldots)$$

Remark :

If the system (S1) allows μ and ν and the a_i of initial conditions to be determined, then (S2) determines the solution completely.

2.2.2 - Solutions belonging to $GF_2(x)$

We seek solutions of the form :

$$v = \sum_{j=0}^{+\infty} a_j(x)_{\nu+j}$$

with $\nu \in \mathbb{C}$. Then the system becomes :

1st system

$$(T1) : \quad \begin{cases} a_o f_o(\nu,\mu) = 0 \\ \vdots \\ a_o f_{m-1}(\nu+m-1,\mu) + \ldots + a_{m-1} f_o(\nu+m-1,\mu) = 0 \end{cases}$$

2nd system

$$(T2) : \quad a_{m+s} f_o(s+m+\nu,\mu) + \ldots + a_s f_m(\nu+m+s,\mu) = 0$$

The same remark as for 2.2.1 are valid.

2.2.3 - Conclusion

Now, we must begin to talk about the feasibility of the method. For that, we must first attempt to classify linear difference equations. We shall outline this in the following paragraph.

3) NEWTON POLYGON OF A LINEAR DIFFERENCE EQUATION AND CLASSIFICATION

3.1 - The Newton polygon

We have seen that the Boole method first supposes the determination of the indices μ,ν .

The values of μ is obtained by searching for zeros of the polynomial :

$$(P5) : \quad f_m(m+\nu,\mu) = 0$$

In fact, this polynomial depends on the unknown ν.
To clarify this point, we are going to study the formation of (P 5) which is called the :

Characteristic equation of the difference equation

Let $L = \sum_{i=0}^{n} a_i \delta^i$ be the initial operator, with $a_i(x) = \sum_{j=0}^{n_i} a_j^i x^j$

The 2nd step of the Boole method leads the operator to be considered as :

$$L_\mu = \sum_{i=0}^{n} b_i(\pi+\rho)\, \mu^{n-i} \rho^i$$

in which the highest power of ρ in the term $b_i(\pi+\rho)\mu^{n-i}\rho^i$ is given by theorem 2 and is

$$a_{n_i}^i \mu^{n-i} \rho^{n+n_i}$$

Then, we place the points (i,n_i), $i = 0,1,\ldots,n$ on an orthogonal axes system. We then consider the concave envelope of these points.

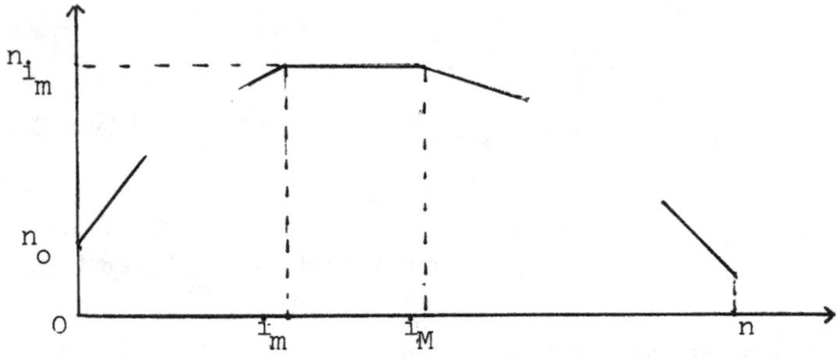

The thus formed polygon is called "the Newton polygon". If this polygon has a null slope with extremities

$$(i_m,n_{i_m}) \text{ and } (i_M,n_{i_M})$$

We obtain as coefficients of $\rho^{n+n_{i_m}}$

$$\mu^{n-i_m} a_{n_{i_m}}^{i_m} + \ldots + \mu^{n-i_M} a_{n_{i_M}}^{i_M}$$

wich immediately gives

$$f_m(m+\nu,\mu) = \mu^{n-i_M}(a_{n_{i_m}}^{i_m} \mu^{i_M-i_m} + \ldots + a_{n_{i_M}}^{i_M})$$

then we have the following lemma

<u>emma 1</u>

The characteristic equation is free of the indice ν, it is a polynomial with coefficients in the ground field.

:t is convenient to note

<u>)efinition 1</u>

A linear difference equation is <u>normal</u> if its Newton polygon has a unique null slope of length n.

Example : The hypergeometric difference equation is

$$\Delta = (b_o x+c_o)\delta^2+(b_1 x+c_1)\delta+(b_2 x+c_2)$$

its polygon is

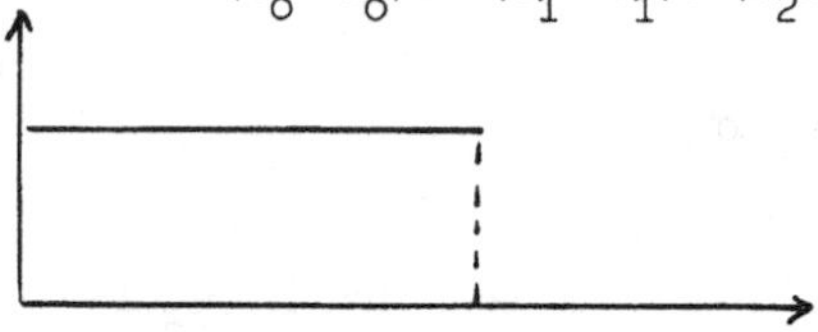

if $b_o . b_2 \neq 0$ we have a normal equation.

3.2 - <u>Regular and irregular normal equations</u>

We consider a linear recurence equation and let μ be a root of the characteristic equation. Then we must determine ν. To do this, we divide the problem into two parts, seeking solutions in $GF_1(x)$ or in $GF_2(x)$.

3.2.1 - <u>Search for solutions in</u> $GF_1(x)$

ν can be determined according to the solution of the second equation

$$a_o\, f_{m-1}(\nu+m-1,\mu)+a_1 \underbrace{f_m(\nu+m-1,\mu)}_{=0} = 0$$

because of the choice of root of the characteristic equation. Thus to determine ν, we have to search for a root of the polynomial

$$f_{m-1}(\nu+m-1,\mu) = 0$$

<u>Study of the polynomial</u>

By successive developments we show that

$$L_\mu = \sum_{i=0}^{n} \mu^{n-i}(a^i_{n_i}(x)_{n+n_i} + (a^i_{n_i}(n+n_{i-1})(\pi-(n+n_{i-1-i})+{}_i(x)_{n+n_{i-1}})$$

where γ_i is a constant.

If we suppose that L is a normal operator, that is to say, all the n are equal, the previous development can be written

$$L_\mu = \left(\sum_{i=0}^{n} a^i_{n_i} \mu^{n-i} \right) (x)_{n+n_i} + \left\{ \left(\sum_{i=0}^{n} a^i_{n_i} (n+n_i-i)\mu^{n-i} \right)\pi + \sum_{i=0}^{n} \theta_i \right\} (x)_{n+n_{i-1}}$$

where θ_i is a constant.

So we establish :

1st - $f_{m-1}(\pi,\mu)$ is a polynomial of degree 1 in π

2nd - ν is determined by $f_{m-1}(\nu+m-1,\mu) = 0$

3rd - ν can be determined by this polynomial of degree 1, only if the coefficient of ν in this polynomial is not null.

4th - Properly, this coefficient is $\sum_{i=0}^{n} a^i_{n_i} (n+n_i-i)\mu^{n-i}$

5th - It is easy to note that the expression is nothing more than $\mu\, f'_m(\mu)$.

6th - The equation $f_m(\mu) = 0$ cannot have a null root, (otherwise the null slope would not be of length n) then can be determined only if $f'_m(\mu) = 0$.

These miscellaneous remark lead to

Definition 2

We say that a normal linear recurence equation is regular if the roots of its characteristic equation are simple, otherwise we say that the equation is irregular.

We then have the following theorem

Theorem 3

For a normal regular equation the Boole method allows μ and ν to be determined.

The problem is then to know if, in that case, we obtain a fundamental system of solutions.

Determination of the coefficients of the development

The study of the system (S1) leads to :

Lemma 2

We can determine the coefficients of the development in series in $GF_1(x)$, if and only if :

$$f_{m-1}(\nu+j) \neq 0 \qquad j = m-2, m-1, \ldots$$

As we know that f is of degree 1 in the normal equation case, therefore

Theorem 4

For a normal regular equation the Boole method associated with the first system enables n formal solutions with the form of power series belonging to $GF_1(x)$, to be determined.

.2.2. - Search for solutions in $GF_2(x)$

The results we have obtained in that direction are less accurate. However, we will present them shortly.

We always start with μ as a root of $f_m(\mu) = 0$. But now, to determine ν , we have to equal $f_o(\nu,\mu)$ to zero.

A detailed study of these equations enables the following lemma, to be establish.

Lemma 3

$$f_o(\nu,\mu) = \mu^n \nu(\nu-1) \ldots (\nu-n+1) a_o(\nu)$$

This lemma 3 illustrates how difficult this method is, because, a priori, with one value of μ we can associate n_o+n values of ν which are free of μ.

However a precise study of the system (T1) shows that :

Lemma 4

We can determine $a_1, a_2, \ldots$ in function of a_o, if and only if $f_o(\nu+j) \neq 0$ for all positive j.

This enables $\nu = 0,1,\ldots,n-2$ to be eliminated in so far as roots of $f_o(\nu) = 0$.
Similarly, it is clear that if two roots of $a_o(\nu)$ differ from each other by an integer, then we can not verify the previous conditions.
If all these conditions are verified, we can determine the coefficients. We shall not go into further detail concerning the classical algorithms.

CONCLUSION

After this outline of the Boole method, there is still much work to do. However, we need to study this problem this way because when global methods (Karr [14]) do not give results, only the perturbative method can provide some information concerning the solutions.

Many problems are still open.

- links between the two systems of solutions
- case of irregular normal equation
- case of irregular equation
- algorithmic development of the method of Birkhoff
- link between the methods of Boole and Birkhoff
- study of linear difference systems
- classification of systems.

This present work is aimed as starting point, we hope will be an opening for different directions in research.

4) THE ALGORITHMS

We are still working on them and there implementation in REDUCE, and their detailed study will be presented later on.

BIBLIOGRAPHY

[1] J. Della Dora, E. Tournier
"Formal solutions of differential equations in the neighborhood of singular points" (SYMSAC 81, P.S. Wang editor, Kent State University)

[2] J. Della Dora, C. Dicresenzo, E. Tournier
"An algorithm to obtain formal solutions of a linear homogeneous differential equation at an irregular singular point".
EUROCAM 82, Springer Verlag p. 273-280.

[3] L. Euler
"Opera omnia - Vol. I - Leibzig Berlin 1924

[4] J.P. Ramis
"Solutions meromorphes d'équations aux différences linéaires.
Rapport de recherche IRMA, Strasbourg (1984 to appear).

[5] A. Galbrun
"Sur certaines solutions exceptionnelles d'une équation linéaire aux différences finies".
Bull. Soc. Math. de France, Vol. 49 (1921) p. 206-241

[6] H. Poincaré
"Sur les équations linéaires aux différentielles ordinaires et aux différences finies". Amer. Jour. Math, t. 7 (1885) p. 213-258

[7] G. Birkhoff
"General theory of linear difference equations"
Trans. Amer. Math. Soc. 12 /1911/ p. 243-284

[8] N.E. Norlund
"Leçons sur les équations linéaires aux différences finies-Paris"
Gauthier Villars et C. Editeurs 1929

[9] N.E. Norlund
"Leçons sur les séries d'interpolation - Paris".
Gauthier Villars et C. Editeurs 1926

[10] G. Boole
"Finite difference" Chelsea Publishing Company, New York.

[11] M. Loday
"Théorèmes d'indices sur les espaces de type Gevrey généralisés".
IRMA - Strasbourg 1983

[12] A. Duval
"Etude asymptotique d'une intégrale analogue à la fonction modifiée".
Lecture Notes in Mathematics 712

[13] A. Duval
"Equations différentielles et systèmes de Pfaff dans C". Springer Verlag.

[14] Karr "Summation in finite terms". J. ACM vol. 28,n°2 April 1981 pp. 305-350.

AN EXPERIMENT TOWARD A GENERAL QUADRATURE FOR SECOND ORDER LINEAR ORDINARY DIFFERENTIAL EQUATIONS BY SYMBOLIC COMPUTATION

Shunro Watanabe
Department of Mathematics, Tsuda College
Kodaira, Tokyo 187, Japan

1. Why experiment?

The second order linear ordinary differential equations (L ODE) is the most important class in ODE. The classical mathematical theories for L ODE had developed in 19th and early 20th centuries. Many mathematicians made the theories and methods to find and solve liouvillian or algebraic solutions for L ODE. However it seems to us they did not offer any general procedure that can solve these equations. ([1])

On the other hand, during the last 15 years many people tried to write programs that can solve the equations in L ODE by Symbolic Computation. For example, J.Golden E.Lafferty and others wrote an solver for ODE on MACSYMA, called ODE, which is a collection of algorithms including Y.Avgoustis' simplification program for hypergeometric equations and P.Schmidt's solver for Riccati's equations with coefficients in Q(x), rational functions of x. ([2], [3])

Recently two papers appeared. They offered general algorithms for these equations. J.Kovacic's algorithm can find and solve all the liouvillian and algebraic solutions for second order L ODE with coefficients in C(x). B.Saunders implemented Kovacic's algorithm. ([4]) M.Singer's algorithm can find and solve all the liouvillian and algebraic solutions for the n-th order L ODE with coefficients in F, a finite algebraic extension of Q(x). ([5])

Even after the appearance of these two papers, if one wants to implement a solver for a large class of equations, the following direction seems to be still valuable: "Given a differential equation whose form or structure is not immediately recognizable, one looks for transformations which will convert the given problem into one which is known." ([6]) In this paper, I shall show an experiment toward a general quadrature for second order L ODE with coefficients in elementary functions.

I wrote a program within the classical knowledge on ODE. ([1],[8],[9]) It consists of some 1400 lines by MACSYMA language and I tested this program on PDP-10 using 542 equations in Kamke's table. In these 542 equations we can use 492 equations as meaningful test data. ([7]) Our program solved 473 equations. It means our solvable rate is more than 96%. The computaion times are almost between 10 seconds and 60 seconds. In this experiment, I found an essential error (2-291th equation) and other errors (2-125c(c) and 2-187a) in Kamke's table. Also our program solved a few equations which are essentially different equations from those in Kamke's table. I printed all the processes of calculations for the 473 equations and others.

2. The strategy for solving.

Our approach for solving Kamke's equations is to find a proper transformation of variables which will convert a given equation to a more simple equation. Usually it is very difficult to determine which equation is more simple. However we can guess as follows : if the coefficients of an equation have $\exp(x^2)$ and the coefficients of another equation have only $\exp(x)$, the latter equation must be more simple than the former equation. When all the coefficients of an equation are rational functions of x we may think that the degree of the difficulties for solving increases as the number or the ranks of the singular points increase. Thus we had rough criterions for simplicity of equations.

Then how can we find proper transformations? I used only one technique for our program. First we will recognize the pattern for the given equation. Here I mean the pattern not only as external form but also as a kind of characterization using the informations obtained by calculation. Then we will get several candidate transformations that have a few undetermined parameters. We will try to determine these parameters by applying the transformations to a given equation. Therefore we used the following strategy for our program.

step 1. If the equation contains elementary transcendental functions and if the arguments in the deepest parts of it have a common rational function k(x) that is not x then we try to remove k(x) by the transformation t=k(x).
If we success then go to step 5, if we fail then go to step 4.

step 2. If the equation contains elementary transcendental functions and if all the arguments of these functions are x then we try to remove these functions by the transformation t=e(x), where e(x) is one of the transcendental functions.
If we success then go to step 5, if we fail then go to step 4.

step 3. If all the coefficients of the equation are rational functions of x and parameters then we count all the singular points and calculate their ranks. If the equation has only three regular singular points or it has one regular singular point and one irregular singular point of rank one or it is the easily solvable equation then we solve it using theories. If the equation is a prototype then we say so. If we success then go to step 6.

step 4. We try to find the proper transformations of the form

u=f(x)y, u=y', or t=g(x)

where f(x) and g(x) are elementary or algebraic function of x. Often f(x) and g(x) have undetermined parameters, and we must determine them so as the transformation can simplify the equation. If we fail we cannot solve it.

step 5. We store this successful transformation of variable to the top of a stack. We replace the new variables u or t in the transformed equation by y or x and we use it as new equation. Go to step 1.

step 6. We calculate the solution of the first equation from the series of transformations on the stack and the solution of the last equation.

When we wrote our program according to the above strategy, we used the following loose princiles : 1) We should prepare enough transformations for solving our equations. But it is better to use pattern matchings in small numbers. 2) We should use back-tracking technique only under the restricted condition. At least the number of trials in an environment must be small.

3. Details on the transformations.

Let us consider step 2 in our strategy. When we find trigonometric functions for a given equation, we try to remove these functions from it using t=sin(x) or t=cos(x). When one transformation succeeded and another transformation failed, we can use the succeeded one. When both of them succeeded, we must select the one which will bring us more simple equation. When both of them failed, we cannot remove trigonometric functions from it.

When we find hyperbolic functions for a given equation, we try to remove these functions from it using t=sinh(x) or t=cosh(x). We can determine which transformation is proper or not using the same procedure as the case of trigonometric functions. When we find exponential or logarithmic functions for a given equation, we try to remove them from it using $t=e^x$ or t=log(x) or t=x(log(x)-1).

Now let us consider step 4 in our strategy. First we try to simplify it using $t=x^r$. For this purpose we try to rewrite our equation to the form $x^2y''+xf(x^r)y'+g(x^r)y=0$. Where r is an undetermined parameter. When r is 2 or 3, or -1 or 1/2, it is not so difficult to determine r. But when r is b or -b or b+1, where b is an another symbol, it is not so eaey to determine r.

Then we try to simplify it using $y=\exp(ax^r)u$, where a and r are two undetermined parameters. By this transformation we can expect two directions for simplification. One is to reduce the rank of the irregular singularity, and another is to transform our equation to easily solvable equation as y''+f(x)y'=0. To reduce the rank we can use the value of rank as r. But to transform our equation to y''+f(x)y'=0 we must look for the value of r around the value of rank. Sometimes we go through this step two or three times. Then we must determine the value r under the condition that the value of the successor must be less than the value of the predecessor.

In this case we have one difficultiy. The undetermined parameter 'a'in $\exp(ax^r)$ satisfies a quadratic equation. So we have two values for candidate. The two transformed equations corresponding to these values have often same simplicity. Therefore the first version of our program asks for us which value is preferable. Of course it is for the memory limitation's sake.

After this transformation, we still try to simplify our equation using $y=(x-a)^k u$, where a and k are undetermined parameters. By this transformation we can expect two directions for simplification. One is to remove an apparent singular point from the equation. For this purpose we must select an apparent singular point as 'a' and one of the characteristic roots as k. It is not necessary to decide whether a singular point is apparent or not, because the possible number of a and k is finite.

Another direction is to transform the equation to $y''+f(x)y'=0$. For this purpose it is not necessary to select a singular point for a. These processes are a kind of pattern matchings and their applications for transformations. Then we try to use more explicit patterns.

4. What are our patterns?

In our problem a data or an equation corresponds to a program which can solve the equation. Now we have 542 relevant equations in Kamke's table. Therefore if I wrote 542 programs, then the collection of these programs is a solver for Kamke's equations. However it is too big to be a practical solver. Then we try to find similar parts in this huge program and try to reduce its size by replacing those similar parts by subroutines. These subroutines correspond to patterns.

For example a few equations in Kamke's table pass through similar route in step 4, then we can use a proper pattern to save calculation time. The equations 2-54 and 2-55 in Kamke's table are such examples. Let us consider the equation 2-189 as next example. It is transformed to Bessel's equation (2-162). Our program can solve it easily. However when we solve all of the 542 equation we will meet them 54 times. Therefore we added the pattern 2-189 to our program to save computation time.

In a practical sense how can we find a pattern? Let us consider the easiest example, equation 2-442. It has the form $f(x)y''+xy'-y=0$. When the equation 2-419 is given to us, let us look at it. It has the form : $x^2y''\cos(x)+(x^2\sin(x)-2x\cos(x))y'+(2\cos(x)-x\sin(x))y=0$. After we divided the both sides by $-(2\cos(x)-x\sin(x))$ we can get $f(x)=x^2/(x\sin(x)-2\cos(x))$. The pattern 2-442 has a special solution x, so we can easily solve it.

Then is it always possible to determine whether a pattern matches to an equation or not? The equation 2-77a has the form : $y''+(f+g)y'+(f'+fg)y=0$, where f and g are arbitrary functions of x. When we tried to match this pattern to $y''+py'+qy=0$, we will see that f must be the solution of a Riccati's equation : $f'+pf-f^2-q=0$. But it is very difficult to solve this equation , it is equivalent to our problem.

. Examples.

Example 1. The following are almost raw print-out for the 2-344th equation.

```
(C3) showtime:true$
Time= 5 msec.

(C4) /* September 10, 1983 */

loadfile(pmain,fasl);

PMAIN FASL DSK SWATAN being loaded
Loading done
Time= 333 msec.
(D4)                                        DONE

(C5) batch(exampl,test);

(C6) /* 2-344 */

K344:X^4*'DIFF(Y,X,2)+(EXP(2/X)-V^2)*Y=0;
Time= 72 msec.
                           2
                        4 d Y        2/X     2
(D6)                   X  --- + (%E      - V ) Y = 0
                            2
                          dX

(C7) /* see 2-162(24) */


Time= 349 msec.
(D7)                                  BATCH DONE

(C8) lode2(k344,0);

           2         2/X     2
          d Y    (%E      - V ) Y
we solve  --- + --------------- = 0
            2          4
          dX          X

            1
we use T = -
            X
                                dY
                   2        2 --
                  d Y        dT        2 T     2
the result is    --- + ---- + (%E     - V ) Y = 0
                    2     T
                  dT
                          dY
             2        2 --
            d Y        dX        2 X     2
we solve   --- + ---- + (%E     - V ) Y = 0
              2     X
            dX

SOLVE FASL DSK MACSYM being loaded
Loading done
we use T = 2 X
                               dY
                  2        2 --        2       T
                 d Y        dT      (V   - %E ) Y
the result is   --- + ---- - ------------- = 0
                   2     T              4
                 dT
                         dY
             2        2 --          X     2
            d Y        dX      (%E   - V ) Y
we solve   --- + ---- + ------------ = 0
              2     X             4
            dX
```

```
                     U
we use Y = -
                     X
                               X     2          2
                         U (%E   - V )       d U
the result is ------------ + --- = 0
                               4               2
                                             dX
                  2        X     2
                 d Y    (%E   - V ) Y
we solve    --- + ------------ = 0
                    2        4
                 dX
                      X
we use T = %E
                                   dY
                      2        --        2
                     d Y      dT    (V   - T) Y
the result is    --- + -- - ----------- = 0
                       2     T            2
                     dT                4 T
                     dY
                  2        --         2
                 d Y      dX    (X - V ) Y
we solve    --- + -- + ----------- = 0
                    2     X           2
                 dX                4 X

           [ INF   ASTERISK     0  ]
           [                       ]
           [                    V  ]
           [  0       - %I    - -  ]
y=P        [                    2  ] (x)
           [                       ]
           [                    V  ]
           [  0        %I       -  ]
           [                    2  ]

y= Y              (SQRT(X))
     B, ABS(V)
the solution of the last eq. is Y              (SQRT(X))
                                          B, ABS(V)
the solution of the first eq. is
Time= 24239 msec.
                                                   1/X
                                    X Y           (%E    )
                                       B, ABS(V)
(D8)                               -------------------
                                            2
```

In the above example $y_{B,n}(x)$ is the general solution of the Bessel's equation : $x^2y''+xy'+(x^2-n^2)y=0$.

Example 2. Print-out for the 2-378a equation in Kamke's table.

```
(C6) /* 378A,522 */

K522:X*(X-1)*(X+1)^2*'DIFF(Y,X,2)+2*X*(X+1)*(X-3)*'DIFF(Y,X)-2*(X-1)*Y=0;
Time= 58 msec.
                                  2
                               2 d Y                        dY
(D6)   (X - 1) X (X + 1)   --- + 2 (X - 3) X (X + 1) -- - 2 (X - 1) Y = 0
                                  2                         dX
                                dX

(C8) lode2(k522,0);
                            dY
        2       (2 X - 6) --
       d Y                  dX          2 Y
we solve --- + ------------ - ------------- = 0
        2          2                3      2
       dX         X  - 1          X  + 2 X  + X

             U
we use Y = --------
                 2
          (X + 1)
                           dU
                         2 --     2
                  2 U      dX    d U
the result is ------ - ----- + --- = 0
                  2      X - 1    2
                 X  - X           dX
                  dY
       2        2 --
      d Y       dX       2 Y
we solve --- - ----- + ------ = 0
        2    X - 1     2
       dX             X  - X

it matched with  k442
we use Y = U X
                                      2
                  dU  2      2       d U
the result is -- (- - -----) + --- = 0
                  dX  X    X - 1      2
                                     dX
                   dY
       2       2 --
      d Y        dX
we solve --- - ------ = 0
        2      2
       dX     X  - X

the solution of the first eq. is
Time= 20291 msec.
                                          1
      X (K1 (- 2 LOG(X) + X - -) + K2)
                                          X
(D8)  ---------------------------------
                          2
                   (X + 1)
```

Example 3. Print-out for the 2-430 equation in Kamke's table.

```
(C6) K430:'DIFF(Y,X,2)*SIN(X)^2+'DIFF(Y,X,1)*SIN(X)*COS(X)
     +(V*(V+1)*SIN(X)^2-N^2)*Y=0;
Time= 93 msec.
                    2
          2        d Y                     dY                    2        2
(D6)    SIN (X) --- + COS(X) SIN(X) -- + (V (V + 1) SIN (X) - N ) Y = 0
                    2                      dX
                  dX

(C8) lode2(k430,0);
```

```
                          dY
         2     COS(X)  --         2            2         2
        d Y            dX    ((V  + V) SIN (X) - N ) Y
e solve --- + --------- + ------------------------- = 0
         2     SIN(X)                    2
        dX                            SIN (X)

OLVE FASL DSK MACSYM being loaded
oading done
e use T = COS(X)
                              dY
              2    2 T.--        2          2    2            2
            d Y        dT    ((T  - 1) V  + (T  - 1) V + N ) Y
he result is --- + ------ - --------------------------------- = 0
              2    2                    4      2
            dT    T  - 1               T  - 2 T  + 1
                       dY
         2     2 X --        2         2    2           2
        d Y        dX    ((V  + V) X  - V  - V + N ) Y
we solve --- + ------ - ----------------------------- = 0
         2    2                   4      2
        dX    X  - 1             X  - 2 X  + 1

it matched with  k372
                            ABS(N)
                            ------
                   2          2
we use Y = U (X  - 1)
              2
            d U    2                          dU         2
the result is --- (X  - 1) + 2 (ABS(N) + 1) -- X  + U (- V  - V + ABS(N) (ABS(N) + 1)) = 0
              2                              dX
            dX
                                         dY
         2     (2 ABS(N) + 2) X --       2                   2
        d Y                       dX   (V  + V - ABS(N) - N ) Y
we solve --- + ------------------ - ------------------------ = 0
         2              2                         2
        dX             X  - 1                    X  - 1

the type is hypergeometric
the solution may be written by Riemann's P-functions as follows
    [      1          - 1            INF         ]
    [                                            ]
y=P [  - ABS(N)   - ABS(N)     ABS(N) - V        ] (x)
    [                                            ]
    [      0           0      V + ABS(N) + 1     ]
do you replace in ABS(N) - V ? type y or n
n;
is - 2 V - 1 an odd integer? type y or n
n;
is 2 V + 1 an odd integer? type y or n
n;
Is ABS(N) a positive integer? type y or n
y;
Is 2 V + 1 a positive integer? type y or n
n;
Is - 2 V - 1 a positive integer? type y or n
n;
   ABS(N)
  d
y= -------- (Y (V, X))
     ABS(N)    L
  dX
where Y (V, X)
       L          is the solution of Legendre's eq:(x^2-1)*y''+2*x*y'-vl*(vl+1)*y=0
the solution of the first eq. is
Time= 29504 msec.
                                                                       ABS(N)
                         ABS(N)                                        ------
                        d                                   2            2
(D7)          (------------- (Y (V, COS(X)))) (COS (X) - 1)
                          ABS(N)    L
              dCOS(X)
```

6. The result of our experiment.

There are 542 second order L ODE in Kamke's table. In these equations we have 39 equations which contain arbitrary functions and 11 equations which contain non elementary transcendental functions. Our program solved 473 equations out of relevant 492 equations. The rate of solved equation is more than 96%. Our program solved 488 equations out of all the 542 equations. The rate of solved equation without any restriction is more than 90%.

When will we say "We could solve it." or "We could not solve it."? When the most simplified equation is proto-type or has a solution that is representable by elementary functions or algebraic functions, the equation was solved.

type	classes \ the number of	solved equat.	unsolved equation	total	the type of last tr.eq.			
					s0	s1	s2	s8
s 0	constant coefficients or first order equation of y'	18	0	18				
s 1	Riemann's equation of confluent type	114	0	114	5	109		
s 2	Riemann's equation	99	1	100	13		86	
s 3	$t=x^s \rightarrow$ s1 or s2	118	0	118	26	66	26	
s 4	coefficients contain exponential functions	15	3	18	4	10	1	
s 5	coefficients contain logarithmic functions	4	2	6	4			
s 6	coefficients contain trigonometric functions	55	2	57	11	13	29	2
s 7	coefficients contain hyperbolic functions	7	0	7			6	1
s 8	other equations with coefficients in Q(x)	43	11	54	19	5	9	10
	sub total	473	19	492	100	203	157	13
s 9	coefficients contain transcendental functions	2	9	11				
s10	coefficients contain any functions of x	13	26	39				
	sub total	15	35	50				
	total	485	57	542				

Table 1.

last equation		number of solutions representable by									
					the solution of the equation of						
last class	number of eq	elemen func	algeb func	ellip func	Kummer	Bessel	Whitta -ker	Legen -dre	Gauss	Mattieu	Others
s0	100	100									
s1	203	87			6	51	59				
s2	157	68	9	3				36	41		
s8	13									6	7
total	473	255									

Table 2.

pattern	transformation	frequency	pattern	transformation	frequency	pattern	transformation	frequency
2- 41		2	2-367	$y=(x^2+1)^{\frac{m}{2}}u$	1	2-218a		1
2- 54	$y=\exp(ax)u$	2	2-372	$y=(x^2-1)^{\frac{m}{2}}u$	11		$y=(x-a)^r u$	9
2- 55	$y=\exp(ax^2)u$	6	2-389	$t=\sqrt{x}$	5		$y=\exp(ax^r)u$	29
2- 78	$y=u/(x^2-1)$	3	2-394	$t=c\log(\frac{x}{ax+b})$	1		$\begin{cases} y=u/\sin(x) \\ y=u/\cos(x) \end{cases}$	8
2-120	(to Whittaker)	39	2-442	$y=(x-a)u$	28		$y=\log(x)u$	1
2-130	$t=\sqrt{x}$	2	2-188a	(prototype)	1		$t=\frac{ax+b}{cx+d}$	31
2-189	(to Bessel)	54	2-231a	$t=\operatorname{asinh}(x)$	1		$t=x^r$	137
2-248	(proto-type)	3	2-wit	(to Whittaker)	28		$\begin{cases} t=\sin(x) \\ t=\cos(x) \end{cases}$	44
2-269	$y=x^r u$	1	2- 79		1		$t=e^x$	11
2-297	$t=\operatorname{asinh}(\sqrt{a}x)/\sqrt{a}$	4	2-128	$y=u/x$	1		$\begin{cases} t=\sinh(x) \\ t=\cosh(x) \end{cases}$	7
2-357	$t=\sqrt{x^2+1}$	5	2-220		2		$t=\log(x)$	1
2-359	$t=1/x$	2	2-221		1		$t=x(\log(x)-1)$	1
2-363	$t=\frac{1}{2}(x+\frac{1}{x})$	4	2-76a		1		$y=\cos(x)u$	1

$$\text{2-wit}: \quad x^2y''-x(2a+2bx)y'+(a(a+1)+(\tfrac{1}{4}-m^2)+2ab+pk)x+(b^2-\tfrac{p^2}{4})x^2)y=0.$$

Table 3.

In table 3 we can read how many times a pattern matched to its equations or how many times a transformation was done in our experiment. For example a pattern 2-wit which we cannot find in Kamke's table matched to 28 equations, and t=sin(x) or t=cos(x) was done 44 times in our experiment.

equation	reason for unsolved	equation	reason for unsolved	equation	reason for unsolved
2- 15	not implemented	2-330	too general	2-427	too special
2- 19	not implemented	2-341	not implemented	2-23a	too difficult
2-127	too special	2-362	not implemented	2-115b	too difficult
2-216	not implemented	2-364	not implemented	2-115c	too difficult
2-261	is not well-known	2-399	not implemented	2-354b	too general
2-267	is not well-known	2-407	too general		
2-283	too special	2-408	not implemented		

Table 4. The list of all the unsolved equations in s1-s8.

7. References.

1. A.Forsyth,"Theory of Differential Equations vol.IV", Dover,(1960).
2. E.Lafferty,"Hypergeometric Reduction-An Adventure in Pattern Matching", Proc. 1979 MACSYMA User Conf, pp.465-481.
3. Y.Avgoustis,"Symbolic Laplace Transforms of Special Functions", Proc. 1979 MACSYMA User Conf. pp.21-40.
4. B.Saunders,"An Implementation of Kovacic's algorithm for solving second order linear homogeneous differential equations", Proc. ACM Symp. SYMSAC'81, pp.105-108.
5. M.Singer,"Liouvillian Solutions of n-th Order Homogeneous Linear Differential Equations", Amer.J.Math. vol.103,no.4, 1980, pp.661-682.
6. R.Pavelle, M.Rothstein, J.Fitch,"Computer Algebra", Scientific American, Dec. 1981, pp.136-146,151-152.
7. E.Kamke,"Differential Gleichungen-Lösungsmethoden und Lösungen", Chelsea,(1959).
8. J.Della Dora, E.Tournier,"Formal Solutions of Differntial Equations in the Neighbourhood of Singular Points", Proc. ACM Symp. SYMSAC'81, pp.25-29.
9. S.Watanabe,"A Technique for Solving Ordinary Differential Equations Using Riemann's P-functions", Proc. ACM Symp. SYMSAC'81, pp.36-43.

8. Acknowledgements.

The work described in this paper was performed with MACSYMA which is supported by the U.S.Air Force under grant F49620-79-020. I am very grateful to J.Moses and the member of Mathlab group in MIT. I could not write my program without the help of J.Golden, E.Golden, and R.Pavelle during the period 4/1/82-9/30/83.

OPERATIONAL CALCULUS TECHNIQUES FOR SOLVING DIFFERENTIAL EQUATIONS

Nikolaos Glinos*

B. David Saunders*

Department of Mathematical Sciences

Rensselaer Polytechnic Institute

Troy N.Y 12181

1. Introduction

The operational calculus theory as developed by J. Mikusinski ([MIKUJ59]) is a mathematical justification of the methods of Oliver Heaviside ([MOORD71]) for solving differential equations. The basic idea of Heaviside was the conversion of the differential equation to an algebraic equation by introducing the differential operator and treating it as an algebraic element.

The approach of Mikusinski was to start with the set of functions of a complex variable x, and make it a commutative ring with the following two operations.

(1) + : ordinary addition of two functions

(2) * : convolution of two functions defined by $f(x)*g(x) = \int_0^x f(x-t)g(t)dt$

Then he embedded this ring in a field of quotients which he calls the field of operators and a member of which is the differential operator D. Other authors (Berg [BERGL67], Krabbe [KRABG70]) have defined the operations of the above ring a little differently but they all develop an algebra of operators for solving differential equations.

In general, methods of the operational calculus have three parts.

(1) Transform the differential equation to an equation in the field of operators.

(2) Solve the transformed equation.

(3) Apply an inverse transformation to obtain an expression of the solution to the original differential equation.

One of the advantages of this approach is that in general the extensive machinery of computer algebra systems for algebraic manipulation and simplification can be applied in step (2). One problem is that the transformations of steps (1) and (3) employ heuristics. In particular the inverse transformation cannot succeed if the original equation has no solution of the desired form. In general, precise description of classes of functions for which these transformations can be guaranteed to succeed is lacking.

* Authors partially supported by National Science Foundation Grant MCS-8314600

In this paper we will outline methods for the closed form solution of certain classes of initial value problems. These methods work when the initial values are indeterminates and thus can yield general solutions to the differential equations involved. In section 2 we will deal with initial value problems of linear systems of ordinary differential equations with constant coefficients. One differential equation is then a special case of such a system. In section 3 we will examine the case of linear differential equations with polynomial coefficients. Finally in section 4 we will present an algorithm for series solution of differential equations with variable coefficients.

2. Initial value problems of linear systems of O.D.E's

We outline a method for the solution of linear systems of ordinary differential equations with constant coefficients and initial conditions, but arbitrary right hand sides. We consider systems of the following form

$$F_i(y_1^{(n_1)},\dots,y_1,\dots,y_k^{(n_k)},\dots,y_k) = f_i(x), \quad i=1,\dots,k \tag{2.1}$$

where F_i, $i=1,\dots,k$ are linear functions with constant coefficients and the initial conditions

$$y_i^{(j_i)}(0) = y_{i0}^{(j_i)}, \quad i=1,\dots,k, \quad j_i=0,\dots,n_i-1, \text{ are given constants.}$$

The method is based on a transformation provided by the operational calculus with the property that when applied it transforms the given system of differential equations into an algebraic one which we can then solve by any of the conventional methods for solving algebraic systems of equations.

If we define by D the differential operator then the operational calculus as developed by Krabbe ([KRABG70]) provides us with the following transformation.

$$y^{(m)} = D^m Y - \sum_{i=0}^{m-1} y^{(i)}(0)D^{m-i} \tag{2.2}$$

where Y is the operator corresponding to the function y(x). Based on this transformation and a few other principles from the operational calculus we can find the equivalent operational form of a function. A very simple example is the exponential function. If we take $y(x) = e^{ax}$ then by (2.2) we have $y'(x) = DY - y(0)D$ and so

$$aY = ae^{ax} = y'(x) = DY - D, \quad \text{which implies} \quad Y = \frac{D}{D-a}, \quad \text{for every } a.$$

We say that $\frac{D}{D-a}$ is the equivalent operational form of the function e^{ax}. Some other functions and their equivalent forms are

$$\frac{x^n}{n!} = \frac{1}{D^n}, \quad \frac{e^{ax}-1}{a} = \frac{1}{D-a}, \quad \sin(ax) = \frac{aD}{D^2+a^2}, \tag{2.3}$$

$$1-\cos(x) = \frac{1}{D^2+1}, \quad \cos(ax) = \frac{D^2}{D^2+a^2}, \quad \int_0^x f(x-t)g(t)dt = \frac{FG}{D},$$

where F, G are the operators corresponding to the functions f(x), g(x).

Many such formulas are given in the operational calculus texts (e.g. see [KRABG70] pages 331-344, or [MIKUJ59] pages 454-459). However no algorithm exists to convert in all cases between operational and functional form of a function by means of such formulas alone. There are many expression to which the formulas cannot be directly applied because the transformation, though linear, doesn't commute with multiplication.

Solution of linear systems of O.D.E'S with constant coefficients

We outline a method for solving systems of o.d.e's

(1) Apply the transformation (2.2) to the given system (2.1). If the right hand sides $f_i(x)$ have operational forms which are rational functions of D then substitute these expressions for each $f_i(x)$. If some $f_i(x)$ has not an equivalent operational form of that type then we use its name as an indeterminant operator form, in which case, at the end we will have to perform convolution operations which involve integrations. For simplicity assume that each $f_i(x)$ has an equivalent operational expression in terms of D (let us say $R_i(D)$).

(2) Step (1) will give us a linear system of equations of the form

$$A(D)\overline{Y} = \overline{P}(D) + \overline{R}(D) \text{ where A is a matrix, and } \overline{Y}, \overline{P}, \overline{R} \text{ vectors}$$

Solve the linear (algebraic) equations and obtain $\overline{Y} = \overline{\pi}(D)$.

(3) Decompose the expression for each Y_i into partial fractions. It may be that along with the partial fractions we are also going to have a quotient part containing positive powers of D. Since D is a pure operator we can conclude in this case that the given equation does not have a closed form solution. After decomposing into partial fractions we transform each fraction to its equivalent functional form, if it is known.

We illustrate the method with the following

Example

We are given the following system of differential equations

$$x'(t) + x(t) + 2y(t) = \sin(t)$$

$$x''(t) + 5x(t) + 3y'(t) = 0$$

$$\text{and initial conditions} \quad x(0) = y(0) = x'(0) = 0.$$

Applying the transformation (2.2) and substituting sin(t) with its operational form (from 2.3) we have after the calculations the following algebraic system

$$(D+1)X + 2Y = \frac{D}{D^2+1}$$

$$(D^2+5)X + 3DY = 0$$

At this point we gave the above system to Macsyma ([MACSYMA]) and we got the following solution

$$X = \frac{3D^2}{D^4+3D^3-9D^2+3D-10}, \quad Y = \frac{D^3+5D}{D^4+3D^3-9D^2+3D-10}$$

Then Macsyma partitioned x,y into partial fractions as follows

$$X = \frac{9D+33}{130(D^2+1)} - \frac{75}{182(D+5)} + \frac{12}{35(D-2)}$$

$$Y = \frac{22D-6}{65(D^2+1)} - \frac{75}{91(D+5)} - \frac{18}{35(D-2)}$$

All the above fractions have equivalent functional forms and so step 3 of the above method gives

$$x(t) = \frac{9}{130}\sin(t) + \frac{33}{130}(1-\cos(t)) + \frac{6}{35}(e^{2t}-1) + \frac{15}{182}(e^{-5t}-1)$$

$$y(t) = \frac{22}{65}\sin(t) - \frac{6}{65}(1-\cos(t)) - \frac{9}{35}(e^{2t}-1) + \frac{15}{91}(e^{-5t}-1)$$

which is the solution to the given system.

Comments

From the outlined method and the worked example we can observe that the original problem was transformed into an algebraic one and that the initial conditions were integrated into the resulting algebraic problem. We also see that it is possible to treat the homogeneous and nonhomogeneous case as one case and it was not necessary to find a general and a particular solution though we could have done so by computing with undetermined initial conditions.

We would also like to observe that if the partial fraction decomposition is carried out with respect to a splitting of the denominator into linear factors (algebraicaly extending the coefficient field if necessary) then the method outlined above would be completely algorithmic since in this case the partial fractions of step 3 would be of the form $\frac{1}{(D-a)^m}$ and for these fractions we do have functional equivalents. However, note that the result was obtained in the above example without the need to factor D^2+1 over an algebraic extension.

3. Differential equations with polynmial coefficients

Given the following differential equation

$$p_n(x)y^{(n)} + p_{n-1}(x)y^{(n-1)} + \dots + p_1(x)y' + p_0(x)y = f(x)$$

where the coefficients are polynomials, we seek transformations that will enable us to transform the above equation into an equivalent differential equation containing operators.

If we expand the above equation we will have terms of the form $cx^m y^{(n)}$ where c is a constant, x is the independent variable and y the unknown function. In the following theorem we give the operational equivalent of such terms.

Definition ([KRABG70] page 269)

The class A_∞ is defined as the class of functions Y(x) such that there exists an integer $\mu(Y)$ and coefficients Y_k, $(k = 0, \pm1, \pm2, \dots)$ such that $Y_k = 0$ for all $k > \mu(Y)$ and $Y(x) = \sum_{k=-\infty}^{\infty} Y_k x^k$. Rational functions of x, for example, belong in this class.

Lemma A. ([KRABG70] pages 275,293)

If g(x) is a function such that its equivalent operator is G(D), G in A_∞ then the equivalent operator of the function xg(x) is $-D\frac{d}{dD}\left(\frac{G(D)}{D}\right)$. □

Theorem A.

If D is the differential operator, and we denote

$$\frac{d^ny}{dx^n} \text{ with } y_x^{(n)} \quad \text{and the operator} \quad \frac{d^nY}{dD^n} \text{ with } Y_D^{(n)} \quad , \quad n \geq 1$$

then the following transformations hold if the operator Y(D) of y(x) is in A_∞.

$$(3.1) \qquad y_x^{(n)} = D^nY - \sum_{i=0}^{n-1} y^{(i)}(0)D^{n-i}$$

$$(3.2) \qquad xy_x^{(n)} = -D^nY_D' - (n-1)D^{n-1}Y + \sum_{i=0}^{n-2}(n-i-1)y^{(i)}(0)D^{n-i-1}$$

$$(3.3) \qquad x^2y_x^{(n)} = D^nY_D'' + 2(n-1)D^{n-1}Y_D' + (n-1)(n-2)D^{n-2}Y - \sum_{i=0}^{n-3}(n-i-2)(n-i-1)y^{(i)}(0)D^{n-i-2}$$

$$(3.4) \qquad x^ny = (-1)^nY_D^{(n)} - (-1)^n \frac{n}{D}Y_D^{(n-1)} + \sum_{i=0}^{n-2}(-1)^{n+i+2}\frac{n!}{(n-i-2)!}\frac{1}{D^{i+2}}Y_D^{(n-i-2)}$$

$$(3.5) \qquad x^ny_x' = (-1)^nDY_D^{(n)}$$

$$(3.6) \qquad x^ny_x'' = (-1)^nD^2Y_D^{(n)} + (-1)^nnDY_D^{(n-1)} \qquad \text{for } n > 1$$

$$= -D^2Y_D' - DY + y(0)D \qquad \text{for } n = 1$$

Proof

Tranformation (3.1) is the basic transformation of operational calculus and follows by induction on the order of the derivative. The proof of the basis, $y'(x) = DY - y(0)D$, for this induction can be found in ([KRABG70] page 86). We can prove (3.2) using lemma A and (3.1). Thus we have

$$xy_x^{(n)} = -D\frac{d}{dD}\left(\frac{D^nY - \sum_{i=0}^{n-1} y^{(i)}(0)D^{n-i}}{D}\right)$$

If we now perform the calculations using the usual differentiation rules we easily find (3.2). Transformation (3.3) can be proved similarily from (3.2) and lemma A.

Transformations (3.4)-(3.6) may be proved by induction. For (3.5) we have

Basis: for n=1 we have $xy_x' = -D\frac{d}{dD}\left(\frac{DY-y(0)D}{D}\right) = -DY_D'$

Assumption: Assume (3.5) is true for n.

Step: $x^{n+1}y_x' = x(x^ny_x') = -D\frac{d}{dD}\left(\frac{(-1)^nDY_D^{(n)}}{D}\right) = -D\frac{d}{dD}\left((-1)^nY_D^{(n)}\right)$

$$= -D(-1)^nY_D^{(n+1)} = (-1)D(-1)^nY_D^{(n+1)} = (-1)^{(n+1)}DY_D^{(n+1)}$$

Transformations (3.4), (3.6) can be proved the same way. □

From the above transformations we can see that after applying them to a given differential equation we get a new differential equation in operational form where the order of the original differential equation and the highest degree of its polynomial coefficients have been interchanged. So a differential equation of any order with up to quadratic coefficients can be transformed into a differential equation which is of at most second order and has coefficients with degrees at most up to the order of the original equation. A side effect however of the above transformations is that we may start with a homogeneous equation and end up with a nonhomogeneous equation.

At this point we can solve the new, lower order, differential equation with some available algorithm, for example, kovacic's ([KOVAJ]), see also Saunders ([SAUND81]), or methods in Macsyma's o.d.e solver ([MACSYMA]). Also, when the order is greater than 2 we can in principle apply Singer's algorithm ([SINGM80]). Finally, we obtain a functional expression of the solution by mapping the operational parts of the solution to their functional equivalents.

Let us illustrate the method with the following

Example.

$$xy^{(4)} - 2y^{(3)} = x^3, \qquad y(0)=a,\ y'(0)=b,\ y''(0)=c$$

We apply transformations (3.1), (3.2) and substitute x^3 with $\frac{6}{D^3}$ which is its operational form. After performing the calculations we have the differential equation

$$Y_D' + \frac{5}{D}y = \frac{5a}{D} + \frac{4b}{D^2} + \frac{3c}{D^3} - \frac{6}{D^7}$$

which is a first order nonhomogeneous equation with respect D. We gave it to the Macsyma o.d.e solver and we obtained

$$Y = a + \frac{b}{D} + \frac{c}{D^2} + \frac{k}{D^5} + \frac{6}{D^6}$$

Substituting now $\frac{1}{D^n}$ with its functional equivalent $\frac{x^n}{n!}$ we have

$$y(x) = a + bx + \frac{c}{2}x^2 + \frac{k}{120}x^5 + \frac{1}{120}x^6$$

which is the solution to the given problem.

4. Series solutions of differential equations

In this section we will develop a method for finding series solutions to initial value problems of differential equations with variable coefficients. The method is very general and the series obtained is a generalized series in the sense that the terms of the series may be arbitrary functions. We will use this method to obtain an efficient algorithm for finding power series solutions to differential equations of the form

$$y^{(n)} + p_1(x)y^{(n-1)} + \dots + p_{n-1}(x)y' + p_n(x)y = f(x) \tag{4.1}$$

in the particular case where the coefficients and the right hand side are polynomials or more generally functions analytic at 0 with a readily obtained Taylor series.

Definitions

1. Let C be the set of all continuous functions f(x) on [0, ∞).
2. Let K be the set of all functions k(x,t) continuous in t and x for $0 \le t \le x$. These functions are usually called kernels.
3. If k(x,t) belongs in K then we define the operator [1+k(x,t)] as follows

$$[1+k(x,t)]f(x) = f(x) + \int_0^x k(x,t)f(t)dt, \quad \text{for all } f(x) \text{ in } C.$$

Thus $[1+k(x,t)] : C \longrightarrow C$.

4. Let k_1 and k_2 be two elements of K. Then we define the generalized convolution of the two kernels k_1 and k_2 as follows

$$k_1(x,t)*k_2(x,t) = \int_t^x k_1(x,\xi)k_2(\xi,t)d\xi$$

and we define $k^{*n} = k*k*...*k$ (n times).

5. We define the application of a kernel k(x,t) in K to a function f in C as follows

$$k(x,t)f(x) = \int_0^x k(x,t)f(t)dt$$

Thus we can use the notation $[1+k(x,t)]f(x) = f(x) + k(x,t)f(x)$. Notice that this definition is a particular case of the generalized convolution where the second kernel is independent of t and the lower limit of integration is 0. It can then be shown that

$$(k_1(x,t)*k_2(x,t))f(x) = k_1(x,t)(k_2(x,t)f(x)), \text{ and that } k^{*n} = k^n,$$

where k^n denotes the operator consisting of n successive applications of k.

Lemma B.

$$|k^{*n}(x,t)| \le \frac{1}{(n-1)!}\theta^n(x-t)^{n-1} \le \frac{1}{(n-1)!}\theta^n X^{n-1}, \quad 0 \le t \le x \le X$$

where X and θ are fixed but arbitrary numbers.

Proof

Since k(x,t) is continuous it must be that $|k(x,t)| \le \theta$ for some arbitrary but fixed number θ. We proceed by induction on n.

Basis: For n=1 the inequality becomes $|k(x,t)| \le \theta$ which is true.

Assumption: Assume the inequality is true for n.

Step: We will prove the inequality for n+1. We have the following

$$|k^{*n+1}(x,t)| = |k(x,t)^{*n}*k(x,t)| = \left|\int_t^x k^{*n}(x,\xi)k(\xi,t)d\xi\right|$$

$$\le \int_t^x |k^{*n}(x,\xi)k(\xi,t)|d\xi \le \int_t^x \frac{1}{(n-1)!}\theta^n(x-\xi)^{n-1}\theta d\xi$$

$$= \frac{1}{(n-1)!}\theta^{n+1}\int_t^x (x-\xi)^{n-1}d\xi = \frac{1}{(n-1)!}\theta^{n+1}\frac{(x-t)^n}{n} = \frac{1}{n!}\theta^{n+1}(x-t)^n$$

The last inequality of the lemma is clearly true since $x-t \le X$. □

Theorem B.

The operators $[1+k(x,t)]$ form a group under the operation (denoted by juxtaposition), (see [BERGL67] pages 250-252),

$$[1+k_1][1+k_2] = [1+k_1+k_2+k_1*k_2], \quad \text{for } k_1, k_2 \text{ in } K.$$

The inverse with respect to this operation is given by

$$[1+k(x,t)]^{-1} = [1 + \sum_{n=1}^{\infty}(-1)^n k^{*n}(x,t)]$$

Proof

We verify that the following group axioms hold.

I. $[1+k_1][1+k_2]$ belongs in the group since $k_1+k_2+k_1*k_2$ belongs in K.

II. The identity operator, $1=[1+0(x,t)]$, is the group identity.

III. The juxtaposition operation on the operators $[1+k]$ is associative. This can be shown by using Dirichlet's formula.

IV. For every operator $[1+k(x,t)]$ the given inverse operator $[1+k(x,t)]^{-1}$ exists, is unique and it is well defined.

To prove IV we have to show that the series $\sum_{n=1}^{\infty}(-1)^n k^{*n}(x,t)$ (σ) converges to an element in K. For this we will use Weierstrass M test for uniform convergence. In every interval $0 \leq t \leq x \leq X$ by lemma B we have the following.

$$|(-1)^n k^{*n}(x,t)| = |(-1)^n||k^{*n}(x,t)| = |k^{*n}(x,t)| \leq \frac{1}{(n-1)!}\theta^n X^{n-1}$$

The series $\displaystyle\sum_{n=1}^{\infty}\frac{1}{(n-1)!}\theta^n X^{n-1} = \theta\sum_{n=1}^{\infty}\frac{1}{(n-1)!}(\theta X)^{n-1} = \theta\sum_{n=0}^{\infty}\frac{M^n}{n!}$, $M = \theta X$

has constant terms and converges to θe^M and therefore we can conclude that the series (σ) converges uniformely to an element in K.

Thus the operator $[1+k(x,t)]^{-1}$ is an element of the group. Furthermore the uniqueness of the inverse operator is easily proven using the fact that the series (σ) converges uniformely. So if $[1+k(x,t)]^{-1}$ had two distinct inverses $[1+k_1(x,t)]$ and $[1+k_2(x,t)]$ then $k_1(x,t) = k_2(x,t)$ since they would be both uniform limits of (σ). It is easy to see that $[1+k(x,t)][1+k(x,t)]^{-1} = 1$ because of the telescoping sum. □

Series solution to voltera integral equations

Assume now that we are given an equation of the form

$$y(x) + \int_0^x k(x,t)y(t)dt = f(x) \qquad \text{(voltera integral equation)}$$

where $y(x), f(x)$ belong to C and $k(x,t)$ belongs to K, then by the above theory we may write $[1+k(x,t)]y(x) = f(x)$ and by applying the inverse operator $[1+k]^{-1}$ we have

$$y(x) = [1+k(x,t)]^{-1}f(x) = f(x) + \int_0^x (\sum_{n=1}^{\infty}(-1)^n k^{*n}(x,t))f(t)dt$$

$$= f(x) + \sum_{n=1}^{\infty}(-1)^n\int_0^x k^{*n}(x,t)f(t)dt = f(x) + \sum_{n=1}^{\infty}(-1)^n k^{*n}(x,t)f(x)$$

and therefore $y(x) = f(x) + \sum_{n=1}^{\infty} (-1)^n k^{*n}(x,t)f(x)$ is a series solution to the given voltera equation.

A very general algorithm

In view of the above theory we can establish an algorithm for finding series solutions to initial value problems for n^{th} order differential equations with variable coefficients. For simplicity however we will work on second order equations

$$y'' + p(x)y' + q(x)y = f(x) \tag{4.2}$$

We will return to the general case a little later. We work as follows. Expanding y and y' partially in Taylor series about 0 we have

$$y(x) = y_0 + xy_0' + \int_0^x (x-t)y''(t)dt \quad \text{and} \quad y'(x) = y_0' + \int_0^x y''(t)dt$$

Substituting in the given differential equation and rearranging terms we have

$$y''(x) + \int_0^x (p(x)+q(x)(x-t))y''(t)dt = f(x) - (p(x)+xq(x))y_0' - q(x)y_0$$

We denote $f(x)-(p(x)+xq(x))y_0'-q(x)y_0$ by $g(x)$ and $p(x)+q(x)(x-t)$ by $k(x,t)$. Then we have an equation of the form

$$y''(x) + \int_0^x k(x,t)y''(t)dt = g(x)$$

which is a voltera integral equation and therefore by our previous discussion

$$y''(x) = g(x) + \sum_{n=1}^{\infty} (-1)^n k^{*n}(x,t)g(x)$$

Having found the second derivative of y we integrate twice and considering also the initial conditions we find the generalized series solution for y(x) up to as many terms as we want. The above algorithm relies on our ability to perform integration. Indeed there is an integration hidden in each term of the sum. Integration therefore is generally the most expensive operation of the algorithm. However in the case of polynomial coefficients the integration steps are all easy to perform.

Special case : Power Series Solutions

For the differential equation (4.2) assume now that p,q,f are polynomials or functions analytic about the origin. In order to make the algorithm more clear we will introduce the following notation. We denote by L the kernel $k(x,t)=1$. That is

$$Lf(x) = \int_0^x f(t)dt$$

Using definitions 4 and 5 of generalized convolution and application it is easy to show that

$$L^{*n} = L^n = \frac{1}{(n-1)!}(x-t)^{(n-1)}. \text{ So for example}$$

$$L^2 f(x) = L(Lf(x)) = \frac{1}{(2-1)!}\int_0^x (x-t)^{(2-1)} f(t)dt = \int_0^x (x-t)f(t)dt.$$

For the second order equation (4.2) we have shown that

$$y''(x) = g(x) + \sum_{n=1}^{\infty} (-1)^n k^{*n}(x,t)g(x)$$

where $k(x,t) = p(x) + q(x)(x-t) = p(x)L + q(x)L^2$. Therefore

$$\begin{aligned} y''(x) &= g(x) - (p(x)L + q(x)L^2)g(x) \\ &\quad + (p(x)L + q(x)L^2)((p(x)L + q(x)L^2)g(x)) \\ &\quad - (p(x)L + q(x)L^2)((p(x)L + q(x)L^2)((p(x)L + q(x)L^2)g(x))) \\ &\quad + \dots \end{aligned}$$

We can clearly observe the iterative form of the calculation of each new term of the series. It appears that this series is time consuming to compute, since the operators L, L^2 involve integration and $g(x)$ may be arbitrary to start with. However in the case where $p(x), q(x), f(x)$ are polynomials or generally functions having Taylor series expansions around 0 we totally avoid explicit integration steps and come up with a simple algorithm to calculate power series solutions for the above initial value problem. Indeed we have

$$(p(x)L + q(x)L^2)g(x) = p(x)Lg(x) + q(x)L^2g(x) =$$

$$p(x)\int_0^x g(t)dt + q(x)\int_0^x (x-t)g(t)dt =$$

$$p(x)\int_0^x (g_m t^m + \dots + g_0)dt + q(x)\int_0^x (x-t)(g_m t^m + \dots + g_0)dt =$$

$$p(x)\int_0^x (g_m t^m + \dots + g_0)dt + xq(x)\int_0^x (g_m t^m + \dots + g_0)dt - q(x)\int_0^x t(g_m t^m + \dots + g_0)dt =$$

$$p(x)\left(\frac{g_m}{m+1}x^{m+1} + \dots + g_0 x\right) + q(x)\left(\frac{g_m}{m+1}x^{m+2} + \dots + g_0 x^2\right) - q(x)\left(\frac{g_m}{m+2}x^{m+2} + \dots + \frac{g_0}{2}x^2\right) =$$

$$p(x)\left(\frac{g_m}{m+1}x^{m+1} + \dots + g_0 x\right) + q(x)\left(\frac{g_m}{(m+1)(m+2)}x^{m+2} + \dots + \frac{g_0}{2}x^2\right).$$

Thus $(p(x)L + q(x)L^2)g(x)$ has the form $p(x)A + q(x)B$ where A and B have been calculated from the coefficients of $g(x)$.

We can observe that the above method could be applied to any order differential equation with polynomial or analytic coefficients and obtain a similar algorithm. In general for

$$y^{(n)} + p_1(x)y^{(n-1)} + \dots + p_{n-1}(x)y' + p_n(x)y = f(x)$$

we have the corresponding kernel

$$k(x,t) = p_1(x)L + p_2(x)L^2 + \dots + p_n(x)L^n$$

and the corresponding $g(x)$ will be

$$\begin{aligned} g(x) = f(x) &- \left(p_1(x) + xp_2(x) + \dots + \frac{x^{n-1}}{(n-1)!}p_n(x)\right)y_0^{(n-1)} \\ &- \left(p_2(x) + xp_3(x) + \dots + \frac{x^{n-2}}{(n-2)!}p_n(x)\right)y_0^{(n-2)} - \dots - p_n(x)y_0 \end{aligned}$$

5. Programming experience

A first implementation in Macsyma, on a VAX 11/780, of the method descibed in section 2 was compared with the ODE2 solver of Macsyma. The following table shows some equations and the time (in seconds) required to obtain general solutions.

Equation	Operators method	ODE2
$y''(x) - 2y'(x) + 5y(x) = \sin(3x)$	11.6	29.2
$y''(x) - 4y(x) = \sin(\frac{3x}{2})\sin(\frac{x}{2})$	20.1	21.0
$y''(x) + 3y(x) = 1$	4.1	8.0
$y''(x) - y'(x) + 3y(x) = f(x)$	8.9	40.0
$y''(x) + 4y(x) = \cos(2x)$	7.1	6.5
$8y'(x) - 6y(x) = \sin(x)$	5.9	6.2
$y''(x) - y'(x) - 6y(x) = 2$	4.6	2.1
$3y''(x) - 2y'(x) + 7y(x) = \cos^3(x)$	67.7	215.0
$y'(x) - 2y(x) = x^2\sin(3x)$	13.4	10.2
$y^{(5)}(x) + 2y^{(3)}(x) + y'(x) = \alpha x + \beta\sin(x) + \gamma\cos(x)$	22.6	can not do it
$z''(x) + 2y'(x) + z(x) = 0$ $z'(x) - y'(x) - 2(z(x) - y(x)) = 1 - 2x$	15.2	""
$w'(x) - y(x) + z(x) = 0$ $y'(x) - w(x) - y(x) = 0$ $z'(x) - w(x) - z(x) = 0$	9.4	""
$y''(x) + 3y'(x) + 2y(x) = \begin{cases} \sin(x), & 0 < x \leq \pi \\ 0, & \text{else} \end{cases}$	13.7	""
$z'(x) + y'(x) - 4y(x) = \begin{cases} 1, & 0 < x \leq \alpha \\ 0, & \text{else} \end{cases}$ $y'(x) - 3y(x) + z(x) = x^2$	14.5	""
$y'(x) + 3y(x) = -2\int_0^x y(t)dt + \begin{cases} 1, & \alpha < x \leq \beta \\ 0, & \text{else} \end{cases}$	8.0	""

One difference between the two programs is that the general solutions given by ODE2 contain arbitrary constants which bear no direct relation to the initial conditions. Therefore if we would like the solution to an initial value problem we would have to solve a system of equations in order to express the unknown constants in terms of the initial conditions. The general solution, however, given by our method has as unknown constants the initial conditions of the problem and so all we have to do is substitute these constants with their values.

One general remark about the methods of sections 2 is that the equations we are trying to solve need not be strictly differential. They can contain also convolution integrals as well as discontinous right hand sides. All these entities can be treated in the same way. For example the problem

$$2y'(x) + y(x) = \int_0^x \sin(x-t)y(t)dt + \begin{cases} 1 & \text{if } 2 < x < 3 \\ 0 & \text{else} \end{cases} \quad \text{with } y(0) = a$$

transforms directly to

$$2DY - 2aD + Y = \frac{D}{D^2 + 1}\frac{1}{D}Y + T_2 - T_3$$

where T_2 and T_3 are displacement operators. We now proceed according to the general method we described and obtain the solution. This example required 17.4 seconds to solve.

For the polynomial coefficients case we don't have enough experimental results due to incomplete implementation. However we were able to solve equations that ODE2 could not.

The power series solution algorithm described in this paper is more efficient to use than the Macsyma series package if of course we only want the initial n terms of the series solution and not the general solution in terms of recurrence relations.

6. References

[BERGL67] L. Berg, Introduction to the Operational Calculus, New York: Interscience, John Willey 1967.

[KOVAJ] J. J. Kovacic, An algorithm for solving second order linear homogeneous differential equations. Private communication.

[KRABG70] G. Krabbe, Operational Calculus, New York-Heidelberg-Berlin, Springer-Verlag 1970

[MACSYMA] Macsyma Reference Manual, MIT Laboratory for Computer Science, Version nine, December 1977.

[MIKUJ59] J. Mikusinski, Operational Calculus, London-New York-Paris-Los Angeles: Pergamon Press 1959.

[MOORD71] D. Moore, Heaviside Operational Calculus, American Elsevier, New York 1971.

[SAUND81] B. D. Saunders, An implementation of Kovacic's algorithm for solving second order linear homogeneous differential equations, Proc. ACM SYMSAC, 1981 pp 105-108.

[SINGM80] M. F. Singer, Liouvillian Solutions of n-th Order Homogeneous Linear Differential Equations, American Journal of Mathematics, Vol. 103, No. 4, pp. 661-682

ON THE APPLICATION OF SYMBOLIC COMPUTATION TO NONLINEAR CONTROL THEORY*

G.Cesareo and R.Marino
Seconda Università di Roma, Tor Vergata
Dipartimento di Ingegneria Elettronica
Via O. Raimondo, I00173 Roma, Italy.

Abstract. Applications of computer algebra to linear partial differential equations of first order and to nonlinear control theory are presented. It is shown how symbolic systems can compute automatically: (i) the dimension of the accessible set from a particular state for a nonlinear control system; (ii) the number of independent solutions for a system of linear partial differential equations of first order. The algorithms are based on the computation of certain distributions given a set of vector fields. Examples of application to robotics and power system equations are briefly discussed.

1. INTRODUCTION

We discuss the application of computer algebra to certain important issues in nonlinear control theory and in the solution of systems of linear partial differential equations of first order.

In nonlinear control theory the following system is often encountered

$$\dot{x} = f(x) + \sum_{i=1}^{m} u_i(t)\, g_i(x) \qquad (\Sigma)$$

where $x \in \mathbb{R}^n$, $f, g_1, \ldots, g_m$ are analytic vector fields on $\mathbb{R}^n$, $u=(u_1, \ldots, u_m) : \mathbb{R}^+ \to \mathbb{R}^n$ is a piecewise continous function. A fundamental tool in the study of (Σ) is the accessible set from x_0, denoted as

* This work was partly supported by MPI (fondi 40%).

implementation are discussed.

2. THE BASIC ALGORITHM

A smooth (analytic) vector field $f(x) = \sum_{i=1}^{n} f^i(x)\partial/\partial x_i$ can be represented as an n-vector whose componenets f^i, $i=1,\ldots,n$, are smooth (analytic) functions. Given a set of m vector fields $\{f_1,\ldots,f_m\}$the problem is to design an algorithm which determines a basis of linearly independent vector fields over the quotient field of smooth (analyti functions. A simple solution is the triangularization of the nxm matrix $(f^i_j(x))$, whose entries are functions on $\mathbb{R}^n$. To this purpose we choos a fraction free algorithm ([4],[5]), which is more suitable than minor expansion: in fact, in general, $m<n$ and an $(m+1)$-th vector field can be easily added and checked to be linearly independent on the previous one The algorithm we propose (see also [6]) computes the rank and a spannin set of a distribution given as $\{f_1,\ldots,f_m\}$; it is described in pseudocode as follows

$^{(0)}f^0_0 := 1$

r :=1 (r gives the number of independent vector fields at each step)

pivoting f_1 so that $^{(1)}f^1_1 = \emptyset$

for i :=2 to m do

begin

for k:=1 to r do

for j:=1 to n do

$^{(k+1)}f^j_i := ({}^{(k)}f^k_k \, {}^{(k)}f^j_i - {}^{(k)}f^j_k \, {}^{(k)}f^k_i) / {}^{(k-1)}f^{k-1}_{k-1}$

if $^{(r+1)}f_i = \emptyset$

then vector i is discarded

else begin

r := r+1

pivoting $^{(r)}f_i$ so that $^{(r)}f^r_i \neq \emptyset$

$^{(r)}f_r := {}^{(r)}f_i$

$A(x_0)$ and defined as the collection of x which can be reached in a positive time by a trajectory of (Σ) driven by an admissible control u: it quantifies the capability of controlling system (Σ) when it is in x_0. Sussmann and Jurdjevic [1] relate $A(x_0)$ to an algebraic object called the accessible distribution L.

Consider also the system of linear partial differential equations of first order

$$X_i\phi = \sum_{j=1}^{n} \alpha_i^j(x)\ \partial\phi/\partial x_i = 0 \qquad i=1,\ldots,m \qquad (P)$$

where X_i are smooth vector fields in $\mathbb{R}^n$ and ϕ is a smooth function $\phi(x) : \mathbb{R}^+ \to \mathbb{R}^n$. One investigates the existence of a solution ϕ on U, an open subset of $\mathbb{R}^n$. Chow [2] (see also Sussmann [3]) shows that (P) admits n-s independent solutions $\phi_{n-s+1},\ldots,\phi_n$, i.e. $|d\phi_i/dx_j|$ non-singular in U, $n-s+1\leq i\leq n$, $1\leq j\leq n$, where s is the constant rank in U of D, the smallest involutive distribution which contains the set of vector fields $\{X_1,\ldots,X_m\}$.

Algorithms which allow the automatic computation of L and D, and in particular the verification of the involutivity of a set of vector fields are not available.

In this note we show how these problems can be solved using a common tool: an algorithm which, given a set of vector fields, produces a basis, linearly independent in U, open subset, over the quotient field of smooth (analytic) functions on U. Symbolic computation is crucial since the vector fields involved are in general not constant; in particular Lie differentiation and matrix calculus over smooth functions are required and they can only be performed by symbolic systems.

The plan of the note is the following. In Section 2 the basic algorithm is presented in detail and it si shown how involutivity can be checked by iterated applications of the same algorithm. In Section 3 it is shown how D can be computed: the solvability of (P) and the number of independent solutions n-s are then automatically determined. In Section 4 L is formally introduced and an algorithm for its computation is presented which generalizes known results when (Σ) is linear (f linear and g_i constant vector fields). In Section 5 examples of application (problems from robotics and power systems) and the corresponding

```
        end
    end if
end
```

This algorithm provides $r \le m$ independent vector fields $\{ {}^{(r)}f_1, \ldots, {}^{(r)}f_r \}$ which span the distribution $\{f_1, \ldots\ldots, f_m\}$. One also obtains the submanifold (open and dense in $\mathbb{R}^n$)

$$C = \{ x \in \mathbb{R}^n : {}^{(r)}f_r^k(x) \neq \emptyset \quad \forall k = R, \ldots, n \}$$

where the matrix $(f_j^i(x))$ has maximum rank.

An additional vector field f_{m+1} on $\mathbb{R}^n$ can be easily checked to be linearly independent on $\{f_1, \ldots, f_m\}$ performing once the main loop of the algorithm with $i = m+1$.

Recall that the Lie bracket of two vector fields X and Y is defined in local coordinates as

$$[X, Y] = [dY/dx]\, X - [dX/dx]\, Y$$

and can be computed by symbolic systems. Recall also that the set of independent vector fields $\{f_1, \ldots, f_r\}$ is involutive in U, open subset of $\mathbb{R}^n$, if there exist $r^2(r-1)/2$ smooth functions $\gamma_{ijk}(x)$ on U such that

$$[f_i, f_j](x) = \sum_{k=1}^{r} \gamma_{ijk}(x) \quad f_k(x)$$

for all x U and $1 \le i < j \le r$; equivalently one can say that $[f_i, f_j](x)$ is dependent on $\{f_1, \ldots, f_r\}$for every $x \in U$ and this can be checked as illustrated above. Thus, in order to check the involutivity of a set of vector fields $\{f_1, \ldots, f_r\}$, one can set up the following algorithm,described in pseudocode, where the input is the matrix $B = (f_i^k)_{n \times r}$ and the output is the value T if the property holds or the value F if the property does not hold.

```
PROCEDURE INVOLUTIVITY (B,n,r)
i:=2
while i < r
do begin
   h:=1
```

```
    while h<i
    do begin
       compute [f_i,f_h]
       triangularize[f_i,f_h] giving [f_i,f_h]^G
       if [f_i,f_h]^G = 0
       then h = h+1
       else begin
            write "Lie bracket of vectors i,h is linearly dependent
            return F
            end
       end if
       end
    i = i+1
    end do
  end-do
  return T
```

Note in fact that

$$[f_i \ , \ f_h] \in \text{span} \ \{f_1,\ldots,f_r\}$$

il and only if

$$[f_i^G \ , \ f_h^G] \in \text{span} \ \{f_1^G,\ldots,f_r^G\}$$

where the superscript G indicates "triangularized";thus the set is involutive if and only if for all i and h , i<h

$$[f_i^G \ , \ f_h^G]^G = 0$$

3. APPLICATION TO LINEAR PARTIAL DIFFERENTIAL EQUATION

According to the results reported by Chow [2]if the involutivity algorithm applied to the set of vector fields $\{X_1,\ldots,X_m\}$ established that they are invólutive and of constant rank in U, open subset of $\mathbb{R}^n$, then there exist n-m independent integrals of (P) $\phi_{n-m+1},\ldots,\phi_n$ such that $[d\phi_i/dx_j]$ $i=n-m+1,\ldots,n$, $j=1,\ldots,n$ is nonsingular in U: they constitute a principal system of integrals. If the algorithm determines that the set is not involutive in U then the number of independent integrals is less than n-m and is precisely n-s where s>m and s is the rank in U of D, the smallest involutive distribution which contains span $\{X_1,\ldots,X_m\}$. D can be computed by the following algorithm

step 0: $r_0 = 0$, $B = 0_{n\times n}$

insert in the first r_1 m columns of B a basis for the set of vector fields $\{X_1,\ldots,X_m\}$;

step j: insert in the k-th column of B each vector $[b_i,b_l]$ independent on the first k-1 columns of B:

$$b_k = [b_i,b_l] \qquad k = r_j+1,\ldots,r_{j+1}$$

$$l = r_{j-1}+1,\ldots,r_j$$

$$i = 1,\ldots\ldots,l-1$$

where b_i denotes the i-th column of B.

step j is iterated until the maximum rank of B is n or no column is added at a specific step: at the end the nonzero column of B constitute a basis for D.

Let s the number of nonzero columns of B at the end of the algorithm. If s=n and B is nonsingular for every $x\in U$, open subset of $\mathbb{R}^n$, there does not exists any smooth function which solves equation (P) in U. The singular set for B is given by the collection of x where all the components of the last nonzero column of B^G vanish. In any case n-s gives the number of integrals of any principal system of integrals.

4. APPLICATION TO NONLINEAR CONTROL THEORY

Sussmann and Jurdjevic [1] introduced two basic distributions for general nonlinear systems of type $\dot{x} = f(x,u)$: the stongly accessible distribution L_0, which for the class of systems (Σ) can be defined as the smallest involutive distribution which contains span $\{ad_f^l g_i : l \geq 0 , 1 \leq i \leq m\}$

where $ad_f g = [f,g]$, $ad_f^l g = [f, ad_f^{l-1} g]$, and the accessible distribution L_0, which is involutive and for system (Σ) can be defined as

span $\{f , L_0\}$

The importance of L is due to the fact that the accessible set from x_0, denoted by $A(x_0)$, has nonempty interior in the integral manifold of L through x_0, denoted as $I(x_0, L)$. If one introduces the distribution $G^0 = \text{span}\{g_1, \ldots, g_m\}$ and the set of vector fields $G_f = \{f, g_1, \ldots, g_m\}$ and defines the distributions

$G^j = \text{span}\{G^{j-1}, [G_f, G^{j-1}]\}$

where $[G_f, G^{j-1}] = \text{span}\{ [X,Y] : X \in G_f, Y \in G^{j-1} \}$, it can be proved (see [6] , [7]) that

(i) if there exists an integer k such that $G^k(x) = G^{k+1}(x)$ for every $x \in V$, open subset in $\mathbb{R}^n$, then $G^k(x) = G^{k+1}(x)$ for any integer $l \geq 0$ and any $x \in V$;

(ii) the integer k always exists and is less than n-1; moreover

$$L_0(x) = G^k(x)$$

for every $x \in N = \{x \in \mathbb{R}^n : G^k(x) \text{ has maximum rank}\}$.

Properties (i) and (ii) allow the computation of L_0, and consequently of L , in a finite number of steps. The recursive symbolic computation of the distributions G^j can be accomplished by an algorithm which employs the basic tool of Section 2 and is similar to the algorithm developed in the preceding Section. Property (i) provides a stopping criterium and property (ii) guarantees the computation of L_0 and L in N in terms of a basis of vector fields.

The algorithm can be summarized as follows:

step 0: set the nxn matrix $B = 0_{nxn}$ and insert the first columns of B a basis for G^0, say of r_1 vector fields;

step j: insert, starting from the first zero column of B each vector

$[f, b_i]$ $\quad i = r_{j-1}, \ldots, r_j$

$[b_i, b_l]$ $\quad i = r_{j-1}, \ldots, r_j \; ; \; l = 1, \ldots, r_1$

if it is independent on the nonzero columns of B, where b_i denotes the i-th column of B;

step j is iterated until all b_i are nonzero or no column is added at step j.

The maximum rank of G^{j-1} is r_j and the first r_j columns of B provide a basis for G^{j-1}. According to (i) and (ii) the nonzero columns of B are a basis for L_0 in N. Moreover a triangularized basis is provided so that the singular points for G^k are singled out. L can be easily computed in N using the equality $L = \text{span}\{f, L_0\}$.

A stronger important property for actual applications ([8], [9] , [10]) called feedback linearizability can be also checked via symbolic systems.

The conditions

(a) $G^k(x) = T_x U_{x_0}$ for every x belonging to U_{x_0}, U_{x_0} neighborhood of x_0 and x_0 such that $f(x_0) \in G^0(x_0)$

(b) G^j is involutive and of constant rank in U_{x_0}

are shown to be necessary and sufficient ([19], [20])for the existence of a state space change of coordinates $\tilde{x} = T(x)$, $T(x_0) = 0$,and a stat feedback control law

$$u_i = a_i(x) + \sum_{j=1}^{m} s_i^j(x)\, v_j$$

such that the system

$$\dot{x} = f(x) + \sum_{i=1}^{m} g_i(x)\, a_i(x) + \sum_{i=1}^{m} \sum_{j=1}^{m} g_i(x)\, s_i^j(x)\, v_j$$

is a linear controllable system

$$\dot{\tilde{x}} = A\tilde{x} + \sum_{j=1}^{m} b_j v_j$$

in the coordinates $(\tilde{x}_1, \ldots, \tilde{x}_n)$.

On the basis of the tools so far developed condition (b) can be checked by applying the involutivity procedure to matrix B at each step j of the algorithm which computes the nested set of distributions G^j.

Consider now the special case when system (Σ) is a linear one, i.e. $f(x) = Fx$, $F_{n \times n}$ constant matrix and g_i are constant vector fields, $1 \le i \le m$

In this case the algorithm for the computation of L_0 is simplified by the fact that $[g_i,g_j] = 0$ for all $1 \leq i,j \leq m$, and $[Fx,X] = -FX$ for every constant vector field X. It follows that only constant vector fields are generated by iterated Lie brackets with Fx. Thus the algorithm reduces to the computation of $\{G, FG, \ldots, F^k G\}$, where $G = (g_1, \ldots, g_m)$, which provides the well-known linear controllable subspace. What can be done by numerical computation in the case of linear control systems must be done by symbolic computation in the general nonlinear case.

5. IMPLEMENTATION AND EXAMPLES OF APPLICATION

Algorithms and procedures previously presented have been implemented in REDUCE 2 [14]on a UNIVAC 1100 system at Rome University. The programs developed have been applied so far to two cases of interest: controllability of elastic robots and of power systems.

In [15]it is shown how every system which can be modeled by Lagrange equations is equivalent to a linear controllable system via feedback transformation if the number of controls (generalized forces) is equal to the number of degrees of freedom of the dynamic system ($m=n/2$ in (Σ)). For kinematic chains this condition implies that a robot with rigid joints and links can be controlled as easily as a linear controllable system if each joint is actuated. However if elasticity at joints is taken into account or not every joint is controlled nothing can be said in general: one has to apply the algorithm described in Section 4 in order to check the accessibility and the feedback linearizability properties. In [15] a structured algorithm implemented in REDUCE is presented which checks accessibility and feedback linearizability of elastic robots given spatial geometry, mass distribution and structural parameters. The examples therein reported show that a spheric elastic joint, modeled by two orthogonal rotary elastic joints connecting two links is feedback linearizable and a planar robot constituted by two rigid links connected by two parallel elastic rotary joints is strongly accessible (rank L_0 = n) but not feedback linearizable.

In [16] it is shown how the problem of locating power controls in in power system networks for stabilizability purposes can be solved by programs based on the algorithm developed in Section 4 and implemented in REDUCE. The programs check if a power system network, given by its incidence matrix, is accessible or feedback linearizable for all possible locations of power controls at the nodes of the network. The case studied in [16]is a network of five nodes: since there are $\binom{5}{2}$ possible ways of placing two controls but some symmetries were present, the program was run six times instead of the $\binom{5}{2}$ times required in genera The system is feedback linearizable in three cases and in the mos convenient one the explicit symbolic expression of a state feedback sta bilizing control law is determined according to the REDUCE program described in [17].

In these examples we found that the limit of application of the programs presented mainly depend on the dimension of the state space (n) and on the complexity of the expressions of the vector fields f, g_1,.. ...,g_m. In fact Lie brackets involve computation of nxn Jacobians which can be very complex if rational functions are involved. More specific problems are given by: waste of CPU time due to garbage collection and expression growing due to absence of simplification routines. However one must say that REDUCE garbage collection algorithm is probably not the fastest available and that UNIVAC 1100 systems do not have virtual memory. Adopting the technique of renaming variables in order to minimize the number of terms in each expression, problems with a maximum of twelve state variables could be solved; this technique cannot be extensively used when many differentiations are involved. Note also that, unfortunately,the algorithms presented are not separable, that is they cannot be split into more subprograms.It is likely that the use of Lisp Machines can be of some help as far as the noted problems are concerned.

5. REFERENCES

[1] SUSSMANN H.J., JURDJEVIC V., Controllability of nonlinear systems, J. Diff. Eq.,12,95-116,1972.

[2] CHOW W.L., Uber systeme von linearen partiallen differentialgleichungen erster ordnung, Math. Ann. 117,98-105,1039.

[3] SUSSMANN H.J., Orbits of families of vector fields and integrability of systems with singularities, Trans. Am. Math. Soc. 180,171-188, 1973.

[4] BAIRESS E.H., Sylvester's identity and multistep integer preserving Gaussian elimination, Mth. Comput. 22,565-578,1968.

[5] SASAKI T., MURAO M., Efficient Gaussian elimination method for symbolic determinants and linear systems, ACM Trans. Math. Software, 8,3,277-289,1982.

[6] MARINO R., CESAREO G., Nonlinear control theory and symbolic algebraic manipulation, Mathematical Theory of Networks and Systems, Spinger Verlag, Lecture Notes in Control and Information Scinces, vol. 58,1984.

[7] MARINO R., BOOTHBY W.M., ELLIOTT D.L., Geometric properties of linearizable control systems, submitted to Int. J. Math. System Theory.

[8] MEYER G., SU R., HUNT L.R., Application of nonlinear transformations to automatic flight control, Automatica 20,1,103-107,1984.

[9] MARINO R., NICOSIA S., On the feedback control of robot manipulators with elastic joints: a singular perturbation approach, submitted to IEEE Transactions on Automatic Control.

[10] MARINO R., On the stabilization of power systems with a reduced number of controls, Sixth Int. Conference on Analysis and Optimization of Systems, INRIA, Nice, 1984.

[11] JACUBCZYK B., RESPONDEK W., On linearization of control systems, Bull. Acad. Pol. Sci. Ser. Sci. Math., 28,9-10,517-522,1980.

[12] HUNT R.L.,SU R., MEYER G., Design for multiinput nonlinear systems, in Differential Geometric Control Theory, R.Brockett et alii eds., 268-298, Birkhauser, 1983.

[13] GRAGERT P.K.H., KERSTEN P.H.M., Implementation of differential geo-

metric objects and functions with applications to extended Maxwell equations, Proc. EUROCAM '82, Lecture Notes on Computer Science, Springer Verlag, 144,294-301,1982.

[14] HEARN A.C., REDUCE-2 User's Manual, University of Utah, Symb. Comp. Group, Tech. Rep. UCP-19,1073.

[15] CESAREO G., MARINO R., On the controllability properties of elasti robots, Sixth Int. Conference on Analysis and Optimization of Systems, INRIA, Nice, 1984.

[16] MARINO R., CASAREO G., The use of symbolic computation for power system stabilization: an example of computer aided design, Sixth Int. Conference on Analysis and Optimization of Systems, INRIA, Nice, 1984.

[17] CESAREO G., Symbolic algebraic manipulation and nonlinear control theory, Tech. Rep. 82-14, Istituto di Automatica, Università di Roma, 1982.

QUARTIC EQUATIONS AND ALGORITHMS FOR RIEMANN TENSOR CLASSIFICATION

J.E. Åman*, R.A. d'Inverno+, G.C. Joly* and M.A.H. MacCallum*

* School of Mathematical Sciences,
Queen Mary College,
Mile End Road,
LONDON E1 4NS, U.K.

\+ Faculty of Mathematics,
University of Southampton,
SOUTHAMPTON SO9 5NH, U.K.

Summary

The Petrov classification of the Weyl conformal curvature and the Plebanski or Segre classification of the Ricci tensor of spacetimes in general relativity both depend on multiplicities of the roots of quartic equations. The coefficients in these quartic equations may be complicated functions of the space-time coordinates. We review briefly the general theory of quartic equations and then consider practical algorithms for determination of the multiplicities of their roots and hence for the classification of Riemann tensors. Preliminary results of tests of computer implementations of these algorithms, using the computer algebra system SHEEP, are reported.

1. Introduction: the d'Inverno - Russell-Clark algorithm

Petrov's algebraic classification of the Weyl tensor plays an important part in the study of solutions of Einstein's equations in general relativity (see e.g. [1]), in particular in the theory and practice of the methods for determining the equivalence of metrics [2-6] which we are using in an attempt to build a database of known solutions. For the full description of a non-vacuum spacetime this classification must be supplemented by a classification of the Ricci tensor and of the relation between the Ricci and Weyl tensors (see e.g. [4, 7-8]). The classification of the Ricci tensor has been considered from a number of points of view, the two best known being that of Plebanski [9] and that by Segre type (see e.g. [1], Ch. 5). The mathematics of these classifications and their refinements has been extensively discussed in recent years; Hall [10] gives a useful review. They are related to the multiplicities of the roots of quartic equations (or, equivalently, of their associated cubics and quadratics), though the refinements consider additional properties. In this paper, we merely state the relevant details without proof (we will discuss them more fully elsewhere).

The Petrov classification depends solely on the multiplicities of the roots of a complex quartic whose coefficients are components of the spacetime curvature, and therefore, in general, functions of the spacetime coordinates; the roots give the 'principal null directions' of the Weyl tensor (see [1]). The Segre classification is concerned with the multiplicity of the eigenvalues of the Ricci tensor, considered as a linear map of tangent vectors to a manifold; however, the nature of the eigenvectors (i.e. whether they are timelike, spacelike or null) is also significant, and to determine this a second tensor (quadratic in the curvature), the Plebanski tensor, which has algebraic properties similar to the Weyl tensor, is studied. Thus there are two quartics arising in the classification of the Ricci tensor, one for the eigenvalues, and one for the principal null directions of the Plebanski tensor.

The theory of quartic equations dates from the sixteenth century and is set out in (e.g.) [11-13]. Suppose we have a quartic equation,

$$a_4z^4 + 4a_3z^3 + 6a_2z^2 + 4a_1z + a_0 = 0, \qquad (1.1)$$

in which the coefficients and the variable z may be complex. By the transformation

$$z' = a_4z + a_3,$$

assuming a_4 is non-zero, the equation reduces to the form

$$z^4 + 6Hz^2 + 4Gz + K = 0 \qquad (1.2)$$

where

$$H = a_4a_2 - a_3^2, \quad G = a_4^2a_1 - 3a_4a_3a_2 + 2a_3^3, \quad K = a_4^2I - 3H^2$$

and

$$I = a_4a_0 - 4a_1a_3 + 3a_2^2.$$

The roots of the quartic are related to the roots of the "reducing cubic" which is

$$y^3 - Iy + 2J = 0, \qquad (1.3)$$

where

$$J = \det \underline{J}, \quad \underline{J} = \begin{bmatrix} a_4 & a_3 & a_2 \\ a_3 & a_2 & a_1 \\ a_2 & a_1 & a_0 \end{bmatrix}.$$

There are several methods of obtaining (1.3) from (1.1). (Elsewhere, we will present a simple geometrical argument which does not seem to be well-known, though a somewhat similar argument has been independently found by Agacy and Clendinning [14]). To make the relationship precise, let the roots of the reducing cubic be $(\alpha^2 + 4H)/2a_4$, $(\beta^2 + 4H)/2a_4$ and $(\gamma^2 + 4H)/2a_4 = (- 8H - \alpha^2 - \beta^2)/2a_4$, so that $(\alpha\beta\gamma)^2 = 16G^2$. If the surds are chosen so that $\alpha\beta\gamma = - 4G$, then the roots of the quartic (1.1) are

$$\begin{aligned} &-(a_3 + (\alpha + \beta + \gamma)/2)/a_4, \quad -(a_3 + (\alpha - \beta - \gamma)/2)/a_4 \\ &-(a_3 + (- \alpha + \beta - \gamma)/2)/a_4, \quad -(a_3 + (- \alpha - \beta + \gamma)/2)/a_4. \end{aligned} \tag{1.4}$$

The further solution of (1.3) can also be done by a number of methods, the oldest being due to Tartiglia (but often ascribed to Cardan) [13]. If one supposes the roots to be of the form p + q where $pq = I/3$, then substitution into (1.3) leads to a quadratic for $t = p^3$, namely

$$t^2 + 2Jt + I^3/27 = 0, \tag{1.5}$$

whence

$$p^3 = - J \pm (J^2 - I^3/27)^{1/2}. \tag{1.6}$$

Let P be the principal cube root for p in (1.6) with the upper sign. Then the three roots of (1.3) are $(P + I/3P)$, $(\omega P + \omega^2 I/3P)$ and $(\omega^2 P + \omega I/3P)$, where ω is a complex cube root of 1.

From the stated relationships between the roots of (1.5), (1.3) and (1.1), it is clear that (1.1):-

(i) has four distinct roots if $C = I^3 - 27J^2$ is non-zero (C is the discriminant of the cubic (1.3)):

(ii) has at least one repeated root if $I^3 = 27J^2$ is not zero; and

  (a) has exactly one such repeated root unless $G = 0 = N$, where $N = a_4{}^2 I - 12H^2$,

  (b) has two distinct pairs of repeated roots if $G = 0 = N$:

(iii) has at least a triply repeated root if $I = J = 0$; and

  (a) has two distinct roots unless $H = G = 0$,

  (b) has just one (quadruply repeated) root if $H = G = 0$.

For consistency with the standard names for the possible Petrov types of the Weyl tensor, we have chosen to refer to the possibilities (i), (ii) (a), (ii) (b), (iii) (a), and (iii) (b) respectively as types I, II, D, III and N; the case where the quartic is identically zero is called type 0.

The notation H, G, K, I, J used above follows [12-13]. It was from these classical results that d'Inverno and Russell-Clark [15] obtained their algorithm for Petrov type determination, and they followed this notation, except that they (cf. [12]) used the equation derived from (1.1) by $z \to 1/z$ or $a_n \leftrightarrow a_{4-n}$, which we refer to as the 'inverse' equation. The quantity N is un-named in [15]. The d'Inverno - Russell-Clark algorithm is presented as Figs. 1 and 2. It follows the route suggested by the above discussion if a_4 is non-zero or (by $z \to 1/z$) if a_4 is zero and a_0 non-zero, while giving a separate treatment for $a_0 = a_4 = 0$, when the roots of (1.1) are 0, ∞, and the roots of

$$4a_3z^2 + 6a_2z + 4a_1 = 0. \qquad (1.7)$$

In the flow diagrams we have used fairly standard conventions, but with some abbreviation. The test implied by a diamond-shaped decision box is whether the named quantity(ies) is(are) identically zero; the horizontal exits always represent non-zero values, the vertical exits zero values. The rectangular procedure boxes contain the resulting Petrov type and a list of those quantities which must be checked for possible undetected simplifications or for degeneracy with special choices of parameters. The EXIT returns these values and appropriate user messages. The division of each algorithm into several numbered Figures is shown by putting a circle containing the appropriate Figure number at the connecting point. Quantities derived from the 'inverse' equation are denoted by a prime, e.g. H', G', as are the 'inverses' of the diagrams actually drawn, e.g. Fig. 2' is the diagram in which each quantity in Fig. 2 is replaced by the corresponding value from the inverse equation. Table 1 defines the quantities A to Z and gives the formulae used to compute them, which utilise the algebraic relations which must exist since all the quantities depend on just the five coefficients in (1.1).

We shall not waste paper by paraphrasing every detail of the flow diagrams in words. Figs. 1 and 2 are particularly self-explanatory, in the light of the above discussion. The one quantity used which is not mentioned above, D, is the discriminant of the quadratic (1.7) in the case where all the coefficients of that equation are non-zero.

2. Our algorithms for multiplicities of roots of quartics

If all the coefficients in (1.1) are numbers, the algorithm above needs only some easy arithmetic (a hand calculator could deal with practical cases). Petrov classification can be reduced to this case by first evaluating the (perhaps complicated) algebraic expressions for the coefficients at particular numerical values of the coordinates, and indeed there may be cases where time and store requirements force this expedient upon us (as they did in some cases in [15]); see also section 4 of this paper. However, the quantities to be tested include invariants whose general expressions (and derivatives) are needed for classification of the spacetime [4-6], so this method is less

Figure 1

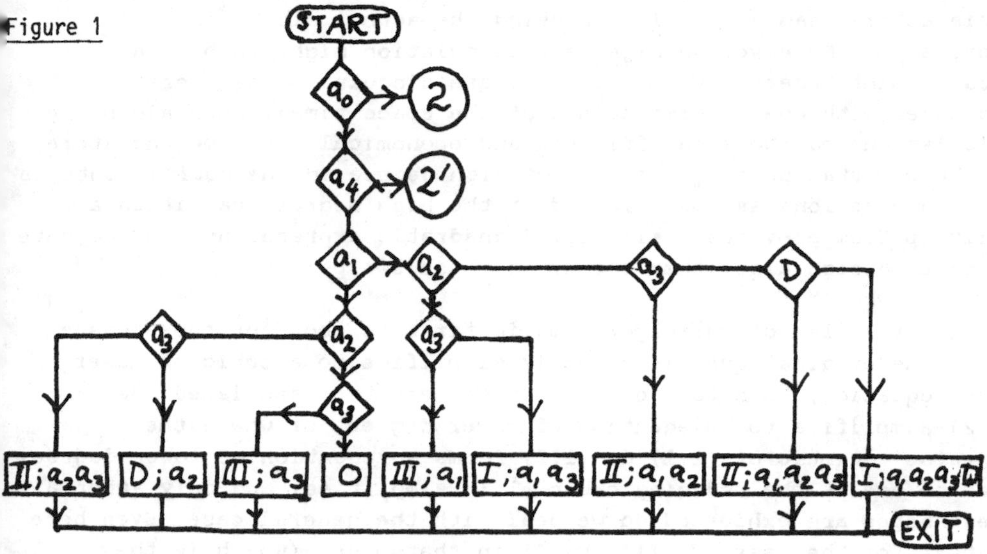

Figure 2

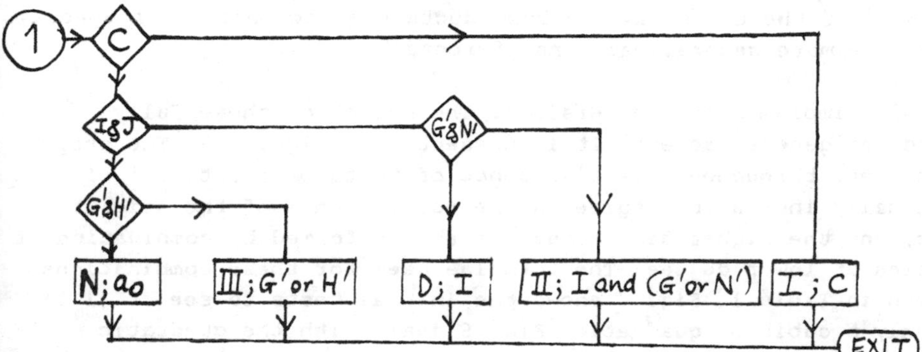

Figure 3

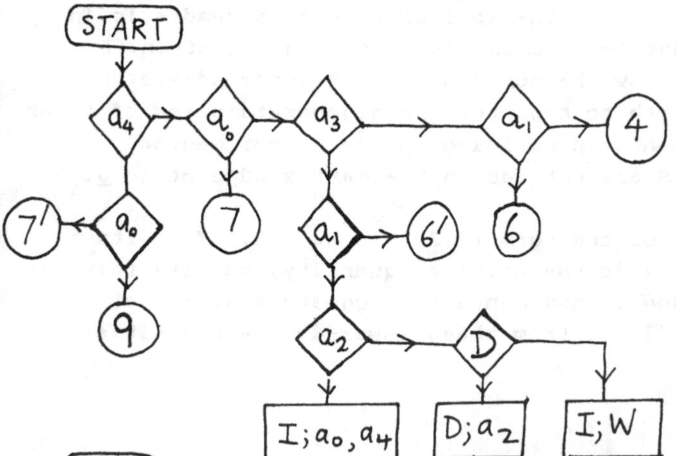

satisfactory than a calculation using the actual algebraic expressions. Moreover an algebraic calculation might enable us to locate points where the coefficients are singular or degenerate (compared with the generic points of the space-time). Such algebraic calculations may be more efficient and economical (in time and store) if the computation of quantities of high degree in the coefficients is postponed as long as possible and if the high degree quantities are built up from previously-simplified quadratic expressions, and we have tried to design algorithms embodying these two points.

The general plan of our algorithms is first to look for those cases where the original quartic directly simplifies to a cubic or lower order equation, then to look for cases where the associated quartic (1.2) simplifies to an equation of lower degree, or where the 'inverse' quartic of (1.1) or (1.2) forms an equation of lower degree, then to see if the reducing cubic (1.3) simplifies, and only after all these hopes are exhausted do we deal with the general case. Even here we test for the cases N, III, D, II in that order (which is the reverse of the one used by d'Inverno and Russell-Clark) since it postpones as long as possible the really unpleasant calculations (e.g. of C); some of the tests have as byproducts the recognition of special cases of the more general patterns of roots.

We actually implemented two versions. The second of these fully embodied our general scheme. It is presented as Figs. 3-9. The steps in it proceed throughout via a sequence of tests of quantities of monotonically increasing degree in the coefficients of the original quartic, and the higher degree quantities are formed by combination of quantities of lower degree. The formulae used for these combinations are given in Table 1. Fig. 3 shows the initial tests to see if (1.1) gives only a cubic or quadratic. Fig. 9 deals with the quadratic (1.7), Fig. 7 the case where the last term of (1.1) is zero (and the equation reduces at least to a cubic), Fig. 6 the case of a quartic (1.1) which is already in the form (1.2) and Fig 4. the general quartic. Fig. 3 also deals with the special case of a quadratic in $w = z^2$, whose discriminant is W; this case occurs quite often. Figs. 4 and 5, and Table 1, show how the construction of intermediate quantities can be used both to test for the degenerate cases of types N, III and D and as elements in building up the higher degree quantities; H, P, Q and S are entries in the matrix adjoint to $\underline{J}$.

In Fig. 6 the quartic is of the form (1.2); if $a_2 = 0$, X is its discriminant; otherwise, Y is the critical quantity, but its form (in Table 1) in terms of W and B (and hence S) suggests a series of special tests as Y is built up from these lower-degree quantities.

Figure 4

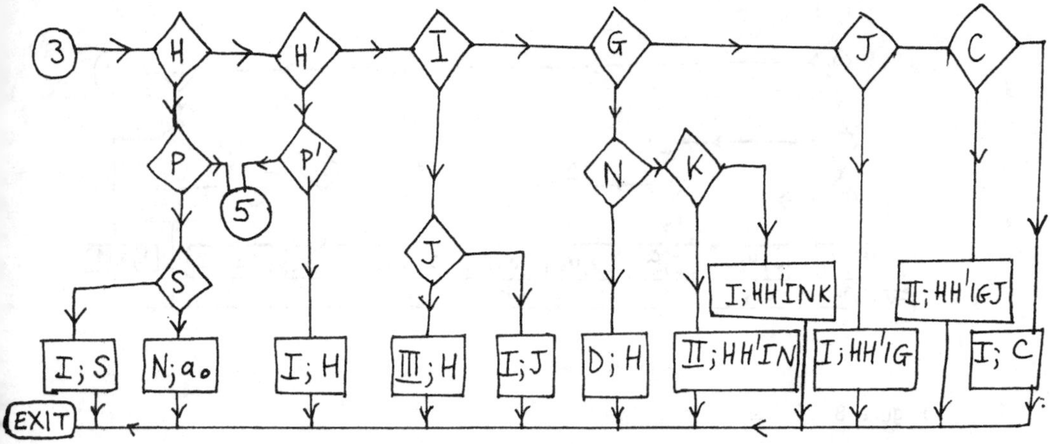

Figure 5

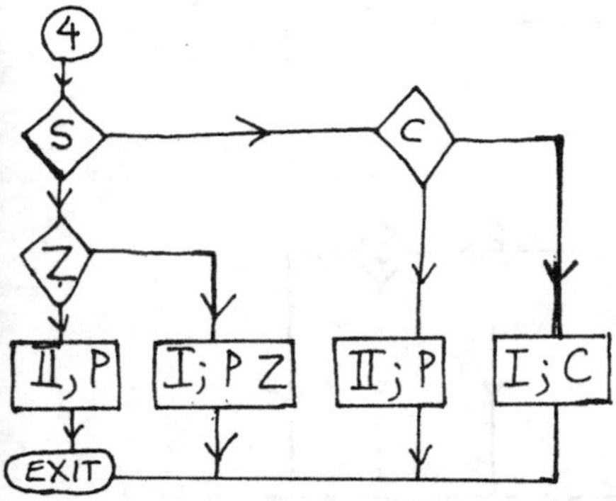

Figure 6

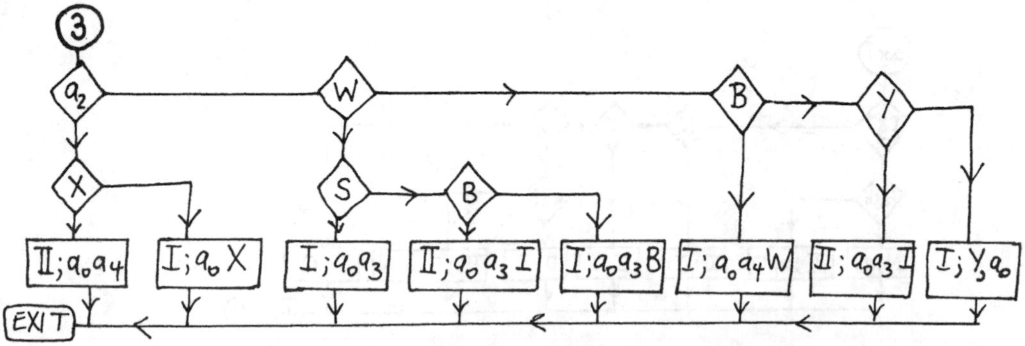

Figure 7

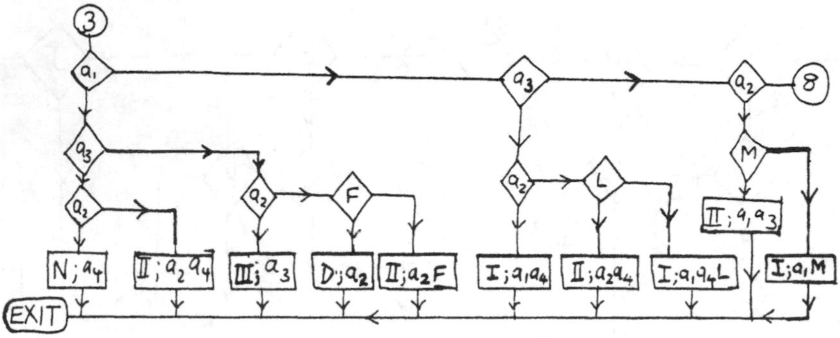

Figure 8

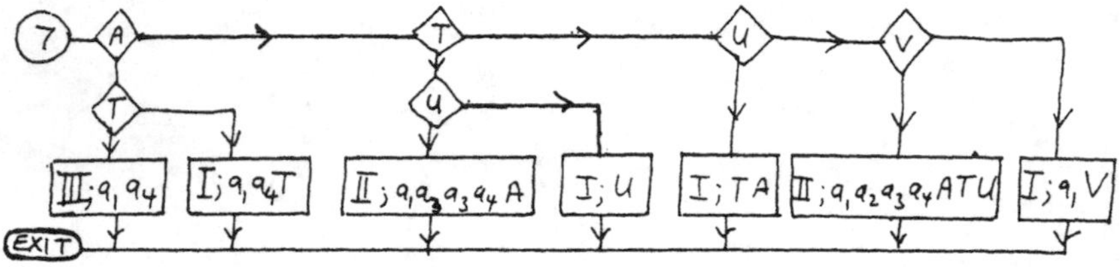

Figure 9

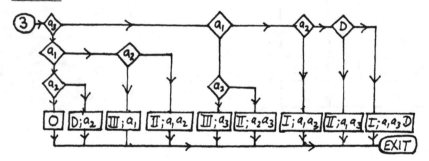

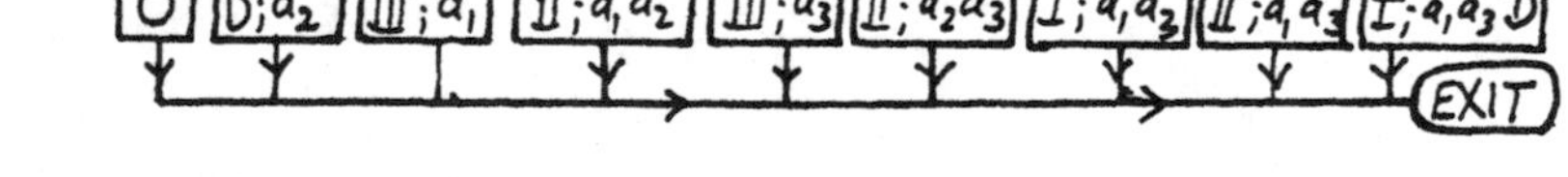

Figure 10

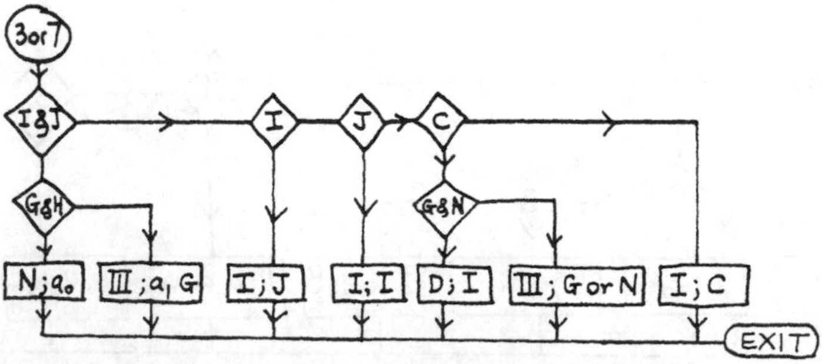

$A = 9H + a_3^2$	$B = a_0(a_3{}^2) - 2a_2S$
$C = I(I^2) - 27J^2$	$D = 9a_2{}^2 - 16a_1a_3$
$F = 2a_3{}^2 - 3a_2a_4$	$G = -a_4P - 2a_3H$
$H = a_4a_2 - a_3{}^2$	$I = S - 4Q$
$J = a_0H + a_1P + a_2Q$	$K = N - 9H^2$
$L = - a_1P + a_2(Q + 3a_2{}^2)$	$M = -27a_1(a_4{}^2) - 64a_3(a_3{}^2)$
$N = a_4{}^2I - 12H^2$	$P = a_2a_3 - a_1a_4$
$Q = a_1a_3 - a_2{}^2$	$S = a_0a_4 - a_2{}^2$
$T = 3a_1a_4 - 2a_2a_3$	$U = 3a_2{}^2 - 4a_1a_3$
$V = - 3T^2 - 2AU$	$W = 9a_2{}^2 - a_0a_4$
$X = a_4{}^2S - 27(a_3{}^2)^2$	$Y = a_4W^2 - 27(a_3{}^2)B$
$Z = - 27a_1a_3 - 37a_2^2$	

Table 1: Definitions of the quantities appearing in the algorithm depicted in the flow diagrams 3-9. The bracketting and the references to other quantities in the Table indicate how the higher degree quantities were computed.

In Fig. 7 (1.1) is at worst a cubic; Fig. 7 itself deals with the possible further reductions to simple forms and Fig. 8. the general case in which all remaining coefficients are non-zero. Here F is the discriminant of the quadratic arising if only the first three terms of (1.1) are present, and L and M are the discriminants of the simplified cubics when the second or third terms vanish but the first and fourth do not. In Fig. 8, A is the coefficient (up to a factor) of y after reduction to the form (1.3); T and U are the other quantities involved in the formula (e.g. [11], page 107) for the discriminant V.

We note that all tests that pick out type I cases involve versions of C, although the special cancellations of coefficients or combinations of coefficients may allow a common factor to be removed so that only a quantity of lower degree must be calculated.

Our first version of a new algorithm was slightly less systematic in calculating low-degree quantities first. It was the same as the algorithm just described except that Figs. 4 and 8 were replaced by Fig. 10, the computations of Fig. 6 involving B, S, W and Y were replaced by immediate calculation of C, L in Fig. 7 was replaced by the more general formula V which reduces to L in this case, and the computations of I and J were done directly from the formulae in section 1 above rather than as in Table 1. (This account of the first new algorithm ignores a few very minor changes.)

3. Some sample timings of the old and new algorithms for Petrov classification as implemented in SHEEP

The extra complexity of the new algorithms, as compared with their predecessors, can only be justified if they show improvements in the speed and economy with which they handle the classification for actual spacetimes. We have applied them to several solutions of Einstein's field equations of general relativity, using programs written for the system SHEEP (which is a small fast system whose facilities are specially adapted to relativity calculations); for some details of SHEEP see [16-17]. The original versions of the Petrov classification programs were written by JEÅ. A related program for Ricci tensor classification has been written (initially by GCJ) but as far as we are aware this program is the first one providing a computerised classification of the Ricci tensor, and we therefore are unable to compare its results with other algorithms.

The discussion given above leads us to expect Figs. 3-9 to improve on Figs. 1-2 in speed and store for cases which enter Fig. 2. but which do not, in Figs. 3-10, involve calculation of C, and we expect the final algorithm (Figs. 3-9) to improve on the intermediate one (using Fig. 10 and the definitions in Section 1) in store if not in time. This is borne out by Table 2, which shows figures from preliminary tests of the algorithms (preliminary in that only a small sample of spacetimes has been tested so far).

The first two lines of Table 2 relate to cases where only the coefficients are tested; in the first line, the values were symbolic (so that the value of a_4 is a_4, etc.), but actual metrics which were in convenient form were used in the second line. The third and fourth lines refer to cases where the d'Inverno and Russell-Clark algorithm tests C but the new algorithms test only coefficients, and the fifth to seventh lines to cases where the d'Inverno and Russell-Clark algorithm tests C but the others test lower degree quantities. In lines 1 to 5, 3 runs of most of the examples were made (to remove some of the fluctuations between one run and another) and the times are averaged over all the cases tried. The results show that the new algorithms are better for those cases which, in the old algorithm, fall into Fig. 2. The intermediate algorithm (the first of the two new versions) does better than the final one on these tests. However, the final algorithm does better on real metrics of the type in line 5 of the Table, as the next two lines show. These refer to the metrics of Chitre et al. ([1], equation 20.11) and the general Weyl-Levi-Civita form ([1], equation 17.20); the asterisk denotes that the algorithm could not perform the calculation within the available store. Finally there are two examples of metrics in which all the algorithms must calculate C. Here the Curzon example ([1], 18.4) shows that when all the algorithms can work within the store limits they are all of about equal speed, while the last line (the Chitre et al. metric in a different reference frame) shows that although the final algorithm is no faster it can do better in its use of store.

These preliminary results thus confirm our expectations, and since all the times are short compared for example with the time to obtain the coefficients from the metric, suggest that the final algorithm is the best choice in that it enables us to handle worse cases. It may be that some compromise between the two new algorithms would be a still better choice.

Input	Algorithm described by Figs. 1-2	3,4,7,9-10	3-9	Notes
Symbolic	135	115	138	Only coefficients
Actual	160	130	197	tested
Symbolic	331	118	166	First column tests C
Actual	661	201	239	Rest test coefficients
Symbolic	474	318	339	First column tests C
Chitre et al	6830	1842	1522	Rest test other
Weyl (see text)	*	7728	6984	combinations
Curzon	17137	17425	18563	All test C
Chitre (see text)	*	*	24571	

Table 2: Some sample timings of the algorithms. Times are CPU times in milliseconds, excluding garbage collection time. For full explanation see text.

4. Further developments

Examples may involve expressions so long that one of the quantities tested in the above algorithms becomes too big to handle; at that point the present implementation simply halts. (Indeed it was the frequency with which this occurred using the algorithm of Figs. 1 and 2 which motivated us to try to improve it.)

We have already pointed out (cf. [15]) that one can go on to use numerical values for the coordinates, or particular choices of arbitrary functions or parameters, because the tests require quantities to vanish identically, and any non-zero value found would exclude this (within some open set if all the functions involved are continuous). Typically one might try to reduce the expression to manageable size by (e.g.) setting one or more coordinates to zero. If the result is non-zero, one can revert to the full form for the next test; if zero, one has to try to establish whether this is identically true or not, which could still prove awkward.

Currently, this type of investigation can only be carried out interactively. However, it might be possible to choose suitable values automatically. The simplest choice is to set one or more of the coordinates to zero, but one might program a selection of suitable non-zero values of coordinates. In such a method, the choice would have to be changed if the expression became indeterminate or unbounded. Only when such automatic checks failed would control be returned to the user. We think that such automated extensions of the algorithm could extend the range of metrics which could be successfully handled.

Acknowledgements

We are grateful to the Science and Engineering Research Council for the computing facilities provided under grants GR/C/19820 (RAdI), GR/C/27030 and GR/C/76335 (MAHM and GCJ) and GR/C/27047 (JEÅ), the last of which also supported JEÅ financially during part of this work, and to the Swedish Natural Science Research Council and the Institute of Theoretical Physics of the University of Stockholm for grants and facilities for JEÅ and, as a visitor, for MAHM. We are also grateful to Dr. I. Frick, author of SHEEP.

References

1. D. Kramer, H. Stephani, M. MacCallum, and E. Herlt (1980). Exact solutions of Einstein's field equations. Deutscher Verlag der Wissenschaften, Berlin, and Cambridge University Press.
2. J.E. Åman and A. Karlhede (1980). Phys. Lett. A **80**, 229.
3. J.E. Åman and A. Karlhede (1980). Proceedings of the ACM conference, Snowbird, Utah
4. A. Karlhede (1980). Gen. Rel. Grav. **12**, 693.
5. A. Karlhede and M.A.H. MacCallum (1982). Gen. Rel. Grav. **14**, 672.
6. M.A.H. MacCallum (1983). In: Unified Field Theories of more than 4 dimensions, including exact solutions, ed. V. de Sabbata and E. Schmutzer. World Scientific: Singapore.
7. L. Witten (1959). Phys. Rev. **113**, 357.
8. S.T.C. Siklos (1976). Ph. D. thesis, University of Cambridge.
9. J. Plebanski (1964). Acta Phys. Polon. **26**, 963.
10. G.S. Hall (1979). Lectures at the Stefan Banach Centre, Warsaw.
11. I. Todhunter (1888). Theory of Equations. Macmillan: London.
12. W.S. Burnside and A.W. Panton (1935). Theory of Equations (10th edn.). Dublin Univ. Press: Dublin and Longmans, Green: London.
13. C.V. Durrell and A. Robson (1956). Advanced Algebra. G. Bell and Sons: London.
14. R.L. Agacy and L.M. Clendinning (1982). J. Math. Phys. **22**, 1445.
15. R.A. d'Inverno and R.A. Russell-Clark (1971). J. Math. Phys. **12**, 1258.
16. I. Frick (1977). The computer algebra system SHEEP, what it can and cannot do in general relativity. Univ. of Stockholm report.
17. R.A. d'Inverno and I. Frick (1982). Gen. Rel. and Grav. **14**, 835.

SYMBOLIC COMPUTATION AND THE DIRICHLET PROBLEM

Ralph W. Wilkerson

Department of Computer and Information Sciences
University of Florida
Gainesville, FL 32611

1. Introduction

One of the most important problems in the theory of harmonic functions is that of finding a harmonic function with given boundary values. This problem is normally referred to as the Dirichlet problem. We say a function u(x,y) is harmonic if it satisfies Laplace's equation: $\nabla^2 u = u_{xx} + u_{yy} = 0$. The Dirichlet problem can be restated more formally as follows: Let D be a domain with boundary ∂D and let f(x,y) be a continuous real valued function defined on ∂D. One wishes to find a function u(x,y) such that u(x,y) is harmonic on D and u(x,y) = f(x,y) at all points of ∂D.

The theory of a function of a complex variable provides the necessary existence and uniqueness conditions for the solution of the Dirichlet problem. While existence and uniqueness theorems are clearly essential to the solution of such problems, they do not provide computationally elegant methods for the more practical problem of explicitly solving the Dirichlet problem. Put more precisely, the exact closed form solution of the Dirichlet problem for any but the simplest domains (e.g., disk or rectangle) is in most cases mathematically infeasible. As a direct result of those difficulties, many numerical methods have been developed to solve these problems such as the method of finite differences and the finite element method.

Almost eighty years ago it was observed by Zaremba [6] that the Dirichlet problem could be solved by the use of complete orthonormal sets of harmonic functions. In what follows, we will explain how his ideas can be used to symbolically calculate an approximate solution of the Dirichlet problem in the form of a harmonic polynomial P(x,y) by orthonormalizing sets of harmonic polynomials. In fact, our approximate solution will be a harmonic polynomial and will provide a value of the solution at every point of D. To find this solution explicitly, we will make extensive use of the symbolic manipulation language FORMAC which makes Zaremba's solution possible in a truly computational sense.

2. Symbolic Solution Method

In what follows, we will develop the necessary mathematical tools which will be used to implement a computer algebra solution to the Dirichlet problem. In particular, we will show how Zaremba's ideas can provide the basis for this solution.

Let us begin by giving a brief summary of Zaremba's observations on this problem. Let $\langle u,v\rangle$ denote the inner product defined by

$$\langle u,v\rangle = \int_D \nabla u \cdot \nabla v \, d\omega$$

where $d\omega$ is the volume element in a two or three dimensional domain D and u and v are functions such that $\langle u,u\rangle$ and $\langle v,v\rangle$ exist. Furthermore let $\{u_i\}$ be a complete set of harmonic functions such that $\langle u_i,u_i\rangle$ is finite over D, which is orthonormalized by $\langle u_i,u_j\rangle = \delta_{ij}$. Zaremba observed that $a_i = \langle u,u_i\rangle$, the Fourier coefficients of a function u harmonic in D and such that $\langle u,u\rangle < \infty$, can be computed in terms of the values of u on the boundary of D [4,6]. If ds is the surface element of ∂D, then

$$a_i = \int_{\partial D} u(\partial u_i/\partial N) \, ds$$

where $\partial u_i/\partial N$ is the normal derivative and hence

$$u(P) = \sum a_i u_i(P)$$

for points P in D.

In the problems we shall consider, we shall assume the domain D is polygonal and the boundary values are at worse piecewise polynomials. To a certain extent this is due to the limitations of FORMAC and its symbolic integration capabilities. If we consider the Dirichlet problem in the plane then for any differentiable functions f and g we define the gradient norm of f and g on D as:

$$\langle f,g\rangle = \int_D \nabla f \cdot \nabla g \, dA \tag{1}$$

where ∇f and ∇g are the gradients of f and g respectively. Now let us recall Green's identity in the plane:

$$\int_D f \, \nabla^2 g \, dA + \int_D \nabla f \cdot \nabla g \, dA = \int_{\partial D} f(\partial g/\partial N) \, ds \tag{2}$$

where $\partial g/\partial N$ is the normal derivative. Let $\{P_m\}$ be a sequence of harmonic polynomials orthonormal on D in the gradient norm, that is

$$\int_D \nabla P_n \cdot \nabla P_m \, dA = \delta_{nm}. \tag{3}$$

Applying Zaremba's results we can write the solution as

$$u(x,y) = \sum c_m P_m(x,y). \tag{4}$$

Taking the gradient of both sides of (4) we obtain

$$\nabla u = \sum c_m \nabla P_m. \tag{5}$$

Next compute the gradient norm of both sides of (4) with P_n and thus we have

$$\langle u,P_n\rangle = \int_D \nabla u \cdot \nabla P_n \, dA = \sum c_m \int_D \nabla P_n \cdot \nabla P_m \, dA$$
$$= \sum c_m \delta_{mn} = c_n.$$

Thus the Fourier coefficients can be expressed as

$$c_n = \int_D \nabla u \cdot \nabla P_n \, dA. \tag{6}$$

Now returning to (2) and setting $f = u$ and $g = P_n$ we obtain

$$\int_D u \, \nabla^2 P_n \, dA + \int_D \nabla u \cdot \nabla P_n \, dA = \int_{\partial D} u(\partial P_n/\partial N) \, ds.$$

The leftmost integral is zero since the P_n are harmonic functions, hence we now have

$$\int_D \nabla u \cdot \nabla P_n \, dA = \int_{\partial D} u(\partial P_n/\partial N) \, ds. \tag{7}$$

Thus combining (6) and (7) we have that the Fourier coefficients can be explicitly expressed as an integral around the boundary of D, that is

$$c_n = \int_{\partial D} u(\partial P_n/\partial N) \, ds. \tag{8}$$

Consequently, the c_n can be easily evaluated since we know the values of u on the boundary and the values of $\partial P_n/\partial N$ are also easily computable since

$$\partial P_n/\partial N = (\partial P_n/\partial x)\cos\alpha + (\partial P_n/\partial y)\sin\alpha$$

as we move along the boundary of D.

In order to complete our preliminary work, we still need a source of orthonormal polynomials. These too are easily calculable by considering the real and imaginary parts of $(x + iy)^n$. It is well known that these polynomials are harmonic. Next we must orthonormalize these polynomials and this can be done by using the Gram-Schmidt process to obtain a set of orthonormal polynomials in the gradient norm. The fact that these polynomials are sufficient for what we want is based on the following theorem due to Walsh [5]: Let $u(x,y)$ be a function of (x,y), harmonic in an open simply connected bounded domain C of the plane. Then $u(x,y)$ can be developed in C in a series of harmonic polynomials in (x,y), which converges almost uniformly on C. Bergmann [1] used similar reasoning and constructed examples.

Thus in order to implement this technique, we begin by generating the necessary harmonic polynomials symbolically by expanding $(x + iy)^n$

and then orthonormalizing these polynomials using the gradient norm. remaining portions of the algorithm involve the symbolic calculation o the line integrals around the boundary of the given domain. Other tha possible difficulties involving the parameterization of the boundary o calculating the normal derivative along each boundary segment, this is a straight forward process. Having calculated the Fourier coefficient associated with each basis polynomial, we need only take their product with the respective basis element and compute the partial sum. Hence the solution is complete.

3. General Observations and Extensions

Numerous examples have been used to test this technique. In parti- cular, consider the following example which is known to be unstable [2] using the usual numerical methods of solving the Dirichlet problem. We wish to solve $\nabla^2 u = 0$ on the rectangular region

$$0 \leq x \leq 1$$
$$0 \leq y \leq 2$$

with boundary conditions

$$u(0,y) = u(1,y) = 0$$
$$u(x,0) = u(x,2) = \sin \pi x$$

The exact solution is known to be

$$u(x,y) = \cosh \pi(y-1) \sin \pi x / \cosh \pi .$$

Using the computer algebra technique, a harmonic polynomial of degree 1 was obtained which approximated the known solution with an error of les than 0.3%.

Determining at what point to stop the approximation is based on th following corollary to the maximum modulus principle. If $u(x,y)$ is a harmonic function on a bounded domain G and continuous on $\bar{G}$, then $u(x,y$ achieves its maximum and minimum on the boundary of G. Hence, after ca culating $P(x,y)$ to some degree we compare the value of $P(x,y)$ at select boundary points to the known boundary values and see if the maximum valu are within some predetermined limit. If not, we need only calculate another orthonormal harmonic basis polynomial and continue the approximation.

As one final observation, we would like to note that the above tech- nique can also be used to solve the Neumann problem. That is, find $u(x,$ such that $\nabla^2 u = 0$ with boundary conditions $\partial u/\partial N = f$, where $\partial u/\partial N$ is the outward normal derivative on the boundary. It is known that the Neumann problem cannot have a solution unless the integral of f over the boundar is zero. Furthermore, any solution we obtain will only be within a constant since we do not have the uniqueness property as in the case of the Dirichlet problem. The derivation utilizes Green's theorem as in the Dirichlet problem except that in (2) we now let $f = P_n$, $g = u$, and thus

$$c_n = \int_{\partial D} P_n (\partial u/\partial N)\, ds.$$

REFERENCES

1. S. Bergmann, Uber die Entwicklung der harmonischen Funktionen der Ebene und des Raumes nach Orthogonalfunktionen, Math. Annalen, 86 (1922), 238-271.

2. D. J. Jones and J. C. Smith, Application of the method of lines to the solution of elliptic partial differential equations (National Research Council of Canada, Ottawa 1979).

3. A. I. Markushevich, Theory of functions of a complex variable (Chelsea, New York, 1977)

4. Z. Nehari, On the numerical solution of the Dirichlet problem, Proceedings of the conference on differential equations held at the University of Maryland (1955), 157-178.

5. J. Walsh, The approximation of harmonic functions by harmonic polynomials and by harmonic rational functions, Amer. Math. Soc. Bulletin, 35 (1929), 499-544.

6. S. Zaremba, L'equation biharmonique et une classe remarquable de fonctions fondementales harmoniques, Bulletin International de l'Academie des Sciences de Cracovie (1907), 147-196.

SIMPLIFICATION OF POLYNOMIALS IN n VARIABLES

G. VIRY
Centre de Recherche en Informatique de Nancy
Campus Scientifique B.P. 239
54506 VANDOEUVRE-LES-NANCY
FRANCE

We denote by $K[x_1,\dots,x_n]$ the polynomial ring in $x_1,\dots,x_n$ over the ring K, and by F a finite subset of $K[x_1,\dots,x_n]$.
The purpose of this paper is to define the automorphisms S of $K[x_1,\dots,x_n]$ that simplify as much as possible the polynomials of F in many senses: decreasing the number of variables, transforming the polynomial into a monic polynomial and lowering as much as possible the degrees of the monomials.
Furthermore we don't want S to increase the number of the monomials of the given polynomials. For this reason we put forward the following condition :

P <u>and</u> S(P) <u>have the same number of monomials for</u> $P \in K[x_1,\dots,x_n]$. (1)

Let us remark that these automorphisms S are generally effective. The number of variables of a generic polynomial obviously will not be decreased, but the degrees of the monomials of a generic polynomial can be decreased.
These automorphisms S are defined by literal transformations on the exponents of the monomials.

I. Definition of the automorphisms S.

For technical reasons, the automorphisms S will be defined on the ring $K[x_1,x_1^{-1},\dots,x_n,x_n^{-1}]$ denoted by $K[G]$ where G is the free group generated by $x_1,\dots,x_n$. The elements of $K[G]$ are called generalized polynomials.
We consider a polynomial of $K[G]$: $P = a_1m_1 + \dots + a_pm_p + \dots$. Let $f:G \longrightarrow \mathbb{Z}^n$ be the mapping that associates the n-uple $(d_1,\dots,d_n)$ to the monomial $x_1^{d_1} \dots x_n^{d_n}$. It is clear that :

f <u>is an isomorphism of</u> G <u>onto the additive group</u> $\mathbb{Z}^n$. (2)

This isomorphism f associates the points $M_1,\dots,M_p,\dots$ of $\mathbb{Z}^n$ to

the monomials $m_1, \ldots, m_p, \ldots$ of P. In the same manner as Ostrowski in [2], we shall call the baric polyhedron of P the hull convex of the points $M_1, \ldots, M_p, \ldots$. This polyhedron will be denoted by $\Pi(P)$.
Since S is an automorphism of K[G], then

$$S: P(x_1, \ldots, x_i, \ldots) \longrightarrow P(S(x_1), \ldots, S(x_i), \ldots)$$

where $S(x_i)$ is a monomial $x_1^{a_{1i}} x_2^{a_{2i}} \ldots x_n^{a_{ni}}$ of G as a consequence of (1). S is defined by its restriction over G which is an isomorphism of G denoted by S_G. Thus the following diagram is commutative:

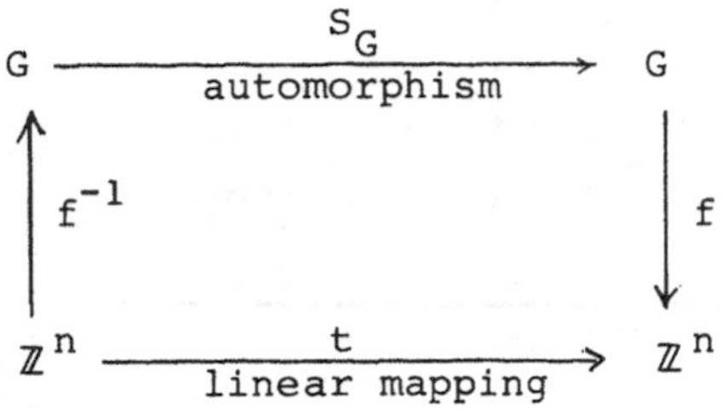

We denote by $T = (a_{ij})$ the matrix of t where $a_{ij} \in \mathbb{Z}$. Any automorphism S of K[G] is so defined by a linear mapping t on the module $\mathbb{Z}^n$ that applies the standard basis $B_\circ$ of $\mathbb{Z}^n$ (the vectors of $B_\circ$ are the unit vectors $\vec{e}_1, \ldots, \vec{e}_n$) on another basis B of $\mathbb{Z}^n$. We can also take a basis B of the vector space $\mathbb{Q}$. Since the components of the vectors of B are integers, then S is a monomorphism of K[G]. In this last case the columns of the matrix T of t must be linearly independent. Moreover, if S is an automorphism, the determinant of T must be equal to 1 or -1.
We denote by F a finite subset $\{P_1, \ldots, P_q\}$ of $K[x_1, \ldots, x_n]$. The images $S(P_i)$ of the polynomials P_i which we get with the matrix T are generalized polynomials of $K[x_1, x_1^{-1}, \ldots, x_n, x_n^{-1}]$. These can also be written as $a.m.S(P_i)^\circ$ where $a \in \mathbb{Z}$ and $m \in G$, and where the $S(P_i)^\circ$ are "relatively prime" polynomials of $K[x_1, \ldots, x_n]$, that is to say no one monomial other than 1 divides all the polynomials $S(P_i)^\circ$. These polynomials $S(P_i)^\circ$ are uniquely determined and they will be called normalized polynomials. We shall denote by S° the automorphisms of K[G] defined by :

$$S^\circ(P) = \frac{S(P)}{a.m} .$$

The image of F belongs to $K[x_1, \ldots, x_n]$.

<u>Example.</u>

$P_1 = 2\,xy^2 - 2\,x^2y - x^3 + 4\,y^3 + x^2y^2 + x^3y - x^2y^3$

$P_2 = 2\,xy^2 - x^3 + xy^4 + 2\,y^4$.

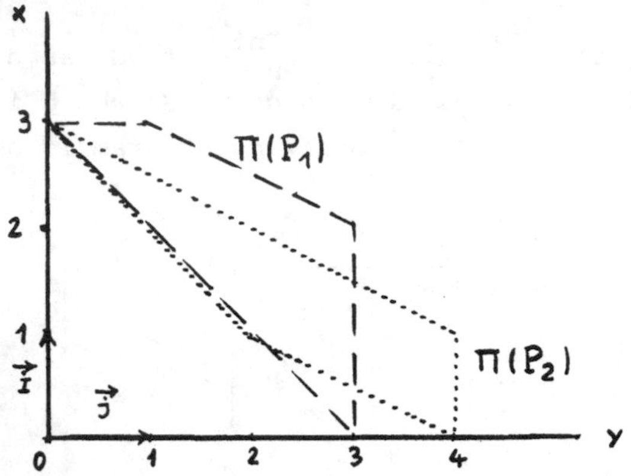

The automorphism $S°$ of $K[x,x^{-1},y,y^{-1}]$ is defined by a basis $B = \{\vec{I},\vec{J}\}$ of $\mathbb{Z}^2$ such that the vectors $\vec{I}$ and $\vec{J}$ are the images of the unit vectors $\vec{i} = (1,0)$ and $\vec{j} = (0,1)$. The choice of the basis B must be adapted at the same time to $\Pi(P_1)$ and $\Pi(P_2)$. For example some vectors of B must be parallel with some edges of $\Pi(P_1)$ or $\Pi(P_2)$ We may thus choose $\vec{I} = (-1,2)$ and $\vec{J} = (-1,1)$; therefore :

$$T = \begin{pmatrix} 1 & 1 \\ -2 & -1 \end{pmatrix}$$

The image of the monomial $x^{d_1} y^{d_2}$ is the monomial $x^{d_1+d_2}\, y^{-2d_1-d_2}$. Therefore we have :

$S(P_1) = x^3y^{-7}(\, y^3 + y^2 + y + y^4 + xy - x - x^2\,) \;=\; x^3y^{-7}\; S°(P_1)$

$S(P_2) = x^3y^{-7}(\, y^3 + y - x^2y - xy^3\,) \;=\; x^3y^{-7}\; S°(P_2)$.

Let us suppose that we want to find the GCD of the polynomials P_1 and P_2. For this it is easier to compute the GCD of $S°(P_1)$ and $S°(P_2)/y$. Indeed, we have :

$S°(P_1) = S°(P_2)/y \;+\; x(\,y^2 + y - 1\,) + y^4 + y^3 + y - 1$

$\qquad = S°(P_2)/y \;+\; (y^2 + y - 1)(x + y^2 + 1)$.

Therefore the GCD of $S°(P_1)$ and $S°(P_2)$ is $D = x + y^2 + 1$. We may compute $S°^{-1}(D)$ with the help of :

$$T^{-1} = \begin{pmatrix} -1 & -1 \\ 2 & 1 \end{pmatrix} .$$

We get $S^{\circ -1}(D) = xy^2 + y^2 + x^2$ which is the GCD of P_1 and P_2.

II. Use of the baric polyhedron $\Pi(P)$.

Let us suppose that $F = \{P\}$. To simplify P is to choose a new basis B that is better adapted to $\Pi(P)$ than the standard basis B°. Moreover, the coordonates of the points of $\Pi(P)$ must be positive. We describe below different ways to simplify P.

a. Simplification of P that decreases the number of the variables.

If the polyhedron $\Pi(P)$ has a dimension $m < n$, then we can choose the new basis B so that the coordonates $x_{m+1},\ldots,x_n$ of the points of $\Pi(P)$ are equal to 0. So the new polynomial $S^\circ(P)$ will have only m variables.

b. Simplification of P so that a constant monomial appears.

We bring B "nearer" to $\Pi(P)$ by taking a vertex $A_\circ$ of $\Pi(P)$ as the origin of B. It is clear that it is always possible to choose a basis B, the origin of which is $A_\circ$ and in which the coordonates of all the vertices of $\Pi(P)$ are positive. So P is transformed into a true (not generalized) polynomial and the monomial associated with the vertex $A_\circ$ becomes a constant monomial.

c. Transformation of P into a monic polynomial.

The polynomial $S^\circ(P)$ will be monic in x_1, that is to say monic as a polynomial in x_1 with coefficients in $K[x_2,\ldots,x_n]$, if the polyhedron $\Pi(P)$ has a point $M_\circ$ with coordonate x_1 greater than the coordonates x_1 of the other points of $\Pi(P)$ and if the coordonates $x_2,\ldots,x_n$ of $M_\circ$ are equal to 0. We can take for $M_\circ$ any vertex of $\Pi(P)$. Then we can take for x_1-axis any edge $AM_\circ$ of $\Pi(P)$ and for hyperplane $x_1 = 0$, any hyperplane H such that $\Pi(P)$ is included between H and the hyperplane H' that is parallel to H and that does not include any point of $\Pi(P)$ other than $M_\circ$.

d. Simplification of P that decreases the degree in x_1.

We must define the face B_1 of B included in the hyperplane $x_1 = 0$ so that it is as near as possible to $\Pi(P)$, or more precisely as near as possible to the set $E(P)$ of the points $M_1,\ldots,M_i,\ldots,M_p$ of $\mathbb{Z}^n$ that are the images $f(m_1),\ldots,f(m_i),\ldots,f(m_p)$ of the monomials of P by the isomorphism f. Furthermore, all the points M_i must be on the same side of B_1, so that the monomials m_i belong to $K[x_1,\ldots,x_n]$. To say that $E(P)$ is near to H, we need define a distance d in $\mathbb{Z}^p$. The distance between two points of $\mathbb{Z}^p$ will be equal to :

$$d_1(M,N) = \sum_{1\le j\le p} |x_j - y_j|$$

where $M = (x_1,\ldots,x_p)$ and $N = (y_1,\ldots,y_p)$. Therefore the distance between H and a point M_i will be equal to :

$$d_1(M_i,H) = \inf_{N\in H} (d_1(M_i,N))$$

and will be the new coordonate x_1 of M_i, denoted by $\partial_1(M_i)$. A distance between H and $E(P)$ can then be defined in two different ways:

$$\begin{cases} d_1(E(P),H) = \sum_{M_i\in E(P)} d_1(M_i,H) \\ d_\infty(E(P),H) = \max_{M_i\in E(P)} (d_1(M_i,H)) \end{cases}$$

If we denote by $\vec{\partial}_1$ the vector $(\partial_1(M_1),\ldots,\partial_1(M_p))$, then the distance between H and $E(P)$ can be defined by one of the two norms :

$$\begin{cases} \|\vec{\partial}_1\|_1 = \partial_1(M_1) + \ldots + \partial_1(M_p) \\ \|\vec{\partial}_1\|_\infty = \max(\partial_1(M_1),\ldots, \partial_1(M_p)) \end{cases}$$

where $\|\vec{\partial}_1\|_1$ is the sum of the degrees in x_1 of the monomials of P and where $\|\vec{\partial}_1\|_\infty$ is the degree of P in x_1. Therefore the problem of decreasing the degree of P in x_1 is reduced to a search for a hyperplane H such that :

$$\begin{cases} \|\vec{\partial}_1\|_1 \text{ or } \|\vec{\partial}_1\|_\infty \text{ is minimum,} \\ \vec{\partial}_1 \ge 0 \quad \text{(that is to say } \partial_1(M_i) \ge 0 \text{ for } 1 \le i \le p). \end{cases}$$

III. Practical resolution.

We suppose we simplify only one polynomial P of $K[x_1,\dots,x_n]$. The monomials of P are written $m_i = x_1^{d_{i1}} \dots x_n^{d_{in}}$ and we consider the matrix associated with P :

$$M(P) = \begin{pmatrix} d_{11} & \dots\dots & d_{1p} \\ \dots & \dots & \dots \\ d_{n1} & \dots\dots & d_{np} \end{pmatrix} \quad \text{where } d_{ij} \in \mathbb{N}.$$

We repeat that P is normalized if no monomial divides any of the monomials of P. In this case every row of $M(P)$ has at least one component equal to 0. We remark that the isomorphism $S°$ transforming P into a simplified normalized polynomial can be defined using the matrix $T°$ quoted below and obtained by adding to T an extra column whose terms are $x_{10},\dots,x_{n0}$:

$$T° = \begin{pmatrix} x_{10} & x_{11} & \dots & x_{1n} \\ \dots & \dots & \dots & \dots \\ x_{n0} & x_{n1} & \dots & x_{nn} \end{pmatrix} \quad \text{where } x_{ij} \in \mathbb{Z}$$

In the same manner we add a row $(d_{01} \dots d_{0p})$ to $M(P)$, and we obtain the matrix :

$$M°(P) = \begin{pmatrix} d_{01} & \dots\dots & d_{0p} \\ \dots & \dots & \dots \\ d_{n0} & \dots\dots & d_{np} \end{pmatrix} \quad \text{where } d_{01}=\dots=d_{0p}=1.$$

We shall find the matrix associated with the simplified polynomial $S°(P)$ by multiplying $T°$ and $M°(P)$. Therefore, the simplification of P amounts to searching for the matrix $T°.M°(P)$ whose coefficients are positive and minimal. The algorithm will have n steps :
at every step we shall compute a new row of $T°$. If we denote by $\vec{d}_0,\vec{d}_1,\dots,\vec{d}_n$ the rows of $M°(P)$, then the simplification of P amounts to finding $x_{i0}, x_{i1},\dots,x_{in}$ such that :

$$\begin{cases} \vec{\partial}_i = x_{i0}\,\vec{d}_0 + \dots + x_{in}\,\vec{d}_n \geq 0 \,, \\ \|\vec{\partial}_i\| \quad \text{minimum.} \end{cases}$$

First, we take $\vec{\partial}_0 = \vec{d}_0$ and we compute $\vec{\partial}_1$. Then we substitute $\vec{\partial}_1$ for $\vec{d}_1$. At step i the rows of $M^\circ(P)$ are $\vec{\partial}_0, \vec{\partial}_1, \ldots, \vec{\partial}_{i-1}, \vec{d}_i, \ldots, \vec{d}_n$ and we compute :

$$\vec{\partial}_i = x_{i0}\,\vec{\partial}_0 + \ldots + x_{i\,i-1}\,\vec{\partial}_{i-1} + x_{ii}\,\vec{d}_i + \ldots + x_{in}\,\vec{d}_n$$

with $x_{ii} = 1$ or -1. Then we substitute $\vec{\partial}_i$ for $\vec{d}_i$. Thus the determinant of T will be equal to 1 or -1 and S° will be an isomorphism. Let us remark that if we took $x_{ii} \geq 1$ or $x_{ii} \leq -1$ (instead of x_{ii} equal to 1 or -1), then the rows $\vec{\partial}_0, \ldots \vec{\partial}_i$ substituted for $\vec{d}_0, \ldots, \vec{d}_i$ would be linearly independent. Thus the determinant of T would be different from 0 (instead of being equal to 1 or -1), and S° would be a monomorphism (instead of an isomorphism). At step i, we have to solve the following program :

$$\begin{cases} \text{Minimum} \quad \|\vec{\partial}_i\| \\ \partial_{i1} = \sum\limits_{0\leq j\leq n} d_{j1}\, x_{ij} \geq 0 \\ \ldots\ldots\ldots\ldots\ldots\ldots \\ \partial_{ip} = \sum\limits_{0\leq j\leq n} d_{jp}\, x_{ij} \geq 0 \\ x_{ii} = 1 \quad \text{or} \quad x_{ii} = -1 \\ x_{ij} \in \mathbb{Z} \end{cases} \tag{3}$$

To solve this integer program we use the method introduced by Garfinkel and Nemhauser in [1]. The quantity $\|\vec{\partial}_i\|$ that we must minimize is called the objective function. The program variables must be positive. We thus suppose that $x_{ij} \geq -M$ where M is a large positive number, and we take $x'_{ij} = x_{ij} + M$ as new positive variables.
The resolution is conditioned by the choice of the norm $\|\vec{\partial}_i\|$ of the objective function.

a. <u>Norm $\|\vec{\partial}_i\|_1 = \partial_{i1} + \ldots + \partial_{ip}$</u>.

The objective function can be written as :

$$Z = \sum_{0\leq j\leq n}\ \sum_{1\leq k\leq p} d_{jk}\, x_{ij} = \sum_{0\leq j\leq n}\ \sum_{1\leq k\leq p} d_{jk}\, x'_{ij} + M \sum_{0\leq j\leq n}\ \sum_{1\leq k\leq p} d_{jk}.$$

The integer program (3) is linear and can be written :

$$\begin{cases} \text{Minimum} \quad Z = Z_0 + M_0\, x'_{i0} + \ldots + M_n\, x'_{in} \\ \sum\limits_{0\leq j\leq n} d_{jk}\, x'_{ij} \geq M \sum\limits_{0\leq j\leq n} d_{jk} \quad \text{for } 1\leq k\leq p \\ x'_{i0}, \ldots, x'_{in} \in \mathbb{N} \\ x'_{ii} = M+1 \quad \text{or} \quad x'_{ii} = M-1 \end{cases} \tag{4}$$

Since $M_\circ, \ldots, M_n \geq 0$, this program can be solved by the usual method (such a program is said dual feasible). In fact we have two programs to solve, one with the constraint $x'_{ii} = M-1$, and the other with the constraint $x'_{ii} = M+1$. We then choose the best solution.

b. Norm $\|\vec{\partial}_i\|_\infty = \max(\partial_{i1}, \ldots, \partial_{ip})$.

We consider the objective function $Z = \max(\partial_{i1}, \ldots, \partial_{ip})$ to be a new variable denoted by m. We have the constraints :

$$m \geq \partial_{i1}, \ldots, m \geq \partial_{ip} \qquad \text{(I)}$$

Let D be a bound of the degrees; we have the constraints :

$$m \leq \partial_{i1} + D(1-\varepsilon_1), \ldots, m \leq \partial_{ip} + D(1-\varepsilon_p) \qquad \text{(II)}$$

where $\varepsilon_1, \ldots, \varepsilon_p$ are new positive integer variables. Finally we have:

$$\varepsilon_1 + \ldots + \varepsilon_p \geq 1 \qquad \text{(III)}$$

It is clear that (I), (II) and (III) conversely imply that m is equal to the maximum of $\partial_{i1}, \ldots, \partial_{ip}$. The linear program (3) can be written:

$$\left\{\begin{array}{l} \text{Minimum} \quad Z = m \\ 0 \leq \partial_{i1} \leq m \leq \partial_{i1} + D(1-\varepsilon_1) \\ \cdots\cdots\cdots\cdots\cdots\cdots \\ 0 \leq \partial_{ip} \leq m \leq \partial_{ip} + D(1-\varepsilon_p) \\ \varepsilon_1 + \ldots + \varepsilon_p \geq 1 \\ x_{ii} = 1 \quad \text{or} \quad x_{ii} = -1 . \end{array}\right. \qquad (5)$$

<u>Example</u>.

$$P = y^2z^2 + xz + xy^2z + x^2y^3 .$$

The matrix associated with P is :

$$M^\circ(P) = \begin{pmatrix} 1 & 1 & 1 & 1 \\ 0 & 1 & 1 & 2 \\ 2 & 0 & 2 & 3 \\ 2 & 1 & 1 & 0 \end{pmatrix}$$

We suppose that $u_i, x_i, y_i, z_i \geq -10$ and we take :

$$u'_i = u_i + 10 , \quad x'_i = x_i + 10 , \quad y'_i = y_i + 10 , \quad z'_i = z_i + 10.$$

The first step is to solve the following program :

$$\left\{\begin{array}{ll} \text{Minimum} \ \|\vec{\partial}_x\|_1 = -190 + 4u_1' + 4x_1' + 7y_1' + 4z_1' & \\ u_1' + 2y_1' + 2z_1' \geq 50 & \\ u_1' + x_1' + z_1' \geq 30 & \text{with } x_1' = 9 , \\ u_1' + x_1' + 2y_1' + z_1' \geq 50 & \text{then with } x_1' = 11. \\ u_1' + 2x_1' + 3y_1' \geq 60 & \end{array}\right.$$

The optimum solution is $\vec{\partial}_x = 0$ with $x_1 = z_1 = -1$ and $y_1 = 0$. Thus the variables x or z can be deleted and the new polynomial can be written : $Q = y^2 + x + xy^2 + x^2y^3$.

The matrix associated with Q is :

$$M^\circ(Q) = \begin{pmatrix} 1 & 1 & 1 & 1 \\ 0 & 1 & 1 & 2 \\ 2 & 0 & 2 & 3 \end{pmatrix}$$

The first step is to take $x_1 = 1$ and we have to solve :

$$\left\{\begin{array}{l} \text{Minimum} \ Z = 4u_1' + 7y_1' - 106 \\ u_1' + 2y_1' \geq 30 \\ u_1' + 3y_1' \geq 38 \\ u_1' \geq 9 . \end{array}\right.$$

The optimum solution $y_1' = 10$, $u_1' = 10$ gives $Z = 4$ and does not lower the degree in x. If we take $x_1 = -1$, the optimum solution is $y_1' = 10$, $u_1' = 12$ and still gives $Z = 4$. Thus it does not lower the degree in x either.

The second step is to take $y_2 = 1$ and to solve the program :

$$\left\{\begin{array}{l} \text{Minimum} \ Z = 4u_2' + 4x_2' - 73. \\ u_2' \geq 8 \\ u_2' + x_2' \geq 20 \\ u_2' + 2x_2' \geq 27 . \end{array}\right.$$

The optimum solution $u_2' = 13$, $x_2' = 7$ gives $Z = 7$ and does not lower the degree in y either. If we take $y_2 = -1$, we obtain the optimum solution : $x_2' = 10$, $u_2' = 13$, $Z = 5$. This last solution lowers the degree in y and the simplified polynomial is :

$$S^\circ(Q) = y + xy^3 + xy + x^2 .$$

IV. Conclusion.

The object of this paper was to find an algorithm decreasing either the degree of a given polynomial P or the sum of the degrees of the monomials of P (this last algorithm being easier to perform).
We can also find other algorithms for the simplifications given at II, b. and c. In particular we can transform a given polynomial into a monic polynomial whose degree is minimum (without increasing the number of the monomials).
We can also define another simplification in order to decrease as much as possible the number of factors of all the monomials of a given polynomial. The simplified polynomial has a constant monomial and several monomials with only one factor.
Further information about such simplifications are given in [3]. But all these simplifications are limited by the size of the integer program we have to solve.

Acknowledgement.
I should like to thank Maurice Mignotte for his helpful comments.

Bibliography.

[1] R.S. GARFINKEL and G.L. NEMHAUSER, Integer Programming, John Wiley, New-York, 1972.
[2] A.M. OSTROWSKI, On multiplication and factorisation of polynomials, Aequationes Math., 13, 1975.
[3] G. VIRY, Simplification des polynômes à plusieurs variables, CALSYF, 3, Ed. Mignotte, Strasbourg, 1983.

ON THE EQUIVALENCE OF HIERARCHICAL AND NON-HIERARCHICAL REWRITING ON CONDITIONAL TERM REWRITING SYSTEMS

M. Navarro
Informatikako Fakultatea
Euskal Herriko Unibersitatea
Donostia, SPAIN

F. Orejas
Facultat d'Informatica (*)
Universitat Politecnica
Barcelona, SPAIN

Since the mid 70's, abstract data types and algebraic specifications have been around playing a fundamental role in different fields related to software design theory and methodology. At first, algebraic specifications were mainly equational, but soon it was proved that the use of (positive) conditional equations was, not only convenient, but also necessary in some cases (ADJ76, ADJ78, ORE79).

Directly related to equational specifications are term rewriting systems, providing means for (effective) equational deduction or for early prototyping of specified software.

When dealing with conditional specifications, a slight generalization is needed, namely conditional term rewriting systems. However, conditional rewriting has not been studied too thoroughly, the authors may only cite BDJ78, PEE81, REM82, REM83, DRO83, BK81.

To avoid certain specific problems (concerning termination) of conditional term rewriting systems, most of the authors cited above work with, the so-called, hierarchical rewriting: the systems are defined in a hierarchical manner (by successive enrichments), the condition part of a given rule should only involve terms of lower hierarchy level, and, finally, when applying a rule the variables occurring in the condition may only be instantiated by terms of lower hierarchy. This should guarantee to avoid the circularity problems that may appear on the evaluation of the conditions.

However, a problem may be raised if using hierarchical rewriting: the congruence induced by the initial algebra semantics may not coincide

---

(*) Current address: C.R.I. Nancy, B.P. 239, 54505 Vandoeuvre-les-Nancy Cedex. FRANCE.

with the congruence induced by this kind of rewriting. This problem was pointed out in BK81 using a counter-example, in which both congruences were shown to be different, but the problem of finding suitable conditions under which the two congruences would coincide was left open. Also, the counter-example was, in a sense, not very appropriate: the hierarchy was not sufficiently complete and, hence, the notion of hierarchical specification, as usually understood (WPPDB83), was lost.

In this paper, we shall obtain conditions which are sufficient to assure that the two conguences coincide. Moreover, we shall prove that if these conditions do not hold, counter-examples may be found in which the congruences fail to be the same.

The organization of the paper is as follows. In section 1, we shall introduce the basic notions concerning conditional term rewriting systems and sketch the circularity problems that may arise when evaluating the conditions. Section 2 is devoted to define hierarchical rewriting as the solution to the problems mentioned in the previous section. Section 3 is the core of the paper, two theorems stating sufficient conditions for the equivalence of hierarchical and non-hierarchical rewriting, and two counter-examples showing the suitability of the previous results, are presented. Finally, in section 4, we shall propose some conclusions and relate our results with previous work.

Acknowledgements

We would like to thank J.L. Remy and J. Hsiang for some valuable conversations and for providing some papers that were essential for the realization of this work. This work has been partially supported by the Comision Asesora de Investigacion Cientifica y Tecnica (ref. 3866-79).

1. Preliminaries

Familiarity with the usual notions concerning abstract data types and term rewriting systems is assumed. For details and notation, see ADJ78a and HO80.

Let F be a signature, and let X be a set of variables disjoint from F. T(F) and T(F,X) will denote, respectively, the ground term and term algebras, i.e. the initial F-algebra and the F-algebra generated by X.

A conditional equation is just a sequence of pairs of terms:

<t=t' <u>if</u> t1=t1' & ... & tn=tn'>

which informally states that, for any instantiation, t=t' has to be satisfied if t1=t1' and ...tn=tn' are satisfied. A conditional specification SP = (F,E) is just a specification in which E is a set of conditional equations.

ADJ have proved (ADJ76) that, if SP is a conditional specification, there is an initial algebra T_{SP} in the category of algebras satisfying SP. Moreover $T_{SP} \cong T(F)/=_E$, where $=_E$ is the least congruence satisfying E.

As with unconditional specifications, we may define conditional term rewriting systems imposing some constraints on the equations: we shall assume that if <t=t' <u>if</u> t1=t1' & ... & tn=tn'> is in E, then $var(t') \subseteq var(t)$ and for all $i=<n$ $var(ti), var(ti') \subseteq var(t)$. We shall indistinctly talk about conditional specifications or term rewriting systems and, in this case, we may speak about conditional rules, instead of equations, and write them < t->t' <u>if</u> t1=t1' & ... & tn=tn'>.

Associated to conditional term rewriting systems, we may define several reduction relations depending on how we interpret the satisfaction of the conditions. We shall use the following definition:

r1 $-->_{SP}$ r2 iff there is a rule <t->t' <u>if</u> t1=t1' & ... & tn=tn'> in E, an address d in r1 and an assignment f, i.e. f:var(t1)--->T(F,X), such that $r1(d)=\bar{f}(t)$ (with $\bar{f}$ being the unique homomorphism from T(F,X) to T(F,X) extending f) $r2=r1[d<-\bar{f}(t')]$ and for all i=<n ti $<-->_{SP}$ ti' (*). Where $<-->_{SP}$ denotes the congruence generated by $-->_{SP}$. Some other authors use reduction relations in which (*) is substituted by ti $\overset{*}{-->}_{SP}$ ti' ($\overset{*}{-->}_{SP}$ denotes the reflexive-transitive closure of $-->_{SP}$), $ti \downarrow_{SP} ti'$ (ti and t1' rewrite into some t"), or some other condition.

Although its circularity, it may be proved that the above definition really defines a relation, moreover $<-->_{SP}$ on ground terms coincides with $=_E$ (NAV83).
Once we have defined the reduction relation associated to SP, we may talk about SP being noetherian or confluent, with the usual definitions. Moreover, we may state the classical results:

- If SP is noetherian and confluent then every term t has a unique normal form, denoted by $|t|_{SP}$.

- If SP is noetherian and confluent then $t1 =_E t2$ iff $|t1|_{SP} = |t2|_{SP}$.

When dealing with unconditional specifications (and/or term rewriting systems) confluency and noetherianity are the conditions to assure the good behaviour of the computation described by the reduction relations (confluency assures the uniqueness of results and noetherianity assures termination). However, when dealing with conditional specifications these conditions may be not enough: certainly, confluency would still assure the uniqueness of results, but noetherianity would just assure termination of the reduction sequence, but in the conditional case this is not the only computation involved, we have also to compute the conditions, and this computation may involve circularities that may lead to non-termination. In general, the problem of knowing if a given rule may be applied to a given term (i.e. if the condition holds) is not recursive, but recursively enumerable (see example 1.2).

Example 1.1

Naturals with le (lower or equal operation) may be easily specified with the following conditional term rewriting system:

sorts	operations	rules
nat, bool	0: ---> nat	le(X,X) -> T
	s: nat ---> nat	le(s(X),X) -> F
	le: nat × nat ---> bool	le(X,s(Y)) -> T <u>if</u> le(X,Y) = T
	T: ---> bool	le(s(X),Y) -> F <u>if</u> le(X,Y) = F
	F: ---> bool	

[]

Example 2.2

Let SP1 be a specification of the naturals with le and mult (multiplication), let f be any (total) recursive function, f: N × N ---> N, let SP2 be a specification including SP1 and f (according to BT80, such specification exists, moreover, considered as a term rewriting system, SP2 can be made noetherian and confluent for ground terms), finally let SP be:

SP2 + operations	rules
ex: nat ---> nat	ex(X) -> 1 <u>if</u> le(ex1(0,X))=F
ex1: nat × nat ---> nat	ex1(X,Y) -> 1 <u>if</u> le(f(X,Y),0) = F

mult(2,ex1(suc(X),Y)) -> ex1(X,Y)
<u>if</u> f(X,Y) = 0

SP is still noetherian (for ground terms), but it may be proved (BBTW81) that ex(n) (for any n) may be rewritten into 1 iff there exists an m iff there exists an m such that f(m,n)>0. Obviously, this relation is, in general non-recursive, but recursively enumerable.

2. Hierarchical term rewriting systems

Hierarchical specification of abstract data types has been advocated, from a methodological point of view, to design structured specifications for complex data types. In this sense, hierarchical means defining a data type from a base type by means of a hierarchy of successive enrichments. These enrichments, usually, have to be consistent and sufficiently complete with respect to the enriched type (WPPDB80), although, sometimes, it may be reasonable to have non-sufficiently complete enrichments, for example for dealing with errors (GOG78).

Similar reasons may be considered to advocate for the use of hierarchical term rewriting systems. Moreover, when dealing with conditional rewriting, the use of hierarchies may serve to avoid the termination problems described in the previous section, if we impose the additional constraint that the condition of a rule should involve terms of lower hierarchy than the rule. Note that this implies that the rules of the base term rewriting system should be unconditional.

If we forget about the methodological reasons, and we concentrate on the use of hierarchies for solving the problems of conditional rewriting, it may be questionable the need for consistency, sufficient completeness or any other condition. In fact, the policy followed by different authors varies, for example, BDJ78, REM82, REM83 and PEE81 assume consistency and sufficient completeness with respect to booleans (the conditions on their rules are boolean), BK81 assumes some kind of consistency (called forward preserving), REM82 also assumes sufficient completeness in a strong sense, finally DRO83 does not assume anything, but although he uses a special kind of hierarchical rewriting, he gets into some problems (see the conclusion).

We think it is reasonable to assume, at least, consistency, since if the idea of hierarchical rewriting is to evaluate the conditions at the appropriate level, at this very same level should be possible to to all the possible reductions on the terms of this level: inconsistent enrichments would force the use of reductions at higher levels. For similar reasons, we will also assume that a term of a given level of hierarchy should not be rewritten on a term of a higher level (this condition is also considered by other authors), since, otherwise we would be again in danger of failing into circularities, and, on the other hand, having consistency is unnecessary to deal with this kind of rules.

Definition 2.1

A hierarchical term rewriting system (htrs) SP is a finite sequence of term rewriting systems, SP = (SP0,...,SPn), such that for every i<n:

1. $SPi \subseteq SPi+1$

2. SPi+1 is consistent with respect to SPi, i.e. if $t1,t2 \in T(Fi,X)$ and $t1 \longleftrightarrow_{SPi+1} t2$ then $t1 \longleftrightarrow_{SPi} t2$.

3. If < t->t' *if* t1=t1' & ... & tm=tm' > is in Ei+1 - Ei then for every j (j=<m) tj,tj' are in T(Fi,X) and t is in T(Fi+1,X)-T(Fi,X).

Note

If we want to deal only with reductions on ground terms, then in the consistency condition it is enough to ask for $t1,t2 \in T(Fi)$

Example 2.2

We may specify finite sets of integers using the following hierarchy: (SP0,SP1,SP2), where SP0 is the boolean specification, SP1 is the integer specification and SP2 is SP1 plus:

sorts	operations	rules
set	0: ---> set	delete(0,X)->0
	insert: set × int ---> set	delete(insert(S,X),X)->delete(S,X)
	delete: set × int ---> set	delete(insert(S,X),Y)-> insert(delete(S,Y),X) *if* eq(X,Y)=F

(eq is an equality operation on the integers). []

Now, to avoid the termination problems in evaluating the conditions, we must define a special 'hierarchical rewriting' by restricting the instantiation of the rules, in such a way that when we are trying to rewrite a term of a given hierarchy level, the conditions to evaluate are of a strict lower level.

Definition 2.3

Let SP = (SP0,...,SPn) be a htrs, then the hierarchical reduction relation $\to_{H,SP}$ associated to SP is defined in the following way: s1 $\to_{H,SP}$ s2 iff there is a rule r = < t->t' *if* t1=t1' & ... & tm=tm' > in some SPi, and an instantiation f: var(t) ---> T(Fn,X), such that:

1) $\bar{f}(t)$ is a subterm of s1 in some address d.
2) s(2) = s1[d<- f($\bar{t}$')]
3) For every j =< m $\bar{f}(tj) \leftrightarrow_{H,SP} \bar{f}(tj')$
4) For every j =< m $\bar{f}(tj)$ and $\bar{f}(tj')$ have lower hierarchy than $\bar{f}(t)$, i.e. if $\bar{f}(t) \in T(Fi+1,X)$ then $\bar{f}(tj),\bar{f}(tj') \in F(Ti,X)$.

Example 2.4

Let SP be a hierarchical specification of finite sets of integers, as the one in example 2.2, but with the operation min: set ---> int, and the appropriate rules, which gives the smallest element of a given set. Then the term delete(insert(0,min(insert(0,0))),1), would not be possible to be reduced to insert(0,min(insert(0,0))) using the rules:

a) delete(insert(S,X),Y) -> insert(delete(S,Y),X) *if* eq(X,Y)=F
b) delete(0,X) -> X

because it is not permitted to instantiate X to min(insert(0,0)), since this would break the hierarchy. Instead, it would be possible to reduce min(insert(0,0)) to 0, using the appropriate rules for min and then reduce delete(insert(0,0),1) to insert(0,0) using rules a and b. []

It may be seen that with the hierarchical reduction we have avoided the problems in evaluating the conditions, since the evaluation of conditions of level i+1 involves only the evaluation of conditions of level i (i>=0), hence the only termination problems we may have would come from the possible non-noetherianity of the system.

3. Equivalence of hierarchical and non-hierarchical reductions

As we have seen in the previous section, hierarchical rewriting may be the way of avoiding the specific problems involved with conditional rewriting. However, if hierarchical rewriting is to be of any value, we must be sure that the congruence induced by it, coincides with the initial algebra congruence or with the deduction associated to the theory presented by the specification (depending on whether we work with ground terms or with terms with variables), or at least, we would have to know under which conditions would they coincide.

As we will see in counter-examples 3.1 and 3.2, in general $<-->_{H,SP}$ does not coincide with $<-->_{SP}$, but theorems 3.3 and 3.4 shall provide sufficient conditions to guarantee their coincidence. However, it is surprising that in previous papers in the subject (BDJ78, PEE81, DRO83) the authors do not even seem to notice the problem, only BK81 prevents about it (counter-example 3.1 was in their paper) and REM82 gives a sufficient condition which is a special case of theorem 3.4.

Counter-example 3.1

Let SP be (SP0,SP1), with

```
SP0 = sorts      s                    SP1 = SP0 + operations  a: s ---> s
      -----                                       ----------
                                                              b:   ---> s
      operations  0: ---> s
      ----------                                              c:   ---> s
                  p: s ---> s
                  q: s ---> s                     rules   a(X)->b if p(X)=0
                                                  -----
      rules       p(q(X)) -> 0
      -----
```

SP is a htrs, moreover it is noetherian and confluent, although SP1 is not sufficiently complete with respect to SP0. Now, we may see that in this case $<-->_{H,SP}$ and $<-->_{SP}$ do not coincide:

$$a(q(c)) <-->_{SP} b \quad \text{but} \quad a(q(c)) <\not-->_{H,SP} b \qquad []$$

Counter-example 3.2

Let SP be (SP0,SP1), with SP0 being the nat specification and SP1 =

```
SP0 + Operations                  rules
      ----------                  -----
      foo: nat x nat ---> nat     foo(X,Y) -> 0 if X=s(Y)
                                  foo(X,Y) -> foo(s(foo(X,Y),foo(X,Y))
```

SP is a htrs, moreover it is sufficiently complete (in fact foo(X,Y) $<-->_{SP}$ 0) and confluent, although it is not noetherian. Now,we may see that in this case $<-->_{H,SP}$ and $<-->_{SP}$ again do not coincide:

$$foo(0,0) <-->_{SP} 0 \quad \text{but} \quad foo(0,0) <\not-->_{H,SP} 0$$

Also, if we change the direction of the arrow in the second rule, we still have a htrs, which is sufficiently complete and noetherian, although not confluent, in which the two congruences are still different. []

Definition 3.3

Let SP=(SP0,...,SPn) be a htrs, then SP is sufficiently complete (resp. sufficiently complete on ground terms) iff for all t in T(Fi+1,X) (resp. T(Fi+1)), if the sort of t is in Fi then there is a t' in T(Fi,X) (resp. T(Fi)) such that $t <\!\!-\!\!->_{SP} t'$.

Theorem 3.4

Let SP be a htrs, then if SP is sufficiently complete, noetherian and confluent then $<\!\!-\!\!->_{H,SP} = <\!\!-\!\!->_{SP}$. Moreover, $-\!\!->_{H,SP}$ is noetherian and confluent and for any t, $|t|_{H,SP} = |t|_{SP}$.

proof

First of all, it may be noted that, under this conditions, if the sort of t is in Fi then $|t|_{SP}$ is in T(Fi,X). Now, if $-\!\!->_{SP}$ is noetherian, so is $-\!\!->_{H,SP}$. Thus it is enough to prove that if t is a normal form under $-\!\!->_{H,SP}$, it is so under $-\!\!->_{SP}$, since $-\!\!->_{H,SP} \subseteq -\!\!->_{SP}$. We proceed by induction on the hierarchy levels:

Case 0 is trivial, since SP0 is unconditional.

Assume t∈T(Fi+1,X) is not a normal form under $-\!\!->_{SP}$, i.e. $t -\!\!->_{SP} t'$, then there is a rule < s->s' <u>if</u> s1=s1' & ... & sn=sn' > in E, an instantiation f:var(s)--->T(F,X) and an address d in t, such that: $t(d) = \bar{f}(s)$, $t'=t[d<\!-\bar{f}(s')]$ and for all j, $\bar{f}(sj) <\!\!-\!\!->_{SP} \bar{f}(sj')$. We have two cases:

1) The instantiation f is appropriate for hierarchical rewriting. Then by induction, for all j, $\bar{f}(sj) <\!\!-\!\!->_{H,SP} \bar{f}(sj')$ and thus $t -\!\!->_{SP} t'$.

2) The instantiation f is not appropriate for hierarchical rewriting. Then, we proceed by subterm induction:

- If t has not proper subterms, then the case is trivial, since it is impossible for f not to be appropriate.

- Assume t has proper subterms, if f is not appropriate this means that for some variable Z occurring in the condition, f(Z)∈T(Fi+1,X) - T(Fi,X). Now, f(Z) is a subterm of t, since Z occurs in the condition its sort must be in Si, hence $|f(Z)|_{SP}$∈T(Fi,X), thus f(Z) may be re-written into its normal form under $-\!\!->_{SP}$, then by subterm induction f(Z) may be rewritten into something under $-\!\!->_{H,SP}$, and thus f(Z) is not a normal form under $-\!\!->_{H,SP}$, but since f(Z) is a subterm of t, t is not a normal form under $-->_{H,SP}$. []

A similar result may be obtained for ground terms.

Definition 3.5

SP is strongly suff. complete (ssp) (resp. ssp on ground terms) iff for all t in T(Fi+1,X) (resp. T(Fi+1)) if the sort of t is in Si then there is a t' in T(Fi,X) (resp. T(Fi)) such that $t<-->_{H,SP}t'$.

Theorem 3.6

If SP is ssp then $<-->_{H,SP} = <-->_{SP}$

proof

It is enough to prove that $t-->_{SP}t'$ implies $t<-->_{H,SP}t'$. Again, we proceed by induction on the levels of the hierarchy.

Case 0 is trivial again.

Case i+1. There is a rule < s->s' *if* s1=s1' & ... & sm=sm'> in E, an instantiation f: var(s)--->T(F,X) and an address d in t, such that $t(d) = \bar{f}(s)$, $t' = t[d<-\bar{f}(s')]$ and for all j, $\bar{f}(sj)<-->_{SP}\bar{f}(sj')$. Again we have two cases: If the instantiation of the rule used is appropriate, then by induction we may use the same rule to rewrite hierarchically t into t'. If the instantiation is not appropriate for hierarchical rewriting then we know that, for every variable Z that occurs in the condition of the rule, there is a term r_Z in T(Fi,X) such that $\bar{f}(Z) <-->_{H,SP} r_Z$. Now, let f1 be an assignment, f1: var(s) ---> T(F,X) defined:

f1(Z) = *if* Z occurs in the condition *then* r_Z *else* f(Z)
then we have: $\bar{f}(s) <-->_{H,SP} \overline{f1}(s) -->_{H,SP} \overline{f1}(s') <-->_{H,SP} \bar{f}(s')$ since we may rewrite hierarchically $\overline{f1}(s)$ into $\overline{f1}(s')$ (f1 is appropriate and the condition must hold). Thus:

$t <-->_{H,SP} t[d<-\overline{f1}(s)] -->_{H,SP} t[d<-\overline{f1}(s')] <-->_{H,SP} t[d<-\bar{f}(s')] = t'$
[]

Again, a similar result may be obtained for ground terms.

Corollary 3.7

If SP is a htrs and SP is not sufficiently complete or confluent or noetherian, then $<-->_{SP}$ may be different than $<-->_{H,SP}$

Corollary 3.8

If SP is not ssc then $<-->_{SP}$ may be different than $<-->_{H,SP}$.

Counter-examples 3.1 and 3.2 would serve to prove these corollaries.

4. Conclusions

Rewriting systems have been considered the operational semantics of equational specifications, this can be so because the congruence associated to the reduction relation coincides with the initial algebra congruence.

When dealing with conditional specifications, hierarchical rewriting seems to be right tool to avoid termination problems when evaluating the conditions. But, as we have seen, semantics may be altered.

Most of the authors dealing with conditional rewriting work with hierarchical systems without bothering about the problems treated in this paper. This seems rather surprising, since it is the validity of the approach which may be questioned. Only BK81, in a paper not so much concerned with hierarchical rewriting, points out the problem, using counter-example 3.1 of this paper, and leaves open the question of finding suitable conditions for solving it, and REM82 which states a theorem which is a restriction of our theorem 3.4.

Finally, while working in this paper, we received DRO83, which is the only one whose definition of hierarchical system is significantly different. The only restriction he poses is that the base specification should be unconditional, also, he does not restrict instantiation of the variables occurring in the conditions, but he restricts the application of the rules depending on the level we are rewriting (evaluating a condition always lowers the level). This approach is, in some sense, more general (and also, sometimes, more restrictive): counter-example 3.2 would not apply, but counter-example 3.1 it would. Also, because of the lack of restrictions, inconsistent specifications may give problems. We believe that, with the appropriate restrictions (at least consistency) this could be the approach to be considered, to which theorem 3.3 (although with changes in the proof) and a variant of theorem 3.4 , would still apply.

6. References

ADJ76 Thatcher, J.W.; Wagner, E.G.; Wright, J.B.
'Specification of abstract data types using conditional axioms', IBM T.J.Watson Res. Center Rep. RC-6214, 1976.

ADJ78 Thatcher, J.W.; Wagner, E.G.; Wright, J.B.
'Data type specification: parameterization and the power of specification techniques', Proc. 10th STOC, 1978.

ADJ78a Goguen, J.A.; Thatcher, J.W.; Wagner, E.G.
'An initial algebra approach to the specification, correctness and implementation of abstract data types', in 'Current Trends in Programming Methodology, Vol IV: Data Structuring' R.T. Yeh (ed.), Prentice-Hall 1978.

BDJ78 Brand, D.; Darringuer, J.A.; Joyner, W.H.
'Completeness of conditional reductions', IBM T.J.Watson Res. Center Rep. RC-7404, 1978.

BBTW81 Bergstra, J.A.; Broy, M.; Tucker, J.V.; Wirsing, M.
'On the power of algebraic specifications', Proc. 10th. MFCS Springer LNCS 118, 1981.

BK81 Bergstra, J.A.; Klop, J.W.
'Conditional rewrite rules: confluency and termination', Math. Centre Amsterdam, Internal report.

BT80 Bergstra, J.A.; Tucker, J.V.
'A characterization of computable and semi-computable data types by means of a finite specification method', Proc. 7th. ICALP, Springer LNCS 85, 1980.

DRO83 Drosten, K.
'Towards executable specifications using conditional axioms' T.U. Braunschweig rep. 83-01, 1983.

GOG78 Goguen, J.A.
'Abstract errors for abstract data types', Proc. Conf. on Formal Description of Programming Concepts, North-Holland 1978.

HO80 Huet, G.; Oppen, D.C.
'Equations and rewrite rules: a survey', in 'Formal Language Theory: Perspectives and Open Problems', R.Book (ed.), Acad. Press, 1980.

NAV83 Navarro, M.
'Conditional term rewriting systems', Master's Thesis, Univ. Complutense, Madrid 1983 (in Spanish).

ORE79 Orejas, F.
'On the power of conditional specifications', Sigplan Notices 14,7 (July 1979).

PEE81 Pletat, U.; Engels, G.; Ehrich H.-D.
'Operational semantics of algebraic specifications with conditional equations', Dortmund Univ. rep 118/81, 1981.

REM82 Remy, J.-L.
'Etude des systemes de reecriture conditionnels et applications aux types abstraits algebriques', these de doctorat, C.R.I. Nancy, 1982.

REM83 Remy, J.-L.
'Proving conditional identities by equational case reasoning, rewriting and normalization', Tech. Rep. CRI Nancy 1982.

WPPDB83 Wirsing, M.; Pepper, P.; Partsch, H.; Dosch, W; Broy, M.
'On hierarchies of abstract data types', Acta Informatica 20,1 pp. 1-34, 1983.

Implementation of a *p-adic* Package for Polynomial Factorization and other Related Operations

*Paul S. Wang**

Department of Mathematical Sciences
Kent State University
Kent Ohio, 44242

ABSTRACT

The design and implementation of a *p-adic* package, called **P**-pack, for polynomial factorization, gcd, squarefree decomposition and univariate partial fraction expansion are presented. **P**-pack is written in FRANZ LISP, and can be loaded into VAXIMA and run without modification. The physical organization of the code modules and their logical relations are described. Sharing of code among different modules and techniques for improved speed are discussed.

1. Introduction

Polynomial factorization, gcd and other related operations have received much attention in the past 15 years or so, because these operations are fundamental in a computer-based symbolic computation system and because there have been steady advancement of new algorithms and improvements for these computations. These techniques are implemented in a number of symbolic computation systems, with varying degrees of completeness. MACSYMA and REDUCE [7] are among the systems with rather extensive implementations of the various new algorithms. Some of the fastest algorithms are based on modular homomorphism and *p-adic* lifting. We present the design and organization of a new, comprehensive software package for polynomial factorization, gcd, squarefree factorization and partial fraction expansion based on *p-adic* techniques. The programs are written in FRANZ LISP [5]. It is a stand-alone package which can be loaded into a VAXIMA system [4] and run without modification. The package implements the state-of-the-art *p-adic* and modular algorithms for these operations. It also includes many recent improvements for increased efficiency. We shall refer to this package as **P**-pack.

---

* Work reported herein has been supported in part by the National Science Foundation under Grant MCS 82-01239, and in part by the Department of Energy under Grant DE-AC02-ER7602075-A010.

The operations implemented include univariate and multivariate factorization, [10], [11], gcd (content) [14], squarefree decomposition [12], and univariate partial fraction decomposition [15]. Most operations can be performed modulo p (p a prime or prime power) and over algebraic extensions of the rationals [18] as well as over the integers, **Z**. These operations are highly interdependent. The code is organized to maximize sharing of common operations. The LISP source is sufficiently documented to be readable.

P-pack consists of 18 LISP modules and one **C** module. Each module implements a well-defined set of operations. The **C** module contains operations whose increased speed is critical for the better performance of the entire package. There is a set of test files which serve two purposes. First, they are used to demonstrate the capabilities provided by **P**-pack and the way to use them. Second, they are used to test **P**-pack after being loaded into VAXIMA at a new site or after a bug fix. **P**-pack will be made available for distribution.

We discuss some important implementational aspects which normally are not elaborated in a description of the underlying algorithms. We show the organizational structure as well as how things fit together.

2. Logical organization

We describe the major interdependencies among the various modules and how they cooperate to achieve the desired functionalities. The modules are individually described in the next section.

2.1. Multivariate gcd, sqfr and factoring

The *p-adic* algorithms for multivariate factoring, gcd and square-free decomposition are similar in approach. The major steps are basically,

- (i) Initialize;
- (ii) Select points of evaluation to reduce the given problem to a corresponding problem in one variable;
- (iii) Obtain solutions to the reduced problem in one variable;
- (iv) Determine leading coefficients;
- (v) Perform multivariate *p-adic* lifting on the univariate solutions;
- (vi) Obtain actual solutions for the given multivariate problem.

Figures 1, 2 and 3 show the relations and dependencies for multivariate factoring, gcd and square-free decomposition respectively. We see there is a great deal of sharing of common operations. Basically, the subst.l and mulift.l are shared by all three computations with the remaining operations provided either by other modules or by the respective driver modules. Operations in <angle brackets> are available in VAXIMA but not contained in **P**-pack.

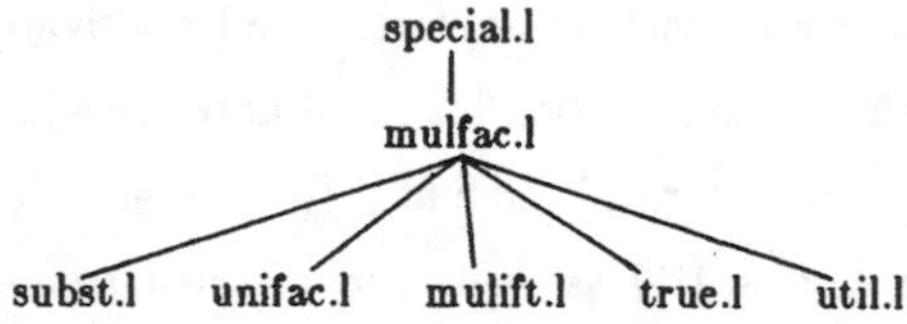

Fig. 1 multivariate factoring modules

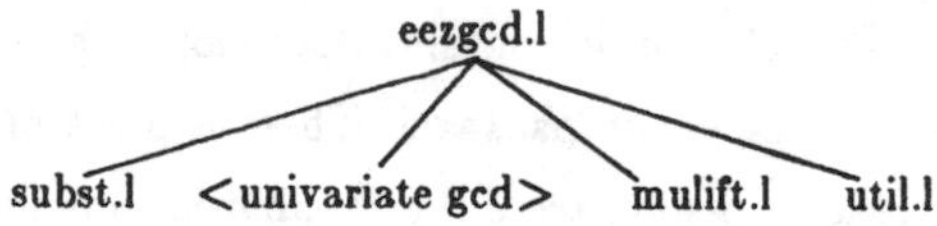

Fig. 2 multivariate gcd modules

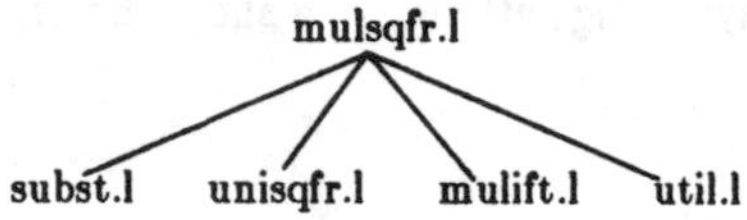

Fig. 3 multivariate square-free decomposition modules

The univariate factoring, partial fraction expansion and multivariate *p-adic* lifting share many common operations as shown in figures 4, 5 and 6.

Again, we see substantial sharing of operations. The routines contained in fac.c and cxprs.l are used in 'inner loops' for many operations and their efficient coding can result in noticeable improvement in performance for the entire package.

The main operations performed by the multivariate *p-adic* lifting are as follows.

(i) Initialize, compute coefficient bound and set modulus.

(ii) Impose coefficients (obtained through leading and other coefficient pre-determination algorithms).

(iii) Compute correction coefficients and lift to next variable.

(iv) Obtain true factors in the variables already lifted (combine extraneous factors).

(v) Use the current partial results in attempting to determine additional coefficients through the coeff.l module (this may result in finding some actual factors).

(vi) Remove any factors completely determined (mainly from step v) from further lifting; re-initialize if necessary; go to step (ii).

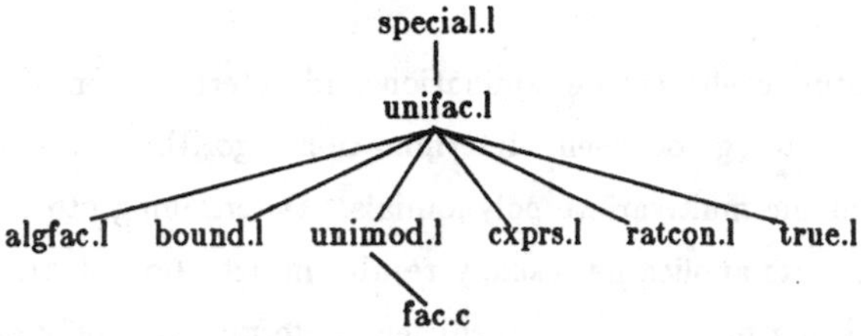

Fig. 4 univariate factoring modules

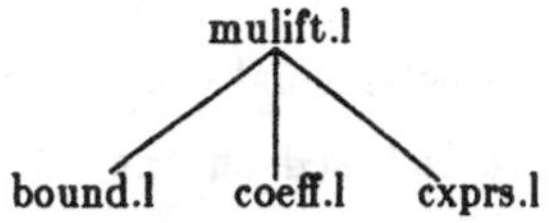

Fig. 5 multivariate *p-adic* lifting modules

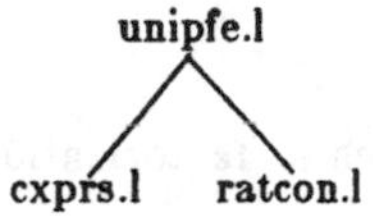

Fig. 6 univariate partial fraction modules

3. Description of the modules

P-pack consists of eighteen LISP modules and a **C** module. Each module implements a set of closely related operations supporting one or a few well-defined functionalities. Each module is described briefly in this section.

3.1. algfac.l

This module contains operations for factoring over large finite fields and algebraic extensions of finite fields $\mathbf{Z}_p$, including Q matrix formation [9], null space basis calculation, and computing *nontrivial* αs [2]. Also contained here are routines for finding integer basis, computing traces, etc.

3.2. bound.l

Programmed here are functions for the computation of coefficient bounds needed in the univariate and multivariate factoring algorithms. See [8] for more information on the computation of bounds for the coefficients of divisors of polynomials.

3.3. coeff.l

Routines for leading coefficient determination and determination of other coefficients are contained here. The leading coefficient determination algorithm is important for computations involving non-monic multivariate polynomials. Determining other coefficients are very important in practice. Its application usually results in detection of true factors early in the multivariate *p-adic* lifting process. Note coefficient determination only applies for operations over **Z**.

3.4. eezgcd.l

Contained here are multivariate polynomial gcd and content routines using *p-adic* algorithms. The algorithm implemented is based on the EZGCD algorithm [10] with improvements as described in [15]. Operations over **Z**, mod p, and algebraic number fields are supported.

3.5. special.l

Special-case factoring routines such as factorization of x^n+a^m using cyclotomic polynomials [3], Eisenstein's irreducibility criterion, etc.

3.6. true.l

Routines for discovering actual factors after *p-adic* lifting are contained here. Principal operations are the restoring of leading coefficients (in the non-monic case) and the recombination of factors (in case there are extraneous factors). Due to the application of coefficient determination, this code is seldom needed in practice for factoring over **Z**.

3.7. interface.l

This module redefines several existing routines in VAXIMA for interfacing to **P**-pack.

3.8. mulfac.l

Multivariate polynomial routines for factoring over **Z** and over algebraic number fields. The main driver routine for multivariate polynomial factoring is here. Other major operations include selection of appropriate points of evaluation, and determination of leading coefficients.

3.9. mullift.l

The *p-adic* lifting algorithm for multivariate factors is implemented by this module. Lifting of all factors is in parallel and one variable at a time. Both the iterative and the recursive algorithm for computing the correction coefficients are available. Detection of true factors is performed at several places for better efficiency. Techniques for the early determination of coefficients are applied.

3.10. unifac.l

This module contains driver routines for univariate polynomial factorization over **Z**, mod p and over algebraic number fields. Three different parallel lifting algorithms are provided that are user-selectable through the setting of the switch 'LIFT'. The early detection of true factors is a feature whose implementation will be described in detail later.

3.11. mulsqfr.l

Multivariate SQFR factoring operations use an efficient algorithm by Wang and Trager [13]. This algorithm is very fast when the given polynomial is squarefree. It is faster than a single gcd operation between the given polynomial and its first derivative when it is not squarefree. SQFR factoring over **Z**, mod p and over algebraic number fields are allowed.

3.12. unisqfr.l

Univariate SQFR factoring over the integers are implemented as described in [13]. SQFR decomposition over algebraic number fields are also provided.

3.13. unimod.l

Implemented here is the Berlekamp algorithm [1] for univariate polynomial factoring modulo a small prime. Operations include forming the Q matrix, finding a basis for the null space of (Q – I), and gcd operations;

3.14. unipfe.l

Univariate partial fraction expansion can be computed using a *p-adic* algorithm [16]. Basically, the incomplete partial fraction expansion can be performed using routines in cxprs.l and then the results can be lifted.

3.15. ratcon.l

Specialized routines for recovering a rational number from its *p-adic* image are in this module. They are used for the early detection of true factors in univariate factorization and in partial fraction expansion.

3.16. cxprs.l

This module is central to the univariate and multivariate lifting process used in **P**-pack. It contains functions for finding $v_i(x)$ satisfying

$$1/f(x) = \sum_i v_i/f_i \pmod p$$

for given $f(x) = \prod f_i$ and prime modulus p. Such congruences can also be lifted to a given power of p. The computation is done through a series of extended PRS operations on partial products of the f_i. For lack of a better term, we call this operation the 'continued extended PRS' (cxprs).

3.17. subst.l

Functions for generating suitable integer substitutions for mapping a multivariate problem down to a univariate problem are here. Zero and small integer substitutions are preferred. This is done by generating (semi-randomly) substitutions modulo a very small modulus (3, for example) and increasing the size of the modulus as needed.

3.18. util.l

This module contains various utility functions that are used in other modules. It also includes functions defined for debugging purposes.

3.19. fac.c

This module is coded in **C**. It implements the null space algorithm for factorization modulo a small prime. Because of declarations in **C**, only polynomials with degree less than or equal to 100 will be handled by this code.

4. Some techniques for improved speed

4.1. A C coded module

This module currently contains the null space algorithm. It is essentially a matrix triangularization algorithm with a double loop on the column and row indices. In factoring over $\mathbf{Z}_p$, p a small prime, the entries of the Q matrix are small integers representable as type *int* in **C**. The repeated access to array entries and arithmetic in $\mathbf{Z}_p$ makes a **C** implementation of the algorithm very much faster than a LISP implementation.

The VAX architecture makes it easy to invoke, from programs written in one language, programs written in a different language. FRANZ LISP provides a 'CFASL' function for loading into LISP compiled foreign function definitions. The foreign subroutine is called through the regular LISP function call mechanism with a LISP atom having already been bound to the desired entry point to the foreign code. It is slightly more complicated if the foreign function is to return a list structure as the null space algorithm would.

For univariate and multivariate factoring over the integers, factoring over $\mathbf{Z}_p$ will be performed for several different p. Thus the speed of the null space code is important. The **C** coded version reduced the total factoring time of the degree 40 polynomial in SIGSAM problem 7 by a factor of 2. Some other key operations may be recoded in **C** in the future.

4.2. Early detection of true factors

Speed can be gained if results of a computation are obtained at the earliest possible opportunity. In **P**-pack this means detection of actual factors as they are formed in the various stages of the entire factoring process, removing any detected factors from the computation, and re-initializing the reduced problem.

For example, in multivariate squarefree factoring, the principal features of the algorithm are (a) the given polynomial being squarefree is detected almost immediately, (b) in case the given polynomial is not square-free, the most repeated part is determined and removed from the problem first, and (c) determining the most repeated part involves multivariate lifting to the base polynomial rather than it raised to the given power. Therefore, the computing time of this squarefree algorithm is, in general, less than a single gcd between the given polynomial and its first derivative.

In univariate factoring, an algorithm for the early detection of actual factors is applied. This algorithm uses a technique for determining rational numbers from their modular images (implemented in ratcon.l) in attempting to determine true factors as the univariate *p-adic* lifting is being carried out. This method is applied to the individual factors being lifted. No recombination of extraneous factors is done. A heuristic bound is used which is the nth root of the coefficient bound (computed by bound.l), where n is the number of factors being lifted. The early detection algorithm is applied after each lifting iteration beyond this heuristic bound. In case true factors are found, the lifting problem and the coefficient bounds are reduced and the lifting of any remaining factors continues after re-initialization.

The re-initialization involves recomputing the polynomials $\alpha_i(x)$ in

$$\sum_i \alpha_i(x) F_i(x) \equiv 1 \pmod{p}. \tag{1}$$

The $F_i(x)$ is a product of all the factors $u_j(x)$ being lifted except $u_i(x)$. That is

$$F_i(x) = \prod_{j=1}^{r} u_j(x) \,/\, u_i(x),$$

where r is the number of factors being lifted. In 'quadratic lifting', initialization must also include lifting the congruence (1) to the correct power of p. Cost of such reinitialization is well worthwhile given the reduction in the overall problem. In the program, the reinitialization is done simply by calling functions in cxprs.l.

In multivariate *p-adic* lifting, true factor detection is performed after lifting each variable. This virtually eliminates the possibility of lifting extraneous factors fully to the last variable, when the computation cost becomes dominant.

4.3. Combining steps in different parts of an algorithm

At several places in **P**-pack, a modulus, q, is needed which must satisfy several conditions. Once q is selected, subsequent computations are conducted modulo q. Often this is needed simply to avoid rational number arithmetic in the subsequent steps. For example, in multivariate gcd computation, after solving the corresponding gcd problem in one variable, a sufficiently large prime or prime power modulus, q, is needed for the multivariate *p-adic* lifting process. This modulus must preserve the relative primeness of the univariate gcd, d(x), and the cofactor, f(x). Such a condition can easily be checked by performing gcd(d,f). However, there is a better way. Since later in multivariate *p-adic* lifting, it is needed to compute $\alpha(x)$ and $\beta(x)$, such that

$$\alpha(x)d(x) + \beta(x)f(x) = 1 \pmod{q}.$$

We can perform this computation which serves as a check and generates useful results for later use.

If the gcd operation being performed is over the integers then there is a better way yet. In this situation, the univariate gcd can be done with a modular method which uses several integer primes for its own purposes, but any one of these primes can be selected and q is then a suitable power of it. In this case there is no need to check and q is guaranteed to work.

A similar situation occurs in univariate partial fraction expansion. There are many other places where an earlier step can be combined with a later step, or an earlier result can be saved for later use. If applied in enough places, this will result in significant savings.

4.4. Reducing garbage collection

In LISP we may use list structure modification functions such as 'rplaca' and 'rplacd' to reuse an old structure and thus avoid using up new list cells. This can be dangerous for newly developed programs but it can reduce the number of garbage collections needed in a given computation.

In univariate *p-adic* lifting, for example, one step in the iteration calls for the exact division of a polynomial by an integer. Another multiplies a polynomial by the previous modulus. We have written special routines for these polynomial operations so that no new list cells are used. Such techniques are used, of course, in many other places.

5. User-settable parameters

For increased flexibility in **P**-pack, we provide quite a few parameters which can be set by the user at the top level. These allow the user to control the list of primes to be used, to select one of three built-in univariate lifting methods, to enable or disable the coefficient determination algorithm, to use the iterative or the recursive algorithm for multivariate correction coefficient computation, etc.

In the LISP level, additional flags are provided for tracing, and debugging. For example, setting one flag to T would cause the semi-random generation of substitutions to always return a pre-set vector. This facilitates debugging because a bug may not show if a different substitution is used.

6. General remarks

The leading coefficient determination and the determination of other coefficients based on the correct leading coefficient and partial results during *p-adic* lifting significantly reduce the practical running times for operations supported in **P**-pack. However, these techniques only work over **Z**. It would be useful if they are extended to help operations over algebraic number fields.

It is hoped that this document, together with the released source code, will prove useful for people interested in these polynomial operations, either as users or as system designers. Although much work has gone into **P**-pack, it, by no means, is beyond improvement or incorporates all techniques known to help. For example, **P**-pack has not implemented the sparse Hensel algorithm [20]. We would also like to see the package contain an efficient integer factorizer for large integers. The package can be made faster by increasing the speed of several key operations as indicated in section 3.

7. Timing Examples

We include here the actual MACSYMA output of some problems done by P-pack. The timing experiments were conducted at Kent State University with VAXIMA on a VAX-11/780 under UNIX (4.1 bsd). The underlying LISP is FRANZ lisp (Opus 38.17). The VAX used has an effective memory cycle time of 300 ns.

```
(c1) G: rat((w^2-1)*(x^2+y)*u^3-(w+1)*x*u^2-w-1)$

(c2) eezcontent(G,u);
Time= 133 msec.
```

(d2)/R/ $[w+1,\ ((w-1)\,y+(w-1)\,x^{2})\,u^{3}-x\,u^{2}-1]$

```
(c3) eezcontent(G,w);
Time= 116 msec.
```

(d3)/R/ $[1,\ (u^{3}\,y+u^{3}\,x^{2})\,w^{2}+(-u^{2}\,x-1)\,w-u^{3}\,y-u^{3}\,x^{2}-u^{2}\,x-1]$

```
(c4) E:rat(X^6*Y^3*Z^2*(29*X+3*X*Y^2+Z^3*W^2-12*X*Y*Z^3*W^2-W^2)
        *(18*Y*X^3+3*Z^3-Y^2+14*Y^2*W^2-8*X*Y^2+2*W*Z))$

(c5) FACTOR(E);
Time= 3916 msec.
```

(d5) $-x^{6}\,y^{3}\,z^{2}\,(3\,z^{3}+2\,w\,z-8\,x\,y^{2}+14\,w^{2}\,y^{2}-y^{2}+18\,x^{3}\,y)$
$(12\,w^{2}\,x\,y\,z^{3}-w^{2}\,z^{3}-3\,x\,y^{2}-29\,x+w^{2})$

```
(c6) Q:(204800000*z^12+4000000*z^11-65536*z^10+638392606720*z^9-1600144375*z^8
     -2735538256*z^7-29990598130*z^6-4987569956250*z^5-7792866074375*z^4
     -21506819503750*z^3+201999140625*z^2+318601500000*z+860343750000)
     *(123456789*z^2+9876543*z+5)*(100000000001*z^2-89*z+234565431)$

(c7) factor(Q);
Totaltime= 14633 msec. GCtime= 3583 msec.
```

(d7) $$(123456789\, z^{2} + 9876543\, z + 5)\,(100000000001\, z^{2} - 89\, z + 234565431)$$

$$(256\, z^{3} + 5\, z^{2} + 798000)\,(3125\, z^{3} - z - 125)$$

$$(256\, z^{6} + z^{3} - 2000\, z^{2} - 3125\, z - 8625)$$

```
/* p40 is the degree 40 polynomial in SIGSAM problem 7 */

(c8) factor(p40);
```

Totaltime= 122733 msec. GCtime= 15200 msec.

(d8) $$(4096\, y0 + 8192\, y^{9} - 3008\, y^{8} - 30848\, y^{7} + 21056\, y^{6} + 146496\, y^{5}$$

$$- 221360\, y^{4} + 1232\, y^{3} + 144464\, y^{2} - 78488\, y + 11993)$$

$$(4096\, y^{10} + 8192\, y^{9} + 1600\, y^{8} - 20608\, y^{7} + 20032\, y^{6} + 87360\, y^{5} - 105904\, y^{4}$$

$$+ 18544\, y^{3} + 11888\, y^{2} - 3416\, y + 1)\,(8192\, y^{10} + 12288\, y^{9} + 66560\, y^{8} - 22528\, y^{7}$$

$$- 138240\, y^{6} + 572928\, y^{5} - 90496\, y^{4} - 356032\, y^{3} + 113032\, y^{2} + 23420\, y - 8179)$$

$$(8192\, y^{10} + 20480\, y^{9} + 58368\, y^{8} - 161792\, y^{7} + 198656\, y^{6} + 199680\, y^{5}$$

$$- 414848\, y^{4} - 4160\, y^{3} + 171816\, y^{2} - 48556\, y + 469)$$

```
(c9) R:X^4+%I*X^3+2*X^3+2*%I*X^2+5*X^2+2*%I*X+6*X+6$

(c10) GFACTOR(R);
```

Time= 3283 msec.

(d10) $$(x - \%i + 1)\,(x + \%i + 1)\,(x^{2} + \%i\, x + 3)$$

```
(c11) Factor(x^10-x^5+1,a^2-a+1);
```

Totaltime= 48733 msec. GCtime= 3783 msec.

(d11) $$(x - a)\,(x + a - 1)\,(x^{4} - a\, x^{3} + x^{3} - a\, x^{2} - x + a - 1)$$

$$(x^4 + a\,x^3 + a\,x^2 - x^2 - x - a)$$

(c12) A:rat((234*x^5+98*x^4-1234*x+8)*(192837*x^5-x^3+1287*x^2-1)
*(999*x^3+765*x^2-x-1))$

(c13) factor(A);

Time= 30616 msec.

(d13) $2\,(999\,x^3 + 765\,x^2 - x - 1)\,(117\,x^5 + 49\,x^4 - 617\,x + 4)$

$$(192837\,x^5 - x^3 + 1287\,x^2 - 1)$$

(c14) B:rat((((x+y)*z^2-x-y+13)^4*(x*y*z^2+z*x-y+10)^2*(x+y+z))$

(c15) sqfr(B);

Totaltime= 173450 msec. GCtime= 24666 msec.

(d15) $(z + y + x)\,(-\,y\,z^2 - x\,z^2 + y + x - 13)^4\,(x\,y\,z^2 + x\,z - y + 10)^2$

(c16) algebraic:true$

(c17) tellrat(a^2+1)$

(c18) gcd (x^2+y^2,x+a*y);

Time= 566 msec.

(d18) $a\,y + x$

8. References

[1] Berlekamp, E. R.: Factoring Polynomials over Finite Fields. Bell System Tech. J., vol. 46, 1853-1859 (1967).

[2] Berlekamp, E. R.: Factoring polynomials over large finite fields. Math. Comp., vol. 24, 713-735 (1970).

[3] Davenport, J.: Factorisation of sparse polynomials. Proceedings, ACM EUROSAM'83 Conference, Kingston Polytechnic, Kingston, England, Mar. 28-30 (1983).

[4] Foderaro, J. K., Fateman, R. J.: Characterization of VAX Macsyma. Proceedings of the 1981 ACM Symposium on Symbolic and Algebraic Computation, 14-19.

[5] Foderaro, J. K., Sklower, K. L.: The FRANZ LISP manual, UNIX Programmer's Manual, vol. 2C, Dept. Electrical Eng. and Computer Science, University of California at Berkeley, **1981**.

[6] Kaltofen, E.: Factorization of Polynomials. *Computer Algebra-Symbolic and Algebraic Computation,* Computing, Suppl. 4, Springer-Verlag, 95-113 (1982).

[7] Knuth, D. E.: *The Art of Computer Programming*, vol. 2:*Seminumerical Algorithms*, 2nd ed., Addison-Wesley, Reading, Mass., USA, **1980**.

[8] Mignotte, M.: Some Useful Bounds. *Computer Algebra-Symbolic and Algebraic Computation*, Computing, Suppl. 4, Springer-Verlag, 259-263 (1982).

[9] Moore, P. M. A., Norman, A. C.: Implementing a Polynomial Factorization and GCD Package. Proceedings of the **1981** ACM Symposium on Symbolic and Algebraic Computation, 109-116.

[10] Moses, J., Yun, D. Y. Y.: The EZGCD Algorithm. Proceedings, **1973** ACM National Conference, 159-166.

[11] Musser, D. R.: Multivariate Polynomial Factorization. JACM, vol. 22, 291-308 (1976).

[12] Wang, P. S.: An Improved Multivariate Polynomial Factoring Algorithm. Mathematics of Computation, vol. 32, No. 144, 1215-1231 (1978).

[13] Wang, P. S., Trager, B. M.: New Algorithms for Polynomial Square-free Decomposition over the Integers. SIAM J. Computing, vol. 8, No. 3, 300-305 (1979).

[14] Wang, P. S.: Parallel *p-adic* Constructions in the Univariate Polynomial Factoring Algorithm. Proceedings, MACSYMA Users' Conference, Cambridge, MA, MIT 310-318 (1979).

[15] Wang, P. S.: The EEZ-GCD Algorithm. SIGSAM Bulletin, vol. 14, No. 2, 50-60 (1980).

[16] Wang, P. S.: A *p-adic* Algorithm for Univariate Partial Fractions. Proceedings of the **1981** ACM symposium on Symbolic and Algebraic Computation, Snowbird, Utah, 212-217.

[17] Wang, P. S., Guy, M., Davenport, J.: *p-adic* Reconstruction of Rational Numbers. ACM SIGSAM Bulletin, vol. 16, 2-3 (1982).

[18] Wang, P. S.: Early Detection of True Factors in Univariate Polynomial Factorization. Proceedings, ACM EUROSAM '83, London, March 28-30, **1983**, 225-235.

[19] Wang, P. S.: Factoring Multivariate Polynomials over Algebraic Number Fields. math. comp., vol. 30, 324-336 (1976).

[20] Zipple, R. E.: Newton's Iteration and the Sparse Hensel Algorithm. ACM SYMSAC , 68-72 (1981).

COMPUTATIONS ON CURVES

Claire DICRESCENZO
IMAG
BP 68
F 38402 St Martin d'Hères Cedex

Dominique DUVAL
Institut Fourier
BP 74
F 38402 St Martin d'Hères Cedex

INTRODUCTION.

We present here an algorithm which, given a projective plane curve C on an algebraic closure $\bar{\mathbb{Q}}$ of the field $\mathbb{Q}$ of rationals, finds all its irreducible components. In algebraic terms, this algorithm factorizes polynomials on several variables with coefficients in $\bar{\mathbb{Q}}$.

We need sub-algorithms which give by themselves interesting results about the curve C. Among them are :

- computing Puiseux expansions at any point on C, and in particular finding all the multiple points on C and the branches of C at these points ;
- determining all the ramification indices in the projection of C on any line L, and as a consequence computing the genus of C if it is irreducible ;
- determining all the rational functions on C having a divisor greater than a given one.

These computations are done with a number of elementary operations which is polynomial in term of the degree of C (and of the given divisor for the last point), and we may replace $\bar{\mathbb{Q}}$ by any algebraically closed field of characteristic zero on which one can compute.

After preliminaries (1), we present the computation of Puiseux expansions and ramifications indices (2), we apply this to Coates algorithm (3), and we end with its application to factorization on $\bar{\mathbb{Q}}$ (4).

1. – NOTATIONS AND FIRST STEPS OF THE ALGORITHM.

From now on, let K be an algebraically closed field of characteristic zero. Let

F(X,Y) be a polynomial in $K[X,Y]$, let m (resp. n) denote the degree of F in X (resp. in Y), and let C be the projective plane curve obtained by completion of the affine curve of equation $F(x,y) = 0$. Let K_0 be the field generated over $\mathbb{Q}$ by the coefficients of F . Thus K_0 is a field of finite type, and we suppose it is "explicitely of finite type" [Da 1] , so that one can compute on it -by this we mean : test equality of two elements of K_0 , make the four elementary operations on K_0 , and factorize in $K_0[X]$ -. For example, K may be an algebraic closure $\overline{\mathbb{Q}}$ of the field $\mathbb{Q}$ of rational numbers, the minimal polynomial over $\mathbb{Q}$ of each coefficient of F being given.

By dividing F by the product of its contents in $(K[X])[Y]$ and in $(K[Y])[X]$ we may suppose that F has no "trivial" factor, i.e. no factor in $K[X]$ or $K[Y]$. Then by applying Yun's algorithm [Yu] we obtain a square-free decomposition of F . So that we may suppose that F has no trivial factor and is square-free.

We denote by $F'_Y(X,Y)$ the derivative of $F(X,Y)$ with respect to Y , by d(X) the discriminant of F(X,Y) in $(K[X])[Y]$ i.e. the resultant of F(X,Y) and $F'_Y(X,Y)$ considered as polynomials in Y , and by $a_i(X)$ $(i = 0,1,\ldots,n)$ the coefficient of Y^i in F(X,Y) . Thus d(X) and the $a_i(X)$ are in $K_0[X]$ and $a_n(X)$ divides d(X) .

A place of C is either a simple point on C or a branch of C at a multiple point. One says that the place is centered at the corresponding point. We project the affine part of C on the x-axis, complete this projection in the natural way to the points at infinity, and denote by ∞ the point at infinity on the x-axis. So that, if α is in K or if α is ∞ , we may speak about the places of C dividing α : it is those places of C which are centered at a point which projects on α . The symbol $\rho|\alpha$ (resp. $\rho\nmid\alpha$) means that ρ divides α (resp. that ρ does not divide α).

2. - PUISEUX SERIES AND RAMIFICATION INDICES.

2.1. Ramification indices.

All ramification indices in the projection of C on the x-axis are equal to 1 , except perhaps for the places of C dividing ∞ or a root of d(X) . First, we compute Puiseux expansions of these places as far as to get their ramification index. We do this in the classical way, using Newton polygons [Wa] :

Replacing $F(X,Y)$ by $F(X+\alpha,Y)$ for the places of C dividing the root α of $d(X)$, and by $X^m F(\frac{1}{X},Y)$ for the places dividing ∞, we may suppose we are computing Puiseux expansions and ramifications indices for the places dividing 0. We draw the Newton polygon of $F(X,Y)$, i.e. the convex envelope of the points (i,j) of the real plane such that the coefficient of X^jY^i in $F(X,Y)$ is not zero. Let Δ be a side of the polygon, γ the opposite of its slope, ϵ the denominator of γ, and i_0 the smallest i such that Δ contains a point (i,j). Let $P(Z)$ be $\sum_{(i,j)} a_{i,j} Z^{(i-i_0)/\epsilon}$ where (i,j) runs among the points on Δ; it is a polynomial in Z. For each root z of $P(Z)$ let u be a root of order ϵ of z, then uX^γ is the first term of Puiseux expansion of at least one place of C dividing 0, and its ramification index is a multiple of ϵ. In order to get the second term of the Puiseux expansion, we replace Y by $(u+Y)X^\gamma$ and divide F by some power of X, and we go on in a similar way but only with the sides of the Newton polygon having a negative slope. As soon as the point $(0,1)$ is on the polygon, i.e. the coefficient of X^1Y^0 is not zero, we stop. The beginning of Puiseux expansion obtained corresponds to exactly one place dividing 0, and its ramification index is the common denominator of the powers of X appearing in these first terms of the expansion.

Notation : from now on, for each place $\wp$ of C we denote by $e_\wp$ its ramification index in the projection of C on the x-axis and by $t_\wp$ the uniformizing parameter at $\wp$ equal to $(x-\alpha)^{1/e_\wp}$ if $\wp$ divides a point α of K, and equal to $(\frac{1}{x})^{1/e_\wp}$ if $\wp$ divides ∞.

2.2. Puiseux expansions.

If we need more terms for these expansions, or expansions for other places, we might use the same method, which would then become much simpler. But if we have many terms to compute, we prefer a "quadratic" method, similar to Newton method for computing approximate values of zeros of functions ; once we know ν terms of the expansion, this method computes directly the ν following terms, see [Li, Ta] .

2.3. Cost (when K is $\overline{\mathbb{Q}}$).

If one uses Lenstra algorithm to factorize polynomials on number fields [Le] , each term of the Puiseux expansions needs a number of operations polynomial in n and m. We can prove -it is nearly done by Coates in [Co] - that the number of terms to compute to obtain the ramification indices is polynomial in n and m too, as well as the degree of the fields on which we factorize. So that, if the number of terms we need is polynomial in n and m -and this will be the case, see (3.2)- all this step of the algorithm is polynomial in n and m .

2.4. Applications.

This part of the algorithm has several geometric applications :

- We have got the multiple points on C and described the different branches of C at these points.
- If one wants to compute ramification indices in the projection of C on any line L , one only needs to make a linear change of variables in F(X, Y) so that L becomes the x-axis.
- If C is known to be irreducible, for example by applying (4.2), one gets its genus by applying Hurwitz formula $g = 1-n-\frac{1}{2}\sum_{\wp}(e_{\wp}-1)$. And a canonical divisor on C is given by

  $$\mathrm{div}(dx) = \sum_{\wp\nmid\infty}(e_{\wp}-1)\wp + \sum_{\wp\mid\infty}(-e_{\wp}-1)\wp .$$

  For these formulae see for example Fulton [Fu] .

3. - COATES'ALGORITHM.

3.1. Sketch of the algorithm.

Let D be a divisor on C , i.e. a formal sum $\sum_{\wp} r_{\wp}\wp$ where $\wp$ runs among the places of C , and the $r_{\wp}$ are integers and all but a finite number of them are zero. For any algebraic function f on C and any place $\wp$ of C we denote by $v_{\wp}(f)$ the valuation of f at $\wp$; this means that f is of the form $t_{\wp}^{v_{\wp}(f)}\cdot g$ where g is an algebraic function on C which is defined at $\wp$ and non zero at $\wp$. Let M*(D) (resp. M(D)) be the set of the algebraic functions f on C such that $v_{\wp}(f) \geq r_{\wp}$ for all $\wp$ not dividing ∞ (resp. for all $\wp$). Then M*(D) is a free module of rank n on K[X] (the ring of polynomials on K in the indeterminate X) and M(D) is a finite-dimensional vector space on K ; this dimension appears in Riemann-Roch theorem (where M(D) is usually written L(-D)) [Fu] . And of course M(D) is made of those f in M*(D) verifying $v_{\wp}(f) \geq r_{\wp}$ for all $\wp$ dividing ∞ .

Coates algorithm computes a basis of M*(D) on K[X] and then "normalize" it with respect to D by conditions at infinity. Once such a "D-normalized" basis of

$M^*(D)$ on $K[X]$ is known, it is very easy to deduce a basis of $M(D)$ on K, and the dimension of $M(D)$ on K. We won't give here a complete description of this algorithm. We refer for this to the original paper by Coates [Co]. When a place above ∞ is ramified, or appears in D with a coefficient $r_{\wp}$ not equal to zero, Coates makes a change of variable which, though very simple and natural, may severely increase the computational time. In this case, we use the modified algorithm of [Du].

Essentially, Coates algorithm computes determinants of $n \times n$ matrices whose elements are some coefficients of the Puiseux expansions of some places of C. If the determinant is zero, the algorithm computes a linear combination of the lines of the matrices which is zero. We have seen in (2) how to compute the elements of the matrices and we use Gauss method for computing determinants and linear combinations of lines.

3.2. Cost.

In view of (2.3) we must verify that the number of terms we need in Puiseux expansions is polynomial in n, m, and the degree $\deg(D)$ of the divisor D, i.e. $\sum_{\wp} r_{\wp}$. This is easy to deduce from [Du].

3.3. Applications.

This algorithm is a basic one in algebraic geometry, it was first used by A. Baker and J. Coates [B-C] on elliptic curves.

J. Davenport used it for integration of algebraic functions and implemented it in some cases [Da 2].

We are trying to implement it in more general cases, together with its application to factorization on algebraically closed fields, see (4).

4. - FACTORIZATION ON ALGEBRAICALLY CLOSED FIELDS OF CHARACTERISTIC ZERO.

4.1. The problem.

On an algebraically closed field, every polynomial in one variable splits into linear factors, so that the factorization problem in one variable is the problem of the representation of the elements of the fields. For algebraic number fields, an answer is given by the primitive element theorem.

On the other hand, if P is a polynomial in $K[X_1, X_2, \ldots, X_\ell]$ with $\ell \geq 3$ one may replace $X_3,\dots,X_\ell$ by some values $x_3,\dots,x_\ell$ in K in order to obtain a polynomial $\tilde{P}$ in $K[X_1,X_2]$. If one gets the factorization of $\tilde{P}$, one may recover the factorization of P by Hensel method [Da 1] .

So that the problem is to factorize a polynomial P in $K[X_1,X_2]$, or F in $K[X,Y]$ to have the same notations as above. If K_1 denotes the extension field of K_0 generated by the coefficients of the factors of F in K , then factorizing F on K is the same as factorizing F on K_1 , which is a finite extension of K_0 , but the difficult point is to determine K_1 [Da 1] . A quite different algorithm is presented in [H-S] which only decides whether F is reducible or not on K , in a number of operations exponential in n and m . Our method is based on Coates algorithm and presented in (4.2).

4.2. <u>The algorithm</u>.

It is based on the two following facts :

- if C has $C_1,C_2,\dots,C_\nu$ as irreducible components, then D is a formal sum $D_1+D_2+\dots+D_\nu$ where each D_h is a divisor on C_h , and $M(D)$ is isomorphic to the direct sum of the $M(D_i)$;
- if C is irreducible then $M(0)$ is K and $M(\wp)$ is 0 if $\wp$ is a place of C .

For the proofs and example, see [Du] . The algorithm runs as follows :

<u>Step 1</u> : compute a basis of $M(0)$ on K -where 0 is the zero divisor on C- by Coates algorithm.

<u>First result</u> : the number of factors of F on K is equal to the dimension of $M(0)$ on K . In particular if it is equal to 1 then F is irreducible and the algorithm stops.

<u>Notation</u> : let $\wp_1,\wp_2,\dots,\wp_s$ be the places of C dividing ∞ .

<u>Step 2</u> : For h running from 1 to s compute $M(\wp_1+\wp_2+\dots+\wp_h)$ by Coates algorithm.

<u>Remarks</u>.

- As $M^*(0) = M^*(\wp_1+\dots+\wp_h)$ for all h , we only need to re-normalize the previous basis.
- We have $M(0) \supset M(\wp_1) \supset M(\wp_1+\wp_2) \supset \dots \supset M(\wp_1+\dots+\wp_s)$, the jump in the dimensions being at most 1 at each step, and $M(\wp_1+\dots+\wp_s)$ is zero. In fact

we stop computations as soon as $M(\rho_1+\rho_2+\dots+\rho_h)$ is one-dimensional over K.

Notation : let $M(0) = \mathfrak{F}_\nu \supset \mathfrak{F}_{\nu-1} \supset \mathfrak{F}_{\nu-2} \supset \dots \supset \mathfrak{F}_1 \supset \mathfrak{F}_0 = 0$ be the set of all the different K-vector spaces obtained at this step (so that ν is the dimension of M(0) on K), and let $\mathcal{B}_h$ be the basis obtained for $\mathfrak{F}_h$ over K $(h = 1 \text{ to } \nu)$.

Step 3 : let $\widetilde{F}_1 = F$. For h running from 1 to $\nu-1$ let f_h run among the elements of $\mathcal{B}_h$ not in $\mathcal{B}_{h-1}$ until $\widetilde{F}_h$ does not divide f_h (this must happen), let $\widetilde{F}_{h+1}$ be g.c.d. (F_h, f_h) for this f_h, and let F_h be $\widetilde{F}_h/\widetilde{F}_{h+1}$. Finally let $F_\nu = \widetilde{F}_\nu$.

Second result : the polynomials $F_1, F_2, \dots, F_\nu$ are the irreducible factors of F on K.

4.3. Cost.

In view of (3.2), and of the fact that s and ν are less than n, the cost of this algorithm is polynomial in n and m.

4.4. Applications.

The geometric meaning of the factorization of F is the decomposition of the curve C in its irreductible components.

This algorithm may be used for more algebraic applications too, for example to study proper values of matrices depending on a parameter.

4.5. Remark.

When computing Puiseux expansions for Coates algorithm, we modify the initial polynomial F, cf. (2.1). If by chance one of these modified polynomials is divisible by Y, then we get at once, by a determinant computation, an irreducible factor of F on K.

CONCLUSION.

We are implementing this algorithm on REDUCE. As we wrote above, when K is $\overline{\mathbb{Q}}$ we may represent any finite family of elements of K as elements of $\mathbb{Q}(\alpha)$ for some α in K, cf[Ze] ; but we are exploring a more appropriate representation.

BIBLIOGRAPHY

[B-C] A. BAKER, J. COATES. Integer points on curves of genus 1 . Proc. Camb. Phil. Soc. 67 (1970), pp. 595-602.

[Co] J. COATES. Construction of rational functions on a curve. Proc. Camb. Phil. Soc. 68 (1970), pp. 105-123.

[Da 1] J. H. DAVENPORT. Calculs dans les corps. Exposé au Colloque de l'Institut Fourier (1983).

[Da 2] J. H. DAVENPORT. On the integration of algebraic functions. Lect. Notes in Computer Sc. 102 (1979).

[Du] D. DUVAL. Une méthode géométrique de factorisation des polynômes en deux indéterminées, to appear in Calsyf 3 (1984 ?).

[Fu] W. FULTON. Algebraic curves. Benjamin (1969).

[H-S] J. HEINTZ, M. SIEVEKING. Absolute primality of polynomials is decidable in random polynomial time in the number of variables. Lect. Notes in Computer Sc. 115 (1981), pp. 16-28.

[Le] A. K. LENSTRA. Lattices and factorization of polynomials over algebraic number fields. Computer Algebra Eurocam'82, Lect. Notes in Computer Sc. 144 (1982), pp. 32-39.

[Li] J. D. LIPSON. Elements of algebra and algebraic computing. Addison-Wesley (1981).

[Ta] E. TAHIRI EL ALAOUI. Solutions formelles d'équation algébrique de deux variables. IMAG R.R. 416 (1983).

[Wa] R. WALKER. Algebraic curves. Springer-Verlag (1978).

[Yu] D.Y.Y. YUN. Fast algorithm for rational function integration. Proc. IFIP 77 (ed. B. Gilchrist) North-Holland (1977), pp. 493-498.

[Ze] H. ZEJLI. Calcul dans les extensions de corps. IMAG, Séminaire 397 (1983).

DETECTING TORSION DIVISORS ON CURVES OF GENUS 2.

T. G. Berry
Departamento de Matemáticas
Universidad Simón Bolívar
Caracas, VENEZUELA

ABSTRACT

We consider the problem of finding an upper bound for the possible torsion of a divisor on a curve of genus 2, when everything is defined over an algebraic number field. Mainly, we show how to write the equation of the Kummer surface of the Jacobian of a curve of genus 2 in terms of the equation of the curve. This allows one to calculate a bound on the torsion which seems better than the bound derived from Riemann-Weil theory. Finally, we discuss briefly a different approach which is valid for all hyperelliptic curves, at the cost of a considerable increase in complexity.

1. INTRODUCTION

In the theory of integration of algebraic functions in finite terms, the major problem is that of detecting torsion divisors: given a divisor D on an algebraic curve, find a positive integer n such that nD is the divisor of a rational function on the curve, or prove that no such n exists. (See [R], [D], [B-D], for expositions of the theory). The only known approach to this problem is to find a bound N for the order of the group of torsion divisors with the same field of definition as D, and to test successively the divisors nD, $n \leq N$. Thus the question becomes that of determining the bound N. For a curve defined over a finite extension of Q (and all other characteristic 0 cases can be reduced to this) there is again just one known approach, that of reduction modulo finite primes ([D], Chaps 5,7,8). The central computation of this method is, given a non-singular curve C defined over the finite field F_q, to estimate the number of F_q-rational points on the Jacobian of C, a number we denote $|J_C(F_q)|$. In all generality one has the bound given by the Riemann-Weil theorem: if C has genus g, then $|J_C(F_q)| \leq (\sqrt{q}+1)^{2g}$. Thus the torsion-divisor problem is in principle solvable in finite terms. However the bound $(\sqrt{q}+1)^{2g}$ - henceforth called the Riemann bound, is usually very coarse. Since the algorithms used in examining divisors tend to be exponential it is worth some trouble to improve the bound. In the case of genus 1, where the curve is essentially its own Jacobian, $|J_C(F_q)|$ can be calculated exactly (and other methods special to genus 1 can also be used. [D], loc.sit). In the case of genus > 1 the problem is that it is difficult to get hold of the Jacobian: it is a variety in higher space defined by equations never explicitly given. In genus 2, however, although the Jacobian is already rather mysterious, there is a quite explicit surface in 3 dimensions associated with it. This is the Kummer surface; it is obtained as the quotient of the Jacobian by the involution $a \to -a$, and it embeds as a quartic surface in $\mathbb{P}^3$, over any basefield of char $\neq 2$. The Jacobian being a double cover of the Kummer, $|J_C(F_q)| \leq 2$(number of F_q-rational points on the Kummer). We call this the Kummer bound. In this paper we derive the equation of the Kummer in terms of the equation of the curve. It turns out that the form of the equation makes it very economical to count points on the Kummer. The results of some experiments are given, which indicate that the Kummer bound is indeed sharper than the Riemann bound.

In the last section we describe briefly a quite different method which is valid for all hyperelliptic curves.

2. THE KUMMER SURFACE ASSOCIATED TO A CURVE OF GENUS 2.

For properties of Kummer surfaces see the original papers in [Ku] [Kl]. In this paper virtually the only properties of Kummer surfaces that we need are that they are quartic surfaces in $\mathbb{P}^3$ with (precisely 16) conical singular points. (A conical singular point on a surface in 3-space is a point such that, if it is taken as the origin of an affine coordinate system, the equation of the surface has the form $0 = f_2(x,y,z)$ + higher terms, where f_2 is a non-degenerate homogeneous quadratic form).

Let C be a curve of genus 2, non-singular model of

$$S^2 = F(U) = U^5+a_1U^4+a_2U^3+a_3U^2+a_4U+a_5 \tag{1}$$

where the $a_i \varepsilon k$, k being any field of char $\neq 2$, and F is a square-free polynomial.

C has a single point at ∞, which we call P_∞. P_∞ is a fixed point of the hyperelliptic involution on C, $(U,S) \to (U,-S)$. The canonical class of C is cut by vertical lines, so $2P_\infty$ is a canonical divisor. Let J be the Jacobian of C; as a group J is {divisors of degree 0 } /linear equivalence. We get at J via the symmetric square of C, $S^2(C)$, i.e. the variety of unordered pairs of points of C. It is well known that $S^2(C)$ is birational to J, in fact is J with one point blown up. Indeed, the map $S^2(C) \to J$, $\{P,Q\} \to Cl(P+Q-2P_\infty)$ where $P,Q \varepsilon C$ and Cl denotes the linear equivalence class of a divisor, has fibre over $0 \varepsilon J$ the linear system $\{\{P,Q\} \mid P+Q$ is a canonical divisor }, (from the description of the canonical class given above) while the fibre over any other point of J is a single point (from some general theory about special divisors). We now identify the function field of $S^2(C)$, which is also the function field of J. Introducing a new indeterminate V, the function field of the Cartesian product CxC is

$$K(U,V, \sqrt{F(U)}, \sqrt{F(V)}) \tag{2}$$

The function field of $S^2(C)$ is the fixed field of (2) under the automorphism given by interchange of U and V, and this is

$$K(U+V, UV, U\sqrt{F(V)} + V\sqrt{F(U)}) \tag{3}$$

as one sees by verifying that (2) has degree 2 over (3), which is evidently contained in the fixed field of the interchange map.

Now the choice of P_∞ as base point implies that the involution $D \to -D$ on J is induced by the hyperelliptic involution on the curve, so that the induced automorphism of the function field (3) is given by changing the sign of the radicals; thus this automorphism changes the sign of $U\sqrt{F(V)} + V\sqrt{F(U)}$ and leaves the other generators fixed. The fixed field is then

$$K(U+V,\ UV,\ \sqrt{F(U)}.\ \sqrt{F(V)}) \tag{4}$$

and this is the function field of the Kummer surface of J.

Let $F(X) = \prod_{i=1}^{5} (X-\alpha_i)$ in an algebraic closure of K.

$$\begin{aligned} \text{Then } F(U)\ F(V) &= \prod_{i=1}^{5} (U-\alpha_i)(V-\alpha_i) \\ &= \prod_{i=1}^{5} (UV - (U+V)\alpha_i + \alpha_i^2) \\ &= \Delta(X,Y) \text{ say, where we set } X=UV,\ Y=U+V. \end{aligned}$$

It is an exercise in symmetric functions to write the coefficients of $\Delta(X,Y)$ in terms of the a_i. The results are given in table 1.

In summary, we have proved the:

<u>Lemma</u>. The Kummer surface of the Jacobian of the curve $S^2 = F(U)$ has function field $K(X,Y,T)$ where $T^2 = \Delta(X,Y) = \prod_{i=1}^{5} (X-\alpha_i Y+\alpha_i^2)$.

If X,Y,T are taken as coordinates in affine space then the equation $T^2 = \Delta(X,Y)$ gives the classical representation of a Kummer surface as a double cover of the plane branched over six lines tangent to a conic (the lines being $X-\alpha_i Y + \alpha_i^2 = 0$, $i=1\ldots5$ and the line at infinity; the conic is $Y^2 = 4X$). Geometrically this comes by projecting the surface away from one of its double points onto a plane not passing through the double point. Taking (X,Y,Z,T) as homogeneous coordinates for $\mathbb{P}^3$, the double point as (0001) and the plane of projection as T=0, the homogeneous equation of the surface must have the form

$$f_2^* T^2 + 2f_3^* T + f_4^* = 0 \tag{5}$$

where f_i^* denotes a homogeneous polynomial in X,Y,Z of degree i. Thus the discriminant $f_3^2 - f_2 f_4$, where $f_i = f_i(X,Y) = f_i^*(X,Y,1)$ should be identical to $\Delta(X,Y)$. This enables us to identify the f_i. (A precisely analagous argument with all details explicit can be found in [EC] where it is proved that any double cover of the plane branched over a non-singular quartic is obtained by projecting a non-singular cubic surface away from a point of itself). Some geometrical reasoning shows that f_2 must be the conic Y^2-4X. On the locus $f_2 = 0$ one has $f_3^2 = \Delta$ so that substituting $X = \frac{Y^2}{4}$ in $\Delta(X,Y)$ allows one to guess f_3. Finally when f_2 and f_3 are given, the equation $\Delta = f_3^2 - f_2 f_4$ yields a (highly overdetermined) set of linear equations for the coefficients of f_4. Details are left to the reader. The results are given in table 2. In summary

Theorem. The Kummer surface associated to the Jacobian of the curve $S^2 = F(U)$ is the quartic in 3-space with equation given by (5), where the f_i^* are the homogenizations of the f_i given in table 2.

Note that it is easy to count F_q-rational points on (5). The plane at infinity $Z = 0$ cuts out the conic $X^2+2YT=0$. (The planes which cut out conics in this way are famous in the theory of Kummer surfaces; there are 16 of them) which, since it has one F_q -rational point, has its full complement $q+1$. In the finite space, (i.e. $Z\neq 0$), there is at most one point over each point of the conic $f_2=0$. This gives q points. It remains to count possible points of the Kummer over the complement in the (X,Y)-plane of $Y^2=4X$. For such a point (a,b), if $\Delta(a,b)$ is not a square in F_q, count 0; if $\Delta(a,b)$ is nonzero square, count 2, and if $\Delta(a,b)=0$, count 1.

3. We give the Kummer and Riemann bound, (and the bounds on torsion thereby obtained) for the mod p reductions of some curves with small integer coefficients, for some small primes p. The results are far from conclusive. One would like to see similar experiments for F_q with q a genuine prime power, not a prime.

4. A quite different method of bounding torsion can be based on the following theorem (attributed to Klein in genus 2 and Miles Reid in general).

Theorem. The Jacobian of

$$Y^2 = \prod_{i=1}^{2g+2} (X-\alpha_i)$$

is isomorphic to the variety of all lines on the intersection of the quadrics

$$\sum_1^{2g+2} X_i^2 = 0 \ ; \qquad \sum_1^{2g+2} \alpha_i X_i^2 = 0;$$

Unfortunately the isomorphism is only defined over an extension of the ground field that contains all the α_i. Moreover, counting the lines is several orders of magnitude more complex than counting points on the Kummer. Nevertheless the matter seems worth pursuing, as the only known alternative to Riemann-Weil in genus greater than two.

Δ_5	$X^5+a_1X^4Y+a_2X^3Y^2 + a_3X^2Y^3 + a_4XY^4 + a_5Y^5$
Δ_4	$(a_1^2 - 2a_2)X^4 + (a_1a_2 - 3a_3)X^3Y + (a_1a_3 - 4a_4)X^2Y^2 + (a_1a_4 - 5a_5)XY^3 + a_1a_5Y^4$
Δ_3	$(a_2^2 - 2a_1a_3 + 2a_4)X^3 + (a_2a_3 - 3a_1a_4 + 5a_5)X^2Y + (a_2a_4 - 4a_1a_5)XY^2 + a_2a_5Y^3$
Δ_2	$(a_3^2 - 2a_2a_4 + 2a_1a_5)X^2 + (a_3a_4 - 3a_2a_5)XY + a_3a_5Y^2$
Δ_1	$(a_4^2 - 2a_3a_5)X + a_4a_5Y$
Δ_0	a_5^2

Table 1. $\Delta(X,Y) = \sum_{i=0}^{5} \Delta_i(X,Y)$, where Δ_i is homogeneous of degree i.

f_2 $\quad Y^2 - 4X$

f_3 $\quad \frac{X^2Y}{2} + a_1X^2 + \frac{a_2}{2}XY + a_3X + \frac{a_4}{2}Y + a_5$

f_4 $\quad \frac{X^4}{4}$

$$- \frac{a_2}{2}X^3 - a_3X^2Y - a_4XY^2 - a_5Y^3$$

$$- a_1a_5Y^2 + (a_5-a_1a_4)XY + \left(\frac{a_2^2}{4} + \frac{a_4}{2} - a_1a_3\right)X^2$$

$$- a_2a_5Y - \frac{a_2a_4}{2}x$$

$$+ \frac{a_4^2}{4} - a_3a_5$$

Table 2. The polynomials f_2, f_3, f_4 .

Y^2 =

A5 + A4*X + ... X^5

	2(34)	3(55)	5(109	7(176)	11(347)	KUMMER BD. ON TORSION	RIEMANN BD. ON TORSION
-1 0 0 0 0 1	G2	22	B5	102	216	544	1088
2-2 3 9 3 1	B2	B3	72	128	314	3454	3817
1-5 0 0 6 1	G2	B3	58	116	308	812	1232
3-4 1 1 6 1	B2	20	72	100	292	360	2725
1 1 1 1 1 1	B2	B3	64	120	302	1600	3817
0 1 3 3 3 1	G2	26	B5	114	B11	544	1088
0 1 0 1 0 1	B2	B3	82	106	258	2050	3817
0 -3 6 0 0 1	B2	B3	66	110	258	1650	3817

Table 3. Numbers in parenthesis are Riemann bounds for number or points on the Jacobian of a curve with good reduction at the corresponding prime.BP indicates bad reduction at P. The first column gives reduction at 2 . Where there is good reduction at 2 the best bound is obtained by taking the Riemann bound at 2 together with a Kummer bound. This is given as the Kummer bound.

BIBLIOGRAPHY

[B-D] F. Baldassari and B. Dwork. "On second order linear differential equations with algebraic solution". In Contributions to Algebraic Geometry, Johns Hopkins Press, Baltimore 1979.

[D] J.H. Davenport. On the Integration of Algebraic Functions. Lecture Notes in Computer Science 102, Springer 1981.

[E-C] F. Enriques. Lezioni sulla teoria delle superficie algebriche, Parte I (Raccolte da L. Campadelli). Padova 1932.

[Kl] F. Klein. Gesammelte Mathematische Abhandlungen. Vol. 1. Berlin, Springer Verlag 1973.

[K] E. Kummer Collected Papers. Berlin, Springer Verlag 1975.

[R] R. Risch. "The Solution of the problem of integration in finite terms". Bull A.M.S. 76 (1970) 605-608.

COMPUTATION IN RADICAL EXTENSIONS

H. Najid-Zejli
Institut IMAG - Laboratoire TIM3
BP 68 - 38402 Saint Martin d'Hères Cedex France

INTRODUCTION

The aim of this paper is to determine computation rules in an extension of Q generated by radicals.

Until now, many works have already been done to solve this problem, and in particular to determine the degree of such extensions (L.J. Mordell, M. Kneser, A. Schinzel,...).

Our study is based on a theorem of A. Schinzel from which we will build an algorithm that enables to find dependence relations between radicals, or the required computing rules to work in the concerned extension.

This work has been wildly oriented by J.H. Davenport. The author wishes to thank Dr. Davenport for his helpful suggestions and informative discussions.

1) HISTORIC - THEOREM OF A SCHINZEL

1.1 Historic

In 1953 L.J. Mordell demonstrated the following theorem :

Theorem

Let K be an algebraic number filed; $a_1,\dots,a_r$ belonging to K ; $n_1,\dots,n_r$ positive integers and $\xi_1,\dots,\xi_r$ elements of an algebraic closure of K such that $\xi_i^{n_i} = a_i$.

If ($\prod_{i=1}^{r} \xi_i^{x_i} \in K$ implies $x_i \quad 0$ modni) and (if the ξ_i are real or K contains n_i-th roots of unity $(1 \le i \le r)$) then $[K(\xi_1,\dots,\xi_r):K] = n_1,\dots,n_r$. [1].

We note that this is only a sufficient condition.

M. Kneser has work on this result to give the following theorem.

Theorem

Let K be a field, $K(\xi_1,\dots,\xi_r)$ a finite separable extension of K, and $K^*\langle\xi_1,\dots,\xi_r\rangle$ the multiplicative group generated by the ξ_i.
$[K(\xi_1,\dots,\xi_r):K] = [K^*\langle\xi_1,\dots,\xi_r\rangle:K]$ if and only if for every prime p, $\zeta_p \in K^*\langle\xi_1,\dots,\xi_r\rangle$ implies $\zeta_p \in K^*$, and $1+\zeta_4 \in K^*\langle\xi_1,\dots,\xi_r\rangle$ implies $\zeta_4 \in K^*$. [2]

$[K^*\langle\xi_1,\dots,\xi_r\rangle:K]$ is the index of K^* in $K^*\langle\xi_1,\dots,\xi_r\rangle$. [4].
ζ_p is a primitive p-th root of unity.

1.2 - Theorem of A. Schinzel

Theorem

Let K be a field.
We consider the extension $K(\xi_1,\dots,\xi_r)$ of K where $\xi_i^{n_i} = a_i \in K^*$, and the characteristic of K that does not divide n_i $(1 \le i \le r)$.
We denote by I_p the set of indices i such that p divides n_i. Then
$[K(\xi_1,\dots,\xi_r):K] = n_1,\dots,n_r \iff$

i) for all primes p, if $\prod_{i\in I_p} a_i^{x_i} = \gamma^p$ for an element γ of K, then $x_i \equiv 0$ mod p for all $i \in I_p$.

and ii) if $\prod_{i\in I_2} a_i^{x_i} = -4\gamma^4$ for a γ of K and if $n_i x_i \equiv 0 \bmod 4$ for all $i \in I_2$, then $x_i \equiv 0 \bmod 4$ for all $i \in I_2$.

Sketch of proof

In general we have $[K(\xi_1,\dots,\xi_r):K] \le [K^*\langle\xi_1,\dots,\xi_r\rangle:K^*] \le n_1,\dots,n_r$
then $[K(\xi_1,\dots,\xi_r):K]=n_1,\dots,n_r \iff [K(\xi_1,\dots,\xi_r):K]=[K^*\langle\xi_1,\dots,\xi_r\rangle:K^*]$
and $[K^*\langle\xi_1,\dots,\xi_r\rangle:K^*] = n_1,\dots,n_r$.

But $[K^*\langle\xi_1,\dots,\xi_r\rangle:K^*] = n_1,\dots,n_r \iff$ (1) $\exists\, y_i \in \mathbb{N}$, $\gamma \in K$, $\gamma\pi\xi_i^{y_i} = 1 \Rightarrow y_i \equiv 0$ mod
and from Kneser

$$[K\langle\xi_1,\dots,\xi_r\rangle:K^*]=[K^*\langle\xi_1,\dots,\xi_r\rangle:K^*] \iff \begin{cases} (1') \text{ for every prime } p \\ \exists\, y_i,\ \gamma/\gamma\pi\xi_i^{y_i} = \zeta_p \Rightarrow \zeta_p \in K^* \\ \text{and } (2')\ \exists\, y_i\ \ \gamma/\gamma\pi\xi_i^{y_i} = 1+\zeta_4 \\ \qquad \Rightarrow \zeta_4 \in K^*. \end{cases}$$

The points (1) and (1') give the condition (i) of the theorem and the point (2') gives the condition (ii) of the theorem [3].

CONCLUSION

Our problem was to determine the relations of dependency between the ξ_i. From the previous proof the two conditions of the theorem come from relations which can exist between the ξ_i if $[K(\xi_1,\dots,\xi_r):K] < n_1\dots n_r$.

So, we shall study the conditions of the theorem, then build an algorithm which tests if these conditions are verified or not.

We shall do this when K is the field Q of rational numbers.

2) STUDY OF THE CONDITIONS OF THE THEOREM OF A.SCHINZEL

2.1 First condition

For all primes p,
If there exists integers x_i $(i \in I_p)$ and a rational number γ such that $\prod_{i\, I_p} a_i^{x_i} = \gamma^p$, then p divides x_i for all $i \in I_p$.

This first condition means that the vector (x_i) $i \in I_p$ null mod p is the unique solution of the following problem : $\prod a_i^{x_i}$ is a p-th power of a rational number.

We now study this problem :

First we decompose the a_i in relatively prime factors (cf. algorithm 1). Let $q_1,\dots,q_\ell$ be these factors, for all i we have $a_i = q_1^{s_{i,1}} \times \dots \times q^{s_{i,\ell}}$ where $(q_i,q_j) = 1$ if $i \neq j$.

Let p be a prime number then $\prod_{i \in I_p} a_i^{x_i} = \gamma^p$ implies $\prod_{j=1}^{\ell} q_j^{\sum_{i \in I_p} \frac{x_i s_{i,j}}{p}} \in Q$, since $\gamma \in Q$.

The q_j are relatively prime, this implies that for all j

$$q_j^{1/p} \in Q \text{ or } \sum_{i \in I_p} x_i\, s_{i,j} \equiv 0 \mod p.$$

We can eliminate the case $q_j^{1/p} \in Q$: when forming the q_j, we replace q_j by $q_j^{1/p}$ and the corresponding $s_{i,j}$ by $p.s_{i,j}$ each time that $q^{1/p} \in Q$.

And then $\prod_{i \in I_p} a_i^{x_i} = \gamma^p \Rightarrow \forall j \sum_{i \in I_p} x_i\, s_{i,j} \equiv 0 \mod p$.

Let X be the matrix (x_i) $i \in I_p$, $S = [s_{i,j}]$ be the matrix having $s_{i,j}$ as elements for $i \in I_p$ and $0 \le j \le \ell$.

$\prod_{i \in I_p} a_i^{x_i} = \gamma^p \Rightarrow XS \equiv 0 \mod p$ (modular linear system of ℓ equations with $\mathrm{card}(I_p)$ unknowns)

To solve this system, we can use a modular Gauss method [5].

If $X \equiv 0 \mod p$ (i.e. $\forall i \in I_p$ $x_i \equiv 0 \mod p$) the first condition is verified for p, else we obtain the relation $\prod_{i \in I_p} a_i^{x_i} = \gamma^p$.

For all the suitable prime p, we repeat this.

2.2 Second Condition of the theorem of A. Schinzel

We deal the same way.

To solve $\prod_{i \in I_2} a_i^{x_i} = -4\gamma^4$, $\gamma \in Q$ and $n_i x_i \equiv 0 \mod 4$.

Remark : If all the a_i $(i \in I_2)$ are positive we can not obtain an equality of the type $\prod_{i \in I_2} a_i^{x_i} = -4\gamma^4$ and then the second condition is verified.
If the (a_i^2) $i \in I_2$ are not all positive we take $q_1 = -1$, $q_2 = 2$.

$$\prod_{i \in I_2} a_i^{x_i} = -4\gamma^4 \Rightarrow \prod_{j=1}^{\ell} q_j^{\sum_{i \in I_2} x_i s_{i,j}} = q_1 . q_2^2 \gamma^4$$

$$\Rightarrow \sum_{i \in I_2} x_i s_{i,1} \equiv 1 \mod 4,$$

$$\sum_{i \in I_2} x_i s_{i,2} \equiv 2 \mod 4,$$

$$\sum_{i \in I_2} x_i, s_{i,j} \equiv 0 \mod 4 \quad \text{for } j = 3,\dots,\ell.$$

In the same way if we take

$$X = (x_i)_{i \in I_2},\ S = [s_{i,j}]_{i \in I_2,\ 1 \le j \le \ell},\quad Y = (1,2,0,..,0)$$

Then

$$\prod_{i \in I_2} a_i^{x_i} = -4\gamma^4 \Rightarrow XS \equiv Y \mod 4.$$

Again we apply the modular gauss algorithm, which gives X the vector solution.

2.3 Conclusion

With the theorem of Schinzel we can know if $Q(\xi_1,\dots,\xi_r)$ is of maximal degree.

. If we find that $[Q(\xi_1,\dots,\xi_r):Q] = n_1,\dots,n_r$, that means that there are not relations of dependence between the ξ_i, and to work in $Q(\xi_1,\dots,\xi_r)$ we just have to introduce the rules $\xi_i^{n_i} = a_i$, (that is done in MACSYMA with the function "tellrat").

. If we find $[Q(\xi_1,\dots,\xi_r):Q] < n_1,\dots,n_r$, that means we have obtained relations with the a_i.

In the following paragraph, we explain how from these relations, we search for the dependence relations between the ξ_i.

3) RELATIONS OF DEPENDENCE BETWEEN THE ξ_i

3.1 Case where the first condition is not verified

We obtain a relation of the type :

(1)
$$\prod_{i \in I_p} a_i^{x_i} = \gamma^p,\ \gamma \in Q,\ \exists\, i_o / x_{i_o} \not\equiv 0 \mod p.$$

$$\Rightarrow \prod_{i \in I_p} \xi_i^{n_i x_i} = \gamma^p.$$

or

(2)
$$\prod \xi_i^{\frac{n_i x_i}{p}} = \zeta_p^j \gamma.$$

We see that this is non trivial relation between the ξ_i as there exists an $i_o \in I_p$ such that $\frac{n_{i_o} x_{i_o}}{p} \not\equiv 0 \bmod n_{i_o}$.

We have then the relation

$$\prod_{i \in I_p} \xi_i^{\frac{n_i x_i}{p}} = \zeta_p^j \cdot \gamma$$

The x_i are given by the algorithm 2.

γ can be computed from (1).

It now remains to determine ζ_p^j (or j) which depends on the ξ_i.

<u>Determination of ζ_p^j</u> :

$\zeta_p^j = e^{\frac{2i\pi j}{p}}$

The complex expressions of a_k, ξ_k, γ are : $a_k = |a_k| e^{i\pi\varepsilon_k}$, $\gamma = |\gamma| e^{i\pi\varepsilon_o}$

$\varepsilon_i = 0$ or 1 according to the sign.

$$\xi_k = \sqrt[n_k]{|a_k|}\; e^{i\pi \frac{(\varepsilon_k + 2\ell_k)}{n_k}} \qquad 0 \le \ell_k < n_k.$$

By substituring these values in (1) and (2) we obtain :

$$\prod_{k \in I_p} |a_k|^{x_k} e^{i\pi\Sigma\varepsilon_k x_k} = |\gamma|^p e^{i\pi\varepsilon_o p}.$$

and

$$\prod_{k \in I_p} |a_k|^{\frac{x_k}{p}} e^{i\pi \sum_{k \in I_p} \frac{\varepsilon_k x_k + 2\ell_k x_k}{p}} = |\gamma|\, e^{2i\pi j/p}\, e^{i\pi\varepsilon_o}$$

By identification of the arguments, we obtain the following identities :

$$\sum_{k \in I_p} \varepsilon_k x_k \equiv \varepsilon_o\, p \mod 2.$$

and

$$\sum_{k \in I_p} (\varepsilon_k x_k + 2\ell_k x_k) \equiv 2j + p\varepsilon_o \mod 2p$$

$$\Rightarrow \qquad j \equiv \sum_{k \in I_p} \ell_k x_k + \frac{\Sigma\varepsilon_k x_k - p\varepsilon_o}{2} \mod p$$

As $\Sigma\varepsilon_k x_k - p\varepsilon_o \equiv 0 \bmod 2$ and $0 \le j < p$, j is well defined.

3.2 <u>Case where the second condition is not verified</u>

We deal the same way

We have

(1) $$\prod_{k\in I_2} a_k^{x_k} = -4\gamma^4,\ \gamma \in Q\ n_k x_k \equiv 0 \bmod 4.$$

and $\exists\, k_o \in I_2 \,/\, x_{k_o} \not\equiv 0 \bmod 4.$

$$\Rightarrow \qquad \prod_{k\in I_2} \xi_k^{\frac{n_k x_k}{4}} = \zeta_n^j \sqrt{2}\, e^{i\frac{\pi}{4}} \gamma$$

By using the complex expressions, and identifying the arguments we obtain for j

$$j \equiv \sum_{k\in I_2} \ell_k x_k + \frac{\Sigma \varepsilon_k x_k - 4\varepsilon_o - 1}{2} \quad \bmod 4$$

3.3 Conclusion

We can prove [6], that the obtained relations are sufficient to work in $Q(\xi_1,\ldots,\xi_r)$. Then it is enough to introduce them with the rules which are for example given by the function tellrat in MACSYMA to obtain the needed simplifications in all the expressions in $\xi_1,\ldots,\xi_r$.

4) CONCLUSION

In the theorem of A. Schinzel, K is any field . Our study of the conditions of this theorem has been done for Q.

For Q, we can propose an extension of Q in which we know how to compute (example : a radical extension of Q), then, again a similar study can be done.

The main difficulties will come from the factorization.

5) ALGORITHMS

5.1 Algorithm 1. Decomposition of an integers familly in relatively prime factors

Input : a[1:r] integer array

Output : q[1:ℓ] vector of relatively prime factors.

s[1:r,1:ℓ] integer array such that

$$a[i] = \prod_{j=1}^{\ell} q[j]\uparrow s[i,j].\ \text{for } i = 1 \text{ until } r.$$

```
1) : q[1]:= -1, for i := 1:r do s[i,1] := if a[i] < 0 then 1 else 0
2) : for i :=2 : r+1 do q[i] := a[i-1]
     ℓ := r+1,
3) : for i := 1 to ℓ-1 do
     (3.1) for j := i+1 to ℓ do
           (3.1.1) while j ≤ ℓ and q[i] = q[j] do
                   - suppress  q[i]
                   - column ith := column ith+column j-th    (columns of S).
                   - ℓ := ℓ-1
           (3.1.2) b := if j ≤ ℓ then GCD (q[i],q[j]) else 1
                   while b≠1 do
                   q[i] := q [i]/b, q[j] := q[j]/b
                   if q[i] ≠ 1
                      then if q[j] ≠ 1
                              then - ℓ := ℓ+1, q[ℓ] := b
                                   - column ℓ-th := column ith+ column j-th
                              else - q[j] := b
                                   - column j-th := column i-th + column j-th
                      else - q[i] := b
                           - column i-th := column j-th + column i-th
                   b := gcd(q[i],q[j]).
```

5.2 Algorithm 2 : test of the first condition

data s[1:r, 1:ℓ] : integer array given by algorithm 1
     a[1:r]   : integer array
     n[1:r]   : integer array

result. The relations which link the a[i] when the first condition of the theorem of A.Schinzel is not verified.

```
(1) p := 2
(2) while p ≤ ℓcm ((n_i)/2) do
    2.1 if p is prime and p| ℓcm(n_i) then
        2.1.1 mod := p (the calculus are computed modulus p)
        2.1.2 choice of a[i] such that p|n[i], and take as S the rows of S corres-
              ponding to these a[i].
        2.1.3 reduction of S (cf : 2.1)
        2.1.4 solve XS ≡ 0 (mod p) using the modular Gauss-algorithm.
        2.1.5 if X ≢ 0 mod p (∃ i_o/x_{i_o} ≢ 0 mod p) then
                - compute γ
                - write "the relation obtained is" Π a_i^{x_i} = γ^p
```

```
2.2 if p=2 then p := 3
         else p := p+2.
```

BIBLIOGRAPHY

[1] L.J. MORDELL On the linear independence of algebraic numbers J. Math. 3 (1953) p. 625-630.

[2] M. KNESER Lineare Abhângigkeit von Wurzeln, Acta Arithmetica 26 (1975) p. 307-308

[3] A. SCHINZEL On linear dependence of roots Acta Arithmetica 28 (1975) p. 161-175

[4] S. LANG Algebra Addison-Wesley Publishing Company, Inc.

[5] J.H. DAVENPORT Private communication.

[6] H. NAJID These de troisime cycle (to appear)

A Primer: 11 Keys to New SCRATCHPAD

Richard D. Jenks

Mathematical Sciences Department
IBM Thomas J. Watson Research Center
Yorktown Heights, New York 10598

This paper is an abbreviated primer for the language of new **SCRATCHPAD**, a new implementation of **SCRATCHPAD** which has been under design and development by the Computer Algebra Group at the IBM Research Center during the past 6 years. The basic design goals of the new **SCRATCHPAD** language and interface to the user are to provide:

- a "typeless" interactive language suitable for on-line solution of mathematical problems by novice users with little or no programming required, and
- a programming language suitable for the formal description of algorithms and algebraic structures which can be compiled into run-time efficient object code.

The new **SCRATCHPAD** language is introduced by 11 keys with each successive key introducing a additional capability of the language. The language is thus described as a "concentric" language with each of the 11 levels corresponding to a language subset. These levels are more than just a pedagogic device, since they correspond to levels at which the system can be effectively used. Level 1 is sufficient for naive interactive use; levels 2-8 progressively introduce interactive users to capabilities of the language; levels 9-11 are for system programmers and advanced users. Levels 2, 4, 6 and 7 give users the full power of **LISP** with a high-level language; level 8 introduces "type declarations;" level 9 allows polymorphic functions to be defined and compiled; levels 10-11 give users an **Ada**-like facility for defining types and packages (those of new **SCRATCHPAD** are dynamically constructable, however). One language is used for both interactive and system programming language use, although several freedoms such as abbreviation and optional type-declarations allowed at top-level are not permitted in system code. The interactive language (levels 1-8) is a blend of original **SCRATCHPAD** [GRJY75], some proposed extensions [JENK74], work by Loos [LOOS74], **SETL** [DEWA79], **SMP** [COWO81], and new ideas; the system programming language (levels 1-11) superficially resembles **Ada** but is more similar to **CLU** [LISK74] in its semantic design.

The presentation of the language in this paper omits many details to be covered in the **SCRATCHPAD** System Programming Manual [SCRA84] and an expanded version of this paper which will serve as a primer for **SCRATCHPAD** users [JESU84].

Notation and Vocabulary. The basic vocabulary of new **SCRATCHPAD** consists of identifiers, reserved words, numbers, strings, and operator symbols. Identifiers are used to name constants, variables, and functions. They must begin with a "$" or a letter but may be followed by letters (upper/lower case is distinguished) or digits, e.g. "a3b4", "a3B4", and "$a3B4" are distinct identifiers. Two reserved words *true* and *false* are boolean constants, others (e.g. *if* and *then*) are operators ("Appendix 4: Scratchpad Operators"), still others are names of functions provided in the **SCRATCHPAD** library. Numbers are of two basic kinds: integers and floats. Integers are written as a sequence of digits. Floats contain a decimal point and/or a scale factor, e.g. 12.34E-12. Many other kinds of numbers are available but must be referenced by parameterized forms (e.g. sqrt(2)) special symbols (e.g. %i), or coercion expressions (e.g. 2@BF to create a BigFloat (floats of arbitrary precision)). Strings are sequences of any printable characters enclosed with double quotes, e.g "a string". Operation symbols (e.g. +,*) are groups of special characters used as operator symbols in the language ("Appendix 4: Scratchpad Operators") When operations are adjacent, grouping is governed by the left- and right-precedence numbers as described in [SCRA84], e.g. "2↑3+4*5" means "((2↑3)+(4*5)". Parentheses are used solely for grouping and have no other significance Curly brackets {} can be used anywhere in a **SCRATCHPAD** program to write comments.

Key #1: Workspace

SCRATCHPAD can be used as a symbolic desk calculator. You simply enter expressions at your terminal as commands to **SCRATCHPAD**. **SCRATCHPAD** will interpret your expressions, do the computation, and output the result. Every expression you enter and every result you create is saved in a *workspace* for later review, editing, and retrieval. You may work on several problems at once, pursue side problems to make experimental definitions and trial substitutions and later undo their effect to return to a previous line of pursuit. The workspace saves all your results for later recall or for a future session.

In the example conversations which follow, user input begins in column 1, system responses are indented to column 4. Anything enclosed in curly brackets is a comment.

```
11+11   {what is 11 plus 11?}

   (1)  22

111↑111 {integer computations remain fully accurate}

   (2)  1073620128884742258012145650466955019598507239942248048047759_
        1117562507619578334702249122617009363462146610374309298696 7_
        7777863300673101594633035586669100910260177855872955396221 4_
        2057315437069730229375357546494103400699864397711

(x+1)↑6  {what is the result of expanding x+1 to the 6th power?}

         6      5       4       3       2
   (3)  x  + 6x  + 15x  + 20x  + 15x  + 6x + 1

factor(deriv(%,x)) {"%" refers to the last expression displayed}

               5
   (4)  6(x+1)
```

A number of *system commands* perform various services for the user. These include: **)edit,)read,** and **)write,** which allow you to edit, read, or write to output files; **)on** and **)off** which turn on/off various system flags such as **FORTRAN** output; **)what,** which provides an interactive query of algebraic facilities; **)compile,** and **)trace** which cause functions to be compiled and traced. Also, command **)undo** un-does all computations back to some point; **)redo** is similar except that commands may be edited and then reexecuted.

```
)undo 3   {undo every command back until after display of (3)}

% {what is the last expression displayed}

         6      5       4       3       2
   (5)  x  + 6x  + 15x  + 20x  + 15x  + 6x
```

Key #2: Expressions

With the exception of the system commands which begin with ")", every input to, and output from, the system is an expression. In addition to the simple arithmetic expressions illustrated thus far, there are numerous infix and prefix operations available in the language. This paper principally focuses on the notion of *sequence*, the only aggregate in top-level SCRATCHPAD. A sequence consists of zero or more expressions separated by commas and enclosed in square brackets [ ].

```
[1,"hoho",[x,true]]  {sequences can have members of any kind}

   (1)  [1,"hoho",[x,true]]

[11,12,13,14,15]  {integer segments are generally abbreviated}

   (2)  [11..15]

[1,1..3,5,8,13,21] {the first 8 Fibonacci numbers}

   (3)  [1,1..3,5,8,13,21]

[2↑i-1 for i in 1,1..3,5,13,21] {a seq. can be made by a for-construct}

   (4)  [1,1,3,7,31,255,8191,2097151]

[2↑i-1 for i in 1..20 | isPrime i] {for-constructs may have filters}

   (5)  [3,7,31,127,2047,8191,131071,524287]

[0..9]-10 {sequences may be added to or multiplied by a scalar}

   (6)  [-10,-9,-8,-7,-6,-5,-4,-3,-2,-1]

{a seq. whose first 50 elements are 0, next 50 are 1}
[1..50 → 0, 51..100 → 1]

   (7)  [1..50 → 0, 51..100 → 1]

[0..] {sequences may be infinite, here the sequence of integers from 0}

   (8)  [0..]

-[0..]+[0..]  {inf. seq. may be added, here to form an inf. seq. of 0's}

   (9)  [0.. → 0]

[1..50 → 0,51.. → 1] {a generalization of an above example}

   (10) [1..50 → 0,51.. → 1]
```

Key #3: Forms

Forms are used to name objects and functions. Forms are symbols which can have 5 kinds of parameters: subscripts, superscripts, pre-superscripts, pre-subscripts or functional arguments. Scripts are enclosed in [ ] brackets which have no preceding blank.

```
{f with 1 subscript, 1 superscript, and two functional arguments}

f[i;j](u,v)

       j
(1)  f (u,v)
       i
```

Two forms with the same leading name and the same number and kinds of scripts/arguments refer to the same function, e.g. the function x with 1 subscript, denoted by x[□]. Examples of use of this function are: x[1], x[k], and x[i+j]. Juxtaposition of a form f to an expression x always means "f applied to x" and may be written "f(x)" or simply "f x". Successive juxtapositions nest to the right, e.g. "f g x" and "f(g(x))" are equivalent. Application is also indicated by infix "." for which successive applications nest to the left, e.g. "x.i.j" and "(x.i).j" are equivalent.

If a function takes two or more functional arguments, its arguments are written as *tuples*: expressions enclosed in parentheses and separated by commas. Tuples do not denote data objects but rather are syntactic denotations for groups of two or more values passed to, or returned from, a function. Inner parentheses are superfluous, e.g. if "g u" returns two values x and y, all the following are equivalent: "f(g u,z)", "f((x,y),z)", and "f(x,y,z)". When applications are mixed with infix and prefix operations, applications are done first. Thus "f x + g (x,y)" and "(f x)+g(x,y)" are equivalent.

Key #4: Rules

Rules have the format: <form> → <expression>. Rules perform no computation; they simply describe how to compute something you later want to ask for. Once the notions of rules and expressions have been mastered, SCRATCHPAD programs can be written to perform any computable function.

To define the Legendre polynomials p(0),p(1),..., one can simply write a recurrence relation using three rules.

```
p(0)  →  1
p(1)  →  x
p(n)  →  (2*n-1)*x*p(n-1)/n-(n-1)*p(n-2)/n when n in 2..
```

These rules cause no computation but simply tell **SCRATCHPAD** how to compute p(i) for each i=0,... . To obtain values for the nth polynomial, one simply types the expression "p(n)". The expression p(n) will then be continually rewritten using the above rules and simplified until no further change is possible. The result is called the "value" of p(n).

```
[p(n) for n in 5..6] {what are p(5) and p(6)?}

                5      3             6       4        2
           63x  - 70x  + 15x   231x  - 315x  + 105x  - 5
   (1)  [-----------------,----------------------------]
                   8                      16
```

> **Key #5: Maps**
>
> Maps provide a general mechanism for representing mappings of source expressions to target expressions. Maps thus represent many things: sequences of rules, finite and infinite sequences, and, indeed, general functions.

```
{The simplest example of a map is a sequence as described under key #2}
[1,1..3,5,8,13,21]   {the mapping 0 → 1, 1 → 1, 2 → 2,...,7 → 21}

   (1)  [1,1..3,5,8,13,21]

{apply map to each element; "□" denotes an undefined value.}
% [1,3,5,7,9]

   (2)  [1,3,8,21,□]

)clear properties p
p(0) → 1     {again define Legendre polynomials}
p(1) → x
p            {the value of p is now the mapping 0 → 1, 1 → x}

   (3)  [1,x]

p(n) → (2*n-1)*x*p(n-1)/n-(n-1)*p(n-2)/n when n in 2..
p           {p's value is a map which tells how to generate values of p}
                                  (2n - 1)x*p(n - 1) - (n - 1)p(n - 2)
   (4)  [1,x,(n | n in 2..) → -------------------------------------]
                                                n

p [0..5] {what are the first 6 Legendre polynomials?}

                2         3          4      2          5      3
             3x  - 1   5x  - 3x   35x  - 30x  + 3   63x  - 70x  + 15x
   (5)  [1,x,--------,----------,----------------,------------------]
                2         2              8                 8
```

```
define a function to generate the Fibonacci series}
:ib 0 → 1; fib 1 → 1; fib n → fib n-1 + fib n-2 when n in 2..
[the value of function fib is a map i → ith Fibonacci number, i=0,..}
:ib
```

(6) `[1,1,(n | n in 2..) → fib(n-1)+fib(n-2)]`

```
{Infinite sequences are obtained by composition with infinite sequences}
:s → fib [1..] {the infinite sequence of Fibonacci numbers}
oddFn → [n for n in fs | isOdd n] {any sequence can be iterated over}
(3*oddFn-1) [2*i for i in 1..3] {or used in arithmetic expressions}
```

(7) `[8,38,101]`

```
{Maps may be defined explicitly}
cover(n) → [0..n → 1, (n+1).. → 0]
{two seq. are equal if they have the same generators}
cover(-1) = [0.. → 0]
```

(8) `true`

```
primes →
  sieve [2..] where sieve [h,:t] → [h,:sieve [y for y in t | h ¬|| y]]

{new notation for 1st n elements of a sequence}
n s → s [0..n-1] when n in 0..
10 primes  {what are the first 10 primes computed using sieve method?}
```

(9) `[2,3,5,7,11,13,17,19,23,29]`

```
primesLessThan n → [x for x in primes while x < n]
primeDivisorsOf n → [p for p in primesLessThan (n//2) | p || n]
divisors → primeDivisorsOf [1..]  {a sequence of sequences}
```

Key #6: Quote Marks

Often you will want to refer to some specific variable or expression which you do not want transformed by existing rules. Any expression preceded by a quote mark (') always stands for itself. Using quotes, you can also write rules which apply only for specific symbolic argument values.

If an argument to a function appearing on the left-side of a rule is a quoted expression, the rule is understood to give the value of the function applied to that symbolic constant.

```
f(x) → 0      {define f(x) = 0 for all x}
f('y) → a     {except let f have the value a at point "y"}
f             {what is f?}
```

(1) `['y → 1, x → 0]`

```
f [0,y] {what are the values of f at 0 and y?}
```

(2) `[0,a]`

The value of a quoted-expression is the expression itself; extra evaluations are performed by the function "ev"; each level of ev will remove exactly one quote-mark.

```
a → ''b; b → 7; [a,ev a,ev ev a]
```

(3) `['b,b,7]`

Key #7: Assignments

Assignments have the syntax: <form> ← <expression>. Assignments always cause <expression> to be immediately evaluated with the result "assigned" to <form>. The next time the value of <form> is requested, that assigned value is immediately returned without re-evaluation. Using assignments, you can permanently capture a computed result and be assured that it never will change.

```
u → [x,y,z]
{the ordering of rules is generally unimportant}
u where (x → y+1; y → z+1; z → 7)
```

(1) `[9,8,7]`

```
{assignments compute values immediately}
u where (x ← y+1; y ← z+1; z ← 7)
```

(2) `[y+1,z+1,7]`

```
{the ordering of assignments is usually critical}
u where (z ← 7; y ← z+1; x ← y+1)
```

(3) `[9,8,7]`

```
{Right and left assignments can always be mixed}
u where (x → y+1; y ← z+1; z → 7)
```

(4) `[z+2,z+1,7]`

```
{Define fib so that all previously computed values are saved}
fib 0 → fib 1 → 1
fib n → fib n ← fib (n-1) + fib (n-2) when n in 2..4
fib
```

(5) `[1,1,(n | n in 2..) → fib n ← fib (n-1) + fib (n-2)]`

```
fib 11

  (6)  144

fib

  (7)  [1,1,2,3,5,8,13,21,34,55,89,144,
          (n | n in 2..) → fib n ← fib (n-1) + fib (n-2)]

{fib can also be defined so as to save only the last two values}
fib 0 → fib 1 → 1
fib n → (fib n ← fib (n-1) + fib (n-2) {compute and store new value};
         fib (n-2) ← □ {delete previously computed value};
         fib n {return new value}) when n in 2..
fib 11

  (8)  144

fib

  (9)  [10 → 89,144,(n | n in 2..) →
          (fib n ← fib n-1 + fib n-2; fib (n-2) ← □; fib n)]

{Assignments could also have been used to create the Legendre
polynomials}

p(0)  ← 1
p(1)  ← 1
p(n)  ← (2*n-1)*x*p(n-1)/n-(n-1)*p(n-2)/n for n in 2..4
p        {what are the first 5 Legendre polynomials?}

                    2             3              4      2
                  3x  - 1       5x  - 3x      35x  - 30x  + 3
   (10) [1,'x,'(---------),'(----------),'(----------------)]
                     2             2                8
```

Key #8: Modes

A *mode* is an expression denoting a set of representations. Using modes, you can preselect output formats, re-format something already computed, or specify an algebraic structure in which a computation will take place. Expression "e @ M" causes expression e to be converted to a representation indicated by mode M.

The example which follows is from [LOOS74].

```
u ← z↑3*(y↑2-1)/(x+%i)+3*z*(x-%i)/(y+%i) -1
u@P[z]□ {display u as a polynomial in z}
```

```
                 2
            3   y  - 1          -3 %i + 3x
(1)  u:  z  (--------) + z(------------) - 1
             %i + x             %i + y
```

The symbol □ stands for a "don't care" mode to be determined by the system. The □ can generally be omitted (e.g. "u@P[z]" in above example). Similarly, "u@P[z]G" will display u as a polynomial in z with Gaussian coefficients; "u@P[z]G(FP)", as a polynomial in z with Gaussian coefficients with real and imaginary parts factored (over the integers); and, "u@P[z]FP", as a polynomial in z with coefficients factored (over the Gaussian integers). A mode which contains no explicit or implicit □ designates a specific algebraic structure called a *domain*. In general, modes only partially specify a domain into which an expression is to be converted with the details of that structure left to be determined by the system. When used as a prefix-operator, □ denotes an arbitrary gap in the domain specification, e.g. "u@□(G I)" means "convert u to any domain over the Gaussian integers." Similarly, "u@P(□I)" means "convert u to a polynomial over any domain whose ground domain is the integers."

A *declaration* "x: M" is used to force any value assigned to x to be first converted to a representation given by M.

```
v: G P[z]   {gaussian expressions with coefficients as polynomials in z}
v ← u       {what is u expressed as a G(P[z])?}
```

(2)

```
        2                                            2
  3  x*y   - x      3x*y - 3                  3 - y   + 1      - 3x - 3y
z   (---------) + z(--------)  - 1 + %i(z  (---------) + z(---------))
        2                2                       2               2
       x  + 1           y  + 1                  x  + 1          y  + 1
```

Declarations may also be used to declare the modes of arguments and return values of functions. For example, in the following definition of Legendre polynomials, the function p is declared to map the non-negative-integers into the domain of polynomials in x over the rational numbers.

```
p: NNI -> P[x]RN
p(0) → 1
p(1) → 1
p(n) → (2*n-1)*x*p(n-1)/n-(n-1)*p(n-2)/n otherwise
)on compile
```

The **)on** system command causes the rules for p to be compiled when first invoked; compiled rules generally run 10-100 times faster than if interpreted. Here again the declaration for p is optional, in the above case, unnecessary. When rules are to be invoked with the compiler option turned on, rules are mode-analyzed. In the above case, the declared mode would be chosen by default.

Declarations are used to declare the *type* of an argument or return value. One example of a type is a mode. Another is a *category*.

Key #9: Categories

In the last section, it was shown how a declaration can be used to declare that an argument or return value of a function is to come from some domain. The concept of *category* allows you to be less specific. Using categories, it is possible to declare arguments and return values of functions to come from any domain with specific algebraic properties. Categories thereby permit the definition and compilation of functions which can be used in the widest possible algebraic context.

The system provides a number of built-in categories. Among these is OrderedSet.

```
D: OrderedSet     {let domain D be a member of category OrderedSet}
x,y: D            {let x and y be members of D}

max(x,y): D → if x < y then y else x
```

Category OrderedSet denotes the class of all domains which have a total-ordering operation "<". This definition of max can be used to compute the maximum of two elements from any domain which is an ordered set.

```
max(3,-3)      {what is the maximum of two integers?}
```

(1) 3

```
max(5.3,3.5) {what is the maximum of two floats?}
```

(2) 5.3

A category designates a class of domains having certain specific operations and algebraic properties as described below. The simplest, most basic algebraic category is Set.

```
)what Set   {what is a Set?}
  3 operations:
      □=□: ($,$) -> Boolean
      coerce: $ -> Expression
      coerce: Expression -> Union($, "failed")
```

The above description of Set may be interpreted as follows: "A domain D is a set (a member of Set, the category of all sets) if it has an operation □=□: (D,D) -> Boolean and the above two coerce operations." The expression appearing to the right of the ":" is called the signature of the operation. In the notation □=□, the □ shows where the arguments go and therefore this means "the infix operation =." Categories are created by functions called *category-constructors,* that is, functions which return a category. The category-constructor for Set is defined as follows:

```
Set: Category → with
   {operations}
     □=□: ($,$) -> Boolean
     coerce: $ -> Expression
     coerce: Expression -> Union($, "failed")
```

The above syntax defines Set to be a category-constructor with no arguments which returns an object of type Category (the class of all categories). In order to assert that the operations of a domain satisfy certain algebraic properties, *attributes* may be included in the category definition. Attributes designate mathematical facts such as axioms and theorems that domains are asserted to have. For example, the category OrderedSet extends Set to include one new operation □<□ and one attribute: total(□<□) (which asserts that the infix operation "<" is total).

```
OrderedSet: Category → Set with
   {operations}
     □<□: ($,$) -> Boolean
   {attributes}
     total(□<□)    {not(x < y) and not(y < x)   implies x=y}
```

Another way of forming a category is by performing the *join* of two other categories, that is, the category formed by directly combining the operations and attributes of one category with those of the other, e.g.:

```
FiniteField: Category → Join(Field,Finite)
```

Categories may also be parameterized, e.g:

```
Algebra(R:SimpleRing): Category → Join(SimpleRing,Module(R)) with
   {operations}
     coerce: R -> $
     ...
```

The category-constuctor Algebra creates the category of all R-algebras, that is, algebras over a given ring R. For example, the function Algebra applied to Integer produces the category of all domains D which are both simple rings and algebras over the integers and which have the additional operation "coerce: Integer -> D."

Categories are organized into a hierarchy as shown in Appendix 3. The definitions of all system categories are interactively accessible. Using the system editor, users can inspect all system categories and define new ones needed for their work. In the current implementation of **SCRATCHPAD**, however, it is not possible to change an existing category without recompiling functions which reference them.

Key #10: Domains

The objects with which you compute (e.g. integers, polynomials, matrices) are members of algebraic structures called *domains*. In **SCRATCHPAD**, domains are objects too! Domains are created by functions called *domain-constructors*. All domain-constructors are interactively accessible for user inspection and modification. By use of the system editor, users can create new domains of their own and modify those provided by the system.

A *domain* consists of two parts:

1. a category — a set of operations and a set of attributes, and
2. a set of functions which implement these operations so as to satisfy the attributes, that is:

Domain = Category + Functions

All domains are created by functions called *domain-constructors*. The return type of a domain-constructor is a category, called the *target category*, which describes the operations and attributes of the domain it produces. A *capsule* part of the domain-constructor definition defines the set of functions which implement the operations described in the target category. Domains provide an abstract datatype component to the language. Whereas the target category provides *public* information about the domain, the capsule part describes a representation for objects of the domain and is *private*. Programs which manipulate objects of the domain are permitted only to use the exported operations of the domain and, in particular, are not permitted to take advantage of any knowledge of how objects of the domain are implemented. The format of a domain-constructor definition closely parallels the above equation for domains.

<Domain-constructor Form>: <Target Category> → add <Capsule>

public part (<Target Category>) — private part (<Capsule>)

Example 1: Gaussian.

A domain-constructor Gaussian (slightly simplified) takes a ring R as an argument and produces the domain "Gaussian over R" (Figure 1). Three special cases are the Gaussian integers (R=Integer), the Gaussian rationals (R=RationalNumber), and the complex numbers (R=Float). Its target category lists the operations which can be performed on Gaussian domains: the ring operations — such as 0,1,+,-,*,↑; scalar multiplication (from Algebra(R)); two functions, real and imag, to select real and imaginary parts; and [a,b], to construct a Gaussian object from 2 members a and b of R.

Inside the domain-constructor definition, the symbol "$" stands for the domain "Gaussians-over-R" which the constructor creates. The capsule (everything following "add") consists of one or more statements to be processed in order. An essential component of a capsule is Rep which describes the representation of the objects of the domain. Rep is always assigned a value which is a predefined domain, here, Record(real:R,imag:R). Records are basic constructors which implement general Cartesian products of domains [SCRA84]. Here, the record type provides operations "x.real" and "x.imag" to select the real and imaginary parts of a record object x, and "[a,b]" to construct a record object from two members a,b of R. Within a capsule — and nowhere else — the set of operations on $ are extended to include the operations of the representation.

The capsule contains a set of declarations followed by a list of rules defining a set of functions, one function for each operation mentioned in TargetCategory. The declarations are useful, for example, to disambiguate the 3 definitions of "*" in the capsule. As with categories, the statements of a capsule are all left-aligned.

Remarks. Definitions of domain-constructors, as well as those of categories and package-constructors (covered later), represent system code which is always compiled, never interpreted. Several freedoms allowed in top-level **SCRATCHPAD** are not allowed in system code where code legibility is considered of paramount importance. For example, within each function definition in a capsule, the following *strong-typing rules* are required:

1. the type of every identifier must be constant and unambiguous and
2. the type of each simple expression must be determinable by its context.

```
Gaussian(R:Ring): TargetCategory → Definition where
  TargetCategory →                    {public part}
    Join(Ring,Algebra(R)) with
      real: $ -> R
      imag: $ -> R
      [□,□]: (R,R) -> $
  Definition → add                    {private part}
    {representation}
      Rep ← Record(real:R,imag:R)
    {declarations}
      x,y: $
      r,i: R
      n: Integer
    {define}
      0 → [0,0]
      1 → [1,0]
      gauss(r,i) → [r,i]
      real(x) → x.real
      imag(x) → x.imag
      x + y → [x.real+y.real,x.imag+y.imag]
      - x   → [-x.real,-x.imag]
      r * x → [r*x.real,r*x.imag]
      n * x → [n*x.real,n*x.imag]
      x * y →
        [x.real*y.real-x.imag*y.imag,x.imag*y.real+y.imag*x.real]
      characteristic → R$characteristic   ...
```

Figure 1. Gaussian Domain-Constructor

```
Localization(N,R,D): TargetCategory → Definition
 where
  R: Ring
  N: Module(R)
  D: SubsetCategory(Monoid,R)
  TargetCategory →                {public part}
    Module(R) with
      if N has OrderedSet then OrderedSet
      if N has Algebra(R) then Algebra(R)
      □/□:($,D) -> $
      numer: $ -> N
      denom: $ -> D
  Definition → add                {private part}
    {representation}
      Rep ← Record(num:N,den:D)
    {declarations}
      x,y: $
      n: Integer
      r: R
      d: D
    {definitions}
      0 → [0,1]
      -x → [-x.num,x.den]
      x=y → y.den*x.num = x.den*y.num
      numer x → x.num
      denom x → x.den
      if N has OrderedSet then
        x < y → y.den*x.num < x.den*y.num
      x+y → [y.den*x.num+x.den*y.num, x.den*y.den]
      n*x → [n*x.num,x.den]
      r*x → if r=x.den then [x.num,1] else [r*x.num,x.den]
      x/d → [x.num,d*x.den]
      if N has Algebra(R) then
        1 → [1,1]
        x*y → [x.num*y.num,x.den*y.den]
        characteristic → N$characteristic
              ...
```

Figure 2. Localization Domain-Constructor

It is never permissible to omit the type of an argument of a function unless uniquely implied by its signature in the target category. Also, unlike conversational **SCRATCHPAD** where it is possible to add a real r to an integer i and get a real result, the conversion of an object from one type to another must be made explicit by use of one of several "conversion" expressions.

Example 2. Localization.

Domain-constructor Localization produces a domain of localizations, fractions for which the numerator domain N and denominator domain D may be different. For example, if N is "polynomials over R," D may be "factored polynomials over R" or "factored integers." Domain

```
QuotientField(D: IntegralDomain): TargetCategory → Definition where
  TargetCategory →                   {public part}
    Join(Field,Algebra(D)) with
      if D has OrderedRing then OrderedRing
      if D has DifferentialRing then DifferentialRing
      □/□: (D,D) -> $
      numer: $ -> D
      denom: $ -> D
  Definition →                       {private part}
    Localization(D,D,D) add
      {representation}
        Rep ← Record(num:D,den:D)
      {declarations}
        x,y: $
        nn,dd: D
        n: Integer
      {definitions}
        recip(x) →
          x.num = 0 => "failed"
          [x.den,x.num]
        nn / dd → [nn,dd]
        if D has DifferentialRing then
          deriv(x) →
            [deriv(x.num)*x.den - x.num*deriv(x.den), x.den↑2]
        if D has UniqueFactorizationDomain then
          {local declarations}
            cancelGcd: $ -> D
            normalize: $ -> $
          {local definitions}
            normalize(x) →
              uca:=unitNormal(x.den)
              x.den:=uca.coef
              x.num:=x.num*uca.associate
              x
            cancelGcd(x) →
              d:=gcd(x.num,x.den)
              x.num:=(x.num exquo d)@D
              x.den:=(x.den exquo d)@D
              d
        ...
```

Figure 3. Quotient Field Domain-Constructor (continued on next page)

N is required to be a module over a ring R in order to allow scalar multiplication. Addition of localizations requires the ability to multiply elements of D into elements of N; D is thus required to be a subset of R. Finally, in order to add localizations, D must be closed under multiplication, that is, D must be a monoid.

The definition of Localization is given in Figure 2. The statements in the where-clause are processed in order. Since the mode of N depends on R, R must be introduced before N. Also, the TargetCategory must occur before the Definition since it tells the compiler what functions must be provided in the Definition.

```
{redefinitions}
  recip(x) →
    x.num = 0 => "failed"
    normalize [x.den,x.num]
  nn / dd → (cancelGcd (z:=[nn,dd]);z)
  x + y  →
     z:=[x.den,y.den]
     d:=cancelGcd(z)
     g:=[z.den*x.num + z.num*y.num, d]
     cancelGcd(g)
     g.den:= g.den * z.num * z.den
     normalize g
  x - y  →
     z:=[x.den,y.den]
     d:=cancelGcd(z)
     g:=[z.den*x.num - z.num*y.num, d]
     cancelGcd(g)
     g.den:= g.den * z.num * z.den
     normalize g
  x * y  →
     (x,y):=([x.num,y.den],[y.num,x.den])
     cancelGcd x; cancelGcd y;
     normalize [x.num*y.num,x.den*y.den]
  n * x →
     y:=[n@D,x.den]
     cancelGcd y
     normalize [x.num*y.num,y.den]
  ...
  if D has DifferentialRing then
     deriv(x) → ...

RationalNumber: TargetCategory → QuotientField Integer where
  TargetCategory → Join(OrderedRing,Field,DifferentialRing) with
                        □/□: (Integer,Integer) -> $
                        numer: $ -> Integer
                        denom: $ -> PositiveInteger
```

Figure 4. Quotient Field Domain-Constructor (continued from previous page)

The meaning of the first if-then clause in target category is "if N has all the operations and attributes of OrderedSet, the domain Localization(N,R,D) has them as well." This if-clause in the target category requires a corresponding one in the capsule in order that the function for "<" be conditionally introduced into the domain. The use of infix $ in the definition of characteristic is needed for type disambiguation. The need for $ is avoidable in other situations. For example, the rule for 0 could have otherwise been defined by "0 → [N$0,D$1]"; but the need for $ in this case is obviated by the uniqueness of the [ ] construct in context.

Example 3. Quotient Field.

This domain-constructor produces the domains of localizations in which numerator and denominator elements come from the the same integral domain. Its target category has two conditional categories: OrderedRing and DifferentialRing. The latter conditional has the interpretation "localizations are differentiable if elements of D are differentiable." The definition c QuotientField has a new form of definition:

<New Constructor>: <Target Category> → <Old Constructor> add <Capsule>

public part (<Target Category>) — private part (<Capsule>)

The domain is initially created by instantiating Localization with A=D=R, then *add*ing in newly required functions and redefinitions. The capsules for Localization and QuotientField are independent and self-contained. On the other hand, because one extends the other, the representations given by Rep in each must be isomorphic. The system checks for such isomorphisms or instantiation.

```
GrobnerPackage(nvars,R,P): TargetCategory → Definition where
  nvars: Integer
  R: Field
  P: GeneralPolynomial(R,DirectProduct(nvars,NonNegativeInteger))
  TargetCategory → with
    reduce: (P,List(P)) -> P
    grobner: List(P) -> List(P)
  Definition → add
    reduce(S:P,Basis:List(P)) →
      j: Integer ← 0
      n ← #Basis-1
      t: Union(Expon, "failed")
      while j <= n repeat
        if not ((t ← degree(S) - degree(Basis.j)) case "failed")
           then
             S ← lc(Basis.j) * S - monom(t, lc(S)) * Basis.j
             j ← 0
           else j ← j+1
       S
         ...
```

Figure 5. Grobner Basis Package-Constructor

Key #11: Packages

All functions which are not defined by domains are are organized into clusters called *packages*. Packages are created by functions called *package-constructors* which generally take domains as well as other types of values as arguments. All system package-constructors are interactively accessible for user inspection or modification. Using the system editor, users can create packages of their own or augment those provided by the system.

In **SCRATCHPAD**, functions (e.g. "factorize") are usually defined in their most general context and are therefore parameterized by one or more domains (e.g. "polynomials over a field F"). Packages are thus simply parameterized collections of functions where the parameters are often domains of some category (e.g. some field F).

All packages are defined by package-constructors which have the same syntax as domain-constructors. There is one difference, however. Whereas a domain-constructor creates a domain $ of computational objects, packages are simply collections of functions. As a consequence, all operations in the target category of a package-constructor are free of $.

Example 4. GrobnerPackage

The skeletal package-constructor for Grobner basis is shown in Figure 5. The package exports two functions: *grobner* which, given a list l of general polynomials over a domain R, produces a Grobner basis for l; and *reduce*, which given an polynomial p and a basis B, will reduce p with respect to B. The definition *grobner*, which requires locally defined data structures and numerous locally defined subfunctions, is omitted.

History and Acknowledgements

The ideas in the new **SCRATCHPAD** language mostly originate from: original **SCRATCHPAD** [JENK74,GRJY75] (workspace, forms, and rules), work by Ruediger Loos [LOOS74], **MODLISP** [JENK79,DAVJE80] (modes, ← and →), **SMP** [COWO81] (maps, I/O), **APL** (e.g. reduction,system commands), and, most importantly, **LISP** (programming style). The particular design of modes, ← and →, iterators, sequences, and maps for the interactive language is due to the author. The design of other aspects of the interactive language and the entire system programming language design [JETR81] is the joint work of the author with Barry M. Trager (IBM Research), and, more recently, Victor S. Miller (IBM Research). The notion of domain-constructors and categories is originally due to David Barton (U. of Cal., Berkeley; Tandem), James H. Davenport (University of Bath), and J. W. Thatcher (IBM Research). This research has greatly prospered through numerous discussions with other colleagues, particularly, Patrizia Gianni, Scott C. Morrison, Michael Rothstein, Christine J. Sundareson, Robert S. Sutor, and especially David Yun (SMU), manager of the Computer Algebra group at IBM until February, 1983. I am also very grateful to Bob Sutor for assistance in the final preparation of this paper.

References

[COWO81] Cole, C. A., Wolfram, S., et al, "SMP: A Symbolic Manipulation Program," Californi Institute of Technology, July, 1981.

[DAVJE80] Davenport, J. H. and Jenks, R. D., "MODLISP," Proceedings of LISP '80 Conference August, 1980 (also available as IBM Research Report RC 8537, October 29, 1980).

[DEWA79] Dewar, Robert B. K., "The SETL Programming Language," Computer Science Depart ment, NYU Courant Institute of Mathematical Sciences, August, 1979.

[GRJY75] Griesmer, J. H., Jenks, R. D., and Yun, D. Y. Y., "SCRATCHPAD User's Manual," IBM Research Report RA 70, June 1975.

[JENK74] Jenks, R. D., "The SCRATCHPAD Language," Proceedings of a Symposium on Very High Level Languages, SIGPLAN Notices, Vol. 9, No. 4, April 1974 (Reprinted in SIGSAM Bulletin, Vol. 8, No. 2, May 1974).

[JENK79] Jenks, R. D., "MODLISP: An Introduction," Proc. EUROSAM 79 (Springer-Verlag Lecture Notes in Computer Science 72) pp. 466 - 480 (also available is slightly modified form as: "MODLISP: A Preliminary Design," IBM Research Report RC 8073, January 18, 1980).

[JESU84] Jenks, R.D., and Sundaresan, C.J., "The 11 Keys to SCRATCHPAD: A Primer," in preparation.

[JETR81] Jenks, R.D., and Trager, B.M., Proceedings of SYMSAC '81, 1981 Symposium on Symbolic and Algebraic Manipulation, Snowbird, Utah, August, 1981 (also published in SIGPLAN Notices, November, 1981 and available as an IBM Research Report RC 8930).

[LISK74] Liskov, B., Snyder, A., Atkinson, R., and Schaffert, C., "Abstraction Mechanisms in CLU," Communications of the ACM, Vol. 20, No. 8, August, 1977.

[LOOS74] Loos, R., "Towards a Formal Implementation of Computer Algebra," Proceedings of Eurosam '74, SIGSAM Bulletin, Vol. 8, No. 3, August 1974, pp. 9-16.

[SCRA84] Davenport, J.H., Gianni, P., Jenks, R.D., Miller, V., Morrison, S., Rothstein, M., Sundaresan, C.J., Sutor, R.S., Trager, B.M., "SCRATCHPAD System Programming Language Manual," in preparation.

Appendix 1: Programming Language Syntax

Expression ::= Conditional | Loop | OperatorExpression
Conditional ::= **if** Expression **then** Expression **else** Expression>
Loop ::= <Iterator...> **repeat** Expression
  Iterator ::= While | Until | For
  While ::= **while** Expression
  Until ::= **until** Expression
  For ::= **for** Primary **in** Expression <Suchthat>
    Suchthat ::= | Expression
OperatorExpression ::= Prefix <InfixOp Expression | SuffixOp>
  Prefix ::= PrefixOp Prefix | Reduction | Application
  PrefixOp ::= {see Appendix 4}
  InfixOp ::= {see Appendix 4}
  SuffixOp ::= {see Appendix 4}
  Reduction ::= ReductionOp Application
    ReductionOp ::= InfixOp /
    Application ::= Composition <Application>
      Composition ::= Primary. ...
Primary ::= Literal | QuadPhrase | Parameter | Sequence | Enclosure
Literal ::= Integer | Float | Boolean | String | Symbol
  Integer ::= Digit...
  Float ::= Mantissa <Exponent>
    Mantissa ::= Digit... <Fraction> | Fraction
    Fraction ::= . Digit...
    Exponent ::= **E** <-> Digit...
  Boolean ::= **true** | **false**
  String ::= " <Any...> "
  Symbol ::= First <Alphanumeric...>
    First ::= **$** | Letter
    Alphanumeric ::= Letter | Digit
QuadPhrase ::= <AnyNonBlank...> QuadString...
  QuadString ::= ⎕ <AnyNonBlank...>
Parameter ::= **#** Digit
Sequence ::= **[** <SequenceSpec> **]**
  SequenceSpec ::= Expression <IteratorTail>
  IteratorTail ::= <**repeat**> Iterator...
Enclosure ::= (Expression)

Appendix 2: Domain Table

Basic Domains

E	Expression	F	Float
I	Integer	N	Name
S	String	SI	SmallInteger

SubDomains

EI	EvenInteger	ESI	EvenSmallInteger
NI	NegativeInteger	NNI	NonNegativeInteger
NNSI	NonNegativeSmallInteger	NPI	NonPositiveInteger
NPSI	NonPositiveSmallInteger	NSI	NegativeSmallInteger
OI	OddInteger	OSI	OddSmallInteger
PI	PositiveInteger	PSI	PositiveSmallInteger
ES	EnumerationSet(vl)		

Basic Constructors

L	List(D)	R	Record(s:D,...)
U	Union(D,...)	V	Vector(n,D)

Number Domains

FI	FactoredInteger	GF	GaloisField(p)
IM	IntegerMod(p,b)	BF	BigFloat(n)
RN	RationalNumber		

Algebraic Domains

A	Algebraic(e,D)	BBT	BalancedBinaryTree(D)
B	Boolean	CF	ContinuedFraction(e,D)
CP	ContentPrimitivepart(D)	DP	DirectProduct(n,D)
DMP	DistributedMultivariatePolynomial(vl,D)	F	Fraction(D,D)
FM	FreeModule(R,S)	FP	FactoredPolynomial(vl,D)
G	Gaussian(D)	IB	IntegralBasis(D)
LA	LocalAlgebra(R,S,D:=S)	M	Matrix(D)
MM	ModMonic(D,D)	P	Polynomial(D,E:=Integer)
PS	PowerSeries(x,D)	PR	PolynomialRing(R,E)
Q	Quaternion	QF	QuotientField(D)
RF	RationalFunction(vl,D)	SM	SquareMatrix(n,D)
SMP	SparseMultivariatePolynomial(f,D,vl)	SUP	SparseUnivariatePolynomial(D)
UP	UnivariatePolynomial(x,D)	VP	VectorPolynomial(D)

Appendix 3: Algebraic Categories

Category	Extends	Operations
Set		=, coerce
AbelianGroup	Set	0, +, -
OrderedSet	Set	<
SemiGroup	Set	*
Rng	AG, SG	
Monoid	SemiGroup	1
Group	Monoid	inv
SimpleRing	Rng, Monoid	characteristic, recip, coerce
Module(R:SimpleRing)	AbelianGroup	scalar multiplication
Algebra(R:SimpleRing)	SR, Module(R)	coerce
Ring	Algebra($)	
DifferentialRing	Ring	deriv
IntegralDomain	Ring	isAssociate, ← exquo.
SkewField	Ring	/
UniqueFactorizationDomain	IntegralDomain	gcd, factor, isPrime
EuclideanDomain	UFD	sizelp, div, quo, rem
Field	ED, SkewField	
Finite	Set	size, random
GaloisField	Field, Finite	
VectorSpace(S:Field)	Module(S)	
QuotientObject(S:Set)	Set	reduce, lift, coerce

Appendix 4: Scratchpad Operators

Key: Each operator with a meaningful relative precedence is accompanied by an *operator precedence code* in the format (XnnY,mm) where:

X = prefix(P), suffix(S) or infix(default) operator
nn = precedence
Y = right(R)-, non(N)- or left(default)-associative
mm = optional right-precedence

Separators

,	(40)	tuple/sequence separator	f(x,y) [a,b]
;	(30)	block separator	(x ← 1; y ← 2; x+y)
where	(70,10)	qualifier	a where b ← 1

Assignment

→	(90R)	delayed	f(x) → x+1; a → b
←	(85R)	immediate	f(x) ← x+1; a ← b
→→	(90N)	macro	f(x) →→ x+1; a →→ b

Conditional

if	(P100)	conditional expression	if a then b else c
then	(P40)		
else	(P40)		
=>	(80N)	exit from surrounding block	a => b ≡ if a then exit b

Logical

and	(150)	evaluate while true	a and b and c
or	(150)	evaluate until true	a or b or c
not	(P160)	logical negation	not a

Compare

<	(180N)	less than	a < b
<=	(180N)	less than or equal	a <= b
=	(180N)	equal	a = b
<>	(180N)	not equal	a <> b
>	(180N)	greater than	a > b
>=	(180N)	greater than or equal	a >= b

Arithmetic

<table>
<tr><td>+</td><td>(200)</td><td>plus</td><td>4 + 3 ≡ 7</td></tr>
<tr><td>-</td><td>(200) (P200)</td><td>difference, minus</td><td>4 - 3 ≡ 1; -3</td></tr>
<tr><td>*</td><td>(210)</td><td>times</td><td>4 * 3 ≡ 12</td></tr>
<tr><td>/</td><td>(210)</td><td>quotient</td><td>24/18 ≡ 4/3</td></tr>
<tr><td>| |</td><td>(210)</td><td>does divide exactly</td><td>3 | | 5 ≡ false</td></tr>
<tr><td>¬| |</td><td>(210)</td><td>does not divide exactly</td><td>3 ¬| | 5 ≡ true</td></tr>
<tr><td>div</td><td>(210)</td><td>quotient and remainder</td><td>11 rem 3 ≡ [quotient: 3,remainder: 2]</td></tr>
<tr><td>rem</td><td>(210)</td><td>remainder</td><td>11 rem 3 ≡ 2</td></tr>
<tr><td>quo</td><td>(210)</td><td>quotient</td><td>11 quo 3 ≡ 3</td></tr>
<tr><td>exquo</td><td>(210)</td><td>exact quotient or "failed"</td><td>4 exquo 2 ≡ 2; 4 exquo 3 ≡ "failed"</td></tr>
<tr><td>↑</td><td>(220)</td><td>exponentiation</td><td>4 ** 3 ≡ 256</td></tr>
</table>

Application

(blank)		apply	(f g) h ≡ f.g.h
.		apply	(f g) h ≡ f.g.h
!		apply each	[f,g]!x ≡ [f x,g x]

Iteration

for	(P100)	do for each element	for x in y repeat ...
until	(P100)	do iterate then test	until x < 0 repeat ...
while	(P100)	test then do iterate	while x > 0 repeat ...
repeat		do forever	repeat ...

Control Exit

exit		exit from a block	(..; if c then exit d; ..)
leave		to leave a loop	while x repeat (.. leave u ..)
return		to return from a function	f(x) → (.. p => return u ..)
case	(180N)	union case branch	if x case A then ...

Connectors

with	(260N) (P260)	category operator	SomeCategory → with ...
add	(180N) (P180)	capsule operator	SomeConstructor → add ...

Mode Operators

:	(230R)	declare	n: Integer
@	(230)	convert	n@ Integer
->		source/target separator	f: Integer -> Integer
has	(180N)	category predicate	if N has Ring then ...

Quote Mark

'	(P240)	quoted expression	x:= '(a+b)

Constructor/Destructor

:	(P120)	segment operator	[a,:b]
is	(180N)	destructuring predicate	if x is ["COND",:pl] then ...
isnt	(180N)	destructuring predicate	if x isnt ["COND",:pl] then ...
=	(P200)	tests equality to variable	pal [a,:b,=a] → pal b

Rule Operators

where	(70)	expression qualifier	a where b ← 3
otherwise	(S50)	gives rule least preference	f(0) → 1; f(n) → 0 otherwise
when	(60N)	rule qualifier	f(x) → 0 when x > 0

Miscellaneous

/		APL-reduction	+/[f(x) for x in S]
#	(P240)	size	#S
$		domain operator qualifier	x:= a R$+ b

A Pure and Really Simple Initial Functional Algebraic Language

J. P. Fitch & J. A. Padget,
School of Mathematics,
University of Bath,
Claverton Down
Bath, England.

Abstract

A medium sized algebra system supporting rational functions and some elementary functions, which is written in the purely functional subset of LISP is described. This is used to investigate the practicability of writing systems in a no-side effect, no property list, pure style. In addition, using the experimental LISP system in Bath that allows for full environment closures, ways have been discovered in which eager (applicative) evaluation and lazy (normal) evaluation strategies can be applied to computer algebra. The system is demonstrated on some well known sample programs.

Introduction

Since the early days of computer algebra, systems have been written in LISP. However in general, they have employed the extended version of LISP that is known as LISP 1.6 [Quam & Diffie68] and its descendants. One feature of all these programs is their use of side effects with both global and fluid variables, and the object-oriented use of the property list. In this way the programming language used has become divorced from the mathematical model of lambda calculus which bore it. More recently, and especially after the Turing lecture by Backus [Backus78], there has been a revival of interest in the pure functional, zero assignment and single assignment languages. Evidence of this is the rise of projects such as SKIM [Clarke et al. 80], ALICE [Darlington & Reeve81], AMPS [Keller et al. 79] on the hardware side, engendered by the work of [Turner79] and [Burton & Sleep82]. A particular reason for this interest is that in this programming style new architectural concepts of reduction machines and parallelism are immediately applicable. This is an alternative to the approach of [Marti & Fitch83].

An open question which has hung over the future of these elegant schemes is whether it is practical to write large systems whilst still remaining within the constraints imposed by functional purity. Viewed from a mathematical standpoint there is no doubt that it is feasible, if only by writing a Turing machine simulator, but the concern of this paper is with the pragmatics of such programs. We wish to discover the practical problems in writing a system with the functional paradigm, both in the resulting efficiency of the code, and the intellectual effort required on our part.

In writing such a demonstration system, the authors had a choice of base language. By building on the ASLISP dialect of LISP (a compatible extension of Cambridge LISP [Fitch & Norman77]) [Padget83] [Padget84], it is possible to delay the decision of whether to use normal order or applicative order evaluation. ASLISP is an experimental system that provides an efficient implementation of full environment closures by a method of environment labelling [Padget & Fitch]. With this new tool we can experiment with mixed eager and lazy evaluation (by explicit closures) in the same program. This is equivalent to the node labelling techniques of Burton [Burton82] in a practical context. Another benefit of the availability of closures is that high order functions can be applied in a sophisticated manner to overcome the self imposed discipline of programming style to provide an elegant solution to problems which do not lend themselves easily to the functional metaphor.

Throughout this paper we have used a MC68000 based computer running the Tripos operating system, both for our new system and for the implementation of REDUCE we use for comparisons [Fitch83].

In order to test the system and compare various evaluation strategies, the now old set of test programs, the f and g series [Sconzo et al. 65], the Y(2n) problem [Campbell72] and the series reversion problem [Hall73] have been coded and run.

System Design and Implementation

In a previous paper Fitch and Marti [Fitch & Marti82] described NLARGE, a small algebra system for use on a microcomputer which manipulates rational forms based on multivariate polynomials. As described in that paper, NLARGE is written in a functional style but not completely pure. It uses a polynomial representation to contruct rationals which it makes canonical by always dividing out the greatest common divisor, and ensuring that the denominator is positive. This system was taken as a starting point for the new functional system and a large number of modifications were made to remove all assignments and the destructive use of the property list of atoms. This involved extensive use of embedded lambda expressions to give the effect of assign-once variables, the passing of functions as arguments and of course a heavy reliance on the compiler for the removal of tail recursions. For the majority of the functions of NLARGE this modification was straightforward. The main areas of difficulty arose in the parsing of the input language, and a section below is devoted to this part of the system. Apart from this, the form used for looping constructs was rather contorted and was hard to follow. As an example we present in figure 1 the function for raising a polynomial to an integer power.

The basic data structure used for polynomials is the same as that in NLARGE, that is the REDUCE variant of the recursive data structure, but extended to allow elementary functions as kernels. This common data structure is obviously well suited for a functional programming style, which to a large extent can be seen in the current REDUCE sources.

The fundamental algorithms of the algebra system are addition, multiplication, subtraction and division. A simple implementation of all these can follow the NLARGE code except where there is a need for the calculation of a gcd. This is the first place in our system where we consider a non trivial algorithm. As the system handles rational forms in canonical representation the gcd algorithm is fundamental to the system. This function in NLARGE was the furthest from the required pure style, and so the opportunity was taken to improve the algorithm used, the reduced PRS algorithm in NLARGE, to the subresultant algorithm in Parsifal (as the new system is called). It is with pleasure that we can report that the functional implementation of the subresultant algorithm is shorter in code than the procedural reduced polynomial remainder sequence (as would be expected), but also took less time to write, and considerably less time to debug.

In this main algebraic part of Parsifal we encountered the first problem. When running interpretively all was well, but when we attempted to compile the system some deficiencies in the compiler were noted. The compiler we use is a descendent of the Portable Lisp compiler [Griss & Hearn81], which deals well with lambda expressions in the function position of a form, and compiles a separate function for lambda expressions as arguments. There are circumstances when the compiler should be forced to declare some variables FLUID, but for good local reasons does not notice. In fact the code shown in figure 1 is such a case: consider the status of the variable fn. This indicates the need for a return to the local functions of LABEL, or some variant of this.

It is apparent that for efficient use of space we are going to need the compiler to be smart about tail recursions. In the simple cases there is no difficulty, but when fluid variables are involved the compiler seems to be over cautious.

In order to make a true algebra system there are a number of other algebraic functions that are needed. So far the only one of these that we have implemented is substitution, which is fairly straightforward, apart from the minor confusion introduced by substituting a rational form into a polynomial.

Parsing and Printing in a Functional Style

Initially it was expected that this would be one of the most difficult tasks, since the use of READ admits side-effects. Of course, sooner or later in any applicative system some form of I/O must be done. It is a question of how well the functional part is insulated from this (i.e. the degree of integration of I/O at the 'implementation' level, or the degree of abstraction viewed at the functional level), and how much of the implementation may be written in a functional style. The obvious model is the stream; however this requires lazy evaluation (explicit coroutining is unacceptable), and hence can only be considered in the second stage system. In the first instance, the programming style is voluntarily limited to being first order functional. This restriction eads to a compromise between purity and expediency.

The solution chosen also serves as some explanation of the remark above regarding insulation/integration. The top-level system driver reads in tokens until a delimiter (';') is encountered. These tokens are constructed into a list and this is handed over to the parser. Hence the parser itself never has to read, and so manages to remain side-effect free. The parser is a straightforward recursive descent method, only complicated slightly by the need to 'read' tokens from the list which is passed down as an argument to each level, and returned as part of the result with the requisite tokens nibbled off. In this way, the non-functional reading process is kept as far removed from the main body of the code as possible.

The system to which we are moving makes extensive use of the closure facility in ASLISP. This is to great advantage in the parsing process. Being able to 'demand' a new token of the input stream permits a more natural style of coding, although it is still necessary to bind the closure at each level or return the continuation as part of the result to ensure that the correct suspension is evaluated. It is altogther more satisfactory that reading is now even further removed from the body of the system; being hidden inside a stream generator.

The general approach to printing has been similar to reading, where at one level the printer generates a stream of characters, which are printed separately. However we have noticed that as we moved to a lazy evaluation system that in order to preserve a natural print style it seems necessary to evaluate the answer in full before it can be formatted.

Results of Initial System

The system we have so far described is capable of running the f and g series, and SIGSAM examples 2 and 3. For these we present in figures 2, 3 and 4 the user level programs, and in table 1 the timing results, and comparisons with REDUCE. While being considerably slower than REDUCE for the recursive function style, for larger iterative programs it performs credibly. These results are preliminary, as we have not yet attempted any extensive optimization of the system. We expect to make some gains from improved algorithms, but will sustain some loss as Parsifal becomes more general. We have determined that in the present implementation a large overhead results from the macro expansion, for example of for loops and blocks, during evaluation.

Use of Normal Order Reduction

One of the advantages claimed for the pure applicative programming style is that one can use normal order reduction, that is, lazy evaluation. The work of Turner on KRCL [Turner80] makes a major point of the freedom of algorithm that lazy evaluation allows, and the perceived performance of SKIM-1 [Clarke et al. 80] is a clear indicator that we should consider whether the system would benefit from judicious use of normal order evaluation. In a previous paper Padget [Padget82] indicated that the use of closures gives access to improved algorithms. Such an algorithm is polynomial multiplication. Despite other algorithms with asymptotically good performance, the best practical multiplication algorithm is Johnson's algorithm [Johnson74]. The basic principle of this algorithm is to delay the production of the terms of the product until there is reason to believe that the term may contribute to the answer chain at the end. Described in this way it is clear that Johnson's algorithm is a suitable starting point for the inclusion of some lazy evaluation. The implementation of this algorithm using closures is given in Appendix 1. In Table 2 comparisons are given for some of our simple problems using the lazy Johnson algorithm and the more normal algorithm. At present the timings are a little disappointing, but this may well be due in part to our inexperience in programming with explicit closure, and in part to poor compilation of context switching. In addition since only the multiplication phase has been coded lazy, there is a fair overhead in conversion between the two forms and very few of the advantages of the method have a chance to become apparent.

There are a number of other places in the system where laziness can be usefully applied. We have already mentioned the parser, and we can see other sections of code where we intend to experiment. Division presents an interesting dilemma; the divide function is expected to return a quotient and a remainder, but when evaluted lazily, the remainder would only appear after all the terms of the quotient have been consumed. It is often the case that an algorithm calls for one expression to divide another exactly (done by checking that the remainder is zero), and then make use of that quotient, which will by then have all been evaluated, thus it must be reconverted into the lazy form. Quotient and remainder by themsleves create no particular problems.

Extended Functional Programming

The pure functional style advocated in this paper is of course limited to the programmer. When the functions are compiled we can expect for the time being that the usual von Neumann machine is being used, and the code will involve assignment to registers and goto instructions. In an analogous way we can contemplate an extended pure style in which we allow certain object style functions to exist as an aid to efficiency without affecting the overall purity. Indeed the outlawing of side effects makes one of the main extended forms possible. We refer to memo functions.

If whenever a function is evaluated in a environment the result is remembered, for example on an association list connected to the function, it is possible to interrogate this memory before evaluating the function body to see if the value in this environment has been calculated already. It is well known that the use of a memo function can modify the expected computational time in a non-trivial way: for example consider the Fibonacci numbers by the naive program or the f and g series where we will be able to convert the recursive times to the iterative ones.

Conclusions

This paper has presented an experimental pure functional algebra system written n a dialect of LISP that supports functional closure. While there are many experiments outstanding we have already seen that once one has learnt the style it is possible to write reasonably efficient programs in a fairly short time. The use of some normal order reduction gives us a wider means of expression that we have not yet fully exploited. The system is of medium size, amounting to 20 pages of LISP, and so we cannot yet answer the question on the practicability of writing large programs, although we have noticed a marked shortening of the function based code. To write a REDUCE replacement, for example, would take considerably more time and intellectual effort, but we feel that we have learnt lessions that make us hopeful that such a task is not impossible.

Among the plans we have for continuing to develop Parsifal are to make a fully lazy version, and to implement it under Miranda, Turner's most recent version of his combinator-based language. We have given some thought to the problems introduced by a pattern matching capability, and forsee this as an exciting area for research.

We wish to acknowledge our debt to Dr J B Marti for allowing us such free access to the latest version of NLARGE, and Dr A C Norman who first raised the question of the practicability of the functional style.

Figures

```
(De P^ (a n)
  (Cond
    ((MinusP n) (P^ (P1/ a) (Minus n)))
    (t ((Lambda (fn) (fn (PCreate 1) 0))
        (Lambda (aa i)
          (Cond
            ((Eq i n) aa)
            (t (fn (P* aa a) (Add1 i)))))))))
```

Figure 1: Raising a polynomial to a power

```
U : - 3 * mu * sig;
V : eps - 2 * sig^2;
W : - eps * (mu + 2*eps);
DbyDt(x) : U*(x DF mu) + V*(x DF sig) + W*(x DF eps);
f(n) : If (n=0, 1, DbyDt(f(n-1)) - mu*g(n-1));
g(n) : If (n=0, 0, DbyDt(g(n-1)) + f(n-1));
f(12);
End;
```

Figure 2: Program for the f and g series (recursively)

```
v[0] : 1;
g[0] : 1;
for(m, 1, 4,
   << v[m] : Sigma(
                Sigma(f[k-s,s] * a^s * c^(k-s)
                      * Sub(gg, b*s+2*(k-s), g[m-k]),
                      s, 0, k),
                   k, 1, m),
      g[m] : Sigma(((gg+1)*k-m)*v[k]*g[m-k], k, 1, m)/m,
      ans[m] : Sub(gg, -2*b, g[m]) >> );
ans[4];
end;
```

Figure 3: Program for SIGSAM Problem 2

```
diff(a, n) :
  sum(e[i]*(a DF e[i-1]), i, 1, n);

wfac(a, b, c, d) :
  if(a=b,
     if(b=c,
        if(c=d, 1, 4),
        if(c=d, 6, 12)),
     if(b=c,
        if(c=d, 4, 12),
        if(c=d, 12, 24)));

y2[0] : 1;
y2[1] : e[0]/2;
sum2[1] : 0;
for(n, 2, 4, <<
    sum2[n] : Sigma(y2[a]*y2[n-a], a, 1, n-1)/2,
    sum4[n] : Sigma(
                 Sigma(
                    Sigma(if((n-b-c-d)<0,0,
                             if(b<(n-b-c-d),0,
                                -wfac(n-b-c-d,b,c,d) * y2[n-b-c-d]
                                 * y2[b] * y2[c] * y2[d]/2 )),
                          b, 0, c),
                       c, 1, d),
                    d, 1, n-1),
    y2[n] : sum2[n] + sum4[n] + e[0]
            * (sum2[n-1]+y2[n-1]) - diff(diff(y2[n-1], n), n)/4
            - diff(diff(sum2[n-1], n), n)/4 + (5/8)
            * Sigma(diff(y2[a], n)*diff(y2[n-1-a], n), a, 1, n-2)
>> );
end;
```

Figure 4: Program for SIGSAM Problem 3

```
y2[1] : (2*e[0]^3 + 6*e[2]*e[0] + 5*e[1]^2)/32

y2[2] : ( - 5*e[0]^4 - 30*e[2]*e[0]^2 + ( - 50*e[1]^2 - 4*e[4])*e[0]
        - 28*e[3]*e[1] - 19*e[2]^2)/128

y2[3] : (14*e[0]^5 + 140*e[2]*e[0]^3 + (350*e[1]^2 + 40*e[4])*e[0]^2
        + (392*e[3]*e[1] + 266*e[2]^2)*e[0] + 442*e[2]*e[1]^2
        + 36*e[5]*e[1] + 96*e[4]*e[2] + 69*e[3]^2)/512

y2[4] : ( - 42*e[0]^6 - 630*e[2]*e[0]^4 + ( - 2100*e[1]^2
        - 280*e[4])*e[0]^3 + ( - 3528*e[3]*e[1] - 2394*e[2]^2
        - 32*e[6])*e[0]^2 + ( - 7956*e[2]*e[1]^2 - 720*e[5]*e[1]
        - 1784*e[4]*e[2] - 1242*e[3]^2)*e[0] - 1105*e[1]^4
        - 1488*e[4]*e[1]^2 - 5564*e[3]*e[2]*e[1] - 1262*e[2]^3
        - 168*e[6]*e[2] - 366*e[5]*e[3] - 234*e[4]^2)/2048
```

Figure 5: Output for SIGSAM Problem 3

		Parsifal	REDUCE
f and g			
(Recursive)	8	58.72	46.66
	12	972.88	757.46
(Iterative)	8	13.18	14.98
	12	81.92	97.50
	18	576.82	730.26
Y(2n)			
	6	6.50	6.64
	8	14.32	9.84
	10	29.22	15.86
Series Reversion			
(Recursive)	4	202.00	89.52
(Iterative)	4	55.06	46.92

Table 1: Timing Results

References

[Backus78]
J Backus
Can Programming be liberated from the von Neumann style?
Comm ACM 21 p613-41

[Burton82]
F W Burton
Annotations to Control Parallelsm and Reduction Order Control in the distributed evaluation of Functional Programs
(Preprint)

[Burton & Sleep82]
F W Burton and M R Sleep
Executing Functional Programs on a Virtual Tree of Processors
Proc. Conf. Functional Programming Languages and Computer Architecture

[Campbell72]
J A Campbell
SISGAM Problem #2: The Y2n Problem
SIGSAM Bulletin 22 p8-9

[Clarke et al. 80]
T J W Clarke, P J S Gladstone, C D McLean and A C Norman
SKIM - The S, K, I Reduction Machine
Proc. 1980 LISP Conference p128-135

[Darlington & Reeve81]
J Darlington and M Reeve
ALICE: A multiprocessor reduction machine for the parallel evaluation of applicative languages
Proc. ACM Conf. on Functional Programming Languages and Computer Architecture, 1981

[Fitch & Marti82]
J P Fitch and J B Marti
NLARGEing a Z80 Microprocessor
Proc. Eurocam 82, Lecture Notes in Computer Science 144 p249-55

[Fitch83]
J P Fitch
Implementing REDUCE on a Microcomputer
Proc. Eurocal 83, Lecture Notes in Computer Science 162 p128-136

[Fitch & Norman77]
J P Fitch and A C Norman
Implementing LISP in a high level language
Software - Practice and Experience, 7 p713-25

[Johnson74]
S C Johnson
Sparse Polynomial Arithmetic
Proc. EUROSAM 74, SIGSAM Bulletin 8 p63-71

[Keller et al. 79]
R M Keller, G Lindstrom and S Patil
A Loosely-Coupled Applicable Multi-Procesor System
NCC AFIP V 48 p613-22

[Hall73]
A Hall
Solution to SIGSAM Problem #3
SIGSAM Bulletin 26 p15-23

[Griss & Hearn 81]
A C Hearn and M R Griss
The Portable LISP Compiler
Software - Practice and Experience 11 p541-605

[Marti & Fitch83]
J B Marti & J P Fitch
The Bath Concurrent LISP Machine
Proc. Eurocal 83, Lecture Notes in Computer Science 162 p78-90

[Padget82]
J A Padget
Escaping from Intermediate Expression Swell: A Continuing Saga
Proc. Eurocam 82, Lecture Notes in Computer Science 144 p256-62

[Padget83]
J A Padget
The Ecology of LISP, or
The case for the preservation of the environment
Proc. Eurocal 83, Lecture Notes in Computer Science 162 p91-100

[Padget84]
J A Padget
PhD Thesis, University of Bath (in preparation)

[Padget & Fitch]
J A Padget & J P Fitch
Closurize and Concentrate
(in preparation)

[Quam & Diffie68]
L Quam & W Diffie
Stanford LISP 1.6 Manual
Stanford AI Laboratory Operating Note 28.7

[Sconzo et al. 65]
P Sconzo, A Le Shack and R Tobey
Symbolic Computation of f and g series by Computer
Astronomical Journal 70 pp269-71

[Turner79]
D A Turner
A New Implementation Technique for Applicative Languages
Software - Practice and Experience 9 p31-49

[Turner80]
D A Turner
Recursion Equations as a Programming Language
CREST-ITG Advanced Course on Functional Programming and its Applications,
Cambridge University Press (ed. Darlington, Henderson and Turner) p1-28

Appendix: Lazy Johnson's Algorithm (univariate case)

```
% in the following code some functions require explanation:
%    term - leading term of polynomial
%    nterm - reductum of polynomial
%    exp - exponent of a term
%    conz - cons which suspends the second argument

% add polynomials a and b
(de p!+ (a b)
  (cond
    ((numberp a)
     (cond
       ((numberp b) (plus a b))
       (t (conz (term b) (p!+ (nterm b) a)))))
    ((numberp b) (conz (term a) (p!+ (nterm a) b)))
    ((equal (exp (term a)) (exp (term b)))
     (conz (t!+ (term a) (term b)) (p!+ (nterm a) (nterm b))))
    ((lessp (exp (term a)) (exp (term b)))
     (conz (term b) (p!+ a (nterm b))))
    (t (conz (term a) (p!+ (nterm a) b)))))

% multiply polynomials a and b
(de p!* (a b)
  (cond
    ((numberp a)
     (cond
       ((numberp b) (times a b))
       (t (pn!* b a))))
    ((numberp b) (pn!* a b))
    (t (p!+ (tp!* (term a) b) (p!* (nterm a) b)))))

% multiply term and a polynomial
(de tp!* (a p)
  (cond
    ((numberp p) (cons (term a) (times (coeff a) p)))
    (t (conz (t!* a (term p)) (tp!* a (nterm p))))))
```

		Parsifal	REDUCE
f and g			
(Iterative)	5	12.20	4.34
	8	102.38	20.54
Series Reversion			
(Iterative)	3	206.88	13.88
Y(2n)			
	6	43.56	6.64
	8	118.16	9.84
	10	307.14	15.86

Table 2: Timing Results with Lazy Multiplication Algorithm

SOME EFFECTIVITY PROBLEMS IN POLYNOMIAL IDEAL THEORY

by M. GIUSTI

Centre de Mathématiques de l'Ecole Polytechnique
Plateau de Palaiseau - 91128 Palaiseau Cedex (France)
"Laboratoire Associé au C.N.R.S. n° 169"

INTRODUCTION.

Let K be a field of characteristic zero. Consider a homogeneous ideal I in $R = K[x_o,\dots,x_n]$ generated by homogeneous elements $f_1,\dots,f_k$ of degree less than d, and the following problems arising in various areas :

1. Hilbert function of $A = R/I$.

Call $(R/I)_s$ the homogeneous part of degree s of the graded ring R/I ; for s large enough, $\dim_K(R/I)_s$ becomes a polynomial in s (the so-called Hilbert polynomial P(s)). Define :

$$H(I) = \mathrm{Inf}\{s_o \in \mathbb{N} \mid \dim_K(R/I)_s = P(s) \quad \text{for} \quad s \geq s_o\} \quad .$$

What is the smallest upper bound H(n,d) of the H(I)'s for all such ideals ?

2. Standard bases of I.

Choose an order < on the monomials, compatible with products ; call $D_{<,x}(I)$ the largest degree of elements of a minimal standard basis of I (relative to <). What is the smallest upper bound D(n,d) of the D(I)'s for all such ideals ?

3. Resolution of R/I.

Consider the R-module of relations among the generators $f_1,\dots,f_k$, i.e. the kernel of $\Phi : R^k \to R$, where $\Phi(g_1,\dots,g_k) = \sum_{i=1}^{k} f_i g_i$. As usual, R^k is graduated so that Φ is homogeneous of degree 0. What is the smallest integer such that this module can be generated by elements of degree less that it ?

More generally, following the notations of B. Angéniol [A] we can introduce the integers $S_i(I)$ $(0 \leq i \leq n+1)$. Let $L^{\cdot}$ be a R-free resolution of A, each L^i being graduated so that $L^i \to L^{i-1}$ is homogeneous of degree 0 ; choose a basis e^i of L^i ; define $S_i(L^{\cdot},e) = \operatorname{Sup}_{h \in e^i} (\deg h) - i + 1$, and $S_i(I) = \operatorname{Inf}_{L^{\cdot},e} (S_i(L^{\cdot},e))$. Finally $S(I) = \operatorname{Sup}_i S_i(I)$.

What is the smallest upper bound $S(n,d)$ for all such ideals ?

Note that among these integers attached to I, $D_{<,x}(I)$ is not intrinsic, and depends not only on the ordering but also on the choice of coordinates. We shall denote it simply by $D(I)$ if we deal with :

- the lexicographic ordering

$(\alpha_o,\ldots,\alpha_n) <_{lex} (\beta_o,\ldots,\beta_n) \Leftrightarrow \exists\, j \quad (0 \leqslant j \leqslant n)$ such that $\alpha_o = \beta_o,\ldots,\alpha_{j-1} = \beta_{j-1}$ and $\alpha_j < \beta_j$.

The exponent of a polynomial $f = \sum_{\alpha \in \mathbb{N}^{n+1}} f_\alpha x^\alpha$ will be $\exp f = \mathrm{Inf}_{lex}\{\alpha \in \mathbb{N}^{n+1} \mid f_\alpha \neq 0\}$.

- generic coordinates

following the notations of Galligo ([GA 1]), for M in GL(n+1) denote by f^M the polynomial defined by $f^M(x) = f(Mx)$, and by I^M the ideal generated by $f_1^M,\ldots,f_k^M$. As usua we shall say that a property is true for I in generic coordinates if there exists a non-empty Zariski-open subset of GL(n+1) such that for all M in it, the property hold for I^M.

All these integers are strongly related, as shown by :

Theorem A : $-1 + \frac{S(n,d)}{2^{n-1}} < S_2(n,d) \leqslant D(n,d) = H(n,d) \leqslant S(n,d) + n.$

The knowledge of this common upper bound (say $D(n,d)$) is essential for these effectivity problems ; computing it exactly seems to be a huge task. Nevertheless we have the following asymptotic behaviour :

Theorem B : $D(n,d)$ is bounded by a polynomial in d, with leading term $6^{2^{n-3}} d^{3.2^{n-3}}$ (for $n \geqslant 3$).

On the other hand a family of examples of Mayr-Meyer [M-M] shows that for an infinite number of values of n this double exponentially growth of $D(n,d)$ cannot be avoided. So it seems natural to introduce the real a

$$a = \mathrm{Inf}\,\{a \mid D(n,d) \leqslant O(d^{a^n}) \qquad n \to +\infty\}$$

Refinements lead to the bounds

$$2^{1/10} = 1.07\ \ldots \leqslant a \leqslant 1.72\ \ldots = \sqrt{3}\ .$$

The same number characterizes the asymptotic behaviour of $S_i(n,d)$ for arbitrary i, and of $S(n,d)$.

In last part we consider analogous problems for non necessarily homogeneous ideals, proving weaker affine versions of Lazard's results [L 2] ; this leads to a pleasant generic linear bound for H(I), D(I) and S(I), contrasting with the double exponentally asymptotic growth of the universal bound. More precisely :

Theorem C : In the finite-dimensional vector space parametrizing the ideals of $K[x_o,\dots,x_n]$ generated by k polynomials of degree less than d, there exists a non-empty Zariski-open subset where H, D and S are bounded by $(n+1)d - n$.

Many thanks to B. Angéniol and D. Lazard for fruitful conversations, and to the referees for pointing out several dark statements.

I - STANDARD BASES AND THE COMPUTATION OF HILBERT FUNCTIONS.

In this part we will deal with the lexicographic ordering on monomials of $K[x_o,\dots,x_n]$, unless specified. The degree $|A|$ of $(A_o,\dots,A_n)$ is $A_o + \dots + A_n$.

1.1 Let E be a subset of $\mathbb{N}^{n+1}$, stable under addition of quadrants ; there exists a finite minimal family S(E) of elements of E, $A^{(1)} < A^{(2)} < \dots < A^{(q)}$ (the stairs of E) such that

$$E = \bigcup_{i=1}^{q} (A^{(i)} + \mathbb{N}^{n+1}) \quad .$$

An example is provided by the subset E(I) of exponents of all elements of a non zero homogeneous ideal $I \subset K[x_o,\dots,x_n]$; a family of elements $f_1,\dots,f_q$ of I which exponents build the stairs of E(I) is called a (minimal) standard basis of I. Define D(E) as $\mathrm{Sup}\,\{|A| \mid A \in S(E)\}$, and naturally for an arbitrary subset of $\mathbb{N}^{n+1}$, its Hilbert function as

$$H_E(s) = \#\,\{A \notin E,\ |A| = s\} \quad .$$

Recall a result of Galligo ([GA 1]), théorème 2) :

1.2 Theorem : There exists a non-empty Zariski-open subset U of GL(n+1) such that $E(I^M)$ is contant for $M \in U$.

We shall from now on use freely combinatorial properties of stairs of ideals for generic coordinates ("generic stairs") stated by Galligo (loc. cit.). For example such generic stairs have a particular shape : consider their sections by 2-dimensional planes obtained by fixing the values of all coordinates except two. Then these stairs of $\mathbb{N}^2$ have steps of height 1 (for precise statements see loc. cit. § 4, A and B).

1.3 For generic coordinates $x_o,\dots,x_{\dim A-1}$ (resp. $x_o,\dots,d_{\mathrm{depth}\, A-1}$) form a sequence of parameters of A (resp. a maximal regular sequence).

We need then the following characterization of dimension and depth of local rings: for a subset $E\subset \mathbb{N}^{n+1}$ stable under addition of quadrants define :

$$d(E) = \mathrm{Sup}\ \{r \mid S(E) \cap (\mathbb{N}^{\{0,\dots,r-1\}}\times\{0\}^{\{r,\dots,n\}}) = \emptyset\}$$

$$p(E) : \mathrm{Sup}\ \{r \mid S(E) \subset (\{0\}^{\{0,\dots,r-1\}} \times \mathbb{N}^{\{r,\dots,n\}})\} .$$

Proposition : Let I be a homogeneous ideal of $K[x_o,\dots,x_n]$. For generic coordinates we have :

$$\dim\ (K[x_o,\dots,x_n]/I) = d(E(I))$$

$$\mathrm{depth}\ (K[x_o,\dots,x_n]/I) = p(E(I)) .$$

Example :

$d(E) = 1$

$p(E) = 0$

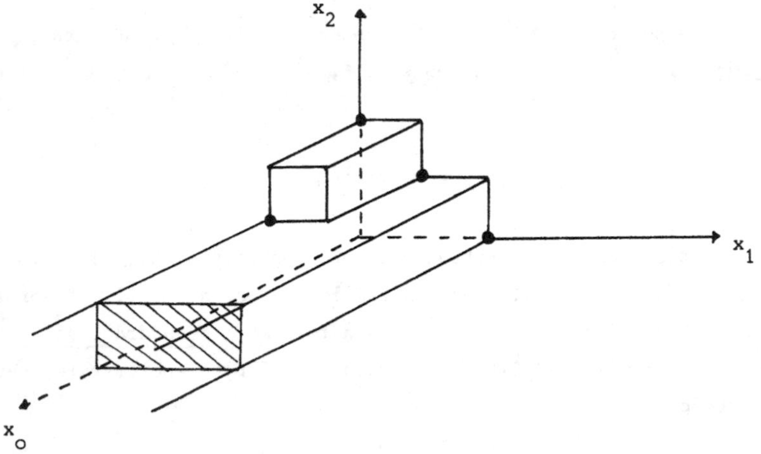

Proof of the proposition : By induction on n, using

$$E(I+(x_o,\dots,x_{r-1})) = E(I) \cap (\{0\}^{\{0,\dots,r-1\}}\times\mathbb{N}^{\{r,\dots,n\}}) .$$

If $S(E)\subset\{0\}\times\mathbb{N}^{\{1,\dots,n\}}$, then x_o is a non zero divisor in $K[x_o,\dots,x_n]/I$, $x_o f\in I$ implies that the exponent of the remainder of the division of f by I is simultaneously in E(I) (hypothesis on S(E)) and not in E(I) (division theorem of Hironaka), hence zero. Conversely, in generic coordinates : if the depth is non zero, x_o is a non zero divisor and trivially $S(E)\subset\{0\}\times\mathbb{N}^{\{1,\dots,n\}}$. x_o is a parameter in $K[x_o,\dots,x_n]/I$ if and only if $S(E)\cap(\mathbb{N}^{\{0\}}\times\{0\}^{\{1,\dots,n\}}) = \emptyset$ (Nullstellensatz). Furthermore in generic coordinates if the dimension is non zero, then x_o is a parameter.

1.4 Remark : As a consequence of the division theorem of Hironaka, the Hilbert function $\dim_K A_s$ is the Hilbert function of the set $E(I)$.

1.5 Proposition : For generic coordinates, the Hilbert function $H_{E(I)}(s)$ becomes a polynomial $P_{E(I)}(s)$ when $s \geq D(E(I)) - \text{depth}\,(R/I)$.

1.5.1 The proof goes by induction on $\dim(R/I) - \text{depth}\,(R/I)$. Call $E_i \subset \mathbb{N}^n$ the section $E \cap \{x_o = i\}$, i_o the first index such that E_i becomes constant ($= E_\infty$) for $i \geq i_o$.

If depth $(R/I) \geq 1$, x_o is a non zero divisor in R/I, and $H(I + x_o) = H(I) + 1$, as can be easily seen on the exact sequence $0 \to A \xrightarrow{x_o} A \to A/x_oA$. But $D(I + i_o) = D(I)$ by 1.3.

If depth $(R/I) = 0$, by a property of generic stairs stated in ([GA]1 Lemme § 4,B) we have, following the notations (loc. cit.) :

$$\mathbb{N}^{n+1} - E(I) = B_{n+1} \amalg (\mathbb{N}^{n+1} - \mathbb{N} \times \pi_o(E_\infty))$$

where B_{n+1} is finite non empty, and π_o is the canonical projection $\mathbb{N}^{n+1} \to \{0\} \times \mathbb{N}^n$.
Thus $H_{E(I)}(s) = H_{\mathbb{N}^{n+1}-B_{n+1}}(s) + H_{\mathbb{N} \times \pi_o(E_\infty)}(s)$ and $P_{E(I)}(s) = P_{\mathbb{N} \times \pi_o(E_\infty)}(s)$.
We have now to study more carefully Hilbert functions of zero-dimensional R/I.

1.5.2 Lemma : If $\dim\,(R/I)$ is zero, then $D(I)$ and $H(I)$ are equal.

By 1.3 $E(I)$ has a finite complementary, hence each E_i also. So $S(E)$ (resp. $S(E_i)$) contains a point A on the x_o-axis (resp. a point $A^{(i)}$ on the x_1-axis). I say that $|A|$ is $D(E)$ ((by induction on n. This is empty for $n = 0$. Then all $A^{(i)}$ form 2-dimensional stairs in $\mathbb{N}^2$; by the property stated in 1.2, $i + D(E_i)$ is a growing function of i, so we are done.)) Moreover all points of $\mathbb{N}^{n+1} - E$ have degrees strictly less than $D(E)$; hence $H_E(s)$ is zero for $s \geq D(E)$. On the other hand $H_E(D(E) - 1) > 0$, as shown by a local study in the neighborhood of A. So 1.5.2 is proved.

1.5.3 End of the proof of 1.5 : By a similar argument to 1.5.2, all points of B_{n+1} have degrees strictly less than $D(E)$; now we conclude by induction on dim A. If $\dim A = 0$, $\mathbb{N}^{n+1} - E(I)$ is reduced to B_{n+1}, so apply 1.5.2. If not, $H_{E(I)}(s)$ is equal to $H_{\mathbb{N} \times \pi_o(E_\infty)}(s)$ for $s \geq D(E)$ since $H_{\mathbb{N}^{n+1}-B_{n+1}}(s)$ is zero, and then to $P_{\mathbb{N} \times \pi_o(E_\infty)}(s)$ ($= P_{E(I)}(s)$) since $\mathbb{N}^n - \pi_o(E_\infty)$ is obtained by substracting from $\mathbb{N}^n - E_o$ a finite subset $\pi_o(B_{n+1})$; so $D(\pi_o(E_\infty)) \leq D(E_o) \leq D(E)$.

1.5.4 Remark : For $H(I) \leq D(I)$ we can deduce another proof from ([L2], proof of theorem 2).

1.6 Call ${}^{r}I$ the ideal generated by I and $x_o,\dots,x_{r-1}$. Recall

<u>Proposition</u> ([A] 3.3.28) : $D(I) = \sup_{\text{depth } A \leqslant r \leqslant \dim A} H({}^{r}I)$.

Let us give a proof by induction on dim A - depth A based on the preceding properties of generic stairs.
Using 1.3, define $D_i(I)$ as $\operatorname{Sup}\{|A| \mid A \in S(E(I)),\ A \notin \{0\}^{\{0,\dots,i\}} \times \mathbb{N}^{\{i+1,\dots,n\}}\}$ (depth $A = p \leqslant i \leqslant n$) so that $D(I) = \sup_{p\leqslant i\leqslant n} D_i(I)$.
Reduce to the depth 0 cutting by the maximal regular sequence $x_o,\dots,x_{p-1}$:

$$D(I) = D^{p}I) = \operatorname{Sup}\,(D_p(I), D({}^{p+1}I)) \quad .$$

The computation of $H_{E({}^{p}I)}$ given in 1.5.1 yields

$$H({}^{p}I) \begin{cases} = D_p(I) & \text{if} \quad D_p(I) \geqslant D({}^{p+1}I) \\ \leqslant H({}^{p+1}I) - 1 & \text{if} \quad D_p(I) < D({}^{p+1}I) \end{cases} \quad .$$

We conclude by induction on $\dim(R/{}^{p}I)$ starting from 1.5.2.

1.7 From 1.5 and 1.6 we deduce $H(n,d) = D(n,d)$.

II - <u>MODULE OF RELATIONS AMONG GENERATORS OF STANDARD BASES AND ALGORITHMS OF CONSTRUCTION.</u>

2.1 A general philosophy says how these two points are related. Given a standard basis $(f_1,\dots,f_q)$ of I, it is easy to find relations among $f_1,\dots,f_q$ by lifting relations among $\exp f_1,\dots,\exp f_q$ (since $K[x_o,\dots,x_n]/I$ is a flat deformation of the associated graded ring quotient by the initial ideal, by the general result of Gerstenhaber [GE]).

Conversely, a description of generators of this module of relations provides an algorithm to construct a standard basis from given generators. Thus the description of Schreyer [S] corresponds to S-polynomials in Buchberger's algorithm [BU 1]: the description of Briançon-Galligo [BG], Galligo [GA 2] corresponds to forbidden products of Galligo (loc. cit.). The improvement given by Buchberger of his algorithm in [BU 2] corresponds also to this last case.

2.2 Let $f_1,\dots,f_q$ be a standard basis of an homogeneous ideal $I \subset K[x_o,\dots,x_n]$ $(n \geqslant 1)$, relative to lexicographic ordering and generic coordinates. Let A be an element of S(E) (1.1). In any 2-dimensional stairs passing through A the <u>predecessor</u> of A is well defined by the lexicographic ordering ; so define the predecessors of A in S(E) (maximum number $\binom{n+1}{2}$).

Let B be a predecessor of A in S(E) : an obvious bilateral relation between the corresponding elements g and f of the standard basis is obtained by lifting the obvious relation between the monomial initial forms $g_B x^B$ and $f_A x^A$. Notice that the degree of this relation is $|A| + 1$ from the property stated in 1.2. Since these last relations generate all relations of the initial ideal $(x^A)_{A \in S(E)}$ we get the following refinement of Schreyer's theorem :

2.3 Theorem : With the notations and assumptions of 2.2, the module of relations among $f_1,\dots,f_q$ is generated by the obvious bilateral relations.

2.4 Remark : With the notations of 2.2, lifting the relation $g_{\exp} \, x^{\exp f \vee \exp g - \exp f} \, in(f) = f_{\exp f} \, x^{\exp f \vee \exp g - \exp g} \, in(g)$ consists to divide the S-polynomial (Buchberger's notation) $S(f,g) = g_{\exp g} \, x^{\exp f \vee \exp g - \exp f} \, f - f_{\exp f} \, x^{\exp f \vee \exp g - \exp g} \, g$ by $f_1,\dots,f_q$ using Hironaka's division algorithm (see the presentations of Bayer [BA] or Galligo [GA 2]).

2.5 Conversely we get the following algorithm to build a standard basis from a given set of generators $f_1,\dots,f_k$ of degrees $d_1 \leqslant \dots \leqslant d_k = d$.

Algorithm : Assume we built the output polynomials in degree less than i. For every pair consisting of one of them (of degree i) and one of its predecessors (if they exist), say (f,g), divide S(f,g) by all previously obtained output polynomials of degree < i. Add to all remainders (of degree i+1) the input polynomials of degree i+1. Expand them on the natural basis of all monomials of degree i+1. The triangulation of their matrix gives the output polynomials in degree i+1.

2.6 Theorem : Under the notations and assumptions of 2.5 the described algorithm yields a (minimal) standard basis of I, which furthermore contains elements in each degree between d and D.

2.7 Idea of the proof of 2.6 : The output polynomials form a standard basis by an argument similar to Buchberger's original one [BU 1] ; it is minimal for a simple matter of degree, and contains elements in each degree between d and D by 2.2 and 2.3.

2.8 Proposition : $S_i(I) \leqslant 2^{i-2}(D(I)+1) - i+1 \quad (i \geqslant 2)$.

$S_2(I) \leqslant D(I)$ is an immediate corollary of 2.3 ; as the obvious bilateral relations form again a standard basis for the module of relations (see e.g. [MO-MO 1] 7.8),

$S_3(I) \leq 2D(I)$ (and conjecturally $D(I)$ if we can transmit genericity).

2.9 Proposition ([A] 3.4.7) : $H(I) \leq \mathrm{Sup}\,\{S_i(I) + i-1 \mid 1 \leq i \leq dh(R/I)\}$.

The proof consists to compute explicitly the Hilbert function of R/I on a free resolution.

2.10 The theorem A follows then from 1.7, 2.8 and 2.9.

Question : Do we have exactly $S(n,d) = D(n,d)$?

2.11 Proof of theorem B : Consider the decomposition of $\mathbb{N}^{n+1} - E(I)$ used in 1.5.1. The volume of $\pi_o(B_{n+1})$ is at most $\prod_{r=o}^{n-1} D({}^rI)$. Call $k(\delta)$ the number $\#\,\{A \in S(E) \mid A_o \neq 0\,,\ |A| = \delta\}$; then $\mathrm{Vol}\ \pi_o(B_{n+1}) \geq \sum_{\delta=d_1}^{D(I)} k(\delta)$. If $D_{n+1}(I) = D(I)$ (see 1.6) this is $\geq D(I) - D({}^1I)$ by 2.6. Finally in all cases we get :

2.11.1 $$D(I) \leq D({}^1I) + D({}^1I) \ldots D({}^nI)$$

and the induction relation on n

$$D(n,d) \leq D(n-1,d) + D(n-1,d) \ldots D(0,d) \quad .$$

At the beginning $D(0,d) \leq d$, $D(1,d) \leq 2d-1$ ([BU 2]), [L2] or 3.9), $D(2,d) \leq 3d-2$ ([L2]) so e.g. $D(3,d) \leq (3d-2)(2d^2-d+1) = 6d^3-7d^2+5d-2$ and $D(n,d)$ is bounded by a polynomial in d with leading term $6^{2^{n-3}}\, d^{3.2^{n-3}}$ $(n \geq 3)$.

2.11.2 Instead of doing induction on n, we can try on the dimension. Define $D(n,d,\delta)$ as the maximum of the $D(I)$'s for all I generated by polynomials in $K[x_o,\ldots x_n]$ of degree less than d such that $\dim(R/I) = \delta$. Then 2.11.1 yields

$$D(n,d,\delta) \leq D(n-1,d,\delta-1) + \prod_{i=1}^{\delta-1} D(n-i,d,\delta-i) \prod_{i=\delta}^{n} D(n-i,d,0) \quad .$$

At the beginning $D(n,d,0) \leq (n+1)d - n$ ([L2] or 3.9). For example a not yet known bound will be :

$$D(n,d,2) \leq n!\, d^n + \ldots . \qquad (n \geq 3)$$

(for $n = 3$ similar results are given by Galligo).

2.11.3 <u>Question</u> : Do we have $\mathrm{Vol}(\pi_o(B_{n+1})) \leq \frac{1}{n!} \prod_{r=1}^{n} D({}^{r}I)$?

This will allow to gain a factor $\frac{1}{n!}$ in the asymptotic leading term, but will unfortunately not change the bound 2 for the ratio a defined in the introduction.

2.12 Let M be a submodule of R^t, generated by elements of degree less than d. Call $E(t,n+1,d)$ the smallest integer so that the module of solutions of the system defined by M, i.e. the kernel of the canonical map $R^t \to R^t/M$, can be generated by elements of degree less than $E(t,n+1,d)$.

<u>Proposition</u> (D. Lazard) : $H(n,d) \leq E(n+1,n+1,d)$.

As $E(t,n+1,d) = O((td)^k)$ $(d \to +\infty)$ with $k = \text{cte}.\ 3^{n/2}$ ([L2], proposition 8) a is upper bounded by $\sqrt{3}$.

2.13 <u>Sketch of proof 2.12</u> : Let x be a generic element of R_1.

$$\begin{aligned} C(I) &\overset{\text{def.}}{=} \mathrm{Sup}\ \{\deg y \mid y \in \mathrm{Ann}\ x = \mathrm{Ker}\ R/I \xrightarrow{x} R/I\} \\ &= \mathrm{Sup}\ \{\deg y \mid y \in \mathrm{Ann}(x_o,\dots,x_n)\} \\ &\leq E(n+1,n+1,d) \quad . \end{aligned}$$

But $H(n,d) = \mathrm{Sup}_I\ C(I)$ ([A], 3.3.28).

2.14 On the other hand, the slightly modified examples of [M-M] yield a family of ideals in 10m+3 variables such that $S_2 \geq (d-2)^{2^m}$ (Lazard, Lecture in Ecole Polytechnique, march 1984). So $a \geq 2^{1/10}$. (Compare with the weaker affine result of [MO-MO 2] in view of 3.2).

2.15 A final word on $D_{<,x}(n,d)$ for an arbitrary choice of ordering and coordinates.

<u>Proposition</u> : $H(n,d) \leq (n+1)\ D_{<,x}(n,d)$
$S_2(n,d) \leq 2\ D_{<,x}(n,d)$.

In particular the double exponentially asymptotic growth of $D_{<,x}$ is unavoidable.

III - AFFINE PROBLEMS.

3.1 Deshomogeneizing the lexicographic ordering of $\mathbb{N}^{n+1}$ gives the diagonal ordering of $\mathbb{N}$ (setting $x_o = 1$), with which we will deal exclusively in this part :

$$\alpha = (\alpha_1,\ldots,\alpha_n) > (\beta_1,\ldots,\beta_n) = \beta \iff \begin{array}{l} \text{i) } |\alpha| > |\beta| \\ \text{ii) } |\alpha| = |\beta| \text{ and } \exists\ i, 1 \leqslant i \leqslant n \end{array},$$

such that $\alpha_n = \beta_n, \ldots, \alpha_{i+1} = \beta_{i+1}$, $\alpha_i > \beta_i$.

Take as exponent of $f = \sum_{\alpha \in \mathbb{N}^n} f_\alpha x^\alpha \in K[x_1,\ldots,x_n]$, $\exp f = \sup \{\alpha \mid f_\alpha \neq 0\}$. In the same way as before we can define for a (non zero) ideal I of $K[x_1,\ldots,x_n]$, E(I), the stairs of I, a standard basis of I, and $D_x(I)$. $E(I^M)$ is constant on a non-empty Zariski-open subset of GL(n). Call D(I) the corresponding value of $D_x(I)$.

Assume from now on that I generated by $f_1,\ldots,f_k$ of total degree $\leqslant$ d.

3.2 In this affine situation, several unpleasant phenomena can happen : constructing a standard basis by anyone of the algorithms yields not necessarily a minimal one ; and another trouble is that the hyperplane at infinity $\{x_o = 0\}$ is fixed thus not necessarily in generic position : i.e. considering the ideal I generated by the homogeneized $\tilde{f}_1,\ldots,\tilde{f}_k$, we cannot deal with generic coordinates.

3.3 Illustration of 3.2 (ex. of Mora)

$I = (x_2^4, x_1^3 x_2 - 1)$

$\tilde{I} = (x_2^4, x_1^3 x_2 - x_o^4)$

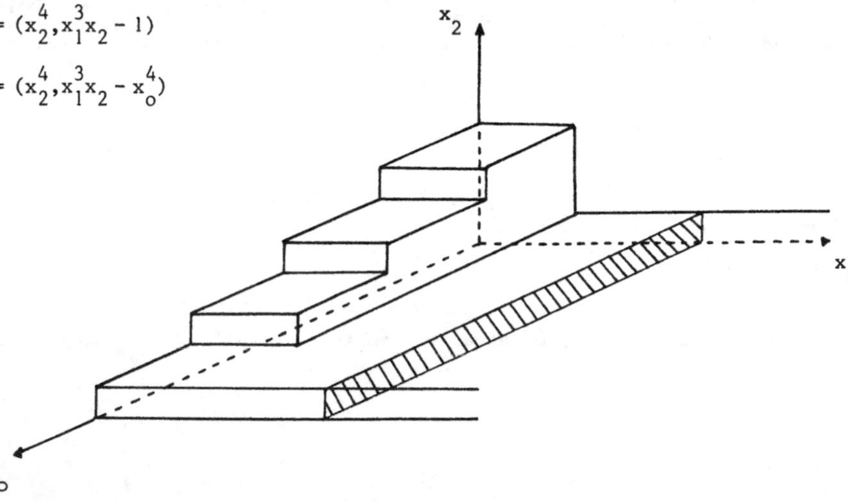

Standard basis of $\tilde{I}$ (automatically minimal) :

$$(x_2^4 , x_1^3x_2 - x_o^4 , x_o^4x_2^3 , x_o^8x_2^2 , x_o^{12}x_2 , x_o^{16}) \quad , \quad \text{so} \quad D_x(\tilde{I}) = 16 \quad .$$

But we shall see further that $D(\tilde{I})$ is actually 7 (3.9).

Building a standard basis of I :

$$(x_2^4 , x_1^3x_2 - 1 , x_2^3 , x_2^2 , x_2 , 1) \quad .$$

Minimal standard basis of I : (1), so $D(I) = 0$. But the maximal degree of intermediate computations is 4. How the affine situation and its homogeneization are related ?

3.4 Let $\tilde{f}_1,\dots,\tilde{f}_q$ be a standard basis of $\tilde{I}$; $A^{(1)},\dots,A^{(q)}$ generate $E(\tilde{I})$. To every $A^{(i)} = (A_o^{(i)},\dots,A_n^{(i)})$ is associated an $\tilde{f}_i$; consider $\tilde{g}_i = x_o^{-A_o^{(i)}} \tilde{f}_i$, and the ideal $\tilde{N}_\infty$ generated by the $\tilde{g}_i$'s.

$E_i(\tilde{I})$ (1.5.1) becomes constant ($= E_\infty(\tilde{I})$) for large i and is minimally generated by $B^{(1)},\dots,B^{(s)}$. To every B corresponds an element A of $S(E(\tilde{I}))$, hence an element $\tilde{g}$; call $\tilde{R}_\infty$ the ideal generated by all these $\tilde{g}$'s. Moreover $B^{(1)},\dots,B^{(s)}$ generate $E(\tilde{R}_\infty)$: if $h = \Sigma\ \lambda_i\ \tilde{g}_i$, as $x_o^i h$ is in $\tilde{I}$ for large i, $\pi_o(\exp h)$ is in $\bigcup_{i=1}^{s} B^{(i)} + \mathbb{N}^{n+1}$.

Finally consider the ascending chain of the ideals $\tilde{T}_i = (\tilde{I} : x_o^i)$ becoming constant ($= \tilde{T}_\infty$) for large i.

3.5 <u>Theorem</u> : With notations of 3.4, $\tilde{R}_\infty$, $\tilde{N}_\infty$ and $\tilde{T}_\infty$ coincide and define the projective closure of the affine variety defined by I. The $\tilde{g}$'s (resp. their deshomogeneizations g's) corresponding to $B^{(1)},\dots,B^{(s)}$ form a minimal standard basis of $\tilde{T}_\infty$ (resp. of I).

3.6 <u>Proof of 3.5</u> : Obviously $\tilde{R}_\infty \subset \tilde{N}_\infty \subset \tilde{T}_\infty$. Now if $x_o^i h$ is in $\tilde{I}$ for large i, so is $x_o^i r$ where r is the remainder of the division of h by $\tilde{R}_\infty$; $B^{(1)},\dots,B^{(s)}$ generating $E(\tilde{R}_\infty)$, r has to be zero. As $x_o^i\tilde{T}_\infty \subset \tilde{I} \subset \tilde{T}_\infty$, their deshomogeneizations coincide with I, and $B^{(1)},\dots,B^{(s)}$ generate $E(I)$.

3.7 <u>Remark</u> : Consider now the suitably modified algorithm 2.5 for homogeneous ideals in non necessarilly generic coordinates (it corresponds to the homogeneous Buchberger's algorithm restricted to "essential pairs" with "normal selection strategy" (Buchberger's terminology)). It provides a minimal standard basis for $\tilde{I}$; setting $x_o = 1$ we obtain an algorithm building $B_1,\dots,B_s$ and the corresponding minimal standard basis of I. In particular the degrees of all intermediate computations are bounded by $D(\pi_o(E(\tilde{I}))) = D(E_\infty(\tilde{I}))$ hence by $D(\tilde{I})$. This shows exactly how the construction of an affine standard basis is as difficult as the general case for homogeneous one.

3.8 Example : If the dimension of the variety defined by I in an algebraic closure of K is negative (resp. 0), degrees of elements of a minimal standard basis are 0 (resp. at most d^n) ; but studying an upper bound for degrees of intermediate computations is exactly solving the problem of affine elimination, on which nothing is known in general, except special cases ([BU 2], [L2]).

3.9 Our aim is now to give a proof without homological algebra of weaker affine version of these last results of Lazard (loc. cit.), using only 3.5 and 3.7.

Theorem : Let I a non necessarily homogeneous ideal in $K[x_1,\dots,x_n]$, generated by $f_1,\dots,f_k$ of degree $\leq d$. Consider the homogeneized $\tilde{f}_1,\dots,\tilde{f}_k$ generating $\tilde{I}$ in $K[x_o,\dots,x_n]$; assume the coordinates $x_o,\dots,x_n$ are generic (which implies in particular that the hyperplane at infinity is in generic position).

If $K[x_o,\dots,x_n]/\tilde{I}$ is Cohen-Macaulay, or if dim $K[x_o,\dots,x_n]/\tilde{I}$ is one, then the degrees of a minimal standard basis of I are at most $1+c(d-1)$, where c is the codimension of the graded ring $K[x_o,\dots,x_n]/\tilde{I}$. The same bound holds for all intermediate computed elements when constructing an affine standard basis of I.

3.10 Proof of 3.9.

3.10.1 Degrees of elements of a standard basis of a homogeneous ideal L of maximal height c in $K[x_1,\dots,x_c]$ are at most $1+c(d-1)$: extracting a regular sequence of maximal length from L, we generate $J\subset L$; and $D(L)\leq D(J)$. But by 1.5.2, D(J) is equal to H(J) ; the resolution of $K[x_1,\dots,x_c]/J$ by the Koszul complex says that H(J) depends only on the degrees of the generators of J, and may be computed easily with the special case $(x_1^d,\dots,x_c^d)$: $1+c(d-1)$.

3.10.2 Assume $K[x_o,\dots,x_n]/\tilde{I}$ is Cohen-Macaulay ; by the characterization of depth 1.3 this case is reduced to the previous one, cutting by a regular sequence of maximal length.

3.10.3 dim $K[x_o,\dots,x_n]/\tilde{I}=1$; x_o is a parameter, thus $E(I+x_o)$ is of maximal height and $D(I+x_o)\leq(n+1)d-n$. As the affine stairs of I are under $S(I+x_o)$, we are done.

3.11 Proof of theorem C : k generic combinations define a complete intersection, so apply 3.10.1 for H and D. The same bound is given for S by the Koszul complex.

REFERENCES

[A] B. ANGÉNIOL, Résidus et effectivité, Preprint Centre de Mathématiques de l'Ecole Polytechnique, 1984.

[BA] D. BAYER, The division algorithm and the Hilbert scheme, PhD thesis, Harvard, Mass., USA (1982).

[BU 1] B. BUCHBERGER, Ein algorithmisches Kriterium für die Lösbarkeit eines algebraischen Gleichungssystems, Aequat. math. 4 (1970), 374-383.

[BU 2] B. BUCHBERGER, A criterion for detecting unnecessary reductions in the construction of Gröbner bases, Eurosam 79, Lect. Notes in Computer Science 72 (1979), 3-21, Springer Verlag.

[BG] J. BRIANÇON, A. GALLIGO, Déformations de points de $\mathbb{R}^2$ ou $\mathbb{C}^2$, Astérisque n° 7-8 (1973), 129-138.

[GA 1] A. GALLIGO, A propos du théorème de préparation de Weierstrass, Lect. Notes in Mathematics 409 (1973), 543-579, Springer Verlag.

[GA 2] A. GALLIGO, Algorithmes de calcul de bases standard, Preprint, Université de Nice, Math. n° 9 (1983).

[GE] M. GERSTENHABER, On the deformations of rings and algebras, Ann. of Math. 79, 1 (1964).

[GI] M. GIUSTI, Bases standard et profondeur, Journées Calcul Formel, Luminy (1983), à paraître dans CALSYF.

[L 1] D. LAZARD, Algèbre linéaire sur $K[x_1,\ldots,x_n]$ et élimination, Bull. Soc. Math. France, 105 (1977), 165-190.

[L 2] D. LAZARD, Gröbner bases, Gaussian elimination and resolution of systems of algebraic equations, Eurocam 83, to appear in Lect. Notes in Computer Sciences (Springer).

[M-M] E. MAYR , A. MEYER, The complexity of the word problems for commutative semi-groups and polynomial ideals, Adv. in Maths. 46 (1982), 305-329.

[MO-MO 1] H. MÖLLER, F. MORA, New constructive methods in classical ideal theory, Preprint, Fernuniversität Hagen, RFA.

[MO-MO 2] H. MÖLLER, F. MORA, Upper and lower bounds for the degree of Gröbner bases, These proceedings.

[S] F.O. SCHREYER, Die Berechnung von Syzygien mit dem verallgemeinerten Weierstrassschen Divisionsatz und eine Anwendung auf analytische Cohen-Macaulay Stellenalgebren minimaler Multiplizität, Diplomarbeit am Fachbereich Mathematik der Universität Hamburg (1980).

UPPER AND LOWER BOUNDS FOR THE DEGREE OF GROEBNER BASES

H.Michael Möller
FernUniversität Hagen
FB Mathematik und Informatik
Hagen, BRD

Ferdinando Mora
Università di Genova
Istituto di Matematica
Genova, Italy

The problem of the complexity of Buchberger's algorithm to compute Gröbner bases has been recently studied by Buchberger [2,3],Bayer[1],and Lazard[7].
Here we present some results on this question,by giving both lower and upper bounds for the maximal degree of the elements of a Gröbner basis of a polynomial ideal,as a function of the degree of a general basis,the number of variables and the dimension of the ideal.
To know the complexity of Buchberger's algorithm,the knowledge of a bound for the degree of the Gröbner basis is not sufficient:also a bound for the degree of the polynomials arising during the intermediate computations is required.Unfortunately we are able to obtain such a bound only under assumptions on the input basis (namely,an H-basis of the ideal must be known).
Our lower bounds are obtained by two classes of examples:
i) in the first one,we present ideals in n variables,which have a Gröbner basis with maximal degree d under a total degree ordering,while under a different total degree ordering (or,after a suitable linear changement of coordinates:just a renaming of the variables) their Gröbner basis contains an element of degree d^{n-1}.Lazard [7] proved that under a total degree ordering the degree bound of a Gröbner basis is linear in the degree of the input basis,if a suitable linear change of coordinates is performed. Our examples show that this condition is unavoidable.
ii) the second class of examples is more related with a kind of basis (H-basis) which has weaker properties than a Gröbner basis and which is widely studied in classical constructive ideal theory.In her well-known paper[6],Hermann gave an incorrect proof that the maximal degree of an H-basis is doubly exponential in the number of variables Here we adapt an example by Mayr and Meyer[8] to show the existence of ideals such that any H-basis (and henceforth any Gröbner basis under a degree compatible term-ordering) contains elements whose degree is doubly exponential in the dimension of the ideal.
As for upper bounds,Bayer[1] proved that the degree of a Gröbner basis is bounded by a coefficient (under a suitable representation) of the Hilbert polynomial of the ideal (the use of Hilbert polynomials to give a bound to the degree of a Gröbner basis has

been suggested also by Lazard in a preliminary version of [7]). By improving on Bayer's result, we are able to prove that the degree of any Gröbner basis is polynomially bounded by the degree of the input basis (the same can be proved for the intermediate polynomials if the input basis is an H-basis) and, under the same conjecture used in [7] we are able to give the explicit bound:

$$\left((n+1)(d+1)+1 \right)^{(n+1)2^{s+1}}$$

d the degree of the input basis, n the number of variables, s the dimension of the ideal. Also the paper contains a simplification to Buchberger's algorithm in the case the input basis is an H-basis.

I - PRELIMINARIES AND MISCELLANEA

1 BUCHBERGER'S ALGORITHM FOR HOMOGENEOUS IDEALS

1.1 If $f \in k[X_1,\dots,X_n]$, denote $M_H(f)$ the homogeneous form of maximal degree appearing in f; for an ideal I denote $M_H(I)$ the ideal generated by $\{M_H(f) : f \text{ in } I\}$.
A basis $\{f_1,\dots,f_r\}$ of I is called H-basis of I iff $\{M_H(f_1),\dots,M_H(f_r)\}$ is a basis of $M_H(I)$ .or, equivalently, iff for each f in I, f can be represented : $f = \Sigma g_i f_i$ and $\deg(g_i f_i) \leqslant \deg(f)$ for each i.
An ideal is called homogeneous iff it is such that if $f \in I$ also the homogeneous summands of f are in I, or equivalently iff it has a basis consisting of homogeneous elements; such a basis is then an H-basis.

1.2 In the following we aim to show how Buchberger's algorithm can be improved when a Gröbner basis is computed for an ideal of which an H-basis is known, with respect to a degree compatible term-ordering $<_T$ (i.e. s.t. $\deg(m_1) < \deg(m_2)$ implies $m_1 <_T m_2$). We will use the notations of [2] and suppose a normal selection strategy [4] is used to choose pairs in B.

1.3 LEMMA *If* $G:=\{f_1,\dots,f_r\}$ *is an H-basis of* I and for each $\{i,j\}$: $1 \leqslant i < j \leqslant r$ *s.t.* $\deg(H(i,j)) < d$, $SP(f_i,f_j) \xrightarrow[G]{*} 0$, *then if* f *is in* I *and* $\deg(f) < d$, $f \xrightarrow[G]{*} 0$.

Proof: $f = \sum_{j=1}^{u} a_j m_j f_{i_j}$, a_j in k , m_j terms, $m_1 H(i_1) \geqslant_T m_2 H(i_2) \geqslant_T \dots \geqslant_T m_u H(i_u)$.

Let $v \leqslant u$ s.t. $j \leqslant v$ iff $m_1 H(i_1) = m_j\ H(i_j)$. Then:

$$f = \left(\sum_{j=1}^{v} a_j\right) m_1 f_{i_1} + \sum_{j=2}^{v} a_j (m_j f_{i_j} - m_1 f_{i_1}) + \sum_{j>v} a_j m_j f_{i_j} = \left(\sum_{j=1}^{v} a_j\right) m_1 f_{i_1} + \sum_{j=2}^{v} a_j m_j' SP(f_{i_j}, f_{i_1}) + \sum_{j>v} a_j m_j f_{i_j} .$$

By assumption $SP(f_{i_j}, f_{i_1}) = \Sigma a_{hj} m_{hj} f_{i_{hj}}$, $m_j' m_{hj} H(i_{h_j}) <_T m_1 H(i_1)$, so that

$$f = (\Sigma a_j) m_1 f_{i_1} + \sum_{h>2} b_h n_h f_{i_h}, \ b_h \text{ in } k, n_h \text{ terms}, \ n_h H(i_h) <_T m_1 H(i_1).$$

If $\Sigma a_j = 0$ the argument can be repeated,otherwise it can be applied inductively to $f - (\Sigma a_j) m_1 f_1$.

1.4. COROLLARY *Under the same assumption,if* $\deg(H(I,J)) = d$, $f := NF(SP(f_I, f_J)) \neq 0$; *then* $\deg(f) = d$.

1.5 COROLLARY *If* $\{f_1,\dots,f_t\}$ *is a G-basis of* I *obtained by a Buchberger algorithm in which a normal selection strategy is used,starting from an H-basis* $\{f_1,\dots,f_r\}$*,redund elements in the G-basis can be found only among* $\{f_1,\dots,f_r\}$

Proof: First,the normal selection strategy is required to guarantee that,when a pair (I,J) is treated with $\deg(H(I,J)) = d$, then $NF(SP(f_i,f_j)) = 0$ if $\deg(H(i,j) < d$.
So if $NF(SP(f_i,f_j)) \neq 0$ its degree is d;therefore $\deg(f_{r+1}) \leq \deg(f_{r+2}) \leq \dots \leq \deg(f$
So assume f_j, $j > r$, redundant,which means there is i, and w.l.o.g. $i < j$, s.t. H(i) divides H(j).But then f_j would not be in normal form w.r.t. $\{f_1,\dots,f_{j-1}\}$,a contradic

1.6.COROLLARY *If* $D := \max\deg\{f_1,\dots,f_t\}$ *,for any polynomial* f *computed during the performance of the algorithm* $\deg(f) \leq 2D$ *(and if S-polynomials of pairs with relatively prime headterms are not computed* $\deg(f) < 2D$).

1.7 COROLLARY *If an H-basis of* I *,*$\{f_1,\dots,f_r\}$ *is given as input to a Buchberger algorithm with normal selection strategy and degree compatible term-ordering,then all S-polynomial computations* $SP(f_i,f_j)$ *can be skipped for which both* $M_H(f_i)$ *and* $M_H(f_j)$ *consist just of the headterms.*

2 REDUCTION OF THE GROEBNER BASIS PROBLEM TO HOMOGENEOUS IDEALS

2.1 In this section we aim to expand some remarks already contained in [7],which show that to discuss degree bounds for Gröbner bases one can restrict to homogeneous ideals in this way being allowed to make use of techniques suited to such ideals,e.g.Hilbert functions.

2.2 Define the mappings ${}^h- : k[X_1,\dots,X_n] \to k[X_0,\dots,X_n]$, ${}^a- : k[X_0,\dots,X_n] \to k[X_1,\dots,X_n$ as follows: ${}^hf := X_0^{\deg(f)} f(X_1/X_0,\dots,X_n/X_0)$, ${}^af := f(1,X_1,\dots,X_n)$ so that ${}^{ah}f = f$, while if f is an *homogeneous* polynomial in $k[X_0,\dots,X_n]$ then $f = X_0^t g$,$g \notin (X_0)$ and ${}^af = {}^ag$, ${}^{ha}f = g$.

2.3 For an ideal I in $k[X_1,\dots,X_n]$ denote ${}^hI := ({}^hf : f \text{ in } I)$ and,if I is given throu a basis $(f_1,\dots,f_r)$ denote ${}^*I := ({}^hf_1,\dots,{}^hf_r)$[7].We remark explicitly that while ${}^hI$ is independent of the choice of a basis, ${}^*I$ depends on it.

Both ideals are homogeneous and the following hold:

i) if f is in I there is t s.t. $X_0^t\,{}^hf$ is in *I; if f is in *I, ${}^af$ is in I

ii) ${}^hI : X_0 = {}^hI$; if *I : X_0 = *I , then *I = ${}^hI$

iii) if I is given through an H-basis *I = ${}^hI$

2.4 Let $<$ any term-ordering (not necessarily degree compatible) on $k[X_1,\dots,X_n]$. Define then the following degree compatible term-ordering $<_h$ on $k[X_0,\dots,X_n]$: $m_1 <_h m_2$ iff $\deg(m_1) < \deg(m_2)$ or $\deg(m_1) = \deg(m_2)$ and ${}^am_1 < {}^am_2$.

2.5 LEMMA <u>If $\{h_1,\dots,h_t\}$ is a G-basis for *I w.r.t. $<_h$ consisting of homogeneous polynomials, then $\{{}^ah_1,\dots,{}^ah_t\}$ is a G-basis for I w.r.t.</u>$<$(however, also if the first is a reduced G-basis, the second could as well be not such)[7]

<u>Proof</u>: If f is in I, there is s s.t. $g := X_0^s\,{}^hf$ is in *I. So $\mathrm{Hterm}(g) = X_0^s\,\mathrm{Hterm}({}^hf) = X_0^t\,\mathrm{Hterm}(f)$. There is i and a term m s.t. $X_0^t\,\mathrm{Hterm}(f) = \mathrm{Hterm}(g) = m\,\mathrm{Hterm}(h_i)$. So $\mathrm{Hterm}(f) = {}^a\mathrm{Hterm}(g) = {}^am\,{}^a\mathrm{Hterm}(h_i) = {}^am\,\mathrm{Hterm}({}^ah_i)$.

3 THE HILBERT POLYNOMIAL OF A HOMOGENEOUS IDEAL

3.1 If I is a homogeneous ideal of $k[X_0,\dots,X_n]$ $I_d := \{f : f \text{ homogeneous}, \deg(f)=d, f \text{ in } I\}$ is a k-vectorial subspace of $P_d := \{f : f \text{ homogeneous}, \deg(f)=d\}$.

The Hilbert function H(I,t) of I is defined: $H(I,t) := \dim_k P_t - \dim_k I_t$.

By the <u>syzygien-formel</u> H(I,t) can be written:

$$H(I,t) := \sum_{i=0}^{K+n} a_i \binom{t+n-i}{n}_+ \qquad (3.1.1.)$$

for suitable integers K and a_i and with $a_0 = 1$, where $\binom{t+n-i}{n}_+$ is the usual binomial coefficient if $t \geq i-n$, is zero otherwise.

If $t \geq K$, H(I,t) is then a polynomial of degree s, $s \leq n$, the <u>Hilbert polynomial</u> of I; the least such K is called the <u>regularity bound</u>, s the <u>dimension</u> of I

3.2 Other representations of the Hilbert polynomial are:

$$H(I,t) = \sum_{i=0}^{s} h_i \binom{t+i}{i} \qquad \text{(SEVERI)} \qquad (3.2.1.)$$

$$H(I,t) = \sum_{i=0}^{s} \binom{t+i}{i+1} - \binom{t+i-m_i}{i+1} \qquad \text{(HARTSHORNE[5])} \qquad (3.2.2.)$$

3.3 REMARK If $I := {}^hJ$, J in $k[X_1,\dots,X_n]$, then $M_H(J)$ is a homogeneous ideal of $k[X_1,\dots,X_n]$, its dimension is one less than the one of I and

$$H(M_H(J),t) = H(I,t) - H(I,t-1).$$

4 BAYER'S BOUND FOR GROEBNER BASIS DEGREE

4.1 In his Ph.D.Thesis[1],Bayer gives a bound for the degree of a Gröbner basis of a homogeneous ideal under some assumptions on it,which applies also to non-homogeneous ideals by 2.5. Now we present his result,improving it by dropping his assumptions and by lowering the bound if the ideal is not homogeneous.

4.2 Let $<$ a term-ordering on $k[X_1,\dots,X_n]$, I an ideal,not necessarily homogeneous. Define $M_T(I) := (\mathrm{Hterm}(f) : f \text{ in } I)$.Then $\{f_1,\dots,f_t\}$is a Gröbner basis of I iff $\{\mathrm{Hterm}(f_1),\dots,\mathrm{Hterm}(f_t)\}$ is a basis of $M_T(I)$.
If I is homogeneous,the Hilbert function of I and $M_T(I)$ are the same.If I is not homogeneous but $<$ is degree compatible,the Hilbert functions of $M_T(I)$ and $M_H(I)$ are the same.

4.3 A homogeneous ideal is <u>saturated</u> iff for any $J \supset I$, J homogeneous, $J_d = I_d$ for sufficiently large d,implies J = I.
If I is not saturated,the largest homogeneous J s.t. $J \supset I$, $J_d=I_d$ for sufficiently large d ,is called the <u>saturation</u> of I, I^{sat} and is a saturated ideal[1].Also,if I is a monomial ideal (i.e.generated by terms) also its saturation is such.

4.4 THEOREM 1 <u>If I is a saturated homogeneous ideal,whose Hilbert polynomial is given by</u> 3.2.2.,<u>then a reduced G-basis of</u> I <u>w.r.t. a degree compatible term-ordering is generated by elements of degree</u> $\leq m_0$.

4.5 COROLLARY <u>If I is a homogeneous ideal,a reduced G-basis of I w.r.t. a degree compatible term-ordering is generated by elements of degree</u> $\leq b := \max(K,m_0)$.
<u>Proof</u>: The Hilbert function and the Hilbert polynomial of $M_T(I)$ have the same value if $t \geq K$.The Hilbert polynomials of $M_T(I)$ and $M_T(I)^{sat}$ are the same,since they have the same value for large t.Finally if $t \geq m_0-1$ the Hilbert polynomial and the Hilbert function of $M_T(I)^{sat}$ have the same value ([1],2.5,10.4) .
So,if $t \geq b$,the Hilbert functions of $M_T(I)$ and $M_T(I)^{sat}$ have the same values,which implies $(M_T(I))_t = (M_T(I)^{sat})_t$.
Suppose $M_T(I)$ has an unredundant generator m of degree $>b$, which can w.l.o.g. be supposed a term. There is then a term m_1 in $M_T(I)^{sat}$,$\deg(m_1) = b$, m_1 dividing m, since $M_T(I)^{sat}$ is generated by elements of degree $\leq m_0$.But then $m_1 \in (M_T(I)^{sat})_b =$
$= (M_T(I))_b$,which is a contradiction.

4.6 REMARK If I is not homogeneous and $<$ degree compatible,let the Hilbert polynomial of ${}^hI$ be given by.3.2.2. Then $M_T(M_H(I)) = M_T(I)$ is generated by elements of degree $\max(K,m_1)$ which is then a bound for the degree of a Gröbner basis of I.This improves on Bayer's suggestion ([1],page102) to reduce the problem to the one for ${}^hI$, for $m_1 \leq m_0$.

II - UPPER BOUNDS FOR GROEBNER BASIS DEGREE

1 A BOUND FOR m_0 IN TERMS OF K

1.1 Let $I \subset k[X_0,\dots,X_n]$ be homogeneous with Hilbert function given by I.3.1 and Hilbert polynomial by I.3.2. Let K denote the regularity bound. We aim to give a bound for m_0 in terms of K,n,s.

1.2 LEMMA $|a_i| \leq \sum_{\nu=0}^{n+1} \binom{n+1}{\nu}\binom{i+n+1-\nu}{n}$, i=0,...,K+n , <u>with</u> a_i <u>as</u> <u>in</u> I.3.1.1

<u>Proof</u>: By definition $0 \leq H(I,t) \leq \binom{t+n}{n}$. Using backwards differences: $\nabla P(t) := P(t)-P(t-1)$, $\nabla^j P := \nabla(\nabla^{j-1} P)$, simple manipulations of binomial coefficients give

$$\nabla^j H(I,t) = \sum_{i=0}^{K+n} a_i \nabla^j \binom{t+n-i}{n}_+ = \sum_{i=0}^{K+n} a_i \binom{t+n-i-j}{n-j}_+$$

Especially, for j=n: $\nabla^n H(I,t) = a_t + a_{t+1} + \dots + a_{K+n}$. Starting now with $H(I,t) \leq \binom{t+n}{n}$ and using $|\nabla P(t)| \leq |P(t)| + |P(t-1)|$, by induction $|\nabla^j H(I,t)| \leq \sum_{\nu=0}^{j}\binom{j}{\nu}\binom{t+n-\nu}{n}$.
Especially with j=n+1, $|a_t| = |\nabla^n H(I,t+1) - \nabla^n H(I,t)| = |\nabla^{n+1} H(I,t+1)| \leq \sum_{\nu=0}^{n+1}\binom{n+1}{\nu}\binom{t+n+1-\nu}{n}$

1.3 LEMMA $\binom{w-p}{m} = \sum_{i=0}^{m} (-1)^{m+i}\binom{p}{m-i}\binom{w-m+i}{i}$

<u>Proof</u>: [9], page 8 (5)

1.4 COROLLARY $h_i = (-1)^{n+i} \sum_{j=0}^{K+n} a_j \binom{j}{n-i}$, i=0...n; <u>especially</u> $h_{s+1} = \dots = h_n = 0$

<u>Proof</u>: By 1.3, I.3.1.1, I.3.2.1

1.5 LEMMA $|h_i| < (n+1)2^{n+1}\binom{2n+1-i}{n+1}\binom{K+2n+2}{2n+2-i}$, i=0...s

1.6 LEMMA $\sum_{i=0}^{\nu-1} (-1)^{\nu-i+1}\binom{m+i}{\nu+1-i}\binom{t+i}{i} = \binom{t+\nu-m}{\nu+1} + m\binom{t+\nu}{\nu} - \binom{t+\nu}{\nu+1}$

<u>Proof</u>: In order to apply 1.3, extend the left hand summation to i=0...ν+1, by adding two summands .

1.7 LEMMA <u>Starting with the Severi constants</u> h_i, <u>and defining</u> $h_{is} := h_i$ i=0...s, $h_{i,\nu-1} := h_i + (-1)^{\nu-i+1}\binom{h_{\nu\nu}+1}{\nu-i+1}$ i=0...ν-1 , ν=s,...,1, <u>then</u>:

$$H(I,t) = \sum_{i=\nu}^{s} \binom{t+i}{i+1} - \binom{t+i-h_{ii}}{i+1} + \sum_{i=0}^{\nu-1} h_{i,\nu-1}\binom{t+i}{i} , \quad \nu=0,\dots,s+1$$

<u>In particular, in</u> I.3.2.2, $m_i = h_{ii}$.

<u>Proof</u>: For ν=s+1, it is I.3.2.1. The induction step from ν+1 to ν is done by 1.6

1.8 PROPOSITION Let $B := (K+2n+2)^{2(n+1)}$. Then the constants m_i of I.3.2.2 are bounded by $m_i < B^{2^{s-i}}$, i=0,...,s.

<u>Proof</u>: We will prove $|h_{i,s-j}| < B^{2^{j-1}(s-i-j+2)}$, which gives for j = s-i the thesis.
For n=s I has dimension n, i.e. I = (0) . Then $h_0 = \dots = h_{n-1} = 0$, $h_n = 1$ and the result holds trivially. So let s < n and j = 0:

$$|h_{is}| = |h_i| < (n+1)\, 2^{n+1} \frac{(2n+1-i)!}{(n+1)!(n-i)!} \frac{(K+2n+2)!}{(2n+2-i)!(K+i)!} <$$

$$< \frac{2^{n+1}}{n!(n-i)!} \frac{1}{2n+2-i} (K+i+1)(K+i+2)\dots(K+2n+2) < (K+2n+2)^{2n+2} = B$$

If $|h_{i,s-j}| < B^{2^{j-1}(s-i-j+2)}$ then

$$|h_{i,s-j-1}| \leqslant |h_{i,s-j}| + \binom{m_{s-j}+1}{s-i-j+1} < B^{2^{j-1}(s-i-j+2)} + B^{2^{j}(s-i-j+1)} \frac{1}{(s-i-j+1)!}$$

and since $C^u \leqslant (u!-1)C^{2u}/u!$,provided $C,u > 1$,we have the desired result.

2 A BOUND FOR GROEBNER BASIS DEGREE

2.1 Let I a not necessarily homogeneous ideal in $k[X_1,\dots,X_n]$,$\{f_1,\dots,f_r\}$ a basis for I, d := maxdeg(f_i) , D the maximal degree of an irreducible H-basis of I (D doesn't depend on the choice of the basis),$<$ a term-ordering,$\{g_1,\dots,g_t\}$ a G-basis of I w.r.t $<$; G := maxdeg(g_i).

2.2 If I is homogeneous, f_i homogeneous,$<$ degree compatible,then d = D ,$G \leqslant (K+2n)^{n2^s}$
By [6] Satz2,K is bounded by a polynomial function of d. So G is bounded by a polynom function of d and,by I.1.6, the same is true of the degree of any polynomial computed by Buchberger's algorithm.

2.3 In [7] Lazard proved that the regularity bound of an homogeneous ideal is actually bounded by a linear function of the degrees of its basis elements: $K \leqslant nd-n+1$.
However his result is partially conjectural:unless a conjecture stated in the same paper (Conjecture 1) holds,the proof works only under some assumptions on the ideal (roughly,the depth of the ideal must not be too low).If his conjecture proves true or if the ideal satisfies any of the other assumptions we have then an explicit bound for G.

2.4 If I is not homogeneous ,but $<$ is degree compatible and an H-basis of I is known, by applying the previous result to $M_H(I)$, we have $G \leqslant (K+2n)^{n2^s}$, G bounded by a polynomial function of D,the degrees of intermediate polynomials bounded by 2G,and again an explicit bound under Lazard's conjecture.

2.5 If I is not homogeneous and either $<$ is not degree compatible or an H-basis of I is not known,since a G-basis of $^*I$ w.r.t. $<_h$ bounds in degree G, we have that G is polynomially bounded by d, $G \leqslant (^*K+2n+2)^{(n+1)2^{s+1}}$,and an explicit bound under Lazard's conjecture, $^*K$ denoting the regularity bound of $^*I$.
It is not known if also the intermediate polynomials are so bounded in degree,since I.1.6 cannot be applied. It is true that it is possible to compute a G-basis of I in such a way that the intermediate polynomials have degree polynomially bounded by d, simply by computing a G-basis for $^*I$;the resulting algorithm seems however to perform

worse.

2.6 The bound of 2.4 is of interest because there are likely situations in which an H-basis of I is known in advance.

For instance,consider the following problem:given G-bases $(f_1,\dots,f_r),(g_1,\dots,g_t)$ of I and J,compute a G-basis of $I \cap J$.If the term-ordering is degree compatible ,a possible solution is: to extend $(f_1,\dots,f_r,g_1,\dots,g_t)$ to a G-basis G:= $(f_1,\dots,f_r,g_1,\dots,g_t,h_1,\dots,h_s)$ of $I \cup J$,obtaining as a by-product of Buchberger's algorithm also an H-basis for the relations among the elements of G,which can then be reduced to an H-basis for the relations among the f_i's and the g_i's;if for any of them, say $\Sigma a_i f_i + \Sigma b_i g_i = 0$ we take $\Sigma a_i f_i = -\Sigma b_i g_i$ we obtain an H-basis of $I \cap J$ which can then be extended to a G-basis (with the simplified algorithm of I.1.7)

3 A BOUND FOR IDEALS IN 3 VARIABLES UNDER A DEGREE COMPATIBLE TERM-ORDERING

3.1 LEMMA <u>Let</u> $I \subset k[X_1,\dots,X_n]$ (n-2)-<u>dimensional</u> (<u>i.e.</u>deg$(H({}^hI,t))$=n-2).<u>Then also</u> $^*I$ <u>is</u> (n-2)-<u>dimensional.</u>

<u>Proof</u>: Since $\dim(^*I) \geq \dim({}^hI)$,we must show that $\dim(^*I) = n-1$ is impossible.

$\dim(^*I) = n-1$ implies $^*I \subset (f)$ for an irreducible f in $k[X_0,\dots,X_n]$, i.e. f divides ${}^hf_i$, for each f_i in a basis of I; so ${}^af$ divides each f_i,and unless it is a constant, this implies $\dim(I) = n-1$. Hence ${}^af$ is constant, f is in (X_0), which is again impossible

3.2 REMARK[7] Let $I := (f_1,\dots,f_r) \subset k[X_1,\dots,X_n]$a (n-1)-dimensional ideal.Then $f :=$ g.c.d.$(f_1,\dots,f_r) \neq 1$. Let $J := (f_1/f,\dots,f_r/f)$; then $\dim(J) < n-1$ and if $(g_1,\dots,g_s)$ is a G-basis of J, then $(fg_1,\dots,fg_s)$ is a G-basis of I.

3.3 Let $I \subset k[X_1,X_2,X_3]$ generated by polynomials of degree at most d;let < a degree compatible term-ordering.Let ${}^hI, M_T(I)$, I as usualand K the regularity bound of ${}^hI$, G the maximal degree of a G-basis of I w.r.t. <.

0) If $\dim(I) = 0$ then $H(M_T(I),t) = 0$,hence $m_1 = 0$ and by I.4.6 $G \leq K$

1) If $\dim(I) = 1$ also $\dim(^*I) = 1$ and since $H(^*I,t) \geq H({}^hI,t)$ (because ${}^hI \supset {}^*I$),if $H({}^hI,t) =: Dt+g$, $H(^*I,t) =: {}^*Dt+{}^*g$, we must have $m_1 = D \leq {}^*D \leq d^2$ ([7]).So,by I.4.6 $G \leq \max(K,d^2)$

2) If $\dim(I) = 2$ by 3.2 $G \leq \max(K,d^2)$

3.4 Lazard's Theorem 4 ([7]) allows one to obtain a bound for K which is linear in the degree of a a basis of ${}^hI$ or,equivalently, in the degree of an H-basis of I.

If we are allowed to conjecture that K is linearly bounded by the degree of <u>any</u> basis of I (say,in the case discussed here: $K \leq 3d-2$) we obtain $G \leq d^2$ as a bound for the G-basis degree of a 3-variable ideal under a degree compatible term-ordering.

III - LOWER BOUNDS FOR GROEBNER BASIS DEGREE

The upper bounds of I.4.5 and I.4.6 are actually sharp;the ones of II.2 are not such, as their derivation clearly shows. We present here examples which show,however,that both the exponential behaviour in n and the doubly exponential one in s are unavoidab

1. AN IDEAL IN 2n+1 VARIABLES,GENERATED BY ELEMENTS OF DEGREE NOT EXCEDING d+1, WITH $G = d^{n-1}(d^2+1)$

1.1 Let $d \geq 2$. Define $g_0 := X_0^{d+1} - X_1^{d-1} Y_1$, $g_1 := X_0^d X_1 - Y_1^d$ and $h_n := X_{n-1} Y_n^{d-1} - X_n^d$ for $n \geq 1$. For any $n \geq 1$,let $I_n \subset k[X_0,\ldots,X_n,Y_1,\ldots,Y_n]$, the ideal generated by $B_n :=$ $:= (g_0,g_1,h_1,\ldots,h_n)$.Under a degree compatible term-ordering $<$ s.t.$X_{i-1}Y_i^{d-1} < X_i^d$ for each i (e.g.under the usual "total degree ordering"[2,7] with $X_0 < X_1 < \ldots < X_n <$ $< Y_1 < \ldots < Y_n$) an easy direct verification shows that B_n is a G-basis of I_n hence an H-basis,so that I.1.7 can be applied in the computation of a G-basis of I_n from B_n under any degree compatible term-ordering.

1.2 Let us introduce some notations.

An "admissible exponent of level n" (an AE(n)) is any $\underline{e} := (e_0,\ldots,e_n) \in \mathbb{N}^{n+1}$ s.t. $e_0 \leq d$ and if $f_1 := d(d-e_0)+1$, $f_i := (f_{i-1} - e_{i-1})\, d$, if $1 < i \leq n$,then $0 \leq e_i < f_i$ if $1 \leq i < n$, $e_n = f_n$ hold.

Let $\mathbb{E}(n) := \{\underline{e} \in \mathbb{N}^{n+1}$, $\underline{e}$ is an AE(n)$\}$.

If $\underline{e} \in \mathbb{E}(n)$ and $0 < a \leq e_n$ define $E(\underline{e},a) := (e_0,\ldots,e_{n-1},e_n-a,ad) \in \mathbb{E}(n+1)$

Then $\mathbb{E}(n+1) = \{E(\underline{e},a) : \underline{e}\ \ \mathbb{E}(n)\ ,0 < a \leq e_n\}$.

Finally to each $\underline{e} \in \mathbb{E}(n)$ associate $f(\underline{e}) \in k[X_0,\ldots,X_n,Y_1,\ldots,Y_n]$,

$$f(\underline{e}) := X_0^{e_0}\ldots X_n^{e_n} - Y_1^{(d-e_0)(d-1)+d}\, Y_2^{(f_1-e_1)(d-1)} \ldots Y_n^{(f_{n-1}-e_{n-1})(d-1)}.$$

Remark that $M_H(f(\underline{e})) = M_T(f(\underline{e}))$

1.3 PROPOSITION Let $G_1 := \{g_0,h_1\} \cup \{f(\underline{e}) : \underline{e} \in \mathbb{E}(1)\}$; $H_n := G_n \cup \{h_{n+1}\}$, $n \geq 1$; $G_{n+1} := H_n \cup \{f(\underline{e}) : e \in \mathbb{E}(n+1)\}$, $n \geq 1$.

Then,under any degree compatible term-ordering s.t. $X_i^d < X_{i-1}Y_i^{d-1}$ (e.g. for the total degree ordering with $X_n < \ldots < X_1 < X_0 < Y_1 < \ldots < Y_n$) G_n is an irreducible G-basis of I_n.

Proof: 1) If $0 \leq i < d$, let $\underline{e}(i) := (d-i,id+1)$; Then $\mathbb{E}(1) = \{\underline{e}(i) : 0 \leq i < d\}$. Also $\text{Hterm}(f(\underline{e}(i))) = X_0^{d-i} X_1^{id+1}$.

2) $g_1 = f(\underline{e}(0))$, $SP(g_0,h_1) = X_1^{d-1} g_1$, $SP(f(\underline{e}(i)),h_1) = f(\underline{e}(i+1))$,$0 \leq i < d$; h_1 and $f(\underline{e}(d))$ have relatively prime headterms.

So: G_1 is a G-basis of I_1

3) Inductively assume: G_{n-1} is a G-basis of I_{n-1} and Hterm$(f(\underline{e})) = X_0^{e_0} \dots X_{n-1}^{e_{n-1}}$ for each $\underline{e} = (e_0,\dots,e_{n-1}) \in \mathbb{E}(n-1)$.

Then for each $\underline{e} \in \mathbb{E}(n-1)$: $SP(f(\underline{e}),h_n) = f(E(\underline{e},1))$, $SP(f(E(\underline{e},a)),h_n) = f(E(\underline{e},a+1))$ if $a < e_{n-1}$, the H-terms of $f(E(\underline{e},e_{n-1}))$ and h_n are relatively prime.

Finally for each j, $1 \leq j < n$, and each $\underline{e} := (e_0,\dots,e_n) \in \mathbb{E}(n)$ s.t; $e_{j-1} \neq 0$, define $\underline{e}' := (e'_0,\dots,e'_n)$ by $e'_{j-1} := e_{j-1}-1$, $e'_j := e_j+d$, $e'_i := e_i$ otherwise; then $\underline{e}' \in \mathbb{E}(n)$ and $SP(f(\underline{e}),h_j) = f(\underline{e}')$.

This proves G_n is a G-basis of I_n ;moreover h_n is homogeneous while $f(\underline{e})$ is not such for every $\underline{e} \in \mathbb{E}(n-1)$, so also any $f(\underline{e})$, $\underline{e} \in \mathbb{E}(n)$, is not homogenous which completely proves the inductive assertion.The irreducibility of G_n is easy to verify.

1.4 LEMMA $(0,\dots,0,d^{n-1}(d^2+1)) \in \mathbb{E}(n)$

1.5 COROLLARY G_n <u>contains an element of degree</u> $d^{n-1}(d^2+1)$

1.6 We want to emphasize that this example shows how the choice of the term-ordering (also if one restricts to total degree orderings) can strongly influence the degree of the G-basis.

2 AN IDEAL IN n VARIABLES,GENERATED BY ELEMENTS OF DEGREE NOT EXCEEDING d,WITH $G = d^{n-1}$

2.1 We presented the previous example for two reasons:firstly it has an interpretation in commutative semigroup theory. Secondly it has a geometrical meaning since I_1 is the ideal of the curve with zero-set $(t^{n^2-n+1}, t^{n^2}, t^{n^2+1})$ and the zero-set of I_n can be obtained by the one of I_{n-1} by taking the cylinder on the latter in the X_n - and Y_n - directions and cutting it by the cone with equation $h_n = 0$.

The following class of examples,in the same line of reasoning, give a better lower bound but are lacking both interpretations.The proof of the assertions is omitted since it is very similar to and easier than the one of the preceding example.

2.2 PROPOSITION $B_n := \{X_n^d\} \cup \{X_0^{d-1}X_i - X_{i-1}^d : i = 2\dots n\}$ <u>is a G-basis for the ideal</u> $I_n \subset k[X_0,\dots,X_n]$ <u>it generates, under any degree compatible term-ordering s.t.</u> $X_0^{d-1}X_i < X_{i-1}^d$ <u>for each</u> i (<u>e.g. the total degree ordering with</u> $X_0 < X_1 < \dots < X_n$)

<u>An irreducible G-basis for the same ideal under any degree compatible term-ordering s.t.</u> $X_{i-1}^d < X_0^{d-1}X_i$ (<u>e.g. the total degree ordering</u> $X_1 < \dots < X_n < X_0$) <u>contains an element of degree</u> d^n <u>v.i.z.</u> $X_1^{d^n}$.

3 AN EXAMPLE BY MAYR AND MEYER

3.1 In [8] an example is given of a class of ideals which shows that "a degree bound growing exponentially in the number of variables is unavoidable" for [6],Satz 2. A suitable modification of their arguments allows to use the same techniques of proof to show the existence of ideals for which any H-basis,and hence any G-basis under deg compatible term-orderings, contains elements whose degree is doubly exponential in th dimension of the ideal. The examples are as follows:

3.2 Define $P_0 := k[S_0, Q_{10}, Q_{20}, Q_{30}, Q_{40}, F_0, C_{10}, C_{20}, C_{30}, C_{40}, B_{10}, B_{20}, B_{30}, B_{40}]$

$P_n := P_{n-1}[S_n, Q_{1n}, Q_{2n}, Q_{3n}, Q_{4n}, F_n, C_{1n}, C_{2n}, C_{3n}, C_{4n}, B_{1n}, B_{2n}, B_{3n}, B_{4n}]$

$I_0 := (S_0 C_{i0} - F_0 C_{i0} B_{i0}^d : 1 \leqslant i \leqslant 4) \subset P_0$

$J_{n-1} := I_{n-1} + (S_n - Q_{1n} S_{n-1} C_{1n-1}, Q_{1n} F_{n-1} C_{1n-1} B_{1n-1} - Q_{2n} S_{n-1} C_{2n-1}, Q_{2n} F_{n-1} C_{2n-1} - Q_{3n} F_{n-1} C_{3n-1}, \{Q_{2n} C_{in} F_{n-1} B_{2n-1} - Q_{2n} C_{in} F_{n-1} B_{3n-1} B_{in} : 1 \leqslant i \leqslant 4\}) \subset P_n$

$I_n := J_{n-1} + (Q_{3n} S_{n-1} C_{3n-1} B_{1n-1}, - Q_{2n} S_{n-1} C_{2n-1} B_{4n-1}, Q_{4n} S_{n-1} C_{4n-1} - F_n, Q_{3n} S_{n-1} C_{3n-1} - Q_{4n} F_{n-1} C_{4n-1} B_{4n-1}) \subset P_n$

$e_n := d^{2^n}$ so that $e_0 = d$, $e_n = e_{n-1}^2$

The dimension of ^hJ_n is then gretaer than to 3n+15.

In [8] ,Mayr and Meyer show that the only term in $P_n \cap (S_n, F_n)$ which is congruent to $S_n C_{in}$ modulo I_n is $F_n C_{in} B_{in}^{e_n}$.

We are able to show the following (proofs are omitted since they are too long to be exposed here; a fùll discussion of these examples,which also shake a conjecture by Renschuch[10] related to syzygies degree bounds, will appear elsewhere):

3.3 LEMMA $Q_{3n+1} C_{in+1} C_{3n} S_n B_{in+1}^{e_n} - Q_{2n+1} C_{in+1} C_{2n} S_n \in J_n$, $n \geqslant 1$

3.4 PROPOSITION <u>Any H-basis of</u> J_n <u>contains an element whose degree is at least</u> $e_n/2 + 4$

<u>Sketch of proof</u>: By the lemma, $\Phi := Q_{3n+1} C_{in+1} C_{3n} S_n B_{in+1}^{e_n} \in M_H(J_n)$.

So any minimal H-basis of I_n whose generators are binomials (there is such an H-basis: a not necessarily minimal one can be obtained by Buchberger's algorithm applied to the given basis w.r.t. any degree compatible term-ordering;from it a minimal H-basis consisting of binomials can be extracted) must contain an element $\Psi - \beta$,Ψ,β terms, $\deg(\Psi) \geqslant \deg(\beta)$, Ψ divides Φ.

The core of the proof consists then to show,by a careful analysis of the congruences between terms modulo J_n, that the only possible choices for Ψ are:

i) if a term α exists not containing neither F_n nor S_n s.t. $\alpha C_{2n} - C_{2n} F_n B_n^k \in I_n$ (this implies $\deg(\alpha) \geqslant 2$)with $\deg(\alpha) \leqslant 2k - e_n - 2$, then $\Psi = Q_{3n+1} C_{in+1} C_{3n} S_n B_{in+1}^j$,with $j \geqslant k \geqslant e_n/2$ and $\beta = Q_{2n+1} C_{in+1} C_{2n} B_{3n}^{e_n - k} B_{in+1}^{j-k}$.

ii) if such an α doesn't exist (which was hard and of scarce interest to check directly then $\Psi = \Phi$.

REFERENCES

[1] D.A.BAYER, The division algorithm and the Hilbert scheme,Ph.D.Thesis,Harvard(1982)

[2] B.BUCHBERGER, A criterion for detecting unnecessary reductions in the construction of Gröbner bases, Proc.EUROSAM 79, L.N.Comp.Sci. 72 (1979) 3-21

[3] B.BUBHBERGER, A note on the complexity of constructing Gröbner bases,Proc.EUROCAL 83, L.N.Comp.Sci.162 (1983)

[4] B.BUCHBERGER,F.WINKLER, Miscellaneous results on the construction of Gröbner bases for polynomial ideals,Bericht 137;Inst.Math.Univ.Linz (1979)

[5] R.HARTSHORNE, Connectedness of the Hilbert scheme,Publ.Math.I.H.E.S. 29(1966),5-48

[6] G.HERMANN, Die Frage der endlichen viele Schritten in der Theorie der Polynomideale,Math.Ann. 95 (1926),736-788

[7] D.LAZARD, Gröbner bases,Gaussian elimination and resolution of systems of algebraic equations, Proc.EUROCAL 83, L.N.Comp.Sci. 162 (1983)

[8] E.W.MAYR,A.R.MEYER, The complexity of the word problems for commutative semigroups and polynomial ideals, Adv.Math.46 (1982),305-329

[9] J.RIORDAN, Combinatorial identities,Wiley,New York,(1968)

[10] B.RENSCHUCH,Elementare und praktische Idealtheorie,DWV Berlin (1976)

[11] M.GIUSTI, Some effectivity problems in polynomial ideal theory, these Proceedings

APPENDIX

Giusti's remark[11] that the elements of a Gröbner basis of $^*I$ provide also the sequence of intermediate computations necessary to build a Gröbner basis of I,implies that if G is a degree bound for a G-basis of $^*I$, 2G bounds the degree of all intermediate computations for a normal selection strategy on I. So in II.2.5. one obtains also such a bound.

On the Complexity of the Gröbner-Bases Algorithm over K[x,y,z] *)

Franz Winkler
Institut für Mathematik
Arbeitsgruppe CAMP
Johannes Kepler Universität
A-4040 Linz, Austria

Abstract

In /Bu65/, /Bu70/, /Bu76/ B. Buchberger presented an algorithm which, given a basis for an ideal in $K[x_1,...,x_n]$ (the ring of polynomials in n indeterminates over the field K), constructs a so-called Gröbner-basis for the ideal. The importance of Gröbner-bases for effectively carrying out a large number of construction and decision problems in polynomial ideal theory has been investigated in /Bu65/, /Wi78/, /WB81/, /Bu83b/. For the case of two variables B. Buchberger /Bu79/, /Bu83a/ gave bounds for the degrees of the polynomials which are generated by the Gröbner-bases algorithm. However, no bound has been known until now for the case of more than two variables. In this paper we give such a bound for the case of three variables.

1. Introduction

In /Bu65/, /Bu70/, /Bu76/ B. Buchberger presented an algorithm which, given a basis F for an ideal in $K[x_1,...,x_n]$ (the ring of polynomials in n indeterminates over the field K), constructs a so-called Gröbner-basis G for ideal(F), the ideal generated by F. A Gröbner-basis G can be characterized by the fact that every polynomial has a unique normal form w.r.t. a certain reduction relation induced by G. A large number of construction and decision problems in polynomial ideal theory can be solved easily once a Gröbner-basis for the ideal has been constructed (see /Bu65/, /Wi78/, /WB81/, /Bu83b/).

*) The results reported in this paper are part of the authors doctoral dissertation at the Johannes Kepler University, Linz, Austria.
The work for this paper was supported by the Austrian Research Fund under grant Nr. 4567.

However, for a long time no bound was known for the complexity of the Gröbner-bases algorithm, especially for the degrees of the polynomials which are constructed by the Gröbner-bases algorithm. In 1979 B. Buchberger /Bu79/ gave such a bound, which was improved in /Bu83a/, for the case of two variables. Lazard /La83/ makes some remarks on this problem but he considers a special class of ideals. In this paper we give a bound for the case of three variables, where absolutely no special properties are required of the ideal.

The problem to be solved is the following:

(P) given a basis F for a polynomial ideal in $K[x,y,z]$
construct a bound b such that the degree of every polynomial which is constructed during the execution of the Gröbner-bases algorithm on F is less than or equal to b.

(P) is solved in the subsequent chapters. Expressed only in D and d, the maximal and minimal degree of the polynomials in F, respectively, we get the bound $(8D+1)\cdot 2^d$. For proofs of the various lemmata we refer to /Wi83/.

2. Reduction of the problem

Throughout this paper, we let the linear ordering $<_t$ on the set of power products be the graduated lexicographical ordering, i.e. power products are ordered according to their degrees and lexicographically within the same degree.

By the "overlap lemma" /KB78/, /Bu79/, /BW79/ it suffices to consider only "essential" pairs of polynomials during the execution of the Gröbner-bases algorithm, where a pair f,g in F is essential if there is no sequence $f=h_1,\dots,h_l=g$ in F such that

$$\mathrm{lpp}(h_i) \text{ divides } \mathrm{lcm}(\mathrm{lpp}(f),\mathrm{lpp}(g)) \quad \text{for all } 1<i<l,$$
$$\deg(\mathrm{lcm}(\mathrm{lpp}(h_i),\mathrm{lpp}(h_{i+1}))) < \deg(\mathrm{lcm}(\mathrm{lpp}(f),\mathrm{lpp}(g))) \quad \text{for all } 1<i<l-1,$$

where lpp(f) denotes the leading power product of f w.r.t. $<_t$ and lcm(p,q) the least common multiple of the power products p,q. So every polynomial h which is added to the basis during the execution of the Gröbner-bases algorithm satisfies the following two conditions:

(i) lpp(h) is not a multiple of lpp(f) for every f, which is already in the basis,

(ii) deg(h) is not greater than the maximal degree of the least common multiples of essential pairs of polynomials in the basis.

We call a sequence of polynomials $h_1,\dots,h_s$ **admissible** w.r.t. F if h_i satisfies these two conditions w.r.t. $F \cup \{h_1,\dots,h_{i-1}\}$ for all i.

Theorem 2.1: Let F be a finite set of polynomials in $K[x_1,\dots,x_n]$. Then every polynomial which is either in F or is generated during the execution of the Gröbner-bases algorithm on F has degree less than or equal to $\max\{\max\{deg(h) \mid h \in H\} \mid H = F \cup \{h_1,\dots,h_s\},\ h_1,\dots,h_s$ admissible w.r.t. $F\}$.

So if we have a bound for the maximal degree of the polynomials in $F \cup \{h_1,\dots,h_s\}$, where $h_1,\dots,h_s$ are admissible w.r.t. F, then we have solved problem (P). Such a bound is constructed in the next chapter. Actually the notion of "admissibility" depends only on the leading power products of the involved polynomials. So instead of sets of polynomials F we consider sets of power products P.

3. A bound for admissible sequences of power products

Let **V**:={x,y,z} denote the set of variables or indeterminates. By **pp3** we denote the set of power products in x,y and z. If $p=x^a y^b z^c$ is a power product then **deg**(p,x)=a, **deg**(p,y)=b, **deg**(p,z)=c and **deg**(p)=a+b+c. By **lcm**(p,q) we denote the least common multiple of the two power products p,q. We write $p \prec q$ for "p **divides** q".
If $P \subseteq$ pp3, $v \in$ **V** and $d \in \mathbf{N}$ then P^* := $\{q \in pp3 \mid p \prec q$ for some $p \in P\}$, **mind**(P,v) := $\min\{deg(p,v) \mid p \in P\}$, and **sect**(P,d) := $\{p \in P \mid deg(p)=d\}$.

Def.: Let $d \in \mathbf{N}$, P a nonempty subset of sect(pp3,d). Then
int(P) := $\{p \in sect(pp3,d) \mid deg(p,v) > mind(P,v)$ for all $v \in V\} - P$.
ext(P) := sect(pp3,d) - (P $\cup$ int(P)).

An important notion in /Bu83a/ is the "essentiality" of pairs of polynomials in some basis F. Since this notion depends only on the leading power products of the polynomials in F, we can define it for sets of power products.

Def.: Let P be a finite subset of pp3. Then
ess(P) := $\{(p,q) \mid p,q \in P,\ p \neq q$, and there are no $r_1,\dots,r_l$ in P such that
$p=r_1,\ r_l=q,$
$r_i \prec lcm(p,q)$ for all $1 \le i \le l$, and
$deg(lcm(r_i,r_{i+1})) < deg(lcm(p,q))$ for all $1 \le i \le l-1\}$.
(**Essential pairs** in P.)

Def.: Let $P \subseteq$ pp3 be finite, $|P| > 1$. Then the **maximal degree of essential least least common multiples** of P is defined as
mdel(P) := $\max\{deg(lcm(p,q)) \mid (p,q) \in ess(P)\}$.

Example 3.1: Let $P = \{x^2yz^6,\ x^3y^2z^5,\ xy^3z^5,\ x^4y^2z^3,\ xy^5z^3,\ x^4y^4z,\ x^3y^5z\}$.

$ess(P) = \{(p_1,p_2),(p_1,p_3),(p_2,p_3),(p_2,p_4),(p_3,p_5),(p_4,p_6),(p_5,p_7),(p_6,p_7)\}$.
For instance (p_1,p_6) is not in ess(P), since $r_1=p_1$, $r_2=p_2$, $r_3=p_4$, $r_4=p_6$ satisfy the condition in the definition of "ess".
So mdel(P)=11.

Def.: Let $P \subseteq pp3$. Then the **width** of P is defined as $\mathbf{w}(P) := \sum_{v \in \mathbf{V}} mind(P,v)$.

Lemma 3.1: Let $P \subseteq pp3$ be finite, $|P| > 1$, $m \geq mdel(P)$, $p \in int(sect(P^*,m))$, $v \in \mathbf{V}$.
If $p.v^k \notin P^*$ for all $k \in \mathbf{N}$,
then for all $w \in \mathbf{V}-\{v\}$ there is a $k \in \mathbf{N}$ such that $p.w^k \in P^*$.

So $int(sect(P^*,m))$ $(m \geq mdel(P))$ can be decomposed into the following four parts.

Def.: Let $P \subseteq pp3$ be finite, $|P| > 1$, $m \geq mdel(P)$.
$\mathbf{ker}(sect(P^*,m)) := \{p \mid p \in int(sect(P^*,m))$ and for all $v \in \mathbf{V}$ there is a $k \in \mathbf{N}$ such that $p.v^k \in P^*\}$.
(**Kernel** of $sect(P^*,m)$.)
For $v \in \mathbf{V}$:
$\mathbf{mar}(sect(P^*,m),v) := \{p \mid p \in int(sect(P^*,m))$ and for all $k \in \mathbf{N}$ $p.v^k \notin P^*\}$.
(**Margin** of $sect(P^*,m)$ at v.)

Example 3.2:
Let P be as in example 3.1, m=11 ($\geq$mdel(P)).

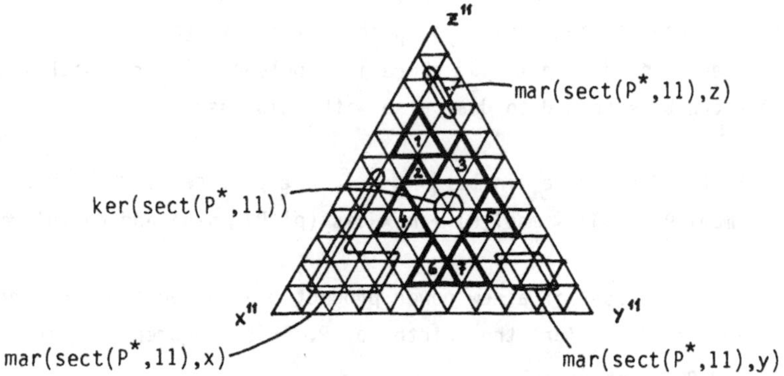

The triangles symbolize the multiples of the indicated power products.

Corollary to lemma 3.1: Let $P \subseteq pp3$ be finite, $|P| > 1$, $m \geq mdel(P)$.
Then
$int(sect(P^*,m))$ is the disjunct union of $ker(sect(P^*,m))$, $mar(sect(P^*,m),x)$, $mar(sect(P^*,m),y)$ and $mar(sect(P^*,m),z)$.

In order to investigate the increase of "mdel" if an "admissible" power product p is added to the set of power products P, we need some means of measuring the "distance" between p and P. The goal, of course, is to specify this "distance" dist(p,P) in such a way that $mdel(P \cup \{p\})$ can easily be expressed in terms of mdel(P) and dist(p,P).

Def.: Let P $\subseteq$ pp3, p ε pp3.
dist(p,P) := max{deg(r) | p.r ε P^* and p.s $\notin$ P^* for all s<r}.
(Distance between p and P.)

Lemma 3.2: Let P $\subseteq$ pp3 be finite, | P | > 1, p ε sect(pp3-P^*,mdel(P)).
Then mdel(P u {p}) = mdel(P) + dist(p,P).

Example 3.3: Let P be as in example 3.1.

Suppose p = p_8 = $x^7y^2z^2$ is added to P.

dist(p,P)=2

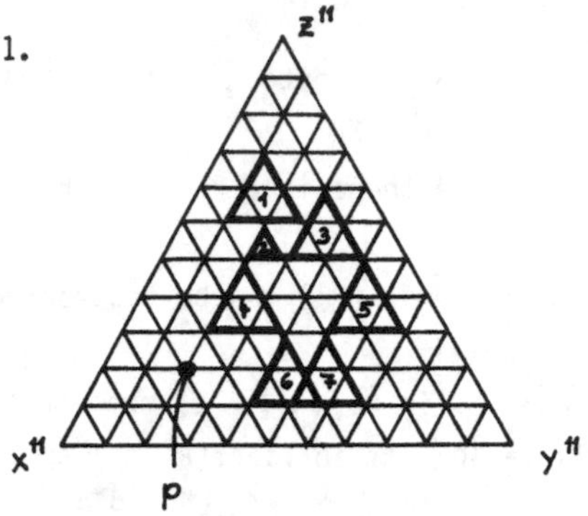

The new essential pairs are (4,8) and (6,8).
So mdel(P u {p}) = 13 = mdel(P) + dist(p,P).

During the execution of the Gröbner-bases algorithm it is well possible that a polynomial h is added to the basis F such that, for p=lpp(h),

deg(p) < mdel({q ε pp3 | there is a polynomial f ε F with lpp(f)=q}.

Lemma 3.2 can be extended to deal also with this case.

Lemma 3.3: Let P $\subseteq$ pp3 be finite, | P | > 1, p ε pp3, deg(p)<mdel(P).
Then mdel(P u {p}) < mdel(P) + max{dist(p',P) | p<p' and deg(p')=mdel(P)}.

While "mdel" increases if a new power product p is added to P, one notices a decrease of the "interior" and (or) the "width" of P. This phenomenon is investigated in detail in the next few lemmata.

Lemma 3.4: Let P $\subseteq$ pp3 be finite, | P | > 1, p ε int(sect(P^*,mdel(P))).
Then
| int(sect((P u {p})*,mdel(P)+dist(p,P))) | < | int(sect(P^*,mdel(P))) | - dist(p,P).

Lemma 3.5: Let P $\subseteq$ pp3 be finite, | P | > 1, p ε ext(sect(P^*,mdel(P))),
t = w(P) - w(P u {p}).
Then
| int(sect((P u {p})*,mdel(P)+dist(p,P))) | <
| int(sect(P^*,mdel(P))) | + t.mdel(P) - (dist(p,P)-t).

Example 3.4: Let P and p be as in example 3.3.

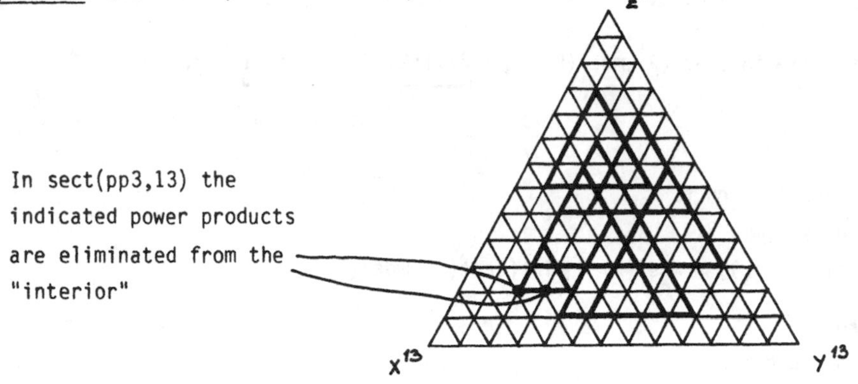

Example 3.5: Let P be as in example 3.1.

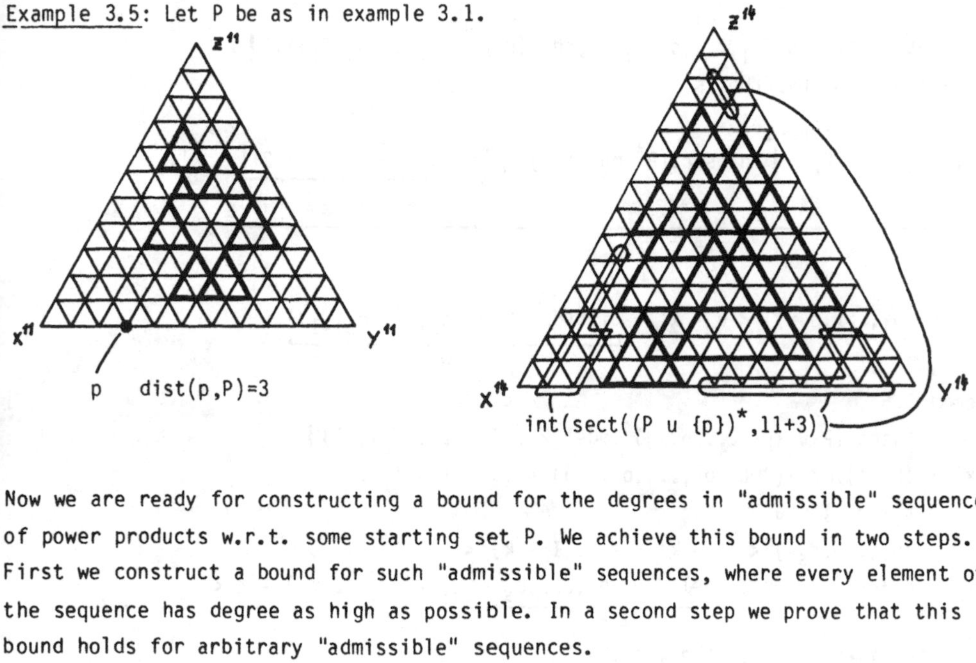

Now we are ready for constructing a bound for the degrees in "admissible" sequences of power products w.r.t. some starting set P. We achieve this bound in two steps. First we construct a bound for such "admissible" sequences, where every element of the sequence has degree as high as possible. In a second step we prove that this bound holds for arbitrary "admissible" sequences.

Def.: Let $P \subseteq pp3$ be finite, $|P| > 1$. Then
a sequence $(p_1,\dots,p_s)$ in pp3 is called **maximal** w.r.t. P
$:\Longleftrightarrow$ for all $1 \le i \le s$:
$\deg(p_i) = \mathrm{mdel}(P \cup \{p_1,\dots,p_{i-1}\})$ and
$p_i \notin (P \cup \{p_1,\dots,p_{i-1}\})^*$.

Lemma 3.6: Let $P \subseteq pp3$ be finite, $|P| > 1$, $(p_1,\dots,p_s)$ maximal w.r.t. P,
$t = w(P) - w(P \cup \{p_1,\dots,p_s\})$,
$k = |\mathrm{int}(\mathrm{sect}((P \cup \{p_1,\dots,p_s\})^*,\mathrm{mdel}(P \cup \{p_1,\dots,p_s\})))|$.

Then

$$\mathrm{mdel}(P \cup \{p_1,\ldots,p_s\}) <$$
$$(\ldots(((\mathrm{mdel}(P)+|\mathrm{int}(\mathrm{sect}(P^*,\mathrm{mdel}(P)))|)\cdot\underbrace{2+1)\cdot 2+1)\cdot\ \ldots)\cdot 2+1}_{t\ \text{times}} - k.$$

Proof: By induction on t.

If t=0 then by lemma 3.4

$$\mathrm{mdel}(P \cup \{p_1,\ldots,p_s\}) < \mathrm{mdel}(P) + |\mathrm{int}(\mathrm{sect}(P^*,\mathrm{mdel}(P)))| - k.$$

Now let $t>0$.

We choose s' such that

$w(P \cup \{p_1,\ldots,p_{s'-1}\}) = w(P)-t' > w(P)-t$ and

$w(P \cup \{p_1,\ldots,p_{s'}\}) = w(P)-t$.

Let

$$k' := |\mathrm{int}(\mathrm{sect}((P \cup \{p_1,\ldots,p_{s'-1}\})^*,\mathrm{mdel}(P \cup \{p_1,\ldots,p_{s'-1}\})))|.$$

Then by induction hypothesis

$$\mathrm{mdel}(P \cup \{p_1,\ldots,p_{s'-1}\}) <$$
$$\underbrace{(\ldots(((\mathrm{mdel}(P)+|\mathrm{int}(\mathrm{sect}(P^*,\mathrm{mdel}(P)))|)\cdot\underbrace{2+1)\cdot 2+1)\cdot\ \ldots)\cdot 2+1}_{t'\ \text{times}}}_{:=\ c} - k'.$$

So

$$\mathrm{mdel}(P \cup \{p_1,\ldots,p_{s'}\}) < c - k' + \underbrace{\mathrm{dist}(p_{s'},P \cup \{p_1,\ldots,p_{s'-1}\})}_{:=\ d}.$$

By lemma 3.5

$$I := |\mathrm{int}(\mathrm{sect}((P \cup \{p_1,\ldots,p_{s'}\})^*,\mathrm{mdel}(P \cup \{p_1,\ldots,p_{s'}\})))| <$$
$$k' + (t-t').\mathrm{mdel}(P \cup \{p_1,\ldots,p_{s'-1}\}) - (d - (t-t')).$$

Now we get from lemma 3.4

$$\mathrm{mdel}(P \cup \{p_1,\ldots,p_s\}) < c - k' + d + (I - k) <$$
$$c - k' + d + k' + (t-t').\underbrace{\mathrm{mdel}(P \cup \{p_1,\ldots,p_{s'-1}\})}_{<\ c} - d + (t-t') - k <$$
$$(\ldots((c\cdot\underbrace{2 + 1)\cdot 2 + 1)\cdot\ \ldots)\cdot 2 + 1}_{(t-t')\ \text{times}} - k <$$
$$(\ldots(((\mathrm{mdel}(P) + |\mathrm{int}(\mathrm{sect}(P^*,\mathrm{mdel}(P)))|)\cdot\underbrace{2 + 1)\cdot 2 + 1)\cdot\ \ldots)\cdot 2 + 1}_{t\ \text{times}} - k.$$

●

<u>Def</u>: Let $P \subseteq pp3$ be finite, $|P| > 1$.

$$b(P) := \max\{\mathrm{mdel}(P \cup \{p_1,\ldots,p_s\}) \mid (p_1,\ldots,p_s)\ \text{maximal w.r.t. } P\}.$$

(Bound for P.)

<u>Theorem 3.1</u>: Let $P \subseteq pp3$ be finite, $|P| > 1$.
Then

$$b(P) < (\ldots(((mdel(P) + |int(sect(P^*,mdel(P)))|)\cdot \underbrace{2 + 1)\cdot 2 + 1)\cdot \ldots)\cdot 2 + 1}_{w(P)\ \text{times}}.$$

Proof: The assertion follows from lemma 3.6 if we set $t=w(P)$ and $k=0$. •

<u>Corollary</u> to theorem 3.1: Let $P \subseteq pp3$ be finite, $|P| > 1$.
Then

$$b(P) < (mdel(P) + |int(sect(P^*,mdel(P)))| + 1)\cdot 2^{w(P)}.$$

Theorem 3.1 gives a bound for the degrees of the power products in a sequence $(p_1,\ldots,p_t)$ which is maximal w.r.t. P. But during the execution of the Gröbner-bases algorithm this maximality usually does not hold. So what remains to be done is to show that b(P) is an upper bound for $mdel(P \cup \{q_1,\ldots,q_s\})$, where the sequence $(q_1,\ldots,q_s)$ is admissible w.r.t. P.

<u>Lemma 3.7</u>: Let $P,Q \subseteq pp3$ be finite, $|P| > 1$, $|Q| > 1$, $P^* \subseteq Q^*$, $mdel(P) > mdel(Q)$, $q \in sect(pp3,mdel(Q))$.
Then there is a $p \in sect(pp3,mdel(P))$ such that

$q < p$ and $dist(q,Q) + mdel(Q) < dist(p,P) + mdel(P)$.

<u>Theorem 3.2</u>: Let $P \subseteq pp3$ be finite, $|P| > 1$, $q_1,\ldots,q_s \in pp3$ such that $deg(q_i) < mdel(P \cup \{q_1,\ldots,q_{i-1}\})$ for all $1<i<s$.
Then there is a maximal sequence $(p_1,\ldots,p_t)$ w.r.t. P such that

$mdel(P \cup \{q_1,\ldots,q_s\}) < mdel(P \cup \{p_1,\ldots,p_t\})$ and
$(P \cup \{p_1,\ldots,p_t\})^* \subseteq (P \cup \{q_1,\ldots,q_s\})^*$.

Proof: By induction on s.

s=1: If $mdel(P \cup \{q_1\}) < mdel(P)$ then the assertion holds with t=0.

If $mdel(P \cup \{q_1\}) > mdel(P)$ then by lemma 3.3 there is a p_1 such that

$deg(p_1)=mdel(P)$, $q_1 < p_1$, $p_1 \notin P^*$ and

$$mdel(P \cup \{q_1\}) < mdel(P) + dist(p_1,P) \underset{\uparrow\ \text{lemma 3.2}}{=} mdel(P \cup \{p_1\}).$$

Obviously $(P \cup \{p_1\})^* \subseteq (P \cup \{q_1\})^*$ holds.

s>1: By induction hypothesis there are $p_1,\ldots,p_{t'}$ maximal w.r.t. P such that

$mdel(P \cup \{q_1,\ldots,q_{s-1}\}) < mdel(P \cup \{p_1,\ldots,p_{t'}\})$ and
$(P \cup \{p_1,\ldots,p_{t'}\})^* \subseteq (P \cup \{q_1,\ldots,q_{s-1}\})^*$.

By lemma 3.7 for every $q \in sect(pp3,mdel(P \cup \{q_1,\ldots,q_{s-1}\}))$ there is a $p \in sect(pp3,mdel(P \cup \{p_1,\ldots,p_{t'}\}))$ such that

$q \leq p$ and

(*) $\mathrm{mdel}(P \cup \{q_1,\ldots,q_{s-1}\}) + \mathrm{dist}(q,P \cup \{q_1,\ldots,q_{s-1}\}) \leq$
$\mathrm{mdel}(P \cup \{p_1,\ldots,p_{t'}\}) + \mathrm{dist}(p,P \cup \{p_1,\ldots,p_{t'}\})$.

So

$\mathrm{mdel}(P \cup \{q_1,\ldots,q_s\}) \leq$
↑ lemma 3.3

$\mathrm{mdel}(P \cup \{q_1,\ldots,q_{s-1}\}) + \max\{\mathrm{dist}(q',P \cup \{q_1,\ldots,q_{s-1}\}) \mid q_s \leq q'$ and
$\deg(q')=\mathrm{mdel}(P \cup \{q_1,\ldots,q_{s-1}\})\ \} \leq$
↑ (*)

$\mathrm{mdel}(P \cup \{p_1,\ldots,p_{t'}\}) + \max\{\mathrm{dist}(p',P \cup \{p_1,\ldots,p_{t'}\}) \mid q_s \leq p'$ and
$\deg(p')=\mathrm{mdel}(P \cup \{p_1,\ldots,p_{t'}\})\ \}$.

If $\mathrm{sect}(\{q_s\}^*,\mathrm{mdel}(P \cup \{p_1,\ldots,p_{t'}\})) \subseteq (P \cup \{p_1,\ldots,p_{t'}\})^*$ then the assertion holds for $t=t'$.

If $A := \mathrm{sect}(\{q_s\}^*,\mathrm{mdel}(P \cup \{p_1,\ldots,p_{t'}\})) - (P \cup \{p_1,\ldots,p_{t'}\})^* \neq \{\}$ then we choose $p_{t'+1}$ in A such that

$\mathrm{dist}(p_{t'+1},P \cup \{p_1,\ldots,p_{t'}\}) = \max\{\mathrm{dist}(p',P \cup \{p_1,\ldots,p_{t'}\}) \mid p' \in A\}$.

Then we have

$\mathrm{mdel}(P \cup \{q_1,\ldots,q_s\}) \leq \mathrm{mdel}(P \cup \{p_1,\ldots,p_{t'}\}) + \mathrm{dist}(p_{t'+1},P \cup \{p_1,\ldots,p_{t'}\})$
$= \mathrm{mdel}(P \cup \{p_1,\ldots,p_{t'},p_{t'+1}\})$
↑ lemma 3.2

and by the induction hypothesis

$(P \cup \{p_1,\ldots,p_{t'},p_{t'+1}\})^* \subseteq (P \cup \{q_1,\ldots,q_s\})^*$. •

<u>Corollary</u> to theorem 3.2: Let $P \subseteq pp3$ be finite, $|P| \geq 1$, $q_1,\ldots,q_s$ such that $\deg(q_i) \leq \mathrm{mdel}(P \cup \{q_1,\ldots,q_{i-1}\})$ for all $1 \leq i \leq s$.
Then $\mathrm{mdel}(P \cup \{q_1,\ldots,q_s\}) \leq b(P)$.

<u>Theorem 3.3</u>: Let F be a finite set of polynomials in $K[x,y,z]$, $|F| \geq 1$, $P = \{p \mid p=\mathrm{lpp}(f)$ for some $f \in F\}$, $h_1,\ldots,h_s$ admissible polynomials w.r.t. F.
Then

$$\max\{\deg(h) \mid h \in F \cup \{h_1,\ldots,h_s\}\ \} \leq b(P).$$

Proof: The leading power products of $h_1,\ldots,h_s$ satisfy the conditions of the corollary to theorem 3.2. So

$\max\{\deg(h) \mid h \in F \cup \{h_1,\ldots,h_s\}\ \} \leq$
$\mathrm{mdel}(P \cup \{\mathrm{lpp}(h_1),\ldots,\mathrm{lpp}(h_s)\}) \leq$
↑ cor. to theorem 3.2
$b(P)$. •

4. Conclusion

Combining theorem 2.1 and the corollary to theorem 3.2 we get

Theorem 4.1: Let F be a finite set of polynomials in $K[x,y,z]$, $|F| > 1$,
$P = \{lpp(f) \mid f \in F\}$,
then every polynomial which is either in F or is generated during the execution of the Gröbner-bases algorithm on F has degree less than or equal to b(P).

From this bound for the degrees of the polynomials generated by the Gröbner-bases algorithm we can get one which only depends on the maximal and minimal degree of the given basis F. This bound is of course much coarser than the one given in the above theorems.

Corollary to theorem 4.1: Let F be a finite set of polynomials in $K[x,y,z]$, $|F| > 1$,
$d = \min\{deg(f) \mid f \in F\}$, $D = \max\{deg(f) \mid f \in F\}$,
then every polynomial which is either in F or is generated during the execution of the Gröbner-bases algorithm on F has degree less than or equal to

$$(8D + 1)\cdot 2^d.$$

Proof: $w(P) < d$, $mdel(P) < 2D$,

$$|int(sect(P^*,mdel(P)))| < |sect(pp3,2D)| = \binom{3 - 1 + 2D}{2D} =$$

$$= \frac{(2D+2).\ \dots\ .3}{2D.\ \dots\ .1} < 2D.3.$$

So by the corollary to theorem 3.1

$$b(P) <$$
$$(mdel(P) + |int(sect(P^*,mdel(P)))| + 1)\cdot 2^{w(P)} <$$
$$(2D + 6D + 1)\cdot 2^d =$$
$$(8D + 1)\cdot 2^d .$$

●

Although the degree of the polynomials in F enters exponentially in the degree bound for the Gröbner-basis, the exponential part depends only on the minimal degree of F. This minimal degree usually drops during the Gröbner-basis computation, thus giving better and better bounds for the actual result of the computation.

References

/Bu65/ B. Buchberger: Ein Algorithmus zum Auffinden der Basiselemente des Restklassenringes nach einem nulldimensionalen Polynomideal, Ph.D. Dissertation, Univ. Innsbruck, Austria, 1965.

/Bu70/ B. Buchberger: Ein algorithmisches Kriterium für die Lösbarkeit eines algebraischen Gleichungssystems, Aequ. Math., vol. 4/3, 374-383, 1970.

/Bu76/ B. Buchberger: A Theoretical Basis for the Reduction of Polynomials to Canonical Forms, ACM SIGSAM Bull., vol. 39, 19-29, 1976.

/Bu79/ B. Buchberger: A Criterion for Detecting Unnecessary Reductions in the Construction of Gröbner-Bases, Proc. Int. Symp. on Symbolic and Algebraic Manipulation, EUROSAM'79, Marseille, 1979, Lecture Notes in Computer Science 72, 3-21, Berlin-Heidelberg-New York: Springer-Verlag, 1979.

/Bu83a/ B. Buchberger: A Note on the Complexity of Constructing Gröbner-Bases, Proc. European Computer Algebra Conf., EUROCAL'83, London, 1983, Lecture Notes in Computer Science 162, 137-145, Berlin-Heidelberg-New York-Tokyo: Springer-Verlag, 1983.

/Bu83b/ B. Buchberger: Gröbner Bases: A Method in Symbolic Mathematics, 5th Intern. Conf. on Simulation, Programming and Mathematical Methods for Solving Physical Problems, Joint Inst. for Nuclear Research, Dubna, USSR, 1983.

/BW79/ B. Buchberger, F. Winkler: Miscellaneous Results on the Construction of Gröbner-Bases for Polynomial Ideals, Techn. Rep. Nr. 137, Inst. für Math., Univ. Linz, Austria, 1979

/KB78/ C. Kollreider, B. Buchberger: An Improved Algorithmic Construction of Gröbner-Bases for Polynomial Ideals, Techn. Rep. Nr. 110, Inst. für Math., Univ. Linz, Austria, 1978.

/La83/ D. Lazard: Gröbner Bases, Gaussian Elimination and Resolution of Systems of Algebraic Equations, Proc. European Computer Algebra Conf., EUROCAL'83, London, 1983, Lecture Notes in Computer Science 162, 146-156, Berlin-Heidelberg-New York-Tokyo: Springer-Verlag, 1983.

/Wi78/ F. Winkler: Implementierung eines Algorithmus zur Konstruktion von Gröbner-Basen, Diplomarbeit, Inst. für Math., Univ. Linz, Austria, 1978.

/Wi83/ F. Winkler: On the Complexity of the Gröbner-Bases Algorithm over K[x,y,z], Techn. Rep. Nr. CAMP 83-25.0, Inst. für Math., Univ. Linz, Austria, 1983.

/WB81/ F. Winkler, B. Buchberger, F. Lichtenberger, H. Rolletschek: An Algorithm for Constructing Canonical Bases (Groebner-Bases) of Polynomial Ideals, Techn. Rep. CAMP 81-10.0, Inst. f. Math., Univ. Linz, Austria, 1981.

ALGORITHMS FOR COMPUTING GRÖBNER BASES OF POLYNOMIAL IDEALS OVER VARIOUS EUCLIDEAN RINGS*

Abdelilah Kandri-Rody
Dept. of Mathematical Sciences
Rensselaer Polytechnic Institute
Troy, New York 12181
and
University Mohammed — V, Rabat, Morocco

Deepak Kapur†
Computer Science Branch
General Electric Company
Corporate Research and Development
Schenectady, New York 12345

ABSTRACT

Algorithms for computing Gröbner bases of polynomial ideals over integers, Gaussian integers and univariate polynomials over a field are discussed. Each of these algorithms takes an ideal specified by a finite set of polynomials as its input; the result is another finite basis of the ideal which can be used to simplify polynomials such that every polynomial in the ideal simplifies to 0 and every polynomial in the polynomial ring simplifies to a unique normal form. These algorithms are closely related to each other and they are extensions of Buchberger's algorithm for computing a Gröbner basis of polynomial ideals over a field. A general theorem exhibiting the uniqueness of a reduced Gröbner basis of an ideal, determined by the ordering used on indeterminates and other conditions, is given.

1. INTRODUCTION

Algorithms are developed for computing Gröbner bases [2] of polynomial ideals in which the coefficients of polynomials are from the rings of integers, Gaussian integers and univariate polynomials over a field. These algorithms are very similar to each other and they are extensions of Buchberger's algorithm [2] for computing a Gröbner basis of a polynomial ideal over a field. The input to the algorithm is an ideal specified by a finite set of polynomials; the algorithm produces another finite basis of the ideal which can be used to simplify polynomials such that every polynomial in the ideal simplifies to 0 and every polynomial in the polynomial ring simplifies to a unique normal form. A reader may wish to refer to [4] for the applications of the Gröbner basis algorithm as well as a brief introduction to the subject.

A polynomial ideal is like an equational theory; the Gröbner basis of the ideal is like a canonical term rewriting system for the equational theory when polynomials are viewed as rewrite rules. New polynomials added to complete a basis (called S-polynomials by Buchberger) are computed between pairs of polynomial in the basis; S-polynomials are analogous to critical pairs between rules in a term rewriting system as pointed in [4].

The paper is organized as follows: The next subsection is a summary of related work. Section 2 gives definitions. Section 3 discusses properties of a Euclidean ring, well-founded orderings on Z, $Z[i]$ and $Q[s]$. Section 4 discusses how to obtain a rewrite rule corresponding to a polynomial. Properties of rewriting relations needed in the paper are also reviewed. The Gröbner basis of an ideal is defined in terms of properties of the rewriting relation induced by polynomials in the basis. A unified view of the approach taken in the paper as well as a general Gröbner basis algorithm patterned after the Knuth-Bendix completion procedure [14] are presented.

Section 5 discusses the algorithms for polynomial ideals over Z, $Z[i]$, and $Q[s]$. In each case, firstly, the rewriting relation on polynomials induced by a polynomial is defined. The rewriting process is shown to terminate using orderings introduced in Section 3. Then, a critical pair and an S-polynomial between a pair of polynomials viewed as rewrite rules are defined. Using these S-polynomials, the Gröbner basis test is discussed as a special case of local confluence test discussed in [5,14]. The algorithm over Z has been implemented in ALDES; an interested reader may look at [10] for detailed discussion of this algorithm as well as for proofs of theorems in case of Z. For each of Z, $Z[i]$, and $Q[s]$, the algorithms and concepts are illustrated using examples. The final section reports a result about the uniqueness of a reduced Gröbner basis of a polynomial ideal over an arbitrary Euclidean ring given an ordering on indeterminates and the canonicals of the Euclidean ring.

---

* Some of the results reported in this paper will appear in Kandri-Rody's doctoral dissertation at RPI, Troy, NY.

† Partially supported by NSF grant MCS-82-11621.

1.1 Related Work

Szekeres showed the existence of a canonical basis for polynomial ideals over a Euclidean ring. According to Lauer, Shtokhamer developed a generalization of the construction suggested by Szekeres to define a canonical basis over a principal ideal domain. Schaller proposed an algorithm for computing a Gröbner basis of a polynomial ideal over a principal ideal domain; at the same time, Zacharias developed a similar algorithm for a polynomial ideal over a ring in which ideal membership and the basis problem for homogeneous linear equations are solvable. In both Schaller's and Zacharias's approaches, new polynomials needed for a complete basis must be computed for every finite set of polynomials in the input basis; this computation needs solving homogeneous linear equations. The reduction process in their approach needs a computation of extended greatest common divisor over many head coefficients in the basis; their algorithms give a Gröbner basis which is not necessarily unique.

The algorithms discussed in this paper were developed during the course of identifying relationship between Buchberger's algorithm for polynomial ideals over rationals and the Knuth-Bendix completion procedure [9]. Our approach is heavily influenced by term rewriting concepts and is similar to the approach taken in [4]. We would like to point out that we have benefited heavily in obtaining these results by conceptualizing the polynomial simplification problem in the framework of rewrite rule theory. We would recommend researchers in the field of algebraic simplification to closely investigate the relationship between algebraic simplification and term rewriting systems.

2. DEFINITIONS

Let $E[x_1, \cdots, x_n]$ be the ring of polynomials with indeterminates $x_1, \cdots, x_n$ over a ring E; it is assumed that $x_1 < x_2 < \cdots < x_n$. A *term* is any product $\prod_{i=1}^{n} x_i^{k_i}$, where $k_i \geqslant 0$; the degree of a term is $\sum_{i=1}^{n} k_i$. A *monomial* is a term multiplied by a nonzero coefficient from R. A *polynomial* is a sum of monomials; such a polynomial is said to be in *sum of products form,* abbreviated as SPF (this form of polynomials has also been called distributive normal form in the literature). If no term appears more than once in a polynomial in SPF, it is said to be in *simplified sum of products form,* abbreviated as SSPF. An arbitrary polynomial which is not in SPF can be transformed into an equivalent polynomial in SSPF using the rules of the polynomial ring. Henceforth, we will assume polynomials to be in SSPF.

The ordering on terms is defined using the degree of a term and terms of the same degree are ordered lexicographically (this ordering is the same as the one used by Buchberger in [1,2]). Terms $t_1 = \prod_1^n x_i^{k_i} < t_2 = \prod_1^n x_i^{j_i}$ if and only if (i) the degree of $t_1 <$ the degree of t_2, or (ii) if the degree of $t_1 =$ degree of t_2, then there exist an $i \geqslant 1$, such that $k_i < j_i$ and for for each $1 \leqslant i' < i$, $k_{i'} = j_{i'}$. This ordering is a total ordering and is well-founded. The results of the paper hold for any total well-founded ordering on terms. Another total well-founded ordering, for example, is the pure lexicographic ordering on terms based on a total ordering on indeterminates in which the degree of terms is not considered.

A quasi-ordering $\lesssim$ on the elements of R induces a quasi-ordering on monomials as follows: Given two monomials $m_1 = c_1 t_1$ and $m_2 = c_2 t_2$, $m_1 \lesssim m_2$ if and only if $t_1 < t_2$, or if $t_1 = t_2$, then $c_1 \lesssim c_2$. And, $m_1 < m_2$ if and only if $t_1 < t_2$, or if $t_1 = t_2$, then $c_1 < c_2$, where $<$ is the partial ordering subcomponent of $\lesssim$. The ordering $<$ on monomials is total and well-founded if the ordering $<$ on R is total and well-founded.

Let $p = m + r$ be a polynomial in SSPF such that the term of the monomial m is greater than those within r; then m is called the *head-monomial* of p, the term of m is called the *head-term* of p and the coefficient of m is called the *head-coefficient* of p. We will call r the *reductum* of p.

The quasi-ordering $\lesssim$ on monomials can be used to define a quasi-ordering on polynomials in the following way: polynomials $p_1 < p_2$ if and only if either (i) $m_1 < m_2$, or (ii) if $m_1 \sim m_2$, then $r_1 < r_2$, where m_i and r_i are, respectively, the head-monomial and reductum of p_i, $i = 1, 2$. If $<$ component of the quasi-ordering $\lesssim$ on monomials is well-founded, then the $<$ component of the quasi-ordering on polynomials is also well-founded.

3. WELL-FOUNDED ORDERING ON EUCLIDEAN RING AND CANONICALS

An element ϵ of a Euclidean ring E is called *unit* if there exists a unit ϵ' in E such that $\epsilon * \epsilon' = 1$. For example, 1 is a unit. A Euclidean ring could have more than one unit. In Z, for example, both 1 and -1 are units. For $Z[i]$, the units are $1, -1, i, -i$. In $Q[s]$, every element in $Q - \{0\}$ is a unit of $Q[s]$. Two elements a and b of E are called *associated* if and only if there exists a unit ϵ such that $a = b * \epsilon$. It is easy to see that associatedness is an equivalence relation on E. In particular, all units are associated.

For many Euclidean rings, it is possible to define a total well-founded ordering on its elements. For examples, elements of Z can be totally ordered as follows:

$$a \ll a' \text{ if and only if } |a| < |a'| \text{ or (if } |a| = |a'|, \text{ then } a > 0 \text{ and } a' < 0),$$

where $|x|$ is the absolute value of x. So, $3 \ll -3$, even though 3 and -3 are associated elements.

Similarly, the elements of $Z[i]$ can be totally ordered using the above ordering $\ll$ on integers and viewing complex integers as 2-tuples: Let $u = a + i\,b$, $v = c + i\,d$ Then, $u \ll v$ if and only if either $b \ll d$ or if $b = d$, then $a \ll c$, where $\ll$ on integers is defined as above. For example, $(-3 + i\,2) \ll (2 + i\,3)$, even though $2 + i\,3$ and $-3 + i\,2$ are associated. Also, $(3 + i\,2) \ll (-3 + i\,2)$.

For $Q[s]$ also, it is possible to define a total ordering as follows. We will represent non-zero elements $<sign>\, a/b$ of Q as a 3-tuple $<a, b, sign>$, where a and b are non-zero natural numbers and *sign* is either positive or negative. The 3-tuple $<0, 1, +>$ represents 0. Many well-founded total orderings on rational can be defined; we only require that (i) $<0, 1, +>$ is the least element immediately followed by $<1, 1, +>$, and (ii) for a, b, $<a, b, +> \ll <a, b, ->$. One such ordering is: $<a, b, sign_{1>} \ll <c, d, sign_{2>}$ if and only if (i) $a < c$, or (i) $a = c$ and $b < d$, or (iii) $a = c$, $b = d$, and $sign_1$ is + whereas $sign_2$ is $-$, where $<$ is less than ordering on natural numbers. A well-founded ordering on rationals induces a total well-founded ordering on polynomials in $Q[s]$ as defined in the previous section. For examples, $u = s^2 - 1 \ll v = s^2 + s + 2$.

Let $\ll$ be a total well-founded ordering on E such that 0 is the least element with respect to $\ll$. Let $canon\colon E \rightarrow E$ be a selection function, called *canonical,* which picks a unique representative for each equivalence class induced by the associatedness relation such that $canon(a)$ is a minimal element with respect to $\ll$ in the equivalence class. So, if a and b are associated, then $canon(a) = canon(b)$. An element a is called *canonical* if and only if $canon(a) = a$. For examples, for Z, the function which selects positive integers is a canonical function; similarly, for $Z[i]$, the function which selects complex numbers $(a + i\,b)$, where (i) $b \ll a$ and $b > 0$, or (ii) if $b = 0$, then $a > 0$, is a canonical function. Similarly, for $Q[s]$, the function which selects a polynomial whose head-coefficient is 1, is a canonical function. Henceforth, we assume that E is a Euclidean ring endowed with a computable *canon* function with respect to some well-founded ordering $\ll$ on E. We will use the canon function for each of Z, $Z[i]$, and $Q[s]$, as defined above.

We are interested in performing division only with respect to canonical elements. Given a canonical c, c induces an equivalence relation on E as follows: $a =_c b$ if and only if there exist k such that $a = k * c + b$. Using this equivalence relation $=_c$, we define the *remainders* with respect to a canonical divisor c (henceforth, called remainder of c) as follows: Consider all elements $\ll c$ and the equivalence relation $=_c$ induced on them. From each equivalence class induced by $=_c$ on elements $\ll c$, the smallest element is a remainder of c. For example, the remainders of a number 5 are $0, 1, -1, 2, -2$, whereas, the remainders of 4 are $0, 1, -1, 2$.

Lemma 3.1: For any non-zero canonical c, for any two distinct remainders r and r' of c, $(r - r') \neq k\,c$ for any k.

Lemma 3.2: For any non-zero canonical c, for every element a in E, there exists a unique q and r such that $a = q\,c + r$ and r is a remainder of c.

4. POLYNOMIALS AS REWRITE RULES AND GRÖBNER BASIS

Informally, a finite set B of polynomials, say $\{p_1, \cdots, p_k\}$, in $E[x_1, ..., x_n]$ is called a *Gröbner basis* for an ideal I generated by B if for any polynomial q, no matter how q is rewritten using the rules corresponding to polynomials in I, the result is always the same, i.e., it is unique [1,2]. An equivalent definition is that for any polynomial p in the ideal I generated by B, $p \rightarrow^* 0$. The Gröbner basis of an ideal generated by a finite set of polynomials is thus like a canonical rewriting system for an equational theory generated by a finite set of axioms.

For examples, consider the ideal I generated by $\{x\,y+1, y^2+x\}$ in $Z[x,y]$; $y - x^2$ is in I but does not reduce to 0, so I is not a Gröbner basis. However, $I' = \{x\,y+1,\ y^2+x,\ x^2-y\}$ is a Gröbner basis. Similarly, the basis $\{(5+i3)\,x^2y - y,\ (3+i2)\,x\,y^2 - x\}$ in $Z[i][x,y]$ is not a Gröbner basis.

In order to precisely define a Gröbner basis of an ideal I, it is necessary to define the rewriting relation induced by a polynomial. Let $p = m_1 + m_2 + \cdots + m_k$ be a polynomial, where $m_1 = c_1\,t_1$ is its head-monomial. The rewrite rule corresponding to p is as follows: let $canon(c_1) = \epsilon\, c_1$, where ϵ is a unit of E and is 1 if c_1 is a canonical, then

$$canon(c_1) * t_1 \rightarrow -\epsilon\, m_2 + \cdots + -\epsilon\, m_k$$

For example, in case of $Z[x,y]$, the rewrite rule corresponding to $-2\,x^2y + y$ is $2\,x^2y \rightarrow y$ since $canon(-2) = 2$. In case E is a field, the rule corresponding to a polynomial always has the head-term of the polynomial as its left-hand side since all elements other than 0 in F are associated and for any $a \neq 0$, $canon(a)$ is 1. In case of $Z[i][x,y]$, the rewrite rule corresponding to $(-2+i3)\,x\,y^2 - i\,x$ is $(3+2i)\,x\,y^2 \rightarrow x$, since $canon((-2+i3)) = (3+2i)$. Similarly, in case of $Q[s][x,y]$, for the polynomial $(2\,s^2 - 2/3)\,x\,y^2 - s\,x$, the rewrite rule is $(s^2 - 1/3)\,x\,y^2 \rightarrow s/2\,x$.

The above rule corresponding to p is used to rewrite polynomials in $E[x_1, x_2, \cdots, x_n]$. In later sections, we define the rewrite relation induced by a finite set of polynomials in case of $E = Z$, $Z[i]$, $Q[s]$. For each case, we will assume that after rewriting by a polynomial, polynomials are always brought back to SSPF, i.e., indeterminates in terms are ordered using the prespecified ordering on indeterminates, equal terms are combined, and terms with zero coefficients are omitted (see also [2]).

Let $T = \{L_1 \rightarrow R_1, \cdots, L_k \rightarrow R_k\}$ be the rule set corresponding to a basis $B = \{p_1, \cdots, p_k\}$ of an ideal I such that $\{L_i \rightarrow R_i\}$ be the rule corresponding to p_i. Let $\rightarrow$ denote the rewriting relation defined by T. We define properties of $\rightarrow$ which are needed for defining a Gröbner basis (an interested reader may want to refer to [4,5] for more details). Let $\rightarrow^*$ be the reflexive and transitive closure of $\rightarrow$ and $\rightarrow^+$ be the transitive closure of $\rightarrow$.

Definition: A relation $\rightarrow$ is *Noetherian* if and only if there does not exist any infinite sequence $x_0 \rightarrow x_1 \rightarrow x_2 \rightarrow \cdots$.

Definition: Two elements x and y are said to be *joinable* if and only if there exists u such that $x \rightarrow^* u$ and $y \rightarrow^* u$,

Definition: A relation $\rightarrow$ is *confluent* if and only if for all x, y, z, such that $x \rightarrow^* y$ and $x \rightarrow^* z$, y and z are joinable.

Definition: A relation $\rightarrow$ is *canonical* if and only if $\rightarrow$ is Noetherian and confluent.

Definition: A basis B is a *Gröbner basis* if the relation $\rightarrow$ induced by B is confluent.

Since we are interested in developing algorithms, we put an additional requirement that $\rightarrow$ be Noetherian. Under these conditions, the test for confluence reduces to a simple local test, called local confluence.

Definition: A relation $\rightarrow$ is *locally confluent* if and only if for each x, y, z, *such that* $x \rightarrow y$ *and* $x \rightarrow z$, y *and* z *are joinable.*

Theorem 4.1 [Newman]: If a relation $\rightarrow$ is Noetherian, then $\rightarrow$ is confluent if and only if $\rightarrow$ is locally confluent.

See [5] for a proof.

In order to develop the Gröbner bases test for polynomial ideals over Z, $Z[i]$, and $Q[s]$, we show in each case that $\rightarrow$ is Noetherian using the total well-founded ordering defined on polynomials in the previous sections induced by a total well-founded ordering on E. Then, we develop a test for local confluence and use the above theorem to check whether a basis is a Gröbner basis.

The test for local confluence is developed in a way similar to the approach developed by Buchberger for polynomial ideals over a field [1,2,3,4]. We define *critical pairs* for a pair of polynomials in a basis. Then it is shown that if these critical pairs are trivial in the sense that the corresponding S-polynomials reduce to 0, $\rightarrow$ is locally-confluent.

From this test, we get a Gröbner basis algorithm similar to Buchberger's algorithm. If a critical pair is not trivial, then we augment the basis by adding the reduced form of the corresponding S-polynomial. As pointed in [1,4,9,10], this completion algorithm is closely related to the Knuth-Bendix completion procedure [14] for term-rewriting systems. The correctness of the Gröbner basis algorithm is demonstrated by (i) showing that the reduced forms of S-polynomials corresponding to critical pairs of a basis are indeed in the ideal generated by the basis and (ii) using the above test for a Gröbner basis.

In the rest of the paper, we discuss Gröbner Bases algorithms for polynomial ideals over Z, $Z[i]$, and $Q[s]$. For each Euclidean ring, we

(i) define the reduction relation $\rightarrow$ defined by a polynomial,

(ii) show that $\rightarrow$ is Noetherian,

(iii) define the critical pair and S-polynomial for a pair of polynomials,

(iv) prove that if all critical pairs of a basis are trivial, then the basis is a Gröbner basis by showing that $\rightarrow$ is locally confluent.

ALGORITHM: Given F, a finite set of polynomials in $E[x_1, \cdots, x_n]$,
find G where $ideal(F) = ideal(G)$ and G is a Gröbner basis.

```
Initialization: T_0 := F; G_0 := { }; i := 0; m := 0;
LOOP
 WHILE T_i ≠ { } DO { reduce polynomial: select polynomial p in T_i
            (hm, red) := normalize(G_i, p);
        ;;;; hm and red are head monomial and reductum of normalized p, respectively.}
 IF hm = 0 THEN { T_{i+1} = T_i − { p };  G_{i+1} := G_i;  i := i+1; }
 ELSE { Add new polynomial: let K be the set of labels k of polynomials of G_i
        whose head term hm_k is reducible by (hm, red);
    T_{i+1} := (T_i − { p }) ∪ {(hm_k, red_k), k belongs to K};  m := m + 1;
    G_{i+1} := {j: (hm_j, red'_j) | j: (hm_j, red_j) in G_i − K } ∪ {m: (hm, red)};
        ;;;; red'_j = normalize(G_i ∪ {m: (hm, red)}, red_j)
      the new polynomial m:(hm, red) is unmarked;
      i := i+1 }
 ENDWHILE;
compute critical pairs: IF all polynomials in G_i are marked THEN EXITLOOP (G_i canonical);
  ELSE {select an unmarked polynomial in G_i, say with label k;
    T_{i+1} := the set of all critical pairs computed between polynomial k and
           any polynomial of G_i of label not greater than k.
    G_{i+1} := G_i, except that polynomial k is now marked;
    i := i+1 }
 ENDLOOP

 G := G_i
```

The general Gröbner basis algorithm patterned after the version of the Knuth-Bendix completion procedure in [6] is given above. For a detailed discussion of the Gröbner basis algorithm over Z, see [10]. We also discuss there an implementation of the algorithm in ALDES and LISP with examples.

5. ALGORITHMS FOR POLYNOMIAL IDEALS OVER VARIOUS EUCLIDEAN RINGS

5.1 RING OF INTEGERS

A rule $L \to R$, where $L = c_1 t_1$ and $c_1 > 0$ rewrites a monomial $c\,t$ to $(c - \epsilon c_1)\,t + \epsilon \sigma R$ where $\epsilon = 1$ if $c > 0$, $\epsilon = -1$ if $c < 0$, if and only if (i) there exists a term σ such that $t = \sigma t_1$ and (ii) either $c > (c_1/2)$ or $c < -(c_1 - 1)/2$. If $-(c_1 - 1)/2 \leqslant c \leqslant (c_1/2)$ or there does not exist any σ such that $t = \sigma t_1$, then then the monomial $c\,t$ cannot rewritten.

A polynomial Q is rewritten to Q' using the rule $L \to R$ if and only if (i) $Q = Q_1 + c\,t$ and $c\,t$ is the largest monomial in Q which can be rewritten using the rule, and (ii) $Q' = Q_1 + (c - \epsilon c_1)\,t + \epsilon \sigma R$, where $\epsilon = 1$ if $c > 0$, $\epsilon = -1$ otherwise. If there is no monomial in Q which can be rewritten using the rule, then Q is *irreducible* or in *normal form* with respect to the rule. For example, using the rule $2x^2y \to y$, the polynomial

$$4x^3y + 5xy^2 - 3x^2y \to 2x^3y + xy + 5xy^2 - 3x^2y \to 2xy + 5xy^2 - 3x^2y.$$

The result can be further reduced as the monomial $-3x^2y$ is reducible:

$$\to 2xy + 5xy^2 - x^2y - y \to 2xy + 5xy^2 + x^2y - 2y.$$

Lemma 5.1.1: The rewriting relation $\to$ induced by any finite basis over $Z[x_1, \cdots, x_n]$ is Noetherian.

Proof: Follows from the fact that for any polynomials Q, Q', such that $Q \to Q'$, $Q' \ll Q$. □

5.1.1 Critical Pairs

Given two rules $L_1 \to R_1$ and $L_2 \to R_2$, where $L_1 = c_1 t_1$ and $L_2 = c_2 t_2$, such that $c_1 \geqslant c_2 > 0$. Its *critical pair* $<p, q>$ is defined as: $p = (c_1 - c_2)\, lcm(t_1, t_2) + f_2 * R_2$, and $q = f_1 * R_1$, where $f_1 * t_2 = f_1 * t_2 = lcm(t_1, t_2)$. Polynomials p and q are obtained from the superposition $c_1\, lcm(t_1, t_2)$ by applying $L_2 \to R_2$ and $L_1 \to R_1$, respectively. Note that the above definition of a critical pair is a generalization of the definition used by Buchberger [1,2,3,4] for a field.

Example: in $Z[x, y]$, consider the basis $B_1 = \{3x^2y \to y,\ 10xy^2 \to x\}$.
The superposition of the two polynomials is $10x^2y^2$, and the critical pair is $<7x^2y^2 + y^2, x^2>$

It is easy to see that for the critical pair $<p, q>$ of two polynomials in an ideal, the polynomial $p - q$ is also in the ideal. So, adding the polynomial $p - q$ to the ideal does not change the ideal.

The *S-Polynomial* corresponding to a critical pair $<p, q>$ is the polynomial $p - q$.

Definition: A critical pair $<p, q>$ is *trivial* if and only if its S-polynomial $p - q$ can be reduced to 0 by applying at every step, among all applicable rules, a rule whose left-hand-side has the least coefficient.

The above restriction is necessary because of the way the rewriting relation is defined above. If we do not have this restriction, then there are bases for which all critical pairs are trivial but the bases are not Gröbner bases. For example, consider the basis $B_2 = \{1.\ \ 6x^2y \to y, 2.\ \ 2xy^2 \to x\}$. Its critical pair is $<4x^2y^2 + x^2, y^2>$, and the two polynomials are joinable if we apply rule 1 first and then rule 2 on the first polynomial.

5.1.2 Gröbner Basis Test

To test whether a given basis is a Gröbner basis, (i) get the rule set corresponding to the basis, and (iii) check whether for each pair of distinct rules, the critical pair $<p, q>$ is trivial. For example, the basis B_1 in the above example is not a Gröbner basis because the two polynomials in the critical pair $<7x^2y^2 + y^2, x^2>$ do not reduce to the same polynomial. The following theorem serves as the basis of this test.

Theorem 5.1.2: A basis B of polynomials in $Z[x_1, \cdots, x_n]$ is a Gröbner basis if and only if for every pair of polynomials in B, the critical pair $<p, q>$ is trivial.

Proof: We show that the relation $\rightarrow$ induced by B is locally confluent if and only if the critical pairs are trivial. The proof is very similar to the one given in [1] for a field. It uses the following lemma:

Lemma 5.1.3: For any two polynomials p and q, if $p - q \rightarrow'^{*} 0$, then p and q are joinable.

The relation $\rightarrow'$ is a subset of the relation $\rightarrow$ and is defined as: A monomial $c\,t \rightarrow' q'$ if and only if $c\,t \rightarrow q'$ using a rule $c_1\,t_1 \rightarrow R_1$ in B such that there does not exist any other rule $c_2\,t_2 \rightarrow R_2$ in B which can be applied on $c\,t$ and $c_2 < c_1$. A polynomial $P \rightarrow' Q$ if and only if Q is obtained from P by rewriting the largest monomial under $\rightarrow'$. The definition of a critical pair being trivial uses the rewriting relation $\rightarrow'$.

The proof of Lemma 5.1.3 is by induction and is similar to the proof of a similar lemma in [1]. It uses the following property of $\rightarrow'$.

Lemma 5.1.4: For any two polynomials p, q, if $p - q \rightarrow' h$ and $h \rightarrow'^{*} 0$, then there exist p', q', such that $h = p' - q'$ and $p \rightarrow^{*} p'$ and $q \rightarrow^{*} q'$.

Proof: Suppose that $p - q$ is reduced to h by a rule $c\,t \rightarrow R$. Let $p = R_p + d_p\,t$, $q = R_q + d_q\,t$, $d = d_p - d_q$. Then $h = (R_p - R_q) + (d_p - d_q - \epsilon\,c)\,t + \epsilon\,\sigma\,R$. There are two cases: (i) $d > c/2$ and (ii) $d < -(c-1)/2$. The proofs in the two cases are similar. Below, the proof for the first case is given.
$d > c/2$ implies $d_p > d_q + c/2$ and $h = (R_p - R_q) + (d_p - d_q - c)\,t + \sigma\,R$. There are two subcases:
Subcase 1: $d_q \geqslant 0$, which implies $d_p > c/2$, hence d_p is not a remainder of c. So, we reduce p to $p' = R_p + (d_p - c)\,t + \sigma\,R$. We take $q' = q$.
Subcase 2: $d_q < 0$: If $d_q < -(c-1)/2$ then we reduce q to $q' = R_q + (d_q + c)\,t - \sigma\,R$ and we take $p' = p$.
If $0 > d_q \geqslant -(c-1)/2$, then $d_p > 0$. If $d_p > c/2$ then we take $p' = R_p + (d_p - c)\,t + \sigma\,R$ and $q' = q$. If $d_p \leqslant c/2$ then $c/2 < (d_p - d_q) \leqslant (c/2 + (c-1)/2)$ and $d_p - d_q - c$ is a remainder of c. This implies that h cannot be reduced to 0 since in $\rightarrow'$, we require that the rewriting be done using a rule with the smallest head-coefficient. This is a contradiction. □

5.1.3 Gröbner Basis Algorithm

If a basis is not a Gröbner basis, it can be completed to get a Gröbner basis. For every non-trivial critical pair $<p, q>$, add a new rule corresponding to a normal form of the polynomial $p - q$ using the relation $\rightarrow'$, thus generating a new basis for the same ideal. This step is repeated until for every pair of polynomials in the basis, its critical pair is trivial. The termination of this process is guaranteed because of finite ascending chain condition of properly contained ideals over a Noetherian ring (since $Z[x_1, \cdots, x_n]$ is a Noetherian ring) (see van der Waerden [21], Vol. II, p. 117); also see [10] for details of the proof. The termination proof holds for any Euclidean ring.

Example: In $Z[x, y]$, consider the basis $B = \{1.\ 2\,x^2\,y \rightarrow y,\ 2.\ 3\,x\,y^2 \rightarrow x\}$, we first add the rule obtained by the critical pair of rules 1 and 2: 3. $x^2\,y^2 \rightarrow -y^2 + x^2$.
From rules 1 and 3, we get the critical pair $<x^2\,y^2 - y^2 + x^2, y^2>$ which gives an additional rule: 4. $3\,y^2 \rightarrow 2\,x^2$.
Using rule 4, rule 2 can be reduced to 2'. $2\,x^3 \rightarrow x$.
The above 4 rules constitute a Gröbner basis because every critical pair is trivial.

5.1.4 Optimization

The above process of generating critical pairs (henceforth called definition CP1) can be optimized by generating the critical pairs as follows:

Definition CP2: The critical pair for two rules $c_1\,t_1 \rightarrow R_1$ and $c_2\,t_2 \rightarrow R_2$, where $c_1 \geqslant c_2$ is: let $t = lcm(t_1, t_2) = f_1\,t_1 = f_2\,t_2$ and $c_1 = a\,c_2 + b$, where b is a remainder of c_2, then the superposition of the two left-hand-sides is the monomial $c_1\,t$ from which by applying the two rules, we obtain the critical pair $<p, q>$, where $p = b\,t + a\,f_2 * R_2$ and $q = f_1 * R_1$.

Definition CP2 can be further optimized using the greatest common divisor (gcd) computation on the elements of a Euclidean ring.

Definition CP3: The critical pair for two rules $c_1 t_1 \rightarrow R_1$ and $c_2 t_2 \rightarrow R_2$, where $c_1 \gg c_2$ or $c_1 \sim c_2$ is defined as follows:

(i) if c_2 divides c_1, we generate the critical pair using the lcm of L_1 and L_2 as the superposition and we obtain p and q by applying the given rules respectively. This case is the same as the definition CP2. Since lcm of c_1 and c_2 is c_1, suppose $c_1 = k\, c_2$, then, $p = f_1 R_1$ and $q = k\, f_2 R_2$; otherwise,

(ii) if c_2 does not divide c_1, we generate the critical pair using the gcd. Let c be the extended gcd of c_1 and c_2; there exist a and b such that $c = a\, c_1 + b\, c_2$. Then the superposition of the two rules is $a\, c_1 f_1 t_1 + b\, c_2 f_2 t_2$, and the critical pair $<p, q>$ is obtained from the superposition by applying the two rules: $p = c\ lcm(t_1, t_2)$ and $q = a\, f_1 R_1 + b\, f_2 R_2$.

The above optimization should work for any Euclidean ring.

5.2 RING OF GAUSSIAN INTEGERS

The Gröbner basis algorithm for polynomial ideals over Gaussian integers is an extension of the algorithm for integers discussed in the last section. We use the total well-founded ordering defined on complex integers and canonicals induced by the ordering, given in Section 3.

A rule $L \rightarrow R$, where $L = c\, t_1$ and $c = (c_1 + i\, c_2)$ is a canonical, rewrites a monomial $m = (a + i\, b)\, t$ to $q' = ((a + i\, b) - \epsilon\, (c_1 + i\, c_2))\, t + \epsilon\, \sigma\, R$ under the following conditions: (1) there exists a term σ such that $t = \sigma\, t_1$, (2) if $c_2 > 0$, then either $b > c_2/2$ or $b < -(c_2 - 1)/2$, and $\epsilon = 1$ if $b > 0$, $\epsilon = -1$ if $b < 0$, and (3) if $c_2 = 0$, then (i) if either $b > c_1/2$ or $b < -(c_1 - 1)/2$, then $\epsilon = i$ if $b > 0$ and $\epsilon = -i$ if $b < 0$, and (ii) if $-(c_1 - 1)/2 \leqslant b \leqslant c_1/2$, and (either $a > c_1/2$ or $a < -(c_1 - 1)/2$), then $\epsilon = 1$ if $a > 0$ and $\epsilon = -1$ if $a < 0$. The monomial m cannot be reduced otherwise. A polynomial Q is rewritten to Q' using the above rule if and only if (i) $Q = Q_1 + (a + i\, b)\, t$ and $(a + i\, b)\, t$ is the largest monomial in Q which can be rewritten using the rule, and (ii) $Q' = Q_1 + ((a + i\, b) - \epsilon\, (c_1 + c_2))\, t + \epsilon\, \sigma\, R$, where ϵ is defined as above.

Lemma 5.2.1: The rewriting relation $\rightarrow$ induced by any finite basis over $Z[i][x_1, \cdots, x_n]$ is Noetherian.

Given two rules $L_1 \rightarrow R_1$ and $L_2 \rightarrow R_2$, where $L_1 = (c_1 + i\, c_2)\, t_1$ and $L_2 = (d_1 + i\, d_2)\, t_2$, such that $(c_1 + i\, c_2) \gg (d_1 + i\, d_2)$ or $(c_1 + i\, c_2) = (d_1 + i\, d_2)$, its *critical pair* $<p, q>$ is defined as: Polynomials p and q are obtained from the superposition $(c_1 + i\, c_2)\ lcm(t_1, t_2)$ by applying $L_2 \rightarrow R_2$ and $L_1 \rightarrow R_1$, respectively.

$$p = ((c_1 + i\, c_2) - \epsilon\, (d_1 + i\, d_2))\ lcm(t_1, t_2) + f_2 * R_2, \quad \text{and} \quad q = f_1 * R_1,$$

where $f_1 * t_1 = f_2 * t_2 = lcm(t_1, t_2)$, where ϵ is defined as above.

Definition: A critical pair $<p, q>$ is *trivial* if and only if its S-polynomial $p - q$ can be reduced to 0 by applying at every step, among all applicable rules, a rule whose left-hand-side has the least coefficient with respect to $\ll$.

Like in case of integers, the above restriction is necessary here also. To test whether a given basis is a Gröbner basis, (i) get the rule set corresponding to the basis, and (iii) check whether for each pair of distinct rules, the critical pair $<p, q>$ is trivial. The following theorem, which is similar to Theorem 5.1.2, serves as the basis of this test.

Theorem 5.2.2: A basis B of polynomials in $Z[i][x_1, \cdots, x_n]$ is a Gröbner basis if and only if for every pair of polynomials in B, the critical pair $<p, q>$ is trivial.

The proof is similar to the proof of Theorem 5.1.2.

If a basis is not a Gröbner basis, it can be completed to get a Gröbner basis of its ideal. For every non-trivial critical pair $<p, q>$, add a new rule corresponding to a normal form of the polynomial $p - q$ obtained by reducing $p - q$ by applying a rule whose left-hand-side has the least coefficient, thus generating a new basis for the same ideal. This step is repeated until for every pair of polynomials in the basis, its critical pair is trivial.

We illustrate the algorithm using the following example. Consider the basis:

1. $(5+i\,3)\,x^2 y \rightarrow y$ and 2. $(3+i\,2)\,x\,y^2 \rightarrow x$.

From rules 1 and 2, we get the superposition $(5+i\,3)\,x^2 y^2$ and the critical pair $<y^2, x^2+(2+i)\,x^2 y^2>$, which gives the following rule: 3. $(2+i)\,x^2 y^2 \rightarrow y^2 - x^2$.
From rules 2 and 3, the superposition is $(3+i\,2)\,x^2 y^2$, which gives the following rule:

4. $x^2 y^2 \rightarrow 2\,y^2 - 3\,x^2$.

Rule 3 now reduces to: 3': $(3+i\,2)\,y^2 \rightarrow (5+i\,3)\,x^2$.
Rule 2 now simplifies to: 2': $(5+i\,3)\,x^3 \rightarrow x$.
The basis consisting of polynomials corresponding to rules 1, 2', 3', and 4' is a Gröbner basis.

We should remark here that another way to get a Gröbner basis algorithm over $Z[i][x_1, \cdots, x_n]$ is to treat i as an additional indeterminate and add the polynomial i^2+1 into the input basis and use the Gröbner basis algorithm over $Z[i, x_1, \cdots, x_n]$.

5.3 RING OF UNIVARIATE POLYNOMIALS OVER A FIELD

As discussed in Section 3, the canonical elements of $Q[s]$ are the polynomials whose head-coefficient is 1. The rewriting relation is defined by just using the standard division algorithm in $Q[s]$. A rule $L \rightarrow R$, where $L = c_1\,t_1$ and $c_1 > 0$ rewrites a monomial $c\,t'$ to $r\,t' + a\,\sigma\,R$ where $c = a\,c_1 + r$, if and only if (i) there exists a term σ such that $t' = \sigma\,t_1$ and (ii) c is not a remainder of c_1. If there does not exist any σ such that $t' = \sigma\,t_1$ or c is a remainder of c_1, then the monomial $c\,t'$ cannot be rewritten. A polynomial Q is rewritten to Q' using the rule $L \rightarrow R$ if and only if (i) $Q = Q_1 + c\,t'$, $c\,t'$ is the largest monomial in Q which can be rewritten using the rule, and (ii) $Q' = Q_1 + r\,t + a\,\sigma\,R$, where a and r are as defined above. If there is no monomial in Q which can be rewritten using the rule, then Q is *irreducible* or in *normal form* with respect to the rule.

Lemma 5.3.1: The rewriting relation $\rightarrow$ induced by any finite basis B on $Q[s][x_1, \cdots, x_n]$ is Noetherian.

Given two rules $L_1 \rightarrow R_1$ and $L_2 \rightarrow R_2$, where $L_1 = c_1\,t_1$ and $L_2 = c_2\,t_2$ such that the degree of the head-term of $c_1 \geqslant$ the degree of the head-term of c_2, its *critical pair* $<p, q>$ is defined as:

$$p = b\ \mathit{lcm}(t_1, t_2) + a\,f_2 * R_2, \quad \text{and} \quad q = f_1 * R_1,$$

where $f_1 * t_2 = f_1 * t_2 = \mathit{lcm}(t_1, t_2)$ and $c_1 = a\,c_2 + b$, where b is the remainder obtained by dividing c_1 by c_2. Polynomials p and q are obtained from the superposition $c_1\ \mathit{lcm}(t_1, t_2)$ by applying $L_2 \rightarrow R_2$ and $L_1 \rightarrow R_1$, respectively.

Definition: A critical pair $<p, q>$ is *trivial* if and only if its S-polynomial $p - q$ can be reduced to 0 by applying at every step, among all applicable rules, a rule whose left-hand-side has the least coefficient.

This restriction on reducing $p - q$ is not needed for $Q[s]$; however, it is retained so as to help us in developing a generalization of these algorithms to an arbitrary Euclidean ring.

Theorem 5.3.2: A basis B of polynomials in $Q[s][x_1, \cdots, x_n]$ is a Gröbner basis if and only if for every pair of polynomials in B, the critical pair $<p, q>$ is trivial.

The proof of this theorem is also similar to the proofs of Theorems 5.1.2 and 5.2.2. It also needs a lemma analogous to Lemma 5.1.4; however, the proof of this lemma is simpler than the proof of Lemma 5.1.4 because for $Q[s]$, for any two remainders r_1 and r_2 of a canonical c, $r_1 - r_2$ is also a remainder.

The above treatment and proofs generalize to an arbitrary Euclidean ring where the remainders of every canonical satisfy the property that the difference of two remainders is a remainder. This property however does not hold in case of Z and $Z[i]$; for example, the remainders of 3 in Z are 0, 1, −1; 1 − (−1) is not a remainder.

If a basis is not a Gröbner basis, it can be completed to get a Gröbner basis of its ideal. For every non-trivial critical pair $<p, q>$, add a new rule corresponding to a normal form of the polynomial $p - q$, thus generating a new basis for the same ideal. This step is repeated until for every pair of polynomials in the basis, its critical pair is trivial.

Consider an example over $Q[s][x,y]$. The basis is:

1. $(s^2 + 2/5\, s - 1/5)\, x^2 y \rightarrow 1/5\, y$ and 2. $(s - 1/3)\, x y^2 \rightarrow 1/3\, x$.

From rules 1 and 2, we get the rule: 3. $x^2 y^2 \rightarrow 9/2\, y^2 - (15/2\, s + 11/2)\, x^2$.
From rules 2 and 3, we get the rule: 4. $(s - 1/3)\, y^2 \rightarrow (5/3\, s^2 + 2/3\, s - 1/3)\, x^2$.
Rule 2 can now be reduced using rule 4 to: 2′. $(s^2 + 2/5\, s - 1/5)\, x^3 \rightarrow 1/5\, x$.

Rules 1, 2′, 3 and 4 constitute a Gröbner basis of the above ideal. Since $Q[s][x,y] = Q[s,x,y]$, the Gröbner basis algorithm over rationals can be run to obtain a Gröbner basis over $Q[s,x,y]$ and we can verify that these two different bases are indeed equivalent.

6. UNIQUENESS OF MINIMAL GRÖBNER BASIS

Definition: A Gröbner basis $B = \{p_1, \cdots, p_m\}$ is *minimal* (or *reduced*) if and only if for each i, $1 \leqslant i \leqslant m$, the head-coefficient of p_i is canonical and p_i cannot be rewritten by any other polynomial in B when viewed as a rewrite rule.

Theorem 6.1: Let $B = (p_1, \cdots, p_m)$ be a basis of an ideal I in $E[x_1, \cdots, x_n]$, where E is a Euclidean ring endowed with a well-founded total ordering $\ll$. Then, a minimal Gröbner basis of I over $R[x_1, \cdots, x_n]$ is unique subject to a total ordering on indeterminates $x_1, \cdots, x_n$ and the selection of a *canon* function on E induced by $\ll$ as discussed in Section 3.

For a proof of the theorem when $E = Z$, see [10]. That proof generalizes using Lemma 3.1 given in Section 3. Similar results about the uniqueness of a reduced canonical system have been reported in Kapur and Narendran [12] for Thue systems and Lankford and Ballantyne [15] for term rewriting systems; see also Lankford and Butler [16].

7. CONCLUDING REMARKS

Gröbner bases algorithms for polynomial ideals over Z, $Z[i]$, and $Q[s]$ have been presented. We conjecture that these algorithms are an instance of a general Gröbner basis algorithm over a Euclidean ring. The unique Gröbner basis of an ideal gives insight into the structure of the ideal under consideration, such as the primality of an ideal and zeros of an ideal, especially when the pure lexicographical ordering on monomials is used to compute the Gröbner basis, see [8,11] for more details.

Computing the Gröbner basis of an ideal over Z solves the uniform word problem (for elementary terms) over a finitely presented commutative ring with unity. If we add additional polynomials which are valid for a boolean ring into a basis, then the Gröbner basis algorithm over Z can be used as a way to prove the unsatisfiability of a conjunctive normal form; this method is closely related to Hsiang's approach [7] for theorem proving in propositional calculus. Computing the Gröbner basis over Z is also related to the uniform word problem and unification problem (for elementary terms) over a finitely presented abelian group. For details, see [10].

ACKNOWLEDGMENT: We are thankful to Paliath Narendran and David Saunders for their helpful comments and suggestions on various drafts of this paper, and to Dallas Lankford for suggesting that there might be a relation between the Gröbner basis computation and word problems over finitely presented commutative rings with unity.

8. REFERENCES

[1] Bachmair, L., and Buchberger, B., "A Simplified Proof of the Characterization Theorem for Gröbner-Bases," *ACM-SIGSAM Bulletin,* 14/4, 1980, pp. 29-34.

[2] Buchberger, B., "A Theoretical Basis for the Reduction of Polynomials to Canonical Forms," *ACM-SIGSAM Bulletin,* 39, August 1976, pp. 19-29.

[3] Buchberger, B., "A Criterion for Detecting Unnecessary Reductions in the Construction of Gröbner-Bases," *Proceedings of EUROSAM 79,* Marseille, Springer Verlag Lecture Notes in Computer Science, Vol. 72, 1979, pp. 3-21.

[4] Buchberger, B. and Loos, R., "Algebraic Simplification," *Computer Algebra: Symbolic and Algebraic Computation* (B. Buchberger, G.E. Collins, and R. Loos, eds.), Computing Suppl. 4, Springer Verlag, New York, 1982, pp. 11-43.

[5] Huet, G., "Confluent Reductions: Abstract Properties and Applications to Term Rewriting Systems," *JACM,* Vol. 27, No. 4, October 1980, pp. 797-821.

[6] Huet, G., "A Complete Proof of Correctness of the Knuth-Bendix Completion Procedure," *JCSS,* Vol. 23, No. 1, August 1981, pp. 11-21.

[7] Hsiang, J., *Topics in Theorem Proving and Program Synthesis,* Ph.D. Thesis, University of Illinois, Urbana-Champagne, July 1983.

[8] Kandri-Rody, A., *Effective Problems in the Theory of Polynomial Ideals,* Forthcoming Ph.D. Thesis, RPI, Troy, NY, May 1984.

[9] Kandri-Rody, A. and Kapur, D., "On Relationship between Buchberger's Gröbner Basis Algorithm and the Knuth-Bendix Completion Procedure," TIS Report No. 83CRD286, General Electric Research and Development Center, Schenectady, NY, December 1983.

[10] Kandri-Rody, A. and Kapur, D., "Computing the Gröbner Basis of Polynomial Ideals over Integers," to appear in *Third MACSYMA User's Conference,* Schenectady, NY, July 1984.

[11] Kandri-Rody, A. and Saunders, B.D., "Primality of Ideals in Polynomial Rings," to appear in *Third MACSYMA User's Conference,* Schenectady, NY, July 1984.

[12] Kapur, D. and Narendran, P., "The Knuth-Bendix Completion Procedure and Thue Systems," *Third Conference on Foundation of Computer Science and Software Engg.,* Bangalore, India, December 1983, pp. 363-385.

[13] Kapur, D. and Sivakumar, G., "Architecture of and Experiments with RRL, a Rewrite Rule Laboratory," *Proceedings of the NSF Workshop on Rewrite Rule Laboratory,* Rensselaerville, NY, September 4-6, 1983.

[14] Knuth, D.E. and Bendix, P.B., "Simple Word Problems in Universal Algebras," *Computational Problems in Abstract Algebras* (J. Leech, ed.), Pergamon Press, 1970, pp. 263-297.

[15] Lankford, D.S. and Ballantyne, A.M., Private Communication, December 1983.

[16] Lankford, D.S. and Butler, G., "Experiments with Computer Implementations of Procedures which often Derive Decision Algorithms for the Word Problem in Abstract Algebra," Technical Report, MTP-7, Louisiana Tech. University, August 1980.

[17] Lauer, M., "Canonical Representatives for Residue Classes of a Polynomial Ideal," *SYMSAC,* 1976, pp. 339-345.

[18] Lausch, H., and Nobaurer, W., *Algebra of Polynomials,* North-Holland, Amsterdam, 1973.

[19] Schaller, S., *Algorithmic Aspects of Polynomial Residue Class Rings,* Ph.D. Thesis, Computer Science Tech., University of Wisconsin, Madison, Rep. 370, 1979.

[20] Szekeres, G., "A Canonical Basis for the Ideals of a Polynomial Domain," *American Mathematical Monthly,* Vol. 59, No. 6, 1952, pp. 379-386.

[21] van der Waerden, B.L., *Modern Algebra,* Vols. I and II, Fredrick Ungar Publishing Co., New York, 1966.

[22] Zacharias, G., *Generalized Gröbner Bases in Commutative Polynomial Rings,* Bachelor Thesis, Lab. for Computer Science, MIT, 1978.

COMPUTATIONS WITH RATIONAL SUBSETS OF CONFLUENT GROUPS

Robert H. Gilman
Department of Pure and Applied Mathematics
Stevens Institute of Technology
Hoboken, N.J. 07030

Abstract

Various problems involving rational subsets of finitely generated free groups can be solved efficiently using a technique related to coset enumeration. We investigate the extension of this method to other finitely generated groups.

1. Introduction

Let $\overline{G}$ be a finitely generated group. Let Σ be a finite set and $\pi:\Sigma^* \to \overline{G}$ a projection of the free monoid Σ^* onto $\overline{G}$. Use bars to denote images in $\overline{G}$. The word problem for $\overline{G}$ is to decide for $w,v \in \Sigma^*$ whether or not $\overline{w} = \overline{v}$. The occurrence problem is to decide if $\overline{w} \in \langle\overline{v}_1,\ldots,\overline{v}_n\rangle$, the subgroup of $\overline{G}$ generated by $\overline{v}_1,\ldots,\overline{v}_n$. These problems and others involve the rational subsets of $\overline{G}$ and can be solved directly if the rational subsets of $\overline{G}$ are amenable to computation. The rational subsets of $\overline{G}$, $\mathrm{Rat}(\overline{G})$, are the projection of the rational (or regular) subsets of Σ^*. Elements of $\mathrm{Rat}(\Sigma^*)$ are described by regular expressions, finite automata or in other well-known ways; and from descriptions of $S,T \in \mathrm{Rat}(\Sigma^*)$ one can compute descriptions of $S+T$ (the union), ST (the product), and S^*, (the submonoid generated by S). We will usually suppress the distinction between $S \in \mathrm{Rat}(\Sigma^*)$ and its description. For $S,T \in \mathrm{Rat}(\Sigma^*)$ inclusion, $S \subseteq T$, is decidable; and $|S|$, the cardinality of S, is computable.

For computations in $\overline{G}$ we use $S \in \mathrm{Rat}(\Sigma^*)$ as a description of $\overline{S} \in \mathrm{Rat}(\overline{G})$. Since π is a homomorphism, $\overline{S} + \overline{T} = \overline{S+T}$, $\overline{ST} = \overline{ST}$, and $\overline{S}^* = \overline{(S^*)}$. Thus sum, product, and submonoid are always computable in $\mathrm{Rat}(\overline{G})$. If inclusion is decidable or cardinality is computable, then the word problem for $\overline{G}$ is solvable, so in general these two problems cannot be solved by algorithms.

If we can solve the inclusion and cardinality problems, then in addition to the word and occurrence problems we can solve the order problem (finding the order of $\overline{w}$) and the power problem (deciding if $\overline{w}$ is a power of $\overline{v}$). We can solve other problems too. For example if $\overline{H}$ and $\overline{K}$ are finitely generated subgroups of $\overline{G}$, then $\overline{H},\overline{K} \in \mathrm{Rat}(\overline{G})$; and we can decide if $\overline{H} \subseteq K$, $\overline{Hw} = \overline{Hv}$, $\overline{HwK} = \overline{HvK}$ etc.

In [3] it is shown that if inclusion is decidable, then whether or not $\overline{w}_1,\ldots,\overline{w}_n$ generate a free submonoid is also decidable. Likewise we can decide if $\overline{w}_1,\ldots,\overline{w}_n$ are free generators of a free subgroup by checking whether the subset of all nontrivial reduced words in $\overline{w}_1,\ldots,\overline{w}_n$ contains the identity.

We say that $\overline{G}$ is confluent if it has a confluent presentation, by which we mean a finite set of reductions

$$w_i \to v_i \qquad 1 \le i \le n \qquad w_i, v_i \in \Sigma^* \tag{1}$$

such that $\overline{w}_i = \overline{v}_i$, either $|w_i| > |v_i|$ (w_i is longer than v_i) or $|w_i| = |v_i|$ and w_i is lexicographically greater than v_i, and finally such that for any $w \in \Sigma^*$ replacing subwords w_i of w by v_i in any order until no further replacements are possible yields a word $w\#$ which depends only on $\overline{w}$.

Given a finite presentation for $\overline{G}$ one may attempt to deduce a confluent presentation by using a procedure described in [9]. If one succeeds, then clearly $\overline{G}$ has a solvable word problem; and in fact the cardinality of $\overline{G}$ can be determined [7]. If $\overline{G}$ is monadic (i.e. if it is confluent with $|v_i| \le 1$ in (1)), then a result of Ronald Book [3] says that inclusion is decidable, although he does not give a specific algorithm.

Free groups are monadic. Indeed if $\overline{G}$ is free on $\overline{a}_1,\ldots,\overline{a}_n$, and $\Sigma = \{a_1, a_1^{-1},\ldots,a_n,a_n^{-1}\}$, then $\overline{G}$ has the monadic presentation.

$$a_i a_i^{-1} \to 1 \qquad a_i^{-1} a_i \to 1 \qquad 1 \le i \le n. \tag{2}$$

Efficient algorithms for computing with finitely generated subgroups of $\overline{G}$ have been given by Charles Sims [13]. We extend these algorithms in the next section to deal with rational subsets of monadic groups, and in section 3 we investigate to what extent we can compute with rational subsets of confluent groups in general.

The solution to the word problem for confluent groups is a generalization of Max Dehn's solution to the word problem for fundamental groups of compact surfaces. Another generalization leads to the solution of the word problem for small cancellation groups [10, chapter V]. See [5] for a connection between these two generalizations.

Several authors have considered rational subsets of free groups and their decision problems. The earliest article we know of is [8]; [1] is another example. For commutative groups and monoids computations with rational sets can always be carried out [6]. Confluent presentations of groups and monoids have also been studied from the point of view of formal languages; see [4] for example.

2. Algorithms for Rational Sets in Monadic Groups

In this section we reformulate the algorithm of Charles Sims [13] in terms of rational sets. As before Σ is a finite set, $\overline{G}$ a group, and $\pi:\Sigma^* \to \overline{G}$ a projection onto $\overline{G}$. We assume that $\overline{G}$ has a finite monadic presentation (1) in terms of the generators $\overline{\Sigma}$. In particular given $w \in \Sigma^*$ we can calculate a representative $w\#$ of $\overline{w}$, and $w\#$ depends only on $\overline{w}$.

Algorithm C

1. Input: A finite directed graph Γ whose edges have labels in $\Sigma \cup \{1\}$. Γ represents $S \in \mathrm{Rat}(\Sigma^*)$ where S is the set of words obtained by reading along directed paths in Γ from a distinguished initial vertex to one of a set of distinguished terminal vertices.
2. While there is a path from vertex p to vertex q with label w_i but no path from p to q with label v_i, add a path from p to q with label v_i.
3. Output: $S\# = S_1 \cap R$ where S_1 is the set represented by Γ upon exiting from step 2 and $R \in \mathrm{Rat}(\Sigma^*)$ is the set of all words not divisible by any w_i.

Because $\overline{G}$ is monadic, all paths which are added have length 1. Thus no vertices are added to Γ, and Algorithm C must terminate. Clearly $\overline{S} = \overline{S}_1$ and $w \in S$ implies $w\# \in S_1$. In addition R and $S\#$ can both be computed. From the definition of confluent group it follows that R is a cross-section for π. Thus π maps $S\#$ bijectively onto $\overline{S}$. In fact $S\# = \{w\# | w \in S\}$. Now we can decide $\overline{S} \subseteq \overline{T}$ by checking $S\# \subseteq T\#$, and since $\overline{S}$ and $S\#$ have the same cardinality, we can calculate the cardinality of $\overline{S}$. As a bonus $\overline{S} \cap \overline{T} = \overline{S\# \cap T\#}$ yields that rational subsets of monadic groups are closed under intersection, and intersection is computable. We have proved

<u>Proposition 1</u>. For rational subsets of monadic groups intersection and cardinality are computable and inclusion is decidable.

Of equal importance from out point of view, we have an algorithm which is suitable for actual computation. By [2, Lemma 3.1] if $S \in \mathrm{Rat}(\Sigma^*)$, then $\langle\overline{S}\rangle$, the subgroup of $\overline{G}$ generated by $\overline{S}$, is finitely generated. In view of Proposition 1 we have

<u>Proposition 2</u>. Finitely generated subgroups of monadic groups are closed under intersection.

In the next section we discuss how large the class of monadic groups is. For an effective version of Proposition 2 we need an algorithm to find generators for $\langle\bar{S}\rangle$ given S. The proof of Lemma 3.1 mentioned above is by induction on rational sets and contains an algorithm implicitly. We sketch an algorithm which is an extension of the method of coset diagrams [10, chapter III §12]. Let Γ represent S as in step 1 of Algorithm C. Delete all vertices of Γ which do not lie on paths from the initial vertex, p_o, to any terminal vertex. Find a directed spanning subtree, Γ_o, with root p_o. For each vertex p let w_p be the label of the path in Γ_o from p_o to p. For each terminal vertex t, $\bar{w}_t \in \bar{S}$. Likewise for any edge of $\Gamma-\Gamma_o$ leading from vertex p to vertex q with label a, $\bar{w}_p\bar{a}\bar{w}_q^{-1} \in \langle\bar{S}\rangle$. The set of all such elements, $\{\bar{w}_t, \bar{w}_p\bar{a}\bar{w}_q^{-1}\}$, generates $\langle\bar{S}\rangle$. This algorithm is a slight extension of the one Sims uses for free groups [13].

There is a connection between Algorithm C and coset enumeration, and this connection becomes clearer if we amend the algorithm to allow identification of two vertices, p and q, whenever there is an edge labelled 1 from p to q and an edge labelled 1 from q to p. Identification of two such vertices does not change the set represented of Γ. Of course after identification there may be vertices r and s such that two or more edges with the same label go from r to s. If so, we remove the superfluous edges. We also remove edges with label 1 from a vertex to itself.

Now suppose $\bar{G}$ is free with presentation (2). Given a finite set of words $T \subseteq \Sigma^*$, construct Γ as follows: Γ has initial vertex p_o, and for each $w \in T$, Γ has a loop from p_o to p_o with label w. For each edge in Γ add another so that whenever vertices r and s are joined by an edge labelled a_i (or a_i^{-1}), then s and r are joined by an edge with label a_i^{-1} (or a_i respectively). Let us called a graph with this property antisymmetric. Γ is antisymmetric and contains no edges with label 1. Further it is easy to see that Γ represents $S \in \mathrm{Rat}(\Sigma^*)$ with $\bar{S} = \bar{T} \cup \{\bar{1}\}$. In particular $\langle\bar{S}\rangle = \langle\bar{T}\rangle$.

Apply the amended form of Algorithm C to the graph of the preceding paragraph. Whenever step 2 adds an edge labelled 1 from vertex p to vertex q, it also adds an edge labelled 1 from q to p. Thus q and p are identified and Γ remains an antisymmetric graph with no edges labelled 1. This procedure is just coset enumeration (the vertices of Γ are the cosets). More generally when $\bar{G}$ is any monadic group and $\Sigma = \{a_i, a_1^{-1}, \dots, a_n, a_n^{-1}\}$, applying the same procedure amounts to a kind of coset enumeration in which relators are applied to some but not all cosets.

3. Rational Sets in Confluent Groups

The preceding section gives a method for computing with rational subsets of monadic groups. Unfortunately there do not seem to be many monadic groups. If $\overline{G}$ is free with presentation (2), then $\overline{G}$ is monadic; and if $\overline{G}$ is finite, then the multiplication table presentation is monadic. Also the union of two monadic presentations gives a monadic presentation for the free product of the corresponding groups. We conjecture that the monadic groups are precisely the free products of free and finite groups. In this section we investigate calculations with rational subsets of confluent groups in general.

By [4, Theorem 2.2] monadic groups are a subclass of groups with a context-free word problem. By [12] context-free groups are essentially just finite extensions of free groups; this fact provides support for the conjecture above. A.V. Anisimov [2] has shown that if $\overline{G}$ had context-free word problem, then (using the notation of the preceding section) if $\overline{S} \in \mathrm{Rat}(\overline{G})$ one can compute $S_1 \in \mathrm{Rat}(\Sigma^*)$ such that $\pi(S_1) = \overline{S}$ and the inverse image in S_1 of any point in $\overline{S}$ is finite.

We do not know how large the class of confluent groups is. It is easy to show that it is closed under free product and direct product. We would like to extend the method of the preceding section to confluent groups, but by [11] the occurrence problem is not solvable for the direct product of two nonabelian free groups. Thus the membership and inclusion problems are unsolvable for rational subsets of confluent groups. However, we can still hope to solve instances of these problems. Indeed the steps in Algorithm C still make sense for confluent groups. The cross-section $R \in \mathrm{Rat}(\Sigma^*)$ can still be computed, and step 2 in Algorithm C can be performed except that now we may add paths of length greater than 1. Thus the number of vertices of Γ may grow, and there is no guarantee that step 2 will terminate. However, if termination occurs, then we obtain a cross-section $S\#$ for $\overline{S}$. If we obtain $S\#$, then membership in $\overline{S}$ is decidable and the cardinality of $\overline{S}$ is computable. Likewise if $S\#$ and $T\#$ are obtained, then $\overline{S} \subseteq \overline{T}$ is decidable.

Experimentation with confluent groups indicates that the amended form of Algorithm C (i.e. with identification of vertices) can be useful. For example the group

$$\overline{G} = \langle a,b;\ (aba^{-1}b^{-1})^7 = (aab)^2 = 1\rangle$$

has a confluent presentation with 26 reducations. Algorithm C was applied to 200 cyclic subgroups $\overline{S} = \langle\overline{w}\rangle$ where w was a random string of length at most 100. In all cases the algorithm converged and computed S#. Consequently it seems likely that Algorithm C solves the occurrence problem for cyclic subgroups of $\overline{G}$, (i.e. the power problem and the problem of finding the order of elements of $\overline{G}$.

It may be that the power and order problems are solvable for all confluent groups. However, Algorithm C is not sufficient for this task: it often fails to terminate when applied to confluent groups which are direct products. In fact it is not hard to find examples for which $\pi^{-1}(\overline{S}) \cap R \not\in \mathrm{Rat}(\Sigma^*)$ so that no $S\# \in \mathrm{Rat}(\Sigma^*)$ exists.

References

1. A.V. Anisimov, Languages over free groups, Springer Lecture Notes in Computer Science 32 1975, 167-171.
2. A.V. Anisimov, to appear.
3. R.V. Book, The power of the Church-Rosser property for string rewriting systems, 6th Conf. on Automated Deduction, New York, 1982, Springer Lecture Notes in Computer Science 138 1982, 360-368.
4. R.V. Book, M. Jantzen and C. Wrathall, Monadic Thue systems, Theor. Comp. Sci. 19 1982, 231-251.
5. H. Bucken, Anwendung von Reduktionssysteme auf das Wort-problem in der Gruppentheorie, Dissertation, Aachen 1979.
6. S. Eilenberg and M.P. Schutzenberger, Rational sets in commutative monoids, J. Alg. 13 1969, 173-191.
7. R. Gilman, Presentations of groups and monoids, J. Alg. 57 1979, 544-554.
8. P. Johansen, Free groups and regular expressions, ACM Symposium on Theory of Computing, May 5-7, 1969, Marina del Rey, CA., 113-128.
9. D.E. Knuth and P.B. Bendix, Simple word problems in universal algebras, in "Computational Problems in Abstract Algebra", J. Leech ed. Pergamon Pr., Oxford 1970, 263-297.
10. R.C. Lyndon and P.E. Schupp, "Combinatorial Group Theory", Springer Verlag, Berlin 1977.
11. K.A. Mihailova, The occurrence problem for direct products of group Mat. Sb. (N.S.) 70 (112) 1966, 241-251.
12. D.E. Muller and P.E. Schupp, Context-free languages, groups, the theory of ends, second order logic, tiling problems, cellular automata, and vector addition systems, Bull. A.M.S. (N.S.) 4 1981, 331-334.
13. C. Sims, Lecture given at Symposium on Computational Group Theory, Durham 1982.

CAMAC2: A PORTABLE SYSTEM FOR COMBINATORIAL AND ALGEBRAIC COMPUTATION

Jeffrey S. Leon*

Department of Mathematics, Statistics, and Computer Science
University of Illinois at Chicago
Chicago, Illinois 60680

1. Introduction

In recent years, computers have come to play an increasingly important role in research in many fields of mathematics, including combinatorics and algebra. They have been used in constructing large combinatorial objects or in proving their nonexistence, in classifying smaller objects up to isomorphism, and in investigating the properties (symmetry group, code weight distribution, etc.) of combinatorial objects of various sizes. Several of the sporadic simple groups were first constructed by computer, character tables of many large groups rely on machine computations, and p-groups of low order have been investigated by computer methods. Perhaps no project of this type has occupied more computer time than the effort to determine if there exists a projective plane of order 10. Many interesting problems in these areas are finite and thus, in principle, solvable by exhaustive search (testing all possibilities). However, such techniques generally require time at least exponential in the object size and thus are feasible only for very small cases. Considerably more sophisticated algorithms have been developed for a number of combinatorial and algebraic calculations. Some of these, though still exponential in the worst case, perform quite well for many interesting objects, even fairly large ones. However, most of them require a good deal of effort to program.

These developments have created a demand for unified computer systems, preferably interactive, for investigating combinatorial and algebraic structures. Such systems differ from the more general symbolic and algebraic manipulation languages in that they have, built into the system, much more of the specific structure of the objects (permutation groups, error-correcting codes, etc.) and more

----

*Work partially supported by National Science Foundation Grant MCS-8201311.

Computing services used in this research were provided by the Computer Center of the University of Illinois at Chicago. Their assistance is gratefully acknowledged.

specialized algorithms for computing with such objects.

The first such systems, oriented toward group-theoretic computation, were developed by Joachim Neubüser [10] at Kiel and John Cannon [1] at Sydney in the 1960s. In the early 70s, Neubuser and Cannon commenced joint work on a more extensive system called GROUP. In 1973 Vera Pless [12] established a system named CAMAC (Combinatorial and Algebraic Machine Aided Computation). Originally an adaptation of GROUP, CAMAC was subsequently extended with many new commmands, especially in the area of coding theory, and with its own facilities to make it easy for anyone to use. More recently, several systems, more extensive or more specialized, have been developed. Probably the most extensive such system is Cayley, developed by John Cannon [3],[4]. Actually Cayley is a programming language for computing with groups, with a very wide range of group theoretic algorithms built in. Joachim Neubüser, H. Pahlings, and W. Plesken [11] have developed CAS (Character Theory System), a system for computing group character tables. R. Laue, J. Neubüser, and U. Schoenwaelder [6] have designed SOGOS for solvable group computations. Working with Vera Pless and several graduate students (Meiliu Lu, Hon Wing Cheng), I have developed CAMAC2. Although influenced by our experience with CAMAC, CAMAC2 is an entirely new system, written in a different language and employing an entirely new set of data structures for representing objects. It is oriented toward computation with combinatorial structures (codes, graphs, designs, (0,1)-matrices or, more generally, matrices over finite fields) and combinatorial aspects of group theory (generators and relators, permutations and permutation groups).

CAMAC2 has been under development for approximately two years, and it is far from complete. The primary purpose of this paper is to describe the design of CAMAC2 (its objectives, the choice of the language in which it is written, and the structuring of the system consistent with the objectives and implementable within the language) rather than to describe in detail its current and projected capabilities; such information can be found in the CAMAC2 User's Manual [8].

2. Objectives of CAMAC2

The primary objective of CAMAC2 is to provide a convenient tool for researchers investigating combinatorial structures (graphs, codes, designs, matrices over finite fields), combinatorial group theory, permutation groups, and the interaction among them. Combinatorial structures and groups are closely related: for any combinatorial structure, there is associated an automorphism group; conversely, given any group, we may wish to study its action on various combinatorial objects. The most effective methods of determining code minimum weights make use of the code automorphism group; conversely the most powerful algorithms for finding code automorphism groups require knowledge of the set of minimum weight vectors. To meet its objective, CAMAC2 must provide not only algorithms for computing with both combinatorial and group-theoretic objects, but also a number of "utility commands" that make it convenient to enter such objects into the system and to modify them once entered. In addition, the following objectives were established for CAMAC2.

1) The system should be easily portable between different computer systems. This mandates that it be written entirely in a higher level language, preferably one widely available and well standardized.

2) It should be suitable for use with microcomputers, especially the newer micros with 16-bit processors and 128-256K or more of memory.

3) The system should be easy to use, even for the researcher who is unfamiliar with it. Whenever a user is required to enter data interactively, a prompting message should be issued by the system, and if the user still does not understand what input is expected, he or she should be able to type a question mark and receive a more detailed explanation.

4) The structure of the system should be kept reasonably simple, even at the cost of some loss of time or space efficiency. Only in this way can we hope to develop a system that is reliable and easily extensible; moreover, we want it to be feasible for users knowledgable in the language in which the system is written (Pascal) to be able to incorporate their own commands into the system without having to devote a great deal of effort to learning its structure.

5) Input/output should be possible from files as well as interactively. These files should be in a standard form so that a user may perform calculations in CAMAC2, write the results out to a file, perform further computations using his or her own specialized programs (possibly in a different language), and then read the results back into CAMAC2 and resume computing in the system.

6) Subject to (4) above, the system should be as time efficient as possible. This is important because many of the calculations (code weight distributions, permutation group structure, etc.) use a substantial amount of time even with very efficient programs. Realistically, algorithms incorporated into a general purpose system cannot be expected to match, in running time, the same algorithms coded to perform specific computations with objects of known size and type. However, our objective is to hold the loss in efficiency to a modest level, say no more than a factor or 2 or 3 over what could be

obtained with special purpose programs coded in a higher level language producing very efficient object code (Fortran, Pascal, etc.).

3. Choice of The Language Pascal

One of the first questions to be resolved was what language, if any, would permit coding of a system consistent with the objectives in Section 2. Ideally the language should be widely available and well standardized, facilitate structured programming, be relatively simple, yet provide data structures adequate for convenient representation of combinatorial and algebraic objects, support recursion, provide dynamic storage allocation under programmer control, and produce reasonably efficient object code.

No language met our requirements entirely. Fortran fails to provide the needed data structures and lacks dynamic storage allocation and recursion, PL/1 is a relatively complex language and is not as widely available as would be desirable, and languages such as Snobol or Lisp would not provide adequate time efficiency. Pascal, despite some deficiencies, meets most of our requirements.

1) Pascal is a relatively simple language, with inexpensive and reliable compilers widely available on microcomputers as well as larger machines.

2) In the last few years, Pascal has become the language most widely taught to students of mathematics and computer science, at least in the United States [5].

3) Many Pascal compilers provide good error checking and generate very efficient object code.

4) Pascal provides the basic tools for structured programming; moreover, it permits recursion and provides pointers and dynamic storage allocation under programmer control (via the NEW statement), and it contains a feature (the variant record) which is particularly useful in representing objects of varying types.

5) ISO and ANSI standards for Pascal exist.

Pascal is a simple language with relatively few features. At first there was some question whether a system as extensive as CAMAC2 could be designed within its limitations. After some initial experimenting, we found that the only serious deficiency in Pascal, from our point of view, was the lack of adjustable dimensions for arrays. Structuring the system within this limitation is discussed in Section 4. In addition, we found a need for several features not present in the

Pascal standard but provided in nearly all implementations; unfortunately, use of such features is a potential impediment to portability.

a) Standard Pascal fails to specify a way for handling interactive input. However, in CAMAC2 such input is confined to a few lines of one procedure, so only these lines may require modification in transporting the system.

b) Standard Pascal makes no provision for direct access files. However, in CAMAC2 direct access IO is required only for two features (libraries and interactive help), which, though convenient, are not essential parts of the system. Also, most versions seem to implement direct access IO in essentially the same way.

c) Standard Pascal makes no provision for separately compiled procedures sharing global variables. From our point of view, this is considerably more serious than (a) or (b) above. A system the size of CAMAC2 (currently 12000 lines of code) requires separate compilation, at least in the development stage. Fortunately, a number of implementations seem to provide for it in ways that are relatively similar. At present, most of the effort in transporting the system involves changing a few statements at the start of each separately compiled section of the program (There are about 50 of these). Most of these changes are fairly routine, and we intend to write a program, perhaps in Snobol, to perform these required changes between several common implementations, and also one to convert the CAMAC2 source code into a single program with no external procedures.

4. The Structure of CAMAC2: Object Tables

In CAMAC2 the user manipulates objects. These objects may be algebraic or combinatorial structures of varying types and sizes. Objects may be created, deleted, and modified; modification of an object may increase or decrease its storage requirements. Ideally there should be no fixed limits on the sizes of objects; actual limits should be determined by the amount of memory available. In practice, however, it has proven useful to establish limits in some cases; this appears to be a reasonable approach provided (1) the limits are quite high (unlikely to be exceeded) and (2) they appear as Pascal constants, and thus can be changed simply by recompiling the system.

Associated with each object is an "object table", containing that information needed to describe the object. Much of memory is devoted to object tables, and comprehending their organization is the key to understanding the internal structure of CAMAC2. In addition to the object tables, there is a directory and a list of "free segments".

The directory contains the number of objects currently defined and one entry for each such object; that entry contains the name of the object, its type (code, graph, etc.), and a pointer to the object table for that object. Actually, as we shall see, object tables are segmented; the directory points to the first segment. A simple linear list, searched sequentially, was chosen for the directory. The maximum directory size is given by a Pascal constant MAXOBJ, and the directory is allocated initially from the stack with space for MAXOBJ entries. The number of objects defined at any one time is nearly always small, so this simple structure leads to only insignificant wastage of time and memory.

The object table for each object is used to store all the information needed to define the object. For example, for an (optionally weighted) graph, the object table would contain the number of vertices, the number of edges, flags indicating whether the graph is directed and/or weighted, and the adjacency matrix. In addition, it may contain symbolic labels for each vertex. In many cases, extra (redundant) information is included because it would be too timetaking to recompute each time it is needed. For example, for a permutation group, not only are the generating permutations included, but their inverses are stored as well.

Object tables must be structured in a manner consistent with the Pascal language. The inclusion of pointers and the ability to allocate storage dynamically at any time from the "heap", as well as the presence of variant records, provide the basic tools necessary. The lack of adjustable dimensions for arrays, however, is a major impediment. Because the Pascal DISPOSE statement for freeing storage is not implemented in some versions, and because there is no guarantee that freed storage will be reclaimed, it was decided to avoid use of this feature. Our objective has been to structure object tables to meet the following objectives:

a) The sizes of object tables must be able to expand or contract (possibly to zero) as objects are created, modified, and deleted; space released upon contraction should be reusable for other objects.

b) The space used by an object table should depend primarily on the object's current size and not on its maximum size (if any is imposed). However, with the trend toward cheaper and larger memories, minor wastage of space would be tolerable if it leads to a simpler structure.

c) Use of single large arrays should be avoided, so the system may be used on a computer with segmented memory (as with certain microprocessors, such as the Intel 8086, with 64K segments).

d) Obtaining information about an object from its object table should be only moderately slower (say at most a factor of two) than obtaining the same information from the most efficient data structure that one would use for an object whose type and exact size is known in advance.

e) object table structures should be reasonably simple.

Some other systems (GROUP, CAMAC, Cayley) have solved the object table problem by a system of garbage collection and storage compaction [2]. This requires the use of assembler routines to allocate and free storage, and subroutine calls to assembler routines are needed to access data in this storage. This approach meets criteria (a), (b), and (c), but our experience with CAMAC leads us to doubt that it can meet (d) (due to the large number of subprogram calls); moreover, it is (in our experience) the most error-prone and least portable part of the system. Accordingly, this approach was rejected for CAMAC2.

I have devised the following system, which appears to meet all our objectives, and has certain other advantages as well.

1) Every object table consists of a varying number of segments; each segment has fixed size SEGSIZE. SEGSIZE is a Pascal constant; it is independent of the type of object. The segments of a table are connected by a doubly linked list.

2) Dynamic storage allocation from the heap (i.e. via the NEW statement) is used only for object table segments.

3) When an object is deleted, or when its size is reduced, any segments no longer needed for its table are added to an (initially empty) linked list of free segments. Note that the DISPOSE statement is never used to free unneeded segments.

4) When a new object is defined, or when an object expands, the new segments needed for its table are taken from the list of free segments; if this list is empty, then they are allocated from the heap via the NEW statement.

5) Each segment is a Pascal record (of type OBJECT) with a variant part; however, such records are allocated without a tag field, so that a segment initially used with one tag field can later be used with another. The fixed part of each segment is very small; it contains pointers to the previous and succeeding segments of the same table, and (for the first segment only) the name of the object and an index giving the position in the directory of its entry. The tag field of the first segment in each table is simply the type of the

object. The tag field of the remaining segments may be of a different type, as appropriate (see below). The variant part of the record is designed, for each possible tag, so that this particular variant will have size as close to SEGSIZE as feasible without exceeding it. Let VARSIZE denote the maximum possible size for the variant part; VARSIZE is nearly SEGSIZE.

This approach totally eliminates problems of memory fragmentation and garbage collection. In a computing system with paged memory, SEGSIZE may be chosen to be the page size, or possibly a multiple or divisor of it, in order to minimize paging operations. I will give two examples (matrices over GF(q) and permutation groups) illustrating that it is feasible to structure object tables in this manner.

The object table for a matrix M is structured as follows. Two Pascal constants, MAXROWS and MAXCOLS, give the maximum number of rows and columns; we shall see that these constants may be given very generous values without significant wastage of memory. The first segment of the table, of type MATRIX, holds the field size, the number of rows (NROWS), the number of columns (NCOLS), and two arrays MPTR and MIDX, which will enable rapid determination of any matrix entry M[i,j] given i and j. Each remaining segment, of type MATRIX2, will hold an integral number of rows of the matrix, the maximum number that will fit, namely r = floor(VARSIZE / (NCOLS*B)), where B is the number of addressable units (e.g. bytes) used to hold one field element. The number of segments of type MATRIX2 is thus ceil(NROWS / r). The variant parts MATRIX and MATRIX2 are as follows (the types OBJPTR, FLDELTYP, and SHORTINT are used for pointers to segments, field elements, and short integers, respectively).

```
MATRIX:  (MFIELD:                        {field size}
          NROWS,                         {no of rows}
          NCOLS:  INTEGER;               {no of columns}
          MPTR:  ARRAY[1..MAXROWS]       {MPTR[i] points to the segment of the }
                 OF OBJPTR;              {  table containing row i of matrix}
          MIDX:  ARRAY[1..MAXROWS]       {row i of the matrix begins in entry }
                 OF SHORTINT);           {  MIDX[i]+1 of segment MPTR[i]^}

MATRIX2:  (MAT:  ARRAY[1..NOMATRIX]      {The constant NOMATRIX is chosen to }
                 OF FLDELTYP);           {  make the size of MAT almost VARSIZE}
```

Now, if P points to the first segment of the matrix table, we can refer to the matrix entry M[i,j], within a WITH P^ statment, as

MPTR^.MAT[MIDX[i]+j].

Although this is somewhat less convenient than writing simply M[i,j], the loss in time efficiency is relatively small. Note that MAXROWS is limited only by the need to fit arrays MPTR and MIDX in slightly less than VARSIZE storage units, and MAXCOLS only by the fact that a single row must fit in VARSIZE units. In a byte-oriented system with 8192-byte segments (reasonable in a large system), MAXROWS and MAXCOLS might exceed 1300 and 8000, respectively. The primary limitation on matrix sizes comes from the need to fit NROWS * NCOLS entries in available memory.

Permutation groups are represented by base and strong generating set, as these concepts, due to Charles C. Sims [13],[14], provide the most effective techniques for permutation group computations. Definitions of these concepts and others that appear in the following example may be found in [13], [14], and [7]. Each object table consists of one segment of type GROUP, as many segments of type GROUP2 as are needed to hold the Schreier vectors and basic orbits, and as many segments of type PSET2 as are needed to hold the strong generators (including inverses). Pascal constants MAXDEG, MAXBASE, and MAXGEN provide bounds on the degree, base size, and number of strong generators, respectively; again, these bounds may be chosen very generously without significant memory wastage. The appropriate variant parts are as follows.

```
GROUP:  (GDEG,                           {degree of permutation group}
         BASESIZE,                       {number of points in base}
         NGEN:    INTEGER;               {number of strong generators}
         BASE:    ARRAY[1..MAXBASE]      {BASE[i] is the ith base point}
                  OF SHORTINT;
         ORBLEN:  ARRAY[1..MAXBASE]      {ORBLEN[i] is length of ith basic orbit}
                  OF SHORTINT;
         INV:     ARRAY[1..MAXGEN]       {generator INV[i] is the inverse of }
                  OF SHORTINT;           {  generator i}
         FMOVED:  ARRAY[1..MAXGEN]       {BASE[FMOVED[i]] is the first base }
                  OF SHORTINT;           {  point moved by generator i}
         SVPTR:   ARRAY[1..MAXBASE]      {SVPTR[i] points to segment containing  }
                  OF OBJPTR;             {  ith Schreier vector and basic orbit}
         SVIDX:   ARRAY[1..MAXBASE]      {The ith Schreier vector begins with }
                  OF SHORTINT;           {  SVPTR[i]^.SV[SVIDX[i]+1]}
         GNPTR:   ARRAY[1..MAXGEN]       {GNPTR[i] points to segment containing }
                  OF OBJPTR;             {  the ith strong generator}
         GNIDX:   ARRAY[1..MAXGEN]       {The ith generator begins with }
                  OF SHORTINT);          {  GNPTR[i]^.PERM[GNIDX[i]+1]}

GROUP2: (SV:  ARRAY[1..NOSVEC]           {The image of j under ith Schreier vector }
         OF SHORTINT;                    {  is SVPTR[i]^.SV[SVIDX[i]+j]}
         ORB:  ARRAY[1..NOSVEC]          {The ith basic orbit consists of }
         OF SHORTINT);                   {  SVPTR[i]^.ORB[SVIDX[i]+j], j=1,2,...}
```

```
PSET2:  (PERM:  ARRAY[1..NOPERM]      {The image of point j under generator i }
         OF SHORTINT);                {  is GNPTR[i]^.PERM[GNIDX[i]+j]}
```

5. Capabilities of CAMAC2

CAMAC2 contains data structures for computing with objects of ten types:

- CODE: a subspace of GF(q)**n, represented internally by a canonical basis,
- VSET: a set of vectors (of the same length) over GF(q)**n,
- GRAPH: a graph, optionally directed or weighted, given by adjacency matrix,
- DESIGN: a set of points and blocks,
- MATRIX: a matrix over GF(q),
- GROUP: a permutation group, given by base and strong generating set,
- PSET: a set of permutations of a common degree,
- GENREL: a set of generators, relators, and subgroup generators,
- COSTAB: a coset table (for use in coset enumerations),
- PARTN: a partition.

Eventually CAMAC2 will contain a rich set of commands for computing with objects of each of these types, and more types may be added. However, at present, only the command set for codes and vsets is reasonably complete, though work is in progress in a number of areas. A single command may interrelate objects of several types. For example, in computing the weight distribution of a code, the vectors of a given weight may be saved in a vset; conversely, given a vset, one may find the code spanned by it. Given a group, one may generate a partition corresponding to its orbits; conversely, given a partition and a group, one may generate the subgroup stabilizing the partition. Given a code, design, or matrix, one may generate a group by computing the automorphism group; given a permutation or permutation group, one may investigate its action on a combinatorial object. The CAMAC2 User's Manual [8] describes in detail the commands currently available in CAMAC2 and discusses many of those which we intend to add.

I will conclude with a brief example of using CAMAC2 in an interesting coding problem. We will use the DEFINE command to define a (73,37) duadic code [9] D73 whose basis consists of cyclic shifts of a vector with ones in positions 1,2,4,...,60,73 (complete list below), the MINWT and PRINT commands to determine that D73 has minimum weight 9 with 73 vectors of this weight (saved in a vset MINVECS), the GENERATE command to find the dimension (28) of the code (MVECSPAN) spanned by the minimum weight vectors, and finally the PRINT command to print out one minimum weight vector (all the others are obtained by cyclic shifts). By theoretical considerations [9], these facts tell us that MINVECS consists of the lines of a cyclic projective plane of order 8. Items typed by the system are shown in lower case; those entered by the user in upper case. The character "+"

is a line continuation character. Although in this case the user entered all operands in response to the prompt for the command name (cmd?), only the name of the command need be entered there; CAMAC2 will prompt the user for any operands not included along with the command name. Any command name or keyword (e.g. DIMENSION) could have been abbreviated by any unambiguous initial substring. If an error had been made in typing in the first basis vector, it could have been corrected easily without retyping the entire vector.

```
cmd? DEFINE  CODE(D73)  FIELD(2)  LENGTH(73)  DIMENSION(37)  BASIS( <1 2 +
          4 8 16 32 37 55 64 3 6 12 19 23 24 38 46 48 5 7 10 14 20 28 39 40  +
          56 11 15 21 22 30 42 44 47 60 73>  CYCLE RIGHT 0/36)

cmd? MINWT  CODE(D73)  WTRANGE(1/14)  VSET(MINVECS)  MAXSAVE(500)
    minimum weight is 9

cmd? PRINT  OBJECT(MINVECS)  ITEM(NOVECS)
    no vecs:  73

cmd? GENERATE  CODE(MVECSPAN)  USING(MINVECS)  NUMBERS(1/73)
    code has dimension 28

cmd? PRINT  OBJECT(MINVECS)  ITEM(VEC 1)
    1: 1010010000000000001000000000000000000000001000100000110000000100000000000
```

REFERENCES

1. J. Cannon, "Computing local structure of large finite groups," Computers in Algebra and Number Theory, Vol. 4, SIAM-AMS Proceedings, Providence, RI, 1971.

2. J. Cannon, R. Gallagher, and K. McAllister, "Stackhandler; A scheme for processing packed dynamic arrays," Dept. of Pure Math., Univ. of Sydney, Sydney, Australia, 1972.

3. J. Cannon, "A language for group theory," Dept. of Pure Math., Univ. of Sydney, Sydney, Australia, 1982.

4. J. Cannon, "An introduction to the group theory language Cayley" (to appear).

5. D. Hill, "Programming languages for service courses and courses for C.S. majors," SIGCSE Bulletin <u>12</u> (1980), 43-45.

6. R. Laue, J. Neubüser, and U. Schoenwaelder, "Algorithms for finite solvable groups and the SOGOS system" (to appear).

7. J. Leon, "On an algorithm for finding a base and a strong generating set for a group given by generating permuations," Math. Comp. 35 (1980), 941-974.

8. J. Leon and V. Pless, "CAMAC2 User's Manual," Dept. of Math., Stat., and Comp. Science, Univ. of Illinois at Chicago, Chicago, Illinois, 1983.

9. J. Leon, J. Masley, and V. Pless, "Duadic codes," I.E.E.E. Trans. Inform. Theory (to appear).

10. J. Neubüser, "Untersuchungen des Untergruppenverbandes endlicher Gruppen auf einer programm-gesteurten elektronischen Dualsmaschine," Numerische Mathematik 2 (1970), 280-282.

11. J. Neubüser, H. Pahlings, and W. Plesken, "CAS: Design and use of a system for the handling of characters of finite groups" (to appear).

12. V. Pless, "CAMAC," SYMSAC 76: Proceedings of the 1976 ACM Symposium on Symbolic and Algebraic Computation, ed. R. D. Jenks, Association for Computing Machinery, New York, 1976.

13. C. Sims, "Computation with permutation groups," in Proceedings of the Second Symposium on Symbolic and Algebraic Manipulation, Association for Computing Machinery, New York, 1971.

14. C. Sims, "Determining the conjugacy classes of a permutation group," in Computers in Algebra and Number Theory (Proc. Sympos. Appl. Math., New York, 1970), SIAM-AMS Proc., Vol 4, Amer. Math. Soc., Providence, RI, 1971.

POLYNOMIAL TIME ALGORITHMS FOR GALOIS GROUPS

Susan Landau

Math Department

Wesleyan University

Middletown, CT. 06457

Abstract:

In this paper we present several polynomial time algorithms for Galois groups. We show:

(i) There are polynomial time algorithms to determine:

   (a) if the Galois group of an irreducible polynomial over Q is a p-group.

   (b) the prime divisors of the order of a solvable Galois group

(ii) Using the classification theorem for finite simple groups, there is a polynomial time algorithm to determine whether an irreducible polynomial over Q has Galois group S_n or A_n.

We consider several techniques for computing Galois groups, including the Chebatorev Density Theorem, and their applicability to polynomial time computations.

Introduction:

In a description of his algorithm to determine whether a polynomial has roots expressible in radicals, Galois wrote, "... the calculations are impractical." Galois's technique involved factoring a polynomial of degree n!. In the century and a half since Galois, research has concentrated on finding the group for polynomials of small degree. Very little work has been done on general techniques, in part because until recently algorithms for factoring polynomials required exponential time. The discovery of a polynomial time algorithm for factoring polynomials over the rationals [L3], and over algebraic number fields [AKL,La] enabled the developement of a polynomial time algorithm for determining solvability by radicals [LaMi.]

It is an easy matter to compute the Galois group of a polynomial f(x), a monic irreducible polynomial over Z; a simple bootstrapping algorithm which consists of factoring f(x) over K=Q[t]/f(t), adjoining a root of f(x) to K, computing a primitive element for this field over Q, and repeating this procedure until f(x) splits completely has a running time which is polynomial in the size of f(x) and the size of its Galois group [La.] And therein lies the difficulty. For if f(x) is of degree n over Q, its Galois group may be as large as S_n. What we seek is an algorithm which has running time a polynomial in the size of f(x).

Although S_n has n! elements, its generating set is polynomial in size. In fact, a transitive group on n elements has a generating set of no more than 2n elements [Ba], thus allowing the possibility of construction of Galois groups in time polynomial in the size of f(x).

In [LaMi] we gave a polynomial time algorithm to determine if f(x), a monic irreducible polynomial over Z, has roots expressible in radicals. We checked the solvability of the Galois group without actually determining the group, its order or structure. In this paper we explore those problems, and give polynomial time solutions to certain questions. Our result in [La Mi] relied heavily on the divide-and-conquer techniques of primitive permutation groups, and we use these ideas again in this paper.

Finite simple groups are the building blocks of finite groups. The success of group theorists is classifying all finite simple groups will undoubtedly bear fruit in many settings; it does so already in the computational one of this paper. Theorems dependent on the classification of finite simple groups will be marked (S.) This paper is organized as follows: II Background, III Polynomial

Time Algorithms for Solvable Groups, IV Other Algorithms for Galois Groups.

II: Background:

Throughout this paper we assume the base field is Q, and the polynomial f(x) is a monic irreducible polynomial over Z. Neither of these assumptions is strictly necessary; running times remain polynomial if the base field is an algebraic number field, and f(x) has coefficients in the number field. The analysis is messier, and we avoid that here. We assume familiarity with the basic concepts of algebraic number theory, including Galois groups. We define:

For $f(t) = t^n+a_{n-1}t^{n-1}+\ldots+a_0$, a polynomial in Z[t], the size of f(t), $|f(t)|$, is $(\Sigma a_i^2)^{1/2}$.

For $f(x)=\beta_m x^n+\beta_{m-1}x^{m-1}+\ldots+\beta_0$, where $\beta_i=\Sigma b_{ij}\alpha^j$, with α the root of a monic irreducible polynomial over Z, the size of f(x) is $\max_i(\Sigma b_{ij}^2)^{1/2}$; we will write it as $[f(x)]$.

We make use of the following results:

Theorem 2.1 [L³]: A polynomial f(x) in Z[x] of degree n can be factored in $O(n^{9+\varepsilon} + n^{7+\varepsilon}\log^{2+\varepsilon}|f(x)|)$ steps.

Theorem 2.2 [La]: Let g(t) be a monic irreducible polynomial of degree m over Z, with discriminant d, and root α, and let f(x) be in $Z(\alpha)[x]$ be of degree n. Then f(x) can be factored into irreducible polynomials over (1/d) $Z(\alpha)[x]$ in $O(m^{9+\varepsilon}\ \ n^{7+\varepsilon}\log^{2+\varepsilon}([f(x)](m|g(t)|)^n\ (mn)^n)$ steps.

Theorem 2.3 [La]: Let f(x) be an irreducible polynomial over Z. The Galois group of f(x) over Q can be computed in time polynomial in ([Splitting field(f(x)):Q], $\log|f(x)|$).

If f(x) is irreducible, its Galois group, G, is a transitive permutation group on the set of roots of f(x),

$$\Omega=\{\alpha_1, . . . , \alpha_m\}.$$

We define:

$$G_\alpha=\{\sigma \in G| \ \sigma(\alpha)=\alpha\},$$

and we call G regular if G is transitive and $G_\alpha=e$ for all α. The action of G on Ω is said to be k-transitive if the induced action of G on ordered k-tuples of distinct elements is transitive. A fundamental way the action of a permutation group on a set breaks up is into blocks: a subset $B\subset\Omega$ is a block iff for every σ in G, $\sigma(\beta)\cap B = B$ or ϕ. It is not hard to see that if B is a block, σB is also. We let G_B be the subgroup of G which fixes B setwise. Every group has trivial blocks: $\{\alpha\}$ and Ω. The nontrivial blocks are called blocks of imprimitivity, and a group with only trivial blocks is a primitive group. The set of all blocks conjugate to B: B, σ_2B, . . . , σ_kB, form a complete block system. If B is a nontrivial maximal block of G, we can consider the induced action of G on $\{B,\sigma_2B, . . ., \sigma_mB\}$. We note the following well-known theorem; a proof and further discussion may be found in [Wie.]

Theorem 2.4: The lattice of groups between G_α and G is isomorphic to the lattice of blocks containing α.

Let f(x) be a monic irreducible polynomial over Z, with roots $\alpha=\alpha_1,...,\alpha_m$ and Galois group G. The subgroup of G which fixes $Q(\alpha)$ is G_α. Each subfield between Q and $Q(\alpha)$ corresponds to a subgroup of G which contains α. Finally each subgroup corresponds to a block of imprimitivity containing α. This statement can be made more precise.

Lemma 2.5: Let K be a field, and let f(x) be an irreducible polynomial over K, with roots $\alpha_1,..., \alpha_m$. Let $B=\{\alpha_1,..., \alpha_k\}$ be a block of roots, and let G be the Galois group of f(x) over K. Then $K(\alpha_1,\ldots,\alpha_m)^{G_B} =$ K(elem. symmetric fcns in $\{\alpha_1,\ldots,\alpha_k\}$).

This lemma was a crucial building block in [LaMi]. We conclude this section with a brief review of some of the techniques used in [LaMi] in determining solvability of the Galois group. There we constructed a sequence of fields $Q \subset Q(\rho_1) \subset \ldots Q(\rho_r) \subset Q(\alpha)$ where the ρ_i's are chosen so that if $g_i(y)$ is the minimal polynomial for ρ_i over $Q(\rho_{i-1})$, the Galois group of the splitting field of $g_i(y)$ over $Q(\rho_{i-1})$ acts primitively on the roots of $g_i(y)$. The $g_i(y)$ are constructed so that $[g_i(y)] \leq m! [f(x)]^{m^4}$. Let $K_1, \ldots, K_{r+1}$ be the Galois group of $g_i(y)$ over Q, . . . , f(x) over $Q(\rho_r)$ respectively. Now G is solvable iff α is expressible in radicals over Q. But α is expressible in radicals over Q iff α is expressible in radicals over $Q(\rho_r)$ **and** ρ_r is expressible in radicals over $Q(\rho_{r-1})$ **and** ... **and** ρ_1 is expressible in radicals over Q. In this way the question of solvability of G has been transformed into the question of the solvability of $K_1, \ldots, K_{r+1}$. This is surprisingly easy to answer, because of:

Theorem 2.6 [Palfy]: If G is a primitive solvable group which acts transitively on n elements, then $|G| < n^{3.24}$.

The polynomials $g_i(y)$ are constructed so that the Galois group of $g_i(y)$ over $Q(\rho_{i-1})$ acts primitively on the roots of $g_i(y)$. Thus if K_i is solvable, it is of small order. In this case, we computed a group table, and checked solvability in polynomial time. If K_i is of small order but not solvable, we discovered that instead. If K_i is of large order (i.e. greater than $(\deg(g_i(y)))^{3.24}$, then K_i is not solvable, and therefore neither is G. But if G is solvable, we have discovered that fact without discovering G's order or structure. It is to these questions we now turn our interest.

III Polynomial Time Algorithms for Solvable Galois Groups

We continue with the notation of the previous section. Let $Q(\gamma_i)$ be the splitting field for $Q(\rho_i)$ over $Q(\beta_i)$, for $i=1,\ldots,r$, and let $Q(\rho_{r+1})$ be the splitting field for $Q(\alpha)$ over $Q(\rho_r)$. Suppose further that the roots of $f(x)$ are numbered so that $\{\alpha_1,\ldots,\alpha_{k_i}\}$ is the block associated with $Q(\rho_i)$. Let H_i be the group of automorphisms of $Q(\alpha_1,\ldots,\alpha_{k_{i-1}})$ over $Q(\gamma_i)$, and let K_i be the Galois group of $Q(\rho_i)$ over $Q(\beta_{i-1})$.

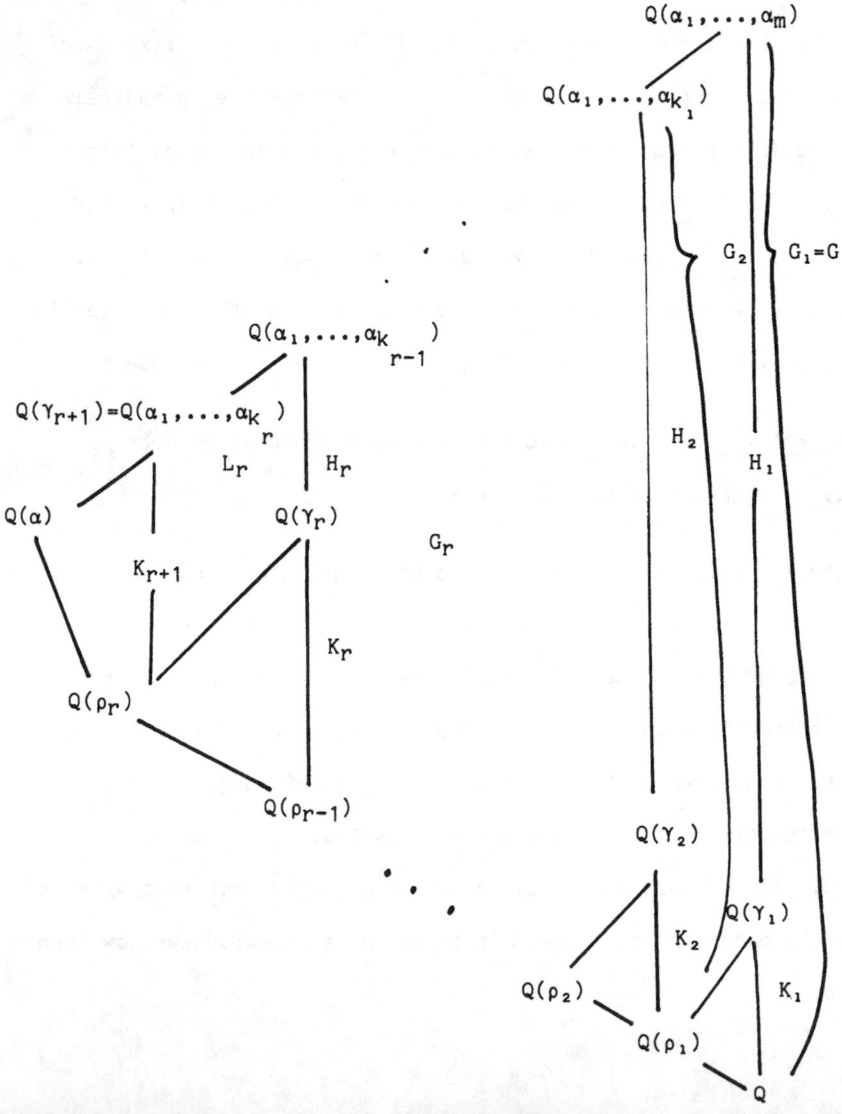

Let $G_1 = G$, and G_i for $1 \leq i \leq r+1$ be the group of automorphisms of $Q(\alpha_1, \ldots, \alpha_{k_{i-1}})$ over $Q(\gamma_i)$. Then $K_i = G_i/H_i$. Let T^n be the direct product of n copies of T, a group. Then:

<u>Theorem 3.1:</u> With notation as above, $H_i \lesssim (G_{i+1})^{k_{i-1}/k_{i-2}}$, where $m = k_0$.

<u>proof:</u> Let L_i be the group of automorphisms of $Q(\alpha_1, \ldots, \alpha_{k_{i-1}})$ over $Q(\rho_i)$. Clearly $H_i \subseteq L_i$. Now $\{\alpha_1, \ldots, \alpha_{k_{i-1}}\} = B$ is the block associated with $Q(\rho_i)$, and let $\{\alpha_{k_{i-1}+1}, \ldots, \alpha_{2k_{i-1}}\}, \ldots, \{\alpha_{jk_{i-1}+1}), \ldots, \alpha_{k_i}\}$ be the conjugate blocks. Suppose $Q(\theta_2), \ldots, Q(\theta_j)$ are the fields conjugate to $Q(\rho_i)$ associated with those blocks. Then the Galois group of $Q(\alpha_1, \ldots, \alpha_{k_{i-1}})$ over $Q(\gamma_i)$, H_i, fixes each of the $Q(\theta_j)$. But this means that $H_i \subset \bigcap_i (\sigma_i)^{-1} G_B \sigma_i$. But $(\sigma_i)^{-1} G_B \sigma_i = G_{\sigma_i B}$. Then we can view $H_i \lesssim (G_B B)^j$. But $G_B B \approx G_i$, and we are done.

<u>Corollary 3.2:</u> With the same notation as above, H_i is solvable if G_{i+1} is, and G_{i+1} is solvable if H_i and K_i are.

<u>proof:</u> By theorem 3.1, it is clear that H_i is solvable if G_{i+1} is. Without loss of generality, we assume r=1. The converse is clear from earliar remarks.

<u>Corollary 3.3:</u> With the same notation as above, G is a p-group iff each of the K_i are.

<u>proof:</u> Without loss of generality, we assume r=1. If G is a p-group, then G is solvable, hence each of the K_i are also. Since K_1 is a factor group of G, K_1 is a p-group, as is L_1. Now $Q(\alpha_1, \ldots, \alpha_m)$ is a normal extension of $Q(\alpha_1, \ldots, \alpha_{k_1})$, G_2 is a factor group of L_1, from which it follows that G_2 is a p-group. Since H_2 is normal in G_2, and $K_2 = G_2/H_2$, we know K_2 is a p-group. Now suppose K_1 and K_2 are p-groups. In particular, $G_2 = K_2$ is a p-group. Since $H_1 \lesssim (G_2)^{k_1/k_2}$, we know that H_1 is a p-group. But $|G_1| = |H_1| \times |K_1|$ implies that G_1 is also a p-group.

Corollary 3.4: Let p be a prime. Then $p \mid |G|$ iff $p \mid |K_i|$ for some i.

proof: Again, without loss of generality, we assume that r=1. Suppose $p \mid |G|$, and $p \nmid |K_1|,\ldots,|K_r|$. Since $p \nmid |K_1|$, we must have $p \mid |H_1|$. Hence $p \mid |G_2|$, since H_1 $(G_2)^{m/k_1}$. But $G_2=K_2$. If $p \mid |K_1|$, then it is clear that $p \mid |G|$. Suppose instead that $p \mid |K_2|$. Then $p \mid |L_1|$, which is a subgroup of G.

Theorem 3.5: Let f(x) be a monic irreducible polynomial over Z, with solvable Galois group G. Then the following can be determined in time polynomial in (log $|f(x)|$,n):

(i) if G is a p-group

(ii) the set of primes p which divide the order of G.

proof: If G is solvable, then the groups $K_1,\ldots,K_{r+1}$ are all of small order ($<n^{3.24}$) by Palfy's theorem. In [LaMi] we showed how to construct a group table for $K_1,\ldots,K_{r+1}$ in time polynomial in (log $|f(x)|$,n). Determining the orders of the K_i can be accomplished in time polynomial in (log $|f(x)|$,n). The theorem follows immediately by the application of Corollaries 3.2,3.3 and 3.4.

Theorem 3.5 is a beginning to determining the order and structure of solvable Galois groups. Unfortunately the techniques of this section do not appear to extend to giving us the order of solvable Galois groups, for Theorem 3.5 yields only the set of primes which divide $|G|$, and not their exponents.

IV Other Algorithms for Galois Groups

In this section we examine several classical techniques for their applicability to efficient Galois group determination. Let f(x) be, as always, a monic irreducible polynomial over Z with Galois group G. Questions we would like to able to answer in polynomial time include:

(i) Is G the alternating or symmetric group?

(ii) Is G simple?

(iii) If G is simple, what is G`s order and structure?

(iv) Is a particular element in in G?

At this time we have a polynomial time answer only to the first question. Techniques which will aid us include the recent classification of finite simple groups and the Chebotarev Density Theorem. The former enables an easy resolution of problem (i).

Theorem 4.1 (S): Let f(x) be a monic irreducible polynomial of degree n over Z. There is an algorithm to determine if the Galois group of f(x) over Q is S_n or A_n, which runs in time polynomial in (n,log|f(x)|).

proof: By the classification theorem, a 6-transitive finite permutation group is symmetric or alternating. Let G be the Galois group of f(x) over Q, and let $\alpha,\beta,\gamma,\delta,\rho$ be five distinct roots of f(x). Then G is 6-transitive iff $G_\alpha \cap G_\beta \cap G_\gamma \cap G_\delta \cap G_\rho$ is (n-5)-transitive. But this condition is equivalent to f(x) having an irreducible factor of degree n-5 over $Q(\alpha,\beta,\gamma,\delta,\rho)$. This of course, can be determined in time polynomial in (n, log|f(x)|). (Note that there is no ambiguity in picking the five roots $\alpha,\beta,\gamma,\delta,\rho$, since f(x) has an irreducible factor of degree n-5 in $Q(\alpha,\beta,\gamma,\delta,\rho)$ only if it has an irreducible factor of degree n-1 in $Q(\alpha)$ and an irreducible factor of degree n-2 in $Q(\alpha,\beta)$, etc.) Thus in polynomial time we can determine that f(x) has Galois group S_n or A_n. To distinguish between these two cases, it suffices to note that $G \subseteq A_n$ iff disc(f(x)) is a square in Z. Since disc(f(x))=Res(f(x),f'(x)), this condition can be checked in polynomial time.

We are not yet able to determine, in polynomial time, the Galois group in the simple case. We do note however that certain simple invariants including the rank and k-transitivity can be computed in polynomial time.

It makes little sense to ask question (iv) without an explicit determination of the roots; rather we should be asking whether <u>any</u> element of a particular conjugacy class C in S_n is in G. A classical technique to do so is the Chebotarev Density Theorem. Let K be the splitting field of f(x) over Q, and let G=Gal[K/Q]. Let p be a rational prime which does not divide disc(f(x)).

<u>Theorem 4.2 (Chebotarev):</u> Let $\pi_C(x)$ denote the number of prime ideals P of K unramified in L, with $p=N_{K/Q}(P)<x$ and the degree partition of f(x) mod p corresponds to an element of C. Then $\pi_C(x) \sim |C|/|G|\ Li(x)$.

On occassion we can determine the Galois group of f(x) by reliance on a the Density Theorem and a judicious choice of primes. In general however there are non-isomorphic groups with the same cycle structure, and factorizations in finite fields give us no way to distinguish between them.

An effective version yields:

<u>Theorem 4.3 (ERH) [LaOd]:</u> For any conjugacy class C G, there is a prime $p < (\text{a constant})(\log d_K)^{2+\varepsilon}$ such that the degree partition of f(x) mod p corresponds to an element of C.

Now $d_K \sim (\mathrm{disc}(f))^{n!}$ in worst case. Therefore $\log d_K \sim n! \log(\mathrm{disc}(f))$. This guarantees us that there is a fixed proportion of primes less than $(\log d_K)^{2+\varepsilon}$ for which f(x) mod p corresponds to a particular cycle structure of G. Then the size of p (i.e. the number of digits of p) ~nlogn loglog disc(f), which is certainly polynomial in (n, log(f(x))). Finding a prime p is the problem; while asymptotically, the number of primes for which the factorization of f(x) mod p corresponds to a particular cycle structure is $|C|/|G|$, certain conjugacy classes may remain sparse past the bounds of Theorem 4.3 [Lapc.] This is quite unsatisfying from a computational viewpoint, leading us to believe that the

Chebatorev Density Theorem is not an appropriate way to pursue a polynomial time solution to the problem.

In our introduction we discussed the possibility of determining Galois groups in polynomial time. We have some partial answers, we raise some difficulties and we have presented several directions from which to pursue the main problem.

References

[BKL] L.Babai, W.Kantor and E.Luks, "Computational Complexity and the Classification of Finite Simple Groups", 24th IEEE Symp. Found. Comp. Sci.

[Ca] P.Cameron,"Finite Permutation Groups and Finite Simple Groups", Bull. London Math. Soc., 13 (1981), pp.1-22.

[LaOd] J.C.Lagarias and A.M.Odlyzko, "Effective Versions of the Chebotarev Density Theorem", Algebraic Number Theory, A. Frolich (ed.), Academic Press, 1977.

[Lapc] J.C.Lagarias, private communication.

[La] S.Landau, "Factoring Polynomials over Algebraic Number Fields", to appear.

[LaMi] S.Landau and G.Miller, "Solvability by Radicals is in Polynomial Time," 15th ACM Symp. on Theory of Computing, pp.140-151.

[AKL] A.K.Lenstra, "Factoring Polynomials with Rational Coefficients", Stichting Mathematisch Centrum, 1W 213/82

[L³] A.K.Lenstra, H.W.Lenstra and L.Lovasz, "Factoring Polynomials with Rational Coefficients", Math. Ann. 261, (1982), pp.515-534.

[Pa] P.Palfy, "A Polynomial Bound for the Orders of Primitive Solvable Groups," Journal of Algebra, July 1982, pp.127-137.

[Wie] H.Wielandt, Finite Permutation Groups, Academic Press, New York, 1964.

Code Generation and Optimization for Finite Element Analysis

Paul S. Wang, T. Y. P. Chang† and J. A. van Hulzen‡*

ABSTRACT

The design and implementation of a software system for automatically generating code for finite element analysis are described. Exact symbolic computational techniques are employed to derive strain-displacement matrices and element stiffness matrices. Methods for dealing with the excessive growth of symbolic expressions in practical computations are discussed. Automatic FORTRAN code generation and optimization are described with emphasis on improving the efficiency of the resultant code. The generated code can be used, without modification, with a FORTRAN-based finite element analysis package.

1. Introduction

Finite element analysis has many applications in structural mechanics, heat transfer, fluid flow, electric fields and other engineering areas. It will play a critical role in modern Computer Aided Design systems. In recent years we have seen increasing interest in using computer-based symbolic and algebraic manipulation systems for computations in both linear and non-linear finite element analysis. Application areas include the symbolic derivation of stiffness coefficients [3], [9], the reduction of tedium in algebraic manipulation, the generation of FORTRAN code from symbolic expressions [10], [11] etc. The strength of this approach lies in the combined use of symbolic and numerical computational techniques. The potential benefits and usefulness of such an approach in finite element analysis as well as other scientific research areas are evident. However, several problems need be solved before this approach can become widely accepted and practiced for finite element work:

(i) the efficiency of the symbolic processor and its ability to handle the large expressions associated with practical problems,

*‡ Work reported herein has been supported in part by the US National Aeronautics and Space Administration under Grant NAG 3-298 and in part by the US Department of Energy under Grant DE-AC02-ER7602075.

† Work reported herein has been supported in part by US National Aeronautics and Space Administration under Grant NAG 3-307.

(ii) the interface between a symbolic system and a finite element system on the same computer, and

(iii) the inefficiencies that are usually associated with automatically generated code.

We describe our on-going research on the design and implementation of a finite element code generator. The functionalities of this generator relies on interfacing the symbolic processing capabilities of VAXIMA [11] and the numerical programs on the same computer. One major goal of this research is to develop symbolic techniques in the context of automatic mathematical derivation interfaced to automatic code generation. Thus the results presented here should be applicable in many other places within and without finite element analysis.

2. Functional Specifications and Design

From a functional point of view, the finite element code generator (F-Generator) will perform the following.

(1) to assist the user in the symbolic derivation of finite elements;

(2) to provide routines for a variety of symbolic computations in finite element analysis, including linear and non-linear applications, especially for shells [4];

(3) to provide easy to use interactive commands for most common operations;

(4) to allow the mode of operation to range from interactive manual control to fully automatic;

(5) to generate, based on symbolic computations, FORTRAN code in a form specified by the user;

(6) to automatically arrange for generated FORTRAN code to compile, link and run with FORTRAN-based finite element analysis packages such as the NFAP package [5];

(7) to provide for easy verification of computational results and testing of the code generated.

In providing the above functions, attention must be paid to making the system easy to use, modify and extend. Our initial effort is focused on the isoparametric element family. Later, the system can be extended to a wider range of finite elements.

3. Generation of Element Stiffness Matrices

Symbolic processing can play an important role in the generation of element matrices, especially for higher order elements. As an example, we shall describe the automatic processing leading to the derivation of the element stiffness matrix [**K**] in the isoparametric formulation. From user-supplied input information such as the element type, the number of nodes, the nodal degrees of freedom, the displacement field interpolation polynomial and the material properties matrix [**D**], the F-Generator will derive the shape functions, the strain-displacement matrix [**B**] and the element stiffness matrix [**K**].

The computation is divided into five logical phases (fig. I) Each is implemented as a LISP program module running under the VAXIMA system. Aside from certain interface considerations, these modules are largely independent.

3.1. Phase I: define input parameters

The basic input mode is interactive with the system prompting the user at the terminal for needed input information. While the basic input mode provides flexibility, the input phase can be tedious. Thus we also provide a menu-driven mode where well-known element types together with their usual parameter values are pre-defined for user selection.

The input handling features include:

(1) free format for all input with interactive prompting showing the correct input form;
(2) editing capabilities for correcting typing errors;
(3) the capability of saving all or part of the input for use later;
(4) the flexibility of receiving input either interactively or from a text file.

3.2. Phase II: Jacobian and [B] matrix computation

The strain-displacement matrix [**B**] is derived from symbolically defined shape functions in this phase. Let n be the number of nodes, then $\mathbf{H} = (h_1, h_2, \ldots, h_n)$ is the shape function vector whose components are the n shape functions h_1 through h_n. The value for the shape functions will be derived in a later phase. Here we simply compute with the symbolic names. Let r, s and t be the natural coordinates in the isoparametric formulation and **HP** be a matrix

$$\mathbf{HP} = \begin{bmatrix} \mathbf{H},r \\ \mathbf{H},s \\ \mathbf{H},t \end{bmatrix}$$

where **H**,r stands for the partial derivative of **H** with respect to r. The Jacobian **J** is then $\mathbf{J} = \mathbf{HP} \,.\, [\mathbf{x},\mathbf{y},\mathbf{z}]$ where **x** stands for the column vector $[x_1, \ldots, x_n]$ etc. Now the inverse, in full symbolic form, of **J** can be computed as

$$\mathbf{J}^{-1} = \frac{\mathbf{invj}}{det(\mathbf{J})}$$

By forming the matrix (**invj** . **HP**) we can then form the [**B**] matrix.

3.3. Phase III: shape function calculation

Based on the interpolation polynomials and nodal coordinates, the shape function vector **H** is derived and expressed in terms of the natural coordinates r, s and t in the isoparametric formulation. Thus the explicit values for all h_i and all their partial derivatives with respect to r, s and t, needed in **HP** are computed here.

3.4. Phase IV: FORTRAN code generation for [B]

A FORTRAN subroutine for the numerical evaluation of the strain-displacement matrix [B] is generated for use with the NFAP package. This NFAP package is a large FORTRAN based system for linear and nonlinear finite element analysis. It is developed and made available to us by P. Chang of the University of Akron. It has been modified and made to run in FORTRAN 77 under UNIX. Details of the FORTRAN code generator will be discussed later.

3.5. Phase V: compute and generate FORTRAN code for [K]

The inverse of the Jacobian, **J**, appears in [**B**]. By keeping the inverse of **J** as **INVJ**/det(**J**), the quantity det(**J**) can be factored from [**B**] and, denoting by [**BJ**] the matrix [**B**] thus reduced, we have

$$[\mathbf{K}] = \int\int\int_{-1}^{1} \frac{[\mathbf{BJ}]^T \cdot [\mathbf{D}] \cdot [\mathbf{BJ}]}{det(\mathbf{J})} \, dr \, ds \, dt$$

The determinant of the Jacobian involves the natural coordinates. This makes the exact integration in the above formula difficult. We elect to evaluate det(**J**) at r=s=t=0 and factor it out of the integral. The resulting integrand involves only polynomials in r, s and t which can be integrated. Comparing computational results obtained using this approximation and those with direct numerical methods using NFAP, we found that they agree. Although more extensive tests are needed, we believe this approximation to be useful. Because the finite element computations in engineering applications seek the overall behavior of the structure at hand rather than very accurate numerical figures. In many cases, an error of five to ten percent tend to be entirely satisfactory [1]. Later we may compute only the integrand symbolically and leave the integration to numerical techniques.

To avoid accumulating large amounts of symbolic expressions, the integrand matrix is not formed all at once, instead each entry is computed and integrated individually. Furthermore, the FORTRAN code of each [**K**] entry is output after it is computed. Usually [**K**] is symmetric and only the upper triangular part need be computed. We use a specially designed integration program to gain speed and efficiency. The integration is organized to

AUTOMATIC GENERATION OF [B] AND [K]

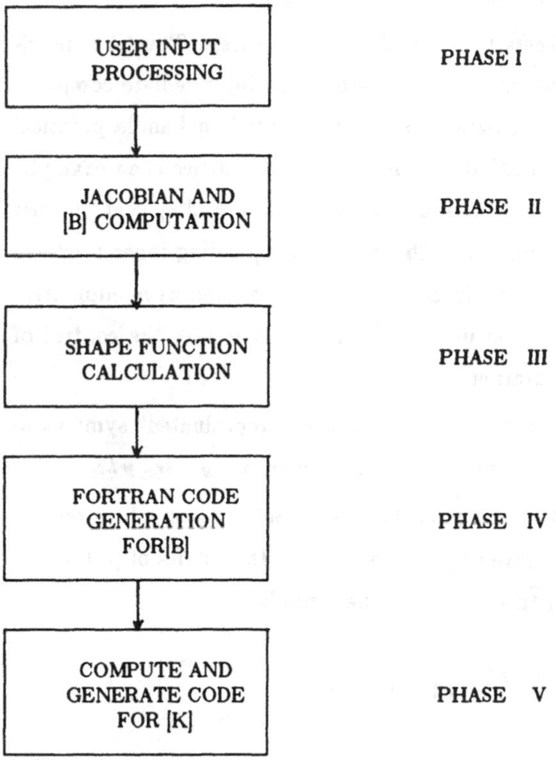

Figure I

combine common subexpressions and produce compact and efficient FORTRAN code. Details on this later.

4. The FORTRAN Code Generator

A separate module is developed for producing FORTRAN code from results derived symbolically (fig. II). This package, called **GENTRAN**, has been developed to satisfy the needs of producing finite element code. However, it is also of independent interest as a general purpose FORTRAN code generator/translator. It can generate control-flow constructs and complete subroutines and functions. **GENTRAN** can generate a program with or without a template file.

5. Expression Growth and Efficiency of FORTRAN Code

Previous work in using systems such as MACSYMA for finite element computation uses user-level programs which do not allow much control over the exact manner in which computations are carried out. As a result, the ability of handling realistic cases in practice is very restricted because of expression growth, a phenomenon in symbolic computation when intermediate expressions become too large for efficient manipulation.

We use LISP programs with direct access to internal data structures. Thus it is possible to construct programs which will avoid expression growth in the intermediate computations as much as possible. Therefore, our programs are better suited to handle practical problems with efficiency. The integration needed to compute the [**K**] entries is an example. None of the top-level integrations in MACSYMA is particularly suited and special purpose integration routines are written which, among other things, avoid expanding inner products involving coordinate vectors. This requires new data representation as well as manipulative routines. It is next to impossible to do at the user level. Let us illustrate the control of expression growth by the [**K**] matrix computation.

First of all, the [**B**] matrix in the integrand is computed with "unevaluated" symbols to keep things small. Thus a typical non-zero entry of [**B**] looks like $hr_2\ hs\ .\ y - hr\ .\ y\ hs_2$, where hr_2 = the second component of **H**, r and $\mathbf{y} = [y_1,\ldots,y_n]$. But these symbols remain un-evaluated at this point. As stated before, we proceed to generate the entries of [**K**] one at a time to keep expressions small. In doing this, we apply the formula,

$$[\mathbf{K}]=\sum_i \sum_j \int\int\int_{-1}^{1} [\mathbf{B}]^T_i\, [\mathbf{D}]_{ij}\, [\mathbf{B}]_j\ dr\ ds\ dt,$$

to collect terms with respect to $[\mathbf{D}]_{ij}$. In the above formula, $[\mathbf{B}]^T_i$ denotes the *ith* row of [**B**] transpose, etc. Coefficients thus obtained are kept in un-expanded form on a list which is

FORTRAN CODE GENERATION

Figure II

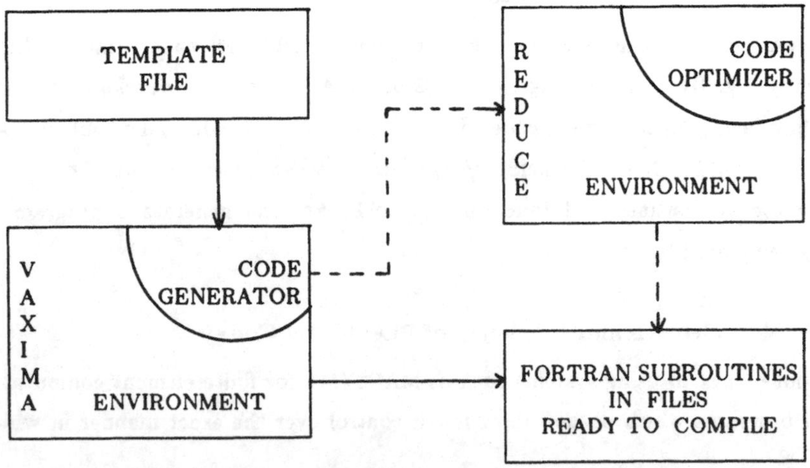

consulted for duplicates whenever a new coefficient is generated. This identifies common (duplicate) subexpressions in different entries of [**K**] and keep the resulting FORTRAN code compact and more efficient. When a new coefficient is formed then it is evaluated and expressed as a polynomial involving the natural coordinates r, s and t. Now a special-purpose integration routine is used. The integration result for each coefficient is converted into FORTRAN code and assigned to a temporary FORTRAN variable. Thus a typical section of the code for [**K**] may look like the following.

```
      t30 = -((16*y3-4*y2-12*y1)*y4+(-12*y2-4*y1)*y3
     1  +4*y2**2+8*y1*y2+4*y1**2)/3.0
      t31 = ((16*x3-4*x2-12*x1)*y4+(-12*x3+4*x2+8*x1)
     1  *y2+(-4*x3+4*x1)*y1)/3.0
      t32 = ((16*x4-12*x2-4*x1)*y3+(-4*x4+4*x2)*y2
     1  +(-12*x4+8*x2+4*x1)*y1)/3.0
      t33 = -((16*x3-4*x2-12*x1)*x4+(-12*x2-4*x1)*x3
     1  +4*x2**2+8*x1*x2+4*x1**2)/3.0
      k(5,7) = 4*(d6*t33+d3*(t32+t31)+d1*t30)/detk
      k(5,8) = 4*(d5*t33+d6*t32+d2*t31+d3*t30)/detk
```

In the above, t30, t31, etc. are the temporary variables and d1, d2, etc. are entries of the material properties matrix [**D**]. Without the techniques mentioned here, the code for each single [**K**] entry will require 5 to 8 continuation lines (for a plane 4-node element).

Experiments on the VAX-11/780 with the NFAP package together with code for the [**B**] and [**K**] matrices generated show that there is a 10% CPU time savings with the above described simplification for the 4-node plane element. The savings will be much greater for larger problems. Among other things, we are currently studying ways to further simplify the expressions for the t's. For three dimensional elements with many degrees of freedom, controlling the size of the intermediate and the resulting code will become critical. Among the techniques we are exploring are: generating FORTRAN functions and subroutines to simplify the code, using any symmetries that may be present in the given problem, and systematically identify and collect subexpressions.

6. Experiments with Code Optimization

Automatically generated code can be further optimized by identifying common subexpressions (CSEs) in one or more expressions used in a subprogram. We experimented with using the existing expression optimization facilities available in REDUCE [8],[13],[14],[15]. This is done by taking the code generated by the F-Generator as input to the REDUCE code optimizer and examining the resulting optimized code. The following was observed.

A1 The REDUCE simplifier helps to reduce the size of the unexpanded input. REDUCE does this by using the simplification strategy [7] of taking the factored rational form, as proposed by Brown [2], or the expanded form, which ever is smaller.

A2 The REDUCE optimizer further reduces the code size and the number of arithmetic operations considerably.

In performing our quick experiments, we decided against the idea of implementing a similar code optimizer in VAXIMA. However, we did have to modify the REDUCE code optimizer to interface with the finite element code generator and to handle large expressions piecewise for better efficiency.

After initialization, the optimization is done on REDUCE-simplified expressions in two phases:

(1) A repeated search for CSEs is carried out until no further reduction can be made. One such iteration step contains four different searches:

 1.1 Search for linear (sub)sums and (sub)monomials, (see [14,15]).

 1.2 An operator search to detect repeated functions such as sines, cosines etc.

 1.3 Discovering CSEs having a multivariate polynomial structure (see [15]).

 1.4 Identifying CSEs by the distributive law, i.e. replacing ab + ac by a(b + c).

(2) Factoring out contents of constant numeric coefficients, and applying Horner's rule for polynomial expressions.

Optimized output is produced, in two steps.

(1) Construction of an association list (called prefix list) consisting of pairs $(N_i \,.\, V_i)$, i = 1,...,m, where N_i is the expression identifier and V_i is the expression in prefix form.

(2) Printing of the sequence of generated assignment statements $N_i = V_i$.

This approach works fast and well for optimizing expressions of moderate size. Simplification in REDUCE becomes a significant problem when the larger expressions produced by the F-Generator were treated.

Improvements are made for the Optimizer to handle large expressions by partitioning them and then optimizing the pieces successively. This mainly involves controlled storing of CSEs found in previous pieces and delaying the application of the "finishing touch" step for all expressions until a later pass. This method is especially suitable for matrices such as the [**K**]. A typical example of the optimized output obtained is shown in Figure III.

Figure III

```
      t1= (((24*(2*((-y8+y7-y6+y5-y4+y3-y2+y1)*(z8+z7-z6-z5-z4-z3+z2+z1
     1 )+(-y8-y7+y6+y5-y4-y3+y2+y1)*(z8-z7+z6-z5-z4+z3-z2+z1)-(y8+y7-y
     2 6-y5-y4-y3+y2+y1)*(-z8+z7-z6+z5-z4+z3-z2+z1)-(y8-y7+y6-y5-y4+y3
     3 -y2+y1)*(-z8-z7+z6+z5-z4-z3+z2+z1))-2*(y8-y7+y6-y5-y4+y3-y2+y1)
     4 *(z8+z7-z6-z5-z4-z3+z2+z1)+2*(y8+y7-y6-y5-y4-y3+y2+y1)*(z8-z7+z
     5 6-z5-z4+z3-z2+z1)-2*(-y8+y7-y6+y5-y4+y3-y2+y1)*(z8-z7+z6-z5-z4+
     6 z3-z2+z1)-2*(-y8-y7+y6+y5-y4-y3+y2+y1)*(z8-z7+z6-z5-z4+z3-z2+z1
     7 )+2*(y8-y7+y6-y5-y4+y3-y2+y1)*(-z8+z7-z6+z5-z4+z3-z2+z1)+2*(y8-
     8 y7+y6-y5-y4+y3-y2+y1)*(-z8-z7+z6+z5-z4-z3+z2+z1))**2+24*(2*(2*(
     9 -y8+y7-y6+y5-y4+y3-y2+y1)*(z8-z7+z6-z5-z4+z3-z2+z1)-2*(y8-y7+y6
     : -y5-y4+y3-y2+y1)*(-z8+z7-z6+z5-z4+z3-z2+z1))+2*(2*(y8-y7+y6-y5-
     ; y4+y3-y2+y1)*(-z8+z7-z6+z5-z4+z3-z2+z1)-2*(-y8+y7-y6+y5-y4+y3-y
     < 2+y1)*(z8-z7+z6-z5-z4+z3-z2+z1)))*(2*((-y8-y7+y6+y5-y4-y3+y2+y1
     = )*(z8+z7-z6-z5-z4-z3+z2+z1)-(y8+y7-y6-y5-y4-y3+y2+y1)*(-z8-z7+z
     > 6+z5-z4-z3+z2+z1))-2*(y8-y7+y6-y5-y4+y3-y2+y1)*(z8+z7-z6-z5-z4-
     ? z3+z2+z1)+2*(y8+y7-y6-y5-y4-y3+y2+y1)*(z8-z7+z6-z5-z4+z3-z2+z1)
     @ -2*(-y8-y7+y6+y5-y4-y3+y2+y1)*(z8-z7+z6-z5-z4+z3-z2+z1)+2*(y8-y
     1 7+y6-y5-y4+y3-y2+y1)*(-z8-z7+z6+z5-z4-z3+z2+z1)))/3+2*(12*(2*((
     2 -y8+y7-y6+y5-y4+y3-y2+y1)*(z8+z7-z6-z5-z4-z3+z2+z1)+(-y8-y7+y6+
     3 y5-y4-y3+y2+y1)*(z8-z7+z6-z5-z4+z3-z2+z1)-(y8+y7-y6-y5-y4-y3+y2
     4 +y1)*(-z8+z7-z6+z5-z4+z3-z2+z1)-(y8-y7+y6-y5-y4+y3-y2+y1)*(-z8-
     5 z7+z6+z5-z4-z3+z2+z1))-2*(-y8+y7-y6+y5-y4+y3-y2+y1)*(z8+z7-z6-z
     6 5-z4-z3+z2+z1)-2*(-y8+y7-y6+y5-y4+y3-y2+y1)*(z8-z7+z6-z5-z4+z3-
     7 z2+z1)+2*(y8+y7-y6-y5-y4-y3+y2+y1)*(-z8+z7-z6+z5-z4+z3-z2+z1)+2
     8 *(y8-y7+y6-y5-y4+y3-y2+y1)*(-z8+z7-z6+z5-z4+z3-z2+z1)-2*(-y8-y7
     9 +y6+y5-y4-y3+y2+y1)*(-z8+z7-z6+z5-z4+z3-z2+z1)+2*(-y8+y7-y6+y5-
     : y4+y3-y2+y1)*(-z8-z7+z6+z5-z4-z3+z2+z1))**2+12*(2*(2*(-y8+y7-y6
     ; +y5-y4+y3-y2+y1)*(z8-z7+z6-z5-z4+z3-z2+z1)-2*(y8-y7+y6-y5-y4+y3
     < -y2+y1)*(-z8+z7-z6+z5-z4+z3-z2+z1))+2*(2*(y8-y7+y6-y5-y4+y3-y2+
     = y1)*(-z8+z7-z6+z5-z4+z3-z2+z1)-2*(-y8+y7-y6+y5-y4+y3-y2+y1)*(z8
     > -z7+z6-z5-z4+z3-z2+z1)))*(2*((-y8-y7+y6+y5-y4-y3+y2+y1)*(z8+z7-
     ? z6-z5-z4-z3+z2+z1)-(y8+y7-y6-y5-y4-y3+y2+y1)*(-z8-z7+z6+z5-z4-z
     @ 3+z2+z1))-2*(-y8+y7-y6+y5-y4+y3-y2+y1)*(z8+z7-z6-z5-z4-z3+z2+z1
     1 )+2*(y8+y7-y6-y5-y4-y3+y2+y1)*(-z8+z7-z6+z5-z4+z3-z2+z1)-2*(-y8
     2 -y7+y6+y5-y4-y3+y2+y1)*(-z8+z7-z6+z5-z4+z3-z2+z1)+2*(-y8+y7-y6+
     3 y5-y4+y3-y2+y1)*(-z8-z7+z6+z5-z4-z3+z2+z1))))/60.0
```

(a)

```
      t1=(128.*(3.*(y8*z7-y8*z6+y8*z3-y8*z2-y7*z8+y7*z5-y7*z3+y7
     . *z2+y6*z8-y6*z5+y6*z3-y6*z2-y5*z7+y5*z6-y5*z3+y5*z2-y3*z8
     . +y3*z7-y3*z6+y3*z5+y2*z8-y2*z7+y2*z6-y2*z5)**2+(y8*z7-y8*
     . z6-y8*z3+y8*z2-y7*z8+y7*z5+y7*z3-y7*z2+y6*z8-y6*z5-y6*z3+
     . y6*z2-y5*z7+y5*z6+y5*z3-y5*z2+y3*z8-y3*z7+y3*z6-y3*z5-y2*
     . z8+y2*z7-y2*z6+y2*z5)**2))/15.
```

(b)

Number of (+,-)-operations : 47
Number of (*)-operations : 15

Number of integer exponentiations : 2

```
g3 = -z7+z6
g6 = -z8+z5
g2 = g6-g3
g5 = -z3+z2
g4 = g6-g5
g7 = g6+g5
g8 = -g5+g3
g9 = g5+g3
g10 = g2*y3
g11 = g2*y2
g12 = -g11+g10
g13 = -y7+y6
g14 = -y8+y5
t1 = (128.*(-g12-g13*g4+g14*g8)**2+384.*(g12-g13*g7+g14*g9)
   **2)/(15.)
```

Number of operations after optimization:
Number of (+,-)-operations : 16
Number of (*)-operations : 9
Number of integer exponentiations : 2

(c)

(a) t1 is a portion of the [K] matrix code
(b) t1 simplified by REDUCE simplifier
(c) FORTRAN code after optimization

REFERENCES

[1] Babuska, I., Rheinboldt W.: Computational Aspects of the Finite Element Method. *Mathematical Software* III, J. R. Rice ed., Academic Press, N.Y., 225-255 (1977).

[2] Brown W. S.: On Computing with Factored Rational Expressions. Proceedings EUROSAM'74, ACM SIGSAM Bulletin Vol. 8, No. 3, 27-34 (1974).

[3] Cecchi, M. M., Lami, C.: Automatic generation of stiffness matrices for finite element analysis. Int. J. Num. Meth. Engng 11, 396-400 (1977).

[4] Chang, T. Y., Sawamiphakdi, K.: Large Deformation Analysis of Laminated Shells by Finite Element Method. Comput. Structures, Vol. 13, (1981).

[5] Chang, T. Y.: NFAP - A Nonlinear Finite Element Analysis Program Vol. 2 - User's Manual. Technical Report, College of Engineering, University of Akron, Akron, Ohio, USA (1980).

[6] Foderaro, J. K., Fateman, R. J.: Characterization of VAX Macsyma. Proceedings, ACM SYMSAC Conference, 14-19 (1981).

[7] Hearn, A. C.: The Structure of Algebraic Computations. Proceedings Saint-Maximin, 1-15 (1977).

[8] Hearn, A. C.: REDUCE Users Manual. The Rand Corporation (1983).

[9] Korncoff, A. R., Fenves, S. J.: Symbolic generation of finite element stiffness matrices. Comput. Structures, 10, 119-124 (1979).

[10] Noor, A. K., Andersen C. M.: Computerized Symbolic Manipulation in Nonlinear Finite Element Analysis. Comput. Structures 13, 379-403 (1981).

[11] Noor, A. K., Andersen C. M.: Computerized symbolic Manipulation in structural mechanics-progress and potential. Comput. Structures 10, 95-118 (1979).

[12] MACSYMA Reference Manual: version nine, the MATHLAB Group, Laboratory for Computer Science, M.I.T., Cambridge, Mass. USA (1977).

[13] Smit, J., van Hulzen, J. A., Hulshof, B. J. A.: NETFORM and Code Optimizer Manual. ACM SIGSAM Bulletin, Vol. 15, No. 4, 23-32 (1981).

[14] van Hulzen, J. A.: Breuer's Grow Factor Algorithm in Computer Algebra. ACM SYMSAC Conference, 100-104 (1981).

[15] van Hulzen, J. A.: Code Optimization of Multivariate Polynomial Schemes: A Pragmatic Approach. Proceedings EUROCAL'83, Springer LNCS series Nr. 162, 286-300 (1983).

T. Y. P. Chang, Department of Civil Engineering, University of Akron, Akron, Ohio, USA 44325

J. A. van Hulzen, Department of Computer Science, Twente University of Technology, P.O. Box 217, 7500 AE Enschede, The Netherlands

Paul S. Wang, Department of Mathematical Sciences, Kent State University, Kent, Ohio, USA 44242

A Comparison of Algorithms for the Symbolic Computation of Padé Approximants

Stephen R. Czapor[1]

Keith O. Geddes [2]

[1] Department of Applied Mathematics
[2] Department of Computer Science
University of Waterloo
Waterloo, Ontario
Canada N2L 3G1

ABSTRACT

This paper compares three algorithms for the symbolic computation of Padé approximants: an $O(n^3)$ algorithm based on the direct solution of the Hankel linear system exploiting only the property of symmetry, an $O(n^2)$ algorithm based on the extended Euclidean algorithm, and an $O(n \log^2 n)$ algorithm based on a divide-and-conquer version of the extended Euclidean algorithm. Implementations of these algorithms are presented and some timing comparisons are given. It is found that the $O(n^2)$ algorithm is often the fastest for practical sizes of problems and, surprisingly, the $O(n^3)$ algorithm wins in the important case where the power series being approximated has an exact rational function representation.

1. Padé approximants and the standard approach

Consider a power series over a field F,

$$A(x) = a_0 + a_1x + a_2x^2 + \cdots \quad \in F[[x]].$$

Roughly speaking, we seek a rational approximant of the form $p(x)/q(x)$ such that:

$$\deg p \leq m \,, \tag{1.1}$$

$$\deg q \leq n \,, \tag{1.2}$$

$$qA - p = O(x^{m+n+1}) \,. \tag{1.3}$$

More formally, we define the (m,n) *Padé approximant to* $A(x)$ as the rational function $p(x)/q(x)$, where (p,q) are a pair of polynomials of lowest degree satisfying (1.1), (1.2), and the following equation (1.3′) for k as large as possible:

This research was supported by the Natural Sciences and Engineering Research Council of Canada under Grant A8967.

$$qA - p = 0(x^k) . \tag{1.3'}$$

Example: For $A(x) = \exp(x) = 1 + x + \frac{1}{2} x^2 + \cdots$, the Padé table is as follows:

deg(p) \ deg(q)	0	1	2	...
0	1	$\frac{1}{1-x}$	$\frac{1}{1-x+\frac{x^2}{2}}$	
1	$1+x$	$\frac{1+\frac{x}{2}}{1-\frac{x}{2}}$	$\frac{1+\frac{x}{3}}{1-\frac{2x}{3}+\frac{x^2}{6}}$	
2	$1+x+\frac{1}{2}x^2$	$\frac{1+\frac{2x}{3}+\frac{x^2}{6}}{1-\frac{x}{3}}$	$\frac{1+\frac{x}{2}+\frac{x^2}{12}}{1-\frac{x}{2}+\frac{x^2}{12}}$	
.				
.				
.				

In the normalized form:

$$\frac{p(x)}{q(x)} = \frac{v_0 + v_1 x + \cdots + v_m x^m}{1 - u_1 x - \cdots - u_n x^n} \tag{1.4}$$

the Padé approximant has the power series expansion ([3])

$$\frac{p(x)}{q(x)} = \sum_{k=0}^{\infty} a_k x^k \tag{1.5a}$$

where

$$a_k = \begin{cases} v_k + \sum_{i=1}^{k} u_i \, a_{k-i} \ , \ 0 \le k \le m & (1.5b) \\ \sum_{i=1}^{n} u_i \, a_{k-i} \ , \ k > m . & (1.5c) \end{cases}$$

Thus, given a power series $A(x)$ we can first obtain the denominator coefficients of the (m,n) Padé approximant by solving the first n equations of (1.5c), then determine the numerator via (1.5b). The linear system of order n determining the denominator is known as a *Hankel system*, and is of the form:

$$H_{m,n}\,\mathbf{u} = \mathbf{a}_{m,n} \tag{1.6}$$

where

$$\mathbf{u} = (u_n, \ldots, u_1)^T,$$

and

$$[H_{m,n} \mid \mathbf{a}_{m,n}] = \begin{bmatrix} a_{m-n+1} & a_{m-n+2} & \cdots & a_m & a_{m+1} \\ a_{m-n+2} & a_{m-n+3} & & a_{m+1} & a_{m+2} \\ \cdot & \cdot & & \cdot & \cdot \\ \cdot & \cdot & & \cdot & \cdot \\ \cdot & \cdot & & \cdot & \cdot \\ a_m & a_{m+1} & \cdots & a_{m+n-1} & a_{m+n} \end{bmatrix}$$

Strictly speaking, it is not necessary that the coefficients a_k lie in a field. If instead they lie in an integral domain D, and we derive the Padé approximant in the form

$$\frac{p(x)}{q(x)} = \frac{b_0 + b_1 x + \cdots + b_m x^m}{c_0 + c_1 x + \cdots + c_n x^n} \tag{1.7}$$

(where $c_0 = |H_{m,n}|$), then it may be computed entirely in D (i.e., the quotient field F_D is avoided). This is of some importance, since many of the applications of Padé approximants involve free parameters. However, the present discussion will be limited to the case of power series over a field.

Geddes [3] describes a fraction-free symmetric elimination algorithm for solving the Hankel system (1.6), yielding an $0(n^3)$ algorithm for computing the Padé approximants. In this paper this algorithm will be referred to as Padé1.

2. The extended Euclidean algorithm

We now discuss an application of the well known extended Euclidean algorithm (EEA) to Padé approximants suggested by McEliece and Shearer ([6]) and Brent, Gustavson and Yun ([2]). Suppose $a(x)$ and $b(x)$ are fixed polynomials over a field F, with $\deg(a) \geq \deg(b)$. We recall that the EEA produces the equation:

$$s(x)\,a(x) + t(x)\,b(x) = g(x)\,, \tag{2.1}$$

where $g := GCD(a,b)$, and sequences $\{s_i\}$, $\{t_i\}$, $\{r_i\}$, $\{q_i\}$ such that $g(x) = r_n(x)$ and

$$s_{-1}(x) = 1,\ t_{-1}(x) = 0,\ r_{-1}(x) = a(x)\,, \tag{2.2a}$$

$$s_0(x) = 0,\ t_0(x) = 1,\ r_0(x) = b(x)\,, \tag{2.2b}$$

$$r_{i-1}(x) = q_i(x) r_i(x) + r_{i+1}(x)\,,\ \deg(r_{i+1}) < \deg(r_i)\,, \tag{2.2c}$$

$$s_{i+1}(x) = s_{i-1}(x) - q_i(x) s_i(x)\,, \tag{2.2d}$$

$$t_{i+1}(x) = t_{i-1}(x) - q_i(x) t_i(x)\,. \tag{2.2e}$$

Further, the EEA possesses the following useful properties (among others).

Property A: $t_i r_{i-1} - t_{i-1} r_i = (-1)^i a, \quad 0 \le i \le n+1.$
Property B: $s_i t_{i-1} - s_{i-1} t_i = (-1)^{i+1}, \quad 0 \le i \le n+1.$
Property C: $s_i a + t_i b = r_i, \quad -1 \le i \le n+1.$
Property D: $\deg(t_i) + \deg(r_{i-1}) = \deg(a), \quad 0 \le i \le n+1.$

These are easily established by induction. In particular, we consider Property C, which can be written:

$$t_i(x)b(x) \equiv r_i(x) \mod a(x) \tag{2.3a}$$

(cf. (1.3)), and Property D which yields

$$\deg(t_i) + \deg(r_i) < \deg(a) \tag{2.3b}$$

since $\deg(r_{i-1}) > \deg(r_i)$. There is a converse result to (2.3a,b), established in [6] via the following.

Lemma 2.1: Given two non-negative integers m, n with $m \ge \deg(GCD(a,b))$ and $m+n = \deg(a)-1$, there exists a unique index j $(0 \le j \le n)$ such that $\deg(r_j) \le m$, $\deg(t_j) \le n$. □

Theorem 2.1: Suppose $t(x)$ and $r(x)$ are non-zero polynomials satisfying

$$t(x)b(x) \equiv r(x) \mod a(x),$$

$$\deg(t) + \deg(r) < \deg(a).$$

Then there exists a unique index j $(0 \le j \le n)$ and a polynomial $\lambda(x)$ such that

$$t(x) = \lambda(x)\, t_j(x),$$

$$r(x) = \lambda(x)\, r_j(x) \quad \square$$

It is now fairly clear how these results apply to Padé approximation. Given a power series $B(x) \in F[[x]]$ and an integer $N \ge 0$, we consider the EEA applied to

$$a(x) = x^{N+1} \tag{2.4}$$

$$b(x) = B_N(x) := b_0 + b_1 x + \cdots + b_N x^N . \tag{2.5}$$

Then the (m,n) Padé approximant to $B(x)$ is obtained from $r_j(x)/t_j(x)$, where r_j, t_j are the polynomials arising when the EEA is applied to a,b and j is fixed uniquely by Lemma 2.1. Note that, in contrast to the standard algorithms (which compute a series of approximants along diagonals of the Padé table), this approach produces a sequence along an *antidiagonal* starting at the $(N,0)$ entry. In practice, one is usually interested in finding only main-diagonal (or near main-diagonal) entries. If the power series $B(x)$ is *normal* (i.e., its Padé approximants are all distinct; see [5]), it is a simple matter to find the (m,n) approximant by checking the degrees of each pair (r_i, t_i) in the EEA sequence until reaching (r_j, t_j). However, this need not be the case; the degrees of $r_j(x)$, $t_j(x)$ may be strictly less than m and n respectively. While it would be possible to identify the desired approximant by checking the degrees of (r_{i-1}, t_{i-1}) and (r_i, t_i) at each step, a less clumsy approach is provided by a result of Brent,

Gustavson and Yun ([2]).

Lemma 2.2: The term r_i/t_i of the EEA gives rise to $\deg(q_i)$ equal entries of the Padé table along the Nth antidiagonal. □

It should also be mentioned that r_j and t_j need not be relatively prime. Fortunately, from Property A we know that any common divisor of r_j, t_j also divides $a(x) = x^{N+1}$. So, if $GCD(r_j, t_j) \neq 1$, then:

$$r_j(x) = x^k\, p(x)\,,$$
$$t_j(x) = x^k\, q(x)\,,$$

with

$$GCD(p, q) = 1\,.$$

We conclude this section by presenting procedure PEA1 (Padé-Euclidean algorithm 1), which computes *one* specified approximant from the antidiagonal sequence.

```
Procedure PEA1 (s, x, m, n)
   N ← m + n ; a(x) ← x^(N+1)
   if deg(s) < N then [input series has insufficient degree]
      print 'warning:...'
   b(x) ← s(x) mod x^(N+1)
   if n = 0 then [trivial case] return (b)
   else begin
      c ← 0 ; d ← 1 ; i ← 0 ; temp ← b
      while b ≠ 0 and i < n do
         q ← quo (a,b) ; r ← rem(a,b)
         for j from 2 to deg(q) do [skip through equal approximants]
            i ← i + 1
         if i ≥ n then [(m,n) approximant found] break
         else begin
            r1 ← c − qd
            i ← i + 1
            if r ≠ 0 then [not at end of sequence] temp ← r/r1
            a ← b ; b ← r
            c ← d ; d ← r1
         end
         return (temp)
   end
end PEA1
```

3. A fast EEA - Padé algorithm

We have seen that it is relatively simple to obtain a sequence of Padé approximants as part of a GCD calculation. In this section we describe part of an asymptotically fast ($O(n \log^2 n)$) polynomial GCD algorithm, and following

Brent, Gustavson and Yun modify it to perform the Padé antidiagonal calculation.

The algorithm in question is the PRSDC1 (polynomial remainder sequence divide and conquer 1) algorithm of [2], which is an extension and improvement of the HGCD (half GCD) routine of Aho, Hopcroft and Ullman ([1]). Both algorithms are based upon the principle that quotients of polynomials of degrees d_1, d_2 $(d_1 > d_2)$ depend only on the leading $2(d_1 - d_2) + 1$ terms of the dividend and the leading $(d_1 - d_2) + 1$ terms of the divisor. Let $u_0(x)$, $u_1(x)$ be polynomials with remainder sequence $\{u_0, u_1, u_2, \ldots, u_k\}$ and consider the task of finding $GCD(u_0, u_1)$. Let $l(i)$ be the unique integer such that

$$\deg(u_{l(i)}) \geq i \tag{3.1}$$

and

$$\deg(u_{l(i)+1}) < i\ . \tag{3.2}$$

Then if $n = \deg(u_0)$, procedure HGCD yields $u_{l(\frac{n}{2})}$, i.e., the last term in the remainder sequence whose degree exceeds half that of u_0. As we shall see with PRSDC1, we may just as easily obtain $u_{l(r)}$ where $\frac{n}{2} \leq r \leq n$. In order to produce this routine, we will require some additional notation, and a pair of lemmas.

Definition ([1]): For u_0, u_1 as above, with quotient sequence

$$\{q_i = \left\lfloor \frac{u_{i-1}}{u_i} \right\rfloor\}_1^k ,$$

we define 2×2 matrices $R_{ij}^{(u_0 u_1)}$ for $0 \leq i \leq j \leq k$ by

$$R_{ii}^{(u_0 u_1)} = \begin{bmatrix} 1 & 0 \\ 0 & 1 \end{bmatrix} ,\ i \geq 0 \tag{3.3a}$$

$$R_{ij}^{(u_0 u_1)} = \begin{bmatrix} 0 & 1 \\ 1 & -q_j \end{bmatrix} \begin{bmatrix} 0 & 1 \\ 1 & -q_{j-1} \end{bmatrix} \cdots \begin{bmatrix} 0 & 1 \\ 1 & -q_{i+1} \end{bmatrix} ,\ j > i \tag{3.3b}$$

It is easy to show that these matrices have the following properties:

Lemma 3.1 ([1]):

$$(a)\ \begin{pmatrix} u_j \\ u_{j+1} \end{pmatrix} = R_{ij}^{(u_0 u_1)} \begin{pmatrix} u_i \\ u_{i+1} \end{pmatrix} ,\ i < j < k \tag{3.4a}$$

$$(b)\ R_{0j}^{(u_0 u_1)} = \begin{bmatrix} s_j & t_j \\ s_{j+1} & t_{j+1} \end{bmatrix} ,\ 0 \leq j < k \tag{3.4b}$$

□

Lemma 3.2 ([1]): Let f, g be polynomials such that $n = \deg(f) > \deg(g)$, and let:

$$f(x) = f_1(x)\, x^k + f_2(x)\ ,\ \deg(f_2) < k\ , \tag{3.5}$$

$$g(x) = g_1(x)\,x^k + g_2(x)\,,\ \deg(g_2) < k\,, \tag{3.6}$$

where

$$k \le 2\deg(g) - \deg(f)\,, \tag{3.7}$$

i.e., $\deg(g_1) \ge \frac{1}{2}\deg(f_1)$.

Then

$$R^{(f,g)}_{0,l(\lceil \frac{n+k}{2} \rceil)} = R^{(f_1,g_1)}_{0,l(\lceil \frac{n-k}{2} \rceil)}\,, \tag{3.8}$$

that is, the quotients of the remainder sequences for (f,g) and (f_1,g_1) agree (at least) until the latter reaches a remainder whose degree does not exceed $\frac{1}{2}\deg(f_1)$ □

Procedure PRSDC1 (u_0, u_1, r)
  $n \leftarrow \deg(u_0)$
  if $\deg(u_1) < r$ or $n = 0$ **then return** $\begin{bmatrix} u_0 & 1 & 0 \\ u_1 & 0 & 1 \end{bmatrix}$

  else begin
    $m \leftarrow \lceil r \rceil$ [assuming $\frac{n}{2} \le r \le n$]
    $u_0 \rightarrow b_0 x^m + c_0,\ \deg(c_0) < m$
    $u_1 \rightarrow b_1 x^m + c_1,\ \deg(c_1) < m$
    $[\underline{U}_1, \underline{W}_1, \underline{V}_1] \leftarrow$ PRSDC1 $(b_0, b_1, \frac{1}{2}\deg(b_0))$
    $\binom{d}{e} \leftarrow \underline{U}_1 x^m + [\underline{W}_1, \underline{V}_1]\binom{c_0}{c_1}$
    if $\deg(e) < r$ **then return** $[\binom{d}{e}, \underline{W}_1, \underline{V}_1]$
    else begin
      $q \leftarrow quo(d,e)$
      $f \leftarrow rem(d,e) = d - qe$
      $k \leftarrow 2m - \deg(e)$
      $e \rightarrow g_0 x^k + h_0,\ \deg(h_0) < k$
      $f \rightarrow g_1 x^k + h_1,\ \deg(h_1) < k$
      $[\underline{U}_2, \underline{W}_2, \underline{V}_2] \leftarrow PRSDC1\,(g_0, g_1, \frac{1}{2}\deg(g_0))$
      return $[\underline{U}_2 x^k + [\underline{W}_2, \underline{V}_2]\binom{h_0}{h_1}, [\underline{W}_2, \underline{V}_2]\begin{bmatrix} 0 & 1 \\ 1 & -q \end{bmatrix}[\underline{W}_1, \underline{V}_1]]$
    end
  end
end PRSDC1

Algorithm PRSDC1 as stated above computes the matrix

$$\left[\begin{matrix} u_j & s_j & t_j \\ u_{j+1} & s_{j+1} & t_{j+1} \end{matrix}\right] \text{ where } j = l(r)\ ,\ \frac{n}{2} \leq r \leq n\ . \qquad (3.9)$$

By Lemma 3.2, if we take the $m = \lceil r \rceil$ leading terms of u_0, u_1 and compute PRSDC1 $(b_0, b_1, \frac{1}{2}\deg(b_0))$, we obtain in effect

$$R^{(b_0, b_1)}_{0,l(\lceil \frac{n-r}{2} \rceil)} = R^{(u_0, u_1)}_{0,l(\lceil \frac{n+r}{2} \rceil)}\ .$$

Then

$$\begin{aligned}\binom{d}{e} &= \underline{U}_1 x^m + [\underline{W}_1, \underline{V}_1] \binom{c_0}{c_1} \\ &= [\underline{W}_1, \underline{V}_1] \binom{b_0}{b_1} x^m + [\underline{W}_1, \underline{V}_1] \binom{c_0}{c_1} \\ &= [\underline{W}_1, \underline{V}_1] \begin{pmatrix} b_0 x^m + c_0 \\ b_1 x^m + c_1 \end{pmatrix} = R^{(u_0, u_1)}_{0,l(\lceil \frac{n+r}{2} \rceil)} \binom{u_0}{u_1} \qquad (cf.(3.4a))\end{aligned}$$

If we then take the $k := 2m - \deg(e)$ leading terms from e and $f := rem(d,e)$, computing PRSDC1 $(g_0, g_1, \frac{1}{2}\deg(g_0))$, we obtain

$$\begin{aligned} R^{(g_0, g_1)}_{0,l(\lceil \frac{\deg(e) - k}{2} \rceil)} &= R^{(e,f)}_{0,l(\lceil \frac{\deg(e) + 2r - \deg(e)}{2} \rceil)} \\ &= R^{(e,f)}_{0,l(\lceil r \rceil)} = R^{(u_0, u_1)}_{l(\lceil \frac{n+r}{2} \rceil + 1),\, l(r)} \end{aligned}$$

Hence

$$\underline{U}_2\, x^k + [\underline{W}_2, \underline{V}_2] \binom{h_0}{h_1} = [\underline{W}_2, \underline{V}_2] \binom{e}{f} = \binom{u_{l(r)}}{u_{l(r)+1}}$$

Now, suppose we have $0 \leq r' < \frac{n}{2}$. Then we can call PRSDC1 with $r = \frac{n}{2}$ until the input polynomials u_j, u_{j+1} satisfy the conditions for PRSDC1, namely

$$\frac{n'}{2} \leq r' \leq n' := \deg(u_j)\ .$$

It is therefore possible to compute *any* term in the remainder sequence. To obtain the (m,p) Padé approximant to $A(x)$ from the $(m+p)^{th}$ antidiagonal, we apply the above algorithm to $u_0 = x^{m+p+1}$ and $u_1 = A \bmod x^{m+p+1}$ with $r = m$. This yields terms (u_j, u_{j+1}) in the remainder sequence such that:

$$\deg(u_j) \geq m, \quad \deg(u_{j+1}) < m \; .$$

Since $A(x)$ may be abnormal, we cannot tell a priori whether u_j or u_{j+1} corresponds to the numerator of the desired approximant; hence both must be considered. Also, since we obtain the denominator of the approximant from one of the comultiplier polynomials ("V_i", or "t_i" in the notation of Section 2), we must update the matrix $[\underline{W}, \underline{V}]$ after each recursive call to PRSDC1. We thus have algorithm PDC (Padé divide and conquer), which computes the (m,p) Padé approximant in $O(n \log^2 n)$ time. (This depends, of course, on using an $O(n \log n)$ algorithm to multiply polynomials; we have avoided methods such as the fast Fourier transform in our implementation of the PDC since for problems of reasonable size, standard polynomial multiplication algorithms are more efficient.)

Procedure PDC (a, m, p)

$n \leftarrow m + p + 1$

if $\deg(a) < n - 1$ **then print** 'warning:...'

$\binom{u_0}{u_1} \leftarrow \binom{x^n}{a \bmod x^n}$

$[\underline{W}, \underline{V}] \leftarrow \begin{bmatrix} 1 & 0 \\ 0 & 1 \end{bmatrix}$

if $\deg(u_1) \leq m$ **then return** (u_1)

else begin

    while not $(\frac{n}{2} \leq m \leq n)$ **do**

        if $m \leq \deg(u_1) < \frac{n}{2}$ **then** [pathological case]

            $q \leftarrow quo\,(u_0, u_1)$; $r \leftarrow rem(u_0, u_1)$

            $\binom{u_0}{u_1} \leftarrow \binom{u_1}{r}$

            $[\underline{W}, \underline{V}] \leftarrow \begin{bmatrix} 0 & 1 \\ 1 & -q \end{bmatrix} [\underline{W}, \underline{V}]$

            $n \leftarrow \deg(u_0)$

        else

            $[\underline{U}_1, \underline{W}_1, \underline{V}_1] \leftarrow PRSDC1\,(u_0, u_1, \frac{n}{2})$

            $\binom{u_0}{u_1} \leftarrow \underline{U}$

            $n \leftarrow \deg\,(u_0)$

            $[\underline{W}, \underline{V}] \leftarrow [\underline{W}_1, \underline{V}_1]\,[\underline{W}, \underline{V}]$

    $[\underline{U}_1, \underline{W}_1, \underline{V}_1] \leftarrow PRSDC1\,(u_0, u_1, m)$

    $[\underline{W}, \underline{V}] \leftarrow [\underline{W}_1, \underline{V}_1]\,[\underline{W}, \underline{V}]$

    if $\deg\,(\underline{U}[0]) \leq m$ and $\deg(\underline{V}[0]) \leq p$ **then return** $(\underline{U}[0]/\underline{V}[0])$

    else return $(\underline{U}[1]/\underline{V}[1])$

end

end PDC

4. Sample Problems

In this section we compare some timings of the Maple [4] implementations of our three Padé routines, Pade1 of section 1, PEA1 of section 2, and PDC of section 3, testing them on three basic problem types. While it is known that algorithm Pade1 is $O(n^3)$, algorithm PEA1 is $O(n^2)$, and algorithm PDC is $O(n \log^2 n)$, for practical purposes this information is of limited usefulness. Before presenting the timing results, we note that we are ignoring the fact that Pade1 and PEA1 can actually compute *sequences* of approximants. This seems practical not only because it puts the routines on an equal footing, but because one approximant is often all that is required. Therefore for each problem we compute only the (n,n) approximant for $n = 2,5,10,15,\dots$.

Problem 1: $s = exp(x) = \sum_{k=0}^{\infty} \dfrac{x^k}{k!}$

This is an example of a function whose power series representation is normal. Also note the rate of growth of the integers $k!$, which determine the series coefficients. The results are largely predictable, with a fairly high "cutoff" point between PDC and PEA1.

		time (s)	storage (Kbytes)
$n = 2$	PDC	6.1	204
	PEA1	2.4	155
	Pade1	3.9	172
$n = 5$	PDC	13.2	282
	PEA1	5.7	196
	Pade1	10.5	237
$n = 10$	PDC	30.4	467
	PEA1	16.9	303
	Pade1	74.8	566
$n = 15$	PDC	66.3	767
	PEA1	39.1	529
	Pade1	551.2	1,891
$n = 20$	PDC	122.9	1,157
	PEA1	95.5	845
	Pade1	---	---
$n = 25$	PDC	238.9	1,749
	PEA1	302.7	1,399
	Pade1	---	---

Problem 2: $s = \sum_{k=0}^{\infty} (k!)x^{4k}$

This type of power series will have degenerate blocks in its Padé table, i.e., groups of approximants which remain equal until the next non-zero term in the series is reached. Because of the sparseness of the series, the simple EEA routine PEA1 is at an advantage here; in fact, no "cutoff" was exhibited as high as $n = 50$.

		time (s)	storage (Kbytes)
$n=2$	PDC	3.4	176
	PEA1	1.4	143
	Padé1	2.0	163
$n=5$	PDC	4.9	188
	PEA1	2.1	147
	Padé1	5.4	188
$n=10$	PDC	8.4	237
	PEA1	3.3	167
	Padé1	17.9	278
$n=20$	PDC	17.7	352
	PEA1	6.6	204
	Padé1	229.0	988
$n=30$	PDC	27.7	475
	PEA1	11.9	274
	Padé1	---	---
$n=40$	PDC	42.0	615
	PEA1	19.1	344
	Padé1	---	---
$n=50$	PDC	55.8	746
	PEA1	31.8	442
	Padé1	---	---

Problem 3:

$$s = \frac{1 + 3x^2 + 10x^3 + x^6 - 5x^7}{1 - 4x + x^2 - 5x^3 + 17x^5 + 2x^7 - 13x^8}$$

$$= 1 + 4x + 18x^2 + 83x^3 + 334x^4 + \cdots$$

Power series of rational functions are of particular interest, since they may provide a method of solving Risch differential equations. The point to note in this problem is that the [inexact] approximants neighbouring (7,8) (i.e., the "exact" one) in the Padé table are rather unwieldy. Since PDC and PEA1 must produce intermediate approximants on the way to the correct one, Padé1 is at an advantage here.

		time (s)	storage (Kbytes)
$n=2$	PDC	8.1	229
	PEA1	4.3	180
	Padeĺ	5.1	192
$n=5$	PDC	33.0	352
	PEA1	15.8	245
	Padeĺ	9.9	241
$n=10$	PDC	321.3	857
	PEA1	333.4	902
	Padeĺ	29.5	377
$n=15$	PDC	---	---
	PEA1	---	---
	Padeĺ	47.9	512

References

1. A.V. Aho, J.E. Hopcroft, and J.D. Ullman, "The Design and Analysis of Computer Algorithms", pp. 300-308, Addison-Wesley, Reading, Mass., 1974.
2. R.P. Brent, F.G. Gustavson, and D.Y.Y. Yun, *Fast Solution of Toeplitz Systems of Equations and Computation of Pade Approximants,* Journal of Algorithms *1,* 259-295, 1980.
3. K.O. Geddes, *Symbolic Computation of Padé Approximants,* ACM TOMS *5,* 2, 218-233, 1979.
4. K.O. Geddes, G.H. Gonnet, and B.W. Char, "Maple User's Manual", third edition, University of Waterloo Res. Rep. CS-83-41, December, 1983.
5. W.B. Gragg, *The Padé table and its relation to certain algorithms of numerical analysis,* SIAM Rev. *14,* 1, 1-62, 1972.
6. R.J. McEliece and J.B. Shearer, *A Property of Euclid's algorithm and an application to Padé approximation,* SIAM J. Appl. Math. *34,* 4, 611-617, 1978.

AUTOMATIC ERROR CUMULATION CONTROL

B.J.A. Hulshof and J.A. van Hulzen
Twente University of Technology, Department of Computer Science
P.O. Box 217, 7500 AE Enschede, the Netherlands

EXTENDED ABSTRACT

Abstract: Algorithmic methods are presented to perform a priori error analysis and error cumulation control. The corresponding programs are implemented in REDUCE as an extension of Sasaki's multiple precision floating point arithmetic package. Ingredients for the method are some concepts of interval arithmetic and a slightly modified precision notion, in both absolute and relative sense. This allows to take second order effects into account and to consider errors as a combination of inevitable propagated errors, due to inaccurate input, and controlable generated errors, due to arithmetic operations. The error control allows to consider these operations as adjustable sources and results in a set of instructions for using the Sasaki-package such that the precision, dictated by the analysis, guarantees to limit error cumulation to admissible, user chosen error bounds.

1. Introduction

An algorithmic method is presented for a priori error analysis and error cumulation control. Its implementation in REDUCE [2] allows to produce instructions for a reliable use of Sasaki's package for multiple precision floating-point arithmetic (MFA) [11], since our method allows to <u>automatically</u> determine the precision, required for each operation in (an)arithmetical expression(s), once accuracy of input data and required precision for the answer(s) are known. In contrast to Olver's [9] and our approach, which resembles Richman's recomputation algorithm [10], most other methods for (round off) error analysis [6,7, 8,13] neglect second order effects. But Olver's proposal to obtain the relative error in an additive expression is too complicated for a systematic use. We are convinced that our method allows a wider range of applications than Richman's algorithm.

Ingredients we use are some concepts from interval arithmetic and a slightly modified precision notion, in both absolute and relative sense. An a priori error analysis, without any knowledge of the actual values, which are going to replace the formal operands in an arithmetical expression, is impossible. We employ interval arithmetic to obtain estimations for (sub)result values and to estimate realistic upperbounds for the absolute and relative error. Our approach to govern error cumulation by a priori determining the precision does not demand very accurate interval bounds; our intervals are not real error intervals. This insensibility is also convenient when initially defining input data intervals.

Before giving a description of our method in section 3, we informally introduce the main concepts in section 2. Then section 4 is used to discuss some interesting aspects, such as precision distribution and recognition of low precision branches. Section 5 deals with aspects of implementation. Possible applications are indicated in the last section.

2. An informal treatement

Our a priori error analysis concentrates on worst case situations. Hence the criteria, produced for using MFA, might be qualified as somewhat pessimistic, i.e. as certainly sufficient to guarantee reliability. We essentially distinguish between (inevitable) propagated errors, i.e. the possibly cumulative effect of inaccurate inputdata, and (reducable) generated errors, i.e. errors caused by performing MFA operations. Our intention is to reduce the generated errors such that they fit into the gap between the propogated error and the allowed error bound.

Like done by others [1,3,6,7,8], our strategy can be vizualized by error data flowgraphs. The nodes of such a directed graph correspond with arithmetic operations. The edges directed to a node represent the error inflow of the operand(s) and the edge directed from a node the error outflow, i.e. the error cumulation resulting from performing the node operation on the operands. Using (M)FA forces to consider the nodes as error sources. Error cumulation control can therefore be viewed as a tool allowing to (partly) regulate the error sources. Hence nodes are adjustable sources, used to suppress generated errors by increasing precision.

Fig. 1 reflects a first impression of a "general"worst case error situation for a binary operation $x_r \leftarrow x_1 \circ x_2$. Here $\beta_i \geq 0$ denotes the total error contribution of the operand x_i to β_i; β_o reflects the β_r-part, due to the MFA operation. Assuming x_r corresponds with one of the future final results we wish to determine β_o such that $\beta_r \leq \varepsilon$, where ε is the totally allowed error bound. Visually this can be illustrated by adding a hypothetical <u>m</u>easure and <u>c</u>ontrol <u>u</u>nit (see Fig. 2). The need for an instrument to describe the influence of operand errors in the result error is also recognized by others. Stummel [13] and Sterbenz [12], for instance, introduced the notion of <u>magnification factors</u> $\gamma_i \geq 0$. Bauer [1] called them partial derivative weights. Such a magnification factor γ_i, associated with

x_i, depends on x_1, x_2, x_r, $\circ$ and the question if absolute or relative error analysis is performed (see theorem 3.3). It expresses that $\beta_i = \gamma_i \delta_i$, where δ_i is

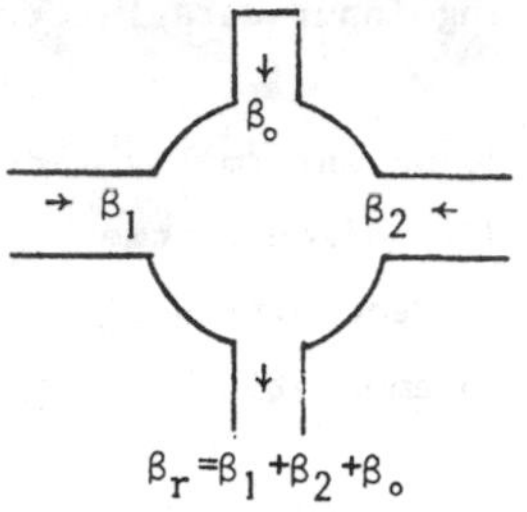

Figure 1

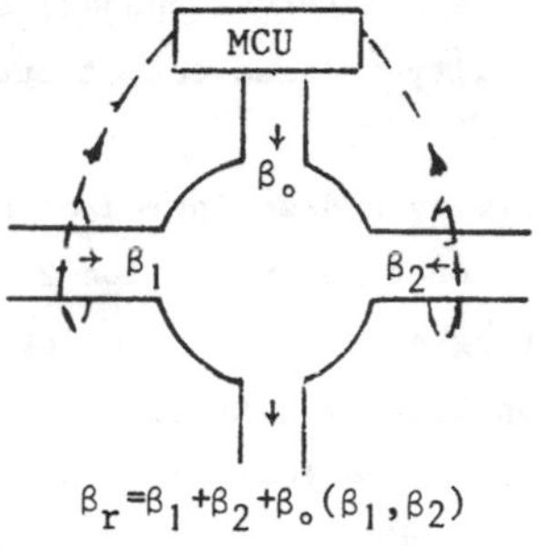

Figure 2

the total error in the computation of x_i. Fig. 3 shows a further refinement of Fig. 1. Obviously δ_i does also contain a generated part, if x_i is not an input value, i.e. $\delta_i = \delta_{ip} + \delta_{ig}$, where δ_{ip} and δ_{ig} denote the propagated and generated error in δ_i, respectively. This stresses the need to trace the history of all generated errors, if we want to control them. The magnitude of these δ_{ig} is in fact not known, since the precision of the MFA operations will result from our

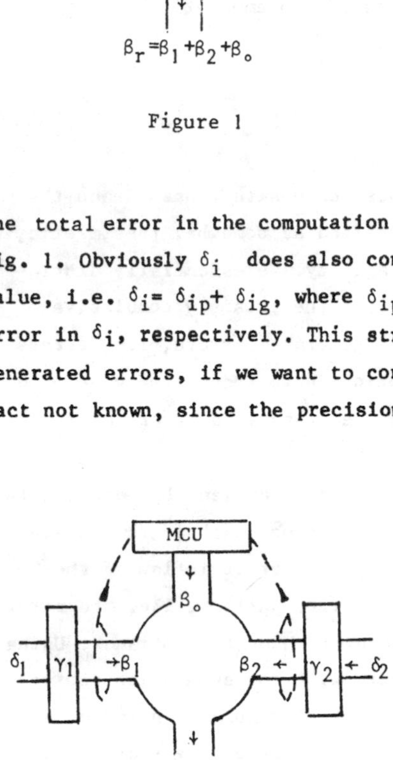

Figure 3

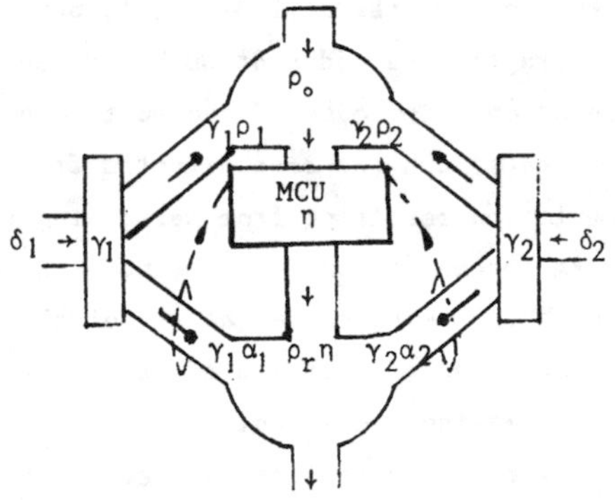

Figure 4 → $\delta_r = \beta_r = \alpha_r + \rho_r \eta$

analysis. We therefore introduce a <u>generated error control factor</u> η, which occurs, during the entire process, as linear factor in all generated errors, as proved by theorem 3.3. The multiplier of η, the <u>generated error indicator</u> ρ_i is actually used to manipulate with the generated errors. So we take $\delta_i = \alpha_i + \rho_i \eta$ ($\alpha_i = \delta_{ip}$ and $\rho_i \eta = \delta_{ig}$) and $\delta_r = \beta_r = \Sigma_i \gamma_i \alpha_i + (\Sigma_i \gamma_i \rho_i + \rho_o)\eta$. <u>All</u> generated errors can now be controlled by choosing a suitable η, i.e. $\delta_r = \beta_r \leq \varepsilon$ can be refined, resulting

in $\eta \le (\varepsilon - \alpha_r)/\rho_r$. This also shows that $\varepsilon \le \alpha_r$, i.e. a total error smaller than the inevitable propagated error, is impossible. Fig. 4 reflects this strategy, where the mcu determines the value of η. Apparently the choice of ρ_o is arbitrary, since it is the product $\rho_o \eta$ which finally matters. However the ρ_i-choices are of essential importance for controlling the "local" precision, as discussed in section 4. In contrast, η can therefore be viewed as a tool controlling the "global" precision. Once η is known the generated error $\rho_o \eta$ for any operator $\circ$, dictates the precision d for performing $\circ$ during the actual computations.
Obviously d must be choosen such that the corresponding generated error is not larger than $\rho_o \eta$. The computation of η is illustrated by the following

Example 2.1: We consider the absolute error for $x_r = x_1 + x_2$, where $x_1 = \frac{1}{3}$ and $x_2 = \frac{1}{7}$ exactly. If the x_i are represented as floating-point numbers in 8 decimal digits, their absolute errors are smaller than $\frac{1}{2} 10^{-8}$. For this simple example the choice of ρ_+ appears to be irrelevant. As is intuitively clear $\gamma_1 = \gamma_2 = 1$, because absolute errors may be added for an addition (see also theorem 3.3). Let $\varepsilon = 10^{-7}$. Then we find the following values:

$x_i : \alpha_i = \frac{1}{2} 10^{-8}, \rho_i = 0 \quad , \gamma_i = 1 \ , \quad i = 1,2.$

$x_r = x_1 + x_2 : \alpha_r = \gamma_1 \alpha_1 + \gamma_2 \alpha_2 = 10^{-8}, \rho_r = \gamma_1 \rho_1 + \gamma_2 \rho_2 + \rho_+ = 1,$ when choosing $\rho_+ = 1$.

So $\eta \le (\varepsilon - \alpha_r)/\rho_r \le (10^{-7} - 10^{-8})/1 = 9.10^{-8}$.

The allowable generated error in $x_1 + x_2$ is $\rho_+ \eta = 9.10^{-8}$, from which the precision d for the addition can be determined (see section 3). Notice that any choice of ρ_+ leads to $\rho_+ \eta = 9.10^{-8}$. □

3. A priori error analysis

All computations required during an a priori error analysis are done in MFA and based on the notion of p-precision numbers and on some concepts of interval arithmetic. Therefore we start introducing these ingredients, using Richman's terminology [10], in combination with our concept of absolute and relative error. Then we discuss error propagation and generation due to a variety of arithmetical operations.

Definition 3.1: A floating point number is called a p-precision number, $p \ge 1$, if its mantissa is p digits long and if its exponent is an arbitrary integer. $\mathbb{F}_p^b \subset \mathbb{R}$ denotes the set of all p-precision numbers with base b. □

The base b is assumed to be fixed and will only be given when explicitly needed. Under- and overflow of the exponent are non existent when using Sasaki's package.

Definition 3.2: Let $s \in \mathbb{R}$ and let ∇_p, Δ_p be postfix operators on $\mathbb{R} \to \mathbb{F}_p$ such that
- $s \nabla_p$ denotes the smallest p-precision number larger than s, if $s \ne 0$.
- $s \Delta_p$ denotes the largest p-precision number smaller than s, if $s \ne 0$.

- $s\nabla_p = s\Delta_p = 0$ if $s=0$. □

Example 3.1: In $\mathbb{F}_4^{10}$ holds $A\nabla_4=1.572$ and $A\Delta_4=1.571$ if $A=\frac{11}{7}$. □

Definition 3.3: Let $I_p(x_i)$, or I_i for short, be a so called a priori approximation interval, or AA-interval for short, bounded by p-precision numbers, for a (fictive) exact value x_i occurring in the actual computations. Let $\circ$ denote a binary operation such that $\circ: \mathbb{F}_p \times \mathbb{F}_p \to \mathbb{F}_q$, $q \geq p$. Let f denote a unary operator such that $f: \mathbb{F}_p \to \mathbb{F}_q$, $q \geq p$. Then the AA-intervals resulting from $x_i \circ x_j$ and $f(x_i)$ are defined as:

$$I_p(x_i \circ x_j) = [(\min_{x\in I_i, y \in I_j} (x\circ y))\Delta_p, (\max_{x\in I_i, y\in I_j} (x\circ y))\nabla_p]$$

and

$$I_p(f(x_i)) = [(\min_{x\in I_i} f(x))\Delta_p, (\max_{x\in I_i} f(x))\nabla_p].$$ □

Although the interval arithmetic, reflected by definition 3.3, not essentially differs from those given by others [4], our intention is different. During the precomputation, i.e. the a priori analysis, the bounds for these AA-intervals need not to be accurate, as long as their most significant digit is a reliable measure for determining the effect of error propagation and for producing criteria for suppressing the influence of error generation -the generated error indicators- during the actual computations. All we need is the gurantee that during the actual computations both x_i and its approximation $\bar{x}_i$ are in the AA-interval $I_p(x_i)$. Theorem 3.1 ensures this for input values. Theorem 3.2 expresses that this guarantee can only be given if the actual computations are at least performed in precision p.

Theorem 3.1 Let $\bar{y}$ be some input value approximating the exact value $\bar{y} \in \mathbb{R}$, then:

a- If y known then $y,\bar{y} \in [y\Delta_p, y\nabla_p]$ if $\bar{y}$ approximates y within precision p.

b- If $|\bar{y}-y| \leq \alpha_y$, where $\alpha_y > 0$, then $y,\bar{y} \in [(\bar{y}-\alpha_y)\Delta_p, (\bar{y}+\alpha_y)\nabla_p]$.

c- If $|(\bar{y}-y|/\bar{y}| \leq \beta_y$, where $\beta_y > 0$, then $y,\bar{y} \in [(\bar{y}-|\bar{y}|\beta_y)\Delta_p, (\bar{y}+|\bar{y}|\beta_y)\nabla_p]$. □

Proof: Straightforward. □

Theorem 3.2: Let the AA-intervals $I_p(y_i)$ for all input values y_i, be computed as shown in theorem 3.1. Let all $\bar{x}_i$ (of the actual computations) approximating x_i be computed in at least precision p, where $I_p(x_i)$ is computed in accordance with definition 3.3. Then $\forall_{x_i,\bar{x}_i} (x_i, \bar{x}_i \in I_p(x_i))$. □

Proof: By straightforward induction on the operations of the actual computations. □

Corollary 3.1: Let $I_p(x)=[xb,xe]$ denote an AA-interval. Let $x\uparrow=\max(|xb|,|xe|)$, $x\downarrow=\min(|xb|,|xe|)$ if $0 \notin I_p(x)$ and let $x\downarrow=0$ otherwise, then $x\downarrow \leq |x| \leq x\uparrow$ and $x\downarrow \leq |\bar{x}| \leq x\uparrow$. □

Proof: Straightforward consequence of theorem 3.2. □

Let us now introduce our notion of absolute and relative precision.

Definition 3.4: Let $x_i \in \mathbb{R}$ and let $\bar{x}_i$ be some approximation of x_i, occurring in the actual computations, then:
The absolute precision of x_i, denoted by $ap(x_i)$, is a pair of non-negative p-precision numbers (α_i,ρ_i), such that $|x_i-\bar{x}_i| \le ap(x_i)=\alpha_i+\rho_i\eta$.
The relative precision of x_i, denoted by $rp(x_i)$, is a pair of non-negative p-precision number (α_i,ρ_i), such that $|(x_i-\bar{x}_i)/x_i| \le rp(x_i)=\alpha_i+\rho_i\eta$.
Here $\eta>0$ denotes the generated error control factor and α_i and ρ_i are upperbounds for the propagated error and generated error indicator, respectively. $\rho_i\eta$ denotes the generated error. □

Theorem 3.3: Let $x_i \in \mathbb{R}$ and $ap(x_i)=\alpha_i+\rho_i\eta$, where $\alpha_i,\rho_i \in (\mathbb{F}_p)^+$. Let $I_p(x_i)$ denote the AA-internal for x_i. Then:

$$ap(x_1 \pm x_2) = (\alpha_1+\alpha_2)\nabla_p + (\rho_1+\rho_2+\rho_\pm)\nabla_p\eta,$$

$$ap(x_1 . x_2) = (\alpha_1 x_2\!\uparrow + \alpha_2 x_1\!\uparrow)\nabla_p + (\rho_1 x_2\!\uparrow + \rho_2 x_1\!\uparrow + \rho_.)\nabla_p\eta,$$

$$ap(x_1/x_2) = (\alpha_1\cdot\frac{1}{x_2\!\downarrow}+\alpha_2\cdot\frac{(x_1/x_2)\!\uparrow}{x_2\!\downarrow})\nabla_p + (\rho_1\cdot\frac{1}{x_2\!\downarrow}+\rho_2\cdot\frac{(x_1/x_2)\!\uparrow}{x_2\!\downarrow}+\rho_/)\nabla_p\eta,$$

assuming $0 \notin I_p(x_2)$,

$$ap(f(x_1)) = (\alpha_1 \cdot \max_{x\in I_p(x_1)}(|f'(x)|))\nabla_p + (\rho_1 \cdot \max_{x\in I_p(x_1)}(|f'(x)|)+\rho_f)\nabla_p\eta,$$

assuming f is continue differentiable on $I_p(x_1)$. □

Proof: We only verify $ap(x_1\cdot x_2)$, since the other proofs are almost similar. $ap(x_i) = \alpha_i+\rho_i\eta$, i.e. $|x_i-\bar{x}_i| \le \alpha_i+\rho_i\eta$. Let $u_i = \bar{x}_i - x_i$, i.e. $|u_i| \le \alpha_i+\rho_i\eta$. Now $|\overline{x_1 . x_2} - x_1 . x_2| \le \varepsilon_g + \varepsilon_p$, where ε_g and ε_p denote the generated and propagated error contribution, respectively. So:

$$\varepsilon_g = |\overline{x_1\cdot x_2} - \bar{x}_1\cdot\bar{x}_2| \le \rho_.\eta \quad \text{and}$$

$$\varepsilon_p = |\bar{x}_1\cdot\bar{x}_2 - x_1\cdot x_2| = |(x_1+u_1)\cdot(x_2+u_2) - x_1\cdot x_2|$$

$$= |x_1\cdot u_2 + \bar{x}_2\cdot u_1| \le I_1\!\uparrow\cdot(\alpha_2+\rho_2\eta) + I_2\!\uparrow\cdot(\alpha_1+\rho_1\eta)$$

Hence:

$$\varepsilon_g + \varepsilon_p \le (\alpha_1\cdot I_2\!\uparrow + \alpha_2\cdot I_1\!\uparrow) + (\rho_1\cdot I_2\!\uparrow + \rho_2\cdot I_1\!\uparrow + \rho_.)\eta$$

$$\le (\alpha_1\cdot I_2\!\uparrow + \alpha_2\cdot I_1\!\uparrow)\nabla_p + (\rho_1\cdot I_2\!\uparrow + \rho_2\cdot I_1\!\uparrow + \rho_.)\nabla_p\eta$$

$$= ap(x_1\cdot x_2).$$ □

The absolute precision of a division is undefined if the divisor AA-interval contains zero. A solution is to increase the precision p, thus atempting to get more accurate and smaller AA-intervals, without zero. For shortness we omit the equivalent of theorem 3.3 for relative precision calculations.
Diasadvantages of the latter over an absolute precision analysis are that the computations become more complex and that zero problems are insuperable.
Observe that the absolute (and also the relative) precision of the result of an $\circ$-operation is given by $\Sigma\alpha_i\gamma_i + (\rho_\circ + \Sigma\rho_i\gamma_i)\eta$. The γ_i are the magnification factors, mentioned earlier. Hence their structure is implicitly given in theorem

3.3., which also shows that η is maintained as a linear factor during the entire precomputation process. The ρ_i's allow to manipulate with generated errors. The ρ_i-cumulation (<u>ρ-stream</u> for short) describes how the generated errors "flow" through the actual computations without knowing their actual values, which depend on the actual MFA operations. For each $\circ$-operation a $\rho_\circ$-contribution has to be added. How to actually determine this contribution is considered in the next section. Let us now formulate how to start up the overall process via theorem 3.4, which is followed by an example illustrating our strategy.

<u>Theorem 3.4</u>: Let $I_p(y)$ be an AA-interval for an input value y in accordance with theorem 3.1. Then:

- a: If y is known then either
    1. there exists a smallest integer $q > 0$, such that $y \in \mathbb{F}_q$, implying that $ap(y)=rp(y)=0+0\eta$, or
    2. y can be computed up to arbitrary precision, i.e. $ap(y)=rp(y)=0+\rho_y\nabla_p\,\eta$, where $\rho_y>0$ is the contribution of y to the ρ-stream.
- b: If $|\bar{y}-y|\le\alpha_y$, where $\alpha_y>0$, then $ap(y)=\alpha_y\nabla_p+0\eta$ and $rp(y)=(\alpha y/y{\downarrow})\nabla_p+0\eta$ if $0\notin I\ (y)$.
- c: If $|(\bar{y}-y)/\bar{y}|\le\beta_y$, where $\beta_y>0$, then $ap(y)=(\beta_y|\bar{y}|)\nabla_p+0\eta$ and $rp(y)=(\beta_y|\bar{y}|/y{\downarrow})\nabla_p+0\eta$ if $0\notin I_p(y)$. □

<u>Proof</u>: We only verify c, since the other proofs are similar.

$|(\bar{y}-y)/\bar{y}|\le\beta_y$. So $|\bar{y}-y|\le\ \beta_y|\bar{y}|\le(\beta_y|\bar{y}|)\nabla_p+0\eta=ap(y)$ and

$|(\bar{y}-y)/y|\le(\beta_y|\bar{y}|)/|y|\le\ (\beta_y|\bar{y}|)/y{\downarrow}\le(\ \beta_y|\bar{y}|/y{\downarrow}\ )\nabla_p+0\eta=rp(y)$. □

<u>Example 3.2</u>: Let $F=A+B.(C-D/E)$, where $A=\frac{11}{7}$, $B=\frac{3}{17}$, $C=\frac{13}{12}$ and $D=E=\frac{1}{3}$.

We assume the corresponding floating values to be known in 8 significant digits, leading to absolute error upperbounds of $\frac{1}{2}10^{-7}$ for A,C and $\frac{1}{2}10^{-8}$ for B,D, and E. Although strickter bounds are possible -we have exact values- we thus simulate operating with computed or measured inputdata. So, instead of applying theorem 3.4.a2 in some $\mathbb{F}_q^{10}$, we use theorem 3.4 b leading to $ap(A)=ap(C)=\frac{1}{2}10^{-7}$ and $ap(B)=ap(D)=ap(E)=\frac{1}{2}10^{-8}$. Then according to theorem 3.1, and operating in $\mathbb{F}_4^{10}$, we have:

$I_4(A)=[1.571,1.572]$, $I_4(B)=[1.764.10^{-1},1.765.10^{-1}]$, $I_4(C)=[1.083,1.084]$ and $I_4(D)=I_4(E)=[3.333.10^{-1},3.334.10^{-1}]$. Now applying definition 3.3 leads to $I_4(r1=D/E)=[9.996.10^{-1},1.001]$, $I_4(r2=C-r1)=[8.199.10^{-2},8441.10^{-2}]$, $I_4(r3=B.r2)=[1.446.10^{-2},1.490.10^{-2}]$ and $I_4(F=A+r3)=[1.585,1.587]$.

For an absolute error analysis certain $\rho_\circ$ choices are needed. We simply take $\rho_\circ=1$ if the $\rho_i=0$ and $\rho_\circ=(\frac{1}{2}\Sigma\rho_i\gamma_i)\Delta_p$ otherwise. Then theorem 3.3 gives:

$$ap(r1) = \left(\frac{1}{3.333.10^{-1}}.5.10^{-9}+\frac{1.001}{3.333.10^{-1}}.5.10^{-9}\right)\nabla_4+$$

$$\left(\frac{1}{3.333.10^{-1}}.0\qquad+\frac{1.001}{3.333.10^{-1}}.0+\rho_/\ \right)\nabla_4\eta$$

$$= \quad 3.002.10^{-8} + 1.001\ \eta \quad (\rho_{/} = 1)$$
$$ap(r2) = \quad 8.003.10^{-8} + 1.502\ \eta \quad (\rho_{-} = 0.5)$$
$$ap(r3) = \quad 1.455.10^{-8} + 3.977.10^{-1}\eta \quad (\rho_{.} = 1.325.10^{-1})$$
$$ap(F) = \quad 6.456.10^{-8} + 5.996.10^{-1}\eta \quad (\rho_{+} = 1.988\ 10^{-1})$$ □

Once the required precision for both intermediate and final results z_i of the future actual computations - the $\alpha_i + \rho_i\eta$ - are calculated η -the control factor- can be obtained, using the admissible errors ε_i for the z_i, from

(3.1) $$\eta = \min_i \left(\eta_i = \left(\frac{\varepsilon_i - \alpha_i}{\rho_i}\right)\Delta_p\right)$$

Eq. (3.1) leads to a minimal η for all computations. If $\varepsilon_i < \alpha_i$ the precision p for the a priori analysis can be increased. Since the α_i are actually upperbounds we can thus try to satisfy $\varepsilon_i > \alpha_i$.

We assume that a generated error, introduced by an actual MFA $\circ$-operation is due to chopping or rounding the result to, say, d digits. Reliable computations are guaranteed if $g_\circ(d) \le \rho_\circ\eta$, where $g_\circ(d)$ is the generated error due to MFA $\circ$-operation. When rounding is performed, d results from (3.2) or from (3.3), depending on an absolute or relative precision analysis, respectively, and assuming $I_\circ$ denotes the AA-interval, associated with the result of $\circ$.

(3.2) $$d \ge \lceil \max \left(\max_{x \in I_\circ} (\log_b |x|) - \log_b |2\rho_\circ\eta| + 1, p\right)\rceil$$

(3.3) $$d \ge \lceil \max (1 - \log_b |2\rho_\circ\eta|, p)\rceil$$

Here $d \ge p$ is imposed by theorem 3.2. The factor 2 must be omitted when chopping is done. The internal word length can, of course, also be taken into account. Since η is minimal d is "maximal". Hence reliability is guaranteed. As said above accurate interval bounds are hardly required. Even wrong most significant digits in $I_\circ$-interval bounds will hardly affect the underbound for d. A simple remedy in doubtful situations is to repeat the analysis with a slightly increased precision.

Since $\rho_\circ\eta$ is merely an upperbound for $g_\circ(d)$ we can try to refine the actual precision rules by employing the difference $r = \rho_\circ\eta - g_\circ(d)$ to increase the generated error upperbound, as reflected by

<u>Theorem 3.5</u>: Let $x_r = x_1 \circ x_2$, where $ap(x_i) = \alpha_i + \rho_i\eta$, i=1,2. Assume $\rho_1 = \Sigma\gamma_j\rho_j + \rho_\theta$ and $\rho_{m,1}\eta = \rho_\theta\eta - g_\theta(d) > 0$, then $\rho_\circ\eta$ may be increased with $\gamma_1\rho_{m,1}\eta$. □

<u>Proof</u>: $\rho_r\eta = (\gamma_1\rho_1 + \gamma_2\rho_2 + \rho_\circ)\nabla_p\eta = (\gamma_1(\rho_{m,1} + \rho_1 - \rho_{m,1}) + \gamma_2\rho_2 + \rho_\circ)\nabla_p$
$= (\gamma_1(\rho_1 - \rho_{m,1}) + \gamma_2\rho_2 + (\gamma_1\rho_{m,1} + \rho_\circ))\nabla_p\eta$. □

<u>Example 3.2</u>: (continued): Given $ap(F) = \alpha_F + \rho_F\eta$ and assuming $\varepsilon_F = \frac{1}{2}10^{-6}$ we find,

using eq. (3.1):

$\eta = ((\varepsilon_F - \alpha_F)/\rho_F)\Delta_4) = ((5.10^{-7} - 6.456.10^{-8})/5.966.10^{-1})\Delta_4 = 7.298.10^{-7}$.

This leads to:

	$\circ$	$g_1 = (\rho_\circ \eta)\Delta_4$	$g_2 = (\Sigma\gamma_i\rho_{m,i}\eta)\Delta_4$	d	$g_\circ(d)$	$r = (g_1 + g_2 - g_\circ(d))\Delta_4$
r1	/	$7.297.10^{-7}$	0	7	5.10^{-7}	$2.297.10^{-7}$
r2	-	$3.648.10^{-7}$	$2.296.10^{-7}$	5	5.10^{-7}	$9.440.10^{-8}$
r3	.	$9.669.10^{-8}$	$1.666.10^{-8}$	6	5.10^{-8}	$6.335.10^{-8}$
F	+	$1.450.10^{-7}$	$6.334.10^{-8}$	8	5.10^{-8}	$1.583.10^{-7}$

This results in $\bar{F}=1.5861344$. It is easily verified that omitting the r-corrections demands d=6 for r2. Then we find F=1.5861345. Since $F=\frac{755}{476}$ we indeed obtain $|F-\bar{F}| \leq \varepsilon$, i.e. $1.5861340 \leq \frac{755}{476} \leq 1.5861350$. □

4. Error cumulation control.

One of the quintessences of our approach is reflected by eq.(3.1). The generated error indicators $\rho_\circ + \Sigma_i\gamma_i\rho_i$ are constructed in accordance with theorem 3.3 (or its equivalent for a relative error analysis). Once choices for $\rho_\circ$ and the ρ_i are made η and d can be computed if ε is known. How to utilize this degree of freedom?

Example 4.1: Let $x_1=10^3$ and $x_2=10^{-3}$. Assume also that $ap(x_1)=10^{-3}+\rho_1\eta$ and $ap(x_2)=10^{-9}+\eta$. Let us now analyse what can happen if we want to compute $r=x_1 \cdot x_2$ with $\varepsilon=10^{-5}$. According to theorem 3.3 holds: $\alpha_r = 2.10^{-6}$, $\gamma_1\rho_1=\rho_1.10^{-3}$ and $\gamma_2\rho_2=10^3$. Let us furthermore take $\rho_\circ=\frac{1}{2}(\gamma_1\rho_1+\gamma_2\rho_2)$. Then $ap(r)=2.10^{-6}+\{\rho_1.10^{-3}+10^3+\frac{1}{2}(\rho_1.10^{-3}+10^3)\}\eta$. So, in accordance with eq.(3.1) holds: $\eta=(\varepsilon-\alpha_r)/\rho_r=(10^{-5}-2\cdot 10^{-6})/(\frac{3}{2}(10^3+\rho_1.10^{-3}))= 5.333.10^{-6}/(10^3+\rho_1.10^{-3})$. If $\rho_1=1$ then $\eta=5.333\cdot 10^{-9}$. But if $\rho_1=10^4$ then $\eta=5.280\cdot 10^{-9}$. This leads to the conclusion that the ε-guarantee is not affected when increasing the generated error in x_1 from $5.333.10^{-9}(\rho_1=1)$ to, for instance, $5.280.10^{-5}(\rho_1=10^4)$. □

The phenomenon, shown in example 4.1, indicates that low precision branches (x_1's) might occur in a computatonal process. To avoid useless expense, computations have to be balanced, i.e. the MFA-precision has to be controlled by increasing error contributions of such low precision branches. Similar phenomena can be observed when $\rho_\circ$ and $\Sigma\gamma_i\rho_i$ considerably differ in size. But increasing the value of $\rho_\circ$ leads to a decrease of η and consequently also to smaller generated errors in the $\circ$-operands, implying that accurately computed $\circ$-operands are subjected to a less accurate $\circ$-operation. So, it is obvious that the $\rho_\circ$-choices influence precision distribution. Our experiments suggested that a good overall balance is obtained by taking $\rho_\circ=1$ if the $\rho_i=0$ and to choose $\rho_\circ=\frac{1}{2}(\gamma_1\rho_1+\gamma_2\rho_2)$ otherwise. But this implies that the generated error correction (theorem 3.5) is atmost $2\rho_\circ\eta$. In view of the stable character of the d-computation it is doubtful if corrections are profitable. This conclusion is confirmed by example 3.2, where the above indicated choice was made.

5. An experimental implementation

Most of the features, discussed so far for performing an absolute precision analysis, are implemented in REDUCE, as extension of Sasaki's MFA-package. The structure of this program is in accordance with the above outlined strategy and can be summarized as a

Precomputation Algorithm

[Input: $(\{u_i, \bar{u}_i, \varepsilon u_i)\}, \{v_i\}, \{(z_i, \varepsilon z_i)\})$

The $u_i, i \geq 1$, form a set of input variable names. The $\bar{u}_i$ and εu_i are the corresponding values and input errors, respectively. The $v_i, i \geq 1$, denote well defined arithmetic assignment statements $w_i = e_i$, where the e_i are expressions formed by operators $\circ$ and f operating on $u_i, i \geq 1$ and eventually $w_1, \ldots, w_{i-1}$ if $\circ \in \{+,-,\cdot,/\}$ and $f \in \{-,\uparrow,\exp,\log,\surd,\sin,\cos,\tan,\text{asin},\text{acos},\text{atan}\}$ with $\uparrow$ denoting integer exponentiation. $\{z_i\} \subseteq \{w_i\}$ is the set of result names and the corresponding εz_i are the admissible errors. Let, finally, $\bar{w}_i, \bar{z}_i$ denote the values resulting from applying v_i on $\bar{u}_j, j \geq 1$, and w_j, $1 \leq j \leq i-1$].

P1: Rewrite the v_i as a sequence of binary and or unary operations, with intermediate names ie_{ij} and result names w_i.

P2: Choose (low)precision p for the a priori computations.

P3: Compute $I_p(\bar{u}_i)$, $i \geq 1$, according to theorem 3.1.
Compute $I_p(\bar{w}_i)$, by successively applying definition 3.3 on the values corresponding with ie_{ij} and w_i.

P4: Determine $ap(\bar{u}_i)$, as imposed by theorem 3.4, and $ap(\bar{w}_i) = \alpha_i + \rho_i \eta$ by successively applying theorem 3.3 on the values corresponding with ie_{ij} and w_i.

P5: Compute for all z_i, if $\varepsilon z_i > \alpha_j$ the η_i. Otherwise failure [Try again for a larger p].

P6: Compute $\eta = \min_i \eta_i$

P7: Compute the precisions d_{ij} for the $\overline{ie}_{ij}$ and the d_i for $\bar{w}_i$, according to (3.2) [and eventually in combination with the correction mechanism given by theorem 3.5].

P8: [Output] Deliver $(\{u_i, \bar{u}_i)\}, \{(ie_{ij}, d_{ij})\}, \{(w_i, d_i)\}, \{z_i\})$. □

The output can be presented in the form of a sequence of instructions to apply Sasaki's package to accomplish the calculations. Low precision branches are recognized and taken into account. Features for operating on blocks of straightline code and for-statements are included, albeit that, at present, the for-statements are expanded.

6. Conclusions

One of the main motives for writing the program in REDUCE is the intention to combine it with our code optimization facilities [14,15]. But in addition we believe such an a priori analysis to be interesting for testing routines for numerical libraries, for computations requiring high (intermediate) precision and for stability analysis, certainly when an analytic stability proof is hard to give or not sufficient due to possible parasitical side effects.

The present program is still limited. Many programs for solving numerical problems demand repeated execution of identical blocks of code, due to iteration techniques or repeated approximation methods. When thinking of template file mechanism [5,16], in combination with code optimization, for the construction of such programs and using a computer algebra system, it suffices to create code describing these blocks. But automatic error control demands more. One has to determine a precision d, such that the admissible error is also guaranteed after these block-execution repetitions. The d can be influenced by the number of passages through blocks as well as by the structure of the computations inside the blocks. Although we are convinced that some modifications of the ρ_0-control strategy, as discussed in section 4, allows error control in such situations, we did not yet implement it.

References

[1] Bauer, F.L.: Computational graphs and rounding error, SIAM J. Numer.Anal. 11, 87-96 (1974).

[2] Hearn, A.C.: REDUCE user's manual. The Rand Corporation (1983).

[3] Johnson, D.B., Miller, W., Minnihan, B., Wrathall, C.: Reducibility among floating-point graphs, J. ACM 26, 739-760 (1979).

[4] Kulish, U., Miranker, W.L.: Computer arithmetic in theory and practice. New York: Academic Press (1981).

[5] Lanam, D.H.: An algebraic frond-end for the production and use of numerical programs, Proceedings SYMSAC '81 (P.S. Wang, ed.), 223-227. New York: ACM (1981).

[6] Larsen, L., Sameh, A.: Efficient calculations of the effect of roundoff errors, ACM TOMS 4, 228-236 (1978).

[7] Miller, W.: Software for roundoff analysis, ACM TOMS 1, 108-128 (1975).

[8] Miller, W.: Spooner, D.: Software for roundoff analysis II, ACM TOMS 4, 369-387 (1978).

[9] Olver, F.W.J.: A new approach to error arithmetic, SIAM, J. Numer.Anal. 15, 368-393 (1978).

[10] Richman, P.L.: Automatic error analysis for determining precision, C. ACM 15, 813-817 (1972).

[11] Sasaki, T.: An arbitrary precision real arithmetic package in REDUCE, Symbolic and Algebraic Computation (E.W. Ng, ed.), LNCS series nr.72, 358-368. Berlin-Heidelberg-New-York: Springer Verlag (1979).

[12] Sterbenz, P.H.: Floating point computation. New York: Prentice Hall (1974).

[13] Stummel, F.: Perturbation theory for evaluation algorithms of arithmetic expressions, Math. of Comp. 37, 435-473 (1981).

[14] van Hulzen, J.A.: Code optimization of multivariate polynomial schemes: a pragmatic approach, Proceedings EUROCAL '83 (J.A. van Hulzen, ed.), LNCS series nr. 162, 268-300. Berlin-Heidelberg-New York: Springer Verlag (1983).

[15] van Hulzen, J.A., Hulshof, B.J.A.: A code optimization package for REDUCE (in preparation).

[16] Wang, P.S., Chang, T.Y.P., van Hulzen, J.A.: Code generation and optimization for finite element analysis (These Proceedings).

Polynomial factorization by root approximation

Arjen K. Lenstra
Centrum voor wiskunde en informatica
Kruislaan 413
1098 SJ Amsterdam
The Netherlands

Abstract

We show that a constructive version of the fundamental theorem of algebra [3], combined with the basis reduction algorithm from [1], yields a polynomial-time algorithm for factoring polynomials in one variable with rational coefficients.

Introduction

In 1982 the first polynomial-time algorithm for factoring polynomials in one variable with rational coefficients was published [1]. The most important part of this factoring algorithm is the so-called *basis reduction algorithm.* This basis reduction algorithm, when applied to an arbitrary basis for an integral lattice, computes in polynomial time a *reduced basis* for the lattice, which is, roughly speaking, a basis that is *nearly orthogonal.* Also, such a reduced basis yields approximations of the successive minima of the lattice, and the first vector in the reduced basis is a reasonable approximation of a shortest non-zero vector in the lattice.

For certain specially constructed lattices it can be shown that the basis reduction algorithm actually computes a shortest non-zero vector in the lattice. This happens for instance in the factoring algorithm from [1]. By means of a sufficiently precise, irreducible, p-adic factor of the polynomial $f \in \mathbf{Z}[X]$ to be factored, an integral lattice is defined that contains a factor of f as shortest non-zero vector. The basis reduction algorithm is then applied to this specially constructed lattice to compute this factor in polynomial time.

Here we show that the lattice for the factoring algorithm can also be constructed in another way. Instead of a p-adic factorization of f, we use approximations of the (real or complex) roots of f to define a lattice with similar properties as the lattice above: its shortest vector leads to a factorization of f, and this shortest vector can be found by means of the basis reduction algorithm. As a result we get a polynomial-time algorithm for factoring univariate rational polynomials, which does not apply the usual Berlekamp-Hensel techniques (to compute the p-adic factors), but which relies on (a constructive version of) the fundamental theorem of algebra.

An outline of our algorithm to factor f is as follows. First, we compute a sufficiently precise approximation $\tilde{\alpha}$ of a root α of f, by means of the algorithm from [3]. The minimal polynomial h of α, which clearly is an irreducible factor of f, can then be found by looking for a $\mathbf{Z}$-linear relation of minimal degree among the powers of $\tilde{\alpha}$. In Section 1 we show that the coefficients of this $\mathbf{Z}$-linear relation are given by the shortest vector in a certain lattice, and in Section 2 we present the factoring algorithm and we analyze its running time.

For a polynomial $f = \sum_i f_i X^i \in \mathbf{Z}[X]$ we denote by δf its *degree,* and by $|f| = (\sum_i f_i^2)^{1/2}$ its *length.* We say that f is *primitive* if the *gcd* of its coefficients equals one. By $\mathbf{Z}$, $\mathbf{Q}$, and $\mathbf{C}$ we denote the set of the integers, the rational numbers, and the complex numbers respectively.

1. Approximated roots and lattices

Let $f \in \mathbf{Z}[X]$ be a primitive polynomial of degree n, and let $\alpha \in \mathbf{C}$ be a zero of f. Obviously, the minimal polynomial $h \in \mathbf{Z}[X]$ of α is an irreducible factor of f. We will show that a sufficiently precise complex rational approximation of α enables us to determine the factor h of f. First, we need the following proposition.

(1.1) **Proposition.** *For any $s \in \mathbf{Z}_{\geq 0}$ and for any $\tilde{\alpha} \in \mathbf{C}$ satisfying $|\alpha - \tilde{\alpha}| < 2^{-s}$, we have $|h(\tilde{\alpha})| < 2^{-s} \delta h |f| (2+|f|)^{\delta h - 1}$.*

Proof. Because $h(\alpha)=0$, and because the $(\delta h + 1)$-th derivative $h^{(\delta h+1)}$ of h is zero, we derive from Taylor's formula and $|\alpha - \tilde{\alpha}| < 2^{-s}$, that

$$|h(\tilde{\alpha})| < \sum_{i=0}^{\delta h} \frac{2^{-si}}{i!} |h^{(i)}(\alpha)|. \tag{1.2}$$

Let $h = \sum_{j=0}^{\delta h} h_j X^j$, then

$$h^{(i)}(\alpha) = \sum_{j=i}^{\delta h} \left(\prod_{k=0}^{i-1} (j-k)\right) h_j \alpha^{j-i}, \text{ for } 1 \leq i \leq \delta h. \tag{1.3}$$

Because h is a factor of f in $\mathbf{Z}[X]$, we have from [2] that $|h_j| \leq \binom{\delta h}{j} |f|$, and because α is a zero of f we have from for instance [3] that $|\alpha| \leq |f|$. Combined with (1.3) this yields

$$|h^{(i)}(\alpha)| \leq |f| \sum_{j=i}^{\delta h} \left(\prod_{k=0}^{i-1} (j-k)\right) \binom{\delta h}{j} |f|^{j-i},$$

so that we get from (1.2) that

$$|h(\tilde{\alpha})| < |f| \sum_{j=1}^{\delta h} \binom{\delta h}{j} \sum_{i=1}^{j} \binom{j}{i} 2^{-si} |f|^{j-i}.$$

Because $\sum_{i=1}^{j} \binom{j}{i} 2^{-si} |f|^{j-i} = (2^{-s} + |f|)^j - |f|^j$, and because $\sum_{j=1}^{\delta h} \binom{\delta h}{j} (2^{-s} + |f|)^j - \sum_{j=1}^{\delta h} \binom{\delta h}{j} |f|^j = (2^{-s} + |f| + 1)^{\delta h} - (|f|+1)^{\delta h}$, we find

$$|h(\tilde{\alpha})| < |f| ((2^{-s} + |f| + 1)^{\delta h} - (|f|+1)^{\delta h}).$$

The proposition now follows from

$$(2^{-s} + |f| + 1)^{\delta h} - (|f|+1)^{\delta h} < 2^{-s} \delta h (2^{-s} + |f| + 1)^{\delta h - 1}. \ \square$$

Suppose that we are given an $s \in \mathbf{Z}_{\geq 0}$ and an $\tilde{\alpha} \in \mathbf{Q}(i)$ such that

$$|\alpha - \tilde{\alpha}| < 2^{-s}, \text{ and } |\tilde{\alpha}| \leq |\alpha|. \tag{1.4}$$

In the sequel we will see how large s should be chosen, i.e. how well α should be approximated.

(1.5) Let m be a positive integer, and let $c \in \mathbf{Q}$ be a positive constant. Suppose that we have computed, for $0 \leq i \leq m$, approximations $\tilde{\alpha}_i \in \mathbf{Q}(i)$ of $\tilde{\alpha}^i$:

$$|\tilde{\alpha}^i - \tilde{\alpha}_i| < 2^{-s}, \text{ for } 0 \leq i \leq m. \tag{1.6}$$

We will identify a polynomial $g = \sum_{i=0}^{\delta g} g_i X^i \in \mathbf{Z}[X]$ of degree at most m with the $(m+1)$-dimensional integral vector $(g_0, g_1, \ldots, g_m) \in \mathbf{Z}^{m+1}$, where $g_{\delta g+1}, g_{\delta g+2}, \ldots, g_m$ are zero. By $\tilde{g}(\tilde{\alpha})$ we will denote $\sum_{i=0}^{\delta g} g_i \tilde{\alpha}_i \in \mathbf{Q}(i)$. For an $(m+1)$-dimensional integral vector $v = (v_0, v_1, \ldots, v_m) \in \mathbf{Z}^{m+1}$ we will denote by $\hat{v} \in \mathbf{Q}^{m+3}$ the $(m+3)$-dimensional rational vector $(v_0, v_1, \ldots, v_m, c(\mathrm{Re}(\sum_{i=0}^{m} v_i \tilde{\alpha}_i)), c(\mathrm{Im}(\sum_{i=0}^{m} v_i \tilde{\alpha}_i)))$. Notice that $|\hat{v}|^2 = |v|^2 + c^2 |\tilde{v}(\tilde{\alpha})|^2$. By L we will denote the lattice $\mathbf{Z}^{m+1}$ embedded in $\mathbf{Q}^{m+3}$ by

$$v \mapsto \hat{v}$$

for $v \in \mathbf{Z}^{m+1}$. The next proposition shows that s and c can be chosen in such a way that a short vector in L leads to an irreducible factor of f.

(1.7) **Proposition.** *Let $g \in \mathbf{Z}[X]$ of degree at most m be such that $gcd(h, g)=1$. Suppose that $\delta h \leqslant m$, and that*

$$2^{\frac{m^2}{2}+\frac{m}{2}+4} B^{\frac{1}{2}+m} |f|^{m-1} \leqslant c \leqslant \frac{2^s}{4m|f|(2+|f|)^{m-1}}, \tag{1.8}$$

where $B=\binom{2m}{m}|f|^2+1$. Then $|\hat{h}|^2<B$, and $|\hat{g}|^2 \geqslant 2^m B$.

Proof. First we will show that $|\hat{h}|^2<B$. Because $|\hat{h}|^2=|h|^2+c^2|\tilde{h}(\tilde{\alpha})|^2$ and $|\tilde{h}(\tilde{\alpha})| \leqslant |h(\tilde{\alpha})| + |h(\tilde{\alpha})-\tilde{h}(\tilde{\alpha})|$, we find

$$|\hat{h}|^2 \leqslant |h|^2+c^2(|h(\tilde{\alpha})|^2 + 2|h(\tilde{\alpha})|\,|h(\tilde{\alpha})-\tilde{h}(\tilde{\alpha})| + |h(\tilde{\alpha})-\tilde{h}(\tilde{\alpha})|^2). \tag{1.9}$$

From Proposition (1.1) and $\delta h \leqslant m$ we know that $|h(\tilde{\alpha})|<2^{-s} m|f|(2+|f|)^{m-1}$, which yields, combined with (1.8)

$$|h(\tilde{\alpha})|<\frac{1}{2c}. \tag{1.10}$$

The polynomial $h=\sum_{j=0}^{\delta h} h_j X^j$ is a factor of f in $\mathbf{Z}[X]$, so that we get from [2] that $|h_j| \leqslant \binom{\delta h}{j}|f|$. With (1.6) and $\delta h \leqslant m$ this gives $|h(\tilde{\alpha})-\tilde{h}(\tilde{\alpha})|<2^{-s}\sum_{j=0}^{\delta h}\binom{\delta h}{j}|f| \leqslant 2^{-s+m}|f|$, and with (1.8)

$$|h(\tilde{\alpha})-\tilde{h}(\tilde{\alpha})|<\frac{1}{2c}. \tag{1.11}$$

From $|h_j| \leqslant \binom{\delta h}{j}|f|$ we also derive

$$|h|^2 \leqslant \binom{2\delta h}{\delta h}|f|^2, \tag{1.12}$$

so that we obtain by combining (1.9), (1.10), (1.11), (1.12), and $\delta h \leqslant m$

$$|\hat{h}|^2<\binom{2m}{m}|f|^2+c^2\left(\frac{1}{4c^2}+\frac{2}{4c^2}+\frac{1}{4c^2}\right)=B.$$

Now we will prove that $|\hat{g}|^2 \geqslant 2^m B$. If $|g|^2 \geqslant 2^m B$, then $|\hat{g}|^2 \geqslant 2^m B$, because $|\hat{g}|^2=|g|^2+c^2|\tilde{g}(\tilde{\alpha})|^2$. Therefore, we may assume that

$$|g|^2<2^m B; \tag{1.13}$$

we will prove that $c^2|\tilde{g}(\tilde{\alpha})|^2 \geqslant 2^m B$, so that $|\hat{g}|^2 \geqslant 2^m B$. From (1.13), (1.6), and $\delta g \leqslant m$ we derive

$$|g(\tilde{\alpha})-\tilde{g}(\tilde{\alpha})| \leqslant 2^{-s+\frac{m}{2}}(m+1)B^{\frac{1}{2}},$$

so that, with $2^{-s}(m+1) \leqslant \frac{1}{c}$ (cf. (1.8)), it suffices to prove that

$$c\,|g(\tilde{\alpha})| \geqslant 2(2^m B)^{\frac{1}{2}}. \tag{1.14}$$

Because $gcd(h, g)=1$, there exist polynomials $a, b \in \mathbf{Z}[X]$ satisfying $\delta a<\delta g$ and $\delta b<\delta h$, such that $ah+bg=R$, where $R \in \mathbf{Z}_{\neq 0}$ denotes the resultant of h and g. Because δh and δg are both at most m, it follows from the definition of the resultant and Hadamard's inequality, that the coefficients of a and b are bounded by $|h|^{m-1}|g|^m$ in absolute value, and therefore by $2^{\frac{m^2}{2}} B^m$ (cf. (1.12), (1.13)). From $|\alpha| \leqslant |f|$ (cf. [3]), $\delta a<m$, $\delta b<m$, and (1.4), we now obtain

$$\text{(1.15)}\qquad \max(|a(\tilde{\alpha})|, |b(\tilde{\alpha})|) \leqslant 2^{\frac{m^2}{2}} B^m \sum_{i=0}^{m-1} |\alpha|^i$$

$$\leqslant 2^{\frac{m^2}{2}} B^m \frac{|f|^m - 1}{|f| - 1}$$

$$< 2^{2+\frac{m^2}{2}} B^m |f|^{m-1},$$

where we use that $|f|-1 \geqslant \frac{|f|}{4}$. From (1.15), Proposition (1.1) and $\delta h \leqslant m$, it follows that

$$|a(\tilde{\alpha})h(\tilde{\alpha})| < 2^{2-s} m |f|^m (2+|f|)^{m-1} 2^{\frac{m^2}{2}} B^m,$$

which gives with (1.8)

$$\text{(1.16)}\qquad |a(\tilde{\alpha})h(\tilde{\alpha})| < \tfrac{1}{2}.$$

Because $R \in \mathbf{Z}_{\neq 0}$ and $a(\tilde{\alpha})h(\tilde{\alpha}) + b(\tilde{\alpha})g(\tilde{\alpha}) = R$, it follows from (1.16) that $b(\tilde{\alpha}) \neq 0$, and that

$$|g(\tilde{\alpha})| \geqslant \frac{1}{2|b(\tilde{\alpha})|}.$$

Combining this with (1.8) and (1.15), we see that (1.14) holds. □

(1.17) **Corollary.** *Let c and s be such that (1.8) holds, and suppose that $\delta h \leqslant m$. Then for any non-zero polynomial $g \in \mathbf{Z}[X]$ satisfying $\delta g < \delta h$ we have $|\hat{g}|^2 \geqslant 2^m B$, where B is as in (1.7).*

Proof. The proof follows from the fact that h is irreducible, so that $gcd(h, g) = 1$, combined with (1.7). □

(1.18) **Corollary.** *Let c and s be such that (1.8) holds, and let $\hat{b}_1, \hat{b}_2, \ldots, \hat{b}_{m+1} \in \mathbf{Q}^{m+3}$ be a reduced basis for the lattice L as defined in (1.5) (cf. [1: (1.4), (1.5)]). If $\delta h = m$, then $|\hat{b}_1|^2 < 2^m B$ and $h = \pm b_1$, where $b_1 \in \mathbf{Z}^{m+1}$ is the $(m+1)$-dimensional vector consisting of the first $m+1$ coordinates of $\hat{b}_1$ (cf. (1.5)), and B is as in (1.7).*

Proof. From (1.7) it follows that $|\hat{h}|^2 < B$. Because $\delta h = m$ we have that $\hat{h} \in L$, so that L contains a non-zero vector of length smaller than $B^{1/2}$. From [1: (1.11)] we derive that $|\hat{b}_1|^2 < 2^m B$, so that, again with (1.7), we conclude that $gcd(h, b_1) \neq 1$. Because $\delta b_1 \leqslant m$, and because h is irreducible we find that $h = t b_1$ for some $t \in \mathbf{Z}_{\neq 0}$, so that $h = \pm b_1$, because $\hat{b}_1$ belongs to a basis for L. □

2. Description of the algorithm

(2.1) Let $f \in \mathbf{Z}[X]$ be a primitive polynomial of degree n. We describe an algorithm to compute the irreducible factorization of f in $\mathbf{Z}[X]$.

First, we choose $s, c \in \mathbf{Z}$ minimal such that (1.8) holds with m replaced by $n-1$:

$$\text{(2.2)}\qquad 2^{\frac{n^2}{2} - \frac{n}{2} + 4} \left(\binom{2(n-1)}{n-1} |f|^2 + 1\right)^{n - 1/2} |f|^{n-2} \leqslant c$$

and

$$\text{(2.3)}\qquad 4(n-1)|f|(2+|f|)^{n-2} c \leqslant 2^s.$$

Next, we apply the algorithm from [3] to compute an approximation $\tilde{\alpha} \in \mathbf{Q}(i)$ of an arbitrary root $\alpha \in \mathbf{C}$ of f, such that (1.4) holds.

Finally, we apply the results from the previous section to determine the minimal polynomial $h \in \mathbf{Z}[X]$ of α. For the values of $m = 1, 2, \ldots, n-1$ in succession we compute a reduced basis $\hat{b}_1, \hat{b}_2, \ldots, \hat{b}_{m+1}$ of the lattice L as defined in (1.5) (this can be done by means of the basis reduction algorithm from [1]). But we stop as soon as we find a vector $\hat{b}_1$ of length less than $2^{\frac{m}{2}}(\binom{2m}{m}|f|^2+1)^{\frac{1}{2}}$.

It follows from the choice of s and c that, if we find such a vector $\hat{b}_1$, then $m \geq \delta h$ according to (1.17); furthermore, because we try the values for m in succession, we find from (1.18) that $h = \pm b_1$ (where b_1 is defined as in (1.18)). If, on the other hand, we do not find such a vector $\hat{b}_1$, then $\delta h > n-1$ according to (1.18), so that $h = f$.

The polynomial h that we find in this way is an irreducible factor of f; the complete factorization of f can be found by applying Algorithm (2.1) to $\frac{f}{h}$.

(2.4) **Theorem.** *Algorithm (2.1) computes the irreducible factorization of any primitive polynomial $f \in \mathbb{Z}[X]$ of degree n in $O(n^6+n^5\log|f|)$ additions, subtractions, multiplications, or divisions of numbers which can be represented by $O(n^3+n^2\log|f|)$ binary bits.*

Proof. The correctness of Algorithm (2.1) follows from its description. We now analyze its running time. From the fact that c and s are chosen minimal such that (2.2) and (2.3) hold, we find

(2.5) $$\log c = O(n^2+n\log|f|), \text{ and } s = O(n^2+n\log|f|).$$

According to [3] and (2.5), the computation of approximations of the n roots of f such that (1.4) holds, satisfies the estimates in (2.4). Obviously, the same is true for the computation of the approximated powers $\tilde{\alpha}_i$ of an approximated root $\tilde{\alpha}$ as in (1.6); these powers have to be computed for the initial basis for L.

The entries of the initial basis for L can be represented by $\lceil \log c + s + \log|\tilde{\alpha}_i| \rceil = O(n^2+n\log|f|)$ bits (cf. (2.5), (1.6); remember from Section 1 that $|\tilde{\alpha}| \leq |f|$). The applications of the basis reduction algorithm for the computation of one irreducible factor h of f can therefore be done in $O(\delta h^4(n^2+n\log|f|))$ operations on $O(n^3+n^2\log|f|)$-bit numbers (cf. [1: (1.26), (1.37), (1.38)], (1.5)).

It follows that the computation of the complete factorization of f satisfies the estimates in (2.4), where we apply that $|\frac{f}{h}| = O(n+\log|f|)$ (cf. (1.12) with h replaced by $\frac{f}{h}$). □

(2.6) **Remark** In [4] A. Schönhage noticed that for the lattice that we use in Algorithm (2.1), a better running time can be proved for the basis reduction algorithm. His observation leads to $O(n^5+n^4\log|f|)$ arithmetic operations on $O(n^2+n\log|f|)$-bit numbers. Furthermore he wins another factor of $O(n)$ by an improved version of the basis reduction algorithm.

References

1. A.K. Lenstra, H.W. Lenstra, Jr., L. Lovász, Factoring polynomials with rational coefficients, Math. Ann. **261** (1972), 515-534.

2. M. Mignotte, An inequality about factors of polynomials, Math. Comp. **28** (1974), 1153-1157.

3. A. Schönhage, The fundamental theorem of algebra in terms of computational complexity, manuscript, 1982.

4. A. Schönhage, Factorization of univariate integer polynomials by diophantine approximation and by an improved basis reduction algorithm, manuscript, 1983.

Effective Hilbert Irreducibility*

Erich Kaltofen

University of Toronto
Department of Computer Science
Toronto, Ontario M5S1A4, Canada

Extended Abstract

1. Introduction

The question whether a polynomial with coefficients in a unique factorization domain is irreducible poses an old problem. Recently, several new algorithms for univariate and multivariate factorization over various coefficient domains have been proposed within the framework of polynomial time complexity. All algorithms in the table below

Polynomial-Time Polynomial Factorization		
Coefficient Domain	Univariate	Multivariate
Finite Fields	Berlekamp [1]	Chistov and Grigoryev [2] Lenstra [12] von zur Gathen and Kaltofen [5]
Rational Numbers	Lenstra et al. [15] Schönhage [16]	Kaltofen [7], [8], [9] Chistov and Grigoryev [2] Lenstra [13]
Algebraic Number Fields	Landau [10] Lenstra [11]	Chistov and Grigoryev [2] Kaltofen [9] Lenstra [14]

are polynomial in $l(n+1)^v$, where l is the number of bits needed to represent the coefficients of the polynomial to be factored, n is its total degree, and v is the number of its variables. The algorithms for finite fields are probabilistic (Las Vegas – always correct and probably fast.) If v is not fixed, $l(n+1)^v$ may not represent the input size since the input polynomial may only consist of a few monomials. In this sparse case, J. von zur Gathen [4] has developed a probabilistic irreducibility test and factorization algorithm, the former of the Monte Carlo kind and polynomial in the degree and the number of non-zero monomials of the polynomial to be tested for irreducibility. Von zur Gathen's

* This research was partially supported by the National Science and Engineering Council of Canada under grant 3-643-126-90.
Author's current address: Rensselaer Polytechnic Institute, Department of Mathematical Sciences, Troy, New York, 12181.

algorithm is based on the Hilbert Irreducibility Theorem, as was our older multivariate to bivariate reduction [7], [9, Sec. 7], and a generalized version of the sparse Hensel lifting scheme of Zippel [18].

In this paper we present a new very effective Hilbert Irreducibility Theorem, which, applied to the rational coefficient case, states roughly the following: If a polynomial $f(x_1, \ldots, x_v)$ is irreducible then the probability that $f(x_1+w_1, c_2(x_1+w_2), \ldots, c_{v-1}(x_1+w_{v-1}), x_2)$ becomes reducible for randomly chosen integers $c_2, \ldots, c_{v-1}, w_1, \ldots, w_{v-1}$ of $O(\deg f - \log \varepsilon)$ digits is less than ε. In [4, theorem 2.E] the integers have $O(\deg^2 f - \log \varepsilon)$ digits and the substitutions are somewhat more complicated ($c_i x_1 + u_i x_2 + w_i$ for x_i.) We also use elementary methods to prove our result whereas von zur Gathen follows the algebraic geometric approach of Heintz and Sieveking [6] which is based on Bertini's theorem.

In section 4 we then use our effective Hilbert Irreducibility Theorem to establish Monte-Carlo irreducibility tests for sparse multivariate polynomials. The tests are similar to probabilistic primality testing except that they definitely establish irreducibility but compositeness only with a small failure probability. For rational coefficients the test runs in polynomial time in the number of non-zero monomials of the input polynomial, its total degree, and its coefficient length. Our theorem also applies to coefficients from a field of positive characteristic p provided the p-th root of any element can be taken within this field. Therefore our theorem includes the important case in which the coefficients lie in a finite field. We propose a different irreducibility test in this case, which, unlike the algorithms by Chistov and Grigoryev [2] and von zur Gathen [4], does not require to work in an algebraic extension of the coefficient domain. All irreducibility tests rely on polynomial-time irreducibility tests for polynomials in two or three variables.

2. Notation and Preliminary Results

By $\mathbf{Z}$ we denote the integers, by $\mathbf{Q}$ the rationals and by $\mathbf{Z}_p$ the prime residues modulo p. D shall denote an integral domain, QF(D) its field of quotients, char(D) its characteristic. $D[x_1, \ldots, x_v]$ denotes the polynomials in $x_1, \ldots, x_v$ over D, $D(x_1, \ldots, x_v)$ the corresponding field of quotients; $\deg_{x_1}(f)$ denotes the highest degree of x_1 in $f \in D[x_1, \ldots, x_v]$, $\deg_{x_1,x_2}(f)$ the highest total degree of monomials x_1 and x_2 in f, and $\deg(f) = \deg_{x_1,\ldots,x_v}(f)$ the total degree of f. The coefficient of the highest power of x_v in f is referred to as the leading coefficient of f in x_v and will be denoted by $\mathrm{ldcf}_{x_v}(f)$. We call f monic in x_v if $\mathrm{ldcf}_{x_v}(f)$ is a unit of D. As is well-known, $D[x_1, \ldots, x_v]$ is a unique factorization domain (UFD) provided that D is a UFD. In this case the content of $f \in D[x_1, \ldots, x_v]$ in x_v, $\mathrm{cont}_{x_v}(f)$, is the greatest common divisor (GCD) of all coefficients of $f(x_v)$ as elements in $D[x_1, \ldots, x_{v-1}]$. The infinity norm of $f \in \mathbf{Q}[x_1, \ldots, x_v]$, the maximum of the absolute values of the rational coefficients of f, will be denoted by $|f|$.

The probability of an event E will be denoted by Prob(E), the cardinality of a set S by card(S).

Now we state a lemma telling that the set of zeros of a multivariate polynomial over an integral domain D is of small measure. (Measure 0 if card$(D) = \infty$.)

Lemma 1 (cf. Schwartz [17]): Assume that $t(y_1, \ldots, y_v) \in D[y_1, \ldots, y_v]$ is a non-zero polynomial of total degree d and let $S \subset D$. Then the probability

$$\mathrm{Prob}(\{t(c_1, \ldots, c_v) = 0 \mid c_i \in S,\ 1 \le i \le v\}) \le \frac{d}{\mathrm{card}(S)}. \quad \Box$$

Secondly, we assert that squarefreeness of an irreducible multivariate polynomial is likely to be preserved by evaluation.

Lemma 2: Let $f(y_1, \ldots, y_v, x) \in F[y_1, \ldots, y_v, x]$ be irreducible in $F(y_1, \ldots, y_v)[x]$, F a field, and assume further that $\partial f / \partial x \neq 0$. Let $n = \deg_x(f)$, $d = \deg_{y_1, \ldots, y_v}(f)$ and $a_n(y_1, \ldots, y_v) = \mathrm{ldcf}_x(f)$. We now select $w_1, \ldots, w_v$ randomly from a subset $S \subset F$. Then the probability

$$\mathrm{Prob}(a_n(w_1, \ldots, w_v) = 0 \text{ or } f(w_1, \ldots, w_v, x) \text{ not squarefree}) \le \frac{(2n+1)d}{\mathrm{card}(S)}. \quad \Box$$

Notice that if char$(F) = 0$, then the condition $\partial f / \partial x \neq 0$ in the previous lemma is automatically satisfied. However, in the case that char$(F) = p > 0$, this condition cannot be omitted. E.g. if F is a finite field with p elements, then $x^p + y$ is irreducible but for every $w \in F$, $x^p + w = (x + w)^p$ is not squarefree. This is also the reason why we must restrict our coefficient field in theorem 2. The following lemma is instrumental to salvage the case in which the coefficient field has finite characteristic. It also shows that, to some extent, the above is the only kind of counter-example possible.

Lemma 3: Let F be a field of characteristic $p > 0$ and let $f(x) = a_n x^n + \cdots + a_0 \in F[x]$ be irreducible. Furthermore, assume that there exists an index i, $1 \le i \le n$, such that for all $b \in F$, $b^p \neq a_i$. Then $f(x^{p^\lambda})$ is irreducible in $F[x]$ for all integers $\lambda \ge 0$. $\Box$

Finally we establish that evaluations rarely allow a GCD of higher degree to occur. This shows that it is unlikely that a content is introduced by our later evaluations of theorems 1 and 2.

Lemma 4: Let $f_1, \ldots, f_k \in F[x_1, \ldots, x_v]$, F a field, with $\deg(f_i) \le \delta$ for $1 \le i \le k$ and $\mathrm{GCD}(f_1, \ldots, f_k) = 1$. Furthermore, assume that $f_1(0, \ldots, 0) \neq 0$. We now select $c_2, \ldots, c_v$ randomly from a subset $S \subseteq F$. Then the probability

$$\mathrm{Prob}(\mathrm{GCD}_{1 \le i \le k}(f_i(x_1, c_2 x_1, \ldots, c_v x_1)) \neq 1) \le \frac{2\delta^2}{\mathrm{card}(S)}. \quad \Box$$

3. The Effective Hilbert Irreducibility Theorem

We proceed to state a random, but very effective version of the Hilbert Irreducibility Theorem for multivariate polynomials over an arbitrary field F.

Theorem 1: Let $f(x_1, \ldots, x_v) \in F[x_1, \ldots, x_v]$, F a field, have total degree δ and be irreducible. Assume that $\partial f / \partial x_v \neq 0$. Let $S \subset F$ and let $c_2, \ldots, c_{v-1}$, $w_1, \ldots, w_{v-1}$ be random elements in S. Then the probability

$$\text{Prob}(f(x_1+w_1, c_2(x_1+w_2), \ldots, c_{v-1}(x_1+w_{v-1}), x_2)$$
$$\text{becomes reducible in } F[x_1, x_2]) \leq \frac{4\delta\, 2^{\delta}}{\text{card}(S)}. \quad \square$$

Remark: The bound $\frac{4\delta\, 2^{\delta}}{\text{card}(S)}$ can be substantially improved if one knows the number r of factors of $f(w_1, \ldots, w_{v-1}, x)$ in $F[x]$. E.g. $\frac{2\delta(2^r + 2\delta)}{\text{card}(S)}$ is a possible upper bound for the probability of failure.

The following theorem removes the condition $\partial f / \partial x_v \neq 0$, which can only fail if $\text{char}(F) = p > 0$, under the assumption that for any element $a \in F$ there exists a $b \in F$ such that $b^p = a$. This requirement is, of course, satisfied if F is a finite field.

Theorem 2: Let $f(x_1, \ldots, x_v) \in F[x_1, \ldots, x_v]$ have total degree δ and be irreducible. Assume that F is a field of characteristic $p > 0$ in which each element possesses a p-th root. Let $S \subset F$ and let $c_2, \ldots, c_{v-1}, w_1, \ldots, w_{v-1}$ be random elements in S. Then the probability

$$\text{Prob}(f(x_1+w_1, c_2(x_1+w_2), \ldots, c_{v-1}(x_1+w_{v-1}), x_2)$$
$$\text{becomes reducible in } F[x_1, x_2]) \leq \frac{4\delta\, 2^{\delta}}{\text{card}(S)}. \quad \square$$

It would be nice to prove theorem 2 without the condition on F. So far we are not quite able to do that though we are convinced that theorem 3 is valid for any field F. The fields for which we proved theorem 3 include, however, the computationally important cases of finite fields and algebraically closed fields, which are used if one wants to test for absolute irreducibility.

4. Probabilistic Irreducibility Testing

We now apply theorem 1 and 2 to construct a probabilistic irreducibility test for a multivariate polynomial $f(x_1, \ldots, x_v) \in F[x_1, \ldots, x_v]$, F an arbitrary field (with the restriction stated in theorem 2 in case that $\text{char}(F) > 0$). Our algorithm outputs "definitely irreducible" or "probably composite" or "failure" where the chance that the irreducibility of f is not recognized as such is less than a given constant $\varepsilon \ll 1$. The algorithm selects random elements in $S \subset F$ and calls an irreducibility test for polynomials in two or three variables, depending on the characteristic of F. Apart from the calls to these unspecified subroutines our algorithm works in polynomially many steps in $\deg(f)$ and monomials(f), where monomials(f) denotes the number of non-zero monomials in f.

If we furthermore specify $F = \mathbf{Q}$ or $\mathbf{Z}_p$, then our algorithm is also of polynomial complexity in $\log 1/\varepsilon$ and in the number of bits needed to encode the coefficients of f. In this case the required polynomial-time subroutines exist. (Cf. Kaltofen [9] for $F = \mathbb{Q}$ and von zur Gathen and Kaltofen [5] for $F = \mathbb{Z}_p$. The later algorithm is unfortunately only a probabilistic one and may, with diminishing probability, take exponential time.)

For char(F) = 0 our algorithm is quite simple:

Algorithm 1:
[Given an irreducible polynomial $f(x_1, \ldots, x_v) \in F[x_1, \ldots, x_v]$, char($F$) = 0, this algorithm attempts to prove the irreducibility of f with a failure chance less than $\varepsilon \ll 1$:]

(R) [Random choices:] From a set $S \subset F$ with card(S) $\geq 4\deg(f)2^{\deg(f)}/\varepsilon$ select random elements $c_2, \ldots, c_{v-1}, w_1, \ldots, w_{v-1}$.

(I) [Irreducibility test:]
$\bar{f}(x_1, x_2) \leftarrow f(x_1+w_1, c_2(x_1+w_2), \ldots, c_{v-1}(x_1+w_{v-1}), x_2)$.
IF $\deg_{x_1}(\bar{f}) < \deg_{x_1}(f)$ THEN RETURN ("failure"). ELSE call an algorithm testing $\bar{f}(x_1, x_2)$ for irreducibility in $F[x_1, x_2]$. IF $\bar{f}$ is irreducible THEN RETURN ("f is definitely irreducible"). ELSE RETURN ("f is probably composite"). □

Complexity analysis for $F = \mathbb{Q}$: We first multiply by a common denominator of all rational coefficients of f. Therefore we may assume that $f \in \mathbb{Z}[x_1, \ldots, x_v]$. Now let $\delta = \deg(f)$ and choose S the interval $\{-2\delta 2^\delta/\varepsilon \leq s \leq 2\delta 2^\delta/\varepsilon\}$. We shall use the shorthands $\underset{\sim}{k}$ and $\underset{\sim}{x}$ for the vectors $(k_1, \ldots, k_v)$ and $(x_1, \ldots, x_v)$ and denote by $|\underset{\sim}{k}| = k_1 + \cdots + k_v$. We evaluate each monomial $b_{\underset{\sim}{k}} \underset{\sim}{x}^{\underset{\sim}{k}}$ of f, $|\underset{\sim}{k}| \leq \delta$, and then add up to get $\bar{f}$. It is easy to see that

$$g_{\underset{\sim}{k}}(x_1, x_2) = b_{\underset{\sim}{k}}(x_1+w_1)^{k_1} c_2^{k_2}(x_1+w_2)^{k_2} \cdots c_{v-1}^{k_{v-1}}(x_1+w_{v-1})^{k_{v-1}} x_2^{k_v}$$

can be computed in $O(v\delta^2)$ integer operations. In fact, the coefficient of x_1^i in $(x_1+w_1)^{k_1} \cdots (x_1+w_{v-1})^{k_{v-1}}$ is

$$\sum_{\substack{i_1+\cdots+i_{v-1}=i \\ 0\leq i_1\leq k_1, \ldots, 0\leq i_{v-1}\leq k_{v-1}}} \binom{k_1}{i_1} \cdots \binom{k_{v-1}}{i_{v-1}} w_1^{k_1-i_1} \cdots w_{v-1}^{k_{v-1}-i_{v-1}}$$

which is $O((i+1)^v 2^{|\underset{\sim}{k}|} (2\delta 2^\delta/\varepsilon)^{|\underset{\sim}{k}|})$ in magnitude. Therefore $\log|g_{\underset{\sim}{k}}| = O(\delta^2 - \delta\log\varepsilon + v\log\delta + \log|f|)$ and $\log|\bar{f}| = O(\log\mu + \log|g_{\underset{\sim}{k}}|)$ where μ = monomials(f). To add up all $g_{\underset{\sim}{k}}$ takes $O(\mu\delta^2)$ integer operations. In summary, algorithm 1 runs in $O(\mu v \delta^2)$ integer operation with integers of

$$O(\delta^2 + \delta\log\frac{1}{\varepsilon} + v\log\delta + \log|f| + \log\mu)$$

digits. The later is also a bound for $\log|\bar{f}|$. The algorithm needs $O(v(\delta - \log\varepsilon))$ random bit choices. This analysis does not account for testing $\bar{f}(x_1, x_2)$ for irreducibility. We can call Algorithm 2 in [9] but the cost of this call might be quite high, $O(\delta^{22}\log^3|\bar{f}|)$, which most likely does not reflect the true behavior of that algorithm. However, the actual cost can be expected to grow quickly with δ. This is why we chose S dependent on ε, the wanted failure probability, and call the bivariate algorithm just once.

We now treat the case in which F has only finitely many elements. Algorithm 1 obviously may run into problems since the sufficiently large subset S of F may not exist. Our approach here is to work in $F(x_1)$ instead of F. We now present the algorithm.

Algorithm 2:
[Given an irreducible polynomial $f(x_1, \ldots, x_v) \in F[x_1, \ldots, x_v]$, card$(F) < \infty$, this algorithm attempts to prove the irreducibility of f with a failure chance less than $\varepsilon \ll 1$:]

(C) [Check for content in $F^* = F[x_1]$:] Rewrite f to $f^*(x_2, \ldots, x_v) \in F^*[x_2, \ldots, x_v]$ and verify that all coefficients of f^* in F^* have no GCD in $F[x_1]$. Otherwise RETURN ("f is definitely composite").

(R) [Random choices:] From a set $S \subset F^*$ with card$(S) \geq 4\deg(f^*)2^{\deg(f^*)}/\varepsilon$ select random elements $c_3, \ldots, c_{v-1}, w_2, \ldots, w_{v-1}$.

(I) [Irreducibility test:]

$$\bar{f}(x_2, x_3) \leftarrow f^*(x_2+w_2, c_3(x_2+w_3), \ldots, c_{v-1}(x_2+w_{v-1}), x_3).$$

IF $\deg_{x_3}(\bar{f}) < \deg_{x_3}(f^*)$ THEN RETURN ("failure"). Compute the GCD of all coefficients of $\bar{f}$ in F^*, $g^*[x_1]$. Set $\hat{f}(x_1, x_2, x_3) \leftarrow \bar{f}(x_2, x_3)/g^*(x_1) \in F[x_1, x_2, x_3]$. Now call an algorithm testing $\hat{f}$ for irreducibility in $F[x_1, x_2, x_3]$. IF $\hat{f}$ is irreducible THEN RETURN ("f is definitely irreducible"). ELSE RETURN ("f is probably composite"). □

The correctness of this algorithm follows from Gauss' lemma stating that if a polynomial $h(x_1, \ldots, x_v) \in D[x_1, \ldots, x_v]$, D a unique factorization domain, is irreducible, it remains irreducible in QF$(D)[x_1, \ldots, x_v]$. We again select a concrete field F to carry out timing estimates.

Complexity analysis for $F = \mathbb{Z}_p$: Let $\delta = \deg(f^*)$ and choose

$$S = \{s(x_1) \mid s(x_1) \in F[x_1] \text{ and } \deg(s) \leq \left\lceil \frac{(\delta+2)\log 2 + \log\delta - \log\varepsilon}{\log p} \right\rceil\}.$$

Notice that card$(S) \geq 4\delta 2^\delta/\varepsilon$. Step (C) takes $O(\mu\delta^2)$ field operations in $\mathbb{Z}_p$, μ = monomials(f). Furthermore, $\bar{f}$ can be computed in $O(\mu v\, \delta^2 \cdot \delta^2 (\frac{\delta - \log\varepsilon}{\log p})^2)$ where the second factor arises from computing powers of c_i and w_i. Also $\deg_{x_1}(\bar{f}) = O(\delta \frac{\delta-\log\varepsilon}{\log p})$ and $\deg_{x_2, x_3}(\bar{f}) \leq \delta$. Hence the calculation of the GCD g^* costs $O(\delta^3 (\frac{\delta-\log\varepsilon}{\log p})^2)$ operations in $\mathbb{Z}_p$. Assuming that $\delta - \log\varepsilon \geq \log p$, algorithm 2 runs in

$$O(\mu\, v\, \delta^4 (\delta + \log\frac{1}{\varepsilon})^2)$$

binary steps. The algorithm needs $O(v\,(\delta - \log\varepsilon))$ random bit choices. Again, we do not account for testing $\hat{f}(x_1, x_2, x_3)$ for irreducibility. We can call the algorithm presented in von zur Gathen and Kaltofen [5]. That algorithm is also random and has a small probability of failure. Furthermore, its complexity in δ is quite high.

In this section we only dealt with irreducibility testing rather than producing a full factorization. Theorem 1 and 2 could, of course, be employed to produce sparse factorizations in the spirit of Zippel [18] and von zur Gathen [4]. In [18] the sparse Hensel lifting is started with $f(c_1, \ldots, c_{v-1}, x_1)$, $c_1, \ldots, c_{v-1} \in F$ whereas in [4] the evaluation is to $f(x_1, x_2, c_3 x_1 + u_3 x_2 + w_3, \ldots, c_v x_1 + u_v x_2 + w_v)$, $c_i, u_i, w_i \in F$. Unfortunately, we have no effective Hilbert Irreducibility Theorem for evaluations in F and neither we nor von zur Gathen [4] choose evaluations in the coefficient field. In order to use a unified Hensel procedure which always evaluates in F we could, however, view theorem 1 and 2 in the following way. Let the coefficient field of $f(x_1, \ldots, x_v)$ be $F(x_1)$ ($F(x_1, x_2)$ for char(F) > 0). Then our algorithm must select random elements in this field which are linear in x_1 (x_2 for char(D) > 0).

5. Conclusion

Though we were able to prove a very effective version for the Hilbert Irreducibility Theorem in the case in which the coefficients came from a transcendental extension of the integers, the classical version with integral coefficients still defies such error estimates. Again the set of evaluation points mapping the irreducible multivariate polynomial into a reducible univariate one is of measure 0 (cf. Dörge [3]). But the first integers preserving irreducibility might be quite large.† However, practical experience indicates that the classical theorem also provides an excellent, though not proven, irreducibility test.

Acknowledgement

I like to thank Joachim von zur Gathen for the many fruitful discussions we have had on this subject. In particular, the subtleties of the finite characteristic case came to light only by his observations.

References

[1] Berlekamp, E.R.: Factoring Polynomials over Large Finite Fields. Math. Comp. **24**, 713-735 (1970).

[2] Chistov, A.L., Grigoryev, D.Y.: Polynomial-Time Factoring of Multivariate Polynomials over a Global Field. Lomi preprint E-5-82, Leningrad 1982.

[3] Dörge, K.: Zum Hilbertschen Irreduzibilitätssatz. Mathematische Annalen **95**, 84-97 (1926).

---

† So far we only can prove that the integers have $(\deg(f)\log|f|)^{O(\deg(f))}$ digits, f being the input polynomial.

[4] von zur Gathen, J.: Factoring Sparse Multivariate Polynomials. Proceedings 1983 IEEE Symposium on Foundations of Computer Science, 172-179.

[5] von zur Gathen, J., Kaltofen, E.: A Polynomial-Time Algorithm for Factoring Multivariate Polynomials Over Finite Fields. Proc. 1983 Internat. Conf. Automata, Languages and Programming. Springer Lec. Notes Comp. Sci. **154**, 250-263.

[6] Heintz, J., Sieveking, M.: Absolute Primality of Polynomials is Decidable in Random Polynomial Time in the Number of Variables. Proc. 1981 Internat. Conf. Automata, Languages and Programming. Springer Lec. Notes Comp. Sci. **115**, 16-28.

[7] Kaltofen, E.: A Polynomial Reduction from Multivariate to Bivariate Integer Polynomial Factorization. Proc. 1982 ACM Symp. Theory Comp., 261-266.

[8] Kaltofen, E.: A Polynomial-Time Reduction from Bivariate to Univariate Integral Polynomial Factorization. Proceedings 23rd Symposium on Foundations of Computer Science. IEEE, 57-64 (1982).

[9] Kaltofen, E.: Polynomial-Time Reductions from Multivariate to Bi- and Univariate Integral Polynomial Factorization. SIAM J. Comp., in press.

[10] Landau, S.: Factoring Polynomials over Algebraic Number Fields is in Polynomial Time. SIAM J. Comp., to appear.

[11] Lenstra, A.K.: Factoring Polynomials over Algebraic Number Fields. Manuscript 1982.

[12] Lenstra, A.K.: Factoring Multivariate Polynomials over a Finite Field. Proc. 1983 ACM Symp. Theory Comp., 189-192.

[13] Lenstra, A.K.: Factoring Multivariate Integral Polynomials. Proc. 1983 Internat. Conf. Automata, Languages and Programming. Springer Lec. Notes Comp. Sci. **154**, 189-192.

[14] Lenstra, A.K.: Factoring Multivariate Polynomials over Algebraic Number Fields. Manuscript 1983.

[15] Lenstra, A. K., Lenstra, H. W., Lovász, L.: Factoring Polynomials with Rational Coefficients. Math. Ann. **261**, 515-534 (1982).

[16] Schönhage, A.: Factorization of Univariate Integer Polynomials by Diophantine Approximation and by an Improved Reduction Algorithm. Manuscript 1983.

[17] Schwartz, J.T.: Fast Probabilistic Algorithms for Verification of Polynomial Identities. J. ACM **27**, 701-717 (1980).

[18] Zippel, R. E.: Newton's Iteration and the Sparse Hensel Algorithm. Proc. 1981 ACM Symp. Symbolic Alg. Comp., 68-72.

GCDHEU: Heuristic Polynomial GCD Algorithm Based On Integer GCD Computation[1]

Bruce W. Char
Keith O. Geddes
Gaston H. Gonnet

Department of Computer Science
University of Waterloo
Waterloo, Ontario
Canada N2L 3G1

Extended Abstract

1. Introduction

The design of algorithms for polynomial GCD computation has been a continuing area of research since the beginning of the development of symbolic computation systems. The earliest efforts were mainly directed at PRS (polynomial remainder sequence) algorithms which are a direct generalization of Euclid's algorithm [1]. The main algorithms of this type are the Reduced PRS algorithm [2] and the Subresultant PRS algorithm [3]. Hearn [4] discusses the use of trial divisions to further improve the performance of PRS algorithms. The first fundamentally different polynomial GCD algorithm was the modular algorithm [5]. To make the modular algorithm competitive for sparse multivariate polynomials, Zippel developed the sparse modular algorithm [6]. Another modular-type algorithm was the Hensel-based EZ GCD algorithm [7] which was later improved as the EEZ GCD algorithm [8].

The present paper discusses a new heuristic algorithm, GCDHEU, which is found to be very efficient for problems in a small number of variables. The heuristic algorithm can be viewed as a modular-type algorithm in that it uses evaluation and interpolation, but only a single evaluation per variable is used. The heuristic algorithm can be incorporated into a reorganized form of the EEZ GCD algorithm such that the base of the EEZ GCD algorithm, rather than a univariate GCD algorithm, is GCDHEU which is often successful for problems in up to four variables.

2. Properties of a Heuristic Procedure

We wish to define precisely our concept of a *heuristic procedure*. A heuristic procedure is composed of a *solver* and a *checker*. The solver receives as input the description of a problem and a random number. Based on this pair it computes a tentative solution to the problem. The checker is a boolean function which receives as input the description of the problem and a proposed solution, and it

[1] This work was supported in part by grants from the Natural Sciences and Engineering Research Council of Canada, and in part by the Academic Development Fund of the University of Waterloo.

determines whether the solution satisfies the problem. Furthermore, the solver solves the given problem with probability p, bounded below by $\epsilon \leq p$, for some distribution of the random input variable but independent of the problem.

In pseudo-code, a heuristic procedure can be described more precisely as:

```
while ( economically_feasible ) do
        soln := solver( problem, rand() );
        if checker( soln, problem ) then RETURN( soln ) fi
        od;
RETURN( deterministic_solver( problem ) );
```

The underlying assumptions of a successful heuristic are:

(i) The solver is at least an order of magnitude faster than deterministic solvers which solve the same type of problem.

(ii) Checking for a correct solution is very efficient, about the same order of magnitude as for heuristically solving the problem.

(iii) The lower bound, ϵ, on the probability is realistically high (say, $\epsilon > \frac{1}{2}$).

In cases where the solver has a wide range of speed ratios compared with a deterministic solver, it may be useful (or mandatory) to estimate this ratio and decide whether the heuristic should be applied or not.

Secondly, the checker may be simplified significantly by knowledge of the type of error which may be introduced by the solver. For example, the GCDHEU algorithm presented in this paper is based on evaluation at integer values and the solver may compute a GCD which is a multiple of the true GCD, but never a sub-multiple. Consequently, for this case the checker's task is simplified. The checker simply ensures that the resulting polynomial divides both input polynomials.

Lazard's algorithm [9] for polynomial factorization is another example of a heuristic solver, where the checker simply expands the product of both polynomials and tests equality with the input polynomial.

3. Integer GCD Computation

A fundamental feature of GCDHEU is that it maps a polynomial GCD problem to an integer GCD problem involving long integers. It might seem that this would be an undesirable transformation given that integer operations generally have a higher asymptotic complexity than polynomial operations. The complexity of computing integer gcds when the size of the problem is n is $O(n^2)$ using the standard algorithms. For univariate polynomials of size n, this can be done in $O(n \log^2 n)$ [10]. It should be noted that for the integer case, the size is given by the number of digits, while for the polynomial case n denotes the number of terms in the *dense* representation of the polynomials.

Our algorithm works in time depending on the number of terms appearing in the expanded representation of the input polynomials and the degree of the result.

The other factor in this analysis is an empirical observation: conventional architectures have hardware for integer arithmetic (which allows direct implementation of efficient methods for long-integer arithmetic), while there is no such assistance for polynomial arithmetic. Thus there is an advantage (i.e., a very small constant in the asymptotic measure of complexity) to relying upon integer instead of polynomial arithmetic, up to problems of a certain complexity.

This paper assumes an integer GCD algorithm, referred to as IGCD, which is typically a standard implementation of the Euclidean algorithm applied to arbitrary-precision integers.

4. Single-Point Evaluation and Interpolation

Consider the problem of computing $g = \mathrm{GCD}(a,b)$ where $a,b \in \mathbf{Z}[x]$ are univariate polynomials of the form

$$\begin{aligned} a &= a_0 + a_1x + a_2x^2 + \cdots + a_mx^m; \\ b &= b_0 + b_1x + b_2x^2 + \cdots + b_nx^n. \end{aligned} \tag{1}$$

Let $\xi \in \mathbf{Z}$ be a positive integer which bounds twice the magnitudes of all coefficients appearing in a and b and in any of their factors. Let $\phi_{x-\xi} : \mathbf{Z}[x] \rightarrow \mathbf{Z}$ denote the substitution $x = \xi$ (i.e., the evaluation homomorphism whose kernel is the ideal $<x-\xi>$) and let

$$\alpha = \phi_{x-\xi}(a), \quad \beta = \phi_{x-\xi}(b).$$

Define $\gamma = \mathrm{IGCD}(\alpha,\beta)$ and suppose for the moment that the following relationship holds (this development will be made mathematically rigorous below):

$$\gamma = \phi_{x-\xi}(g).$$

Our problem now is to reconstruct the polynomial g from its image γ under the evaluation $x = \xi$.

The reconstruction of g from γ will be accomplished by a special kind of interpolation which exploits the fact that ξ is assumed to be larger than twice the magnitudes of the coefficients appearing in g. The required interpolation scheme is equivalent to the process of converting the integer γ into its ξ-adic representation:

$$\gamma = g_0 + g_1\xi + g_2\xi^2 + \cdots + g_k\xi^k, \tag{2}$$

where k is the smallest integer such that $\xi^{k+1} > 2\,|\gamma|$, and $-\frac{1}{2}\xi < g_i \le \frac{1}{2}\xi$ for $0 \le i \le k$. This can be accomplished in linear time by the simple loop:

```
e := γ;
for i from 0 while e ≠ 0 do
    g_i := φ_ξ(e);
    e := (e − g_i) / ξ
od
```

where $\phi_\xi : \mathbf{Z} \rightarrow \mathbf{Z}_\xi$ is the standard "mod ξ" function using the "symmetric representation" for the elements of $\mathbf{Z}_\xi$. Our claim is that, under appropriate conditions yet to be specified, the coefficients g_i are precisely the coefficients of the desired GCD

$$g = g_0 + g_1 x + g_2 x^2 + \cdots + g_k x^k.$$

The method outlined above generalizes immediately to multivariate GCD's through recursive application of evaluation/interpolation. For suppose the problem is to compute $g = \mathrm{GCD}(a,b)$ where $a,b \in \mathbf{Z}[x_1,x_2,\ldots,x_v]$. By choosing x_v as the main variable, we may view the polynomials a,b as univariate polynomials of the form (1) (identifying x with x_v) with polynomial coefficients $a_i,b_i \in \mathbf{Z}[x_1,x_2,\ldots,x_{v-1}]$. Again, let $\xi \in \mathbf{Z}$ be a positive integer which bounds twice the magnitudes of all integer coefficients appearing in the multivariate polynomials a and b and in any of their factors. The evaluation homomorphism $\phi_{x_v-\xi}$ corresponding to the substitution $x_v = \xi$ yields polynomials

$$\alpha = \phi_{x_v-\xi}(a),\ \beta = \phi_{x_v-\xi}(b) \ \in \mathbf{Z}[x_1,x_2,\ldots,x_{v-1}].$$

Recursively, let $\gamma = \mathrm{GCD}(\alpha,\beta)$. The ξ-adic representation (2) for γ can again be computed by the program loop specified below equation (2), where the mapping ϕ_ξ is naturally extended to polynomials by applying it to the integer coefficients. One can view this as a parallel ξ-adic expansion of each of the integer coefficients appearing in the polynomial γ. Again our claim is that, under appropriate conditions, the coefficients $g_i \in \mathbf{Z}[x_1,x_2,\ldots,x_{v-1}]$ appearing in equation (2) will be the desired coefficients of the multivariate GCD

$$g = g_0 + g_1 x_v + g_2 x_v^2 + \cdots + g_k x_v^k. \tag{3}$$

This construction will be made precise by Theorem 1. In the theorem, we use the following

Definition.

For a polynomial $P \in \mathbf{Z}[x_1,x_2,\ldots,x_v]$, the *height* of P will be denoted by $|P|$ and it is defined to be the maximum over all terms in the expanded form of P of the magnitudes of the integer coefficients. □

In the following theorem, we note that it is possible for γ computed by the method described earlier in this section to be larger than $\phi_{x_v-\xi}(g)$, so we denote the polynomial reconstructed from γ by G which may differ from g. The theorem proves that a simple division check will determine whether or not G is a greatest common divisor of a and b.

Theorem 1.

Let $a,b \in \mathbf{Z}[x_1,x_2,\ldots,x_v]$ be nonzero polynomials. Let $\xi > 2$ be a positive integer which bounds twice the *height* of a, b, and any of their factors in the domain $\mathbf{Z}[x_1,x_2,\ldots,x_v]$. Let $\gamma = \mathrm{GCD}(\alpha,\beta)$ where $\alpha = \phi_{x_v-\xi}(a)$ and $\beta = \phi_{x_v-\xi}(b)$, and let G denote the polynomial formed as in (3) such that

$$\phi_{x_v-\xi}(G) = \gamma. \tag{4}$$

G is a greatest common divisor of a and b if and only if

$$G \mid a \text{ and } G \mid b. \tag{5}$$

5. Choosing a Small Evaluation Point

In order to develop an efficient heuristic algorithm for GCD computation, let us note some properties of the algorithm implied by Theorem 1. For multivariate polynomials a and b, suppose that the first substitution is $x_v = \sigma$ for $\sigma \in \mathbf{Z}$. After the evaluation of a and b at $x_v = \sigma$, the algorithm will be applied recursively until an integer GCD computation can be performed. The size of the evaluation point used at each level of recursion depends on the size of the polynomial coefficients at that level. This can grow rapidly with each recursive step. Specifically, if the original polynomials contain v variables and if the degree in each variable is d, then it is easy to verify that the size of the integers in the integer GCD computation at the base of the recursion is $O(\sigma^{d^v})$. Thus it is clear that this algorithm will be unacceptable for problems in many variables with nontrivial degrees. An important aspect of the heuristic is that it must check and give up quickly if proceeding would generate unacceptably large integers.

It must be noted, however, that integers which contain hundreds of digits can be manipulated relatively efficiently in most symbolic computation systems. Thus, we find in practice that the algorithm described here becomes noncompetitive only when the size of the integers grows to a few thousand digits. For example, if $v = 2$, $d = 5$, and $\sigma = 100$ in the above notation then the integers will grow to approximately 50 digits in length. Solving such a problem by the method of this paper would be relatively trivial on conventional systems.

In view of the above remarks on the growth in the size of the integers, it is important to choose the evaluation point reasonably small at each stage of the recursion. In particular, we will not choose a standard upper bound [12] on the size of the coefficients that can appear in the factors as might be implied by Theorem 1. Our heuristic algorithm is allowed to have some probability of failure, and the only essential condition is that the division checks of Theorem 1 must be guaranteed to detect incorrect results. So we pose the question: "How small can we choose the evaluation point ξ and yet be guaranteed that division checks are sufficient to detect incorrect results?" For example, suppose we have

$$a = x^3 - 9x^2 - x + 9 = (x - 1)(x + 1)(x - 9);$$
$$b = x^2 - 8x - 9 = (x + 1)(x - 9).$$

If we choose the evaluation point $\xi = 10$, then $\phi_{x-10}(a) = 99$, $\phi_{x-10}(b) = 11$, and $\gamma = \text{IGCD}(99,11) = 11$. The ξ-adic representation of 11 is simply $1 \times 10 + 1$ and therefore $G = x + 1$ is computed as the proposed $\text{GCD}(a,b)$. Doing division checks, we find that $G \mid a$ and $G \mid b$. However, G is not the correct answer but is only a factor of the true GCD. What has happened is that the factor $H = x - 9$ has disappeared under the mapping since $\phi_{x-10}(H) = 1$.

Theorem 2 proves that division checks are guaranteed to detect incorrect results as long as the evaluation point is chosen to be strictly greater than $1 + \min(|a|,|b|)$. (Note that in the above example $\xi = 1 + \min(|a|,|b|)$, which is not a *strict* bound). This is a much weaker requirement than Theorem 1 since we no longer need to deal with the ***height*** of each possible factor of a

and b.

Theorem 2.

Let $a,b \in \mathbf{Z}[x_1,x_2,\ldots,x_v]$ be nonzero polynomials and let $\xi \in \mathbf{Z}$ be a positive integer satisfying

$$\xi > 1 + \min(|a|,|b|).$$

Let $\gamma = \mathrm{GCD}(\alpha,\beta)$ where $\alpha = \phi_{x_v-\xi}(a)$ and $\beta = \phi_{x_v-\xi}(b)$, and let G denote the polynomial formed as in (3) such that

$$\phi_{x_v-\xi}(G) = \gamma.$$

G is a greatest common divisor of a and b if and only if

$$G \mid a \text{ and } G \mid b.$$

6. The Heuristic GCD Algorithm

Theorem 2 places a lower bound on the size of the evaluation point which guarantees recognition of incorrect results by the *checker*. However, there exist problems where the *solver* fails to find the true GCD via the method of section 4, no matter what evaluation point is used. We now wish to correct the algorithm so that there will always be a reasonable probability of success for any problem.

As an example, suppose that

$$a = (x - 2)(x - 1)x \quad \text{and} \quad b = (x + 1)(x + 2)(x + 3)$$

whose expanded forms have *heights* $|a| = 3$ and $|b| = 11$. Then by Theorem 2 we can choose $\xi = 5$. We get $\phi_{x-5}(a) = 60$, $\phi_{x-5}(b) = 336$, and $\gamma = \mathrm{IGCD}(60,336) = 12$. The ξ-adic representation of 12 is $2\times5 + 2$ and therefore $G = 2x+2$ is computed as the proposed $\mathrm{GCD}(a,b)$. Of course the true GCD is 1 and division checks will detect that this result is incorrect. But the point is that polynomials of the form a and b will *always* have a common factor, when evaluated, of at least 6. When a small evaluation point is chosen, as above, then this extraneous integer factor will be interpolated to an extraneous polynomial factor, yielding an incorrect result.

Carrying on with the above example, let's see what happens if we choose a much larger evaluation point, say $\xi = 20$. We get $\phi_{x-20}(a) = 6840$, $\phi_{x-20}(b) = 10626$, and $\gamma = \mathrm{IGCD}(6840,10626) = 6$. The ξ-adic representation of 6 is 6 and therefore $G = 6$ is computed as the proposed $\mathrm{GCD}(a,b)$. Again the division checks will detect that 6 is not a factor of the original polynomials. The general point to be seen from this example is that if the evaluation point is sufficiently large then any extraneous integer factor will remain as an integer content in the interpolated polynomial.

We are therefore led to the concept of removing the integer content from the polynomials. Let us impose the condition that the input polynomials a and b are *primitive with respect to* $\mathbf{Z}$ (i.e., the integer content has been removed from a and from b). Correspondingly, we will remove the integer content from the computed polynomial G before test dividing because the divisors of a primitive polynomial must be primitive (see [1]). Now it becomes crucial for us to ensure that when we remove the integer content from G we are not removing any factors that correspond to factors of the true GCD g. For if a factor of g evaluates to an integer that is small relative to ξ (specifically, less than $\frac{1}{2}\xi$) then such an integer may remain as part of the integer content in the interpolated polynomial and will be discarded. We are then back to the situation where the division checks may succeed even though the computed G is not a greatest common divisor. Theorem 3 shows how large we must now choose ξ so that, even when the integer content is removed, the division checks will be a true *checker* for the heuristic GCD algorithm.

Theorem 3.

Let $a,b \in \mathbf{Z}[x_1,x_2, \ldots ,x_v]$ be nonzero polynomials which are primitive with respect to $\mathbf{Z}$. Let $\xi \in \mathbf{Z}$ be a positive integer satisfying

$$\xi > 1 + 2\min(|a|,|b|). \tag{11}$$

Let $\gamma = \mathrm{GCD}(\alpha,\beta)$ where $\alpha = \phi_{x_v-\xi}(a)$ and $\beta = \phi_{x_v-\xi}(b)$, and let G denote the polynomial formed as in (3) such that

$$\phi_{x_v-\xi}(G) = \gamma.$$

With $\mathrm{pp}(G)$ denoting the result of dividing G by its integer content, $\mathrm{pp}(G)$ is a greatest common divisor of a and b if and only if

$$\mathrm{pp}(G) \mid a \text{ and } \mathrm{pp}(G) \mid b.$$

It remains to prove that the probability of successful termination of this algorithm can be made arbitrarily close to 1. As described, the algorithm may fail due to the following causes:

(a) The computation promises to be too expensive compared to more "standard" methods.

(b) $\xi/2 < |g|$ and the interpolation of g from γ will fail.

(c) $\xi/2 \geq |g|$ but $\gamma = L\,g$ where L is a spurious integer gcd such that $\xi/2 < L\,|g|$, so that we are not able to interpolate g from γ because of the factor L.

Failing because of (a) is an economic choice, so it is not a concern of this analysis. Failures of type (b) or (c) appear indistinguishable to the algorithm: the division check fails. Fortunately, a good solution to both is to increase the value of ξ. Increasing the value of ξ is the obvious answer for (b), and for (c) we can prove the following results.

Theorem 4.

If ξ is chosen randomly in the interval $N/2 \ldots N$ then the expected value of L is

$$E[L] = O((\log N)^K)$$

where K is a constant depending only on the degrees of the input polynomials. □

Theorem 5.

For fixed a, b, g, and choosing ξ randomly between $N/2...N$, the probability of L exceeding $\frac{\xi}{2|g|}$ is

$$Pr\{L > \frac{\xi}{2|g|}\} = O(\frac{(\log N)^K}{N}). \quad □$$

The result of Theorem 5 shows that the probability of failure of type (c) is strictly decreasing in N. For example, multiplying ξ by 2 in successive applications of the heuristic would deterministically solve the failure due to (b) in a finite number of iterations. It would also decrease the probability of failure due to (c) by roughly one half per iteration.

We are now ready to present algorithm GCDHEU. The algorithm assumes that the input polynomials are primitive and that the integer content will be removed from the output returned. The evaluation points are chosen a little larger than the minimum size given by Theorem 3 in order to decrease the probability of failure. The function "divide" being used in the algorithm returns "true" or "false" based on division of polynomials over the *field of rational numbers*, which is equivalent to removing the integer content from the divisor and then doing test division over the integers (noting that the dividend is already primitive).

Failures of type (a) are detected by a check on the size of the integers that would be generated if the computation were allowed to proceed, and the return mechanism in the algorithm is, in this case, indicated by RETURN_TO_TOP_LEVEL. This needs to be a more "drastic" return mechanism than the ordinary RETURN's appearing otherwise in the algorithm because of the recursive nature of the algorithm and the fact that there is no point in continuing computation on a problem that has lead to such large integers. In Maple [13] , the RETURN_TO_TOP_LEVEL mechanism is achieved by an ERROR return which can be "trapped" in the calling routine (the calling routine is the front-end gcd function). Failures of type (b) and (c) are detected by the division checks, and in the case of such failures the algorithm proceeds with a larger evaluation point. Rather than using an exact doubling of the evaluation point, some randomness is introduced by multiplying by a fraction greater than two chosen to be approximately the square of the golden ratio, performing the arithmetic using the "iquo" (integer quotient) function.

In the algorithm description, the following primitive functions are specific to the Maple language: indets is a function which returns a set of the indeterminates appearing in its argument, the "+" operator applied to sets denotes set union, the selector notation *vars*[*i*] applied to a set *vars* extracts the *i*th element of the set, the length function on an integer returns the number of digits in its decimal representation, and the construct "**to 4 do** · · · **od**" is a loop which will execute four times. The choice of four iterations here is arbitrary; if the first evaluation is lucky then only one iteration will be executed. Another function used here is "height" which is assumed to be a procedure to compute the *height* of a polynomial as defined in section 4.

```
procedure GCDHEU(a, b)

vars := indets(a) + indets(b);
if vars = { } then
        RETURN( IGCD(a,b) )
else
        x := vars[1]
fi;

ξ := 7 × min(height(a), height(b)) + 1;

to 4 do
        if length(ξ) × max(degree(a,x), degree(b,x)) > 3000 then
                RETURN_TO_TOP_LEVEL(fail_flag)
        fi;
        γ := GCDHEU(φ_{x-ξ}(a),φ_{x-ξ}(b));
        if γ ≠ fail_flag then
                g := genpoly(γ, ξ, x);
                if divide(a,g) and divide(b,g) then RETURN(g) fi
        fi;
        ξ := iquo ( ξ × 7778742049, 2971215073 )    # golden-ratio squared
od;
RETURN(fail_flag)
end
```

Figure 1. Procedure GCDHEU

where procedure "genpoly" is the program loop appearing below equation (2), coded as follows:

```
procedure genpoly(γ, ξ, x)

poly := 0;
e := γ;
for i from 0 while e ≠ 0 do
        g_i := φ_ξ(e);
        poly := poly + g_i × x^i;
        e := (e − g_i) / ξ
od;
RETURN(poly)
end
```

Figure 2. Procedure genpoly

7. Some Timing Comparisons

Tables 1 and 2 below list timings (in seconds) for the Maple implementation of GCDHEU, and for the routine gcdeh which is the current Maple implementation of the "extended Hensel" algorithm (corresponding to Wang's EEZ GCD algorithm without coefficient pre-determination). We also give timings for Macsyma's two main gcd algorithms, the sparse modular and the EEZ algorithm, an implementation of GCDHEU written in Franz Lisp [14] to run in Macsyma, and the Reduce gcd routine. The problems were run on a Vax 11/780 running Berkeley Unix 4.2, using Maple (version 3.2), Vaxima (version 2.04), and Reduce 3.0, respectively.

In the context of the preceding sections, it is important to note that the "heuristic" timings are not just timings for the *solver* but, of course, the cost of the *checker* is also included. Another significant point is that the algorithms coded in Maple are written in the user-level Maple language and are interpreted, while the Vaxima and Reduce codes are compiled Lisp. As the development of Maple evolves, some additional critical functions will be moved to the internal kernel (which is currently only about 135K bytes on the VAX) and this evolution will significantly improve the performance of gcdeh, in particular.

Table 1 compares the performance of the algorithms on a set of seven test files. These problems are taken from the tests which versions of Maple are put through before distribution. The source files of the Maple tests are indicated in parentheses in the first column below. Some of these tests involve the computation of several gcd problems in sequence while others involve a single gcd problem.

	Maple		Vaxima			Reduce
test #	heuristic	gcdeh	heuristic	spmod	eez	gcd
1 (t03)	3.1	11.1	1.8	2.1	2.7	0.4
2 (t07)	16.2	174.8	2.1	26.3	14.7	167.2
3 (t08)	11.3	108.8	8.1	25.8	12.7	10.2
4 (t17)	(1)	55.1	(1)	134.7	64.5	297.5
5 (t18)	(1)	294.6	(1)	193.8	196.8	(2)
6 (t19)	(1)	21.9	(1)	60.2	36.5	36.9
7 (t20)	(1)	34.6	(1)	44.7	10.3	234.6

Table 1: Summary of gcd computations for 7 Maple gcd test files.

Notes:

(1) The size check in the heuristic prevents execution on this problem.

(2) Program executed for ten cpu minutes without finishing.

Problem statistics:

1 (t03): one gcd, 3 variables, degree 4 in each variable.

2 (t07): 12 gcd's, all univariate, degrees range from 2 to 48, integer coefficients range from single-digit to 32 digits.

3 (t08): 3 gcd's, 3 variables each, degrees range from 2 to 9 in each variable.

4 (t17): one gcd, large univariate, degree 17, integer coefficients up to 269 digits.
5 (t18): one gcd, large univariate, degree 42, integer coefficients up to 116 digits.
6 (t19): one gcd, 6 variables, degree 12 in each variable.
7 (t20): one gcd, 7 variables, degree 4 in each variable.

The problems in Table 2 are multivariate problems taken from Paul Wang's article on the EEZ-GCD Algorithm [8], and originally come from Zippel's and Yun's theses. Since these are multivariate problems, in many cases they represent problems for which GCDHEU is not expected to be competitive. It is also not surprising that the current implementation of Maple's Hensel-based routine gcdeh is not competitive on some of these problems, since the component of Wang's EEZ algorithm known as "coefficient predetermination" has not yet been incorporated into gcdeh.

	Maple		Vaxima			Reduce
test #	heuristic	gcdeh	heuristic	spmod	eez	gcd
1	(1)	35.3	(1)	14.1	3.2	1.4
2	(1)	97.5	(1)	49.4	5.8	0.3
3	(1)	124.5	(1)	81.1	6.6	0.8
4	7.9	89.5	5.1	24.5	7.8	12.2
5	(1)	388.1	(1)	19.8	49.1	(2)
6	29.0	53.4	76.6	86.8	27.0	0.7
7	26.6	119.8	46.1	25.7	13.2	13.5
8	(1)	267.0	(1)	41.9	18.2	20.2
9	16.5	95.5	4.8	13.2	24.0*	5.1
10	70.7	(2)	44.1	44.0	77.1*	129.7

Table 2: Summary of gcd computations for 10 multivariate gcd problems.

Notes:
(1) The size check in the heuristic prevents execution on this problem.
(2) Program ran out of space.
* Test run at Berkeley on a Vax 11/780 running Berkeley Unix 4.2, since our Vaxima had a bug.

Acknowledgements

The students and staff associated with the Maple project have contributed to this work in various ways. We particularly thank Greg Fee and Michael Monagan for reading an earlier draft of this paper and suggesting several improvements. We also wish to thank John Foderaro at the University of California, Berkeley, for assistance with Vaxima.

References

1. Donald Knuth, *The Art of Computer Programming, vol. 2, 2nd ed.*, Addison Wesley (1981).

2. G.E. Collins, ``Subresultants and Reduced Polynomial Remainder Sequences,'' *Journal of the ACM* **14**, pp. 128-142 (1967).

3. W.S. Brown, ``The Subresultant PRS Algorithm,'' *ACM Transactions on Mathematical Software* **4**(3), pp. 237-249 (1978).

4. Anthony Hearn, ``Non-modular computation of polynomial GCD's using trial division,'' *Proceedings of Eurosam 79*, pp. 227-239, Springer-Verlag (1979). Springer-Verlag Lecture Notes in Computer Science no. 72.

5. W.S. Brown, ``On Euclid's Algorithm and the Computation of Polynomial Greatest Common Divisors,'' *Journal of the ACM* **18**(4), pp. 478-504 (1971).

6. Richard Zippel, ``Probabilistic Algorithms for Sparse Polynomials,'' *Proceedings of Eurosam 79*, pp. 216-226, Springer-Verlag (1979). Springer-Verlag Lecture Notes in Computer Science no. 72.

7. Joel Moses and David Y.Y. Yun, ``The EZ GCD Algorithm,'' pp. 159-166 in *Proceedings of the ACM Annual Conference* (August 1973).

8. Paul Wang, ``The EEZ-GCD Algorithm,'' *SIGSAM Bulletin* **14**(2), pp. 50-60 (May 1980).

9. D. Lazard, ``Factorization des Polynomes,'' in *Proceedings of the 4th Journees Algorithmiques*, Poitiers (1981).

10. A.V. Aho, J.E. Hopcroft, and J.D. Ullman, *The Design and Analysis of Computer Algorithms*, Addison-Wesley, Reading, Massachusetts (1974).

11. Joachim von zur Gathen, ``Factoring Sparse Multivariate Polynomials,'' pp. 172-179 in *Proceedings of the 24th Annual Symposium on Foundations of Computer Science*, IEEE (Nov. 1983).

12. M. Mignotte, ``Some Useful Bounds,'' pp. 259-263 in *Computer Algebra: Symbolic and Algebraic Computation*, ed. B. Buchberger, G.E. Collins, and R. Loos, Springer-Verlag (1982).

13. Keith O. Geddes, Gaston H. Gonnet, and Bruce W. Char, *Maple User's Manual, 3rd edition*, University of Waterloo Computer Science Department Research Report CS-83-41, December, 1983.

14. John Foderaro, *The FRANZ LISP Manual*, Computer Science Division, U. of Calif., Berkeley (1980). For FRANZ LISP version Opus 34b.

A NEW LIFTING PROCESS
FOR THE MULTIVARIATE POLYNOMIAL FACTORIZATION

D. LUGIEZ
LIFIA ENSIMAG BP 68 38402 ST MARTIN D'HERES

1 INTRODUCTION

We propose a new lifting process for multivariate polynomial factorization. Its main feature is to consider the lifting process as a partial fraction decomposition. denoted by p.f.d. in the following. This approach has yet been done in the univariate case and the results are described in Lugiez (4). In section 2 we recall briefly the scheme of the classical method using Wang's presentation. For a more detailled description one is referred to the original paper of Wang (6). We rewiew the solutions given to the three major problems arising in the multivariate polynomial factorization the leading coefficient problem. the occurence of extraneous factors and the bad zero problem. Then the design of an algorithm due to Viry (5) based on p.f.d. is given and shortly discussed. In section 3, we present two versions of the new algorithm. First we describe a serial approach which solves the leading coefficient problem in the simplest way. for the sake of simplicity. Then the parallel version which solves the leading coefficient problem as the classical algorithm does is schemed. In section 4 , we give another new algorithm which allows us to perform the change of variable required to solve the bad zero problem wihout any expansion of terms. Finally. in section 5 we give the numerical results get in a first implementation of the algorithm ; then we discuss the problems yielded by the recursive representation of the polynomials.

2 PROBLEMS AND CLASSICAL SOLUTIONS

2.1 Preliminaries and notations

P is a primitive squarefree polynomial in (m+1) variables

$x, x_1, \ldots, x_m$ with integer coefficients.
n is the degree of P in the main variable x. n_i is the degree of P in x_i.
p is the global degree of P in the variable $x_1 \ldots . x_m$.
V_n is the leading coefficient of P considered as a polynomial in the main variable x. then $V_n \in Z[x_1 \ldots . x_m]$.
M is a coefficient bound .i.e for any integer coefficient c of any factor of P . $2|c| < M$.
I is the ideal of $Z[x_1 \ldots . x_m]$ generated by the set F = $(x_1^{n1+1} \ldots . x_m^{nm+1})$.

For instance if $P(x.x1.x2.x3) = x^2x_1 + xx_3x_2^4 + x_1^3 + 2$ then : $n=2$. $n_1=3$. $n_2=4$, $n_3=1$. $p=5$.

I_i is the ideal generated by the homogeneous polynomials of degree i in the variables $y_1 \ldots . y_m$ where $y_i = x_i - a_i$ with a_i an integer

For instance. if $a_1 = a_2 = 1$ and $i=2$. then I_2 is the ideal generated by $((x_1-1)^2.(x_2-1)^2.(x_1-1)(x_2-1))$.

$Z[x.x1, \ldots .xm]/J$ is the quotient ring of the ring $Z[x.x1, \ldots .xm]$ by the ideal J.

2.2 Problems

The classical algorithms for the multivariate polynomial factorization go through three main steps

First step Choose some suitable prime integers $a_1 \ldots . a_m$ and factorize $P(x.a_1 \ldots . a_m)$ over $Z[x]$

Second step Compute the coeficient bound M and lift the factorization over the integers by an Hensel's type algorithm.

Third step · Reconstruction of the true factors of P from the factors modulo M and I obtained in step two.

The lifting process requires the change of variables $y_i = x_i - a_i$

and the computation of $P(x.y_1+a_1 .\quad y_m+a_m)$. This substitution leads to the expansion of terms such as $(y_1+a_1)^{i_1} . .(y_m+a_m)^{i_m}$ which is time consuming when the a_i are not zero. This problem is known as the bad zero problem. Another difficulty comes from the occurence of extraneous factors i.e. factors of $P(x.a_1 . \quad .a_m)$ which do not give a factor of P after the lifting process. The third problem is the leading coefficient one. When the leading coefficient of the polynomial is not an integer we get factors correct up to units of $Z[x.x_1 . \ldots .x_m]/I$ during the lifting process therefore the computations are complicated by these units coming from the inversion of the leading coefficient problem in $Z[x.x_1 \ldots .x_m]$

2.3 Classical solutions

The bad zero problem is perhaps the most important one because its solution leads to heuristic solutions of the two others. The procedure suggested by Wang (6) is to perform a variable by variable lifting process. Thus the main difficulty is to compute a polynomial $C(x.x_1 . \ldots x_{k-1})$ such that :

$$U(x.x_1 \ldots .x_k) = (x_k-a_k)^1 C + R(x.x_1 \ldots .x_k)$$

with degree of R in (xk-ak) lesser than 1.

U is a polynomial given by the algorithm.

This is performed by using differentiation and by evaluating the polynomial U without any expansion of terms. But this approach prevent us from lifting all the variables simultaneously.

The heuristic solution of the extraneous factor's problem is to compute several factorizations $P(x.a_1 . \ldots .a_m)$ by choosing several sets $(a_1 . \ldots .a_m)$. and to keep the factorization which gives the smallest number of factors. This method greatly reduces the number of extraneous factors. Nethertheless. the only algorithm which solves this problem is Lenstra's one (3) . which uses reduced basis in lattices. But this method is not yet competitive with Wang's one.

To solve the leading coefficient problem. we factorize this coefficient and we try to identify the factors obtained when they are evaluated in $a_1 . \ldots a_m$ to the integer leading coefficients of the factors of $P(x.a_1 . \ldots a_m)$.

For example :

$$P(x.y\ z) = x^2(6 + 4y + 3z + 2yz) + x(5 + 5y + 3z + z^2 + 2y^2) + 1 + y + z + yz$$

The leading coefficient V_n is $6 + 4y + 3z + 2yz$ which factorizes in $(3 + 2y)(2 + 3z) = v_1\ v_2$

$P(x.0.0) = (2x + 1)(3x + 2)$ and we get $v_1(0.0)=3$,$v_2(0.0)=2$.

Then the leading coefficient of the first factor of P is $3 + 2y$ corresponding to the factor $3x + 1$ and we know that this factor is equal to $(3 + 2y)x + 1 + \ldots$

The second factor is equal to $(2 + z)x + 1 + \ldots$

This solution of the leading coefficient problem requires that there is no extraneous factor.

2.4 An algorithm based on p f.d.

Viry (5) suggests an algorithm for the multivariate polynomial factorization which is based on p.f.d. Let P be the polynomial to be factored. First, this algorithm gets a monic polynomial Q from P by the change of variable $x_i \leftarrow x_i + p_i x$. Then the leading coefficient problem is avoided. The factorization of Q is computed from the factorization of $Q(x.0.\ldots.0)$ by lifting all the variables simultaneously and by using the p.f.d. of the fraction $(Q(x.x_1.\ldots.x_m) - Q_{1j}\ldots Q_{rj})/Q_{10}\ldots Q_{r0}$ where the Q_{ij} are the factors obtained at step i ; at step 0 .they are the factors of $Q(x.0.\ldots.0)$. This p f.d. requires only the computations of the p.f.d. of $x^j/Q_{10}\ldots Q_{r0}$ for $0 \leqslant j < l$, with l the degree of Q in x.

Serial or parallel versions of this algorithm can be designed. The most important problem one is faced with in this algorithm. is that of the change of variable. because it leads to many expansions of terms and because it increases the degree of the polynomial to be factored and the probability of getting extraneous factors. The rewarding feature is that the leading coefficient problem is avoided and that all the variables are lifted simultaneously.

3 THE PROPOSED ALGORITHM

The new method is based upon p.f.d. as in Viry's one. We also lift all variables simultaneously. but the change of variables is the classical one. The new expression for the polynomial is computed by a new algorithm based on Euler's identity described in section 4. First, we present the serial version of the algorithm for the sake of simplicity Two serial methods. related to two different solutions of the leading coefficient problem. can be designed; we give here the simplest one. Then the parallel version of the algorithm is described.

3.1 The serial algorithm

The leading coefficient of P has been factored but nothing is known about the leading coefficients of the factors of P. All the computations are done modulo M and I as defined in 2.1. even when it is not explicitly said.

The Algorithm

Step 1 · Choose suitable integers $a_1 \ldots a_m$ and factorize $P(x.a_1 \ldots .a_m)$ over Z[x]. Compute the homogeneous part of degree i of P in $y_1 \ldots .y_m$ where $y_i = x_i - a_i$ by the mean of the new algorithm described in section 4

Step 2 · Compute the coefficient bound M and lift the congruence P = A.B mod(M.I) ,where A is a monic factor of P. After this lifting process set P = P/A and repeat this step until all the factors of P are lifted.

Step 3 · Reconstruction of the true factors of P.

This scheme is similar to the classical one. now we describe the new lifting process.

The new lifting process

(1) i=0. H_0=A . Q_0=B . k is the degree of B.

(2) Compute the partial fraction decomposition of x^j/Q_0H_0 for $0 \leqslant j < n$

(3) Set $Q'_o = V_1 x^k$ where V_i is the homogeneous part of degree i of the leading coefficient V_n of P. Q'_o is the corrective part related to the leading coefficient.

$H1 = Ho$. $Q1 = Q_o + Q'_o$. i=1

(4) While $i \leqslant p$ the degree of P in $y_1, ..y_m$ do

begin

(4.1) $S_i = (P - H_i Q_i)_i$ the homogeneous part of degree i of $P - H_i Q_i$

(4.2) Compute $H_i"$ and $Q_i"$ the p.f.d. of

$S_i/HoQo = H_i"/Ho + Q_i"/Qo$

(4.3) Compute $Q_i' = V_{i+2} x^{k_i}$ the corrective part related to the leading coefficient.

(4.4) $H_{i+1} = H_i + H_i"$; $Q_{i+1} = Q_i + Q_i" + Q_i'$; i=i+1.

end

end

We give an example before proving the algorithm.

Example : $P(x.y.z) = x^2(6 + 4y + 3z + 2yz)$
$+ x(5 + 5y + 3z + z^2 + 2y^2) + 1 + y + z + yz$

$a_1 = a_2 = 0$

$P(x.0.0) = (3x + 1)(2x + 1)$

The bound choosen is $M = 17^2 = 289$.

$A = x + 145$. $B = 6x + 2$

$1/AB = -1/A + 6/B$

$x/AB = 145/A + 287/B$

$Qo' = x^2(4y + 3z)$ then $Q1 = (6 + 4y + 3z)x + 2$

1st iteration $S_1 = (P \quad HoQo)_1 = x(3y + 146z) + y + z$ then

$H_1 = x + 145 + 145y + 72z$

$Q_1 = x(6 + 4y + 3z + 2yz) + 2 + 3z$

2nd iteration : $S_2 = (P - H_1Q_1)_2 = x(74z^2 + 143yz) + 73z^2 + 144yz$ then

$H_2 = x + 145 + 145y + 72z - 36z^2 + 72yz$

$Q2 = x(6 + 4y + 3z + 2yz) + 2 + 3z + z^2$

As the degree of P in y.z is 2 , we stop the lifting process and we try to get the true factors of P from H_2 and Q_2.

$V_n H_2 = (3 + 2y)(x(2 + z) + 1 + y)$ mod I_3 where V_n is the leading coefficient of P and I_3 is the ideal $(y^3.z^3.zy^2.z^2y)$. Then we get the factor $x(2 + z) + 1 + y$ which divides P.

Proof of the correctness of the algorithm.

We shall proove that $P = H_iQ_i \mod(I_{i+1}.M)$ at the iteration i. For i=1 . the result comes from the asumptions.
We suppose that the result is true at iteration i-1.
We can write $P = N.M \mod(I_{i+1}.M)$ with $N = H_i + N_i$

$$M = Q_i + M_i$$

We must show that N_i and M_i and equal.modulo I_{i+1} to the quantity H_i'' and $Q_i' + Q_i''$ respectively. As Q_i' equals zero modulo I_{i+1}. we must show that $N_i = H_i''$. $M_i = Q_i$.

$$P = (H_i + N_i)(Q_i + M_i) \mod I_{i+1}$$

$$P - H_iQ_i = H_iM_i + Q_iN_i \mod I_{i+1}$$

Because of the corrective part related to the leading coefficient. we know that the degree of $P - H_iQ_i$ in x is stricly less than the degree of P in x.

From the previous equaliy. we get the following equality between the homogeneous part of degree i in $y_1.....y_m$

$$(P \quad H_iQ_i)_i = HoM_i + QoN_i$$

because N_i and M_i are of degree i and because Ho and Qo are of degree 0 in $y_1...y_m$. and no term but this one has degree i.

$$S_i = HoM_i + QoN_i \text{ leads to } S_i/HoQo = N_i/Ho + M_i/Qo$$

with the condition $\deg(S_i) < \deg(HoQo)$. $\deg(N_i) < \deg(Ho)$. $\deg(M_i) < \deg(Qo)$ where deg(G) is the degree of G in the variable x.

Then N_i and M_i are the solution of the p f.d. of the fraction $S_i/HoQo$ which is unique and we get $N_i = H_i''$. $M_i = Q_i''$.
C.Q.F.D.

Remark : The p f.d. is easily computed as $S_i = \sum A_j x^j$ where the A_j are polynomials of $Z[y_1....y_m]$. Then the p f.d. is computed as $S_i/HoQo = \sum A_j \; x^j/HoQo$ using the p f.d. of $x^j/HoQo$ over $Z_M[x]$ which are computed once at the very begining of the algorithm by a modular version of Kung and Tong's algorithm. This can be done without any problem when the bound M is equal to p^k . with p a suitable prime.

The polynomial S_i is easily computed because S_i is equal to $P_i - \sum_{l+m=i} H_l''Q_m''$ where H_l'' (resp Q_m'') is the homogeneous part of degree l. (respetively m) of H_i (resp Q_i); $H_l'' = H_l''$ and $Q_m'' = Q_m'' + Q_{m-1}'$

When the factor A of P has been lifted . the algorithm is

applied recursively to a factor of $B = P/A$. But no computation is needed to get the homogeneous parts of degree i of B, because they have been computed yet during the lifting of the factor A.

3.2 The parallel algorithm

We present the algorithm which lifts simultaneously all the factors of P and which solves the leading coefficient problem as the classical algorithm does. Then we suppose that the leading coefficients of the factors of P have been computed.

The algorithm

(1) Compute the factors $R_1 \ldots R_r$ of $P(x, a_1, \ldots, a_m)$ over $Z[x]$.

(2) Compute the leading coefficients of the factors of P over $Z[x, x_1, \ldots x_m]$.

(3) Compute the p.f.d. of $x^j / R_1 \ldots R_r$ for $j=0,\ldots p-1$.

(4) $R_{j1} = R_j + R_j'$ where R_j' is the corrective part related to the leading coefficient. i=1.

(5) While $i \leqslant p$ do

begin

(5.1) $S_i = (P - R_{1i} \ldots R_{ri})_i$ .the homogeneous part of degree i in $y_1, \ldots y_m$.

(5.2) Compute the R_{ji}' the solution of the p.f.d. of $S_i / R_{10} \ldots R_{r0}$

(5.3) For $j=1\ldots r$ compute R_{ji}'' the corrective part related to the leading coefficient.

(5.4) For $j=1,\ldots r$ set $R_{ji+1} = R_{ji} + R_{ji}' + R_{ji}''$

end

end

4 THE ALGORITHM TO CHANGE VARIABLES

We present first an algorithm which computes the homogeneous part P_i of degree i of the polynomial P in the new variables $y_1 \ldots y_m$ where $y_1 = x_1 - a_1$. Then we show how to realize the effective change of variables $y_1 = x_1 - a_1$.

4.1 Computation of the P_i's

P is a polynomial of $A[x_1,\dots x_m]$ where $A = Z[x]$. Hence in the following, P is considered as a polynomial in m variables. The aim of the algorithm is to compute the P_i's, the homogeneous part of degree i of P in $y_1,\dots,y_m$ where $y_l=x_l-a_l$.

For instance : $P(x_1,x_2) = x_1^2 - 2x_1x_2 + 2x_2 + x1 - 1$

$y_1=x_1-1$, $y_2 = x_2-1$

Then $P_0 = 1$ homogeneous part of degree 0 in y_1,y_2

$P_1 = y_1 + y_2$ " " " 1

$P_2 = y_1^2 - 2y_1y_2$ " " " 2

We first give the mathematical underpining of the algorithm. The basis is Euler's identity :

If Q is an homogeneous polynomial of degree k in $x_1,\dots x_m$ then

$$\sum_l x_l\, DQ/Dx_l = kQ$$

where DQ/Dx_l is the partial derivative of Q with respect to x_l.

As $y_l=x_l-a_l$, $DQ/Dx_l = DQ/Dy_l$; then we get :

$$\sum_l (x_l-a_l)\, DP/Dx_l = \sum_i iP_i$$

As $P_0=P(x,a_1,\dots,a_m)$ is easily computed, we suppose that we work with polynomials such that $P_0 = 0$.

By iterating the previous identity, we find the following linear system :

$$P_1 + P_2 + \dots + P_p = G_0$$
$$P_1 + 2P_2 + \dots + pP_p = G_1$$
$$\dots\dots\dots\dots\dots\dots$$
$$P_1 + 2^{p-1}P_2 + \dots + p^{p-1}P_p = G_p$$

where $G_0 = P$ and $G_j = \sum_i (x_i-a_i)\, DG_{j-1}/Dx_i$

Hence the P_i's are the solutions of this linear system and $Pi = D_i/D$ where D and D_i are the determinants given by Cramer's rule.

We set $b_i = i$ for $i=1,\dots,p$. Then D is the Van der Monde determinant :

$$D = \begin{vmatrix} 1 & \cdot & \cdot & 1 \\ b_1 & \cdot & \cdot & b_p \\ \cdot & \cdot & \cdot & \cdot \\ b_1^{p-1} & \cdot & \cdot & b_p^{p-1} \end{vmatrix} = \prod_{l \neq k} (b_l - b_k)$$

D_i is obtained by substituing the column i $\begin{vmatrix} 1 \\ b_i \\ \cdot \\ \cdot \\ b_i^{p-1} \end{vmatrix}$ by $\begin{vmatrix} G_0 \\ G_1 \\ \cdot \\ \cdot \\ G_{p-1} \end{vmatrix}$

Hence the coefficient of G_i is the coefficient of b_i in the determinant D and we know that ·

$$D = (-1)^{p-1} \prod_{l \neq i} (b_i - b_l) \prod_{l \neq k . k \neq i . l \neq i} (b_l - b_k)$$

Then we compute the polynomial $R(X) = \prod_{j=1..m} (X - j)$

and the polynomials $R_i(X) = R(X)/(X-i)$.

Let us denote by A_i the polynomial obtained by substituing X^j into G_j in $R_i(X)$. We set $r_i = \prod_{j \neq i}(i-j) = R_i(i)$

Then we can write $P_i = A_i/r_i$; and we have given the proof of the following algorithm which computes the P_i's

The Algorithm

P is a polynomial such that $P_0 = 0$; if not $P \leftarrow P - P_0$ with P_0 equal to $P(x.a_1 .... a_m)$. We compute P_i's the homogeneous part of degree i in $y_1 . .. y_m$ where $y_l = x_l - a_l$.

(1) Compute $G_0 .... G_{p-1}$ with $G_0 = P$, $G_j = \sum (x_l - a_l) DG_{j-1}/Dx_l$. p is the degre of P in $y_1 .... y_m$.

(2) Compute the polynomial $R(X) = \prod_{i=1....p} (X-i)$

(3) For i=1....p compute the polynomials $R_i(X) = R(X)/(X-i)$ and $r_i = R_i(i)$.

(4) For i=1....p set $P_i = A_i/r_i$ where A_i is the polynomial equal

to R_i when X^j has been substitued into G_j.

end

An example.

$P(x1,x2) = 3 + 6x_1 + x_2 + x_1x_2 + 4x_1^2 + x_1^3$

$y_1 = x_1 + 1$. $y_2 = x_2 + 1$ hence $a_1 = a_2 = -1$

$P_0 = P(-1,-1) = 0$

we compute $G_0 = 3 + 6x_1 + x_2 + x_1x_2 + 4x_1^2 + x_1^3$

$G_1 = 7 + 15x_1 + 2x_2 + 2x_1x_2 + 11\,x_1^2 + 3x_1^3$

$G_2 = 17 + 39x_1 + 4x_2 + 4x_1x_2 + 31x_1^2 + 9x_1^3$

we compute $R(X) = (X\;1)(X\;2)(X\;3)$

$R_1(X) = X^2 - 5X + 6$

$R_2(X) = X^2 - 4X + 3$

$R_3(X) = X^2 - 3X + 2$

$r_1=2$. $r_2=-1$. $r_3=2$.

Finally we get $P_1 = 0$. $P_2 = x_1^2 + x_1x_2 + 3x_1 + x_2 + 1$.

$P_3 = x_1^3 + 3x_1^2 + 3x_1 + 1$

The next part will help us to show how to point out that $P_1=0$. $P_2 = y_1^2 + y_1y_2$. $P_3 = y_1^3$.

4.2 The change of variables

We show how to perform the effective change of variables when we know all the P_i's.

(1) From each P_i. pick up the monomials of degree i in $x_1 \ldots x_m$.

(2) Substitute x_1 into y_1 in these monomials . let $R_i(y_1 \ldots y_m)$ be the result of this substitution . then $P_i = R_i$.

Proof : As P_i is a polynomial of degre i in $y_1 \ldots y_m$. and as $y_1=x_1-a_1$, the term of degree i in $y_1 \ldots y_m$ of P_i is equal to the the term of degree i in $x_1 \ldots x_m$ after that the substitution x_1 <- y_1 has been performed.

Example . $P_2 = x_1^2 + x_1x_2 + 3x_1 + x_2 + 1$. The term of degree 2 of P_2 is $x_1^2 + x_1x_2$. then P_2 is equal to $y_1 2 + y_1y_2$.

5 COMPARISON WITH THE CLASSICAL METHOD AND PROBLEMS

We did not give any study of complexity . because little is known about the average complexity of the multivariate polynomial factorization algorithm . see Kaltofen (1) for example. The algorithm can be exponential in the worst case. but it is easy to see that the lifting process is polynomial in the number of factors over Z[x] . the degree of the polynomial and the number of variables.

We have implemented the serial version without the predetermination of the leading coefficients and we compared it with the classical method without the predeterminetion of the coefficients. In order to avoid the leading coefficient problem . we have factorized monic polynomials. The computations were done using ALDES/SAC 2 implemented on a DPS 68 under MULTICS.

This first implementation was not satisfying because of the recursive representation of the polynomials. This structure does not suit the new algorithm . specially the algorithm to change variables. For instance. the computation of terms such as $\sum$ (xl-al)DP/Dxl is very difficult to achieve efficiently with such a recursive form.

These numerical experiments showed two facts. The first one is that the new change of variable is worse than the classical algorithm which uses the Horner's rule. This fact is strongly related to the recursive representation of the polynomials. The second one is that the new algorithm appeared to be more efficient than the classical one . even with the bad implementation of the algorithm to change variable.

A typical example is the following one :

P(x.y z) = (x3 + xyz + 2)(x2 + z2 + 1)

The time required for the choice of the a_i's and for the factorization of $P(x.a_1.a_2)$ is T = 10078 milliseconds , the time for the change of variables y -> y . z->z is 106ms by the classical algorithm and 1689ms by the new algorithm. But the classical lifting process requires 20028 ms and the new algorithm only requires 5084 ms.

Then .the new algorithm looks promising and it would be valuable to implement it using a new polynomial representation which suits its iterative structure. The main advantage of this algorithm is that we perform less iterations than the classical algorithm because the degree of the polynomial.p. is lesser or equal to the sum of the partial degrees $n_1 + .. + n_m$ and because the early detection of the factors is allowed. Another improvment is that no correction coefficients are computed unless at the very begining of the algorithms and these computations are easily performed because they take place in $Z_M[x]$.

References ·

(1) E.KALTOFEN "Factorization of Polynomials" , Computer Algebra . BUCHBERGER et all editors p95-113

(2) H.T. KUNG and D.M TONG "Fast Algorithms for Partial Fraction Decomposition " SIAM J.of COMP. p582-592 (1977)

(3) A.K. LENSTRA "Lattices and Factorization of Polynomials" Mathematisch Centrum . AMSTERDAM report IW 190/81

(4) D LUGIEZ "Factorisation des polynomes" These de 3 Cycle INP GRENOBLE (1984)

(5) G. VIRY " Factorisation des polynomes a plusieurs variables" RAIRO Informatique Theorique Vol 14 p209-223 (1980)

(6) P.S. WANG "An improved Multivariate Polynomial Factoring Algorithm " Math. of Comp. vol 32 p1215-1231 (1978)

Explicit Construction of the Hilbert Class Fields of Imaginary Quadratic Fields with Class Numbers 7 and 11

Erich Kaltofen[*]

University of Toronto
Department of Computer Science
Toronto, Ontario M5S1A4, Canada

and

Noriko Yui[*]

University of Toronto
Department of Mathematics
Toronto, Ontario M5S1A1, Canada

Extended Abstract

In this note we summarize the progress made so far on using the Computer Algebra System MACSYMA [10] to explicitly calculate the defining equations of the Hilbert class fields of imaginary quadratic fields with prime class number. Our motivation for undertaking this investigation is to construct rational polynomials with a given finite Galois group. The groups we try to realize here are the dihedral groups D_p for primes p. These groups are non-abelian groups of order $2p$ and are generated by two elements

$$\sigma = (1\ 2\ 3 \cdots p) \text{ and } \tau = (1)(2\ \ p)(3\ \ p-1) \cdots (\tfrac{p+1}{2}\ \ \tfrac{p+3}{2})$$

with the relation $\tau\sigma\tau = \sigma^{-1}$, as subgroups of the permutation groups of degree p. These groups are solvable and thus can be realized as Galois groups. The problem is to construct, for a given prime p, an integer polynomial with Galois group D_p.

1. C. U. Jensen and N. Yui have found the following effective characterization for polynomials to have Galois group D_p.

Theorem (cf. Jensen and Yui [7, Theorem II.1.2]): Let $f(x)$ be a monic integral polynomial of degree p, where p is an odd prime. Assume that $p \equiv 1$ modulo 4 and that the Galois group of f is not the cyclic group of order p (*resp. assume that $p \equiv 3$ modulo 4*). Then necessary and sufficient conditions that the Galois group of f is D_p are:

---

* This research was partially supported by the National Science and Engineering Research Council of Canada under grant 3-643-126-90 (the first author) and under grant 3-661-114-30 (the second author).

First author's current address: Rensselaer Polytechnic Institute, Department Mathematical Sciences, Troy, New York, 12181.

(1) f is irreducible over the ring $\mathbf{Z}$ of integers.

(2) The discriminant of f is a perfect square (*resp. is not a perfect square*).

(3) The polynomial $g(x) = \prod_{1 \le i < j \le p}(x - \alpha_i - \alpha_j)$, α_i being the roots of f, which is of degree $p(p-1)/2$ and has all integral coefficients, decomposes into a product of $(p-1)/2$ distinct irreducible polynomials of degree p over $\mathbf{Z}$. □

Given an integral polynomial of degree p, it is quite easy to test whether conditions (1) – (3) are satisfied. Both the computation of the discriminant of f and that of the polynomial g can be accomplished by resultant calculations. The exclusion of the cyclic group of order p in the case that $p \equiv 1$ modulo 4 may be more involved but it is, for example, sufficient to establish that f does not have p real roots. For $p = 3$, 5, and 7 polynomials with Galois group D_p are known for at least a century (cf. Weber [12, Sec. 131]).

Unfortunately, extensive search for polynomials of degree 11 satisfying conditions (1) – (3) has not yet produced even one such polynomial. This is, to some extent, not surprising since the polynomial g will, for randomly chosen coefficients, almost always be irreducible due to the Hilbert irreducibility theorem. In order to construct such polynomials we therefore, at the moment, have to rely on the Hilbert class field theory. We shall briefly summarize the theoretic background of our computations.

2. We consider an imaginary quadratic number field $\mathbf{Q}(\sqrt{m})$ with discriminant d over the field $\mathbf{Q}$ of the rational numbers. Let $ax^2 + bxy + cy^2$, $a > 0$, $\mathrm{GCD}(a, b, c) = 1$, be a positive definite primitive quadratic form with discriminant $d = b^2 - 4ac$. The integral matrix $\begin{bmatrix} \alpha & \beta \\ \gamma & \delta \end{bmatrix}$ with determinant $\alpha\delta - \gamma\beta = 1$ transforms the quadratic form by replacing x by $\alpha x + \beta y$ and y by $\gamma x + \delta y$ into an equivalent one of the same discriminant d. The class number $h(d)$ of $\mathbf{Q}(\sqrt{m})$ is equal to the the number of such defined equivalence classes of positive definite primitive quadratic forms of discriminant d. A unique reduced form for each equivalence class can be selected with

$$-a < b \le a < c \quad \text{or} \quad 0 \le b \le a = c.$$

These conditions imply that $|b| \le \sqrt{|d|/3}$ and hence $h(d)$ is finite.

Now let $SL_2(\mathbf{Z})$ be the modular group:

$$SL_2(\mathbf{Z}) = \left\{ \begin{bmatrix} a & b \\ c & d \end{bmatrix} \mid a, b, c, d \in \mathbf{Z},\ ad - bc = 1 \right\},$$

and let H denote the upper half complex plane:

$$H = \{ z = x + iy \in \mathbf{C} \mid y > 0 \},$$

where $\mathbf{C}$ is the field of complex numbers. $SL_2(\mathbf{Z})$ acts on H by

$$\begin{bmatrix} a & b \\ c & d \end{bmatrix}(z) = \frac{az + b}{cz + d}.$$

A *fundamental domain* F for $SL_2(\mathbb{Z})$ in H is defined to be a subset of H such that every orbit of $SL_2(\mathbb{Z})$ has one element in F, and two elements of F are in the same orbit if and only if they lie on the boundary of F. Then F is given by the set

$$F = \{ z = x + iy \in \mathbb{C} \mid |z| \geq 1, \ |x| \leq \frac{1}{2} \}.$$

We now introduce the *elliptic modular j-invariant*. For each complex number z with non-negative imaginary part, let $q = e^{2\pi i z}$ and let

$$E_4(z) = 1 + 240 \sum_{n=1}^{\infty} \sigma_3(n) q^n, \quad \sigma_3(n) = \sum_{\substack{t \mid n \\ t > 0}} t^3.$$

Furthermore, let

$$\eta(z) = q^{\frac{1}{24}} \prod_{n=1}^{\infty} (1 - q^n) = q^{\frac{1}{24}} \left[1 + \sum_{n=1}^{\infty} (-1)^n \left(q^{\frac{n(3n-1)}{2}} + q^{\frac{n(3n+1)}{2}} \right) \right].$$

The j-invariant $j(z)$ is defined as

$$j(z) = \left(\frac{E_4(z)}{\eta(z)^8} \right)^3.$$

It is well-known that $j(z)$ satisfies the following properties:

(i) $j(i) = 1728$, $j((\pm 1 + i\sqrt{3})/2) = 0$,

(ii) $j(x + iy)$ and $j(-x + iy)$ are complex conjugates for any $\pm x + iy \in F$, and

(iii) $j(q) = \frac{1}{q} + 744 + 196884q + 21493760q^2 + 864299970q^3 + \cdots$.

3. The following theorem now shows how to construct an integral polynomial with dihedral Galois group of prime degree.

Theorem (cf. Deuring [2]): Let $\mathbf{Q}(\sqrt{m})$ be an imaginary quadratic field with discriminat d, and with class number $h(d) = p$, p an odd prime. For each reduced positive definite primitive quadratic form $a_k x^2 + b_k xy + c_k y^2$ of discriminant d, $1 \leq k \leq p$, let $\vartheta_k = (-b_k + \sqrt{d})/(2a_k)$ be the root of $a_k \vartheta^2 + b_k \vartheta + c_k = 0$ belonging to F. Furthermore, let the class equation H_d be defined as

$$H_d(x) = \prod_{k=1}^{p} (x - j(\vartheta_k))$$

Then $H_d(x)$ is an irreducible integral polynomial whose Galois group over $\mathbf{Q}$ is the dihedral group D_p. □

4. We constructed $H_d(x)$ for selected imaginary quadratic fields $\mathbf{Q}(\sqrt{m})$ with $-m$ a prime and $h(d) = 7$ or 11. First we wish to make some comments encountered during our calculations. In all cases we knew the class number in advance. Therefore it was quite easy to calculate the ϑ_k, $1 \leq k \leq p$. Indeed,

for $|b_k| \le a_k < c_k$, we get two roots $\vartheta_k = (\mp b_k + \sqrt{d})/(2a_k)$, and for $0 \le b_k \le a_k = c_k$, one root $\vartheta_k = (-b_k + \sqrt{d})/(2a_k)$, belonging to F. Using the above mentioned properties of j we only had to evaluate $j(\vartheta_k)$ for $(p+1)/2$ different values of ϑ_k. The evaluation of each $j(\vartheta_k)$ was done to high floating point precision. We experienced that the Taylor series of j evaluated at q converged extremely slowly. Therefore we evaluated the Taylor series of E_4 and η separately at q, then raised the value $\eta(q)$ to the eighth power, divided $E_4(q)$ by this result, and finally raised the quotient to the third power. This process yields $j(q)$ to high precision fairly quickly.

In each case there were two parameters to choose: The floating point precision and the order of the Taylor expansions. We decided to choose the same order for both E_4 and η. The constant coefficient of each polynomial turned out to be the one of largest size. Therefore we chose the floating point precision typically 20 digits more than the number of digits in that coefficient. In all cases we then could read off the correct corresponding integer from its approximation. It turns out that the constant coefficient $H_d(0)$ must be a perfect cube. Verifying this condition proved to be a valuable test to see whether the order of the Taylor approximation was high enough. If not, we incremented the order by 5 and tried again. A further confirmation for the correctness of all coefficients is to factor both $H_d(0)$ and the discriminant $\Delta(H_d)$ of H_d both of which surprisingly have only small prime factors. A full explanation for this phenomenon has been found only very recently by B. Gross and D. Zagier. With their permission, we state a version of their theorem best suited for our discussion.

Theorem (Gross and Zagier [3]): Let q be a prime. For a positive integer $n \in \mathbf{N}$ such that $(\frac{n}{q}) \neq +1$, define the function $F_q(n)$ by

$$F_q(n) = \begin{cases} l^{k r_1 \cdots r_t} & \text{if } n = l^{2k-1} l_1^{2n_1} \cdots l_s^{2n_s} q_1^{r_1-1} \cdots q_t^{r_t-1} \\ & \text{where } (\frac{l}{q}) = (\frac{l_i}{q}) = -1,\ (\frac{q_i}{q}) = +1 \\ & \text{with } k, r_i > 1 \text{ and } n_i \ge 0, \\ 1 & \text{if } n = l_1^{2k_1-1} l_2^{2k_2-1} \cdots l_s^{2k_s-1} t \\ & \text{where } (\frac{l_i}{q}) = -1 \text{ with } k_i \ge 1,\ s \ge 3 \\ & \text{and } t \in \mathbf{N}. \end{cases}$$

(a) Let $\mathbf{Q}(\sqrt{m})$, $m < 0$ and $-m$ a prime $\equiv 3 \pmod 4$, be an imaginary quadratic field of discriminant d and of class number $h(d) = h$, an odd prime. Let $Q_k(x,y) = a_k x^2 + b_k xy + c_k y^2$, $a_k > 1$, $b_k > 0$, $k = 1, 2, \ldots, (h-1)/2$ be the reduced positive definite primitive quadratic forms of discriminant d associated with $\mathbf{Q}(\sqrt{m})$. Let $H_d(x)$ be the class equation of $\mathbf{Q}(\sqrt{m})$. Then

$$\Delta(H_d) = I^2 (-m)^{\frac{h-1}{2}} \quad \text{where } I = I_1 \cdots I_{\frac{h-1}{2}}$$

and

$$I_k = \prod_{n=1}^{-m-1} F_{-m}(-m-n)^{r_k(n)},$$

$$r_k(n) = \frac{1}{2}\#\{(x,y) \in \mathbf{Z}\times\mathbf{Z} \mid Q_k(x,y) = n\}.$$

In particular, the largest prime dividing $\Delta(H_d)$ does not exceed $-m$, and all its prime factors except $-m$ appear in even powers.

(b) Let z, $z' \in F$ be imaginary quadratic numbers belonging to two distinct imaginary quadratic fields $\mathbf{Q}(\sqrt{m})$ and $\mathbf{Q}(\sqrt{m'})$, respectively, where $-m$ and $-m'$ are primes $\equiv 3 \pmod 4$. Then

$$|Norm(j(z) - j(z'))| = \left[\prod_{\substack{0<x<\sqrt{mm'} \\ x \text{ odd}}} F_{-m'}\left(\frac{mm'-x^2}{4}\right)\right]^{\frac{w(m')}{2}},$$

where the *Norm* is taken over $\mathbf{Q}$ and $w(m')$ denotes the number of units in $\mathbf{Q}(\sqrt{m'})$.

In particular, taking $z = \dfrac{1+\sqrt{m}}{2}$ and $z' = \dfrac{1+\sqrt{-3}}{2}$, we have

$$|H_d(0)| = |Norm(j(\frac{1+\sqrt{m}}{2}))| = \left[\prod_{\substack{0<x<\sqrt{-3m} \\ x \text{ odd}}} F_{-3}\left(\frac{-3m-x^2}{4}\right)\right]^3$$

and therefore, the largest prime dividing $H_d(0)$ does not exceed $-m$. □

The table below summarizes the cases we considered.

m	$h(d)$	Order of Taylor exp.	Floating point precision	CPU time (VAX 780)
−71	7	25	50	123 sec.
−151	7	25	70	177 sec.
−223	7	25	70	164 sec.
−251	7	25	70	187 sec.
−463	7	25	100	219 sec.
−167	11	25	100	340 sec.
−271	11	30	100	431 sec.
−659	11	40	120	663 sec.

We shall illustrate our construction by two examples: $\mathbf{Q}(\sqrt{-251})$ and $\mathbf{Q}(\sqrt{-659})$. The remaining polynomials can be found in the full paper [8]. In each case we list quadratic form representatives as well as the polynomials H_d thus obtained. We factored out powers of primes ≤ 1000 dividing the coefficients. We also present the factored discriminant $\Delta(H_d)$.

$\mathbf{Q}(\sqrt{-251})$

Reduced quad. form			ϑ
x^2	$+xy$	$+63y^2$	$\frac{-1+\sqrt{-251}}{2}$
$3x^2$	$\pm xy$	$+21y^2$	$\frac{\mp 1+\sqrt{-251}}{6}$
$7x^2$	$\pm xy$	$+9y^2$	$\frac{\mp 1+\sqrt{-251}}{14}$
$5x^2$	$\pm xy$	$+13y^2$	$\frac{\mp 3+\sqrt{-251}}{10}$

$H_{-251}(x)$	
	x^7
$+\ 2^{17}\cdot 29\cdot 1086122234032811$	x^6
$-\ 2^{30}\cdot 3^4\cdot 7\cdot 13\cdot 8364869403342457$	x^5
$+\ 2^{49}\cdot 3^2\cdot 23\cdot 9113559120635943109$	x^4
$+\ 2^{60}\cdot 5\cdot 1381976650295197345607$	x^3
$+\ 2^{77}\cdot 11^3\cdot 2066916598433853809$	x^2
$-\ 2^{90}\cdot 11^6\cdot 817072976407817$	x^1
$+\ (2^{36}\cdot 11^3\cdot 29\cdot 47)^3$	

The discriminant is:

$$\Delta(H_{-251}) = -2^{664}11^{42}19^{24}29^{14}37^{10}43^8 47^8 53^8 59^6 61^6 71^6 107^2$$
$$\times 127^2 139^2 151^2 167^4 191^4 199^2 223^2 239^2 251^3.$$

$\mathbf{Q}(\sqrt{-659})$

Reduced quad. form			ϑ
x^2	$+xy$	$+165y^2$	$\frac{-1+\sqrt{-659}}{2}$
$3x^2$	$\pm xy$	$+55y^2$	$\frac{\mp 1+\sqrt{-659}}{6}$
$5x^2$	$\pm xy$	$+33y^2$	$\frac{\mp 1+\sqrt{-659}}{10}$
$11x^2$	$\pm xy$	$+15y^2$	$\frac{\mp 1+\sqrt{-659}}{22}$
$9x^2$	$\pm 5xy$	$+19y^2$	$\frac{\mp 5+\sqrt{-659}}{18}$
$13x^2$	$\pm 11xy$	$+15y^2$	$\frac{\mp 11+\sqrt{-659}}{26}$

$H_{-659}(x)$	
	x^{11}
$+\ 2^{16}\cdot 11\cdot 14690154361125471419369330393 9$	x^{10}
$-\ 2^{31}\cdot 3^{2}\cdot 11\cdot 23567595172557916437683376079427685 1$	x^{9}
$+\ 2^{46}\cdot 5\cdot 317\cdot 21253848824657244505372416849107899401473 3$	x^{8}
$-\ 2^{63}\cdot 433\cdot 677\cdot 1435389610078937172050502007367846700195 11$	x^{7}
$+\ 2^{76}\cdot 7\cdot 4588870126997653122952459557806209542390458567209$	x^{6}
$-\ 2^{91}\cdot 7\cdot 17\cdot 29\cdot 985109212020450689538604327952847403118219453$	x^{5}
$+\ 2^{106}\cdot 1759326328545462166944141915014487335482392315767$	x^{4}
$-\ 2^{120}\cdot 131\cdot 375056357736805200252366198765553414702693592 3$	x^{3}
$+\ 2^{138}\cdot 3^{2}\cdot 23\cdot 409\cdot 2744949824891485086917113543657720541419 7$	x^{2}
$-\ 2^{162}\cdot 3\cdot 41^{6}\cdot 227\cdot 281\cdot 226354343774362753281177 1$	x^{1}
$+\ (\ 2^{60}\cdot 29\cdot 41^{2}\cdot 47\cdot 71\cdot 101\cdot 113\ )^{3}$	

The discriminant is:

$$\Delta(H_{-659}) = -2^{1746}7^{222}29^{42}31^{36}41^{26}43^{28}47^{26}53^{20}67^{14}71^{18}83^{10}97^{6}101^{10}$$
$$\times\, 103^{10}113^{8}131^{12}137^{4}151^{6}191^{6}193^{4}197^{4}199^{4}223^{2}227^{4}263^{6}$$
$$\times\, 359^{6}367^{2}383^{4}419^{4}431^{4}439^{4}467^{2}479^{6}503^{4}599^{4}607^{2}647^{2}659^{5}.$$

Using a different modular function, the class equations with much smaller coefficients have been constructed by M. Hanna [5] for the imaginary quadratic fields $\mathbf{Q}(\sqrt{-167})$ and $\mathbf{Q}(\sqrt{-191})$ (class number 13) and by G. N. Watson [11] for the fields $\mathbf{Q}(\sqrt{-383})$ (class number 17) and $\mathbf{Q}(\sqrt{-311})$ (class number 19). The given polynomials are actually the h degree integral factors of $x^h H_d((x-16)^3/x)$, where h is the class number and H_d the equation corresponding to the modular function used. We can also carry out this transformation on our class equations resulting in polynomials with much smaller coefficients. Following we give Hanna's polynomial for $\mathbf{Q}(\sqrt{-167})$ which has also passed the test for having Galois group D_{11} described at the beginning of this paper:

$$x^{11}+x^{10}+5x^{9}+4x^{8}+10x^{7}+6x^{6}+11x^{5}+7x^{4}+9x^{3}+4x^{2}+2x-1.$$

Appendix

The Explicit Form of the Modular Equation of Prime Order

Let $j(z)$ be the elliptic modular invariant. It is a classical result going back to Kronecker (see, e.g. Weber [12, Sec. 69]) that *if $z = x + iy \in \mathbf{C}$ belongs to an imaginary quadratic field with $y > 0$, then $j(z)$ is an algebraic integer.* This was proven by showing that $j(z)$ satisfies an algebraic equation with integral coefficients, called the *modular equation* (of order n for some $n > 1$).

However, the explicit form of the modular equation has not been known, except for few cases (cf. Fricke [3, II.4]).†

In this appendix, we shall discuss how to determine explicitly the modular equations of order p where $p = 5$ and 7. For a prime p, let

$$A = \left\{ \begin{bmatrix} p & 0 \\ 0 & 1 \end{bmatrix}, \begin{bmatrix} 1 & i \\ 0 & p \end{bmatrix} \text{ with } 0 \le i < p \right\}.$$

For $\alpha = \begin{bmatrix} a & b \\ c & d \end{bmatrix} \in A$ and for $z = x + iy \in \mathbf{C}$, $y > 0$, we write $j \bullet \alpha$ for

$$(j \bullet \alpha)(z) = j(\alpha(z)) = j(\frac{az+b}{cz+d}),$$

and form the polynomial

$$\Phi_p(x) = \prod_{\alpha \in A} (x - j \bullet \alpha) = \prod_{\alpha \in A} (x - j(\alpha(z)).$$

We can view $\Phi_p(x)$ as a polynomial in two variables x and j over Z,

$$\Phi_p(x) = \Phi_p(x, j) \in \mathbf{Z}[x, j],$$

and we call it the *modular polynomial of order* p The importance of this polynomial is that there exists a prime p such that $\Phi_p(j(z), j(z)) = 0$. Since the leading coefficient of $\Phi_p(x, x)$ is $-x^{2p}$ $j(z)$ must be an algebraic integer. The equation $\Phi_p(x, j) = 0$ is called the *modular equation of order* p.

The modular equations of order p can be very difficult to determine explicitly as the cases $p = 2$ and 3 already suggest (cf. [3]). We shall make use of the following result.

Theorem (Yui [13]): Let $j^*(z) = j(pz)$ with $z = x + iy$, $y > 0$. Then

$$0 = \Phi_p(j^*, j) = (j^{*p} - j)(j^* - j^p) - p \sum_{m=1}^{p} \sum_{n=0}^{m-1} d_{m,n}(j^{*m} j^n + j^{*n} j^m)$$

$$- p \sum_{m=0}^{p-1} d_{m,m} j^{*m} j^m,$$

where $d_{m,n}$ and $d_{m,m}$ are integers. □

The coefficients $d_{m,n}$ and $d_{m,m}$ can be determined by noting that $j^*(q) = j(q^p)$ and then comparing the coefficients of the q-expansions of the identity in the above theorem. In order to obtain an equation for $d_{0,0}$ one must expand the this equation from q^{-p^2-p} through q^0. Therefore one needs the q-expansion of j to the order $p^2 + p - 1$. Using this algorithm we could successfully determine Φ_5 and Φ_7. We present the explicit form of Φ_7, again primes $\le$ 1000 factored out of the coefficients. Φ_5 is given in the full paper [8].

---

† It was brought to our attention after we had completed our computations that W. Berwick [1] already determined Φ_5 and O. Herrmann [6] Φ_7. Their results coincide with ours but it appears to us that our methods are much more efficient.

$$
\begin{aligned}
\Phi_7(j^*,j) = 0 = \\
& j^{*8} + \cdot 2^3 \cdot 3 \cdot 7 \cdot 31 \cdot (j^6 \cdot j^{*7} + j^7 \cdot j^{*6}) \\
& - 13553 \cdot 2^2 \cdot 3^3 \cdot 7 \cdot (j^5 \cdot j^{*7} + j^7 \cdot j^{*5}) \\
& + 2^5 \cdot 5^2 \cdot 7^2 \cdot 11 \cdot 43 \cdot 509 \cdot (j^4 \cdot j^{*7} + j^7 \cdot j^{*4}) \\
& - 1067425727 \cdot 2 \cdot 3 \cdot 7^2 \cdot 13 \cdot (j^3 \cdot j^{*7} + j^7 \cdot j^{*3}) \\
& + 263733037 \cdot 2^4 \cdot 3^4 \cdot 7^2 \cdot 43 \cdot (j^2 \cdot j^{*7} + j^7 \cdot j^{*2}) \\
& - 6866816589877 \cdot 2^3 \cdot 7^2 \cdot 13 \cdot (j \cdot j^{*7} + j^7 \cdot j^{*}) \\
& + 26891 \cdot 2^{16} \cdot 3^7 \cdot 5^3 \cdot 7 \cdot 31 \cdot (j^{*7} + j^7) - j^7 \cdot j^{*7} \\
& + 32268467570786329 \cdot 2^4 \cdot 7^3 \cdot (j^5 \cdot j^{*6} + j^6 \cdot j^{*5}) \\
& + 379331842110025370170 7 \cdot 2^3 \cdot 3 \cdot 7^2 \cdot (j^4 \cdot j^{*6} + j^6 \cdot j^{*4}) \\
& + 37855451213001141 1 \cdot 2^4 \cdot 3^5 \cdot 5 \cdot 7^2 \cdot 197 \cdot 227 \cdot (j^3 \cdot j^{*6} + j^6 \cdot j^{*3}) \\
& + 18798746666818144486823766 7 \cdot 2^2 \cdot 7^2 \cdot 29 \cdot (j^2 \cdot j^{*6} + j^6 \cdot j^{*2}) \\
& + 100209091554964896 83 \cdot 2^{17} \cdot 3^7 \cdot 5^3 \cdot 7^2 \cdot 59 \cdot (j \cdot j^{*6} + j^6 \cdot j^{*}) \\
& + 1323331291097 \cdot 2^{30} \cdot 3^{10} \cdot 5^6 \cdot 7 \cdot 397 \cdot (j^{*6} + j^6) \\
& + 8389943 \cdot 3^2 \cdot 7^2 \cdot 13 \cdot 67 \cdot 97 \cdot j^6 \cdot j^{*6} \\
& + 356412911341706617863901 3 \cdot 2^5 \cdot 3^4 \cdot 5^2 \cdot 7^2 \cdot 11 \cdot 113 \\
& \cdot (j^4 \cdot j^{*5} + j^5 \cdot j^{*4}) \\
& - 2300115592182896081319172688113678807 \cdot 2^3 \cdot 7^2 \\
& \cdot (j^3 \cdot j^{*5} + j^5 \cdot j^{*3}) \\
& + 1782990756994387786210993942 69 \cdot 2^{19} \cdot 3^9 \cdot 5^3 \cdot 7^2 \\
& \cdot (j^2 \cdot j^{*5} + j^5 \cdot j^{*2}) \\
& - 3492578772271181253826420 1 \cdot 2^{33} \cdot 3^{11} \cdot 5^6 \cdot 7^2 \cdot (j \cdot j^{*5} + j^5 \cdot j^{*}) \\
& + 1811220973714061 53 \cdot 2^{47} \cdot 3^{16} \cdot 5^9 \cdot 7^2 \cdot 13 \cdot 31 \cdot (j^{*5} + j^5) \\
& - 1037461288985651353819150 7 \cdot 2^2 \cdot 3^2 \cdot 7^2 \cdot j^5 \cdot j^{*5} \\
& + 3893394856539704079067727101 \cdot 2^{16} \cdot 3^7 \cdot 5^4 \cdot 7^2 \cdot 37 \cdot 43 \cdot 661 \\
& \cdot (j^3 \cdot j^{*4} + j^4 \cdot j^{*3}) \\
& + 6234974029742652978204929527 9 \cdot 2^{31} \cdot 3^{11} \cdot 5^6 \cdot 7^2 \cdot 17 \\
& \cdot (j^2 \cdot j^{*4} + j^4 \cdot j^{*2}) \\
& + 4893785884751115482052 1 \cdot 2^{46} \cdot 3^{17} \cdot 5^9 \cdot 7^2 \cdot 13 \cdot (j \cdot j^{*4} + j^4 \cdot j^{*}) \\
& + 1323331291097 \cdot 2^{60} \cdot 3^{19} \cdot 5^{12} \cdot 7^2 \cdot 17^3 \cdot 397 \cdot (j^{*4} + j^4) \\
& + 912019631831096138476499139089037899 \cdot 2 \cdot 5 \cdot 7^2 \cdot 197 \cdot j^4 \cdot j^{*4} \\
& + 6095183243739692415286 63 \cdot 2^{46} \cdot 3^{16} \cdot 5^9 \cdot 7^2 \cdot 409 \cdot (j^2 \cdot j^{*3} + j^3 \cdot j^{*2})
\end{aligned}
$$

$$
\begin{aligned}
&-88980809456419 \cdot 2^{61} \cdot 3^{19} \cdot 5^{12} \cdot 7^{2} \cdot 17^{3} \cdot 19 \cdot 487 \cdot (j \cdot j^{*3} + j^{3} \cdot j^{*}) \\
&+ 26891 \cdot 2^{76} \cdot 3^{25} \cdot 5^{15} \cdot 7^{3} \cdot 17^{6} \cdot 31 \cdot (j^{*3} + j^{3}) \\
&- 5559535565766995052158900399 1731 \cdot 2^{31} \cdot 3^{10} \cdot 5^{6} \cdot 7^{2} \cdot j^{3} \cdot j^{*3} \\
&- 22541 \cdot 2^{76} \cdot 3^{25} \cdot 5^{15} \cdot 7^{2} \cdot 17^{7} \cdot 947 \cdot (j \cdot j^{*2} + j^{2} \cdot j^{*}) \\
&+ 2^{90} \cdot 3^{27} \cdot 5^{18} \cdot 7^{3} \cdot 17^{9} \cdot (j^{*2} + j^{2}) \\
&- 98755869850221841 \cdot 2^{61} \cdot 3^{20} \cdot 5^{12} \cdot 7^{2} \cdot 17^{3} \cdot j^{2} \cdot j^{*2} \\
&+ 2^{91} \cdot 3^{27} \cdot 5^{18} \cdot 11 \cdot 13 \cdot 17^{9} \cdot j \cdot j^{*} + j^{8}.
\end{aligned}
$$

The computation of Φ_5 took 982 seconds and the one of Φ_7 4091 seconds CPU time on a VAX 780. During the computation of Φ_{11} we ran out of virtual storage after approximately 7 hours of CPU time. We have recently developed a modified version of the above algorithm for computing Φ_p which is much less space consuming and which has already successfully computed the explicit form of Φ_{11} [9].

The modular polynomial $\Phi_p(x, x)$ factors into the product of powers of some class equations (cf. Weber [12, Sec. 116]). For $p = 7$, the factorization is the following.

$$
\begin{aligned}
\Phi_7(x, x) = &-x^2 (x - 3^3 \cdot 5^3 \cdot 17^3)(x - 2^4 \cdot 3^3 \cdot 5^3)^2 \\
&\times (x + 3^3 \cdot 5^3)(x + 2^{15} \cdot 3^3)^2 (x + 2^{15} \cdot 3 \cdot 5^3)^2 \\
&\times (x^2 - 2^7 \cdot 3^3 \cdot 1399 x + 2^{12} \cdot 3^6 \cdot 17^3)^2.
\end{aligned}
$$

Acknowledgement

We wish to thank the Department of Mathematics at Kent State University for allowing us to use their research VAX 780 for carrying out our computations. In particular, we are indebted to Professor Paul Wang for his advice on the usage of MACSYMA. We also wish to thank all colleagues who commented on an earlier version of this paper. Especially, we thank Professor Don Zagier for explaining us his joint results with Professor Benedict Gross. We also thank Professor David Chudnovsky and Professor Gregory Chudnovsky for bringing the work of M. Hanna and G. N. Watson to our attention.

References

[1] W. E. H. Berwick, "An invariant modular equation of the fifth order," *Quarterly J. Math.*, 47, 1916, pp. 94-103.

[2] M. Deuring, "Die Klassenkörper der komplexen Multiplikation," *Enzyklopädie Math. Wiss.* v. 12 (Book 10, part II), Teubner, Stuttgart, 1958.

[3] R. Fricke, *Lehrbuch der Algebra, Bd.* 3, Braunschweig, 1928.

[4] B. Gross and D. Zagier, in preparation.

[5] M. Hanna, "The modular equations," *Proc. London Math. Soc.*, 28, 1928, pp. 46-52.

[6] O. Herrmann, "Über die Berechnung der Fourierkoeffizienten der Funktion $j(\tau)$," *J. Reine Angew. Math.* 274/275, 1974, pp. 187-195.

[7] C. U. Jensen and N. Yui, "Polynomials with D_p as Galois group," *J. Number Theory* v. 15, 1982, pp. 347-375.

[8] E. Kaltofen and N. Yui, "Explicit construction of the Hilbert class fields of imaginary quadratic fields with class numbers 7 and 11," *Math. Comp.*, submitted.

[9] E. Kaltofen and N. Yui, "On the Modular Equation of Order 11," manuscript 1984.

[10] MACSYMA, Reference Manual, v. 1 and 2, the Mathlab Group, Laboratory for Computer Science, MIT 1983.

[11] G. N. Watson, "Singular Moduli (4)," *Acta Arith.*, 1, 1935, pp. 284-323.

[12] H. Weber, *Lehrbuch der Algebra, Bd.* 3, Braunschweig, 1908.

[13] N. Yui, "Explicit form of the modular equation," *J. Reine Angew. Math.*, 299/300, 1978, pp. 185-200.

On A Simple Primality Testing Algorithm

Ming-Deh A. Huang

Department of Electrical Engineering and Computer Science

Princeton University, Princeton, New Jersey 08544

1. Introduction

Primality testing has long been a subject of research interest. A major progress in recent years was reported in a paper of Adleman [A], and a subsequent paper of Adleman, Pomerance, and Rumely [APR]. The primality testing algorithm reported in [APR] (we will call it the *APR-test*) stands for the first successful attempt to bring dowm the complexity of primality testing to within a sub-exponential bound $O(logn^{O(logloglogn)})$.

In the APR-test, a number in question is tested against pairs of "small" testing primes - the *initial primes* and the *Euclidean primes*. A number that passes a series of such tests can be proved to have a very small set of possible divisors. Such a set is then computed, and the testing is finally reduced to trivial trial division. The sub-exponential bound on the running time is essentially a bound on the product of the initial primes, which also provides a bound on the number of pairs of testing primes used in the algorithm.

Mathematically speaking, APR-test is a delicate application of reciprocity laws. It motivated a series of new approaches to the primality testing [Le1], [Le2], which then lead to algorithms that achieve various degrees of simplification. All these algorithms fall under the similar scheme for the choice of testing primes. Therefore, the asymptotic sub-exponential time bound remain unchallenged. However, they indicate that there is still much room for improvement even under the APR-scheme of choosing testing primes.

Most recently, Cohen and Lenstra [CL] reported a probabilistic primality testing algorithm which is very efficient in practical terms, although the expected running time stays in the same sub-exponential bound. Besides practical improvement on the APR-test, the Cohen-Lenstra test is also of theoretical interest. In the original APR-test, the central stage is devoted to testing the following kind of property:

$\text{ind}_q(r) \equiv k \cdot \Theta \bmod p$, for some $k \in N$,

where r is a prime factor of the tested number n, p is an initial prime, q is an Euclidean prime with $p \mid q-1$, $\text{ind}_q(r)$ is the index of r in $(Z/qZ)^*$ with respect to a chosen generator of the group, and Θ is a computed number depending on p and q. In the final stage, it has to solve, for every Euclidean prime q, systems of congruences with the initial primes dividing $q-1$ as moduli. It then has to solve systems of congruences with the Euclidean primes as moduli in order to determine the set of all possible divisors of n not exceeding $n^{1/2}$. In [CL], it is shown that the following stronger property can indeed be tested in the central stage:

(1.2) There is some $m > n^{1/2}$, and $o(n \bmod m)$ in the group $(Z/mZ)^*$ is bounded by $\log n^{c\log\log\log n}$ for some constant c, so that for every $r \mid n$, $r \equiv n^a \bmod m$ for some $a \in N$.

The fact that (1.2) can be tested in the central stage reduces the final stage to simple trial division. This can be taken as an important factor for the practical efficiency of the Cohen-Lenstra test. Also in this test, a more flexible choice of testing primes is allowed. One distint feature of this test is that it replaces the use of higher reciprocity laws by elementary properties of Gauss sums. Therefore, it is a simplified primality test without the use of reciprocity laws.

In this paper, we present a simplified primality testing algorithm that uses reciprocity laws. The simplification is resulted from a refined analysis that incorporates Artin symbols, reciprocity laws, and valuational ideas. We show that the stronger property (1.2) can be tested in a simple way. The need for solving bulk systems of congruences is eliminated, the final stage is reduced to trial division, and the central stage is also simplified considerably. For this simplified probabilistic version of APR-test, the same upper bound for the expected running time, $O(\log n^{O(\log\log\log n)})$, can be established.

2. Overview

As the test described in [APR], we will choose, for the tested number n, a set E of *Euclidean primes* and a set I of *initial primes* that satisfy the following properties:

i) For every Euclidean prime $q \in E$, $q-1$ divide the product of the initial primes, and is therefore square free.

ii) $m = \prod_{q \in E} q > n^{1/2}$.

By a result due to Odlyzko and Pomerance [APR], E and I can be chosen so that $\prod_{p \in I} p < \log n^{c_0\log\log\log n}$, where c_0 is an effectively computable constant.

The main task in the first stage of our algorithm is to prepare the set of Euclidean primes and the set of initial primes.

The central stage of our algorithm is devoted to testing the following property:

(2.1) For each initial prime $p \in I$ and each prime factor r of n, there is $a_r \in N$ such that for every Euclidean prime q with $p \mid q-1$, we have

$$\mathrm{ind}_q(r) \equiv \mathrm{ind}_q(n)a_r \pmod p$$

where ind_q is defined with respect to a chosen generator of $(Z/qZ)^*$

After (2.1) is tested, a small set that contains all the possible prime factors of n is determined. Finally by simple trial division, we will be able to determine whether n is prime or not.

The property (2.1) is actually equivalent to the property that

(2.2) For all $r \mid n$, $r \equiv n^i \pmod m$ for some $i \in N$, where $m = \prod_{q \in E} q$.

We prove this in the following lemma.

(2.3) **Lemma** (2.1) => (2.2)

Proof Suppose (2.1) holds, by Chinese Remainder Theorem, there is $a \in N$ such that

(2.4) $a \equiv a_r \pmod p$ for all $p \in I$.

From (2.1) and (2.4), we have $\mathrm{ind}_q(r) \equiv \mathrm{ind}_q(n)a \pmod p$ for all $q \in E$ with $p \mid q-1$. Therefore,

(2.5) $\mathrm{ind}_q(r) \equiv \mathrm{ind}_q(n)a \pmod{q-1}$

Let t_q be the chosen generator for $(Z/qZ)^*$, then (2.5) => $t_q^{\mathrm{ind}_q(r)} \equiv t_q^{\mathrm{ind}_q(n)a} \pmod q$. Therefore, $r \equiv n^a \pmod q$ for all $q \in E$, and $r \equiv n^a \pmod m$, where $m = \prod_{q \in E} q$ ▪

In Section 3 to Section 5, we will develop the theoretical results on which the testing algorithm will be based. The algorithm will be presented in Section 6.

3. Testing properties regarding Artin symbol and residue class degree

Suppose a number n is prime, then the following is trivially true:

(3.1) For any prime p, and for any prime r dividing n, $r \equiv n^i \pmod p$ for some $i \in N$.

In this section, we will discuss how this property can be tested. In the primality testing algorithm, it will be tested with p being an initial prime.

Let us start with some consideration regarding cyclotomic fields and Artin symbols. Let $m \in N$ and ζ_m be a primitive m-th root of unity. Let $G = Gal(Q(\zeta_m)/Q)$ be the Galois group of the cyclotomic field $Q(\zeta_m)$ over Q, and let $(Z/mZ)^*$ be the group of units in the ring Z/mZ. We know that there is a natural isomorphism between G and $(Z/mZ)^*$ which sends σ_r to $r \bmod m$ for r coprime to m, where σ_r is the *Artin symbol* for r which is characterized by $\sigma_r : \zeta_m \to \zeta_m^r$. For prime r that doesn't divide m, let $H_r = < \sigma_r >$ be the group generated by σ_r, then H_r is the decomposition group for every prime ideal γ above r in $Q(\zeta_m)$. Since r doesn't divide m, it is unramified in $Q(\zeta_m)$, therefore H_r is isomorphic to $Gal\,((Z[\zeta_m]/\gamma)/(Z/rZ))$ for all $\gamma | r$ in $Q(\zeta_m)$.

Let $f(\gamma/r)$ denote the residue class degree of the prime γ above r in $Q(\zeta_m)$, then we have

(3.2) $f(\gamma/r) = [\, Z[\zeta_m]/\gamma : Z/rZ \,] = [\, H_r : 1 \,] = o(r \bmod m)$ in $(Z/mZ)^*$.

We shall need the following *Kummer Theorem* which gives explicit description of the decomposition of a prime in an algebraic number field. We will use it for testing (3.1) which is closely related to Artin symbols and residue class degrees.

(3.3) **Theorem** Let A be a Dedekind ring with quotient field F, K be a finite algebraic extension of F and B be the integral closure of A in K. Suppose $B=A[\alpha]$ with $\alpha \in B$. Let $f(x)$ be the irreducible polynomial of α over F. Let r be a non-zero prime ideal in A, $\overline{f}$ be the reduction of f mod r, and let $\overline{f} = \overline{t_1}^{e_1} \cdots \overline{t_g}^{e_g}$ be the factorization of $\overline{f}$ into powers of irreducible factors with leading coefficients 1 in $(A/r)[x]$. Then $rB = \gamma_1^{e_1} \cdots \gamma_g^{e_g}$ is the factorization of p in B into powers of prime ideals above r in B, where $e_i = e(\gamma_i/p)$, $f_i = f(\gamma_i/p) = deg(\overline{t_i})$, $i=1,\ldots,g$.∎

The following Proposition can be proved using Theorem(3.3).

(3.4) **Proposition** Suppose the following is true

(3.5) p is a prime that does not divide n, and $\Phi_p \equiv \prod_{i=1}^{g} h_i(x) \bmod n$ where h_i are integral polynomials with leading coefficients 1, and degree$(h_i) = f$ with $f = o(n \bmod p)$ in $(Z/pZ)^*$.

Then for any prime r dividing n, putting $f_r = o(r \bmod p)$, we have

(3.6) $r \bmod p \in < n \bmod p >$, and $f_r | f$.

4. Valuation test

In this section, we discuss the testing of a valuational property which will also be needed in the algorithm. Throughout this section, we fix a cyclotomic field $Q(\zeta_p)$, where p is a prime and ζ_p is a primitive p-th root of unity. We let ν_p denote the p-adic valuation in Q, that is, if we express a rational number a as $a = p^k \frac{x}{y}$, where $k, x, y \in Z$, and p does not divide x and y, then $\nu_p(a) = k$. We let Z_p denote the valuation ring of ν_p in Q, that is, $Z_p = \{ a \in Q \mid \nu_p(a) \geq 0 \}$. We also fix a number $n \in N$ not divisible by p, and let $f = o(n \bmod p)$ in $(Z/pZ)^*$. For a prime factor r of n, we let

$$f_r = o(r \bmod p) \text{ in } (Z/pZ)^*$$

$$= f(\gamma/r), \text{ the residue class degree of any prime } \gamma \mid r \text{ in } Q(\zeta_p).$$

We shall show how to test the following property which holds if n is prime:

(4.1) $\nu_p(r^{f_r}-1) \geq \nu_p(n^f-1)$, for any prime $r \mid n$.

For prime $r \mid n$, since $f_r = f(\gamma/r)$ for any prime $\gamma \mid r$ in $Q(\zeta_p)$, $Z[\zeta_p]/\gamma = F_{r_1}$, where $r_1 = r^{f_r}$. So for $\beta \in Z[\zeta_p]$ that is coprime to γ, we have $\beta^{r^{f_r}-1} \equiv 1 \pmod{\gamma}$. Since $r^{f_r} \equiv 1 \pmod{p}$, it follows that

(4.2) $\beta^{(r^{f_r}-1)/p} \equiv \zeta_p^{i(r)} \pmod{\gamma}$, for some $i(r) \in N$.

Notice that the right hand side of (4.2) is nothing but the power residue symbol $\left(\frac{\beta}{\gamma}\right)_p$ which is uniquely defined.

(4.3) **Lemma** Let $\hat{n} = (n, h_i(\zeta_p))$ where h_i is a factor in the decomposition of $\Phi_p \bmod n$ in (3.5). Let $\beta \in Z[\zeta_p]$. Suppose $\beta^{(n^f-1)/p} \equiv \zeta_p^{j(n)} \pmod{\hat{n}}$, for some $j(n) \in N$, $j(n) \not\equiv 0 \pmod{p}$. Then $\nu_p(r^{f_r}-1) \geq \nu_p(n^f-1)$, for any prime $r \mid n$. ▪

For $p = 2$, $Z[\zeta_p] = Z$, $f = f_r = 1$, and $\zeta_p = -1$, so Lemma (4.3) is simplified to:

Corollary Let b be a natural number less than n. Suppose $b^{\frac{n-1}{2}} \equiv -1 \pmod{n}$. Then $\nu_p(r-1) \geq \nu_p(n-1)$ for any prime $r \mid n$.

(4.4) **Lemma** For $\beta \in Z[\zeta_p]$, $\beta^{(r^{f_r}-1)/p} \equiv 1 \pmod{\gamma} \Rightarrow \beta \in (Z[\zeta_p]/\gamma)^{*p}$ ▪

Since $[\,(Z[\zeta_p]/\gamma)^* : (Z[\zeta_p]/\gamma)^{*p}\,] = p$, by Lemma (4.4), if we choose $\beta \in Z[\zeta_p]$ randomly, then with probability $1-\frac{1}{p}$, $\beta^{(r^{f_r}-1)/p} \not\equiv 1 \pmod{\gamma}$.

The following technical lemma will be used later on.

(4.5) **Lemma** Suppose $n = \prod_{\text{prime } r \mid n} r^{k(r)}$, with $k(r) \in N$. Suppose $\nu_p(r^{f_r}-1) \geq \nu_p(n^f-1)$, and $f_r \mid f$ for all $r \mid n$. Let $c_r = \frac{f}{f_r}$. Then $\sum_{r \mid n} \frac{(r^{f_r}-1)c_r k(r)}{(n^f-1)} \equiv 1 \bmod p$

5. Main results

We first recall the definitions of *power residue symbol*, *Jacobi sums*, and some basic properties regarding reciprocity laws. The readers are referred to [APR], [AT], or [CF] for detailed information.

(5.1)*power residue symbol* $\left(\ \right)_p$: Let r, p be two different prime numbers, and γ be a prime ideal above r in $Q(\zeta_p)$. Then for $\alpha \in Z[\zeta_p]$ which is not divisible by γ, there is a unique p-th root of unity $\left(\frac{\alpha}{\gamma}\right)_p$ such that $\alpha^{(N(\gamma)-1)/p} \equiv \left(\frac{\alpha}{\gamma}\right)_p \bmod \gamma$, where $N(\gamma) = [Z(\zeta_p]/\gamma : 1]$ is the absolute norm of γ. Note that since $f_r = o(r \bmod p) = f(\gamma/r)$, $N(\gamma) = r^{f_r}$, and $\alpha^{(r^{f_r}-1)/p} \equiv \left(\frac{\alpha}{\gamma}\right)_p \bmod \gamma$.

(5.2) The definition of power residue symbol can be extended multiplicatively. Namely, for a set S of prime ideals that do not divide p, and for α not divisible by any prime ideal in S, define

$$\left(\frac{\alpha}{\prod_{\gamma \in S} \gamma}\right)_p = \prod_{\gamma \in S} \left(\frac{\alpha}{\gamma}\right)_p .$$

In particular, if $\beta \in Z[\zeta_p]$ is coprime to α and p, let $\beta = \prod_{\gamma | \beta} \gamma^{n_\gamma}$, then

$$\left(\frac{\alpha}{\beta}\right)_p = \prod_{\gamma | \beta} \left(\frac{\alpha}{\gamma}\right)_p^{n_\gamma} .$$

(5.3) The following properties are easily verified:

(a) $\sigma \in Gal(Q(\zeta_p)/Q)$, then $\sigma\left(\frac{\alpha}{\gamma}\right)_p = \left(\frac{\sigma\alpha}{\sigma\gamma}\right)_p$.

(b) For $\alpha_1, \alpha_2 \in Z[\zeta_p]$ not divisible by γ, $\left(\frac{\alpha_1\alpha_2}{\gamma}\right)_p = \left(\frac{\alpha_1}{\gamma}\right)_p \left(\frac{\alpha_2}{\gamma}\right)_p$.

(5.4) *Jacobi sums*: Let p, q be two different prime numbers, $\hat{q}$ be a prime ideal above q in $Q(\zeta_p)$. For $a, b \in Z$, we define the Jacobi sum

$$J_{a,b}(\hat{q}) = \sum{}' \left(\frac{x}{\hat{q}}\right)_p^{-a} \left(\frac{1-x}{\hat{q}}\right)_p^{-b} .$$

where $\sum'$ denotes the sum over a set of representatives of $Z[\zeta_p]/\hat{q}$ other than o, $1 \bmod \hat{q}$.

(5.5) Suppose $a, b \in Z$ with $ab(a+b) \neq 0 \pmod p$. For $u \in Z$, let

$$\vartheta_{a,b}(u) = [\ \frac{a+b}{p}u\ ] - [\ \frac{a}{p}u\ ] + [\ \frac{b}{p}u\ ].$$

where $[x]$ denotes the largest integer not exceeding x (so $\vartheta_{a,b}(u) = 0$ or 1). Then

$$(J_{a,b}(\hat{q})) = \prod_{u=1}^{p-1} \sigma_u^{-1}(\hat{q})^{\vartheta_{a,b}(u)}.$$

Note that $\vartheta_{a+kp,b+lp}(u) = \vartheta_{a,b}(u)$ for $k,l \in Z$.

(5.6) If $p>2$, then there are $a,b \in Z$, $ab(a+b) \neq 0$ (mod p), such that

$$\sum_{u=1}^{p-1} \vartheta_{a,b}(u)u^{-1} \neq 0 \ (\bmod p)$$

where $uu^{-1} \equiv 1$ (mod p). We denote the above expression by $\hat{\vartheta}_{a,b}$.

(5.7) Let $J = -J_{a,b}(\hat{q})$, where a,b are chosen as in (5.6). Then for $r \in N$ that is not divisible by q, and $p>2$,

$$\left(\frac{r}{J}\right)_p = \left(\frac{J}{r}\right)_p.$$

(5.8) Suppose p, q are different prime numbers and $p \mid q-1$. Let t_q be a generator of $(Z/qZ)^*$ that we chose to define ind_q. Let $\hat{q}$ be the "canonical" prime ideal above q with respect to t_q:

$$\hat{q} = (\, q,\ \zeta_p - t_q^{(q-1)/p}\,).$$

Then for $r \in N$ not divisible by q,

(a) $$\left(\frac{r}{\hat{q}}\right)_p = \zeta_p^{\text{ind}_q(r)}.$$

(b) $$\left(\frac{r}{J}\right)_p = \left(\frac{r}{\hat{q}}\right)_p^{\hat{\vartheta}_{a,b}} = \zeta_p^{\text{ind}_q(r)\hat{\vartheta}_{a,b}}. \quad \blacksquare$$

Now we start to derive the main results we need for testing primes.

Case $p>2$

Assume p is a prime and $p>2$. For an integer r that is not divisible by p, any prime ideal in $Q(\zeta_p)$ containing r is unramified, so by (5.2), we have

(5.9) $$\left(\frac{J}{r}\right)_p = \prod_{\gamma \mid r}\left(\frac{J}{\gamma}\right)_p.$$

Let

(5.10) $G = Gal(Q(\zeta_p)/Q) = \{\, \sigma_i \mid \sigma_i : \zeta_p \to \zeta_p^i,\ i = 0,\dots,p-1 \,\}$.

For integer r prime to p, let

$H_r = <\sigma_r>$ = the decomposition group for every prime $\gamma | r$ in $Q(\zeta_p)$.

We can express G as

(5.11) $\quad G = \bigcup_{i=1}^{g_r} \sigma_{a_i} H_r$, where $g_r = \frac{p-1}{f_r}$ with $f_r = o(r \bmod p) = [H_r{:}1]$, and σ_{a_i} are the coset representatives of G/H_r.

(5.12) **Lemma** Let

(5.13) $\quad \alpha = J^{\sum_{i=0}^{p-1} \sigma_i^{-1} i}$

Then

(5.14) $$\zeta_p^{\mathrm{ind}_q(r)(-\hat{\vartheta}_{a,b})} = \left(\frac{\alpha^{g_r}}{\gamma}\right)_p \equiv \alpha^{(r^{f_r}-1)g_r/p} \bmod \gamma,$$

for any prime ideal $\gamma | r$, consequently $\zeta_p^{\mathrm{ind}_q(r)(-\hat{\vartheta}_{a,b})} \equiv \alpha^{(r^{f_r}-1)g_r/p} \bmod rZ[\zeta_p]$.

Proof

$$\left(\frac{J}{r}\right)_p^{f_r} = \left(\prod_{\gamma | r}\left(\frac{J}{\gamma}\right)\right)^{f_r} = \prod_{i=1}^{g_r}\left(\frac{J}{\gamma^{\sigma_{a_i}}}\right)^{f_r} = \prod_{i=1}^{g_r}\prod_{\sigma \in H_r}\left(\frac{J}{\gamma^{\sigma\sigma_{a_i}}}\right) \quad \text{by (5.11)}$$

$$= \prod_{i=0}^{p-1}\left(\frac{J}{\gamma^{\sigma_i}}\right) = \prod_{i=0}^{p-1}\sigma_i\left(\frac{J^{\sigma_i^{-1}}}{\gamma}\right) = \prod_{i=0}^{p-1}\left(\frac{J^{\sigma_i^{-1}}}{\gamma}\right)^i \quad \text{by (5.3)(a), (5.10)}$$

$$= \prod_{i=0}^{p-1}\left(\frac{J^{\sigma_i^{-1} i}}{\gamma}\right) = \left(\frac{\left(\prod_{i=0}^{p-1} J^{\sigma_i^{-1} i}\right)}{\gamma}\right) \quad \text{by (5.3)(b)}$$

$$= \left(\frac{J^{\sum_{i=0}^{p-1}\sigma_i^{-1} i}}{\gamma}\right) = \left(\frac{\alpha}{\gamma}\right)$$

On the other hand, by (5.8)(b), $\left(\frac{r}{J}\right)^{f_r} = \zeta_p^{\mathrm{ind}_q(r)\hat{\vartheta}_{a,b} f_r}$. Therefore,

(5.15) $$\left(\frac{\alpha}{\gamma}\right) = \zeta_p^{\mathrm{ind}_q(r)\hat{\vartheta}_{a,b} f_r}.$$

Since $f_r g_r = p-1 \equiv -1 \bmod p$, rasing both sides of (5.15) to the g_r-th power, we have $\zeta_p^{\mathrm{ind}_q(r)(-\hat{\vartheta}_{a,b})} = \left(\frac{\alpha}{\gamma}\right)^{g_r} = \left(\frac{\alpha^{g_r}}{\gamma}\right)$

(5.16) **Proposition** Let n be a natural number, r be a prime factor of n. Suppose $f_r \mid f$,

(5.17) $\quad \nu_p(r^{f_r}-1) \geq \nu_p(n^f-1)$, and

(5.18) $\quad \alpha^{(n^f-1)g/p} \equiv \zeta_p^{\,j(n)} \bmod nZ[\zeta_p]$, where $j(n) \in N, fg = p-1$,

and α is defined by (5.13).

Then $\mathrm{ind}_q(r) \equiv \mathrm{ind}_q(n)\cdot a_r \bmod p$, where $a_r \in N$ and $a_r \equiv \dfrac{(r^{f_r}-1)c_r}{(n^f-1)} \bmod p$ with $c_r = \dfrac{f}{f_r}$.

Proof Since $g, g_r < p$, $\nu_p((r^{f_r}-1)g_r) = \nu_p(r^{f_r}-1) \geq \nu_p(n^f-1) = \nu_p((n^f-1)g)$. Therefore,

(5.19) $$\frac{(r^{f_r}-1)g_r}{(n^f-1)g} = \frac{a_r}{b_r} \text{ where } a_r, b_r \in N, \text{ and } b_r \equiv 1 \bmod p.$$

Putting $i(r) = \mathrm{ind}_q(r)(-\hat{\vartheta}_{a,b})$ in (5.14), by (5.14), (5.18) and (5.19),

$$\zeta_p^{\,i(r)} = \zeta_p^{\,i(r)b_r} \equiv \alpha^{(r^{f_r}-1)g_r b_r/p} \bmod \gamma$$

$$\equiv \alpha^{(n^f-1)g a_r/p} \equiv \zeta_p^{\,j(n)a_r} \bmod \gamma. \text{ So,}$$

(5.20) $$\zeta_p^{\,i(r)} = \zeta_p^{\,j(n)a_r}$$

If $n = \prod_{r \mid n} r^{k(r)}$, then $\prod_{r\mid n} \zeta_p^{\,i(r)k(r)} = \prod_{r\mid n} \zeta_p^{\,j(n)a_r k(r)} = \zeta_p^{\sum_{r\mid n} i(r)k(r)} = \zeta_p^{\,j(n)\sum_{r\mid n} a_r k(r)}$, and

$$\sum_{r\mid n} i(r)k(r) = (-\hat{\vartheta}_{a,b})\sum_{r\mid n}\mathrm{ind}_q(r)k(r) \equiv (-\hat{\vartheta}_{a,b})\mathrm{ind}_q(n) \bmod q-1.$$

Since $p \mid q-1$, we have $\sum_{r\mid n} i(r)k(r) \equiv (-\hat{\vartheta}_{a,b})\mathrm{ind}_q(n) \bmod p$. Now, (5.19) => $a_r \equiv \dfrac{r^{f_r}-1}{n^f-1}\dfrac{g_r}{g} \bmod p$, and $\dfrac{g_r}{g} = \dfrac{f}{f_r} = c_r$. So,

$$\sum_{r\mid n} a_r k(r) \equiv \sum_{r\mid n} \frac{r^{f_r}-1}{n^f-1} c_r k(r) \equiv 1 \bmod p, \text{ by Lemma (4.5). Therefore,}$$

Therefore,

(5.21) $$\zeta_p^{(-\hat{\vartheta}_{a,b})\mathrm{ind}_q(n)} = \zeta_p^{\,j(n)}.$$

Now, (5.20),(5.21) =>

(5.22) $\zeta_p^{\,\mathrm{ind}_q(r)(-\hat{\vartheta}_{a,b})} = \zeta_p^{\,(-\hat{\vartheta}_{a,b})\mathrm{ind}_q(n)a_r}$.

Since $-\hat{\vartheta}_{a,b}$ is invertible, there is $w \in N$ so that $(-\hat{\vartheta}_{a,b})w \equiv 1 \bmod p$. Raising both sides of (5.22) to w-th power, we have $\zeta_p^{\,\mathrm{ind}_q(r)} = \zeta_p^{\,\mathrm{ind}_q(n)a_r}$. Therefore, $\mathrm{ind}_q(r) \equiv \mathrm{ind}_q(n)a_r \bmod p$ ▪

Case $p = 2$

Now we discuss the case where $p = 2$. First we observe that if q is an Euclidean prime, then q is odd and $q-1$ is square free, from this it is easy to see that $q \equiv 3 \pmod 4$ and for any prime r different from q, $\left(\frac{r}{-q}\right) = \left(\frac{-q}{r}\right)$.

(5.23) **Proposition** Suppose $\nu_2(r-1) \geq \nu_2(n-1)$, and $(-q)^{\frac{n-1}{2}} \equiv (-1)^{j(n)}$ where $j(n) = 0$ or 1. Then $\mathrm{ind}_q(r) \equiv \mathrm{ind}_q(n)a_r \pmod 2$ ▪

6. Algorithm

Now we present the algorithm for testing primes. For practical purposes, one can assume that the tested number n already passed the pseudo-primality test. In the algorithm described below, if n fails at any of the testing step, it halts and output 'composite'.

(6.1) **First stage**:

(a) Prepare the set E of Euclidean primes and the set I of initial primes as explained in Section 2.

(b) Fix a generator t_q of $(Z/qZ)^*$ for every Euclidean prime q.

(c) For initial primes $p > 2$, for every $q \in E$ with $p \mid q-1$, compute $J = -J_{a,b}((\hat{q}))$, where $\hat{q} = (q, \zeta_p - t_q^{(q-1)/p})$ and a,b are as chosen in (5.6). (Note that there is no need to actually compute $\hat{q}$)

(6.2) **Central stage**

(a) Test if none of the primes in I and E divides n.

(b) · For every $p \in I$, if $p > 2$, do the following:

1. Compute $f = o(n \bmod p)$ in $(Z/pZ)^*$, $g = \frac{p-1}{f}$.

2. Test if $\Phi_p \equiv \prod_{i=1}^{g} h_i \bmod n$, with $h_i \in Z[x]$ monic, degree$(h_i) = f$, $i = 1,\ldots,g$. Choose one h_i and let $\hat{n} = (n, h_i(\zeta_p))$.

3. For each $q \in E$ with $p \mid q-1$, let $\alpha = J^{\sum_{i=1}^{p-1} \sigma_i^{-1} i}$. Test if $\alpha^{(n^f-1)g/p} \equiv \zeta_p{}^{j(n)} \bmod nZ[\zeta_p]$, for some $j(n) \in N$.

4. If there is no $q \in E$ with $p \mid q-1$ such that $\alpha^{(n^f-1)g/p} \not\equiv 1 \bmod nZ[\zeta_p]$, then randomly search for $a \in Z[\zeta_p]$ such that $a^{\frac{n^f-1}{p}} \equiv \zeta_p{}^{j(n)} \bmod \hat{n}$, with $j(n) \not\equiv 0 \bmod p$.

If $p = 2$, then do the following:

1. For every $q \in E$, let $\alpha = -q$, test if $\alpha^{\frac{n-1}{2}} = (-1)^{j(n)} \bmod n$ for some $j(n) \in N$.

2. If there is no $q \in E$ such that $\alpha^{\frac{n-1}{2}} \equiv -1 \bmod n$, then randomly search for $a < n$ such that $a^{\frac{n-1}{2}} \equiv -1 \bmod n$.

(6.3) **Final stage**: Compute $t = o(n \bmod m)$ with $m = \prod_{q \in E} q$. Test if none of $n^i \bmod m$ divide n for $i = 1,\ldots,t-1$. Output 'prime'. ▪

Proof of correctness If n is prime, by Kummer Theorem, Lemma (5.2), Fermat Little Theorem, and Lemma (4.4), n must pass the central stage. Conversely, suppose n passes the central stage. Then for all prime $r \mid n$, by Proposition (3.4), $f_r \mid f$; by Lemma (4.3), $\nu_p(r^{f_r}-1) \geq \nu_p(n^f-1)$; by Proposition (5.16) and (5.23), $\mathrm{ind}_q(r) \equiv \mathrm{ind}_q(n) a_r \bmod p$ for some $a_r \in N$; by Lemma (2.3), $r \equiv n^i \pmod m$ for some $i \in N$.

Therefore, the set $\{ n^i \bmod m \mid i = 1,\ldots,t-1 \}$ contains all the possible prime divisors of n not exceeding $n^{1/2}$. Therefore, the final stage of trial division determines if n is prime or not. ▪

Since $n^{q-1} \equiv 1 \bmod q$, $n^K \equiv 1 \bmod q$ where $K = \prod_{p \in I} p$. So $n^K \equiv 1 \bmod m$, so $t \leq K \leq \log n^{c_0 \log\log\log n}$. Since t, $|E|$, $|I|$ are all bounded by $\log n^{c_0 \log\log\log n}$, the total expected running time is bounded by $O(\log n^{O(\log\log\log n)})$

Acknowledgement

This work was supported in part by NSF Grant ECS-8120037, U.S. Army Research Office-Durham Grant DAAG 29-82-K-0095, and DARPA contract N00014-82-K-0594. I would like to thank Professor H. W. Lenstra for his comments.

REFERENCES

[A] L.M.Adleman, "On Distinguishing Primes from Composite Numbers"(Abstract), *Proc. 21st Annual IEEE Symposium on Foundations of Computer Science*, 1980, 387-406.

[AM] L.M.Adleman, R.Mcdonnell, "An Application of Higher Reciprocity to Computational Number

Theory"(Abstract),*Proc. 23rd Annual IEEE Symposium on Foundations of Computer Science*, 1982, 100-106.

[APR] L.M.Adleman,C.Pomrerance,and R.S.Rumely,"On Distinguishing Primes from Composite Numbers", *Annal of Math.*, 117(1983), 173-206.

[AHU] A.V.Aho,J.E.Hopcroft,and J.D.Ullman,"*The Design and Analysis of Algorithms*", Addison-Wesley,Reading,MA 1974.

[B] E.R.Berlekamp,"Factoring Polynomials over Large Finite Fields",*Math. Comput.*,24(1970),713-735.

[CF] J.W.S.Cassel, A. Fröhlich(editors),*Algebraic Number Theory*, Thompson(Washington, D.C.), 1967.

[CL] H.Cohen, H.W.Lenstra,Jr., "Primality Testing and Jacobi Sums", to appear in *Math. Comput.*

[La] S.Lang,"*Algebraic Number Theory*",Addison-Wesley Publishing Company,1970.

[Le1] H.W.Lenstra,Jr.,"Primality Testing Algorithms"(after Adleman,Rumely and Williams), Seminar Bourbaki,33(1980-81),no.576,Lecture Notes in Math,Springer,243-257.

[Le2] H.W. Lenstra,Jr.,"Primality Testing with Artin Symbols", *Number theory related to Fermat's last theorem*, Progress in Math., 341-347.

[M] G.L.Miller,"Rieman Hypothesis and Tests For Primality",*J.C.S.S*,13,1976,300-317.

[R1] M.O.Rabin,"Probabilistic Algorithms",*Algorithms and Complexity,New Directions and Recent Results*, Academic,Press,21-40.

[R2] M.O.Rabin,"Probabilistic Algorithms in Finite Fields",*SIAM J.Comput.*,Vol.9,no.2,1980,273-280.

[S] J.Serre,"*Local Fields*",Springer-Verlag,Grad. text. 67

[SS] R.Solovay,V.Strassen,"Fast Monte-Carlo Tests for Primality",*SIAM J.Comput.* 1977,84-85.

[W] L.C.Washington,"*Introduction to Cyclotomic Fields*",Springer-Verlag,Grad. Text. 83.

A CRITERION FOR THE EQUIVALENCE OF TWO IDEALS

Johannes Buchmann
Mathematisches Institut
Universität zu Köln
Weyertal 86-90
5000 Köln 41

1. INTRODUCTION

A well known method of computing the class number of an algebraic number field K is to calculate the number of pairwise non equivalent integral ideals below the Minkowski bound of K. In order to apply this method one needs an effective algorithm for testing whether two ideals of K are equivalent or not.

For cubic fields such an algorithm was given by Voronoi [9] and Delone/Fadeev [5] and using this algorithm Angle [1], [2] calculated the class numbers of all cubic fields with discriminant less than 10^5 and recently Ennola [6] corrected and extended Angle's table to all cubic fields of discriminant less than $5 \cdot 10^5$.

The criterion of Voronoi/Delone/ Fadeev is very closely related to Voronoi's unit algorithm which the author generalized to all algebraic number fields of unit rank 1 and 2 [3], [4].

In this paper the criterion of Voronoi/Delone/Fadeev for the equivalence of two ideals of a cubic field is generalized to all algebraic number fields of unit rank 1 and 2 and several examples are given which show the effectiveness of the generalized algorithm.

2. BASIC NOTATIONS

In this paper we denote by

- K an algebraic number field of degree
- $n = s + 2t$ where
- s is the number of real and
- t is the number of pairs of complex conjugate fields of K
- $m = s + t$
- R the maximal order of K
- E the group of units of K
- D the discriminant of K

For the number $\alpha \in K$ we denote by

$\alpha^{(1)},\dots,\alpha^{(s)}$ the real and by

$\alpha^{(s+1)},\overline{\alpha^{(s+1)}},\dots,\alpha^{(m)},\overline{\alpha^{(m)}}$ the complex conjugates of α.

3. BASIC DEFINITIONS AND RESULTS

In this section we recall and generalize some definitions and results of [3] and [4]. All the statements can be proved exactly as in [3] and [4]. There we introduced the <u>CA-mapping</u> as follows:

$$\underline{} : \begin{cases} K \rightarrow \mathbb{R}^m \\ \alpha \rightarrow \underline{\alpha} := \begin{bmatrix} |\alpha^{(1)}| \\ \vdots \\ |\alpha^{(s)}| \\ |\alpha^{(s+1)}|^2 \\ \vdots \\ |\alpha^{(m)}|^2 \end{bmatrix} \end{cases}$$

By the definition

$$\bigwedge_{\alpha,\beta \in K} \alpha * \underline{\beta} := \underline{\alpha\beta}$$

the image $\underline{K}$ in a natural way was made a K-modul and for a point $\vec{y} = (y_1,\dots,y_m)^t \in \mathbb{R}^m$ the set

$$Q(\vec{y}) := \{\vec{y}\,' \in \mathbb{R}^m \mid 0 \leq y_i' \leq |y_i|,\ i=1,\dots,m\}$$

was called the <u>normed body of $\vec{y}$</u>.

Further the ordering $<_i$ of $\mathbb{R}^m$, depending on the coordinate direction i, was defined in the following way:

For two different points $\vec{y}, \vec{y}' \in \mathbb{R}^m$ compare the coordinates y_k and y'_k starting with $k = i$ up to $k = m$ then for $k = 1$ up to $k = i-1$. Then there is a first number k_1 with $y_{k_1} \neq y'_{k_1}$. If $y_{k_1} < y'_{k_1}$ we write

$$\vec{y} <_i \vec{y}' .$$

Now for the rest of this section let $\mathfrak{M}$ be an ideal of K different from (0). Then the image $\underline{\mathfrak{M}}$ is a discrete set in $\mathbb{R}^m$ and a point $\vec{y} \in \underline{\mathfrak{M}}$ different from $\underline{0}$ is called a <u>minimal point of $\mathfrak{M}$</u>, if its normed body $Q(\vec{y})$ does not contain any points of $\underline{\mathfrak{M}}$ different from $\underline{0}$ and $\vec{y}$. If α is a number in $\mathfrak{M}$ of minimal norm (in abs. value), then $\underline{\alpha}$ is a minimal point of $\underline{\mathfrak{M}}$. The set of all minimal points in $\underline{\mathfrak{M}}$ is denoted by $M_{\mathfrak{M}}$. The <u>i-neighbour</u> of a minimal point $\vec{y}$ is the minimal point of the set

$$\{\vec{y}' \in M_{\mathfrak{M}} \mid \vec{y}' \neq \vec{y} \ \wedge \ y'_k \leq y_k \ \text{ for } k \neq i\}$$

which is minimal with respect to $<_i$. It is denoted by $\varphi_i(\vec{y})$. As in [3] we can prove that for every minimal point and every coordinate direction i the i-neighbour exists and can be calculated in a finite number of steps.

Further for $\vec{y} \in M_{\mathfrak{M}}$ the chain

$$<\vec{y}>_i := (\varphi_i^k(\vec{y}))_{k\in\mathbb{N}_o}$$

is called the <u>i-chain of $\vec{y}$</u> and such an i-chain is always of the periodic form

$$(*) \qquad <\vec{y}>_i = \vec{y}_o, \vec{y}_1, \ldots, \vec{y}_{j_o}, \ldots, \vec{y}_{j_1}, \varepsilon * \vec{y}_{j_o}, \ldots, \varepsilon * \vec{y}_{j_1}, \ldots$$

where ε is a unit of K and $j_o, j_1 \in \mathbb{N}_o$, $j_1 \geq 1$. If the numbers j_o and j_1 are minimal, then $\{\vec{y}_{j_o}, \ldots, \vec{y}_{j_1}\}$ is called the <u>primitive period</u> and ε is called a <u>primitive unit</u> of the chain $<\vec{y}>_i$.

If $|\varepsilon^{(k)}| = 1$, then $<\vec{y}>_i$ is called <u>degenerated in k-direction</u>. By definition $<\vec{y}>_i$ is never degenerated in i-direction and it can be proved that $<\vec{y}>_i$ is also not degenerated in at least one direction $k \neq i$.

Finally, if the unit rank of K is 1, then all the neighbour chains in $\underline{\mathfrak{a}}$ are purely periodic.

4. THE CRITERIA AND ALGORITHMS

Remark: Note that the following theorems not only hold for integral but also for fractional ideals.

Theorem 4.1

Let K be of unit rank 1, $\mathfrak{a}, \mathfrak{b}$ ideals of K different form (0), ,
$\alpha,\beta \in K$ such that $\underline{\alpha}$ and $\underline{\beta}$ are minimal points of $\underline{\mathfrak{a}}$ and $\underline{\mathfrak{b}}$ resp., $n \in \{1,2\}$. Then $\mathfrak{a}$ and $\mathfrak{b}$ are equivalent, iff there exists a number $\beta' \in K$ with $\underline{\beta}'$ in the primitive period of $<\underline{\beta}>_n$ and

$$(*) \qquad \frac{1}{\alpha}\mathfrak{a} = \frac{1}{\beta'}\mathfrak{b}$$

Proof:

a) If (*) holds for a number $\beta' \in K$, then the equivalence of $\mathfrak{a}$ and $\mathfrak{b}$ is obvious.

b) Let $\mathfrak{a}$ and $\mathfrak{b}$ are equivalent, i.e. $\mathfrak{a} = \gamma\mathfrak{b}$, $\gamma \in K$ and therefore $M_{\mathfrak{a}} = \gamma * M_{\mathfrak{b}}$.
For the unit rank of K is 1 the sets of minimal points $M_{\mathfrak{a}}$ and $M_{\mathfrak{b}}$ by [3] (7.5) each consist of only one two-sided chain. Thus there is a number $\beta' \in K$ with $\underline{\beta'}$ in the primitive period of $<\underline{\beta}>_n$ and $\underline{\alpha} = \gamma * \underline{\beta'}$, i.e. $\alpha = \varepsilon\gamma\beta'$ where ε is a unit of K. This means that that

$$\frac{1}{\alpha}\mathfrak{a} = \frac{1}{\varepsilon\gamma\beta'}\mathfrak{a} = \frac{1}{\gamma\cdot\beta'}\mathfrak{a} = \frac{1}{\beta'}\mathfrak{b}.$$

Theorem 4.2

Let K be of unit rank 2, $\mathfrak{a}, \mathfrak{b}$ ideals of K different from (0), $\alpha,\beta \in K$ such that $\underline{\alpha}$ and $\underline{\beta}$ are minimal points of $\underline{\mathfrak{a}}$ and $\underline{\mathfrak{b}}$ resp., $\{u,v,w\} = \{1,2,3\}$, $<\alpha>_u$ not degenerated in w-direction.
Then $\mathfrak{a}$ and $\mathfrak{b}$ are equivalent, iff there exist numbers α' and β' with $\underline{\alpha}'$ and $\underline{\beta}'$ in the primitive periods of $<\underline{\alpha}>_u$ and $<\underline{\beta}>_v$ resp. and

$$(*) \qquad \frac{1}{\alpha'}\mathfrak{a} = \frac{1}{\beta'}\mathfrak{b}.$$

Proof:

a) If (*) holds for numbers $\alpha', \beta' \in K$, then the equivalence of $\mathfrak{a}$ and $\mathfrak{b}$ is obvious.

b) Let $\mathfrak{a}$ and $\mathfrak{b}$ are equivalent, i.e. $\mathfrak{a} = \gamma \cdot \mathfrak{b}$, $\gamma \in K$ and therefore $M_{\mathfrak{a}} = \gamma * M_{\mathfrak{b}}$.
By our assumptions and by [4] (3.16) it follows that the primitive periods of $\langle\underline{\alpha}\rangle_u$ and $\langle\gamma * \underline{\beta}\rangle_v$ contain elements $\underline{\alpha}'$ and $\underline{\tilde{\beta}}$, $\alpha', \tilde{\beta} \in K$, which are associated.
Now obviously $\tilde{\beta} = \gamma\beta'$ with $\beta' \in K$ and $\underline{\beta}'$ in the primitive period of $\langle\underline{\beta}\rangle_v$ and thus

$$\alpha' = \varepsilon \cdot \gamma \cdot \beta'$$

where ε is a unit of K.
This means that

$$\frac{1}{\alpha'}\mathfrak{a} = \frac{1}{\varepsilon \cdot \gamma \cdot \beta'}\mathfrak{a} = \frac{1}{\gamma \cdot \beta'}\mathfrak{a} = \frac{1}{\beta'}\mathfrak{b}.$$

Thus we get the following

Algorithm (for testing whether two ideals $\mathfrak{a}$ and $\mathfrak{b}$ are equivalent or not)

1. Calculate minimal points $\vec{a} \in M_{\mathfrak{a}}$, $\vec{b} \in M_{\mathfrak{b}}$ (e.g. by calculating vectors of minimal length in the corresponding lattices, see [10])
2. Calculate the primitive period of $\langle\vec{a}\rangle_1$:
$$\{\underline{\alpha_1}, \dots, \underline{\alpha_k}\}$$
3. Let
$$v = \begin{cases} 1 & \text{if } m = 2 \\ 3 & \text{if } m = 3 \wedge \langle a\rangle_1 \text{ not degenerated in 2-direction} \\ 2 & \text{if } m = 3 \wedge \langle a\rangle_1 \text{ is degenerated in 2-direction} \end{cases}$$
4. Calculate the primitive period of $\langle\vec{b}\rangle_v$
$$\{\underline{\beta_1}, \dots, \underline{\beta_\ell}\}$$
5. For $k' = 1$ to k and $\ell' = 1$ to ℓ :
If
$$\frac{1}{\alpha_{k'}} = \frac{1}{\beta_{\ell'}}$$
then $\mathfrak{a}$ and $\mathfrak{b}$ are equivalent and the algorithm stops.

If none of the equations in 5. holds, then $\mathfrak{a}$ and $\mathfrak{b}$ are not equivalent and the algorithm stops.

5. EXAMPLES

The algorithm works in the following cases:

$n = 2$:	$s = 2,\ t = 0$		
$n = 3$:	$s = 1,\ t = 1$	and	$s = 3,\ t = 0$
$n = 4$:	$s = 0,\ t = 2$	and	$s = 2,\ t = 1$
$n = 5$:			$s = 1,\ t = 2$
$n = 6$:			$s = 0,\ t = 3$

In the case $n = 3$ the algorithm is Voronoi's algorithm. For examples in this case see [1], [2] and [6]. For each of the "new" cases $n = 4$, $n = 5$, $n = 6$ we give an example:

Let $K = \mathbb{Q}(\rho)$, where ρ is a route of the equation

$$x^n + k_1 x^{n-1} + \ldots + k_n = 0 .$$

Let D be the discriminant of K, $\omega_1,\ldots,\omega_n$ an integral basis of K with

$$\omega_j = W_{1,j} + W_{2,j}\rho + \ldots + W_{n,j}\rho^{n-1},\ j = 1,\ldots,n,\ W_{ij} \in \mathbb{Q}$$

and R the maximal order of K. In this field we consider the ideal $\mathfrak{a} = \mathbb{Z}\gamma_1 + \ldots + \mathbb{Z}\gamma_n$ with

$$\gamma_j = c_{1,j}\omega_1 + \ldots + c_{n,j}\omega_n , \qquad j = 1,\ldots,n,\ c_{ij} \in \mathbb{Z}$$

and using our algorithm we test whether $\mathfrak{a}$ is a principal ideal or not, i.e. whether $\mathfrak{a}$ and R are equivalent or not.

The input data were taken from [7] and [8]. All computations were carried out on the Control Data Cyber 76 of the Computer Center of the University of Cologne.

In all examples the CPU-time was less than 0,02 s .

0) Input				
n	4	4	5	6
s	2	0	1	0
t	1	2	2	3
$k_1, \ldots, k_n$	1, 0, 3, -1	1, 2, -1, 1	0, -1, 0, 2, 1	1, 2, 3, 2, 1, 1
D	-775	225	3089	-21296
(W_{ij})	$\begin{matrix} 1 & 0 & 0 & 1/2 \\ 0 & 1 & 1 & 0 \\ 0 & 0 & 1 & 1 \\ 0 & 0 & 0 & 1/2 \end{matrix}$	$\begin{matrix} 1 & 0 & 1 & 1/2 \\ 0 & 1 & 1 & 1 \\ 0 & 0 & 1 & 1 \\ 0 & 0 & 0 & 1/2 \end{matrix}$	$\begin{matrix} 1 & 0 & 0 & 0 & 0 \\ 0 & 1 & 0 & 0 & 0 \\ 0 & 0 & 1 & 0 & 0 \\ 0 & 0 & 0 & 1 & 0 \\ 0 & 0 & 0 & 0 & 1 \end{matrix}$	$\begin{matrix} 1 & 0 & 0 & 0 & 0 & 0 \\ 0 & 1 & 0 & 0 & 0 & 0 \\ 0 & 0 & 1 & 0 & 0 & 0 \\ 0 & 0 & 0 & 1 & 0 & 0 \\ 0 & 0 & 0 & 0 & 1 & 0 \\ 0 & 0 & 0 & 0 & 0 & 1 \end{matrix}$
$(c_{i,j})$	$\begin{matrix} 2 & 1 & 0 & 0 \\ 0 & 1 & 0 & 0 \\ 0 & 0 & 1 & 0 \\ 0 & 0 & 0 & 2 \end{matrix}$	$\begin{matrix} 2 & 0 & 0 & 1 \\ 0 & 2 & 0 & 1 \\ 0 & 0 & 1 & 0 \\ 0 & 0 & 0 & 1 \end{matrix}$	$\begin{matrix} 3 & 0 & 0 & 0 & 2 \\ 0 & 3 & 0 & 0 & 0 \\ 0 & 0 & 3 & 0 & 0 \\ 0 & 0 & 0 & 3 & 1 \\ 0 & 0 & 0 & 0 & 1 \end{matrix}$	$\begin{matrix} 2 & 0 & 1 & 1 & 0 & 1 \\ 0 & 2 & 1 & 0 & 1 & 1 \\ 0 & 0 & 1 & 0 & 1 & 1 \\ 0 & 0 & 0 & 1 & 0 & 0 \\ 0 & 0 & 0 & 0 & 1 & 0 \\ 0 & 0 & 0 & 0 & 0 & 1 \end{matrix}$
1) Minimal points $\vec{a}$ of $\mathfrak{a}$	$\underline{\gamma_3}$	$\underline{\gamma_4}$	$\underline{\gamma_5}$	$\underline{\gamma_3}$
$\vec{b}$ of R	$\underline{1}$	$\underline{1}$	$\underline{1}$	$\underline{1}$
2) Primitive period of $\langle\vec{a}\rangle_1$	$\{\underline{\gamma_3}\}$	$\{\underline{\gamma_4}\}$	$\{\underline{\gamma_5}\}$	$\{\underline{\gamma_3}\}$
3) v	3	1	3	3
4) Primitive period of $\langle\vec{b}\rangle_v$	$\{\underline{1}\}$	$\{\underline{1}\}$	$\{\underline{1}\}$	$\{\underline{1}\}$
5) $\mathfrak{a}$ and R equivalent?	$\frac{1}{\gamma_3}\mathfrak{a} = R$	$\frac{1}{\gamma_4}\mathfrak{a} = R$	$\frac{1}{\gamma_5}\mathfrak{a} = R$	$\frac{1}{\gamma_3}\mathfrak{a} = R$

REFERENCES

[1] Angell, I.O. A table of complex cubic fields
Bull. Lond. Math. Soc. 5 (1973) p. 37-38

[2] Angell, I.O. A table of totally real cubic fields
Math. Comput. 30 (1976) p. 184-187

[3] Buchmann, J. A generalization of Voronoi's unit algorithm I
to appear in J. Number Theory

[4] Buchmann, J. A generalization of Voronoi's unit algorithm II
to appear in J. Number Theory

[5] Delone, B.N., Fadeev, D.K. The irrationalities of the third degree
Am. Math. Soc. Transl. of Math. Monographs 10 (1964)

[6] Ennola, V. A table of cubic fields of discriminant less than $5\ 10^5$
to appear

[7] Pohst, M., Weiler, P., Zassenhaus, H. On effective computation of fundamental units II
Math. Comput. 38 (1982) p. 275-328

[8] Trede, V. Die Berechnung der Klassenzahl eines algebraischen Zahlkörpers nach einer Idee von H. Zassenhaus
Diplomarbeit, Köln 1983

[9] Voronoi, G. Über eine Verallgemeinerung des Kettenbruchalgorithmus
Dissertation, Warschau 1896 (russian)

[10] Pohst, M., Fincke, U. Some applications of Cholescy type methods in algebraic number fields
to appear

$y' + fy = g$

James H. Davenport,
School of Mathematics,
University of Bath
Claverton Down,
Bath BA2 7AY,
England

Abstract. In this paper, we look closely at the equation of the title, originally considered by Risch, which arises in the integration of exponentials. We present a minor improvement of Risch's original presentation, a generalisation of that presentation to algebraic functions f and g, and a new algorithm for the solution of this equation. Full details of the last two are to appear elsewhere.

1. Introduction

Integration of functions expressible purely in logarithms has been understood at least since Ostrowski [1946]. The major contribution of Risch's [1969] fundamental paper on integration in finite terms, the paper that has been called the foundation of the modern theory, was the recognition that the problem of integrating $g\ e^F\ dx$ was that of solving the equation $y'+fy = g$, where $F' = f$. Risch furthermore gave an algorithm for solving this equation, which we have also called the *Risch differential equation*, when f,g and the solution lay in an elementary transcendental extension of $K(x)$. Risch in fact considered the slightly more general equation $y'+fy = \Sigma c_i g_i$, where the g_i are known functions and the c_i are unknown constants, but this generalisation was only needed to facilitate Risch's induction, and, while being conceptually straightforward, does complicate the notation, so we shall ignore it. The alternative induction of [Davenport, 1983] does not require this extra generality.

In section 2 we present some fairly straight-forward modifications to Risch's original algorithm, which improve performance and, in many cases, eliminate the necessity of considering systems of linear equations in order to prove that a function does not have an elementary integral. Section 3 outlines the extension of Risch's method from rational f and g to algebraic f and g, full details of which will appear elsewhere [Davenport, 1984]. Sections 4 and 5 consider an alternative approach, based on partial fractions, to the solution of Risch differential equations. The entire approach is too complicated to explain here (see Davenport, 1983), but we give the high-lights, and mention the major difficulties.

2. Minor Modifications

In this section, we present various minor modifications to Risch's original [1969] argument. The first one is concerned with Risch's derivation of various degree or multiplicity bounds. We will concentrate on the first of these [Risch, 1969, p. 181], since the same modification will apply, *mutatis mutandis*, throughout. Bounding the denominator involves bounding the multiplicity of each factor.

Suppose that, in $y'+fy = g$, we wish to bound the multiplicity of an irreducible polynomial p in the denominator of y. We perform p-adic expansions of all the elements of this equation, writing

$$y = \frac{A}{p^{\alpha} q_1}, \quad f = \frac{B}{p^{\beta} q_2} \quad \text{and} \quad g = \frac{C}{p^{\gamma} q_3},$$

where A, B, C and the q_i are polynomials not divisible by p. Let a be the coefficient of the first term of the p-adic expansion of y, i.e. Aq_1^{-1} (modulo p), and b and c the corresponding terms for f and g. In this notation, the p-adic expansion of y' begins $-\alpha p'a/p^{\alpha+1}$, that of fy begins $ab/p^{\alpha+\beta}$, while that of g begins c/p^{γ}. There may be cancellation between the leading terms on the left of the Risch differential equation, and we handle this case as Risch does, observing that this only occurs when $\beta=1$, and that $\alpha = b/p'$ in this case (we will need this result in Section 4). If cancellation does not occur, Risch deduces that $\alpha \leq \max(\gamma-1, \gamma-\beta)$, from the observation that either $\alpha+1 \leq \gamma$ or $\alpha+\beta \leq \gamma$. Let us take a closer look at this argument. The multiplicities of p on the two sides of $y'+fy = g$ must agree, so that

$$\max(\alpha+1,\ \alpha+\beta) = \gamma.$$

Hence

$$\alpha + \max(1,\beta) = \gamma,$$

i.e.

$$\begin{aligned} \alpha &= \gamma - \max(1,\beta) \\ &= \gamma + \min(-1,-\beta) \\ &= \min(\gamma-1,\ \gamma-\beta). \end{aligned}$$

We can apply this improved bound to the problem of integrating

$$\int e^{x^2} dx$$

which reduces to the equation

$$y'+2xy = 1. \qquad (1)$$

y has to be a polynomial, since there is no cancellation of denominators and the right-hand side has no denominator. At this point, Risch [1969, pp. 187-188] reduces the problem to a set of linear equations. In this case, we can argue that α, the degree of y, satisfies $\alpha = \min(0-1,0+1)$ (where Risch deduced $\max(0-1,0+1)$). Therefore $\alpha = -1$, an impossible degree for a polynomial. This agrees with the intuitive feeling that no polynomial can satisfy (1).

There is another modification that can be made to Risch's argument. Unlike the previous change, it does not lead to any improvement in the conclusions, but it does simplify certain deductions. Whatever the main variable θ of y, f and g is, Risch deduces bounds on the numerator by a separate, though similar, argument to that for the denominator. But, if θ is x or an exponential, the substitution $\phi = 1/\theta$ converts the problem into a denominator one, since $\deg_\theta(\mathrm{num}(y))-\deg_\theta(\mathrm{den}(y))$ = multiplicity of ϕ in $\mathrm{den}(y)$. Of course, the equation determining y as a function of ϕ is not the same as that determining it in terms of θ, but the change consists of a factor of $\partial\phi/\partial\theta$ multiplying the y' term. This factor can be divided out, reducing the equation to one of the form of the title.

3. Algebraic Functions.

The modifications suggested in the previous section to Risch's argument enable us to regard that argument as bounding the degrees of the pole of y at each place, including the place at infinity. This argument generalises straightforwardly from the case of rational f, g, y to the case of algebraic f, g, y [Davenport, 1984]. Rather than discuss the complete theory here, let us look at an example:

$$\int \frac{x\sqrt{x^2-1}+x}{\sqrt{x^2-1}}\, e^{\sqrt{x^2-1}}\, dx .$$

This is equivalent to the Risch differential equation

$$y' + \left[\frac{x}{\sqrt{x^2-1}}\right] y = \frac{x\left[\sqrt{x^2-1} + 1\right]}{\sqrt{x^2-1}} .$$

Obviously, as far as a denominator of y is concerned, the only problems are the zeros of the denominators of f and g, viz. the roots of x^2-1. If we substitute $\xi = x-1$, we will have $\sqrt{\xi}$ in various places, so let us instead substitute $\xi^2 = x-1$ (ξ is then a local parameter at $x=1$).

$$\frac{dy}{d\xi}\frac{d\xi}{dx} + \left[\frac{\xi^2+1}{\xi\sqrt{\xi^2+2}}\right] y = \frac{\left[\xi^2+1\right]\left[\xi\sqrt{\xi^2+2}+1\right]}{\xi\sqrt{\xi^2+2}} .$$

Since $dx/d\xi = 2\xi$, we can eliminate $d\xi/dx$, and have an equation connecting y and $dy/d\xi$, viz.

$$\frac{dy}{d\xi} + \frac{2\left[\xi^2+1\right]}{\sqrt{\xi^2+2}} y = \frac{2\left[\xi^2+1\right]\left[\xi\sqrt{\xi^2+2}+1\right]}{\sqrt{\xi^2+2}} .$$

Since there is no ξ term in the denominators of either f or g in this equation, there can be no ξ term in the denominator of y. An identical argument can be applied to the other root of x^2-1, with the substitution $\xi^2 = x+1$.

This leaves us with the question of bounding the degree at infinity. Let us write $\zeta = 1/x$, so that ζ is a local parameter at infinty, and then investigate the multiplicity of a pole of ζ in y.

$$\frac{dy}{d\zeta}\frac{d\zeta}{dx} + \frac{1}{\sqrt{1-\zeta^2}}\, y = \frac{\sqrt{1-\zeta^2} + \zeta}{\zeta\sqrt{1-\zeta^2}} .$$

Since $dx/d\zeta = -1/\zeta^2$, we can eliminate $d\zeta/dx$, and obtain an equation relating $dy/d\zeta$ and y, viz.

$$\frac{dy}{d\zeta} + \frac{-1}{\zeta^2\sqrt{1-\zeta^2}}\, y = \frac{-\sqrt{1-\zeta^2} - \zeta}{\zeta^3\sqrt{1-\zeta^2}} .$$

Applying the formula of the previous section, we see that y has ζ in its denominator with multiplicity at most $\min(3-1, 3-2) = 1$.

Hence y is a form with no finite poles, and degree at most one at infinity, and hence has to be of the form $\lambda x + \mu\sqrt{(x^2-1)} + \nu$, for some, unknown, constants λ, μ and ν. We can substitute this form into the Risch differential equation, resulting in

$$\left[\frac{d}{dx} + \frac{x}{\sqrt{x^2-1}}\right]\left[\lambda x + \mu\sqrt{x^2+1} + \nu\right] = \frac{x\left(\sqrt{x^2-1} + 1\right)}{\sqrt{x^2-1}} .$$

Evaluating the differential application leads to the following equation:

$$\lambda\frac{x^2}{\sqrt{x^2-1}} + \mu\left[\frac{x}{\sqrt{x^2-1}} + x\right] + \nu\frac{x}{\sqrt{x^2-1}} = \frac{x\left(\sqrt{x^2-1} + 1\right)}{\sqrt{x^2-1}} ,$$

from which the deduction $\lambda = \nu = 0$, $\mu = 1$ is easy. The general algorithm is to note that the above equation is always linear in the unknowns, and hence the equation reduces to a linear system. This then determines our final integral as being

$$\sqrt{x^2-1}\; e^{\sqrt{x^2-1}} + c,$$

where c is a constant of integration.

Clearly, we have chosen a relatively simple example, and one that can, if fact, be integrated by existing algorithms after a rationalising substitution, such as $x = \cosh y$. Nevertheless, the method is equally applicable to integrals containing algebraic functions of x which can not be rationalised. It also requires very little additional work if one already has algorithms for integrating algebraic functions and a general implementation of Risch [1969].

4. Partial Fractions (Base Case)

The solution techniques discussed in the previous two sections rely on reducing a Risch differential equation to a system of linear equations. The induction technique in Risch [1969] relies on reducing a Risch differential equation in $K[\theta_1,\ldots,\theta_n]$ to a diagonal system of Risch differential equations in $K[\theta_1,\ldots,\theta_{n-1}]$, which can be solved one at a time. Similarly, integration of rational functions can be done by solving linear equations. However, since the discovery of fast algorithms for square-free decomposition [Yun, 1977] and the computation of partial fraction decompositions [Kung & Tong, 1977; Abdali et al., 1977], it is more usual to integrate rational functions by means of partial fractions (Hermite's algorithm). This poses (more precisely, this caused Mr. Trager to put to me) the problem of solving Risch differential equations by partial fractions, rather than by systems of linear equations. This can in fact be done. The details are rather complicated, and are to appear elsewhere [Davenport, 1983], so we will describe the main results and their significance, rather than giving detailed proofs of the various results.

The major problem in solving the Risch differential equation is that of cancellation. It is quite possible for g to have no denominator, f to have only a linear dominator, but y to have an arbitrarily large denominator. The classic example of this is

$$y' + \left[1 + \frac{5}{x}\right] y = 1 ,$$

whose solution is

$$y = \frac{x^5-5x^4+20x^3-60x^2+120x-120}{x^5} .$$

It can be asserted that this is an "unfair" example, since it arises from the integration of $e^{x+5\log x}$, which is probably better expressed as x^5e^x. It follows from the arguments of Risch [1969], that, in the notation of Section 2, $\alpha = b/p'$. But b/p' is the residue of f at the zeros of p. Since α has to be a positive integer for us to have cancellation, we can conclude that f has a positive integral residue, either at a finite value of x (which gives us cancellation in the denominator) or at infinity (cancellation in the numerator). But this implies that the integral of f has a logarithmic term with a positive integral coefficient, which may then be brought out of the exponential, as in the example above. (We have ignored the possiblity that the integral residue may be at infinity, as in

$$e^{\left[\frac{-1}{2} \log \left[x^2+1\right] + \frac{1}{x}\right]} .$$

Bringing this logarithm out of the exponential would introduce an algebraic expression of $\sqrt{(x^2+1)}$. However, we can transform this integrand to

$$\frac{e^{\left[\frac{1}{2}\log\left[x^2+1\right]+\frac{1}{x}\right]}}{x^2+1},$$

and now the residue at infinity is −1, and the integrand is still purely transcendental.)

This motivates the following definition. An element f of a differential field $D(\phi)$ is said to be *weakly normalised* with respect to ϕ if:

a) it has an integral which is elementary over $D(\phi)$;

b) no logarithm whose argument depends on ϕ occurs linearly in that integral with a positive integral coefficient (the integral being written so that the arguments of all the new logarithms are square-free elements of $D[\phi]$);

c) the sum of the coefficients of the logarithms occurring linearly in the integral (weighted by their degrees in ϕ) is not a negative integer.

In the case of a rational function, conditions (b) and (c) are equivalent to saying that the integrand f should have no integer residues.

If f is weakly normalised, it is possible to find y, or prove that the Risch differential equation is insoluble, by a partial fraction argument. The details are in [Davenport, 1983]. This argument can also be used to prove the $\min(\gamma-1,\gamma-\beta)$ result of section 2 independantly of [Risch 1969].

5. Partial Fraction (Induction).

Suppose we have a Risch differential equation in a transcendental variable θ, for example $\theta = \log x$ or $\theta = e^x$, and our differential equation has this as the main variable, for example

$$y' + \frac{\log x - 1}{\log^2 x}\, y = \frac{(2x+1)\log^2 x + (x^2-x)\log x - x^2}{x \log^2 x}.$$

Then very similar partial-fraction techniques as are used in the rational function case can be used in this case. Comparison of denominators indicates that y has no denominator (which follows also from Section 2). y is therefore a polynomial in $\theta = \log x$. Since cancellation does not occur (a result that is a little messy to prove), then the degrees in θ of y' and fy have to be zero. f has degree −1 in θ, so this constrains the degree in θ of y to be at most one. In fact the coefficient of θ must be a constant, else y' would have also have degree one. Therefore $y = r(x) + c \log x$, where r is an unknown rational function, and c is an unknown constant. Substuting this in, and looking only at the terms that do not involve $\log x$, we have that

$$r'(x) + \frac{c}{x} + c = \frac{2x+1}{x}.$$

r' is the derivative of a rational function, and so has no residues, while c/x and $1/x$ have residues of c and 1 at x=0 respectively. Hence c=1. Therefore r'=1, and $r = x + d$, where d is another unknown constant. Back-substituting implies that d=0 as well. This process may seem somewhat *ad hoc*, but there is a complete algorithm, based on partial fractions for the denominator and equating like terms for the numerator, in [Davenport, 1983].

Occasionally, such term-by-term analysis may lead to a Risch differential equation problem in the field below θ. For example, if our integrand is

$$\frac{(2x^3+x)\log^3 x + (2x^2+x)\log^2 x - x\log x - 1}{x\log^2 x}\, e^{x^2} + 1/\log x,$$

we are left with the Risch differential equation

$$y' + \left[2x + \frac{1}{x\log^2 x}\right] y = (2x^2+1)\log x + (2x+2) - \frac{x\log x + 1}{x\log^2 x}.$$

As in the previous example, y has to be a polynomial of degree one in θ, say $y = y_1\theta + y_0$. Substituting this in, and collecting just the coefficients of the linear terms in θ, gives us

$$y_1' + 2xy_1 = 2x^2 + 1,$$

whose solution is readily seen to be $y_1 = x$. Substituting this in and collecting the θ^0 terms gives us a Risch differential equation for y_0, with the left-hand side looking exactly the same, viz.

$$y_0' + 2xy_0 = 2x.$$

The solution of this is $y_0 = 1$, and substituting this value in cancels the rest of the equation. Hence our integrand is indeed integrable, and its integral is

$$(x\log x + 1)\, e^{x^2} + 1/\log x.$$

There is one major problem with this recursion: are we guaranteed that the solutions of the Risch differential are always unique? The solutions will be unique unless e^F lies in the field under consideration, where F is the integral of f. This can never happen initially, since the equation arises from trying to integrate a multiple of e^F, but it might happen on the recursion. To deal with this possibility, Risch introduces his whole system of undetermined constants c_i. Can it happen?

The answer is yes, and, when it happens, all the "nice" degree bounds that one would like fail to be observed. Consider

$$\int e^{\frac{1}{e^x+1} - 10x} \frac{2581284541e^x + 1757211400}{111e^{3x} + 3.111e^{2x} + 3.111e^x + 111} dx$$

[Davenport, 1983]. The differential equation that has to be satisfied in $K[x, e^x]$ is $y' - 10y = 2581284541/111$, and this clearly has mutiple solutions. This multiple solutions complicate the integration process substantially, and the final integral is

$$e^{\frac{1}{e^x+1} - 10x} \frac{111e^{11x} + 19948400e^{9x} - \ldots - 175721140}{111e^x + 111}.$$

The solution adopted in [Davenport, 1983] is to insist that our differential fields be written in such a way that this can not occur. In the example just given, if the $-10x$ were pulled out, rather than written as part of the nested exponential, there would be no problem. This leads to the following definition. An element η of a differential field $K(x, \theta_1, \ldots, \theta_n)$ is said to be *exponentially reduced* if:

a) the constant (in the sense of not depending on θ) term η_0 of η, when η is written in the form polynomial(θ_n) + constant term + proper rational fraction(θ_n), does not satisfy

$$\eta_0 \in \overline{K(x, \theta_1, \ldots, \theta_{n-1})}$$

unless it is actually a constant ($\eta_0' = 0$). (equivalently, η_0 is not a linear combination with rational coefficients of the logarithms and arguments of exponentials in $\theta_1, \ldots, \theta_{n-1}$);

b) η_0 is exponentially reduced as an element of $K(z, \theta_1, \ldots, \theta_{n-1})$.

A field $K(x, \theta_1, \ldots, \theta_{n-1})$ is said to be *exponentially reduced* if K is its field of constants, $x'=1$ and each θ_i is transcendental over $K(x, \theta_1, \ldots, \theta_{i-1})$ with one of the following two holding:

a) there is a non-constant η in $K(x, \theta_1, \ldots, \theta_{i-1})$ such that $\theta'_i = \eta'/\eta$ (θ_i is a logarithm over $K(x, \theta_1, \ldots, \theta_{i-1})$).

b) there is a non-zero, exponentially reduced, element η of $K(x, \theta_1, \ldots, \theta_{i-1})$ such that $\theta'_i = \eta'\theta_i$ (θ_i is an exponential over $K(x, \theta_1, \ldots, \theta_n)$) and such that no logarithm occurs linearly in η with a rational coefficient (arguments of logarithms always being square-free polynomials, and including the case at infinity).

Then in an exponentially reduced field, all the f which occur in the Risch differential equations which arise in integration are weakly normalised, since no logarithm occurs linearly with a rational coefficient. Furthermore, the conditions that the η be exponentially reduced means that each Risch differential equation has at most one solution, and there is no need for Risch's undetermined coefficients.

Every exponentially reduced field is a field generated by *regular monomials* in the sense of Risch [1969], but the converse is not true. In fact, there are four possibilities.

i) The presentation of the field given by the monomials may indeed be reduced, as in $K(x,\theta_1,\theta_2)$, where $\theta'_1 = \theta_1$ ($\theta_1 = \exp(x)$) and $\theta'_2 = 2\theta_1^2\theta_2$ ($\theta_2 = \exp(\exp(2x))$).

ii) The presentation given may not be exponentially reduced, but there may be another presentation of the same field which is. Consider $K(x,\phi_1,\phi_2)$, where $\phi'_1 = \phi_1$ ($\phi_1 = \exp(x)$) and $\phi'_2 = (1+2\phi_1^2)\phi_2$ ($\phi_2 = \exp(x+\exp(2x))$). This corresponds to the same field as the previous example, with $\phi_1 = \theta_1$ and $\theta_2 = \phi_2/\phi_1$. The presentation is not exponentially reduced, since the argument of ϕ_2 is not.

iii) The field may not have an exponentially reduced presentation, but it may be a sub-field of a field with an exponentially reduced presentation. Consider $K(x,\phi_1,\phi_2)$, where $\phi'_1 = 2\phi_1$ ($\phi_1 = \exp(2x)$) and $\phi'_2 = (1+2\phi_1)\phi_2$ ($\phi_2 = \exp(x+\exp(2x))$). This field does not have an exponentially reduced presentation, but it is a sub-field of the field of the first example, with $\phi_1 = \theta_1^2$ and $\phi_2 = \theta_1\theta_2$. The inclusion is strict, since θ_1 is in the field of the first example, but not in this field.

iv) There may be no exponentially reduced field containing the given field, as in $K(x,\phi_1,\phi_2)$, where $\phi'_1 = 4x^3/(x^4+1)$ ($\phi_1 = \log(x^4+1)$) and $\phi'_2 = (1+2x^3/(x^4+1))\phi_2$ ($\phi_2 = \exp(x + (1/2)\log(x^4+1))$). In order for the argument to the exponential to contain no logarithms with rational coefficients, we have to introduce $\surd(x^4+1)$, and, as is well known, this can not be rationalised.

It is only the fields of case (iv) that cause us any concern, since the others can all be embedded in exponentially reduced fields in which all the calculations can be carried out. In the case of fields of type (iv), it may be necessary to perform a change of presentation part way through the integration process in order to keep the partial integrands weakly normalised and to avoid non-unique Risch differential equations, but this can always be done without introducing new algebraic elements. For example, we can integrate $g\phi_2$ quite happily, since the argument of ϕ_2 is weakly normalised, having residues of 1/2 at the roots of $x^4+1=0$ and -2 at infinity. We can not integrate $g\phi_2^2$ that way, since, regarding ϕ_2^2 as an exponential, it is not weakly normalised, having residues of 1 at the roots of $x^4+1=0$. Therefore we transform the problem to $g\psi(x^4+1)$, where $\psi' = 2\psi$ ($\psi = \exp(x) = \phi_2^2/(x^4+1)$). Fields of this type can be termed *crypto-algebraic*, since the most natural way of representing them would seem to involve algebraic extensions. Other example sof problems caused by non-normalised fields can be found in Cherry [1983].

6. Conclusions

We have looked in various ways at the equation of the title. We have seen that, while Risch certainly recognised its importance, and gave the first algorithms for solving it, he did not necessarily give the most efficient or the most general. There is clearly far more to do, in particular extending the work of section 4 from algebraic extensions of $K(x)$ to general mixed elementary fields. This is clearly one of the stumbling blocks in the way of the extension of the theory of integration to this area.

7. References

[Abdali et al., 1977] Abdali, S. K., Caviness, B. F. & Pridor, A., Modular Polynomial Arithmetic in Partial Fraction Decomposition. Proc. 1977 MACSYMA Users' Conference (NASA Publ. CP-2012) pp. 253-261.

[Cherry, 1983] Cherry, G. W., Algorithms for Integrating Elementary Functions in Terms of Lagarithmic Integrals and Error Functions. Ph.D. Thesis, University of Delaware, August 1983.

[Davenport, 1983] Davenport, J. H., The Risch Differential Equation. Manuscript, Aug. 1983. Submitted to SIAM J. Comp.

[Davenport, 1984] Davenport, J. H., Integration Algorithmique des fonctions elementairement transcendantes sur une courbe algebrique. To appear in Annales de l'Institut Fourier, 34(1984).

[Kung & Tong, 1977] Kung, H. T. & Tong, D. M., Fast Algorithms for Partial Fraction Decomposition. SIAM J. Comp. 6(1977) pp. 582-593. MR 58(1979) #13919.

[Ostrowski, 1946] Ostrowski, A. M., Sur l'integrabilite elementaire de quelques classes d'expressions. Comm. Math. Helvet. 18(1946) pp. 283-308.

[Risch, 1969] Risch, R. H., The Problem of Integration in Finite Terms. Trans. AMS 139(1969) pp. 167-189. MR 38(1969) #5759.

[Yun, 1977] Yun, D. Y. Y., Fast Algorithms for Rational Function Integration. Proc. IFIP 1977, North-Holland, 1977, pp. 493-498.

Integration In Finite Terms With Special Functions: A Progress Report[*]

G. W. Cherry[**]
B. F. Caviness
University of Delaware
Newark, Delaware

ABSTRACT

Since R. Risch published an algorithm for calculating symbolic integrals of elementary functions in 1969, there has been an interest in extending his methods to include nonelementary functions. We report here on the recent development of two decision procedures for calculating integrals of transcendental elementary functions in terms of logarithmic integrals and error functions. Both of these algorithms are based on the Singer, Saunders, Caviness extension of Liouville's theorem on integration in finite terms [Ssc81]. Parts of the logarithmic integral algorithm have been implemented in Macsyma and a brief demonstration is given.

1. INTRODUCTION

Since the publication, in 1969, of a decision procedure for finding elementary integrals of transcendental elementary functions [Risch69], there has been an interest in possible generalizations[Mos71],[Nor79]. One such generalization is the inclusion of familiar yet nonelementary functions in either the integrand, the integral, or both. For instance, integration software should ideally be able to recognize error functions, polylogarithms, logarithmic integrals, etc. and should be able integrate expressions involving these functions. There are some hueristics in the Macsyma integration code for generating error functions and polylogarithms but no claims are made concerning their effectiveness which is, in fact, limited.

We shall report here on two decision procedures. The first determines if an element in a transcendental elementary field has an integral which can be written in terms of elementary functions and logarithmic integrals. The second, which considers a large subset of the transcendental elementary functions, determines if an integral can be written in terms of elementary functions and error functions. In each case we shall state the main results and offer a few remarks.[***] Following this is a brief Macsyma demonstration of the logarithmic integral algorithm.

(*) This work was supported in part by the System Development Foundation grant # 301.

(**) Present address: Tektronix, Inc., P.O. Box 500, Beaverton, Oregon, 97077.

(***) For the complete work the reader is referred to [Cher83a] and [Cher83b].

2. THE LOGARITHMIC INTEGRAL

The classical logarithmic integral function, $li(x)=\int_0^x \frac{1}{\log(x)}dx$, can be used to define a generalization of the elementary extensions as follows: Let F be a differential field of characteristic zero with derivation $'$ and constants C. We say that a differential extension E of F is a li-elementary extension of F if $F=F_0 \subseteq F_1 \subseteq \cdots \subseteq F_n = E$ such that $F_i = F_{i-1}(\theta_i)$ where for each i, $1 \le i \le n$, one of the following holds:

(i) θ_i is algebraic over F_{i-1}.

(ii) $\theta_i' = u'\theta_i$ for some u in F_{i-1}. (i.e. $\theta_i = \exp(u)$).

(iii) $\theta_i' = u'/u$ for some nonzero u in F_{i-1}. (i.e. $\theta_i = \log(u)$).

(iv) $\theta_i' = \frac{u'}{v}$ for some nonzero u and v in F_{i-1} such that $v' = u'/u$. In this case we write $\theta_i = li(u)$.

One of the theoretical foundations for this work is a recent generalization of Liouville's theorem on integration in finite terms [Ssc81]. The following is a corollary of this theorem.

Theorem 2.1: Let F be a liouvillian extension of its field of constants C. Assume C is algebraically closed and has characteristic zero and let γ be an element of F which has an integral in some li-elementary extension of F. Then there exist constants c_i and d_i in C and elements w_i, u_i and v_i in F such that

$$\gamma = w_0' + \sum c_i \frac{w_i'}{w_i} + \sum d_i \frac{u_i'}{v_i} \qquad (2.1)$$

where $v_i' = u_i'/u_i$.

In addition to the above theorem, the decision procedure for logarithmic integrals makes use of the following notions concerning the generators of the elementary field containing the integrand. Let $F = C(x, \theta_1, \theta_2, \ldots, \theta_n)$ be a transcendental elementary field. We say that F is *factored* if for each logarithmic extension, $\theta = \log(a)$, a is an irreducible polynomial in $C[x, \theta_1, \ldots, \theta_{i-1}]$. A simple induction shows that any transcendental elementary field can be imbedded in a factored transcendental elementary field. Next let F be a general elementary field, (i.e. allow any of the θ's to be algebraic), and rearrange the θ's into a tower $C(x) = F_0 \subseteq F_1 \subseteq \cdots \subseteq F_r = F$ where $F_i = F_{i-1}(\theta_{i1}, \ldots, \theta_{ik_i})$ for $i=1,\ldots,r$ and where one of the following holds for each θ_{ij}:

(i) θ_{ij} is algebraic over F_{i-1} but transcendental over F_{i-2}.

(ii) $\theta_{ij}' = \frac{u_{ij}'}{u_{ij}}$ for some nonzero u_{ij} in F_{i-1} where u_{ij} is not in F_{i-2}.

(iii) $\theta_{ij}' = \theta_{ij} u_{ij}'$ for some u_{ij} in F_{i-1} where u_{ij} is not in F_{i-2}.

We define the *rank* of a tower of transcendental elementary fields $F = C(x, \theta_1, \ldots, \theta_n)$, denoted $rank(F)$, to be the tuple $(m_r, \cdots, m_1, 1)$ where m_i is the transcendence degree of F_i over F_{i-1}. We can also define the rank of a particular element in F. Let $F_0, \ldots, F_r$ be as above. An element a in F has rank k if a is an element of F_k and a is not an element of F_{k-1}. Next let F be as above and let $\theta_i = \exp(a_i)$ be an exponential monomial of rank k. Suppose that $a_i = \sum \frac{p_j}{q_j}\theta_j + \gamma$, where p_j and q_j are integers, the θ_j are logarithmic monomials of rank $k-1$ and $rank(\gamma) < k-1$. We shall call such monomials *normalized* if, for all j,

$0<\frac{p_j}{q_j}<1$ and say that F is normalized if each exponential monomial with the above format is normalized. Once again it is easy to show that every transcendental elementary field can be imbedded in (actually, is isomorphic to) a normalized transcendental elementary field.

The main theorem for logarithmic integrals follows.

Theorem 2.2: Let $C(x)$ be a differential field of characteristic zero where x is transcendental over C, a solution to $x'=1$, and C is an algebraically closed subfield of constants. Let $E=C(x,\theta_1, \ldots ,\theta_n)$, $n\geq 0$, be a transcendental elementary extension of $C(x)$ that is factored and normalized. Given γ in E, one can decide in a finite number of steps if γ has an antiderivative in some li-elementary extension of E, and if so, find constants c_i and d_i and elements w_i, u_i, v_i in E satisfying (2.1).

It is important to note that the definitions for exponentials and logarithms used in differential algebra are more general than the corresponding notions in classical analysis. For example, the function $\ln(x)+c$, where $\ln(x)$ denotes the unique solution to $y'-\frac{1}{x}=0, y(1)=0$, is a logarithm of x for any constant c. The following example shows where this generality occurs in the above theorems.

Example: Let $\overline{Q}$ denote the algebraic closure of the rationals and let $F=\overline{Q}(x,\ln(x))$. Then $\gamma=\frac{1}{\ln(x)+1}$ has an antiderivative in an li-elementary extension of F since (2.1) is satisfied with $u_1=x$, $v_1=\ln(x)+1$, $d_1=1$ and $w_i=c_i=0$. Notice, however, that by introducing a transcendental constant we can choose a new value for u_1, say $\tilde{u}_1=ex$, and write $\int\gamma$ as $\frac{1}{e}\int\frac{(ex)'}{\log(ex)}dx=\frac{1}{e}li(ex)$ which has the added property that $v_1=\ln(\tilde{u}_1)$. □

It is easy to show that a similar adjustment can be made in the general case and, in fact, this was done in our implementation of the algorithm. (See the appendix).

The proof of Theorem 2.2 is broken down into cases many of which are resolved using the Main Theorem part (b) from [Risch69]. The remaining cases are each reduced to the calculation of what we have termed Σ-decompositions. This type of decomposition, which can be thought of as a generalization of the p-adic decomposition of a rational function (where there are a number of irreducible multivariate polynomials), is demonstrated in the following examples.

Example: Consider $\int\frac{x^3}{\log(x^2-1)}dx$. First the integrand must be rewritten as $\frac{x^3}{\log(x+1)+\log(x-1)}$ with the factored tower of monomials $C(x,\theta_1=\log(x-1),\theta_2=\log(x+1))$. In the course of the algorithm it becomes necessary to determine a Σ-decomposition for $(2x^4-3x^2+1)/2$; i.e. to determine if there exist integers r_i, $\tilde{r}_i$ and constants β_i so that (among other things)

$$\frac{2x^4-3x^2+1}{2} = \sum\beta_i(x+1)^{r_i}(x-1)^{\tilde{r}_i} .$$

If such rational numbers exist then

$$\int\frac{x^3}{\log(x^2-1)}dx = \sum\frac{\beta_i}{r_i}li((x+1)^{r_i}(x-1)^{\tilde{r}_i})$$

and if they do not exist then the integral can not be written in terms of elementary functions and logarithmic integrals. However, such values do exist: $r_1=\tilde{r}_1=1$, $\beta_1=\frac{1}{2}$, $r_2=\tilde{r}_2=2$ and $\beta_2=1$, and hence,

$$\int \frac{x^3}{\log(x^2-1)}\,dx = \frac{1}{2}li(x^4-2x^2+1)+\frac{1}{2}li(x^2-1) \ .$$

Similarly when integrating $\int \frac{x^2}{\log(x^2-1)}\,dx$, one must find values r_i, $\tilde{r}_i$ and β_i so that

$$\frac{3x^4-4x^2+1}{4x} = \sum \beta_i (x+1)^{r_i}(x-1)^{\tilde{r}_i}$$

In this case no such decomposition exists and so $\int \frac{x^2}{\log(x^2-1)}\,dx$ can not be written in terms of elementary functions and logarithmic integrals. □

3. THE ERROR FUNCTION

We begin again with a generalization of the elementary extensions. Let F be a differential field of characteristic zero with derivation $'$ and constants C. We say that a differential extension E of F is a erf-elementary extension of F if $F=F_0 \subseteq F_1 \subseteq \cdots \subseteq F_n=E$ such that $F_i=F_{i-1}(\theta_i)$ where for each i, $1 \le i \le n$, one of the following holds:

(i) θ_i is algebraic over F_{i-1}.

(ii) $\theta_i{}'=u'\theta_i$ for some u in F_{i-1}. (i.e. $\theta_i=\exp(u)$).

(iii) $\theta_i{}'=u'/u$ for some nonzero u in F_{i-1}. (i.e. $\theta_i=\log(u)$).

(iv) $\theta_i{}'=u'v$ for some u and v in F_{i-1} such that $v'=(-u^2)'v$. In this case we write $\theta_i=erf(u)$.

The Liouville theorem for erf-extensions was first stated in [Ssc81]:

Theorem 3.1: Let F be a liouvillian extension of its field of constants C. Assume C is of characteristic zero and algebraically closed and let γ be an element of F. If γ has an antiderivative in some erf-elementary extension of F, then there exist constants c_i and d_i in C, elements w_i in F, and elements u_i and v_i algebraic over F such that

$$\gamma = w_0{}' + \sum c_i \frac{w_i{}'}{w_i} + \sum d_i u_i{}' v_i \tag{3.1}$$

where $v_i{}'=(-u_i^2)'v_i$ and u_i^2, v_i^2 and $u_i{}'v_i$ are in F.

Notice that this is a weaker result than Theorem 2.1.

Our decision procedure for error functions does not hold for all transcendental elementary fields but only to those which are *reduced*. We say that a transcendental elementary field, F, is reduced if no algebraic extension of F has a lower rank*.

(*) The ordering relation used here is the following: $(m_r, \ldots, m_1, 1) < (\overline{m}_s, \ldots, \overline{m}_1, 1)$ if $r < s$ or if $r = s$ and $(m_r, \ldots, 1) < (\overline{m}_s, \ldots, 1)$ the usual lexicographic ordering.

Example: The field $F=C(x,\log(x),\exp(\frac{1}{2}\log(x)+x))$ is not reduced since $rank(F)=(1,1,1)$ and $\tilde{F}=C(x,\sqrt{x},\log(x),\exp(x))$, which is algebraic over F, has a rank of (2,1). □

The main theorem for error functions can now be stated.

Theorem 3.2: Let $C(x)$ be a differential field of characteristic zero where x is transcendental over C, a solution to $x'=1$, and C is an algebraically closed subfield of constants. Let $E=C(x,\theta_1, \ldots, \theta_n)$, $n \geq 0$, be a transcendental elementary extension of $C(x)$ that is factored and reduced. Given γ in E, one can decide in a finite number of steps if γ has an antiderivative in some erf-elementary extension of E, and if so, find constants c_i and d_i, elements w_i in E and u_i, v_i algebraic over E satisfying (3.1).

The proof of this theorem uses similar techniques to those employed in Theorem 2.2. That is, the basic subprocedures are, once again, the Main Theorem part(b) from [Risch69] and the procedure for determining Σ-decompositions.

4. CONCLUSIONS

Certainly the importance of the results presented here depends on whether these ideas can be extended to other special functions. However, it is well-known that the exponential integral, sin integral and cosine integral can be written in terms of the logarithmic integral and that the Fresnel integrals can be written in terms of error functions[Bat53]. Thus a number of other special functions are indirectly covered here. (See examples (c8) and (c9) in the Appendix). Still there are others, such as the dilogarithm, which appear to be fundamentally different. Even in these more radical cases, however, we hope that notions such as rank, reduced and normalized fields will be useful.

ACKNOWEDGEMENTS

We wish to thank David Saunders and Michael Singer for many helpful discussions and Richard Fateman for his help with the Vaxima integration code.

REFERENCES

[Bate53] H. Bateman, *Higher Transcendental Functions*, McGraw-Hill, New York, 1953.

[Cher83a] G. Cherry, *Algorithms for Integrating Transcendental Elementary Functions in terms of Logarithmic Integrals and Error Functions*, PhD dissertation, Univ. of Delaware, 1983.

[Cher83b] G. Cherry, Integration in Finite Terms with Special Functions: The Logarithmic Integral, submitted SIAM J. of Computing.

[Mos71] J. Moses, Symbolic Integration, the Stormy Decade, Communications of the ACM, 14, 1971, pp. 548-560.

[Nor79] A. C. Norman and J. H. Davenport, Symbolic Integration - The Dust Settles?, in *Symbolic and Algebraic Computation*, E. W. Ng (ed.), Springer-Verlag, 1979, pp. 398-407.

[Risch69] R. H. Risch, The Problem of Integration in Finite Terms, Trans. of the A.M.S., 139, 1969, pp. 167-189.

[Ssc81] M. F. Singer, B. D. Saunders, and B. F. Caviness, An Extension of Liouville's Theorem on Integration in Finite Terms, SIAM J. of Computing, to appear. Extended Abstract in *Proceedings of the 1981 ACM Symposium on Symbolic and Algebraic Computation*, P. S. Wang (ed.).

APPENDIX

The following Macsyma session demonstrates a partial implementation of Theorem 2.2.

```
(c1) int(x/log(x)^2,x):
```

Time= 1216 msec.

$$\int \frac{x}{\log(x)^2}\, dx = 2\,\mathrm{li}(x^2) - \frac{x^2}{\log(x)} \tag{d1}$$

```
(c2) /* The following example shows how transcendental constants
   can be introduced. Int first
   calculates the values u1=x, v1=log(x)+3 and d1=1.
   In the last stage of the computations u1 is replaced with
   e^3x and d1 is replaced
   with 1/e^3. */

int(1/(log(x)+3),x);
```

Time= 983 msec.

$$\int \frac{1}{\log(x)+3}\, dx = e^{-3}\mathrm{li}(e^3 x) \tag{d2}$$

```
(c3) /* An example the generation of a number of logarithmic integrals */

int(x^2/log(x+1),x);
```

Time= 1900 msec.

$$\int \frac{x^2}{\log(x+1)}\, dx \tag{d3}$$

$$= \mathrm{li}(x^3+3x^2+3x+1) - 2\,\mathrm{li}(x^2+2x+1) + \mathrm{li}(x+1)$$

(c4) /* It follows from Theorem 2.2 that any expression of the form $\int u' g(\log(u))dx$ where g is a rational function with constant coefficients can be integrated in terms of elementary functions and logarithmic integrals. For example */

```
int((log(x)^2+3)/(log(x)^2+3*log(x)+2),x);
```

Time= 2233 msec.

$$\int \frac{\log(x)^2+3}{\log(x)^2+3\log(x)+2}\,dx = -7e^{-2}\mathrm{li}(e^2x)+4e^{-1}\mathrm{li}(ex)+x \qquad (d4)$$

(c5) /* Macsyma can also differentiate expressions involving logarithmic integrals. ('%' refers to the previous expression) */

```
li(x/log(x)*exp(x));
```

Time= 50 msec.

$$\mathrm{li}\left(\frac{xe^x}{\log(x)}\right) \qquad (d5)$$

(c6) ratsimp(diff(%,x));

Time= 516 msec.

$$\frac{(x+1)e^x\log(x)-e^x}{\log(x)^2\log\left(\frac{xe^x}{\log(x)}\right)} \qquad (d6)$$

(c7) /* Now integrate this expression: */

```
int(%,x);
```

Time= 8266 msec.

$$\int \frac{(x+1)e^x\log(x)-e^x}{\log(x)^2\log\left(\frac{xe^x}{\log(x)}\right)}\,dx = \mathrm{li}\left(\frac{xe^x}{\log(x)}\right) \qquad (d7)$$

(c8) /* Since li(u)=ei(e^u), where ei(v)=$\int \frac{v'e^v}{v} dx$
is the exponential integral, int will use the 'ei' notation
in these situations. For example */

```
int(exp(x)/(x+1)^2,x);
```

Time= 3350 msec.

$$\int \frac{e^x}{(x+1)^2}\, dx = e^{-1} ei(x+1) - \frac{e^x}{x+1} \tag{d8}$$

(c9) /* The sine integral can be integrated in terms of logarithmic
integrals: */

```
int(sin(x)/x,x);
```

Time= 8216 msec.

$$\int \frac{\sin(x)}{x}\, dx = -\frac{i ei(ix) - i ei(-ix)}{2} \tag{d9}$$

(c10) /* as well as a number of other trigonometric integrands: */

```
int(cos(x)^2/x^3,x);
```

Time= 8750 msec.

$$\int \frac{\cos(x)^2}{x^3}\, dx = -\frac{2x^2 ei(2ix) + 2x^2 ei(-2ix) - 2x\sin(2x) + \cos(2x) + 1}{4x^2} \tag{d10}$$

(c11) /* Any expression of the form $\int u'e^u g(u) dx$ where g
is a rational function with constant coefficients
can be integrated in terms of logarithmic integrals: */

```
int((x^2+3)/(x^2+3*x+2)*exp(x),x);
```

Time= 6800 msec.

$$\int \frac{(x^2+3)e^x}{x^2+3x+2}\, dx = -7e^{-2} ei(x+2) + 4e^{-1} ei(x+1) + e^x \tag{d11}$$

A Note on the Risch Differential Equation*

Erich Kaltofen

University of Toronto
Department of Computer Science
Toronto, Ontario M5S1A4, Canada

Abstract

This paper relates to the technique of integrating a function in a purely transcendental regular elementary Liouville extension by prescribing degree bounds for the transcendentals and then solving linear systems over the constants. The problem of finding such bounds explicitly remains yet to be solved due to the so-called third possibilities in the estimates for the degrees given in R. Risch's original algorithm.
We prove that in the basis case in which we have only exponentials of rational functions, the bounds arising from the third possibilities are again degree bounds of the inputs. This result provides an algorithm for solving the differential equation $y' + f'y = g$ in y where f, g and y are rational functions over an arbitrary constant field. This new algorithm can be regarded as a direct generalization of the algorithm by E. Horowitz for computing the rational part of the integral of a rational function (i.e. $f' = 0$), though its correctness proof is quite different.

1. Introduction

The problem of finding an elementary integral of a function in a regular elementary Liouville extension, that is a function composed recursively by the four basic arithmetic operations and applications of logarithms and exponentials, but not algebraics, ultimately leads to solving the differential equation y' + $f'y = g$ in y, where f, g and y are elements in the field of the integrand itself. (cf. Risch [9]; for further motivation, see also Rosenlicht [5, p. 160]). It is at this stage of the decision procedure at which the size of the answer can become unproportionally large compared to the integrand. An example, stated by several authors, is $\int \exp(x+100 \log x)\, dx$, the closed form of which is a polynomial with 101 terms in x times $\exp(x)$. This blow-up is accounted for in Risch's original proof by the so-called third possibilities in the estimates for the degrees of the answer. However, these bounds can only be calculated if one has, in addition to just performing arithmetic in the constant field C of the integrand including testing for equality to 0, some specialized routines for

* This research was partially supported by the National Science and Engineering Council of Canada under grant 3-643-126-90.
Author's current address: Rensselaer Polytechnic Institute, Department Mathematical Sciences, Troy, New York, 12181.

C. Risch's original algorithm requires polynomial factorization over the constant field as well as testing for integrality, but it has been shown by M. Rothstein [7, 8] that the computation of integral roots of polynomials over C is sufficient.†

It is the subject of the so-called parallel Risch algorithm to compute these bounds without eliminating the exponentials or logarithms in succession (cf. Norman and Moore [4]). Unfortunately, no complete algorithm is known though progress has been made in special cases, e.g. by Davenport [1] who focuses on logarithmic extensions. In this note we will prove that in the basis case the third possibilities for the degree estimates of y in $y' + f'y = g$, f, g, $y \in C(x)$, if the arise give also bounds expressible in the degrees in f and g. An immediate consequence of this result is, that for size blow-up to occur the nested logarithm in the previous example is essential. It also eliminates the need for the special purpose routines for C. The result may explain why the heuristic bounds (cf. Fitch [2]) appear so robust, in practice.

Another interpretation of our result is possible. E. Horowitz [3] has given an algorithm for finding the rational part of a rational function integral by solving a linear system without performing the squarefree factorization of the integrand's denominator. Our result leads to an equivalent algorithm which by setting $f' = 0$, has Horowitz' approach as a special case.

Our paper is arranged in the following way. Section 2 introduces some notation and establishes preliminary facts needed for the proof. Section 3 contains the formulation and proof of the main result as well as links this result to Horowitz' algorithm.

2. Notation and Preliminary Results

The ring $C[x]$ of polynomials with coefficients in the field C becomes a differential ring with derivation $'$ if we prescribe that $c' = 0$ for any $c \in C$ and $x' = 1$. Its field of quotients, $C(x)$, is of course the field of rational functions over C. We always assume that C is a field of characteristic 0. By $\mathrm{ldcf}(f)$ we denote the leading coefficient of a polynomial $f \in C[x]$ and we call f monic if $\mathrm{ldcf}(f) = 1$. As is well known, every polynomial $q \in C[x]$ can be decomposed by GCD computations into a product $q_1 q_2^2 \cdots q_r^r$ of squarefree polynomials q_i with $\mathrm{GCD}(q_i, q_j) = 1$ for $i \neq j$. This squarefree decomposition is also unique up to a scalar factor in C. Furthermore, every rational function p/q, $p, q \in C[x]$, q monic, can be uniquely expanded into partial fractions with respect to the squarefree decomposition of q, namely

$$\frac{p}{q} = p_0 + \sum_{i=1}^{r} \sum_{j=1}^{i} \frac{p_{ij}}{q_i^j}, \quad p_0, p_{ij} \in C[x], \deg(p_{ij}) < \deg(q_i).$$

† It appears to me that this claim extends to the problem of deciding whether an integral of a function in a transcendental Liouville extension is elementary or not. However, the argument seems fairly complicated (cf. Rothstein [7, pp. 46-47]).

The following lemma will be applied in various places of our argument.

Lemma 1: Let $u, v \in C[x]$, $\mathrm{GCD}(u, v) = 1$ and let $(u/v)' = p/q, p, q \in C[x]$, $\mathrm{GCD}(p, q) = 1$. Assume that $w \in C[x]$ is squarefree such that w divides q. Then w divides v and if r is the multiplicity of w in v, w^{r+1} must divide q.

Proof: First it is easy to realize that we can restrict ourselves to w being irreducible. Otherwise, since w is squarefree, applying the lemma for all irreducible factors of w leads to the one for w itself. Notice that r is the minimal multiplicity with which any irreducible factor of w occurs in q. Now, since

$$\left(\frac{u}{v}\right)' = \frac{u'v - uv'}{v^2} = \frac{p}{q}$$

it is clear that w must divide v. Assume now that $v = w^r \hat{w}$ with $\mathrm{GCD}(w, \hat{w}) = 1$. We show that w^r does not divide $u'v - uv'$. Suppose the contrary. Since w^r divides $u'v$ and $\mathrm{GCD}(w, u) = 1$, w^r then would have to divide $v' = rw^{r-1}w'\hat{w} + w^r\hat{w}'$, hence w needed to divide $w'\hat{w}$. But this is impossible since w is irreducible. Therefore w^{r+1} must remain in the reduced denominator of $(u/v)'$. □

This very elementary lemma provides us with quite a powerful tool. To demonstrate this, consider the rational integral

$$\int \frac{p(x)}{q(x)} dx, \quad p, q \in C[x], \deg(p) < \deg(q).$$

Set $\bar{q} = \mathrm{GCD}(q, q')$ and $q^* = q/\bar{q}$, i.e. q^* is the largest squarefree factor of q. We can show that there exist unique polynomials $g, h \in C[x]$ such that

$$\int \frac{p(x)}{q(x)} dx = \frac{g(x)}{\bar{q}(x)} + \int \frac{h(x)}{q^*(x)} dx, \quad \deg(g) < \deg(\bar{q}), \quad \deg(h) < \deg(q^*). \tag{2.1}$$

For, differentiating (2.1) and multiplying by the common denominator q gives

$$p = q^* g' - \frac{q^* \bar{q}'}{\bar{q}} g + \bar{q} h \tag{2.2}$$

where

$$\frac{q^* q'}{q} = \frac{q^*}{q}\left(\frac{q}{q^*}\right)' = \frac{q'}{q} - q^{*\prime} \in C[x],$$

since $\bar{q}$ divides q'. Plugging unknown coefficients for g and h into (2.2) and equating the coefficients of equal powers of x^i, $0 \le i \le \deg(q) - 1$, we get a linear system in $\deg(q)$ equations and $\deg(q)$ unknows. This system has a unique solution if the only solution for $p = 0$ is $g = h = 0$. This follows from lemma 1 since $(g/\bar{q})' = -h/q^*$ has no non-trivial solution because q^* is squarefree. We have incidentally also shown that $\int h/q^*$ cannot be a rational function.

Setting up and solving the linear system resulting from (2.2) is Horowitz' algorithm. It should be noted that neither the full squarefree factorization of

q nor Hermite's reduction is needed in this method, the latter not even in the correctness proof.

3. Main Result

We now show how to solve the differential equation $y' + f'y = g$ in y, where $f, y, g \in C(x)$. We first repeat Risch's original argument, enhanced by Rothstein's observations.

Theorem 1: Let $C(x)$ be the transcendental extension of the constant field C with $x' = 1$. Assume that f and $g \in C(x)$ are given. Then we can solve

$$y' + fy = g, \; y \in C(x) \tag{3.1}$$

in a finite number of arithmetic operations in C, including computing integer roots of polynomials over C.

Proof: We represent, by GCD computations,

$$f(x) = \frac{F(x)}{q_1(x)^{k_1} \cdots q_n(x)^{k_n}}, \quad g(x) = \frac{G(x)}{q_1(x)^{l_1} \cdots q_n(x)^{l_n}}$$

where $F, G, q_1, \ldots, q_n \in C[x]$, $q_1, \ldots, q_n$ monic, squarefree and pairwise relatively prime, $k_i \geq 0$, $l_i \geq 0$ for $1 \leq i \leq n$. From lemma 1 we conclude that if $y(x)$ solves (3.1) then

$$y(x) = \frac{Y(x)}{q_1(x)^{j_1} \cdots q_n(x)^{j_n}}$$

with $Y(x) \in C[x]$, $j_i \geq 0$ for $1 \leq i \leq n$. We first compute a bound $\overline{j_i}$ for j_i, $1 \leq i \leq n$, and then a bound $\bar{\alpha}$ for $\deg_x(Y)$. Let

$$y(x) = \frac{A_{i,j_i}(x)}{q_i(x)^{j_i}} + \cdots, \; f(x) = \frac{B_{i,k_i}(x)}{q_i(x)^{k_i}} + \cdots, \; g(x) = \frac{D_{i,l_i}(x)}{q_i(x)^{l_i}} + \cdots.$$

be the partial fraction expansion of y, f, and g with A_{i,j_i}, B_{i,l_i}, $D_{i,l_i} \in C[x]$ non-zero and $\deg_x(A_{i,j_i}) < \deg(q_i)$ unless $j_i = 0$, $\deg(B_{i,k_i}) < \deg(q_i)$ unless $k_i = 0$. Substituting these expansions into (3.1) we get

$$-\frac{j_i q_i' A_{i,j_i}}{q_i^{j_i+1}} + \cdots + \frac{B_{i,k_i} A_{i,j_i}}{q_i^{j_i+k_i}} + \cdots = \frac{D_{i,l_i}}{q_i^{l_i}} + \cdots.$$

We first observe that $j_i + 1 \leq l_i$ is equivalent to $j_i + k_i \leq l_i$ since otherwise one of the leading terms could not cancel on the left-hand side. The third possibility is that $j_i + 1 = j_i + k_i > l_i$. In this case,

$$k_i = 1 \text{ and } q_i \text{ divides } -j_i q_i' A_{i,j_i} + B_{i,k_i} A_{i,j_i},$$

which implies that $\mathrm{GCD}(-j_i q_i' + B_{i,k_i}, q_i) \neq 1$. Therefore, j_i must be a root of the resultant

$$R(z) = \mathrm{resultant}_x(B_{i,k_i}(x) - z\, q_i'(x), q_i(x)) \in C[z].$$

First of all, $R(z) \neq 0$ because otherwise for some root β of $q_i(x)$, $B_{i,k_i}(\beta) - z\, q_i'(\beta) = 0$ meaning $q_i'(\beta) = 0$ which contradicts the squarefreeness of q_i. Let m_i be the largest positive integral root of $R(z)$, if any, otherwise let $m_i = 0$. Then

$$j_i \leq \bar{j_i} = \max(\min(l_i - 1,\, l_i - k_i),\, m_i).$$

We now set

$$y(x) = \frac{Y(x)}{q_1(x)^{\bar{j_1}} \cdots q_n(x)^{\bar{j_n}}} = \frac{Y(x)}{\bar{q}(x)}$$

and substitute into (3.1). Multiplying out with a common denominator we get

$$u\, Y' + v\, Y = t \tag{3.2}$$

with

$$Y(x) = y_\alpha x^\alpha + \cdots + y_0,\quad u(x) = a_\beta x^\beta + \cdots + a_0 \in C[x],$$
$$v(x) = b_\gamma x^\gamma + \cdots + b_0 \text{ and } t(x) = d_\delta x^\delta + \cdots + d_0 \in C[x].$$

Again it behooves us to determine a bound for α. Substitution in (3.2) gives

$$(a_\beta x^\beta + \cdots)(\alpha y_\alpha x^{\alpha-1} + \cdots) + (b_\gamma x^\gamma + \cdots)(y_\alpha x^\alpha + \cdots) = d_\delta x^\delta + \cdots. \tag{3.3}$$

Thus $\alpha + \beta - 1 \leq \delta$ if and only if $\alpha + \gamma \leq \delta$ or the third case $\alpha + \beta - 1 = \alpha + \gamma > \delta$ which implies that $\alpha a_\beta + b_\gamma = 0$. Let ρ be $-b_\gamma / a_\beta$ if this is a positive integer, otherwise let $\rho = -1$. Then

$$\alpha \leq \bar{\alpha} = \max(\min(\delta - \beta - 1,\, \delta - \gamma),\, \rho).$$

If $\bar{\alpha} < 0$ then (3.3) and thus (3.1) has no solution. Otherwise we multiply (3.3) out with $\alpha = \alpha$ and equate powers of x^i. We thus obtain a linear system in the y_i's with coefficients in C which we then solve. □

We now further inspect the third possibilities in the case that f is the derivative of a rational function.

Theorem 2: If one applies the algorithm given in the proof of theorem 1 to the differential equation $y' + f'y = g$, the third possibility for the bound $\bar{j_i}$ can never occur and the only time the third possibility for the bound $\bar{\alpha}$ can happen is when $\rho = \deg(\bar{q})$.

Proof: Assume that $j_i + 1 > l_i$ which implies that $k_i = 1$. Thus the partial fraction expansion

$$f'(x) = \frac{B_{i,k_i}(x)}{q_i(x)} + \cdots$$

which is impossible as shown in lemma 1. Now let

$$y(x) = \frac{Y(x)}{\bar{q}(x)},\quad f'(x) = \frac{p(x)}{\hat{q}(x)},\quad g(x) = \frac{s(x)}{q(x)}.$$

Notice that $\bar{q}(x)$ divides $q(x)$. Substituting into our differential equation $y' + f'y = g$ we get

$$\frac{Y'(x)}{\bar{q}(x)} + \left[\frac{p(x)}{\hat{q}(x)} - \frac{\bar{q}'(x)}{\bar{q}(x)}\right]\frac{Y(x)}{\bar{q}(x)} = \frac{s(x)}{q(x)} \tag{3.4}$$

Since the bound $\bar{\alpha}$ depends only on the difference $\delta - \beta$ and $\delta - \gamma$ as well as the quotient b_γ / a_β it does not matter for the determination of $\bar{\alpha}$ if we multiply (3.4) with a larger than the least common denominator. We get

$$(\bar{q}\,\hat{q}\,q)\,Y' + q\,(p\,\bar{q} - \hat{q}\,\bar{q}')\,Y = \bar{q}^2\hat{q}\,s.$$

The third possibility implies that

$$\beta = \deg(\bar{q}\,\hat{q}\,q) = \gamma + 1 = \deg(q\,(p\,\bar{q} - \hat{q}\,\bar{q}')) + 1.$$

If $\deg(p) \geq \deg(\hat{q})$, this is clearly impossible. Thus $\deg(p) < \deg(\hat{q})$ which, since

$$\frac{p}{\hat{q}} = f' = (\frac{d}{e})' = \frac{d'e - de'}{e^2}, \quad d, e \in C[x],$$

implies that we may choose $\deg(d) < \deg(e)$ and thus get $\deg(p) \leq \deg(\hat{q}) - 2$. Therefore, $a_\beta = \mathrm{ldcf}(\bar{q}\,\hat{q}\,q) = 1$, $b_\gamma = \mathrm{ldcf}(q\,(p\,\bar{q} - \hat{q}\,\bar{q}')) = \mathrm{ldcf}(-\bar{q}')$ and thus $-b_\gamma / a_\beta = \rho = \deg(\bar{q})$. □

We now present an example showing that the case $\deg(Y) = \deg(\bar{q}) > \min(\delta-\beta-1,\ \delta-\gamma)$ can occur.

Example: Let $f' = -1/x^2$, $g = -(x+1)/x^4$. Then $q_1 = x$, $k_1 = 2$, $l_1 = 4$, $\bar{j_1} = \min(l_1-1,\ l_1-k_1) = 2$ and

$$(\frac{Y}{x^2})' - \frac{1}{x^2}\,\frac{Y}{x^2} = -\frac{x+1}{x^4} \quad \text{with } \bar{q}(x) = x^2.$$

This leads to

$$x^2\,Y' - (2x+1)\,Y = -x - 1.$$

Thus, $\beta = 2$, $\gamma = 1$, $\delta = 1$ and

$$\bar{\alpha} = \max(\min(\delta-\beta-1,\ \delta-\gamma),\ \deg(\bar{q})) = \max(\min(-2, -1), 2) = 2.$$

Solving for $Y = y_2x^2 + y_1x + y_0$ we get $y_2 = 1$, $y_1 = -1$, $y_0 = 1$. Hence

$$\int \frac{x+1}{x^4}\exp(\frac{1}{x}) = -\frac{x^2-x+1}{x^2}\exp(\frac{1}{x}). \quad \square$$

It is surprisingly easy to show that the solution to $y' + f'y = g$, $f' \neq 0$, is unique. Suppose the contrary that is y_1 and $y_2 \in C[x]$ solve the differential equation. Then with $\bar{y} = y_1 - y_2 \neq 0$ we must have $\bar{y}'/\bar{y} = -f'$. It is easy to see from $\int \bar{y}'/\bar{y} = \log(\bar{y})$ that $\bar{y}'/\bar{y}$ can be written as h/q^* with $h, q^* \in C[x]$ and q^* squarefree. But as mentioned in section 1, $\int h/q^*$ cannot be the rational function $-f$.

We now derive from theorem 2 an algorithm for solving

$$y' + f'y = g, \quad f' = \frac{p}{\hat{q}} \in C[x], \quad g = \frac{s}{q} \in C(x)$$

equivalent to Horowitz' rational function integration algorithm. We choose $\bar{q} = \mathrm{GCD}(q, q')$ as the denominator of y. This choice is equivalent to setting $\bar{j_i} = l_i - 1$, which is not necessarily the sharpest bound but which avoids computing the full squarefree factorization of $\bar{q}$ and q. Then we calculate the bound $\bar{\alpha}$ for degree of the numerator of y and solve the resulting linear system as discussed in the proof of theorem 1. One upper bound for $\bar{\alpha}$ is

$$\bar{\alpha} \le \max(\deg(\bar{q}) - \deg(q) + \deg(s) - 1, \deg(\bar{q}))$$

which is slightly pessimistic but which, we hope, exhibits the similarity to Horowitz' algorithm.

Due to M. Rothstein [7, 8], the degree bound $\bar{\alpha}$ for Y in $u\,Y' + v\,Y = t$ can be further reduced in the following way. If $\mathrm{GCD}(u, v) \neq 1$ then we divide u, v and t by this GCD. Obviously, if the division of t leaves a remainder then the differential equation has no solution. Thus we may assume that $\mathrm{GCD}(u, v) = 1$ and we can find unique polynomials d, $e \in C[x]$ with

$$u\,d + v\,e = t, \quad \deg(e) < \deg(u).$$

Now $Y = \bar{Y} u + r$, $\deg(r) < \deg(u)$, if and only if

$$r = e \quad \text{and} \quad u\bar{Y}' + (u' + v)\bar{Y} = d - e'.$$

Thus solving for $\bar{Y}$ with $\deg(\bar{Y}) = \bar{\alpha} - \beta$ is sufficient. Of course, we can repeat this process until either $\deg(\bar{Y}) < \beta$ or $\deg(u) = 0$. In the first case $u\bar{Y}' + v\bar{Y} = t$ implies $\bar{Y} \equiv t\,v^{-1}$ modulo u. Thus we only need to invert v modulo u. The second case must be handled by solving linear systems as discussed above.

One could argue that so far we have only shown that no exponent blow-up due to "third possibilities" occurs when integrating elements in $C(x, \exp f(x))$, $f(x) \in C(x)$. It is relatively easy to show that this remains true when we integrate elements in

$$C(x)[\exp f_1(x), \ldots, \exp f_n(x)], \quad f_i(x) \in C(x). \tag{4.1}$$

We assume that the $\exp f_i$ are algebraically independent over $C(x)$ and introduce no new constants. An element in (4.1) can be written as

$$\sum g_{e_1, \ldots, e_n}(x) \exp(e_1 f_1(x) + \cdots + e_n f_n(x)), \quad g_{e_1, \ldots, e_n}(x) \in C(x),\ e_i \in \mathbb{Z}. \tag{4.2}$$

By our assumption, the arguments to the exponentials in (4.2) cannot differ by just a constant. It now is an old result by Liouville (cf. Rosenlicht [6, p.295]) that the integral of (4.2) is elementary if and only if each

$$\int g_{e_1, \ldots, e_n}(x) \exp(e_1 f_1(x) + \cdots + e_n f_n(x))$$

is elementary. This integral leads, of course, to solving a differential equation of type (3.1). Therefore, theorem 2 implies that the exponents in the integral of an integrand in (4.1) depend only on the exponents in the integrand.

Our conclusions partially generalize in the case in which C is replaced by a regular elementary purely transcendental Liouville extension of $C(x)$ and x is replaced by a logarithm or exponential. However, as we have already exemplified in the introduction, bounds for the third possibilities cannot be derived from the input degrees alone, in general.

4. Conclusion

The complexity of R. Risch's algorithm for deciding whether a function in an elementary purely transcendental Liouville extension field possesses an elementary integral is little understood. The fact that one seems to need the closed form solution for just recognizing elementary integrals indicates that the given decision procedure might not even be elementary recursive. Here we have settled two questions. Firstly, we have shown that even in the basis case third possibilities can arise. Secondly, however, we have put this basis case into the class of polynomial-time problems.

Acknowledgement

I like to express my gratitude to the students and colleagues in my integration course at University of Toronto for their many thoughts on the subject. James Davenport pointed out an improvement in the bound computation what I wish to acknowledge. Thanks go also to Guy Cherry whose trick of summing up arguments to exponentials I have used in section 4.

References

[1] Davenport, J. H.: The parallel Risch algorithm (I). Proc. EUROCAM '82. Springer Lec. Notes Comp. Sci. **144**, 144 - 159 (1982).

[2] Fitch, J.: User based integration software. Proc. SYMSAC '81. ACM, 245 - 248 (1981).

[3] Horowitz, E.: Algorithms for partial fraction decomposition and rational function integration. Proc. SYMSAM '71. ACM, 441 - 457 (1971).

[4] Norman, A.C., and Moore, P.M.A.: Implementing the new Risch algorithm. Proc. Conf. Adv. Comp. Methods in Theoretical Physics at St. Maximin, 99 - 110 (1977).

[5] Rosenlicht, M.: Liouville's theorem on functions with elementary integrals. Pacific J. Math. **24**, 153 - 161 (1968).

[6] Rosenlicht, M.: Differential extension fields of exponential type. Pacific J. Math. **57**, 289-300 (1975).

[7] Rothstein, M.: Aspects of Symbolic Integration and Simplification of Exponential and Primitive Functions. Ph.D. thesis, Univ. Wisconsin 1976.

[8] Rothstein, M.: A new algorithm for integration of exponential and logarithmic functions. Proc. Macsyma Users' Conference. NASA, 263 - 274 (1977).

[9] Risch, R.H.: The problem of integration in finite terms. Trans. Amer. Math. Soc. **139**, 167 - 189 (1969).

Approximation by Continued Fraction of a Polynomial Real Root

Klaus Thull
Hauptstrasse 76
D-6900 Heidelberg

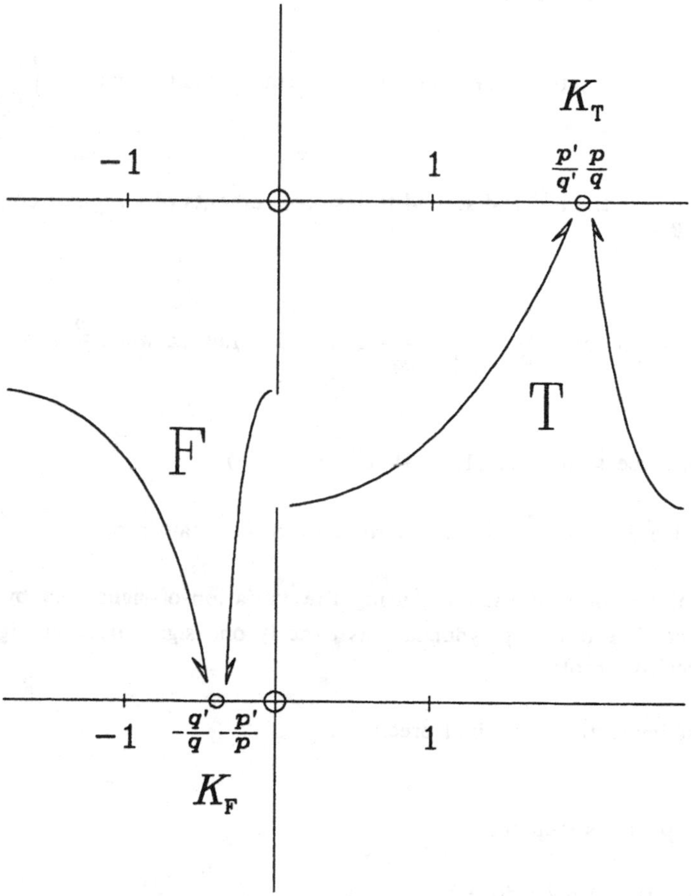

Theorems 1a and 1b on the Complex Plane

Abstract:

A new algorithm is presented which by experiment has proven to be faster by a factor of 3-4 than Newton's algorithm, and faster, too, than the stepwise approach used until now.

Keywords: polynomials, algebraic numbers, continued fraction, rational linear substitution, approximation, real roots.

Introduction

Note: In this paper, all the polynomials are univariate integral polynomials, if not specified otherwise.

The Problem

Given a univariate integral polynomial B, and a desired precision ε.

For each root α of B, compute the rational linear transformation matrix $\begin{pmatrix} p & p' \\ q & q' \end{pmatrix}$ such that:

> $\frac{p}{q}$ and $\frac{p'}{q'}$ are the last and second to last convergents of a *regular* continued fraction $(a_1, a_2, \dots, a_m)$;
>
> If $\neg(\alpha = \frac{p}{q})$ then $\left|\frac{p}{q} - \frac{p'}{q'}\right| = \frac{1}{qq'} < \varepsilon$, and α lies between $\frac{p}{q}$ and $\frac{p'}{q'}$ with respect to ∞.

This is done in three steps (See [1,2,3,4] for reference):

I. Factorize B into $B_1^{e_1} B_2^{e_2} \dots$ where each B_i is squarefree;

II. Isolate the roots of each B_i, using the variation-of-signs rule by *Lagrange* and *Vincent*. The output polynomial has exactly one sign variation, signifying exactly one positive root;

III. Approximate to the desired precision.

Subject of this paper is step III.

Until now, step III has been done by:

> while (desired precision is not reached) do
> (Compute $a = \text{FLOOR}\,\alpha$, where α is the one positive root of B;
> $B(x) \rightarrow B\left(a + \frac{1}{x}\right)$;
> Queue a onto the partial quotient chain).

Until now papers have concentrated on the fast computation of FLOOR α.

In this paper, however, a completely new method for step III is presented.

The Continued Fraction Transformation (CFT)

The theory of continued fractions is presented thoroughly in *Perron*[5]. See the textbooks on projective geometry, and those on the theory of functions, about rational linear substitutions (projectivities) in general [6,7].

Here I shall just state the definitions and theorems I need - mostly without proof.

Definition 1:

Let $(a_1, a_2, \ldots, a_m)$, where the a_i's are positive integers, and $m > 2$, be the partial quotient chain of a *regular* continued fraction. This chain defines a chain of rational linear transformations t_i and their inverses f_i on a 1-dimensional projective space by

$$z_{i-1} = t_i(z_i) = a_i + \frac{1}{z_i}, \text{ and } z_i = f_i(z_{i-1}) = \frac{1}{z_{i-1} - a_i}.$$

These rational linear substitutions are represented by 2×2 -matrices of determinant -1:

$$\begin{pmatrix} z_{i-1} \\ 1 \end{pmatrix} \cong \begin{pmatrix} a_i & 1 \\ 1 & 0 \end{pmatrix} \begin{pmatrix} z_i \\ 1 \end{pmatrix}, \text{ and } \begin{pmatrix} z_i \\ 1 \end{pmatrix} \cong \begin{pmatrix} 0 & 1 \\ 1 & -a_i \end{pmatrix} \begin{pmatrix} z_{i-1} \\ 1 \end{pmatrix}$$

where $\cong$ means: The left hand vector and the right hand product represent the same projective point.

The product of a chain of transformations is represented by the product of the corresponding matrices. Both matrices and fractions may be used equally well.

The Invariance of the Circular Ordering under a Rational Linear Substitution

Let P_1, P_2, P_3, P_4 be points of a 1-dimensional projective space which may be real or complex. The real line or the complex plane, then, is closed by the point ∞. P_2, P_3, and P_4 are pairwise different. On the closed complex plane any circle, of which a line is just a special case, is a mapping of the real axis under some rational linear substitution.

Lemma 1:

The Double Ratio $\mathrm{DR}(P_1,P_2;P_3,P_4)$ is invariant under any rational linear substitution T, where $\mathrm{DR}(P_1,P_2;P_3,P_4)$ is $\left(\frac{P_1 - P_3}{P_1 - P_4}\right) : \left(\frac{P_2 - P_3}{P_2 - P_4}\right)$.

Lemma 2:

If, on the closed complex plane, P_1, P_2, P_3, P_4 lie on a circle then $\mathrm{DR}(P_1,P_2;P_3,P_4)$ is real and vice versa.

Lemma 3:

If $DR(P_1,P_2;P_3,P_4)$ is real and negative then the pairs (P_1,P_2) and (P_3,P_4) separate each other in the sense of the circular ordering on the closed real line.

In this case, P_1 lies *between* P_3 and P_4 with respect to P_2. When P_2 is ∞ then we have the usual between-relation on a real line or its mapping on the complex plane.

The elementary rational linear substitutions are the substitutions $z \to z + a$; $z \to cz$; $z \to \frac{1}{z}$.

Corollary 1:

Any rational linear substitution keeps the between-relation in the sense of lemma 3 invariant.

Corollary 2:

A circle K_1 divides the points of the closed complex plane that are not on K_1 into two equivalence classes: Two points P_1 and P_2 are of different classes, or not, if some circle K_2 through P_1 and P_2 intersects K_1 in P_3 and P_4, and P_1 and P_2 separate P_3 and P_4, or not. One point of reference defines one of these classes as the "outside", the other as the "inside" of K_1. If the point of reference is ∞ then we have the usual inside-outside-relation on the complex plane.

This relation is also invariant under a rational linear substitution.

The Real Continued Fraction on the Closed Complex Plane

Definition 2a:

The continued fraction $(a_1,a_2, \ldots ,a_m)$ of definition 1 can be expressed and evaluated as

$$\begin{pmatrix} z_0 \\ 1 \end{pmatrix} \cong \begin{pmatrix} a_1 & 1 \\ 1 & 0 \end{pmatrix} \begin{pmatrix} a_2 & 1 \\ 1 & 0 \end{pmatrix} \cdots \begin{pmatrix} a_m & 1 \\ 1 & 0 \end{pmatrix} \begin{pmatrix} z_m \\ 1 \end{pmatrix}$$

so we obtain a product $T(z_m)$, defined as

$$T(z_m) = \begin{pmatrix} z_0 \\ 1 \end{pmatrix} \cong \begin{pmatrix} p & p' \\ q & q' \end{pmatrix} \begin{pmatrix} z_m \\ 1 \end{pmatrix}.$$

Written as a fraction, this is

$$z_0 = T(z_m) = \frac{pz_m + p'}{qz_m + q'}.$$

Lemma 4:

p, p', q, and q' are integers, and $p > p' > q'$, $p > q > q'$, and $q' > 0$.

Lemma 5:

$\frac{p}{q}$ and $\frac{p'}{q'}$ are the last and the second to last convergents.

Lemma 6:

The determinant D of T is $(-1)^m$; $\frac{p}{q} - \frac{p'}{q'} = \frac{D}{qq'}$; and $\frac{q'}{q} - \frac{p'}{p} = \frac{D}{pq}$.

Definition 2b:

The inverse of T is $F(z_0)$, defined as

$$F(z_0) = \begin{pmatrix} z_m \\ 1 \end{pmatrix} \cong \begin{pmatrix} q' & -p' \\ -q & p \end{pmatrix} \begin{pmatrix} z_0 \\ 1 \end{pmatrix}.$$

Written as a fraction, this is

$$z_m = F(z_0) = -\frac{q' z_0 - p'}{q z_0 - p}$$

As a rational linear substitution, the CFT maps the system of complex circles and lines onto itself. As a real one, it keeps the real axis invariant, and is invariant against conjugation:

$$\overline{F(z_0)} = F(\overline{z_0})$$

As a result, the symmetry about the real axis of a set of points is invariant under CFT.

Theorem 1a:

Given a CFT T and its coefficients p, p', q, q' as defined by definition 2a. Then

let I_T be the real open interval with $\frac{p}{q}$ and $\frac{p'}{q'}$ as endpoints, and length $\frac{1}{qq'}$;

let K_T be the interior of the complex circle having I_T as diameter:

Then T will map the complex halfplane $\mathrm{Re}(z) > 0$ *onto K_T, the imaginary axis onto its circumference, and the positive real half-axis onto I_T.*

Proof:

$$T(0) = \frac{p'}{q'};$$

$$T(\infty) = \frac{p}{q};$$

$$T(1) = \frac{p + p'}{q + q'};$$

$$T(-\frac{q'}{q}) = \infty.$$

This gives us the two endpoints, one on the interior of I_T, and a reference point in the sense of lemma 3 and corollaries 1 and 2. The invariance against conjugation gives us the fact that the image of the imaginary axis under T is a circle symmetric about the real axis, and so I_T is, indeed, its diameter and we thus complete the proof.

Theorem 1b:

Given T's inverse F and its coefficients p, p', q, q' as defined by definition 2b. Then

let I_F be the real open interval with $-\frac{q'}{q}$ and $-\frac{p'}{p}$ as endpoints, and length $\frac{1}{pq}$;

let K_F be the interior of the complex circle having I_F as diameter:

Then F will map the complex halfplane $\mathrm{Re}(z) < 0$ *onto K_F, the imaginary axis onto its circumference, and the negative real half-axis onto I_F.*

Proof:

$$F(0) = -\frac{p'}{p};$$

$$F(\infty) = -\frac{q'}{q};$$

$$F(-1) = -\frac{q' + p'}{q + p};$$

$$F(\frac{p}{q}) = \infty.$$

Then the proof corresponds to that of theorem 1a.

Front figure demonstrates theorems 1a and 1b in case $D = +1$.

Polynomials under the Continued Fraction Transformation

Let

$$B(z) = b_n z^n + b_{n-1} z^{n-1} + \dots + b_0$$

with deg $n \geq 1$ be a univariate integral polynomial with real or complex roots α_l, where $l = 1, \dots, n$. Let T and F be any pair of rational linear transformations such that

$$\alpha_l^{\mathrm{F}} = \mathrm{F}(\alpha_l), \text{ and } \quad \alpha_l = \mathrm{T}(\alpha_l^{\mathrm{F}}).$$

Then we obtain a new (the transformed) polynomial

$$B^{\mathrm{T}}(z) = B(\mathrm{T}(z)) = b^{\mathrm{T}}{}_n z^n + b^{\mathrm{T}}{}_{n-1} z^{n-1} + \dots + b^{\mathrm{T}}{}_0$$

which has the α_l^{F} as its roots.

Definition 3:

Let $B(z)$ be a univariate integral polynomial of deg $n \geq 1$ where

- the roots $\alpha_1, \dots, \alpha_{n-1}$ are negative or have nonpositive real parts;
- the root α_n (hereafter in this paper called α) is real and > 1.

Theorem 2:

Let $B(z)$ be a polynomial as in definition 3;

let T and its inverse F be the CFT of definitions 2a and 2b;

let I_{T}, I_{F}, and K_{F} be those of theorems 1a and 1b;

let finally α of definition 3 be $\in I_{\mathrm{T}}$.

Then $B^{\mathrm{T}}(z) = B(\mathrm{T}(z))$ is a polynomial having the roots $\alpha_l^{\mathrm{F}}, \dots, \alpha_{n-l}^{\mathrm{F}}$ in the interior or on the circumference of K_{F} (excluding the real endpoints of I_{F}), and α^{F} is real and > 0.

Proof:

follows easily from definition 3, and from theorems 1a and 1b.

Theorem 3:

Given the same conditions as for theorem 2, then $S = \sum_{l=1}^{n-1} \alpha_l^{\mathrm{F}}$ *is real and lies in the interior of the interval* I_S *as specified by the endpoints*

$$-(n-1)\frac{p'}{p} \text{ and } -(n-1)\frac{q'}{q};$$

furthermore $-(n-1) < S < 0$.

Proof:

Following theorem 2, the α_l^{F}'s are

- if real, then each one on the interior of I_{F};
- else pairs of conjugate complex numbers. Their real parts also are on the interior of I_{F}. In the above sum formula, now, one substitutes the real parts for the numbers and thus completes the proof.

Theorem 4:

Given the same conditions as for theorem 2, then α^{F} *lies on the interior of the interval* E *as specified by the endpoints*

$$e_1 = -\frac{b^{\mathrm{T}}_{n-1}}{b^{\mathrm{T}}_n} + (n-1)\frac{p'}{p}, \text{ and } e_2 = -\frac{b^{\mathrm{T}}_{n-1}}{b^{\mathrm{T}}_n} + (n-1)\frac{q'}{q}$$

Proof:

$$-\frac{b^{\mathrm{T}}_{n-1}}{b^{\mathrm{T}}_n} = S + \alpha^{\mathrm{F}}, \text{ or, } \alpha^{\mathrm{F}} = -\frac{b^{\mathrm{T}}_{n-1}}{b^{\mathrm{T}}_n} - S$$

where S is the sum introduced in theorem 3. The between-relation is invariant against negation and translation so we find: the interior of E is the interior of I_S of theorem 3, negated and translated.

Theorem 5:

Given the same conditions as for theorem 2. Now, let t *with* f *be a new, non-empty CFT such that* e_1 *and* e_2 *of the previous theorem transform to* e_1^{f} *and* e_2^{f}, *both of which are* >1 *and* $<\infty$.

Then the product transform T^*t (with its inverse f^*F) yields a new polynomial $B^{T^*t}(z)$, a new set of p, p', q, q', and a new set of I_{T^*t}, I_{f^*F}, and K_{f^*F}. This product and this polynomial fulfill all the conditions of theorems 2 - 4 and thus allow another application of theorem 5.

Proof:

The item of real interest is the new I_{T^*t} in connection with the new value of α^{f^*F}. From theorem 4 we know that α^F is on the interior of E. We know further, from the corollaries 1 and 2 in connection with theorems 1a and 1b, that any point interior to E stays interior to E^f. We conclude that α^{f^*F} stays interior to E^f and, every point of E^f being >1 and $<\infty$, α^{f^*F}, too, is >1 and $<\infty$. Since α^{f^*F} is on the interior of the positive real axis, α, then, is on the interior of I_{T^*t}. This completes the proof.

Note: The condition e_1^f and $e_2^f > 1$ shall ensure that the algorithm will yield a *regular* continued fraction.

The Algorithm

Now, out of theorems 2 - 5, we can outline the new step-III- algorithm:

```
Algorithm  IPRCF1 $(Integral Polynomial, Real root by
                    Continued Fraction, main algorithm)

Input:     B (z) as specified in definition 3;
           eps the precision we want.

Output:    The partial quotient chain C;
           Its matrix T;
           The transformed polynomial BT = B (T (z)).

(1)        $(prepare)
           Set T = Identity, C = empty, BT = B, n = deg (B).
(2)        $(proceed)
           While ((q*q' le 1/eps) and (deg (BT) = n)) do
             ( IPRPQC (BT, T; t, c);
               if c = empty then
                    IPRSPQ (BT, T, C; t, c);
               set C = conc (C, c), T = T*t, BT = IUPRLS (BT, t);
               extract q and q' from T )..
```

IPRPQC (Integral Polynomial, Real root, Partial Quotient Calculation) computes e_1 and e_2 from B^T and T, then computes their longest common continued fraction that satisfies the condition for theorem 5. c is its partial quotient chain, t its matrix. c may be empty.

IPRSPQ (Integral Polynomial, Real root, Single Partial Quotient) computes a single partial quotient when IPRPQC fails. It computes FLOOR$(-(b_{n-1} / b_n))$ if $C =$ empty or LAST$(C) \le 0$, else FLOOR$(-(b_{n-1} / b_n) + (1 / (\text{LAST}(C) + 1)))$ which after theorem 4 is a reasonable starting point, and starts searching for FLOOR(α) from there.

IUPRLS (Integral Univariate Polynomial, Rational Linear Substitution) applies a rational linear substitution on a univariate integral polynomial.

***Theorem** 6:*

Algorithm IPRCF1 is finite.

Proof:

The finiteness follows from the fact that the CFT t will never be the identity. Therefore the product qq' is strictly monotonic during the process and will eventually exceed $1 / \varepsilon$, thus completing the proof, if α does not happen to be rational anyway.

Obreschkoff's Theorem

We still need an interface between the old step II and the entry to our new step III since *Lagrange*'s 1-sign rule does ***not*** include definition 3 which is the entry condition for our new algorithm, except if $n < 4$ or all roots are known to be real.

To achieve this we may use a theorem by *Obreschkoff*[8] which is an extension of the *Budan-Fourier*-theorem, and which I quote without proof.

***Theorem** 7 (**Obreschkoff's Theorem**):*

Given a real univariate polynomial $B'(z)$ with degree n and sign variations V; given the sector S of the complex plane with $|\arg(z)| < \frac{\pi}{n - V}$; then the number of roots of B' on S is $V - 2k$ for some $k \ge 0$.

In our application now where $V = 1$, $k = 0$ necessarily, and the one root is α. Thus, if $n > 3$, one way to make sure of our condition for theorem 2 is, in following theorem 1a, to find some circle $K_{T'}$ (belonging to a CFT T' with its coefficients as in definition 2a) containing α which fits into S and then to transform accordingly starting our main algorithm from there.

Thus, if a_0 is such that $0 < a_0 \le$ FLOOR α, a sufficient condition for T' will be

$$\frac{1}{2qq'} \le a_0 \tan \frac{\pi}{n-1}$$

Now, instead of computing the tangent and π, we substitute the condition

$$\frac{1}{2qq'} \le a_0 \frac{3}{n-1}, \quad \text{or:} \quad qq' \ge \frac{n-1}{6a_0}.$$

Thus, the interface may be:

```
Algorithm  IPRCFO $(Integral Polynomial, Real root by
                     Continued Fraction, Obreschkoff's theorem)

Input    B' with one sign variation.

(1)      set G = 0, B = B', T' = unity, C' = empty, n = degree (B).
(2)      if n > 3 then while G = 0 or q*q' lt G do
            ( IPRSPQ (B, T', C'; t, c'); set a = first (c');
              if (G = 0 and a ne 0)
                       then set G = ceiling ((n - 1)/6*a);
              set B = IUPRLS (B, t), C' = conc (C', c'), T' = T'*t;
              extract q and q' from T' )..

Output   B, then, will be valid input for IPRCF1.
```

Acknowledgement:

Special thanks to W. Böge and R. Gebauer for reading and discussing this paper. Thanks also to M. Salmony for proofreading.

References

[1] Akritas, A.G.: Exact Algorithms for Polynomial Real Root Approximation Using Continued Fractions, *Computing 30* (1983) pp. 63-76.

[2] Lagrange, J.L.: Traité de la Résolution des Équations Numériques, (Paris, 1778).

[3] Vincent, A.J.H.: Sur la Résolution des Équations Numériques, *Journal de Mathématiques Pures et Appliquées 1* (1836) pp. 341-371.

[4] Uspenski, J.V.: Theory of Equations, *McGraw-Hill* (New York, 1948).

[5] Perron, O.: Die Lehre von den Kettenbrüchen, vol I, *Teubner* (Stuttgart, 1977).

[6] Heffter, L.: Grundlagen und analytischer Aufbau der Geometrie, *Teubner* (Stuttgart, 1958).

[7] Kneser, H.: Funktionentheorie, *Vandenhoek & Ruprecht* (Göttingen, 1966).

[8] Obreschkoff, N.: Verteilung und Berechnung der Nullstellen reeller Polynome, *VEB Deutscher Verlag der Wissenschaften* (Berlin, 1963) pp. 48-87.

ON THE AUTOMATIC RESOLUTION OF CERTAIN DIOPHANTINE EQUATIONS

by Maurice Mignotte
Université Louis Pasteur
Centre de Calcul de l'Esplanade
7, rue René Descartes
67084 Strasbourg Cédex, France

We consider equations of the general form

$$(1) \qquad X^2 - k = a^n$$

where a and k are fixed integers, $a > 1$ and not a square, and X and n are unknown positive integers, for example

$$X^2 + 1 = 2^n ;$$

and we give an algorithm to solve completely such equations which works very well in practice and uses only rational arithmetic.

I. Theoretical study.

1. First reduction.

When n is even, say $n = 2m$, equation (1) is equivalent to the system of the two equations

$$\begin{cases} X^2 - Y^2 = k , \\ Y = a^m ; \end{cases}$$

the resolution is obvious since $(X-Y)(X+Y) = k$ and there is only a finite number of solutions. In the sequel we consider only the case n odd, $n = 2m+1$; then equation (1) is equivalent to the system

$$\begin{cases} X^2 - a\,Y^2 = k & (1') \\ Y = a^m & (1'') . \end{cases}$$

2. The equation $X^2 - a\,Y^2 = k$.

The theory of this equation is well-known : there exists a finite set of solutions $S = \{(x^{(i)}, y^{(i)}) ; i \in I\}$ such that every solution is given by some formula

(2) $x + y\sqrt{a} = (x^{(i)} + y^{(i)}\sqrt{a})\,\varepsilon^s$, $s \in \mathbb{Z}$,

where ε is a fundamental unit of the quadratic field $\mathbb{Q}(\sqrt{a})$, $\varepsilon > 1$; moreover it is possible to compute effectively such a set S and the unit ε .

From equation (2) one deduces

$$2\,y\sqrt{a} = (x^{(i)} + y^{(i)}\sqrt{a})\,\varepsilon^s - (x^{(i)} - y^{(i)}\sqrt{a})\,\tilde{\varepsilon}^s ,$$

where $\tilde{\varepsilon}$ is the conjuguate of ε .

3. Resolution of the system.

Considering the previous value of y and equation (1'') one gets a relation like

(3) $\alpha_i\,\varepsilon^s + \beta_i\,\tilde{\varepsilon}^s = a^m$, $i \in I$,

where the unknows are the integers m and s .

Baker's theory enables us to determine an integer N such that equation (3) implies $\max\{m, |s|\} \leq N$. Indeed relation (3) implies

$$|s \operatorname{Log} \varepsilon - m \operatorname{Log} a + \operatorname{Log} \alpha_i| \ll \varepsilon^{-s}$$

and one knows that such an inequality can be true only for m and $|s|$ bounded by $N(\varepsilon, a, \alpha_i)$. Consequently, equation (1) has only a finite number of solutions and one can -in principle - determine all these solutions.

But the upper bounds of $N(\varepsilon, a, \alpha_i)$ are so big (often something like 10^{50} or more) that it seems almost impossible to cover such a range. The aim of the sequel is to solve this problem and to show that our solution is quite efficient in practice.

II. An algorithm.

We work in two steps :

- the determination of the solutions of (1'),
- the computation of the solution of the system (1'), (1'').

1. Resolution of equation $x^2 - a\,y^2 = k$.

We use only the fundamental following result.

THEOREM. - If k and d are integers with $d > 0$ and $|b| < \sqrt{d}$, and d is not a square, all the positive solutions of the Pell-Fermat equation

$$x^2 - d\,y^2 = b$$

are such that x/y is a convergent of the continued fraction expansion of $\sqrt{d}$.

This result is very well-known, a proof can be found - for example - in Leveque, Topics in Number Theory (v. 1, Th. 9.8), noted [L].

If k satisfies $|k| < \sqrt{a}$ we can apply this theorem ; if not we consider an equation of the form $x^2 - a^{2r+1} y^2 = k$ where r is positive and large enough, and in the sequel we suppose that this transformation has been done, so that the new system is

$$\begin{cases} x^2 - d\,y^2 = k \ , \quad d = a^{2r+1} \ (r \geq 0) \ , \quad |k| < \sqrt{d} \ , \\ y = a^m \ . \end{cases}$$

Then the precise resolution of the equation

$$(4) \qquad x^2 - d\,y^2 = k$$

is the following :

- compute the partial quotients $a_0, a_1, a_2, \ldots, a_n$ of the continued fraction expansion of $\sqrt{d}$ until a period is found (see [L], chap. IX for details) ;

- if $p_0/q_0, p_1/q_1, \ldots, p_n/q_n$ are the principal convergents of $\sqrt{d}$ then

  $$p_n^2 - d\,q_n^2 = \pm 1$$

  and if $\eta = p_n + q_n\sqrt{d}$ then all the solutions (p, q) of the equation

  $$|p^2 - d\,q^2| = 1$$

  are given by

  $$p + q\sqrt{d} = \pm (p_n \mp q_n\sqrt{d})^s \ , \quad s \in \mathbb{Z} \ ;$$

- if $p_n - d\,q_n^2 = 1$ then all the positive solutions of equation (4) are given by

(5) $$x + y\sqrt{d} = (p_i + q_i\sqrt{d})\eta^s\ ,\quad s \ge 0\ ,$$

with $i \le n$ and $p_i - d\,q_i^2 = k$;

- if $p_n - d\,q_n^2 = -1$ then all the positive solutions of equation (4) are given by the two formulas

(5') $$x + y\sqrt{d} = (p_i + q_i\sqrt{d})\eta^{2s}\ ,\quad s \ge 0\ ,\ i \le n\ ,\ p_i^2 - d\,q_i^2 = k\ ,$$

or

(5'') $$x + y\sqrt{d} = (p_i + q_i\sqrt{d})\eta^{2s+1}\ ,\quad s \ge 0\ ,\ i \le n\ ,\ p_i^2 - d\,q_i^2 = -k\ .$$

In the case of the example $x^2 + 1 = 2^n$ we get that the positive solutions (x, y) of the associated equation (1') satisfy

$$x + y\sqrt{2} = (1 + \sqrt{2})^{2s+1}\ ,\quad s \ge 0\ .$$

2. Resolution of the system.

Let $p_i + q_i\sqrt{d}$ be fixed in one of the equations (5), (5') or (5'') and denote by y_s the value of y corresponding to the integer s. Then (y_s) is a binary linear recursive sequence, it satisfies a relation

$$y_s = A\,y_{s-1} - y_{s-2}$$

where

$$A = \eta + \tilde{\eta}\ ,\ \text{in case (5)}\ ,$$

and

$$A = \eta^2 + \tilde{\eta}^2\ ,\ \text{in case (5') and (5'')}\ .$$

So the sequence (y_s) is completely determined when y_0, y_1 and A are known, which can be done easily as we saw above.

Then the problem reduces to find all the elements of a given binary recursive sequence which are powers of a. To solve this problem we consider the associated equations modulo "well-chosen" numbers q. Modulo any integer q the sequence (y_s) is periodical and the set Y_q of its values can be computed easily. The sequence (a^m) is also periodical modulo q, let P_q be this period ; the set $A_q := \{a^m \bmod q \, , \, m \geq 0\}$ contains P_q elements. The computation of $A_q \cap Y_q$ gives informations on the integers m and s such that the equation $y_s = a^{mq}$ is possible. Of course the interesting q's are the integers such that Y_q or A_q (or better both) are small ; whereas we get no information when $P_q = q-1$. In this way after j steps we find conditions like

$$m \in E_j \text{ modulo } M_j$$

and

$$s \in F_j \text{ modulo } S_j .$$

When $\max\{M_j, S_j\} \geq N$ we have found all the solutions of equation (1). But in practice, since N is very big, it is better to "guess" a small integer N' such that equation (1) has no solution $n \geq N'$ (very often $N' = 5$ is correct), to consider the system

$$\begin{cases} X^2 - a^{2r+1} Y^2 = k \, , & \text{with } 2r+1 \geq N' \, , \\ Y = a^m \, , & m \geq 0 \, , \end{cases}$$

and then, using congruences, to prove that this system is impossible ; in this case after a certain number of steps (and generally a small number) one gets $E_j = \emptyset$.

In the very simple example

$$x^2 + 1 = 2^n$$

noticing that the equation

$$x^2 + 1 \equiv 0 \bmod 4$$

has no solution we get that

$$x^2 + 1 = 2^n \Rightarrow (x, n) = (0, 0) \text{ or } (x, n) = (\pm 1, 1) .$$

We now consider a less trivial example to show how the previous algorithm works in a concrete case. Moreover the computation involved is rather simple and there is no need of a big computer, we used a home computer T.I. 99.

III. The equation $x^2 + x + 1 = 13^n$.

Notice that the equation

$$x^2 + x + 1 = 13^n \quad , \; x \geq 0 ,$$

has the solutions $(x, n) = (0, 0)$ and $(x, n) = (3, 1)$, whe shall show that there is no other solution.

The equation

$$x^2 + x + 1 = y^2$$

has the only solution $(x, y) = (0, \pm 1)$: we suppose (without loss of generality) that $x > 0$ and $y > 0$, then the equation implies $x < y < x+1$ so that y cannot be an integer. This shows that the equation

$$x^2 + x + 1 = 13^n \quad , \quad n > 1 ,$$

is equivalent to the system of equations

$$\begin{cases} x^2 + x + 1 = 13\, y^2 & (7') \\ y = 13^m \quad , \quad m > 0 & (7'') . \end{cases}$$

If $X = 2x + 1$ and $Y = 2y$ then equation (Y') is equivalent to

$$X^2 - 13\, Y^2 = -3 .$$

The first part of the algorithm shows that the positive solutions X, Y of this last equation are given by the conditions

$$X + \sqrt{13}\, Y = (7 + 2\sqrt{3})(18 + 5\sqrt{13})^{2s} \quad , \; s \geq 0 .$$

This shows that the positive solutions y of equation (7') are given by $y = y_s$ where

$$y_0 = 1 \quad , \quad y_1 = 1279 \quad , \quad y_s = 1298 y_{s-1} - y_{s-2} .$$

Now we consider the following congruences.

modulo 13

The sequence (y_s) has the period 26

s	0	1	2	3	4	5	6	7	8	9	10	11	12	13	14	15	16	17	18	19	20	21	22	23	24	25	26	..
y_s	1	5	2	4	3	3	4	2	5	1	6	0	7	-1	8	-2	9	10	10	9	11	8	-1	7	0	6	1	..

so that $y_s \equiv 0 \bmod 13$ implies

$$s \equiv 11 \bmod 13 .$$

mod 53

The period of the (y_s) is 13 :

s	0	1	2	3	4	5	6	7	8	9	10	11	12	...
y_s	1	7	22	35	40	51	14	48	15	24	26	16	19	...

and we know that $s \equiv 11 \bmod 13$, so we get $y_s \equiv 16 \bmod 53$.

The period of $(13^m) \bmod 53$ is also 13 :

m	0	1	2	3	4	5	6	7	8	9	10	11	12	...
13^m	1	13	10	24	47	28	46	15	36	44	42	16	49	...

and this table shows that we must have

$$m \equiv 11 \bmod 13 .$$

mod 79

The period of (y_s) mod 79 is again 13 :

s	0	1	2	3	4	5	6	7	8	9	10	11	12	...
y_s	1	15	35	69	20	58	56	29	61	70	28	13	19	...

and $s \equiv \bmod 13$ implies $y_t \equiv 13 \bmod 79$.

But the order of 13 modulo 79 is 39, so the condition $13^m \equiv 13 \bmod 79$ implies $m \equiv 1 \bmod 39$. This contredicts the condition $m \equiv 11 \bmod 13$. Our claim is proved.

Note (March 84) : J.P. Serre has proved that the equation $x^2 + x + 1 = y^n$ has only the solutions $(x, y, n) = (0, 1, n), (3, 13, 1), (-4, 13, 1), (2, 7, 1), (-3, 7, 1), (18, 7, 3), (-19, 7, 3)$; his proof uses p-adic analysis.

On Pseudo-Resultants (*)

Michael Rothstein

Dept. of Mathematical Sciences
Kent State University
Kent, OH 44242

ABSTRACT

Given an integral domain D and an indeterminate X over D, there exist many functionals mapping $D[X] \times D[X]$ into D that are similar to the resultant. If D is a Unique Factorization Domain, a specific functional, called the "minimal resultant", could be useful in many places where a resultant would be required, and also for solving certain Diophantine Equations.

(*) Work supported in part by the National Science Foundation under Grants MCS 82-02671 and MCS 78-02234 and by the Department of Energy under Grant DE-AS02-ER7602075-A010

On Pseudo-Resultants (*)

Michael Rothstein

Dept. of Mathematical Sciences
Kent State University
Kent, OH 44242

Key words: resultants, Sylvester Matrix, commutative algebra, Unique Factorization Domains, P-adic Methods.

1. Introduction

Having so many useful properties, resultants have become almost required tools in many branches of Symbolic and Algebraic Computation. Some of their uses include:

a) Elimination of an unknown from a system of equations, see [YUN 73].

b) Computation of satisfying polynomials for algebraic numbers given by algebraic operations on other algebraic numbers with known satisfying polynomials, see [LoC 73] or [BCL 82].

c) Resultants can be used to set up equations on a parameter whose solutions yield solutions to other problems, like integration, see [Rot 76].

Unfortunately, no p-adic algorithms (see [LAU 83] for a definition) have appeared in the literature for computing resultants: to be precise, the only methods known for computing resultants are the modular algorithm [Col 71], (of which a sparse variant could be developed along the lines suggested in [Zip 79]), the sub-resultant p.r.s. algorithm [Col 67], and Expansion of Bezout's or Sylvester's Determinant by one of several methods, see [KuA 69] and [Gri 78].

In this paper, we generalize the concept of resultant, study some of its properties, and choose one special representative of this generalized class of "pseudo-resultants" which, we conjecture, is easier to compute. We will sketch a p-adic algorithm for computing a "minimal resultant" and suggest some applications.

(*) Work supported in part by the National Science Foundation under Grants MCS 82-02671 and MCS 78-02234 and by the Department of Energy under Grant DE-AS02-ER7602075-A010

2. Pseudo-Resultants

In this section we will define pseudo-resultants and study some of its properties. Let us start with a definition:

DEFINITION: Given an integral domain R, an indeterminate X over R, let A, B be polynomials in X with coefficients in R. We shall call a pseudo-resultant of A and B an element p of R for which there exist two polynomials U and V, with $deg(U) < deg(B)$ and $deg(V) < deg(A)$ such that:

$$UA + VB = p$$

We shall also call U and V the co-determinants for p.

It may be thought that the ideal of pseudo-resultants of the polynomials A and B is simply the set $(A,B) \cap \mathrm{R}$. The following example, where R is the set of integers, shows that this is not the case in general: Let $A=2X+5$ and $B=2X+7$. Then, the ideal of pseudo-resultants is the set of all p in R such that for some u, $v \in \mathrm{R}$, $uA+vB \in \mathrm{R}$. But:

$$uA+vB = u(2X+5) + v(2X+7) = p \in \mathrm{R}$$

so that

$$u = -v \text{ and } p = 5u + 7v = 7v - 5v = 2v$$

and p MUST be even. Even so,

$$(X+3)(2X+5) + (-X-2)(2X+7) = 1$$

On the other hand, the existence of pseudo-resultants is guaranteed by the existence of resultants over the fraction field: the only necessary step is clearing denominators. In a similar fashion, it is easy to prove:

Theorem 1: Let R be an integral domain, let X be an indeterminate over R, let A, B be polynomials in X with coefficients in R. Then the following statements are equivalent:

a) there exist non-zero u, v in R such that uA and vB have a common factor of positive degree.

b) there exist non-zero polynomials U, $V \in \mathrm{R}[X]$ such that $deg(U) < deg(B)$, $deg(V) < deg(A)$ and $UA + VB=0$.

c) all pseudo-resultants of A and B are 0.

Proof:

All results follow immediately from similar results for fields after clearing denominators.

The presence of u and v in part a) of the theorem above is necessary. For example, if there is an element w in the domain R that has two distinct factorizations that is, $w = ab = cd$ are two distinct factorizations of w, (not necessarily into primes, but there may not be any common factors between the two factorizations) then for the two polynomials:

$$ax + c$$

and

$$dx + b$$

the only possible pseudo-resultant is 0, and yet they do not have a common factor. However, $(ax+c)b=(dx+b)c$.

Let A and B be fixed polynomials in X over a domain R. It is then easy to see that the set of pseudo-resultants of A and B is an ideal in R. The question is, what kind of an ideal is it? The following elaboration should help:

Let:

$$A = a_n x^n + a_{n-1} x^{n-1} + \cdots + a_0$$

and

$$B = b_m x^m + b_{m-1} x^{m-1} + \cdots + b_0$$

If we let r be a pseudo-resultant of A and B, then, there exist

$$U = u_{m-1} x^{m-1} + u_{m-2} x^{m-2} + \cdots + u_0$$

and

$$V = v_{n-1} x^{n-1} + v_{n-2} x^{n-2} + \cdots + v_0$$

such that $AU + BV = r \in$ R. If we regard this as a linear system in the a_i, b_j, with unknowns u_i, v_j we obtain the following:

$$
\begin{pmatrix}
a_n & 0 & \cdots & 0 & b_m & 0 & \cdots & 0 \\
a_{n-1} & a_n & \cdots & . & b_{m-1} & b_m & \cdots & . \\
. & . & \cdots & . & . & . & \cdots & . \\
. & . & \cdots & 0 & . & . & \cdots & . \\
. & . & \cdots & a_n & . & . & \cdots & 0 \\
a_0 & a_1 & \cdots & a_{n-1} & . & . & \cdots & b_m \\
0 & a_0 & \cdots & . & b_0 & b_1 & \cdots & b_{m-1} \\
. & 0 & \cdots & . & 0 & b_0 & \cdots & . \\
. & . & \cdots & . & . & 0 & \cdots & . \\
. & . & \cdots & . & . & . & \cdots & . \\
0 & 0 & \cdots & a_0 & 0 & 0 & \cdots & b_0
\end{pmatrix}
*
\begin{pmatrix}
u_{m-1} \\ u_{m-2} \\ . \\ . \\ . \\ u_0 \\ v_{n-1} \\ . \\ . \\ v_0
\end{pmatrix}
=
\begin{pmatrix}
0 \\ 0 \\ . \\ . \\ . \\ . \\ . \\ . \\ . \\ 0 \\ r
\end{pmatrix}
$$

Notice how the matrix for this system is the Sylvester matrix. If we apply Cramer's rule and expand the numerators of the u_i, v_j, we can deduce that the ideal of pseudo-resultants consists of exactly those r for which $\alpha_1 r, \alpha_2 r, \ldots, \alpha_k r$, are all divisible by a number u (the resultant of A and B) where $\alpha_1, \alpha_2, \ldots, \alpha_k$ are fixed elements of R dependent only of A and B.

As a corollary, we obtain the well-known fact that the resultant of two polynomials is a pseudo-resultant, but this reasoning also hints that there should be something like a "minimal pseudo-resultant". However, the following theorem, shows that this is only the case under strict conditions:

Theorem 2: Let R be a Noetherian domain, X an indeterminate over R. Then, the following conditions are equivalent:

a) For any polynomials A and B in R[X] , the ideal of pseudo-resultants is principal.

b) For any $q, r, u, v \in$ R, if $q|ur$ and $q|vr$, then, there is a $w \in$ R such that $w|u$, $w|v$, and $q|wr$.

c) R is a unique factorization domain (UFD).

d) For any $q, r_1, \ldots, r_n, a, b \in$ R, if $q|ar_1, q|ar_2, \ldots, q|ar_n$ and $q|br_1, q|br_2, \ldots, q|br_n$ then, there exists a $c \in$ R such that $c|a$, $c|b$, and $q|cr_1, q|cr_2, \ldots, q|cr_n$.

Proof:

Let us first assume (a) that for any two polynomials A and B in R[X] , their ideal of pseudo-resultants is principal, and let q, r, u and v be elements of R such that $q|ur$ and $q|vr$. Now, let

$$A = (r-q)x + 1$$

and

$$B = rx + 1$$

Then, the equation satisfied by the pseudo-resultant is:

$$\alpha A + \beta B = \bar{r}$$

which implies:

$$\alpha(r-q) + \beta r = 0$$

$$\alpha + \beta = \bar{r}$$

If we solve this system for α and β we obtain:

$$\alpha = \frac{r\bar{r}}{q}$$

$$\beta = \frac{\bar{r}(q-r)}{q}$$

Then $\bar{r}$ is a pseudo-resultant of A and B if and only if $q|r\bar{r}$ and $q|\bar{r}(r-q)$, or equivalently, the ideal of pseudo-resultants is the set of all $x \in$ R such that $q|rx$. By hypothesis, u and v belong to this ideal, and by condition (a), this ideal is principal, so let the ideal of pseudo-resultants be generated by w. This means:

i) $w|u$

ii) $w|v$ and

iii) $q|wr$ as required.

Now, let us assume (b) that for any $q, r, u, v \in$ R, if $q|ur$ and $q|vr$, then there is a $w \in$ R such that $w|u$, $w|v$, and $q|wr$. We want to prove that R is a Unique Factorization domain.

The proof will rest mainly on the lemma: If π is a prime element in a ring R satisfying (b), and if $\pi|ab$ where $a, b \in$ R then π divides at least one of a or b, which can be proven by assuming that π does not divide into a, so that any common divisor that π and a would have must be a unit. Applying statement (b) with $q = \pi$, $r = b$, $u = \pi$ and $v = a$, we obtain a $w \in$ R such that $w|\pi$, $w|a$ and $\pi|wb$. But since π and a cannot have a non-trivial common factor, w must be a unit. But this implies that $\pi|b$, as needed.

The remaining steps in a proof that R is a Unique Factorization Domain are that any element of R factors into primes (a trivial consequence of it being a Noetherian domain), and that the factorization is unique, a classical proof (see for example [Her 64] Theorem 3.E, pp 108-109).

The proof of statement (d) follows immediately from the statement that R is a unique factorization domain, so we only have to prove that statement (d) implies statement (a). The proof is as follows: Let A and B be elements of the domain R. Since R is a Noetherian domain, the ideal of pseudo-resultants of A and B will have a finite number of generators. However, if there are two or more generators, we apply the construction done above the theorem statement to find the $r_1, r_2, \ldots, r_k$ and the resultant q and apply statement (d) to two of the generators, (say) a and b , to obtain a c dividing a and b and also in the ideal. This means that we were able to reduce the number of generators of the ideal by 1, which implies that there can only be one generator, i.e. the ideal is principal.

This element, whose existence was just proven (modulo units) deserves a name:

Definition

Let R be a unique factorization domain, X an indeterminate over R, A and B polynomials in X with coefficients in R, and let m be a generator of the ideal of pseudo-resultants of A and B . Then, m will be called a minimal resultant of A and B .

It is this minimal resultant that should be easy to compute in applications, as seen below.

3. Applications

3.1. Computation of the Minimal Resultant.

Recently, [WGD 82] and [Mio 82] have shown how to reconstruct rational numbers from their p-adic expansion, a result that was necessary to complete a p-adic algorithm for computing partial fraction expansions. This algorithm can be used to compute minimal resultants as follows: Given $A, B \in R[X]$ find the partial fraction expansion of $\frac{1}{AB}$ as:

$$\frac{1}{AB} = \frac{u}{B} + \frac{v}{A}$$

so that

$$1 = uA + vB$$

If finding such u and v is not possible, there is no non-zero pseudo-resultant and the minimal resultant is 0. Also, if the fractions in the partial fraction expansion are in lowest terms, the common denominator in the last expression will be the required minimal resultant. (This "algorithm" can be simplified somewhat: in particular the "failure" case, which means that the minimal resultant is 0, can be detected much earlier than indicated here).

3.2. As a Replacement for the Resultant

Many applications (like equation elimination or algebraic number arithmetic) require the computation of a resultant to determine sufficient conditions for two polynomials to have a common factor. It is here suggested that a minimal resultant will do just as well in those cases. An example should help: it is suggested in [LoC 73] and [BCL 82] that, given algebraic numbers α and β, whose defining polynomials are given by $p(X)$ and $q(X)$, a method to obtain a polynomial satisfied by $\alpha+\beta$ is to compute the resultant of $p(X)$ and $q(X-Y)$ with respect to X. However, the minimal resultant will do just as well in this case.

3.3. Solution of certain Diophantine Equations

Often, a solution to an equation of the form: $AU+BV = C$ is required for U and V for given polynomials A and B over some unique factorization domain, and with suitable restrictions on the degrees of U and V, similar to those imposed on pseudo-resultants. One algorithm (which would also check whether A and B are relatively prime) would be to find the minimal resultant r for A and B (and the respective co-determinants $\bar{U}$ and $\bar{V}$) multiply both $\bar{U}$ and $\bar{V}$ by C and then divide $\bar{U}C$ by B (it is well known how to perform this operation without doing rational arithmetic; see [Knu 69] on "pseudo-division" pp. 368-369.) U is then the remainder of this division (divided by r), and $V = \dfrac{QA+\bar{V}C}{r}$, where Q is the quotient in the division mentioned above. In this way, we can find the solution to this equation without doing any rational arithmetic, an operation that can be costly.

4. Conclusions

We have shown that since, given two polynomials over a domain R there are many elements of R which are their pseudo-resultants, it is impossible to find their resultant using only the defining equation for pseudo-resultants, so a p-adic algorithm would have to use some additional information. We have also shown, however, that any pseudo-resultant would serve the same purposes as the resultant in most cases. Added by-products were a new algorithm for computing solutions to certain diophantine equations and another characterization of Unique Factorization Domains.

Acknowledgements

The author hereby gratefully acknowledges many useful discussions with Dr. Stephen Gagola, Dr. Francis Sandomierski, Dr. Paul S Wang and Dr. Olaf P. Stackelberg. This paper owes its present form and its very existence to those discussions. He also acknowledges the comments of the referees.

BIBLIOGRAPHY

[BCL 82] Buchberger, B., Collins, G. E. and Loos, R. editors, *Computer Algebra, Symbolic and Algebraic Computation* Springer-Verlag, Vienna, 1982, pages 173-188.

[Col 67] Collins, G. E. "Subresultants and Reduced Polynomial Remainder Sequences" *ACM Journal,* January 1967, Vol 14 Nr. 1

[Col 71] --- "The Calculation of Multivariate Polynomial Resultants" *ACM Journal,* October 1971, Vol 18 Nr. 4

[Gri 78] Griss, Martin L. "Using an Efficient Sparse Minor Expansion Algorithm to Compute Polynomial Subresultants and GCD" *IEEE Transactions on Computing,* C-27 (1978), 945-950.

[Her 64] Herstein, I. N. *Topics in Algebra* Blaisdell Publishing Co. Waltham, Mass, 1964

[Knu 69] Knuth, Donald E. *The Art of Computer Programming* Volume 2/Seminumerical Algorithms, Addison-Wesley Publishing Co., Reading, Mass., 1969.

[KuA 69] Ku, S. Y. and Adler, R. J. "Computing Polynomial Resultants: Bezout's Determinant vs Collins' Reduced PRS Algorithm" *CACM* Vol 23 Nr 12 (Dec 1969)

[LAU 83] Lauer, Markus "generalized p-Adic Constructions" *SIAM J. Computing* Vol 12 Nr 2, (May 1983), 395-410.

[LoC 73] Loos P and Collins, G. E. *"Resultant Algorithms for Exact Arithmetic on Algebraic Numbers"* Paper presented at SIAM 1973 Natl Mtg, Hampton, Va.

[Mio 82] Miola, Alfonso M. "The Conversion of Hensel Codes to their Rational Equivalents (or how to solve the Gregory's open problem)" *SIGSAM Bulletin* Number 64 (Vol 16 Number 4, November 1982)

[Rot 76] Rothstein, M *Aspects of Symbolic Integration and Simplification of Exponential and Primitive Functions* Ph D Thesis, University of Wisconsin, Madison, 1976, (114 pages) Available from University Microfilms.

[VdW 71] van der Waerden B L, *Algebra I,* Heidelberger Taschenbucher Nr 12, Springer-Verlag, Berlin, 1971 (German)

[WGD 82] Wang, Paul S., Guy, M.J.T. and Davenport, J. H. "P-adic Reconstruction of Rational Numbers" *SIGSAM Bulletin*, Issue Number 62 (Volume 16, Nr. 2, May 1982)

[YUN 73] Yun, David Y "On Systems for Solving Systems of Polynomial Equations" *SIGSAM Bulletin*, Nr 27 (Sept. 1973)

[Zip 79] Zippel,, R. E. "Probabilistic Algorithms for Sparse Polynomials", in *Symbolic and Algebraic Computation* (E. W. Ng, Ed.), Springer Verlag, Heidelberg (1979), pp 216-226.